CATALOGUE

OF THE

LIBRARY

OF THE

LINONIAN SOCIETY,

YALE COLLEGE,

JUNE, 1860.

CATALOGUE

OF THE

LIBRARY

OF THE

LINONIAN SOCIETY,

YALE COLLEGE,

JUNE, 1860.

NEW HAVEN:
J. H. BENHAM, PRINTER, GLEBE BUILDING.

MDCCCLX.

PREFACE.

The Linonian Society was founded in September, A. D., 1753. To the members of the Society of the class of 1769, and of the classes immediately following, we are indebted for the foundation of the Library. In the records of the Society at that time is found a vote of thanks to Timothy Dwight, Nathan Hale, and James Hillhouse, for the first contribution of books.

From the records and catalogues we are enabled to show the number of volumes at different periods. In 1770 there are stated to be nearly 100 volumes; 1780, 152 volumes; 1790, 330 volumes; 1800, 475 volumes; 1811, 724 volumes; 1822, 1187 volumes; 1831, 3505 volumes; 1837, 5581 volumes; 1841, 7500 volumes; 1846, 10,103 volumes. The present catalogue numbers 11,300 volumes.

No labor has been spared to make this a convenient and useful catalogue. While the arrangement is made with especial reference to the ready finding of any known title, care has also been taken that, as far as possible, the title and subject may be suggestive of each other. Many, who use this Library, more frequently want a book on a *particular* subject than a *particular* book. The Classified Index, though valuable, is not alone sufficient for such readers. But if, whenever it is possible, that word of the title which will suggest the subject is made initial, many valuable books will be found and read, which otherwise would seldom or never be taken from the shelves. The Tables of Contents, throughout the Catalogue, will also be found of no inconsiderable convenience. When, however, all has been done in this direction that can be, in a catalogue proper, an Index of Miscellaneous Subjects, would make the Library much more valuable to the mass of students.

Every title is inserted under the name of the author, so far as could be ascertained, and again under at least one of its most prominent words—frequently more. Great pains has been taken to insure accuracy, though owing to the disadvantages under which the proof-sheets were read, an occasional error was unavoidable. It is however believed that there are few, if any, which which will be found of practical inconvenience.

CATALOGUE.

A.

Abbot, The. W. Scott. Boston, 1820. 8°. 1096
The same. Hartford, 1822. 8°. 1086
The same. Philadelphia, 1826. 2 v. 12°. 594
Abbott, J. The Corner Stone. Boston, 1834. 12°. 6159
Hoaryhead. Boston, 1838. 18°. 1695
Summer in Scotland. New York, 1848. 12°. 9246
The Teacher. Boston, 1834. 12°. 3921
The Young Christian. New York, 1833. 12°. 6556
The same. 5247
Abbott, J. S. C. History of Cleopatra. New York, 1851. 12°. . . 8073
History of N. Bonaparte. New York, 1855. 2 v. 8°. . . . 7530
History of Josephine. New York, 1851. 12°. 8389
Abeel, D. Residence in China from 1829–33. New York, 1834. 12°. . 9804
Abeillard and Heloisa, Lives of. J. Berington. London, 1818. 4°. . 11256
Abel, Death of. S. Gessner. Trans. London, 1802. 16°. . . . 11286
Abercrombie, James. Lectures on the Catechism. Philadelphia, 1811. 8°. 5108
Abercrombie, John. Intellectual Powers, &c. New York, 1841. 12°. . 5540
Religious Essays. New York, 1845. 16°. 4299
Philosophy of Moral Feelings. New York, 1840. 12°. . . . 5874
The same. New York, 1833. 16°. 8765
Abipones, An Equestrian Race of Paraguay. Trans. London, 1822. 3 v. 8°. 7389
Aborigines of America, Traits of. Mrs. L. H. Sigourney. Camb. 1832. 12°. 2282
American, Costumes, Habits, &c. of. Illust. N. York, 1841. 12°.
Abraham, C. J. Lectures on Ancient and Modern Hist. Eton, 1845. 8°. 6713
Absentee, The. Miss M. Edgeworth. Washington, 1812. 12°. . . 1650
Abyssinia, History of. London, 1781. 8°. 7058
Life in. M. Parkyns. New York, 1854. 2 v. 12°. . . . 9560
Egypt and Nubia, Travels in. J. Conder. London, 1827. 2 v. 18°. 9337
The same. 9655
and Nubia, History of. M. Russell. New York, 1840. 12°. . . 5877
The same. New York, 1833. 16°. 6626
The same. 8766
Academician, The. Ed. A. and J. W. Picket. London, 1818. 8°. . . 3125
Accum, F. Theoretical and Practical Chemistry. Phila. 1814. 2 v. 8°. . 5965
Achilli, G. Dealings with the Inquisition. New York, 1851. 12°. . 5404

Acts of the Apostles, Lectures on. R. Stack. Annapolis, 1815. 8°. . . 6391
Notes on. A. Barnes. New York, 1841. 12°. 6179
Adam, A. Latin Grammar. Ed. C. D. Cleaveland. Hartford, 1836. 12°. 3389
The same. Ed. B. A. Gould. Boston, 1835. 12°. . . 3396
The same. Boston, 1833. 12°. 4849
Roman Antiquities. (Two copies.) New York, 1833. 8°. . . 11339
Adams, A. Summary of Geography and History. London, 1802. 8°. . 6769
Adams, G. Lectures on Natural Philosophy. London, 1799. 4 v. 8°. . 5967
Plates to Illustrate the Lectures. London, 1799. 4 v. 12°. . . 5994
Adams, J. History of Rome. Dublin, 1792. 2 v. 8°. 7678
Adams, Jasper. Elements of Moral Philosophy. New York, 1837. 8°. . 6306
Adams, John. Defence of the Constitution of the U. S. Phil. 1797. 3 v. 8°. 10774
Letters of. Boston, 1841. 2 v. 12°. 3378
and W. Cunningham. Correspondence between. Boston, 1823. 8°. 10667
and Washington. Adminis. of. Ed. G. Gibbs. N. Y. 1846. 2 v. 8°. 10936
Works, with Life, by C. F. Adams. Boston, 1856. 10 v. 8°. . 10971

Vol. 1. Life.
2, 3. Diary and Autobiography.
3. Essays and Controversial Papers of the Revolution.
4. Controversial Papers of the Revolution.
4-6. Works on Government.
7-9. Official Letters, Messages and Public Papers.
9, 10. General Correspondence; General Index.

Adams, J. Q. Life. Wm. H. Seward. Auburn, 1849. 12°. . . . 8017
Adams, J. W. Sermons. Syracuse, 1851. 12°. 5392
Adams, Miss A. Journal and Correspondence of. New York, 1841. 12°. 4880
Adams, Mrs. A. Letters of. Boston, 1840. 12°. 3377
Adams, M. Biographical Dictionary. London. 8°. 8860
Addison, C. G. Damascus and Palmyra. London, 1838. 2 v. 8°. . . 9407
Addison, J. Evidences of Christianity. Philadelphia, 1805. 12°. . . 6580
The same. London, 1753. 12°. 6606
Life. Lucy Aikin. London, 1843. 2 v. 12°. 8576
Poems. London, 1777. 2 v. 12°. 2290
Remarks on several parts of Italy. London, 1705. 8°. . . . 9820
Select Poetical Works, with Life, by E. Sanford. Phila. 1819. 18°. 2127
Works. New York, 1811. 5 v. 12° 3640
The same. New York, 1855. 3 v. 8°. 59

Vol. 1, 2. Spectator.
3. Tatler; Guardian; Freeholder; Whig; Examiner; Lover; Dialogues on Medals; Remarks on Italy; Present State of the War; Count Tariff; Evidences of Christian Religion; Poems, &c.

Addison, J. R. Steele and others. Guardian. London, 1823. 3 v. 12°. 3676
The Spectator. New York, 1810. 9 v. 12°. 3579
The same. London, 1823. 8 v. 12°. 3668
Duplicate of Vol. I. 3709
The same. Philadelphia, 1819. 12 v. 16°. 3980
The same. London. 8 v. (vol. 4 missing.) 12°. . . . 3908
Tatler. London, 1823. 4 v. 12°. 3664
Addisoniana. London, 1804. 2 v. 16°. 4308

Adeline Mowbray. Boston, 1827. 18°. 908
Adler, G. S. Greek Grammar. New York, 1846. 12°. 2980
Adolphus, J. Biog. Memoirs of the French Revolution. Lon. 1789. 2 v. 8°. 6709
Memoirs of J. Bannister. London, 1829. 2 v. 8°. 7911
Adshead, J. Prisons and Prisoners. London, 1845. 8°. 10666
Advent, a Mystery. A. C. Cox. (2 copies.) New York, 1837. 12°. . . 1945
Adventurer, The. J. Hawkesworth and others. London, 1823, 3 v. 12°. 3683
The same. London, 1756. 3 v. 12°. 11932
Adventures of an Actor. Ed. T. Hook. London, 1842. 2 v. 8°. . . 1135
Adventures of Capt. Singleton. D. De Foe. Edin. 1810. 2 v. 16°. . 329
Adventures of Capt. Bonneville. W. Irving. New York, 1856. 12°. . 539
Adversaria. R. Porsonus. London, 1812. 8°. 397
Advice of a Lady of Quality to her Children. Newburyport. 2 v. 18°. 4953
to a new Married Couple. J. Bean. Greenfield, 1821. 16°. 11290
to the Teens. I. Taylor. Boston, 1820. 18°. 4950
to Young Men. W. Cobbett. New York, 1831. 12°. 4980
The same. 4988
Ælianus. Varia Historia. Lipsiæ, 1829. 16°. 10341
Æschines. Opera. Lipsiæ, 1829. 16°. 10333
Æschylus. Tragœdiæ. Lipsiæ, 1829. 16°. 10332
Æschylus. Trans. R. Potter. New York, 1834. 18°. 3062
The same. New York, 1839. 12°. 5261
The same. Philadelphia, 1823. 18°. 2117
Æsop Junior in America. New York, 1834. 12°. 199
Æsopus. Fabulæ. Lipsiæ, 1829. 16°. 10347
The same, with Latin Notes. Boston, 1812. 12°. 1623
Affghanistan, Disasters in, a Journal of. Lady Sale. London, 1843. 11°. 9788
Affecting Scenes. New York, 1836. 2 v. 16°. 3975
Affections, Religious, Treatise on. J. Edwards. Abridged. N. York. 18°. 5224
Afgans of Hindostan, History of the. C. Hamilton. London, 1787. 8°. 6762
Afloat and Ashore. J. F. Cooper. Philadelphia, 1844. 4 v. 12°. . . 1537
Africa and the American Flag. A. H. Foote. New York, 1854. 12°. . 9229
Central, Journey to. B. Taylor. New York, 1856. 12°. . . . 8887
Description of, J. Conder. London, 1827. 3 v. 16°. 9658
Discoveries and Travels in. H. Murray. Edinburg, 1818. 2 v. 8°. 9110
Discovery and Adventure in. L. Jameson & others. N. Y., 1840. 12°. 5518
The same. New York, 1831. 16°. 6611
History of. London, 1781. 5 v. 8°. 7057
Loss of brig Commerce on Coast of. A. Robbins. Roch. 1818. 12°. 8736
The same. 9026
Politics, Intercourse and Trade of the Ancient Nations of. A. H. L. Heeren. Trans. Oxford, 1832. 2 v. 8°. 10686
South, Five years in. R. G. Cummings. New York, 1850. 2 v. 12° 9577
South, Travels in. J. Barrows. New York, 1802. 8°. . . . 9457
South. Wanderings and Adventures in. A. Steedman. London, 1835. 2 v. 8°. 9405
Southern. History of. R. M. Martin. London, 1843. 12°. . 5819
Southern, Missionary Labors in. R. Moffat. New York, 1843. 12°. 8938

Africa, Travels in. R. and J. Lander. New York, 1821. 2 v. 12°. . . 5538
Travels in. M. Park. Philadelphia, 1800. 8°. 9179
Travels in, in 1803–7. Ali Bey. Philadelphia, 1816. 2 v. 18°. . 9505
Travels and Discoveries in. D. Denham and others. Boston, 1826. 8°. 9460
Arabia, &c., Voyages to Explore the Shores of. W. F. W. Owen. New York, 1833. 2 v. 12° 9251
Western, its Condition, &c. D. J. East. London, 1844. 12°. . 8699
Western, Excursions in. J. E. Alexander. London, 1840. 2 v. 8°. 9098
African and East India Missions. C. Buchanan. Boston, 1811. 8°. . 9173
West, Sketches. G. R. Collins, and C. Maccarthy. London, 1824. 12°. 9299
Agassiz, L. and A. A. Gould. Principles of Zoology. Boston, 1848. 12°. 6053
and J. E. Cabot. Lk. Superior, Phys. Character, &c., of. Bost. 1850. 8°. 5956
Age of Benevolence. C. Wilcox. New York, 1822. 16°. 11292
Agnel, H. R. Book of Chess. New York, 1839. 12°. 1143
Agnes de Mansfeldt. T. C. Grattan. Philadelphia, 1836. 2 v. 12°. . 962
Agricultural Chemistry and Geology. J. F. W. Johnston. N. Y. 1847. 12°. 6076
Society, New York State, Transactions of. Vols. 7–9. Alb. 1848. 8°. 10464
Agriculture, Elements of Scientific. J. P. Norton, Albany, 1850. 12°. . 3001
and the Arts, Reports to Congress on. See U. S. public documents.
Agrippa, H. C. Uncertainty and Vanity of the Arts & Sciences. 1675. 12°. 3352
Aguilar, Grace. Home Scenes and Heart Studies. New York, 1853. 12°. 1200
Mother's Recompense. New York, 1851. 12°. 1199
The same. New York, 1851. 8°. 48
Vale of Cedars. New York, 1851. 12°. 1198
Woman's Friendship. New York, 1851. 12°. 1201
Women of Israel. New York, 1851. 2 v. 12°. 1196
Ahasuerus. A Poem. R. Tyler. New York, 1842. 12°. 2349
Aids to English Composition. R. G. Parker. Boston, 1844. 12°. . . 2997
to Reflection. S. T. Coleridge. Burlington, 1829. 12°. . . 5350
The same. 6430
The same. New York, 1841. 12°. 6133
Aikin, J. Annals of the Reign of George III. London, 1816. 2 v. 8°. . 7931
British Poets. Jonson to Beattie. Philadelphia, 1839. 8°. . . 1848
Letters on English Poetry. New York, 1806. 12°. . . . 4929
Memoir. Lucy Aikin. Philadelphia, 1824. 8°. 7926
Song Writing, with English Songs. London, 1810. 12°. . . 2226
The same. London, 1816. 12°. 1916
Aikin, Lucy. Life of Joseph Addison. London, 1843. 2 v. 12°. . . 8576
Memoirs of the Court of Charles I. Philadelphia, 1833. 2 v. 8°. . 8531
Memoirs of the Court of Queen Elizabeth. Boston, 1821. 2 v. 8°. 7635
Ainsworth, N. Latin and English Dictionary. Philadelphia, 1825. 8°. . 1056
Ainsworth, W. Researches in Assyria, Babylonia, &c. Lond. 1838. 8°. . 9777
Air. R. Mudie. London, 1835. 12°. 6106
Aird, T. Othuriel, and other Poems. Edinburg, 1840. 8°. 1835
Airs of Palestine, and other Poems. J. Pierpont. Boston, 1840. 18°. . 2401
Akenside, M. Poems. Philadelphia, 1822. 16°. 3058
Select Poems, with Life by S. Johnson. Philadelphia, 1822. 18°. 2140
Alarm to the Unconverted. J. Alleine. Charlestown, 1807. 12°. . . 6113

Alarm to the Unconverted. J. Alleine. Philadelphia, 1829. 18°. . . 4617
Albany Institute, Transactions of. Vol. I. Albany, 1830. 8°. . . 10643
Albigenses, Crusades against the. J. C. L. S. DeSismondi. Bost. 1833. 12°. 6505
The same. 6833
Alciphron, or the Minute Philosopher. G. Berkeley. London, 1767. 12°. 6433
Alcott, W. A. Moral Reformer and Teacher on the Human Constitution. Boston, 1835. 12°. 3014
The House I Live In; or, the Human Body. Boston, 1837. 16°. . 4893
Alcuin. Life. F. Lorenz. Trans. Jane M. Slee. 12°. London, 1827. 12°. 7734
Alden, T. Collection of American Epitaphs. New York, 1814. 5 v. 16°. 10030
Alexander the Great. Life. J. Williams. New York, 1839. 16°. . . 8758
The same. New York, 1841. 12°. 5509
Alexander, J. A. Psalms. Translated and Explained. N. Y. 1851. 3 v. 12°. 5394
Alexander, J. E. Excursions in Western Africa. London, 1840. 2 v. 8°. 9098
North and South America and the West Indies. Phila. 1833. 8°. 9092
Alexander, W. Hist. of Women from the Earliest Ages. Lond. 1782. 2 v. 8°. 6925
Alexandri Expeditio. Arrianus. Lipsiæ, 1829. 16°. 10340
Alfieri, V. Autobiography. Trans. C. E. Lester. New York, 1845. 12°. 8339
Algebra and Arithmetic. W. Hopkins. London, 1833. 8°. 5096
First Lessons in. C. Davies. Baltimore, 1839. 12°. 3933
German. J. A. C. Michelsen. Berlin, 1788. 12°. . . . 4896
Key to W. Colburn's. Boston, 1833. 12°. 3313
Treatise on. S. Simpson. London, 1782. 8°. 3290
Alger, W. R. Oriental Poetry. Boston, 1856. 12°. 1939
Algerine Captive. U. Underhill. Hartford, 1816. 18°. 8448
Algiers, Sketches of. W. Shaler. Boston, 1826. 8°. 9126
Alhambra, The. W. Irving. Philadelphia, 1832. 2 v. 12°. 991
The same. New York, 1851. 542
Ali Bey. Travels in Morocco, Egypt, &c., in 1803–7. Phil. 1816. 2 v. 8°. 9505
Ali Pacha. Life. London, 1823. 8°. 11314
Alice, or the Mysteries. E. L. Bulwer. New York, 1837. 2 v. 12°. . 690
Alison, A. Essays on Taste. Dublin, 1790. 8°. 2699
Sermons. Boston, 1815. 8°. 5374
Alison, A., (Jr.) History of Europe from 1189–1815. Lond. 1835. 10 v. 8°. 7641
Second series. From 1815 to 1802. N. Y. 1855. 2 v. 8°. . 7255
Allan, G. Life of Sir W. Scott. Philadelphia, 1835. 8°. 8128
Alleine, J. Alarm to the Unconverted. Charlestown, 1807. 12°. . 6113
The same. Philadelphia, 1829. 18°. 4617
Allen, B., Jr. Urania, or the true Use of Posey, a Poem. N. Y. 1814. 18°. 2767
Allen, D. O. Account of Ancient and Modern India. Boston, 1856. 8°. 7543
Allen, E. Life. H. Moore. Plattsburgh, 1834. 12°. 7781
The same. 8378
Life. J. Sparks. Boston, 1834. 12°. 8068
Autobiography, &c. Boston, 1845. 16°. 7773
Allen, P. History of the American Revolution. Balt. 1842. 2 v. 8°. . 6903
Allen, W. A Decade of Addresses. Boston, 1830. 12°. 6447
American Biographical Dictionary. Cambridge, 1809. 8°. . . 8853
Allen, Z. Philosophy of the Mechanics of Nature. New York, 1852. 8° 394

Allibone, S. A. Dictionary of British and American Authors, and of English Literature. Philadelphia, 1859. 2 v. 4°. 9673
Allston, W. Lectures on Arts and Poems. New York, 1850. 12°. . 10158
Almacks. New York, 1827. 2 v. 12°. 989
Revisited. New York, 1828. 2 v. 12°. 1413
Alps and the Rhine. J. T. Headley. New York, 1845. 12°. . . . 9854
Alton Locke. C. Kingsley. New York, 1856. 12°. 1222
Amaranth, Literary. N. C. Brooks. Philadelphia, 1840. 12°. . . 3009
Amazon, Exploration of the Valley of. W. M. Herndon. Wash. 1853. 2 v. 8°. 10452
Voyage up the. W. H. Edwards. New York, 1847. 12°. . . 8933
Amazonian Republic. New York, 1842. 12°. 11194
Amber Witch, or Trial for Witchcraft. W. Meinhold. Tr. N. Y. 1845. 12°. 1596
Ambitious Student. E. L. Bulwer. New York, 1832. 12°. . . . 1591
The same. 1658
Amelia. H. Fielding. New York, 1816. 2 v. 12°. 3601
Amelia. Poems by. New York, 1848. 12°. 1937
Amenities of Literature. J. D'Israeli. London, 1841. 3 v. 8°. . . 721
The same. New York, 1845. 2 v. 12°. 512
America, and the American People. F. Von Raumer. Tr. N. Y. 1846. 8°. 9105
Annals of, from 1492 to 1826. A Holmes. Cambridge, 1829. 2 v. 8°. 6986
The same. 11330
and England, Comparison between. New York, 1834. 8°. . . 9177
and Europe. A. G. de Gurowski. New York, 1857. 12°. . . 7392
Buccaneers of, History of the. New York, 1826. 3 v. 18°. . . 11276
Commerce of, with Europe. J. P. Brissot. Tr. N. Y. 1795. 12°. 11179
Democracy in. A. De Tocqueville. Trans. N. Y. 1845. 2 v. 8°. 10985
The same. New York, 1838–40. 2 v. 8°. 10061
Diary in. H. Maryatt. Philadelphia, 1839. 12°. 9007
Second series. Philadelphia, 1840. 12°. 9815
European Settlements in. E. Burke. London, 1757. 2 v. 12°. . 7089
The same. Boston, 1835. 8°. 11325
Female Poets of. R. W. Griswold. Philadelphia, 1849. 8°. . . 1789
Fruits and Fruit Trees of. A. G. Downing. New York, 1849. 12°. 2978
General Survey of. A. H. Everett. (2 copies.) Phil. 1827. 8°. . 9766
Hist., Statis. and Descrip. J. S. Buckingham. Lond. 1840. 3 v. 8°. 6935
History of. London, 1783. 3 v. 8°. 7080
History of. W. Robertson. Philadelphia, 1821–2. 2 v. 8°. . . 7007
The same. Dublin, 1777. 2 v. 8°. 7691
The same. Abridged. New York, 1848. 12°. . . 5259
Impressions of. T. Power. Philadelphia, 1836. 2 v. 12°. . . 10144
Its Realities and Resources. H. Wyse. London, 1846. 3 v. 8°. . 9390
Living Orators in. E. L. Magoon. New York, 1849. 12°. . . 8669
Men and Manners in. T. Hamilton. Phil. 1833. 2 v. 12°. . . 8940
North, History of. Rev. Mr. Cooper. Albany, 1815. 12° . . 7443
The same. Lansingburgh, 1795. 12°. 11935
North, Hist. of Disc. and Trav. in. H. Murray. Lond. 1829. 2 v. 8°. 6959
North, Memoirs of the N. W. Coast of. R. Greenhow. N. Y. 1840. 8°. 11319
North, Rambler in. C. J. Latrobe. New York, 1835. 2 v. 12°. . 9631

America, North, Remarks during a Journey through, in 1819–21. A. Hodgson. New York, 1823. 8°. 9726
North and South, History of. C. A. Goodrich. Hart. 1851. 8°. 7597
North and South, and West Indies. J. E. Alexander. Phil. 1833. 8°. 9092
North, Three years in. J. Stuart. New York, 1833. 2 v. 12°. . 9813
North, Topo. Desc. of the W. Ter. of. G. Imlay. Lond. 1792. 8°. 9489
North, Travels in. J. Carver. Philadelphia, 1796. 8°. . . 9214
North, Travels in. B. Hall. Philadelphia, 1829. 2 v. 12°. . . 9280
North, Travels in. C. Lyell. New York, 1845. 12°. . . . 9255
North, Travels in. C. A. Murray. New York, 1839. 2 v. 12°. . 9834
Notes on. C. Dickens. New York, 1844. 8°. 9087
Poets of, Illustrated. Ed. J. Keese. (2 copies.) New York, 1842. 12°. 2328
Poets and Poetry of. R. W. Griswold. Philadelphia, 1842. 8°. 1787
Progress of Discovery on the Northern Coasts of. N. Y. 1841. 12°. 5869
Prose Writers of. R. W. Griswold. Philadelphia, 1847. 8°. . . 28
Researches concerning the Ancient Inhabitants of. A Von Humboldt. Trans. Helen M. Williams. London, 1814. 2 v. 8°. . . 9507
Society in. Harriet Martineau. New York, 1837. 2 v. 12°. . 9611
South, Miranda's Revolution in. Boston, 1810. 12°. . . . 7125
South, Travels in 1799–1804. A. Von Humboldt. Phil. 1815. 8°. 9169
South, Travels in, in 1832. A. R. Terry. Hartford, 1834. 12°. . 9282
South, Voyage to, in 1817, 18. H. M. Brackenridge. Balt. 1819. 2 v. 8°. 9159
South, &c., Wandering Sketches to. W. M. Wood. Phil. 1849. 12°. 8917
Spanish, Outline of the Revolution in. New York, 1817. 12° . 7444
Progress of. J. Macgregor. London, 1847. 2 v. 8°. . . . 7798
The Stranger in. F. Lieber. Philadelphia, 1835. 8°. . . . 9420
American Aboriginese, Costumes, Habits, &c. of. Illust. N. Y. 1841. 12°.
Almanac, vols. 1–16. Boston, 1830–45. 12°. 4207
Annals of Education for 1831. Boston, 1831. 8°. 2193
Annual Register for 1825–33. New York, 1827–35. 8 v. 8°. . . 2178
Antiquarian Society, Cat. of the Library of. Worcester, 1837. 8°. 9707
Antiquarian Society, Transactions of. Worcester, 1820. 8°. . . 10067
Antiquit. and Origin of Red Race. A. W. Bradford. N. Y. 1841. 8°. 7594
Association of Geologists and Naturalists, Transactions of 1840–2. Boston, 1843. 8°. 5960
Biography. J. Belknap. New York, 1846. 3 v. 12°. . . . 5212
The same. Boston, 1794. 2 v. 8°. 8588
Biography.—See J. Sparks.
Biographical Dictionary. W. Allen. Cambridge, 1809. 8°. . . 8853
Bravery Displayed in the Capture of 1400 Vessels of War and Commerce. J. Butler. Carlisle, 1816. 12°. 11471
Chesterfield. New York, 1827. 18°. 4938
The same. Philadelphia, 1828. 18°. 11271
Churches, Visit to. A. Reed and R. Matheson. N. Y. 1835. 2 v. 12°. 8904
Colonies, History of. J. Marshall. Philadelphia, 1824. 8°. . . 7226
Common Place Book of Prose. Ed. G. B. Cheever. Bost. 1832. 12°. 3355
The same. Boston, 1828. 12°. 4892
Constitutions. New York, 1813. 18°. 11151

American, Courage and Enterprise. New York. 2 v. 12°. 5251
Eclectic. vols. 1–8. New York, 1841–4. 8°. 4747
Facts. G. P. Putnam. London, 1845. 12°. 10813
Farmer, Letters from an. J. H. St. John. Philadelphia, 1793. 12°. 8737
First Class Book. Boston, 1823. 12°. 4870
Fruit Garden Companion. E. Sayers. Boston, 1839. 12°. . . 3016
Hist., Arts &c., Discourses on. G. C. Verplanck. New York, 1825. 8° 782
Journal of Science. Vols. 1–49. New Haven, 1818–45. 8°. . . 2865
Second Series. Vols. 1–26, (continued.) N. H. 1846–49. 8°. 2914
Indians. See Indians.
in England. A. S. Mackenzie. New York, 1835. 2v. 12°. . 8690
Institute, Boston, Lectures before the. Boston, 1833. 8°. . . 11679
Institute, N. Y., Reports of the, for 1846, 7. Albany, 1847. 2 v. 8°. 10069
Laborer, Protection to Home Industry, and Statistics of U. States. H. Greeley. New York, 1843. 8°. 10928
Lady, Memoirs of an. Mrs. A. Grant. New York, 1806. 12°. . 8679
Law, Commentaries on. J. Kent. New York, 1840. 4 v. 8°. . 10714
Life, Traits of. Mrs. S. J. Hale. Philadelphia, 1835. 12°. . . 9635
Lit. Cyclopœdia of. E. A. & G. L. Duyckinck. N. Y. 1855. 2 v. 4°. 8796
Literature, Guide to. N. Trübner. London, 1859. 8°. . . 8833
Literature, Introduction to. E. L. Rice. Cincinnati, 1846. 12°. . 515
Lit. &c., Views and Reviews in. W. G. Simms. N. Y. 1845. 12°. 854
Loyalists to England in the Revolution. L. Sabine. Bost. 1857. 8°. 7833
Monthly Magazine. Vols. 1–4. New York, 1818. 8°. . . . 4787
Museum. Vols. 1–6, 8, 9, 11–13. Phila. 1791. 8°. . . . 2194
Naval Battles. Boston, 1837. 8°. 11446
Naval Heroes. S. P. Waldo. Hartford, 1823. 8°. . . . 8493
Orator, Ed. I. Cooke. (3 copies.) Hartford, 1814. 12°. . . 3348
The same. (2 copies.) 3033
The same. 4854
Orator, Introduction to. Ed. I. Cooke. New Haven, 1812. 12°. 3351
Poems. Litchfield. 12°. 2333
Poetry. Essays on. S. Brown, N. H., 1818. 12°. . . . 3915
Poetry, Specimens of. S. Kettell. Boston, 1829. 3 v. 12°. . 2402
Poets, Selections from. Ed. W. C. Bryant. New York, 1841. 12°. 5573
The same. 5574
Preacher. New Haven, 1793. 8°. 5636
Pulpit, Annals of. W. B. Sprague. New York, 1857–9. 5 v. 8°. 5040
Quarterly Observer. Vols. 1–3. Boston, 1833, 4. 8°. . . 3818
Quarterly Register. Vols. 2-8. Andover, 1830–6. 8°. . . 2583
Quarterly Review. Vols. 1–20. Philadelphia, 1827–36. 8°. . 4493
Register. Vols. 1–7. Philadelphia, 1806–10. 2186
Rejected Addresses. New York, 1855. 12°. 2005
Review. R. Walsh, Jr. Philadelphia, 1811, 12. 8°. . . . 2962
Revolution, Border Wars. W. L. Stone. New York, 1845. 2 v. 12°. 5217
Revolution, Dip. Corresp. of. Ed. J. Sparks. Bost. 1829. 12 v. 8°. 11035
Revolution, Hist. of. P. Allen. Baltimore, 1822. 2 v. 8°. . . 6903
Revolution, Hist. of. C. Botta. Trans. Phila. 1820. 3 v. 8°. . 7213

Ancient Lit. and Art, Essays on. B. Sears and others. Bost. 1849. 12°. . 470
Régime. G. P. R. James. New York, 1842. 2 v. 12°. . . 1566
World; or Sketches of Creation. D. T. Ansted. Phil. 1847. 12°. 6054
Ancients, Essays and Wisdom of. Lord F. Bacon. London, 1836. 12°. . 3356
Anderson, A. History of Commerce. Dublin, 1790. 6 v. 8°. . . 10760
Anderson, Æ. British Embassy to China. New York, 1795. 12°. . . 9044
Anderson, F. Zenaida. Philadelphia, 1858. 12°. 559
Anderson, Jas. The Bee, or Weekly Intelligencer. Edin. 1791–3. 18v. 12°. 4248
Anderson, John. The Course of Creation. Cincinnati, 1851. 12°. . . 6064
Anderson, R. Observations upon the Greek Islands and Peloponnesus, in 1829. Boston, 1830. 12°. 8988
Andersson, C. J. Lake Ngami. New York, 1856. 12°. 9593
Andrew Wylie. New York, 1822. 2 v. 12°. 1390
Andrews, E. A. Latin Exercises. Boston, 1839. 12°. 3928
Slavery in the United States. (Two copies.) Boston, 1836. 12°. . 11166
and S. Stoddard. Latin Grammar. Boston, 1844. 12°. . . 3387
Andrews, S. P., and F. Boyle. Phonographic Reader. N. Y. 1850. 12°. . 4872
Andryane, A. Memoirs of a Prisoner of State. London, 1842. 2 v. 8°. . 8285
Anecdote, Encyclopædia of. W. Oxberry. London, 1821. 3 v. 12°. . 860
Anecdotes. S. and R. Percy. See Percy.
Apician, or Tales of the Table, Kitchen and Larder. N. Y. 1836. 12°. 3341
Biographical, Literary and Political. London, 1797. 3v. 8°. 7969
Historical. J. Barrington. Folio. London, 1809. . . . 11248
Literary and Political. W. King. Boston, 1819. 12°.. . . 11697
of Literature and Scarce Books. W. Beloe. London, 1807. 6v. 8°. 447
Religious, &c. C. Buck. New York, 1841. 12°. 6149
Anglo-Saxon Chronicle. London, 1847. 12°. 5440
Poems. Beowulf and others. Original, with a Trans. of Beowulf, by J. M. Kemble. London, 1835. 2 v. 12°. 2025
Anglo-Saxons, History of the. F. Palgrave. London, 1837. 16°. . . 8760
History of. S. Turner. Philadelphia. 1841. 2 v. 8°. . . . 7579
Animal Chemistry. J. Liebig. Cambridge, 1842. 12°. 6051
Kingdom. G. Cuvier and P. A. Latreille. New York, 1831. 4 v. 8°. 10128
Mechanism and Physiology. J. H. Griscom. New York, 1841. 12°. 5543
Animals, Geography and Classification of. W. Swainson. Lond. 1835. 12°. 9971
Habits and Instincts of. W. Swainson. London, 1840. 12°. . 9979
History of. N. Webster, Jr. New Haven, 1812. 12°. . . . 10173
History and Habits of. W. Kirby. Philadelphia, 1836. 8°. . . 6385
The same. vol. 1. London, 1852. 12°. 5488
in Menageries. W. Swainson. London, 1838. 12°. . . . 9975
Annals of the American Pulpit. W. B. Sprague. N. Y. 1851. 5 v. 8°. . 5040
of the Parish. M. Balwhidder. Philadelphia, 1821. 12°. . . 3375
of the Stage. J. O. Collier. London, 1831. 3 v. 12°. . . . 1109
The same. 1112
Anne of Austria. Memoirs. Mad. de Motteville. Trans. Lond. 1726. 5 v. 12°. 7783
Anne of Geierstein. W. Scott. Philadelphia, 1839. 8°. 44
The same. Philadelphia, 1826. 2 v. 12°. 609
The same. Boston, 1834. 12°. 279

Anne of Geierstein. Philadelphia, 1829. 2 v. 12°. 624
The same. 626
Anne Grey. New York, 1835. 12°. 1252
Queen, Court of. Mrs. A. T. Thomson. London, 1839. 2 v. 8°. 7866
Annual Register. vols. 1–69 and 72–74. London, 1758 to 1832. 8°. . 2610
Index to the same. 2 vols. In the Rack.
Review. A. Aikin. vols. 1–3. London, 1803. 8°. 2205
of Scientific Discovery. Ed. D. A. Wells and G. Bliss. Boston, 1850, 1. 2 v. 12°. 6066
Anquetil, L. P. Memoirs of Court of France, 1643, 1723. Edin. 1791. 2 v. 8°. 8521
Anson, G. Voyage round the World. Edin. 1776. 2 v. 12°. . . 8722
Life. J. Barrow. London, 1839. 8°. 7896
Ansted, D. T. Ancient World, or Sketches of Creation. Phil. 1847. 12°. . 6054
Antar. A Bedoueen Romance. Trans. T. Hamilton. Lond. 1820. 4 v. 12°. 236
Anthologia Græca. Lipsiæ, 1829. 2 v. 16°. 10337
Anthology. Greek Collections from. R. Bland. Lond. 1813. 8°. . 1879
Anthon, C. Greek Grammar. New York, 1838. 12°. 3388
Anthon, C. E. A Pilgrimage to Treves. New York, 1845. 12°. . . 8692
Anthos, or Scriptural Anthology. N. C. Brooks. Phila. 1837. 16°. . 2083
Anti-Christ, Trial of, for High Treason against the Son of God. New York, 1817. 12°. 6546
Antigone of Sophocles. Ed. T. D. Woolsey. Cambridge, 1835. 8°. . 2219
See also Sophocles.
Anti-Jacobin Review. vols. 1–5. London. 1799. 8°. 2171
or Weekly Examiner. vols. 1–2. London, 1799. 8°. . . 2176
Anti-Masonry. See Masonic and Masonry.
Anti-Papal Spirit. See Reformation.
Antiquary, The. W. Scott. Boston, 1834. 12°. 269
The same. Boston, 1845. 12°. 287
The same. Philadelphia, 1826. 2 v. 12°. 581
The same. Boston, 1820. 8°. 1091
The same. Hartford, 1823. 8°. 1084
Antiquities, American, and Origin and Hist. of the Red Race. A. W. Bradford. New York, 1841. 8°. 7594
Encyclopædia of. T. D. Fosbroke. London, 1843. 2 v. 8°. . . 8793
of the Anglo-Saxon Church. J. Lingard. Phila. 1848. 8°. . . 5076
of the Christian Church. L. Coleman. Andover, 1841. 8°. . . 5024
of Great Britain, Popular. J. Brand. London, 1841. 3 v. 12°. . . 1183
The same. London, 1848. 3 v. 12°. 5437
of Nations, Rise & Fall of States. P. Pezron. Tr. Lond. 1809. 16°. 11298
Antiquity, Hist. of the States of. A. H. L. Heeren. Trans. Oxford, 1833. 8°. 7361
The same. Trans. G. Bancroft. New York, 1828. 8°. . 7320
Anti-Slavery. See Slavery.
Antommarchi, F. Derniers Momens de Napoleon. Paris, 1825. 2 v. 8°. . 8209
Antonius, M. A. Commentaria. Lipsiæ, 1829. 16°. 10854
Meditations of. Trans. Bath, 1792. 12°. 3316
Anxious Enquirer after Salvation. J. A. James. New York, 1834. 16°. 6574
Apician Anecdotes, or Tales of the Table, Kitchen, &c. N. Y. 1836. 12°. 3341

Apollodorus. Bibliothecæ. Lipsiæ, 1832. 16°. 10352
Apollonius Rhodius. Argonautica. Lipsiæ, 1829. 16°. 10350
Apostles, Lives of the. D. F. Bacon. New Haven, 1835. 8°. . . . 5023
Lives of the. W. Cave. London, 1834. 2 v. 12°. . . . 5777
Appeal in behalf of the New Jerusalem Church. S. Noble. Bost. 1845. 12°. 5642
Appianus, A. Historiæ. Lipsiæ, 1829. 2 v. 16°. 10569
Appleton, J. Works. Andover, 1837. 2 v. 8°. 6330
Appleton's Cyclopædia of Biography.—See Cyclopædia.
Apprentice, Monitor for. I. Watts and others. Boston, 1808. 8°. . . 3907
Arabella Stuart. A Romance. G. P. R. James. New York, 1844. 8°. . 9
Arabia, Description of. J. Conder. London, 1825. 16°. 9650
The same, ... 9657
History of. A. Crichton. New York, 1834. 2 v. 16°. . . . 6239
Arabian Night's Entertainments. Tr. E. W. Lane. Lond. 1841. 3 v. 8°. . 38
The same. Trans. J. Scott. Philadelphia, 1826. 6 v. 24°. 1739
Arabians, History of the. Abbe de Marigny. Trans. Lond. 1758. 4 v. 8°. 6777
Arabs, Dominion of, in Spain. J. A. Condé. Trans. Lond. 1854. 12°. 3 v. 5186
in Spain. London, 1840. 2 v. 12°. 7682
Residence among the. Mrs. Bradley. Boston, 1820. 12°. . . 8728
The same. Boston, 1821. 12°. 11890
and Turks. History of the. Lond. 1780. 3 v. 8°. . . . 7047
Arasmenes, the Seeker. A Tale. E. L. Bulwer. N. Y. 1833. 18°. . 1690
Ararat, Journey to. F. Parrot. New York, 1846. 12°. 9600
Araucanians, The; or Tour in South. Chili. E. R. Smith. N. Y. 1855. 12°. 9592
Architecture, Painting, &c., Hist. of. J. S. Memes. Boston, 1831. 12°. 10148
The same. 10155
and Painting. Lectures on. J. Ruskin. New York, 1856. 12°. . 10160
Seven Lamps of. J. Ruskin. New York, 1849. 12°. . . . 10159
Arctic Advent. in Search of Sir J. Franklin. E. Sargent. Bost. 1857. 12° 9595
Explorations in Search of Franklin. E. K. Kane. Phila. 1856. 8°. 9396
Second Expedition. Phila. 1857. 2 v. 8°. 9416
Journal, Leaves from. S. Osborn. New York, 1852. 12°. . . 9002
Land Expedition, Narrative of. G. Back. London, 1836. 8°. . 9138
Regions, Voyages in. J. Barrow. New York, 1846. 12°. . . 9268
Argentine Repub. Twenty-four Years in. J. A. King. N. Y. 1846. 12°. 6792
Ariosto, L. Orlando Furioso. Trans. J. Hoole. Lond. 1783. 5 v. 8°. . 1870
Aristophanes. Clouds. A Comedy. Ed. C. C. Felton. Camb. 1841. 8°. 2220
Comœdiæ. Lipsiæ, 1842. 2 v. 16°. 10825
The same. Trans. C. A. Wheelright. Lond. 1837. 2 v. 8°. 1846
The same. Trans. T. Mitchell. Philadelphia, 1822. 2 v. 18°. 2113
Aristotle. Opera. Lipsiæ, 1831. 8v. 16°. 10557
Rhetoric, Ethics and Politics. Trans. T. Taylor. Lond. 1818. 2 v. 8°. 755
Arithmetic, Higher. J. B. Thomson. New York, 1848. 12°. . . . 3335
Practical. G. Wilson. Canandaigua, 1838. 12°. 3037
Treatise on. D. Lardner. London, 1836. 12°. 9956
Arkansas, Travels in. T. Nuttall. Philadelphia, 1821. 8°. . . . 9783
and Missouri, Nat. Hist. of. H. R. Schoolcraft. N. Y. 1819. 8°. . 5984
Armenia, Persia, &c., Tour through. H. Southgate. N. Y. 1840. 2 v. 12°. 9627

Armenia, Persia, &c. Tour through. H. Southgate. N. Y. 1840. 2 v. 12°. 9570

Arminius, J. Life. N. Bangs. New York, 1834. 16°. 8459

Armstrong, J. Life of R. Montgomery. Boston, 1834. 12°. 8068

Life of A. Wayne. Boston, 1834. 12°. 8071

Armstrong, J., (Dr.) The Art of Preserving the Health. Walpole, 1808. 16°. 2476

The same, with other Poems and Life. Phila. 1822. 18°. 2143

Armstrong, J. (Gen.) Notices of the War of 1812. N. Y. 1840. 2 v. 12°. 6799

Armstrong, J. S. and E. S. Trevor. Report of the case of the Queen *vs.* D. O'Connell and others. Dublin, 1844. 8°. 10653

Army, British, Regulations and Orders for. London, 1822. 8°. 11690

British, List of Officers of the. 1824. 8°. 10050

of the U. S., Uniform and Dress of. Philadelphia, 1851. Folio.

Arnault, A. V. and others. Biographie des Contemporains. Paris, 1820. 20 v. 12°. 8862

Memoirs of N. Bonaparte. Trans. (Two copies.) Bost. 1828. 2 v. 16°. 7763

Arnold, B. Life. J. Sparks. Boston, 1834. 12. 8070

Arnold, J. S. Poems. Providence, 1797. 12°. 3043

Arnold, T. History of Rome. London, 1840. 3 v. 8°. 7355

History of the Later Roman Commonwealth. N. Y. 1846. 8°. 7245

Lectures on Modern History. Lond. 1843. 8°. 6995

The same. Ed. H. Reed. New York, 1845. 12°. 6793

Life and Correspondence. A. P. Stanley. N. Y. 1845. 12°. 8319

Miscellaneous Works. New York, 1845. 8°. 58

Rugby School Sermons. (Two copies.) New York, 1846. 12°. 6604

Arnold, W. D. Oakfield; or, Fellowship in the West. Bost. 1855. 12°. 571

The same. 572

Arnott, N. Elements of Physics. Philadelphia, 1831. 2 v. 8°. 5982

Arrianus. Expeditio Alexandri. Lipsiæ, 1829. 16°. 10340

The same. 11285

Art and Industry, World of. B. Silliman, Jr. and others. Illustrated. New York, 1854. 4.°.

Art, Criticisms on. W. Hazlitt. 1843. 2 v. 12°. 10179

of being Happy. J. Droz. Trans. Boston, 1832. 12°. 3392

and Poems, Lectures on. W. Allston. N. Y. 1850. 12°. 10158

of Preserving Health. J. Armstrong. Walpole, 1808. 16°. 2476

of Speaking. London, 1784. 8°. 3292

Artist Life, or, Sketches of American Painters. H. T. Tuckerman. New York, 1847. 12°. 10152

Arthur Arundel. H. Smith. New York, 1844. 8°. 17

Arthur Clenning, Life and Adventures of. Philadelphia, 1828. 2 v. 12°. 1333

Arthur Mervyn. A Tale. C. B. Brown. Boston, 1827. 2 v. 12°. 1000

The same. 1426

Arthur, T. S. Insubordination, and other Tales. Phila. 1844. 8°. 18

Artillery Tactics. Boston, 1829. 12°. 3323

Arts and Artists. Anecdotes, Relics, &c. of. J. Elmes. Lond. 1825. 3 v. 16° 10246

Fine. History of the. B. J. Lossing. N. Y. 1840. 18°. 5563

Manufactures, and Mines. Dictionary of. A. Ure. N. Y. 1843. 8°. 8811

of Design in the U. S., Hist of. W. Dunlap. N. Y. 1844. 2 v. 8°. 10107

Arts of the Ancients. C. Rollin. Trans. London, 1767. 3 v. 8°. . . 10116
and Sciences, Uncertainty and Vanity of the. H. C. Agrippa. 1675. 12°. 3352
and Sciences, Emporium of. Philadelphia, 1812–14. 4 v. 8°. . 2967
Useful, with the Applications of Sci. J. Bigelow. Bost. 1840. 12°. 10150
Vegetable substances used in. Boston, 1830. 12°. . . . 6196
Ashmun, J. Memoirs. R. R. Gurley. Washington, 1835. 8°. . . 7899
The same. 8138
Asia, Discoveries and Travels in. H. Murray. Edin. 1820. 3 v. 3°. . 9107
History, Antiquities, Arts, Sciences, &c. of. W. Jones and others. Vols. 2–5. London, 1796. 8°. 11386
History, Geography, &c. C. Ritter and others. Lond. 1842. 12°. 5935
Minor, Description of. J. Conder. London, 1824. 2 v. 16°. . . 9647
The same. 9667
South-Eastern, Travels in. H. Malcom. Boston, 1829. 2 v. 12°. 9568
Travels in, See Clarke, E. D.
Asiatic Annual Register, 1799–1811. London. 13 v. 8°. 2570
Nations, Ancient. Politics, Intercourse and Trade of. A. H. L. Heeren. Trans. Oxford, 1837. 3 v. 8°. 10683
Asmodeus at Large. E. L. Bulwer. Philadelphia, 1833. 12°. . . . 246
The same. 1131
Assyria. J. B. Fraser. New York, 1845. 12°. 5209
Babylonia, &c., Researches in. W. Ainsworth. London, 1838. 8°. 9777
Assyrians, History of the. London, 1779. 8°. 7031
Astoria. W. Irving. Philadelphia, 1836. 2 v. 8°. 9187
The same. New York, 1851. 12°. 535
Astræa. O. W. Holmes. Boston, 1850. 12°. 2330
Astronomer, The Practical. T. Dick. New York, 1846. 12°. . . . 6093
Astronomical Expedition to the S. Hemisphere. See U. S. Pub. Documents.
Astronomy, &c. applied to Nat. Theol. W. Whewell. Phila. 1833. 12°. 6485
Compendium of. J. Vose. Boston, 1834. 12°. 6091
Grammar of. J. Bryan. New York, 1825. 12°. 6096
Improved. N. Strong. New Haven, 1784. 12°. 4558
Introduction to. J. Ferguson. Philadelphia, 1805. 12°. . . 6097
Introduction to. D. Olmsted. New York, 1839. 8°. 5985
Manual of. A. Pettengill. New Haven, 1826. 16°. 4284
Recent Progress of. E. Loomis. New York, 1850. 12°. . . . 5998
Treatise on. J. Farrar. Cambridge, 1827. 8°. 5942
Treatise on. O. Gregory. Cambridge, 1811. 8°. 6003
Treatise on. J. F. W. Herschell. London, 1838. 12°. . . . 9957
and Geology. First Lessons in. H. L. Smith. Cleveland, 1848. 12°. 6071
Athanasion, and other Poems. A. C. Coxe. New York, 1842. 12°. . 2216
Atheists, Voltaire and Rousseau against the. Trans. N. Y. 1845. 12°. . 5672
The same. 5676
Athenæus. Deiphnosophistæ. Lipsiæ, 1834. 2 v. 16°. 10565
Atheneum, 1817-25. vols. 1-16. Boston. 8°. 4074
by the Students of Yale. New Haven, 1814. 8°. . . . 2973
Athenian Captive. T. N. Talfourd. New York, 1838. 12°. 2334

Athens. Public Economy of. A. Bœckh. Trans. London, 1842. 8°. . 7605

Atkinson, J. Epitome of the Art of Navigation. London, 1762. 12°. . 4878

Atonement and Sacrifice, Discourses on. W. Magee. N. Y. 1839. 2 v. 8°. 5050

Atterbury, F. (Bishop.) Sermons. London, 1723. 2 v. 8°. . . . 6449

Attila. G. P. R. James. New York, 1837. 2 v. 12°. 995

Atwater, C. Tour to Prarie du Chien. Columbus. 1831. 12°. . . 9304

Augustine, St., Confessions of. New York, 1844. 12°. 6141

The same. 6145

Augustinism and Pelaginism. G. F. Wiggers. Trans. R. Emerson. New York, 1840. 8°. 6378

Augustus, the Ambitious Student. London, 1820. 8°. 130

Aurelius, Victor S. Historia Romana. Lipsiæ. 1829. 16°. . . . 10857

Aurora Leigh. Mrs. E. B. Browning. New York, 1857. 12°. . . . 1984

Austen, Miss J. Mansfield Park. Philadelphia, 1832. 2 v. 12°. . . 1515

Northanger Abbey. Philadelphia, 1833. 2 v. 12°. 928

The same. 1451

Novels. Philadelphia, 1838. 8°. 37

Persuasion. Philadelphia, 1832. 2 v. 12°. 1440

Sense and Sensibility. Philadelphia, 1833. 2 v. 12°. . . . 1517

Austin, J. T. Life of E. Gerry. Boston, 1828. 8°. 7921

Austral-Asia, History of. R. M. Martin. London, 1839. 12°. . . . 5821

Australia, Two Expeditions into, in 1828-31. C. Sturt. Lond. 1834. 2 v. 8°. 9397

Australia, Felix, Impressions of. R. Howitt. London, 1845. 12°. . 9028

Australian Expedition. T. L. Mitchell. London, 1839. 2 v. 8°. . . 9437

Austria, Anne of. Memoirs. Mad. de Motteville. Tr. Lond. 1726. 5 v. 12°.

as it is, or Sketches of Continental Courts. London, 1828. 8°. . 8975

in 1848-49. W. H. Stiles. New York, 1852. 2 v. 8°. 9412

The House of. 1218-1792. W. Coxe. London, 1847. 3 v. 12°. . 5163

Travels in. P. E. Turnbull. London, 1840. 2 v. 8°. . . . 9140

Authors, Dictionary of. S. A. Allibone. Philadelphia, 1859. 2 v. 4°. . 9673

Autobiography. London, 1830–2. (vols. 25, 27, 32 missing,) 33 v. 16°. . 7480

Vol. 1. C. Cibber.
2. D Hume, W. Lilly, F. M. A. de Voltaire.
3, 4. J. Marmontel.
5. R. Drury.
6. G. Whitefield, J. Ferguson.
7. Mrs. M. Robinson, Mrs. C. Charke.
8. Lord Herbert of Cherbury, Prince Eugene of Savoy.
9, 10. A Von Ko tzebue.
11. S. Creichton, W. Gifford, T. Ellwood.
12. L. Holberg.
Vol. 13. J H. Vaux.
14, 15. E. Gibbon.
16, 17. B Cellini.
18. J. Lackington.
19 T. W. Tone.
20, 1. Margravine of Bareith.
22. G. B. Doddington.
23, 4. C. Goldoni.
25-- 8. E. F. Vidocq.
29 -32. Madame du Barri.
33. W. Sampson.

The same, (vols. 1–11.) 7745

Autobiographic Sketches. T. De Quincey. Boston, 1855. 12°. . . 880

Ava, Embassy to. J. Crawfurd. London, 1834. 7v. 8°. 9136

Embassy to, in 1795. M. Symes. Ed. H. G. Bell. Edin. 1827. 2 v. 9993

Avianus, F., Fabulæ. M. Lipsiæ, 1829. 16°. 10858

Aytoun, W. E. Life and Times of Richard the First. Lond. 1840. 16°. . 8769

B.

Babajee, the Converted Brahmun, Memoirs. H. Read. N. Y. 1836. 2 v. 12°. 5693
Babbage, C., A Fragment, or Infidelity Refuted. Philadelphia, 1841. 8°. 6386
Babington, T. Christian Education. Boston, 1819. 12°. . . . 6550
Babylonians, History of the. London, 1779. 8°. 7031
Bacchus. Prize Essay. R. B. Grindrod. New York, 1840. 12°. . . 514
Bachelor of the Albany. M. W. Savage. New York, 1848. 12°. . . 1568
Bachelor of Salamanca. A. R. Le Sage. Tr. Philadelphia, 1854. 2 v. 12°. 360
Bachelors, The. S. L. Knapp. New York, 1836. 12°. 1227
Back, G. Arctic Land Expedition in 1833–5. London, 1836. 8°. . . 9138
Backus, C. Doctrine of Regeneration. Hartford, 1800. 12°. . . . 6600
Bacon, D. F. Lives of the Apostles. New Haven, 1835. 8°. . . . 5023
Bacon, F. Essays. Moral, Political, &c. Boston, 1820. 18°. . . 4631
The same. London, 1804. 16°. 4297
The same. New York, 1823. 18°. 4637
The same. New York, 1845. 12°. 5221
The same. Boston, 1828. 18°. 4614
Essays, with Annotations, by R. Whately. New York, 1857. 8°. . 25
Essays, and Wisdom of the Ancients. London, 1836. 16°. . . 3356
Novum Organum. Trans. London, 1802. 2 v. 16°. . . . 4977
Works, with life. London, 1824. 10 v. 8°. 6013

Vol. 1. Life; Proficiency and Advancement of Learning, Divine and Human; Sylva Sylvarum, or a Natural History.
2. Sylva Sylvarum concluded; Physiological and Medical Remains; Moral and Theological Works.
3. Political Works.
4. Law Tracts.
5. Historical Works.
6. Letters, Speeches, Charges, Advices, &c.; Index to the first six volumes.
7. Auctoris Vita; De Dignitate, et Augmentis Scientiarum.
8. Novum Organum; Historia Naturalis et Experimentalis; Fragmentum, etc.; Historia Ventorum; Historia Vitæ et Mortis.
9. Historia Densi et Rari, etc.; Historia Sulphuris Mercurii et Salis. Articuli Quæstionum circa Mineralia; Cogitationes de Natura Rerum. Cogitata et Visa; Descriptio globi Intellectualis; Historia Regni Henrici Septimi.
10. Sermones Fideles; Epistolæ; Index in Voluminibus, VII.—X.

Writings, and Philosophy of. Ed. G. L. Clark. Lond. 1846. 2 v. 12°. 7166
Bacon, J. Life and Times of Francis I. London, 1830. 2v. 8°. . . 7519
The same. 7521
Bacon, L. Historical Discourses on the colony of N. H. N. H. 1839. 8°. 7638
Manual for Young Church Members. New Haven, 1838. 16°. . 6225
Occasional Essays on Slavery. New York, 1846. 12°. . . . 5421
Bacon, Miss D. Bride of Fort Edward. New York, 1839. 12°. . . 1569
Tales of the Puritans. New Haven, 1831. 12°. 651
Bacon, W. T. Poems. Boston, 1837. 12°. 2355
Bailey, P. J. Festus, a Poem. Boston, 1845. 12°. 2275
Mystic and other Poems. Boston, 1855. 12°. 1995
Baillie, Joanna. Plays and Poetical Works. Philadelphia, 1832. 8°. . 1820
Baines, E. History of the Wars of the French Revolution, with maps. Philadelphia, 1835. 3 v. 8°. 7276

Baird, H. M. Residence in Modern Greece. New York, 1856. 12°. . 9584
Baird, R. Christian Retrospect and Register. New York, 1851. 12°. . 5771
Life of R. Monsalvatge. New York, 1845. 16°. 8460
Visit to Northern Europe. New York, 1841. 2 v. 12°. 8918
The same. 8978
Baker, D. E. and others. Biographia Dramatica, to 1811. Lond. 1812. 4 v. 8°. 8856
Bakewell, R. Introduction to Geology. New Haven, 1829. 8°. . . . 5955
Balboa, V. N. de, Life of. Boston, 1840. 16°. 7774
Baldwin, E. Annals of Yale College. New Haven, 1831. 8°. . . . 11338
The same. 11350
Baldwin, T. Balloon Excursion. Narrative of. London, 1786. 8°. . 9724
Ballads, Old, Historical, &c. T. and R. H. Evans. Lond. 1810. 4 v. 16°. 1978
Pictorial Book of. Ed. J. S. Moore. Philadelphia, 1847. 2 v. 8°. 1844
Ballard, G. Memoirs of Several Literary Ladies of Eng. Ox. 1752. 8°. . 7807
Balloon Excursion, Narrative of. T. Baldwin. London, 1786. 8°. . 9724
Ballston Springs, a Poem. New York, 1806. 12°. 3053
and Saratoga, A Poem on the Waters of. R. Sears. Balls. 1819. 16°. 3069
Balmes, J. Protestantism and Catholicity of Europe. Balt. 1851. 8°. . 5046
Baltimore, Siege of, and other Poems. A. Umphraville. Balt. 1817. 12°. 11891
Balwhidder, M. Annals of the Parish. Philadelphia, 1821. 12°. . . 3375
Bampton Lectures. E. Hawkins. Oxford, 1840. 8°. 5036
Bancroft, G. History of United States from 1492. Bost. 1841–58. 7 v. 8°. 7566
Literary and Historical Miscellanies. New York, 1855. 8°. . . 35
Bandit's Bride, The. S. S. Stanhope. 1831. 3 v. 18°. 334
Banditti and Robbers of all Nations, Lives. C. Mac Farlane. Phil. 1833. 12°. 8078
The same. Philadelphia, 1839. 2 v. 12°. 8685
Banfield, T. C. Industry of the Rhine. London, 1846. 16°. . . . 7179
Bangs, N. Life of Arminius. New York, 1834. 16°. 8459
Banim, J. Croppy. Philadelphia, 1839. 2 v. 12°. 1314
Mayor of Wind-Gap. Philadelphia, 1835. 12°. 261
The same. New York, 1835. 12°. 1316
The same. 1317
The Smuggler. New York, 1832. 2 v. 12°. 1011
Banking in America, History of. J. W. Gilbart. London, 1837. 8°. . 10495
Practical Treatise on. J. W. Gilbart. London, 1836. 8°. . . 10060
Bankrupt Stories. Harry Franco. New York, 1844. 8°. 1053
Banks, J., and others, Letters from Iceland. London, 1780. 8°. . . 9455
Banks of Europe and America, History of. T. H. Goddard. Lond. 1836. 8°. 10662
and Money. Theory of. G. Tucker. Boston, 1839. 12°. . . 10812
of Wye. R. Bloomfield. London, 1823. 12°. 2028
The same. New York, 1812. 18°. 11284
Bannister, J. Memoirs. J. Adolphus. London, 1839. 2 v. 8°. . . 7911
Bannockburn, Miss J. Porter. Philadelphia, 1822. 2 v. 12°. . . . 1409
Banvard, J., Life of D. Webster. Boston, 1853. 12°. 8072
Baptism, Debate on. A. Campbell and J. Walker. Steubenville, 1820. 12°. 6492
Exposition of. E. Hall. New York, 1840. 16°. 6226
Baptists in America. F. A. Cox and J. Hoby. New York, 1836. 12°. . 5393
The same. 5391

Barbary States, Hist. and Present Condition of. M. Russell. N.Y. 1835. 12°. 5884
The same. New York, 1835. 16°. 8770
Travels in. M. M. Noah. New York, 1819. 8°. 9178
Barbacovi, F. V. Literary History of Italy. Trans. Edin. 1835. 12°. . 4882
Barbauld, Anna L. Works, with Memoir. New York, 1826. 2 v. 12°. . 4865
Barber, J. Grammar of Elocution. New Haven, 1830. 12°. . . . 3332
Barber J. W. Historical Collections of Massachusetts. Worcester, 1841. 8°. 6690
Interesting Events in the Hist. of the U. States. N. Haven, 1828. 12°. 6848
and H. Howe. Historical Collections of N. J. New York, 1844. 8°. 6689
Barca, Madame C. de La. Life in Mexico. Boston, 1843. 2 v. 12°. . 9244
Bards of the Bible. G. Gilfillan. New York, 1851. 12°. . . . 5406
Bareith, Margravine of. Autobiography. London, 1828. 2 v. 18°. . . 7499
Barlow, J. Columbiad. Philadelphia, 1807. 4°. . . . . . .
The same. Philadelphia, 1809. 2 v. 12°. 2323
Vision of Columbus. Hartford, 1787. 12°. 1905
The same . . . . . , ... 2430
The same . . . . . . , ... 2450
Barnabee's Journal. London, 1818. 12° 2491
Barnaby Rudge. Charles Dickens. Philadelphia. 8°. 68
The same. New York, 1842. 12°. 658
Barnard, H. Conn. Com. School Journal for 1838–42. Hart. 1842. 4°. 9701
Journal of the R. I. Institute of Instruction. Providence, 1846. 8°. 10088
Normal Schools, &c. Hartford, 1851. 8°. 10090
Report of Public Schools of Rhode Island for 1845. Prov. 1846. 8°. 10086
Tribute to T. H. Gallaudet. Hartford, 1852. 8°. 11311
Barnes, A. Defense before the 2d Presbytery of Phila. N. Y. 1836. 12°. 5707
Notes on the Acts of the Apostles. New York, 1841. 12°. . . 6179
Notes on I. Corinthians. New York, 1841. 12°. 5727
Notes on II. Corinthians and Galatians. New York, 1841. 12° . 5728
Notes on the Gospels. New York, 1841. 2 v. 12°. 5735
Notes on Hebrews. New York, 1843. 12° 5729
Notes on Isaiah, with a New Translation. Boston, 1840. 3 v. 8°. . 5017
Notes on Revelation. New York, 1852. 12°. 5737
Notes on Romans. New York, 1841. 12°. 5726
Practical Sermons. Philadelphia, 1841. 12°. 5680
Scriptural View of Slavery. Philadelphia, 1846. 12°. . . . 5417
Sermons on Revivals. New York, 1841. 12°. . . . 6211
Trial of. New York, 1836. 12°. 6559
Way of Salvation, a Sermon. New York, 1836. 12°. . . . 5707
Barnet, F. Autobiog. and Review of "No Fiction." Bost. 1823. 2 v. 16°. 8444
Barnham, R. H. D. My Cousin Nicholas. London, 1848. 2 v. 12°. . 1457
Barnum, H. L. The Spy Unmasked. New York, 1828. 8°. . . . 8569
Barnum, P. T. Autobiography. New York, 1855. 12°. 8340
Baron, J. Life of E. Jenner. London, 1838. 2 v. 8°. 7525
Barrett, Elizabeth B. Drama of Exile, &c. New York, 1845. 2 v. 12°. . 2013
See also, Browning. Mrs. E. B.
Barri, Madame Du. Autobiography. (vol. 4 missing.) London, 1830. 4 v. 16°. 7506
Barrington, D. Possibillity of approaching the North Pole. N. Y., 1818. 8°. 10081

Barrington, J. Historical Anecdotes. London, 1809. Folio. . . . 11248
Barrow, I. Sermons. London, 1830. 5 v. 12°. 5757
Treatise on the Pope's Supremacy. New York, 1844. 8°. . . 5316
Barrow, J. Life of Lord G. Anson. London, 1839. 8°. 7896
Life of Admiral Howe. London, 1838. 8°. 7897
Life of Peter the Great. New York, 1841. 12°. 5881
Pitcairn's Island and its Inhabitans. New York, 1832. 16°. . . 6616
The same. New York, 1840. 12°. 5532
Travels in China. Philadelphia, 1805. 8°. . , ... 9454
Travels in South Africa. New York, 1802. 8°. 9457
Voyages in the Arctic Regions. New York, 1846. 12°. . . 9268
Barrows, E. P., Jr. Memoirs of E. Judson. Boston, 1852. 12°. . . 8335
Barry, J. J. Opie and H. Fuseli. Lectures on Painting. Lond. 1848. 12°. 5486
Barry, Cornwall. See Proctor, W. B.
Bartlett, D. W. What I Saw in London. Auburn, 1852. 12°. . . . 8891
Bartlett, J. R. Explorations in Texas, California, &c. N. Y. 1854. 2 v. 8°. 9376
Bartlett, M. R. Practical Reader. New York, 1822. 12°. . . . 3041
Basil Barrington and his Friends. London, 1830. 3 v. 12°. . . . 140
Bastile and its Captives, History of the. R. A. Davenport. Lond. 1839. 16°. 7479
Bates, W. Spiritual Perfection Unfolded and Enforced. Lond. 1834. 12°. 5779
Battle of Life. Charles Dickens. New York, 1846. 8°. 97
Battle of Finnes-Burh. Anglo-Saxon Poem. London, 1835. 12°. . . 2025
Summer. D. G. Mitchell. New York, 1850. 12°. 216
The same. New York, 1859. 12°. 213
Bausset, L. F. J. de. Life of Fenelon. Trans. London, 1810. 2 v. 8°. . 7947
Memoirs of the Court of Napoleon Bonaparte. Tr. Phil. 1828. 8°. 7509
Baviad and Mæviad. W. Gifford. New York, 1800. 16°. . . . 2490
Baxter, G. R. W. Humor and Pathos. London, 1842. 12°. . . . 1127
Baxter, R. Call to the Unconverted. New York, 1839. 16°. . . . 6230
Christian Directory. London, 1678. Folio. 11243
Dying Thoughts. London, 1834. 12°. 5781
The same. New York. 18°. 5227
Enquiry into the Nature of the Soul. London, 1745. 2 v. 8°. . 6411
Appendix to the same. London, 1750. 12°. 5667
Jesuit Juggling, Forty Popish Frauds Detected and Disclosed. (Two copies.) New York, 1835. 12°. 6444
Reformed Pastor. 1776. 12°. 6516
Saints' Rest. Abriged. Ed. B. Fawcett. New York. 16°. . . 5226
The same. Philadelphia, 1831. 16°. 6232
Bayley, J. History of the Tower of London. London, 1830. 8°. . . 7537
Beach, A. B. Claret and Olives. New York, 1852. 12°. 1186
Beach, S. B. Escalala, a Tale. Utica, 1824. 12°. 2286
Beale, T. Natural History of the Sperm Whale. London. 1839. 12°. . 3923
Bean, J. Advice to a New Married Couple. Greenfield, 1821. 16°. . 11290
Beattie, J. Account of Life and Writings. W. Forbes. New York, 1807. 8°. 8518
Dissertations. Dublin, 1783. 2 v. 8°. 6402
Essays on Poetry. London, 1779. 8°. 154
Essays on Truth. Dublin, 1783. 12°. 4321

Beattie, J. Minstrel. Philadelphia, 1787. 18°. 2478
The same, with other Poems. New York, 1802. 16°. . . 2481
Moral Science, Elements of. vol. 1. Dublin, 1787. 8°. . . . 6409
Poetical Works. (Two copies.) Philadelphia, 1836. 8°. . . 1858
Select Poems and Life. Philadelphia, 1822. 18°. 2144
Beattie, W. Life and Letters of Thos. Campbell. New York, 1850. 2 v. 12°. 7993
Beaumarchais and His Times. L. de Loménie. Trans. N. Y. 1857. 12°. 7395
Beaumont, F., and J. Fletcher. Selections. Ed. L. Hunt. Lond. 1855. 12°. 5169
Works of. London, 1840. 2 v. 8°. 1804
Beaumont, G. de. Ireland, Social, Political, &c. Ed. W. C. Taylor. London, 1839. 2 v. 12°. 9552
and A. de Tocqueville. Penitentiary System of U. S. Phil. 1833. 8°. 10068
Beaumont, Madame Le Prince de. Farmer's, &c., Magazine. Translated. New York, 1812. 2 v. 16°. 3088
Beaumont, W. Observ. on Gastric Juice, Digestion, &c. Bost. 1834. 8°. 401
Beauties of the British Poets. New York, 1827. 16°. 3090
of Burke. Ed. A. Howard. London. 18°. 4946
of Byron. Philadelphia, 1826. 16°. 2074
of Chesterfield. Boston, 1828. 18°. 4620
The same. 11150
of the Magazines. London, 1772. 12°. 4895
of the Poets. Ed. Roach. London, 1794. 12°. 3054
of Scott and Moore. Ed. B. F. French. Philadelphia, 1828. 16°. 2075
of Shakespeare. Ed. W. Dodd. Philadelphia, 1830. 16°. . . 3081
of the Waverly Novels. Boston, 1828. 24°. 1750
of White. Boston, 1827. 16°. 2072
Beccaria, C. B. Crimes and Punishments. Edinburgh, 1788. 12°. . . 3893
Beche, H. T. DeLa. Geological Manual. Philadelphia, 1832. 8°. . . 5986
Beck, L. C. Mineralogy of New York. Albany, 1842. 4°. . . . 13106
Becker, W. A. Charicles, or Private Life of Greeks. Tr. Lond. 1844. 8°. 11404
Gallus, or Roman Scenes. Trans. F. Metcalfe. London, 1844. 8°. 11403
Beckford, W. Excursion to the Monasteries. Philadelphia, 1835. 12°. . 9617
Italy, with Sketches of Spain and Portugal. Phil. 1834. 2 v. 12°. 9293
Beckman, J. History of Inventions and Discoveries. Trans. W. Johnston. London, 1817. 4 v. 8°. 762
The same. London, 1846. 2 v. 12°. 5161
Beckworth, J. P. Life and Adventures. T. D. Bonner. N. Y. 1856. 12°. 8016
Becon, T. Writings of. London. 12°. 5661
Bede, The Venerable. Ecclesiastical Hist. of England. Lond. 1847. 12°. 5440
Bedell, G. T. Memoirs. S. H. Tyng. Philadelphia, 1836. 12°. . . 8309
The same. 8681
Bee, The. A Collection of Essays. O. Goldsmith. Boston, 1820. 18°. . 4629
or Weekly Intelligencer. J. Anderson. Edin. 1791, 2. 18 v. 12°. . 4248
Beecher, H. W. Lectures to Young Men. Salem, 1846. 12°. . . . 1158
The same. 1159
Life Thoughts. Boston, 1858. 12°. 5722
Star Papers. New York, 1855. 12°. 5772
Beecher, L. Lectures on Scepticism. Cincinnati, 1835. 12°. . . . 6122

Beecher, L. Plea for the West. New York, 1835. 12°. 6176
Sermons. New York, 1842. 8°. 5065
Six Sermons on Intemperance. Boston, 1830. 16°. . . . 4288
Views in Theology. Cincinnatti, 1836. 5708
Works of. Boston, 1852. 3 v. 12°. 5716

Vol. 1. Lectures on Political Atheism; Six Lectures on Intemperance.
2. Sermons on Various Occasions.
3. Views of Theology; Trial before Presbytery; Remarks on the Princeton Review.

Beechey, H. Memoirs of Sir J. Reynolds, London, 1835. 16°. . . 7735
Bees, Natural History of. F. Huber. London, 1841. 12°. . . . 10156
Beethoven, L. V. Life. I. Moscheles. London, 1841. 2 v. 12°. . . 8272
Beilby, T. Evidences of Christian Revelation. New York, 1801. 12°. . 3904
Belden, L. W. Account of Miss J. C. Rider. Springfield, 1834. 12°. . 8439
Belgium. J. E. Tennent. London, 1841. 2 v. 12°. 9541
and Western Germany, in 1833. Mrs. Trollope. Phil. 1834. 8°. . 9103
Holland, &c., Tour through. J. Mitchell. Lond. 1816. 8°. . 9769
Belisarius. Life. Lord Mahon. Philadelphia, 1832. 12°. . . . 8411
Belisarius, a Romance. Madame de Genlis. Philadelphia, 1810. 12°. . 1506
Bellknap, J. American Biography. Boston, 1794. 2 v. 8°. . . . 8588
The same. New York, 1846. 3 v. 12°. 5212
History of New Hampshire. Boston, 1792. 3 v. 8°. . . . 6781
Bell, C. Mechanism of the Hand. Philadelphia, 1833. 12°. . . . 6484
Bell, H. G. Life of Mary, Queen of Scots. New York, 1831. 2 v. 16°. 6637
The same. New York 1840. 2 v. 12°. 5525
Phenomena of Nature. Edinburgh, 1827. 16°. 9997
Bell, J. Discourses on Nature and Cure of Wounds. Walpole, 1807. 2 v. 8°. 426
Bell, R. History of Russia. London, 1836. 12°. 9871
Life of G. Canning. New York, 1846. 12°. 7729
Lives of the English Poets. London, 1849. 2 v. 12°. . . . 9945
Bell, S. Tales of Travel West of the Mississippi. Boston, 1830. 16°. . 9321
Bells and Pomegranates. R. Browning. London, 1841. 8°. . . . 1790
Belles Lettres, Method of Studying. C. Rollin. London, 1759. 2 v. 12°. 4908
Sexagenarian. London, 1818. 2 v. 8°. 757
Beloe, W. Anecdotes of Literature and Scarce Books. London, 1807. 6 v. 8°. 447
Belsham, W. Memoirs of George III. Dublin, 1796. 2 v. 8°. . . 8224
Belshazzar, a Dramatic Poem. H. H. Milman. London, 1840. 18°. . . 2031
Ben Brace. F. Chamier. Philadelphia, 1836. 2 v. 12°. . . . 1289
Beneficence, Divine Law of. P. Cooke. 16°. 6215
Benevolence, Philosophy of. P. Church. New York, 1836. 12°. . . 6465
Benger, Miss E. O. Memoirs of Anne Boleyn. Philadelphia, 1822. 8°. . 8245
Bennett, John. Letters to a Young Lady. New York, 1830. 24°. . 11283
Bentham, J. Defense of Usury, &c. London, 1818. 12°. . . . 11187
The same. Philadelphia, 1796. 16°. 11154
Principles of Legislation. Boston, 1830. 2 v. 8°. . . . 11139
Works. Edinburgh, 1838–43. 22 v. 8°. 10938

Vol. 1. Principles of Morals and Legislation; Essay on the Promulgation of Laws; Influence of Time and Place in Legislation; Table of the Springs of Action; Fragment on Government.

2. The last concluded; Principles of the Civil Code; Principles of Penal Law.
3. View of the Hard-Labour Bill; Panopticon; Plea for the Constitution; Draught of a Code for a Judicial Establishment in France.

Bentham, J. Works. Edinburgh. 1838–43. (*Continued.*)

4. Bentham's Draught compared with the Assembly's; Emancipate your Colonies; Houses of Peers and Senates; Codification Proposal.
5. Scotch Reform; View of the Plan of a Judicatory; Art of Packing Juries; Swear not at all; Truth *versus* Ashhurst; King against Edmonds, &c.; King against Wolseley, &c.; Official Aptitude Maximized—Expense minimized.
6. The Last Concluded; Commentary on Humphrey's Real Property Code; Plan of a General Register of Real Property; Justice and Codification Petitions; Lord Brougham Displayed.
7. Principles of Judicial Procedure: Rationale of Reward; Leading Principles of a Constitutional Code; Liberty of the Press.
8. Political Tactics; Book of Fallacies; Anarchical Fallacies; Principles of International Law; Junctiana Proposal; Protest againt Law Taxes; Supply without Burden; Tax with Monopoly.
9. Defense of Usury; Manual of Political Economy; Conversion of Stock into Note Annuities; Restrictive and Prohibitory Commercial System; View of a Complete Code of Laws; Pannomial Fragments; Nomography; Logical Arrangements.
10. Equity Dispatch Court Proposal; Equity Dispatch Court Bill; Plan of Parliamentary Reform; Radical Reform Bill; Radicalism not Dangerous.

11—14. Rationale of Judicial Evidence.
15. Chrestomathia; Fragment on Ontology; Essay on Logic.
16. Language; Universal Grammar; Tracts on Poor Law; Tracts on Spanish and Portuguese Affairs; Letters on the Spanish Code; Reformation Projects in Relation to Tripoli.
17—18 Constitutional Code.
19—20. Memoirs of Bentham by J. Bowring, including Autobiographical Conversations and Correspondence.
21. The same Concluded.; General Index.
22. The last Concluded; Introduction to the Study of Bentham's Works, by J. H. Burton.

Benthamiana, or Extracts from J. Bentham. J. H. Burton. Phil. 1844. 12°. 781
Bentley's Miscellany. Amer. Ed. vols. 3–6, 8, 9. New York, 1837–42. 8°. 3748
Bentley, R. Works. Ed. A. Dyce. London, 1836. 3 v. 8°. . . . 378
The same. 381

Vol. 1. Dissertations upon the Epistles of Phalaris.
2. Theological Works.

Benton, T. Thirty year's View, or History of the American Government for thirty years. New York, 1854. 2 v. 8°. 10934
Benvenuto, Cellini. Memoirs of Himself. Tr. T. Roscoe. Lond, 1850. 12°. 5424
The same. London, 1847. 12°. 5425
Beowulf. Anglo-Saxon Poem. Ed. J. M. Kemble. London, 1835. 12°. 2025
The same, Translated by J. M. Kemble. Lond. 1835. 12°. 2026
Benyowsky, M. A. de. Memoirs and Travels in Poland, Siberia, &c. Trans. Dublin, 1790. 2 v. 8°. 9185
Beranger, P. J. de. Songs. Trans. Philadelphia, 1844. 12°. . . 2342
Berber, The. A Tale of Morocco. W. S. Mayo. New York, 1850. 12°. 250
Berg, J. F. Lectures on Romanism. Philadelphia, 1840. 12°. . . 5715
Berington, J. Lives of Abellaird and Heloisa. London, 1815. 4°. . . 11256
Literary Hist. of the Middle Ages. London, 1846. 12°. . . 5496
Berkeley, Elizabeth. Autobiography. London, 1826. 2 v. 8°. . . 7964
Berkeley, G. Alciphron, or the Minute Philosopher. London, 1767. 12°. . 6433
Works. Complete in one vol. London, 1837. 8°. . . . 6324
Works. London, 1820. 3 v. 8°. 6035
Berkeley, Mrs. H. Memoirs of Madame D'Arblay. New York, 1844. 12°. 7454
Berlin, Secret Hist. of Court of. H. G. R. Mirabeau. Tr. Dublin, 1789. 8°. 6742

Bermingham, J. Memoir of T. Matthew. New York, 1841. 12°. . . 11455
Bernier, F. Travels in the Mogul Empire. London, 1826. 2 v. 8°. . . 9486
Berri, Duchess of, in La Vendee. Gen. Dermoncourt. Tr. Lond. 1833. 8°. 7917
Berthollet, C. L. Laws of Chemical Affinity. Trans. Balt. 1809. 12°. 6090
Bethel Flag, The. G. Spring. New York, 1848. 12°. 5419
Bethune, G. W Sermons. Philadelphia, 1846. 8°. 5307
Beveridge, W. Thoughts on Religion & Christ. Life. Lond. 1834. 2 v. 12°. 5783
Beza, T. Life of J. Calvin. Trans. Philadelphia, 1836. 12°. 8687
Bible, Apology for, in Letters addressed to T. Paine. R. Watson. New York, 1835. 8°. 6424
Commentary on. A. Clarke. (vol. 2 missing.) N. Y. 1840. 5 v. 4°. 4992
in the Counting House. H. A. Boardman. Phil. 1859. 12°. . 6151
Dictionary of. A. Calmet. Ed. E. Robinson. Bost. 1832. 8°. . 8795
Exposition of. M. Henry. New York, 1831. 6 v. 8°. . . 5301
The same. Philadelphia, 1833. 6 v. 8°. 5295
in the Family. H. A. Boardman. Philadelphia, 1859. 12°. . . 6150
Historical Geography of. L. Coleman. Philadelphia, 1850. 12°. . 3310
History of the. G. R. Gleig. New York, 1833. 2 v. 16°. . . 6247
The same. New York, 1830. 2 v. 16°. 6249
The same. New York, 1841. 2 v. 12°. 5514
History of the. R. Sears. (2 copies.) New York, 1844, 5. 8°. . 7598
History of the Eng. Trans. Mrs. H. C. Conant. N. Y. 1856. 12°. 5773
History of Prayer. Hartford, 1848. 12°. 5645
Inspiration of the. S. R. L. Gaussen. Trans. N. Y. 1842. 12°. . 5710
with Notes and Observations. Ed. T. Scott. Boston, 1830. 6 v. 4°. 4998
Obligations of the World to. G. Spring. New York, 1839. 8°. . 5586
Religion of the. T. H. Skinner. New York, 1839. 12°. . . 5704
Society, British and Foreign Hist. of. J. Owen. New York, 1817. 8°. 6423
Study of. T. H. Horne. Boston, 1837. 12°. 6118
The same. New York, 1833. 12°. 6153
Thoughts on the. H. Melvill. New York, 1841. 16°. . . 5241
See also Scriptures.
Biblical Archæology. J. Jahn. Trans. T. C. Upham. N. Y. 1832. 8°. . 5077
Literature. Cyclopædia of. J. Kitto. N. Y. 1846. 2 v. 8°. . . 8807
Repository. vols. 1, 2, 11, 12. Andover and N. Y. 1831–8. 8°. . 2535
New Series. vols. 1–12. N. Y. 1839–44. 8°. 2539
Third Series. See Bibliotheca Sacra.
Researches in Palestine, &c., 1838. E. Robinson. Bost. 1841. 3 v. 8°. 9074
The same, with Maps. Boston, 1856. 4 v. 8°. 9378
Theology. T. C. Storr and C. C. Flatt. Trans. And. 1826. 2 v. 8°. 5352
Bibliomania. T. F. Dibdin. London, 1809. 8°. 425
Bibliotheca Sacra. 3d Series of Biblical Repository. vols. 1–16. (Continued.) N. Y. 1845–59. 8° 2550
Bibliotheque Ancienne et Modern. (vol. 2 missing.) Ams. 1714. 29 v. 16°. 11214
Bickersteth, E. Christian Student. Boston, 1830. 12°. 6158
Memoirs of S. Wilhelm. New Haven, 1819. 16°. 8451
Bigelow, J. Elements of Technology. Boston, 1831. 8°. 5991
Jamaica, in 1850. New York, 1851. 12°. 7434

Bigelow, J. Memoirs of J. C. Fremont. New York, 1856. 12°. . . . 8650
Useful Arts with the Applications of Science. Bost. 1840. 12°. . 10150
Bigland, J. Geog. and Hist. view of World. Ed. J. Morse. Bost. 1811. 5 v. 8°. 6918
Biglow Papers, The. Ed. H. Wilbur. Cambridge, 1848. 12°. 1942
Bingham, H. History of the Sandwich Islands. Hartford, 1847. 8°. . 9368
Biographia Dramatica. D. E. Baker and others. London, 1812. 4 v. 8°. 8856
Literaria. S. T. Coleridge. Boston, 1834. 8°. 8499
Navalis. J. Charnock. London, 1794–8. 6 v. 8°. 8812
Biographical Essays. T. De Quincey. Boston, 1850. 12°. . . . 893
Biographical and Hist. Sketches. T. B. Macaulay. N. Y. 1857. 12°. . 834
Dictionary. M. Adams. London. 8°. 8860
Dictionary. H. J. Rose, London, 1857. 12 v. 8°. 8834
Dictionary. American. W. Allen. Cambridge, 1809. 8°. . . 8853
Sketches of Statesmen. S. L. Knapp. Boston, 1821. 8°. . . 8537
Boigraphie des Contemporains. A. V. Arnault and others. Paris, 1820. 20 v. 12°. 8862
Biography, American. J. Belknap. Boston, 1794. 2 v. 8°. . . . 8588
The same. New York, 1846. 3 v. 18°. 5212
American. See Sparks, J.
Cyclopædia of. Ed. F. L. Hawks. Appleton's. New York, 1856. 8°. 8800
Female. Mary Hays. London, 1803. 6 v. 12°. 8404
Romance of. Mrs. A. Jameson. London, 1837. 2 v. 12°. . . 8646
Sacred, or the Hist. of the Patriarchs. H. Hunter. Bost. 1794. 3 v. 8°. 8528
of Self-taught Men. B. B. Edwards. Boston, 1832. 12°. . . 8336
Universal. J. Lempriere. New York, 1810. 2 v. 8°. . . . 8851
The same, with additions, by E. Lord. 1825. 2 v. 8°. . 8854
Universal. J. Platt. London, 1825. 5 v. 8°. 8846
Universal. Handbook of. P. Godwin. New York, 1852. 12°. . 8884
Bion, Theocritus. Moschus. Idyls, Tr. M. J. Chapman. Lond. 1836. 12°. 1915
Bird, R. M. Calavar. Philadelphia, 1835. 2 v. 12°. 227
Hawks of Hawk Hollow. Philadelphia, 1835. 2 v. 12°. . . 1504
The Infidel. Philadelphia, 1835. 2 v. 12°. 1525
The same. 1533
Robin Day. Philadelphia, 1839. 2 v. 19°. 1495
The same. 1601
Birds, Architecture of. Boston, 1831. 12°. 6203
and Flowers. Mary Howitt. Boston, 1839. 12°. 2374
Natural History of. New York, 1840. 12°. 5558
Nat. Hist. and Classification of. W. Swainson. Lond. 1836. 2 v. 12°. 9973
See also, Naturalist's Library.
Birmah, Description of. J. Conder. London, 1826. 16°. 9646
The same. 9657
Births, Deaths and Marriages. T. Hook. Paris, 1839. 8°. . . . 11683
Black, J. Elements of Chemistry. Philadelphia, 1807. 3 v. 8°. . . 5975
Black Dwarf. W. Scott. New York, 1817. 12°. 315
The same. Boston, 1845. 12°. 289
The same. Boston, 1820. 8°. 1093
Blackford, Mrs. Annals of the Family of M'Roy. N. Y. 1831. 2 v. 12°. 8288

Blacklock, T. Select Poems and Life. Philadelphia, 1822. 18°. . . . 2147
Blackmore, R. Creation, a Philosophical Poem. Phil. 1806. 12°. . . . 2444
Select Poems, with Life, by E. Sanford. Philadelphia, 1819. 16°. 2128
Blackstone, W. Commentaries on the Laws of England. Lond. 1783. 4 v. 8°. 10745
The same. vols. 3, 4. Dublin, 1794. 12°. 11185
The same. Ed. J. Chitty, and others. N. Y. 1845. 2 v. 8°. 10712
Blackwood's Edinburgh Magazine. vols. 1–85, (con.) Edin. 1817–59. 8°. 3126
Duplicates for 1834, 5. Edinburgh, 8°. 3094, 3108
Blair, A. Life. Boston, 1822. 12°. 11886
Blair, H. Lectures on Rhetoric and Belles Lettres. New York, 1815. 8°. 748
Sermons. London, 1781. 2 v. 8°. 5619
Blair, R. Poems, with Life. Philadelphia, 1819. 18°. 2133
Blake, J. L. Conversations on Natural Philosophy. Hartford, 1823. 12°. 6094
Blake, M. Hist. of the Mendon Association. Boston, 1853. 12°. . . 6124
Blakeman, R. Credulity and Superstition. New York, 1849. 12°. . 3927
Blanc, L. France under Louis Philippe. Tr. Phil. 1848. 2 v. 8°. . 7362
Blanchard, L. Sketches from Life. New York, 1846. 12°. . . . 9847
Blanche of Navarre, a Play. G. P. R. James. New York, 1839. 12°. . 2409
Blaquiere, E. Letters from Greece. London, 1828. 8°. . . . 9459
Blaz de Bury, Mad. Racine and the French Drama. London, 1845. 16°. 6884
Bleak House. C. Dickens. Philadelphia. 8°. 72
Blessington, Countess of. Confessions of an Elderly Lady and Gentleman.
Philadelphia, 1838. 2 v. 12°. 1465
The Idler in France. Philadelphia, 1841. 2 v. 12°. 9012
The Idler in Italy. Paris, 1839. 8°. 9453
Life and Correspondence. R. R. Madden. New York, 1856. 2 v. 12°. 8020
Bliss, L., Jr. Hist. of Rehoboth, Seekonk, Pawtucket, (Mass.) Bost. 1836. 8° 7310
Bloodgood, S. D. Life of J. Hogg. New York, 1834. 12°. 8468
Bloomfield, R. Banks of Wye. London, 1823. 12°. . . . 2028
The same. New York, 1812. 18°. 11284
Poems and Remains. London, 1822–27. 4 v. 12°. 2027
Blucher, Marshal. Life and Campaigns. Gen. Gneisenau. Tr. Lond. 1815. 8°. 7952
Blue Laws of Connecticut. Hartford, 1838. 12°. 11137
Lights, or the Convention, a Poem. J. M. Scott. N. Y. 1817. 18°. 2778
Blunt, J. J. Veracity of the Gospels, and Acts. Boston, 1829. 12°. . 6121
Boaden, J. Life of J. P. Kemble. Philadelphia, 1825 .8°. 8183
The same. 8189
Boarding School, The. Boston, 1829. 16°. 3974
Boardman, H. A. Bible in the Counting House. Philadelphia, 1859. 12°. 6151
in the Family. Philadelphia, 1859. 12°. 6150
Great Question. Philadelphia, 1858. 12°. 6132
Quarter-Century Discourse. Philadelphia, 1858. 12°. , . 6126
Boase, H. S. Treatise on Primary Geology. London, 1834. 8°. . . 5943
Boccacio's Decameron, or Ten Days' Entertainm't. Tr. Lond. 1822. 4 v. 24°. 1745
Body and Soul. Philadelphia, 1824. 2 v. 12°. 637
The, in relation to Mind. J. Moore. New York, 1848. 12°. . . 4240
Bœckh, A. Public Economy of Athens. Tr. Lond. 1842. 8°. . . 7605
Bogue, D. Divine Authority of the N. Testament. New York. 16°. . 5240

Bogue, T. and J. Bennett. History of Dissenters. London, 1833. 2 v. 8°. 5613

Bogue, D. (Editor.) European Library. London, 1846–48. 13 v. 12°.

No. 5489. M. Luther. Table Talk. Tr. by W. Hazlitt.
5490. Life of Michel Angelo, by R. Duppa; Life of Raffaello. Q. DeQuincy.
5491. Life of Cardinal Wolsey. J. Galt.
5492. Counter Revolution in England under Charles II, and James II. A. Carrel. Tr. by W. Hazlitt; Reign of James II. C. J. Fox.
5493. History of the French Revolution from 1789—1814. F. A. Mignet.
5494. History of the Roman Republic J. Michelet. Tr. by W. Hazlitt.
5495. History of Spanish Literature. F. Bouterwek. Tr. by S. Ross.
5496. Literary History of the Middle Ages. J. Berington.
5497, 8. Conquest of England by the Normans. A. Thierry. Tr. by W. H.
5499–5501. History of Civilization. F. Guizot. Trans. by W. Hazlitt.

Bohn, H. G. (Editor.) Antiquarian Library. Lond. 1847–49. 10 v. 12°.

No. 5437–39. Brand, J. Popular Antiquities of Great Britain.
5440. Bede, The Venerable. Ecclesiastical History of England ; Anglo-Saxon Chronicle.
5441. William of Malmesbury. Chronicle of the Kings of England.
5442. Fenn, J, (Editor.) Paston Letters.
5443, 4. Roger of Wendover. History of England from 447–1235, Tr. by J. A. Giles.
5445. Wright, T. (Editor.) Early Travels in Palestine.
5446. Joinville, Lord John de, and others. Chronicles of the Crusades.

Illustrated Library. London, 1850–2. 12 v. 12°.

No. 5474. White, G., Natural History of Selborne. Edited by E Jesse.
5475. Eaton, Charlotte A. Rome in the Nineteenth Century, (vol. 1.)
5476. Three Courses and a Dessert.
5477. Kitto, J. Scripture Lands.
5478–85. Lodge, E. Portraits of Illustrious Personages.

Standard Library. London, 1846–56. 111 v. 12°.

No. 5122–24. Lanzi, A. L. History of Painting in Italy. Tr. by T. Roscoe.
5124–26. Sismondi, J. C. L. S. de. Life ; Literature of the South of Europe. Trans. by T. Roscoe.
5127. Schlegel, F. von. Life ; Philos. of Hist. Tr. by J. B. Robertson.
5128. Machiavelli, N. History of Florence and other Writings.
5129–32. Cyclopædia of Political Knowledge.
5133. Guizot, F. History of Representative Government in Europe. Trans. by A. R. Scoble.
5134. Hutchinson, Mrs. L. Autobiography. Life of Col. J. Hutchinson ; Siege of Lathom House.
5135. Roscoe, W. Memoir. Life of Lorenzi de'Medici.
5136. Hall, R. Life, by O. Gregory ; Estimate of Character and Writings, by J. Foster ; Works.
5137–38. Roscoe, W. Life of Leo the Tenth.
5139–43. Vasari, G. Lives of Eminent Painters, Sculptors, &c. Trans. by Mrs. J Foster.
5144–46. Ranke, L. History of the Popes. Tr. by E. Foster.
5147–49. Menzel, W. History of Germany. Tr. by Mrs. G. Horrocks.
5427–29. The same.
5150. Sheridan, R. B. Life ; Dramatic Works.
5151–53. Milton, J. Prose Works.
5154–57. Schiller, F. von. Historical and Dramatic Works.
5158–60. Goëthe, J. W. von. Autobiography. Trans. by J. Oxenford ; Travels ; Trans. by A. J. W. Morrison ; Dramatic Works. Trans. by Anna Swanwick, and Sir W. Scott.
5161, 2. Beckmann, J. History of Inventions, &c, Tr. by W. Johnston.
5163–68. Coxe, W. History of the House of Austria ; Memoirs of the Duke of Marlborough.
5169. Beaumont and Fletcher. Select Works, Ed. by L. Hunt.
5170–71. Reynolds, Sir J. Life by H. W. Beechy ; Literary Works.
5172–78. Lamartine, A. de History of the Girondists. Trans. by H. T. Ryde ; Restoration of the Fr. Monarchy. Tr. by Capt. Rafter.
5179. Gregory, O. Evidences, &c. of the Christian Religion.
5180. Naples under Spanish Dominion. Tr. by A. de Reumont.
5181–84. Foster, J. Lectures ; Life, by J. E. Ryland.
5185. De Lolme, J. L. Constitution of England.
5186–88. Condé, J. A. Arabs in Spain. Tr. by Mrs. J. Foster.
5189. Smith, A. Memoir by D. Stewart ; Theory of Moral Sentiments.
5190–3. Smyth, W. Lect. on the Fr. Revolution ; Lect. on Mod. History.

5194. Schlegel, A. W. von. Lectures on Dramatic Art and Literature. Trans. by J. Black.
5195. Schlegel, F. Von. Æsthetic and Miscellaneous Works. Tr. by E. J. Millington.
5196. Fuller, A. Memoir, by A. G. Fuller; Principal Works.
5197–5200. James, G. P. R. Life of Louis XIV; Life Richard Cœur-de-Lion.
5201–2. Kelly, W. History of Russia.
5203–6. Bremer, Frederika. Works. Trans. by Mary Howitt.
5207. Neander, A. Christian Life in the Early and Middle Ages. Tr. J. E. Ryland.
5208. Ranke, L. History of Servia and the Servian Revolution. Tr. Mrs. A. Kerr.
5423. Goëthe, J. W. von. Novels and Tales. Tr. by R. D. Boylan.
5424–5 Cellini, Benvenuto. Autobiography. Tr. by Roscoe. (2 copies.)
5426. Butler. J. Analogy of Religion.
5430–31. Junius. Letters, &c. of. Edited by J. Wade.
5432. Hungary and its Revolutions; Memoir of Kossuth.
5434–36. Herodotus. Trans. by H. Cary. (3 copies.)
5447. Taylor, J. Holy Living and Dying.
5448, 49. Thierry, A. Conquest of Eng. by the Normans. Tr. W. Hazlitt.
5469. Schiller, F. von. Early Dramas and Romances. Tr. by H. G. Bohn. (See 5154.)
5470, 71. Cowper, W. Works. Edited by R. Southey. (vols. 7, 8.)
5372. Mignet, F. A. History of the French Revolution from 1789–1814.
5473. De Foe, D. Plague in London; Fire in London; Storm; True-Born Englishman.
5486. Barry, Opie, and Fuseli. Lectures on Painting.
5487. Humboldt, A. von. Views of Nature. Trans. by E. C. Ottè and H. G. Bohn.
5488. Kirby, W. Wisdom, &c. of God Manifested in Animals. (vol. 1.)
1161. Staunton, H. Chess-Player's Companion.

Bohemia, History of. London, 1783. 8°. 7078
Boileau Despréaux. Œuvres. (2 copies.) Paris, 1813. 2 v. 16°. . . 11207
Bokhara, Narrative of a Mission to. J. Wolff. New York, 1845. 8°. . 9415
Bokum, H. Introduction to the Study of the German Lan. Phil. 1832. 12°. 3384
Boleyn, Anne. Memoirs. Miss Benger. Philadelphia, 1822. 8°. . . 8245
a Dramatic Poem. H. H. Milman. London, 1840. 16°. . . 2032
Bolingbroke, Lord, Collection of Political Tracts. London, 1769. 8°. 10777
Letters to W. Windham, and to A. Pope. London, 1763. 8°. . 10779
Life and Dissertation on Parties. London. 8°. 10780
Remarks on the History of England. London. 8°. . . . 10778
Works. vols. 4–7. London, 1770. 8°. 6038
The same. vol. 3. Philadelphia, 1841. 371
Bolivar, S. Memoirs. H. L. V. D. Holstein. Boston, 1829. 8°. . . 8221
Bolmar, A. Colloquial Phrases. Philadelphia, 1836. 4961
The same. Philadelphia, 1835. 16°. 4962
French Grammar. Philadelphia, 1839. 12°. 3400
Bombet, L. A. C. Lives of Haydn and Mozart. Trans. Boston, 1839. 12°. 8043
Bonaparte, C. L., and A. Wilson. Ornithology. Edinburgh, 1831. 4 v. 12°. 10175
Bonaparte, L. Charlemagne, or Church Delivered. Tr. Phil. 1815. 2 v. 18°. 2752
Government of Holland. Tr. London, 1820. 3 v. 8°. . . . 7662
Autobiography. New York, 1836. 12°. 8360
Bonaparte, N. Campaign in Germany and France in 1813, 14. J. Philippart, London, 1814. 2 v. 8°. 9514
Campaign in Russia. E. Labaume. Tr. Philadelphia, 1815. 8°. . 9493
The same. Hartford, 1816. 8°. 9498
Campaign in Russia. Events that followed. W. Dunlap. Hartford, 1814. 12°. 6824
Campaigns of, By an American. Boston, 1835. 12°. 8500
Conf. Correspondence with J. Bonaparte. New York, 1856. 2 v. 12°. 4533

Bonaparte, N. Court and Camp of. New York, 1841. 12°. . . 5530
The same. New York, 1833. 16°. 6621
Derniers Momens de. F. Antommarchi. Paris, 1825. 2 v. 8°. . 8209
in Exile. B. E. O'Meara. Boston, 1823. 2 v. 12°. . . . 7452
Expedition to Russia in 1812. P. de Segur. New York, 1842. 2 v. 12° 7435
France during reign of. Dictated to his Gen'ls. Lond. 1823. 7 v. 8°. 7887
History of. J. S. C. Abbott. New York, 1855. 2 v. 8°. . . 7530
History of. L. De L'Ardeche. Trans. New York, 1842. 2 v. 8°. . 8135
History of. J. G. Lockhart. New York, 1830. 2 v. 16°. . . 6630
The same. New York, 1840. 2 v. 12°. 5506
The same. New York, 1833. 2 v. 16°. 6639
and Josephine. Con. Correspondence of. Ed. Abbott. N. Y. 1856. 12°. 4520
Journal of the Private Life of, at St. Helena. Count de Las Cases. Paris, 1824. 8 v. 12°. 6808
The same. Tr. London, 1823. 8 v. 8°. 6660
Life of, by an American. Elizabethtown, 1820. 8°. . . . 7510
The same. 8215
Life of, W. Hazlitt. New York, 1849. 3 v. 12°. . . . 8652
Life of, W. Scott. New London, 1834. 3 v. 8°. 8212
The same. Philadelphia, 1827. 3 v. 8°. 7511
and his Marshals. J. T. Headley. New York, 1846. 2 v. 12°. . 8301
Memoirs. A. V. Arnault and others. Tr. Boston, 1828. 2 v. 16°. 7765
The same. Boston, 1839. 2 v. 16°. 7763
Memoirs. F. de Bourrienne. Philadelphia, 1832. 8°. . . . 8211
Memoirs. J. Rapp. London, 1823. 8°. 7875
Military, Maxims of. Trans. J. Akerly. New York, 1845. 12°. . 3922
Opinions and Policy. N. L. Bonaparte. Tr. London, 1840. 8°. 10725
Private Memo's of Court of. L. F. J. de Bausset. Tr. Phil. 1828. 8°. 7509
Reply to Scott's History of. L. Bonaparte. Tr. Philadelphia, 1829. 8°. 11361
Sayings and Deeds of. A. Vieusseux. London, 1846. 2 v. 16°. . 7206
Surrender of. F. L. Maitland. Boston, 1826. 12°. 11412
and his Times. A. A. L. de Caulincourt. Philadelphia, 1838. 2 v. 12°. 8366
Voyage to St. Helena. W. Warden. New Haven, 1817. 12°. . 8399
Bonaparte Family. History of, or Napoleon Dynasty. 1852. 8°. . . 7845
Bondman, The. Times of Wat Tyler. New York, 1835. 12°. . . . 1249
Bonner, T. D. Life and Adventures of. J. C. Beckwourth. N. Y. 1856. 12°. 8016
Bonnycastle, J. Mensuration and Practical Geometry. Lond. 1806. 12°. 4560
Book of Ballads. New York, 1852. 12°. 2357
for a Corner. L. Hunt. New York, 1852. 12°. 1187
of Nature, The. J. M. Good. Boston, 1826. 8°. 423
of Snobs. W. M. Thackeray. New York, 1853. 12°. . . . 961
Without a Name. Sir T. C. and Lady Morgan. N. Y. 1841. 2 v. 12°. 1449
Boone, D. Life. J. M. Peck. Boston, 1847. 12°. 8065
Booth, D. Principles of English Composition. London, 1831. 12°. . 3039
Border Warfare of New York. W. W. Campbell. New York, 1849. 12°. 11460
The same. New York, 1831. 12°. 11365
Borneo, Expedition of H. M. S. Dido to. H. Keppel. N. York, 1846. 12°. 8985
Borrow, G. Lavengro: The Scholar, Gipsy and Priest. N. Y. 1851. 12°. 547

Borrow, G. Lavengro: The Scholar, Gipsy and Priest. N. Y. 1851. 12°. 548
Borrow, G. The Zincali, or Gipsies of Spain. London, 1841. 2 v. 12°. . 11410
Bossange, H. Catalogue de Livres Français. Paris, 1845. 8°. . . 8810
Bossuet, M. History of France. Tr. Edinburgh, 1762. 4 v. 12. . . 7438
Histoire Universelle. Paris, 1828. 2 v. 16°. 11211
The same. Translated. Edinburgh, 1762. 8°. . . . 11348
Boston, a Trip to. E. C. Wines. Boston, 1838. 12°. 8739
Boston Bard. R. S. Coffin. Providence, 1826. 8°. 1892
Book for 1837. Ed. B. B. Thatcher. Boston, 1837. 12°. . . 700
Boston, T. Discourses on Human Nature. Air., 1797. 12°. . . . 6609
Boswell, J. Account of Corsica. Glasgow, 1768. 8°. 9238
Life of S. Johnson. Boston, 1824. 5 v. 12°. 8082
The same. New York, 1837. 2 v. 8°. 7532
Tour to the Hebrides with S. Johnson. Philadelphia, 1810. 8°. . 9171
Botanical Grammar. A. Eaton. Albany, 1828. 12°. 3325
Harmony. J. H. B. St. Pierre. Translated. Worcester, 1797. 8°. 5993
Text Book. A. Gray. New York, 1845. 12°. 6065
Botany, for Beginners. Mrs. A. H. Phelps. New York, 1841 16°. . 4553
Descriptive and Physiological. J. S. Henslow. Lond. 1836. 12°. 9985
Physiology and Chemistry. London, 1831. 8°. 5099
Botta, C. History of American Revolution. Tr. Phil. 1820. 3 v. 8°. . 7213
The same. New Haven, 1842. 2 v. 8°. 7217
Bourke, T. History of Moors in Spain. London, 1811. 4°. . . . 11257
Bourne, G. Lorette, History of a Canadian Nun. N. Y. 1834. 18°. . 1691
Picture of Slavery. Middletown, 1834. 16°. 11156
Boursault. Œuvres. Paris, 1811. 2 v. 18°. 10885
Bourrienne, F. de. Life of Bonaparte. Philadelphia, 1832. 8°. . . 8211
Bouterwek, F. Spanish Literature. London, 1847. 12°. 5495
The same, with Portuguese Literature. Tr. Lond. 1823. 2 v. 8°. 729
Bowditch, N. Practical Navigator, &c. New York, 1817. 8°. . . 1054
Memoir. Boston, 1841. 12°. 8042
Bowdler, H. M. Life and Charac. of Miss E. Smith. Burlington, 1811. 12°. 8380
Bowdler, Miss. Poems and Essays. New York, 1811. 12°. . . . 2359
The same. Boston, 1827. 12°. 858
Bowen, F. Essays on Speculative Philosophy. Boston, 1842. 12°. . 789
Life of B. Lincoln. Boston, 1847. 12°. 8065
Life of J. Otis. Boston, 1844. 12°. 8054
Life of Sir W. Phips. Boston, 1837. 12°. 8049
Bowen, H. L. Memoir and Speeches of T. Burges. Providence, 1835. 8°. 8501
Bower, A. Life of Martin Luther. Philadelphia, 1824. 8°. . . . 11309
Bower of Spring. Philadelphia, 1817. 16°. 11293
Boyle, I. Historical View of the Council of Nice. Phil. 1840. 8°. . 5075
Boyle, R. Treatises on Veneration Due to God, &c. London, 1835. 12°. 5791
Boyse, S. Select Poems, with Life. Philadelphia, 1822. 18°. . . 2143
Bracciolini, P. Life. W. Shepherd. Liverpool, 1802. 8°. . . . 11252
Brace, C. L. Hungary in 1851. New York, 1852. 12°. 7103
Norse-Folk, a Visit to Norway and Sweden. New York, 1857. 12°. 8939
Bracebridge Hall. W. Irving. New York, 1822. 2 v. 12°. . . . 923
The same. New York, 1851. 12°. 538

Brackenridge, H. M. Voyage to S. America in 1817, 18. Balt. 1819. 2 v. 8°. 9159
Bradford, A. History of Massachusetts from 1775–89. Boston, 1825. . 11329
Bradford, A. W. American Antiquities, and Origin and History of the Red Race. New York, 1841. 8°. 7594
Bradford, J. Writings of. London. 12°. 5660
Bradford, J. A. Notes on the North West. London, 1846. 12°. . . 805
Bradley, Mrs. Narrative of a Residence among the Arabs. Bost. 1820. 12°. 8728
The same. Boston, 1821. 12°. 11890
Brainard, J. G. C. Literary Remains of. Hartford, 1832. 12°. . . 2362
Poems. New York, 1825. 12°. 2283
Brainerd, D. Life. J. Styles. Boston, 1821. 12°. 7457
Life. J. Edwards. New Haven, 1822. 8°. 8513
The same. New York. 16°. . . , ... 5228
The same. 8447
Life. W. B. O. Peabody. (Two copies.) Boston, 1837. 12°. . 8050
Brambletye House, or Cavaliers and Roundheads. H. Smith. Boston, 1826. 3 v. 12°. 306
The same. 1252
The same. New York, 1835. 12°. 229
Brand, J. Popular Antiquities of Great Britain. Lond. 1841. 3 v. 12°. 1183
The same. London, 1848. 3 v. 12°. 5437
Brande, W. T. Encyclopædia of Science, Literature and Arts, New York, 1844. 4°. 8801
The same. New York, 1848. 4°, ... 8802
Brandenburg, Memoirs of the House of. London, 1751. 12°. . . 8375
Brant, J. (Thayendanegea.) Life. W. L. Stone. N. Y. 1838. 2 v. 8°. 7938
Bray, Mrs. A. E. Traditions of Devonshire. London, 1838. 12°. . . 11415
Bray, W. Memoirs of J. Evelyn. London, 1827. 5 v. 8°. . . . 7972
Braybrooke, R. Memoirs of S. Pepys. London, 1828. 5 v. 16°. . . 7977
Bravo. J. F. Cooper. Philadelphia, 1831. 2 v. 16°. 1027
Brazil, Description of. J. Conder. London, 1825. 2 v. 16°. . . . 9642
Life in. T. Ewbank. New York, 1856. 8°. 9367
Residence and Travels in. D. P. Kidder. Phil. 1845. 2 v. 8°. . 9517
Travels in. J. B. Von Spix, and C. F. P. Von Martius. London, 1824. 2 v. 8°. 9466
Brazilian Valley. Residence in. A. R. M. Payne. New York, 1852. 12° 8989
Bremer, Frederika. Four Sisters. Philadelphia, 12°. 573
Home ; or, Family Cares and Joys. New York, 1843. 8°. . . 8
Works. Trans. Mary Howitt. London, 1853. 4 v. 12°. . . 5203
The same. New York, 1844. 2 v. 8°. 12

1. President's Daughter.
2. H—— Family; Tralinnan; Axel and Anna; Hopes; Twins; The Solitary; The Comforter; Neighbors.

Brenton, E. P. Naval History of Great Britain, from 1783–1836. London, 1837. 2 v. 8°. 7269
Brewer, J. Patmos, and the Seven Churches of Asia. Ed. J. W. Barber. Bridgeport, 1851. 8°. 5089
Residence at Constantinople in the year 1827. N. H. 1830. 12°. . 9274

Brewer, J. Residence at Constantinople in the year 1827. N. H. 1830. 12°. 9279
Brewster, D. Letters on Natural Magic. New York, 1832. 16°. . . . 4956
The same, ... 5866
The same. 6617
Life of Isaac Newton. New York, 1840. 12°. 5528
The same. New York, 1831 16°. 6619
Martyrs of Science. New York, 1841. 12°. 5906
Treatise on Optics. London, 1835. 12°. 9959
The same. With Notes. Philadelphia, 1833. 12°. . . . 6087
Brewster, W. Life. A. Steele. Philadelphia, 1857. 8°. 7874
Bride of Abydos. Lord Byron. Philadelphia, 1814. 18°. 11288
Fort Edward. Miss D. Bacon. New York, 1839. 12°. . . . 1569
of Lammermoor. W. Scott. Boston, 1845. 12°. 291
See also Scott, W.
Bridges, Sir E. See Brydges, Sir E.
Bridgewater Treatises, on the Power, Wisdom and Goodness of God, as manifested in Creation. Treatises 1–9. London and Phil. 8°.

No. 6382. Adaptation of External Nature to the Moral and Intellectual Constitution of Man. T. Chalmers.
6383, 4. Animal and Vegetable Physiology considered with reference to Natural Theology. P. M. Roget.
6385. History, Habits, &c. of Animals. W. Kirby.
5488. The same. vol. 1.
6386. A Fragment, or Infidelity Refuted. C. Babbage.
6387. Geology considered with reference to Nat. Theology. W. Buckland.
6388. The same.
6483. Chemistry, Meteorology, and the Function of Digestion. W. Prout.
6484. The Mechanism of the Hand, &c. C. Bell.
6485. Astronomy and General Physics. W. Whewell.
6486. Nature, &c. adapted to the Physical Condition of Man. J. Kidd.

Briggs, C. Adventures of Harry Franco. New York, 1839. 2 v. 12°. 1499
Brigham, A. Influence of Ment. Cultiv'n upon Health. Hart. 1832. 12°. 3287
The same. 4886
The same. Boston, 1833. 12°. 3924
The same. 4877
Brisbane, A. Social Destiny of Man. Philadelphia, 1840. 12°. . . . 3302
The same. 11148
Brisson, M. De. Captivity in Africa, A. D. 1785. Edin. 1827. 16°. . 9996
Brissot, J. P. Commerce of America with Europe. Tr. N. Y. 1795. 12°. 11179
Bristed, C. A. Five years in an English University. N. Y. 1852. 2 v. 12°. 823
Bristed, J. Agricult'l, Commerc. &c., Resources of the U. S. N. Y. 1818. 8°. 7368
Britain, under the Roman Emperors. F. Thackeray. Lond. 1843. 2 v. 8°. 6969
British Admirals, to 1672. Lives of. R. Southey. London, 1833–40. 12°. 9927
Admirals, to 1816. Lives. J. Campbell & others. Lond. 1817. 8 v. 8°. 8554
America, History of. H. Murray. Edinburgh, 1839. 3 v. 12°. . 5849
The same. Abridged. New York, 1840. 2 v. 12°. . . . 5561
Association for the Advancement of Science, Reports of the. 1831–42. London, 1835. 11 v. 8°. 10670
Classics. New York, 1813. 85 v. 12°. . . . .

No. 3579–3587. Spectator.
3588–3593. Sterne.
3594–3605. Fielding.
3606–3628. Swift.
3629–3634. Shakspeare.
No. 3635–3639. Goldsmith.
3640–3644. Addison.
3645–3652. Pope.
3653–3663. Johnson.

British Colonial Library, See Martin, R. M.

Constitution. H. Lord Brougham. London, 1844. 8°. 10055

Costume. J. R. Planché. London, 1846. 12°. 3011

Critic. vols. 1–42. London, 1793–1813. 8°. 4790

Index to vols. 1–22 of the same. In the rack.

New Series. vols. 1–14. (vol. 10 missing.) Lond. 1814–20. 8°. 4832

Drama; Tragedies, Comedies, Operas, & Farces. Lond. 1824. 2 v. 8°. 1884

Eloquence. W. Hazlitt. Brooklyn, 1810. 2 v. 8°. 11057

Eloquence, Common Place Book of. London, 1827. 18°. . . 11149

Empire, Tour Through. P. Wakefield. Phil. 1804. 12°. . . 11931

Essayists, with Prefaces, by J. Ferguson. Lond. 1823. 40 v. 12°. 3664

Vol. 1—4. The Tatler.
5—12. The Spectator.
13—15. The Guardian.
16—18. The Rambler.
19. The Idler.
20—22. The Adventurer.
23—25. The World.
Vol. 26—27. The Connoisseur.
28—29. The Mirror.
30—31. The Lounger.
32—34. The Observer.
35—37. Knox, V. Essays.
38—40. Winter Evenings.

History, Biography & Manners in Reign of Henry VIII, Edward VI, Mary & Elizabeth, and James I. E. Lodge. Lond. 1838. 3 v. 8°. 7581

India. See India.

Manufactures, Textile, Chemical, &c. G. Dodd. Lond. 1844. 6 v. 16°. 7466

Military Commanders, Eminent, Lives of. G. R. Gleig. Lond. 1831–2. 3 v. 12.° 9924

Monachism, or Manners, &c., of Monks of England. T. D. Fosbroke. London, 1843. 8°. 5007

Naval History. See Naval.

Plutarch, or Lives of Eminent Brit. Characters. Lond. 1791. 8 v. 12°. 8104

Poets. Works with Lives, by E. Sanford, S. Johnson, and others. Ed. R. Walsh, Jr. Philadelphia, 1819–22. 42 v. 18°. . . 2113

No. 2113, 4. Translations from Aristophanes by T. Mitchell.
2114. Translations from Terence by G. Colman; from Persius by W. Gifford.
2115, 6. Translation of Tasso's Jerusalem Delivered by J. H. Hunt.
2117. Translations from Æschylus and Euripides by R. Potter; and from Sophocles by T. Francklin.
2118. G. Chaucer, J. Gower, J Skelton, T. Wyatt, (Earl of Surrey,) G. Gascoigne.
2119. J. Davies, J. Donne, J Hall, Earl of Sterling, R. Corbet, T. Carew.
2120. A. Cowley, E. Waller, J. Denham.
2121, 2. J. Milton.
2123, 4. S. Butler.
2124. Earl of Rochester, Earl of Roscommon, T. Otway, T. Pomfret.
2125, 6. J. Dryden.
2127. J. Addison, S. Garth, J. Hughes, J. Sheffield, (Duke of Buckingham,) W. Congreve, E. Fenton, W. Pattison.
2128. M. Prior, R. Blackmore.
2129. J. Gay.
2130. T. Tickell, Lord Landsdowne, T. Yalden, M. Green, J. Hammond, W. Somerville.
2131. R. Savage, J. Dyer.
2132, 3. A. Pope, R. Blair, C. Pitt.
2134. J. Thomson.
2135. I. Watts, W. Collins, E. Moore.
2136. W. Shenstone, J. Cawthorn.
2137, 8. E. Young.
2138. R. Dodsley, D. Mallet, A. Ramsay.
2139. C. Churchill, W. Falconer. J. Grainger.
2140. M. Akenside, J. G. Cooper, W. Thompson.
2141. T. Gray, T. Chatterton, W. Harte.
2142. O. Goldsmith, J. Langhorne, C. Smart.
2143. S. Johnson, J. Armstrong, C. Shaw, George (Lord) Lyttleton, S. Boyse.

2144. J. Beattie, J. Scott, J. Cunningham, S. Jenyns.
2145. R. Glover, T. Smollett.
2146. W. J. Mickle, J. Warton, T. Warton.
2147. W. Jones, T. Blacklock, N. Cotton.
2148. W. Cowper.
2149. W. Cowper, R. Lloyd, R. Fergusson, —— Richardson, W. Blackstone, R. Jago, W. Whitehead ; J. Logan, R. Craggs, S. Bishop, J. Bamfylde, T. Russell, R. Lovell, E. Lovibond, M. Bruce, W. H. Roberts. R. Porteus, R. Glynn.
2150, 1. R. Burns.
2151. H. MacNeill.
2152, 3, Translation of Homer's Iliad by A. Pope.
2154. Translation of Homer's Odyssey by A. Pope, with other Miscellaneous Pieces.

British Poets, Beauties of the. New York, 1827. 16°. 3090
Chaucer to Jonson. Select Works & Lives. R. Southey. Lon. 1831. 8°. 1898
Falconer to Scott. Select Works & Lives. J. Frost. Phil. 1838. 8°. 1849
Jonson to Beattie. Select Works & Lives. J. Aikin. Phil. 1839. 8°. 1848
Selections from. Ed. F. G. Halleck. N. Y. 1840. 2 v. 12°. . 5575
Southey to Croly. Select Works & Lives. J. Frost. Phil. 1843. 8°. 1843
Possessions in Indian & Atlan. Oceans. R. M. Martin. Lond. 1837. 12°. 5820
Possessions in the Mediteranean. R. M. Martin. London, 1837. 12°. 5823
Prose Writers. Boston, 1820. 8 v. 18°. 4627

Vol. 1. H. Walpole. Reminiscences and Walpoliana.
2. R. Burns. Letters.
3. O. Goldsmith. Essays and the Bee.
4. T. Gray. Letters.
5. F. Bacon and E. H. Clarendon. Essays.
6. Lady R. Russell. Letters.
7. A. Cowley and W. Shenstone. Essays.
8. S. Johnson. Sermons.

Pulpit. W. Suddards. vol. 2. Philadelphia, 1839. 8°. . . . 5595
Reformers, Lives and Writings of. London. 8 v. 12°. 5656

Vol. 1. T. Cranmer, J. Rogers, L. Saunders, R. Taylor, J. Careless.
2. N. Ridley, J. Philpot.
3. J. Knox.
4. J. Hooper.
5. J. Bradford.
6. T. Becon.
7. H. Latimer.
8. W. Tindall, J. Frith, R. Barnes.

Stage, Biography of the. New York, 1824. 12°. 8398
Statesmen, Eminent. See Lardner, D.
Theatre ; a Collection of Dramas. vol. 4. London, 1794. 8°. . 1899
Theatre ; a Collection of Dramas. Ed. Mrs. Inchbald. Lond. 9 v. 16°. 2459
Treaties with other Powers. London, 1790. 2 v. 8°. 11062
Worthies. See Cabinet Portrait Gallery.
Broad Stone of Honor. K. H. Digby. London, 1844. 12°. 1174
Brocklesby, J. Elements of Meteorology. New York, 1849. 12°. . . 6081
Brockway, T. Gospel Tragedy, a Poem. Worcester, 1795. 12°. . . 2051
Brontë, Miss C. Jane Eyre, an Autobiography. New York, 1856. 12°. 177
Life. Mrs. E. C. Gaskell. New York, 1857. 2 v. 12°. 8345
The Professor. New York, 1857. 12°. 180
Shirley, a Tale. New York, 1856. 12°. 179
Villette. New York, 1856. 12°. 178

Brontë, Miss A. Tenant of Wildfell Hall. New York, 1857. 12°. . . . 182
The same. New York, 1848. 12°. 183
Brontë, Miss E. Wuthering Heights. New York, 1826. 12°. 181
Brook, B. History of Religious Liberty. London, 1820. 2 v. 8°. . . 5355
Brooke, H. The Fool of Quality. London, 1777. 3 v. 12°. 694
Brooke and Brooke Farm. Miss H. Martineau. Boston, 1832. 16°. . 10028
Brookiana. London, 1804. 2 v. 16°. 4306
Brooks, J. G., and Miss M. E. Rivals of Este and other Poems. N.Y. 1829. 12°. 2284
Brooks, M. Zóphiël, or the Bride of Seven. Boston, 1834. 12°. . . . 2435
Brooks, N. C. Anthos, or Scriptural Anthology. Philadelphia, 1837. 16°. 2083
History of the Church, a Poem. Baltimore, 1841. 12°. . . . 2325
Literary Amaranth. Philadelphia, 1840. 12°. 3009
Brougham, H. British Constitution. London, 1844. 8°. 10055
Discourses on Natural Theology. Philadelphia, 1835. 12°. . . 6143
Instinct and Fossil Osteology. London, 1844. 16°. 7196
Men of Letters and Science, of Time of George III. Phil. 1845. 12°. 8631
Second series. Phil. 1846. 12°. 8010
Miscellanies. Philadelphia, 1841. 2 v. 12°. 803
Opinions on Politics, Theology, Law, Science, &c. Paris, 1841. 8°. 11019
Political Philosophy. London, 1844. 3 v. 8°. 10708
Sketches of Public Characters. Philadelphia, 1839. 2 v. 12°. . 8701
Speeches. Edinburgh, 1838. 4 v. 8°. 11053
Statesmen of the Time of George III. Philadelphia, 1839. 2 v. 12°. 8497
The same. 8601
Second series. Philadelphia, 1839. 2 v. 12°. 8327
Third series. London, 1845. 2 v. 16°. 7204
Brown, C. B. Arthur Mervyn. Boston, 1827. 2 v. 12°. 1000
The same. 1426
Clara Howard. Boston, 1827. 12°. 1004
The same. 1430
Edgar Huntly. Boston, 1827. 12°. 1005
The same. 1428
The same. Philadelphia, 1801. 3 v. 12°. 1292
Jane Talbot. Boston, 1827. 12°. 1003
The same. 1429
Ormond, or the Secret Witness. Boston, 1827. 12°. . . . 1002
The same. 1430
Wieland, and Memoir of. Boston, 1827. 12°. 1425
Life. W. H. Prescott. Boston, 1834. 12°. 8068
Brown, S. Poems. New Haven, 1818. 12°. 3915
Brown, T. Philosophy of Human Mind. Hallowell, 1829. 2 v. 8°. . 6374
Brown, T., (Capt.) Butterflies, Sphinges & Moths. London, 1834. 3 v. 16°. 10253
Browne, D. Experiences in Foreign Parts. Boston, 1857. 12°. . . 9829
Browne, J. R. Etchings of a Whaling Cruise. New York, 1846. 8°. . 9370
Yusef, or Journey of the Frangi. New York, 1855. 12°. . . 9589
Browne, Sir T. Christian Morals. London, 1756. 16°. 7769
Works and Life. Ed. S. Wilkin. London, 1836. 4 v. 8°. . . 384

Vol. 1. Memoirs; Correspondence and Journal.
2. Religio Medici; Enquiries into Vulgar and Common Errors.
3. The Last Concluded; Garden of Cyrus. Hydriotaphia; Brampton Urns.
4. Repertorium; Letter to a Friend. Miscellanies.

Brownie of Bodsbeck. J. Hogg. New York, 1818. 12°. 925
Browning, E. B. Aurora Leigh. New York, 1857. 12°. 1984
Poems. New York, 1858. 2 v. 12°. 1982
Prometheus and other Poems. New York, 1851. 12°. 1947
Browning, R. Bells and Pomegranates. London, 1841. 8°. 1790
Paracelsus. London, 1835. 12°. 2396
Sordello. London, 1840. 12°. 2399
Browning, W. S. Hist. of Huguenots, 1598–1838. London, 1839. 8°. . 5589
Brownlee, W. C. Catholic Controversy. New York, 1834. 8°. . . 6427
Brownson, O. A. Charles Ellwood. Boston, 1840. 12°. 1643
Bruce, J. Life and Adventures. F. B. Head. New York, 1841. 12°. . 5904
Travels to Discover the Source of the Nile. Dublin, 1790. 6 v. 8°. 9192
Brummel, G. Life. Capt. Jesse. Phil. 1844. 8°. 8190
Brunton, Mary. Emmeline, and other Pieces. New York, 1819. 12°. . 949
Bryant, E. What I saw in California. Phil. 1848. 12°. 9603
Bryant, W. C. Fountain and other Poems. New York, 1842. 12°. . . 2343
Letters of a Traveler. New York, 1850. 12°. 9799
Poems. New York, 1832. 18°. 1959
Poems. New York, 1857. 2 v. 12°. 1934
(Editor.) Selections from the American Poets. New York, 1841. 12°. 5573
The same. 5574
Miscellanies. New York, 1832. 3 v. 16°. 4289
Brydges, E. Autobiography. London, 1834. 2 v. 8°. 7929
Brydone, P. Tour through Sicily and Malta. New York, 1813. 12°. . 9273
Bubbles from the Brunnen of Nassau. F. B. Head. N. Y. 1845. 12°. . 9846
Buccaneers, The. New York, 1827. 2 v. 12°. 317
The same. 1669
of America, History of the. New York, 1826. 3 v. 18°. . 11276
Buchanan, C. Discourses on African and East India Missions. Bost. 1811. 8°. 9173
Memoir. H. Pearson. New York, 1846. 16°. 5238
The same. Boston, 1818. 12°. 8034
Buchanan, J. Life. R. G. Horton. New York, 1856. 12°. 8651
Buchanan, G. Hist. of Scotland. Trans. and continued by J. Watkins. London, 1836. 2 v. 8°. 6941
Buck, C. Religious Anecdotes. New York, 1841. 12°. 6149
Theological Dictionary. Phil. 1824. 8°. 5327
Treatise on Religious Experience. Boston, 1810. 12°. . . . 6109
Works. New Haven, 1833. 8°. 5326
Bucke, C. Beauties, Harmonies, and Sublimities of Nature. London, 1837. 3 v. 8°. 759
The same, abridged. New York, 1842. 12°. 5917
Ruins of Ancient Cities. New York, 1841. 2 v. 12°. 5909
Buckingham, J. S. Claims against the E. India Co. London, 1836. 8°. 10758
America, Hist., Statistical and Descriptive. Lond. 1840. 3 v. 8°. 6935
Lectures on the East. New York, 1838. 16°. 9320

Buckingham, J. T. Reminiscences, Anecdotes, &c. Boston, 1850. 2 v. 8°. 460
Buckland, W. Geology and Miner. in Ref. to Nat. Theol. Phil. 1837. 8°. 6387
The same. 6389
Buckminster, J. and J. S. Memoirs. Eliza B. Lee. Boston, 1851. 12°. . 8572
Budington, W. I. Hist. of 1st Church, Charlestown. Boston, 1845. 8°. 7627
Buenos Ayres, Travels in. J. Conder. London, 1825. 16°. 9642
Buffier, C. First Truths & Origin of Opinions Expl'd. Tr. Lond. 1780. 8°. 5386
Buffon, G. L. L. Nat. Hist. (vol. 1 missing.) Bost. 1831. 5 v. 16°. . 10241
The same, abridged. Dublin, 1791. 8°. 10166
Bulfinch, S. G. Contemplations of the Savior. Boston, 1833. 12°. . 5664
Bulwer, E. L. Alice, or the Mysteries. New York, 1838. 2 v. 12°. . 690
Ambitious Student. New York, 1832. 12°. 1591
The same. 1658
Arasmenes, the Seeker. New York, 1833. 18°. 1690
Asmodeus at large. Phil. 1833. 12°. 246
The same. 1131
Calderon, the Courtier. Phil. 1838. 12°. 1335
The same. 1559
Caxtons. London, 1855. 12°. 554
Chairolas, Prince of Paida. Phil. 1836. 12°. 1240
Devereaux. New York, 1829. 2 v. 12°. 1346
Duchess De La Valliere, a Play. New York, 1836. 12°. . . 2392
England and the English. New York, 1833. 2 v. 12°. . . . 9031
Ernest Maltravers. New York, 1837. 2 v. 12°. . . . 660
Eugene Aram. New York, 1832. 2 v. 12°. 1025
The same. 1274
France, Social, Literary and Political. N. Y. 1834. 2 v. 12°. . 8944
Godolphin. New York, 1840. 2 v. 12°. 1486
Last of the Barons. New York, 1843. 8°. 1043
Last Days of Pompeii. New York, 1835. 12°. 927
The same. London, 1854. 12°. 553
The same. New York, 1835. 12°. 1249
Leila, or the Siege of Grenada. New York, 1838. 12°. . . . 1545
Miscellanies. Philadelphia, 1841. 2 v. 12°. 471
The same. 478
My Novel. London, 1855. 2 v. 12°. 551
Night and Morning. New York, 1841. 2 v. 12°. 1557
Not so Bad as We Seem, a Comedy. New York, 1851. 16°. . . 340
Paul Clifford. New York, 1830. 2 v. 12°. 1330
The same. 1342
The same. 1775
Pilgrims of the Rhine. New York, 1834. 12°. 687
The same. 1503
Rienzi. Philadelphia, 1836. 2 v. 12°. 1338
The same. New York, 1836. 12°. 666
Robber. New York, 1838. 2 v. 12°. 997
Siamese Twins, and other Poems. New York, 1831. 12°. . . 1910
What Will He Do with It. New York, 1859. 8°. 12094
Zanoni. New York, 1842. 2 v. 12°. 1476

Bulwer, Lady L. Cheveley, or Man of Honor. New York, 1837. 2 v. 12°. 1541
Bunsen. Life and Letters of B. G. Niebuhr. New York, 1852. 12°. . 8571
Bunyan, J., Life, Times, &c., of. R. Philip. New York, 1839. 12°. . 8291
Pilgrim's Progress. Hartford, 1826. 8°. 5375
The same. Exeter, 1829. 16°. 6646
The same. New York. 12°. 5225
Burdell, H. and J. The Structure and Diseases of Teeth. N. Y. 1838. 8°. 11669
Burder, H. F. Mental Discipline, &c. New York, 1830. 12°. . . . 4241
Burder, S. Oriental Customs, or Illustrat's of Scripture. Phil. 1807. 2 v. 8°. 9464
Burges, T. Memoir and Speeches. H. L. Bowen. Providence, 1835. 8°. 8501
Burgh, J. Dignity of Human Nature. 8°. 3289
Political Disquisitions. (vol. 1 missing.) Philadelphia, 1775. 3 v. 8°. 10809
Burgoyne, J. Dramatic Works. London, 1808. 2 v. 12°. 1574
Burke, E. Beauties of. Ed. A. Howard. London. 18°. 4946
Correspondence from 1744–1797. London, 1844. 4 v. 8°. . . 10701
European Settlements in America. London, 1757. 2 v. 12°. . . 7089
The same. Boston, 1835. 8°. 11325
Life. J. Prior. Philadelphia, 1825. 8°. 8241
Works. Dublin, 1792. 3 v. 8°. 11089
Works. Boston, 1806. 6 v. 8°. 10485

Vol. 1. Vindication of Natural Society; Philosophical Inquiry into the origin of our Ideas of the Sublime and Beautiful; Account of a Short Administration; Observations on the Publication "The Present State of the Nation;" Cause of the Present Discontents; American Taxation.
2. Speeches and Letters.
3. Reflections on the Revolution in France; Letters.
4. Thoughts, Remarks and Letters on French Affairs; Observations on the conduct of the Minority; Thoughts on Scarcity.
5. An Abridgment of English History; Miscellaneous Letters and Fragments of Speeches.
6. Report of a Committee on the Affairs of India; Articles of Charge against Warren Hastings

Burke, J. W. Life of R. Emmett. Philadelphia, 1852. 12°. 7732
Burkhard, I. G. Elementary Phil. of Natural Hist. London, 1804. 12°. 10174
Burlamaqui, J. J. Prin. of Nat. and Polit. Law. Tr. Dub. 1776. 2 v. 12°. 11177
Burmese Empire, Account of. M. Symes. Edinburgh, 1826. 2 v. 16°. . 9993
War, Narrative of the. J. J. Snodgrass. London, 1827. 8°. . 7232
Burnap, G. W. Life of L. Calvert, (Lord Baltimore.) Boston, 1846. 12°. 8061
Burnet, G., The Thirty-nine Articles. New York, 1845. 8°. 5309
History of his own Times. Edinburgh, 1753. 6 v. 12°. 6816
History of the Reforma. of the Church of Eng. Lond. 1825. 6 v. 16°. 6868
Life of M. Hale, and J. Wilmot, Earl of Rochester. Lond. 1820 16°. 7775
Burnet, J. Early Settlements of N. W. Territory. New York, 1847. 8°. 7237
Burnet, T. Sacred Theory of the Earth. Glasgow, 1753. 12°. . . . 6527
Burney, C., Memoirs of. Madame F. D'Arblay. Philadelphia, 1833. 8°. 8174
The same. 11333
Burney, Miss F. Cecilia. Boston, 1803. 3 v. 16°. 344
Camilla, or a Picture of Youth. Boston, 1797. 3 v. 16°. . . . 347
Evelina. New York, 1832. 2 v. 12°. 1577
Burns, R., and Clarinda, Correspondence between. New York, 1843. 12°. 4222
Letters. Boston, 1820. 18°. 4628
Life and Land of. A. Cunningham and others. New York, 1841. 12°. 8370

Burns, R. Life. J. G. Lockhart. New York, 1831. 18°. 8438
Poems and Life. Philadelphia, 1822. 2 v. 18°. 2150
Works and Life by A. Cunningham. Boston, 1834. 4 v. 16°. . 2440
The same. Philadelphia, 1834. 8°. 1856
The same. Boston, 1852. 8°. 1795
Burnside, R. Different Sentiments as to the Sabbath. Schenect. 1827. 12°. 6545
Burr, A. Life. M. L. Davis. New York, 1836. 2 v. 8°. 8495
Private Jour. of, in Europe. Ed. M. L. Davis. N. Y. 1838. 2 v. 8°. 10706
Reports of the Trials of. D. Robertson. Philadelphia, 1808. 2 v. 8°. 10734
Burroughs, S. Autobiography. Albany, 1811. 12°. 8719
Burton, E. Description of Antiquities, &c., of Rome. Lond. 1828. 2 v. 12°. 9530
History of the Christian Church. New York, 1839. 12°. . . 5687
Burton, J. H. Life and Correspondence of D. Hume. Edin. 1846. 2 v. 8°. 7869
Burton, R. Anatomy of Melancholy. London, 1826. 2 v. 8°. . . 119
Burton, T. Parliamentary Diary from 1656–59. 4 v. 8°. 10694
Bury, Madame Blaz de. J. Racine and the French Drama. Lond. 1845. 12°. 6884
Busby, T. History of Music and Essays on the Works and Lives of Eminent Composers. London, 1819. 2 v. 8°. 10120
Bush, G. Anastasis, or the Resurrection of the Body. New York, 1846. 8°. 5632
Life of Mohammed. New York, 1846. 12°. 5512
Notes on Exodus. New York, 1840. 2 v. 12°. 5743
The same. New York, 1830. 16°. 6614
Notes on Genesis. New York, 1840. 2 v. 12°. 5741
Treatise on the Millennium. New York, 1832. 12°. 6498
Bush Ranger of Van Dieman's Land. C. Rowcroft. New York, 1846. 8°. 7
Bushnell, H. Christ in Theology. Hartford, 1851. 12°. 5413
Nature and the Supernatural. New York, 1859. 8°. . . . 5085
Sermons for the New Life. New York, 1859. 12°. 5734
Butler, C. Life of H. D'Aguesseau. London, 1830. 8°. 8165
Life of D. Erasmus. London, 1825 8°. 8151
Life of Fenelon. Philadelphia, 1811. 12°. 8087
Life of H. Grotius. London, 1826. 8°. 8160
Reminiscences. New York, 1825. 12°. 3917
Second series. Boston, 1827. 12°. 7719
Butler, F. History of the United States. Hartford, 1821. 3 v. 8°. . . 7374
Sketches of Universal Hist., Sacred and Profane. Hart. 1819. 12°. 7129
Butler, Mrs. F. Star of Seville, a Drama. New York, 1837. 12°. . 2391
Butler, Frances Anne. Journal of. Philadelphia, 1835. 2 v. 12°. . 4527
A Year of Consolation. New York, 1847. 12°. 5714
Butler, James. American Bravery Displayed. Carlisle, 1816. 12°. . 11471
Butler, Joseph. Analogy of Religion to Nature. Boston, 1809. 8°. . 5387
The same. 5627
The same. New Haven, 1822. 12°. 6119
The same, with Sermons. London, 1852. 12°. . . 5426
The same. London, 1834. 12°. 5781½
The same, with Essay by Barnes. (2 copies.) N. Y. 1857. 12°. 5738
Fifteen Sermons, and a Charge to the Clergy. London, 1836. 12°. 5799½
Works. London, 1834. 8°. 5330

Butler, S. (Rev.) Ancient Geography. New York, 1821. 12°. . . . 3374
Butler, S. Hudibras. Edinburgh, 1799. 16°. 2486
Poems, with Life by E. Sanford. Philadelphia, 1819. 2 v. 16°. . 2123
Selections from. Ed. A. Ramsay. London, 1846. 16°. . . . 7161
Butt, G. The Spanish Daughter. Boston, 1824. 2 v. 18°. . . . 1757
Butterflies, Sphinges and Moths, Book of. T. Brown. Lond. 1834. 3 v. 16°. 10253
Buttman, P. Elements of Greek Gram. Tr. E. Everett. Bost. 1831. 8°. 2690
Buxton, T. F. African Slave trade. New York, 1840. 12°. . . . 11147
Memoirs. C. Buxton. Philadelphia, 1849. 8°. . . . . . 7963.
Byron, G. G. (Lord.) Beauties of. London, 1827. 16°. 2074
Bride of Abydos. Philadelphia, 1814. 18°. 11288
Cain, a Mystery. New York, 1822. 16°. 3075
Conversations with. J. Kennedy. Philadelphia, 1853. 12°. . 3382
Conversations with. T. Medwin. Baltimore, 1825. 12°. . . 4853
The same. New York, 1824. 12°. 3898
The same. 8081
The same. 4548
Correspondence of. Philadelphia, 1825. 12°. 3383
The Island. New York, 1823. 16°. 3083
Life. J. Galt. New York, 1832. 16°. 6634
The same. New York, 1841. 12°. 5260
The same. New York, 1830. 16°. 6635
Life, Letters and Journal. T. Moore. New York, 1830. 2 v. 8°. 8191
Sardanapalus. New York, 1822. 16°. 2081
and his Contemporaries. L. Hunt. London, 1828. 2 v. 8°. . . 8145
Works. Philadelphia, 1824. 8 v. 16°. 2093
The same. New York, 1825. 7 v. 18°. 2736
The same. Boston, 1852. 8°. 1793
The same, with Life. (vol. 8 missing.) Lond. 1832. 17 v. 12°. 2307

Vol. 1–6. Life.
6. Miscellaneous Pieces in Prose.
7. Hours of Idleness, English Bards and Scotch Reviewers; Occasional Pieces.
9. Hints from Horace: Curse of Minerva; The Waltz; The Giaour; Bride of Abydos; The Corsair; Occasional Pieces.
10. Ode to Napoleon; Lara; Hebrew Melodies; Siege of Corinth; Domestic and Occasional Pieces; Prisoner of Chillon; The Dream.
11. Manfred; Lament of Tasso; Beppo: Mazeppa; Ode on Venice; Morgante Maggiore; Prophecy of Dante; Occasional Pieces.
12. Francesca of Rimini; Stanzas to the Po, &c.; The Blues; Marino Faliero, Doge of Venice; Vision of Judgment; Occasional Pieces.
13. Heaven and Earth; Sardanapalus; The Two Foscari; The Deformed Transformed.
14. Cain; Werner; Age of Bronze; The Island; Stanzas, To a Hindoo Air, &c.
15. Testimonies of Authors concerning Don Juan; Byron's Observations upon the same.
15–17. Don Juan.

C.

Cabinet Cyclopædia. D. Lardner and others. See Lardner, D.
of Curiosities. Hartford, 1822. 2 v. 12°. 3328
Portrait Gallery of British Worthies. London, 1846. 5 v. 16°. . 6887
The same. vols. 6, 7 and 8. 7201

Vol. 1. Henry II; R. Bacon; Wicliffe; Chaucer; William of Wykeham.
2. Henry V; James I, of Scotland; Dr. J. Colet; Cardinal Wolsey; Sir T. More.
3. T. Cromwell; H. Howard; Earl of Surrey; Lady Jane Gray; Cranmer; Latimer; J. Knox.
4. Sir T. Graham; J. Buchanan; Sir P. Sidney; Sir F. Drake; Lord Burghley; E. Spencer.
5. Queen Elizabeth; W. Shakspeare; Sir Walter Raleigh; Camden; F. Bacon; Ben. Jonson.

Cabot, S. Memoirs. Philadelphia, 1831. 8°. 8500
Cæsar, C. J. Commentaria. Lipsiæ, 1829. 16°. 10608
Ed. D. Patterson. New York, 1833. 12°. 7432
Trans. W. Duncan. New York, 1840. 2 v. 12° 5265
Duplicate of vol. 2. New York, 1835. 16°. 8746
Cæsar Borgia. Life. A. Gordon. London, 1729. Folio. . . . 11244
Cæsars, The. T. De Quincey. Boston, 1851. 12°. 891
Cæsars. The first 12. Lives. Elisha Rogers. London, 1811. 5 v. 8°. . 7377
The first 12. C. Suetonius Tranquillus. Tr. Lond. 1796. 8°. . 8564
Cain, a Mystery. Byron G. G. Lord. New York, 1822. 16°. . . 3075
Cairo, Jerusalem, &c., Excursions to. G. Jones. New York, 1836. 12°. . 9630
Journey from Cornhill to. W. M. Thackeray. New York, 1846. 12°. 9846
Calavar, or the Knight of the Conquest. R. M. Bird. Phil. 1835. 2 v. 12°. 227
Calculus, Integral and Differential. W. Hopkins. London, 1833. 8°. . 5096
Calderon, the Courtier. E. L. Bulwer. Philadelphia, 1838. 12°. . . 1559
Caldwell, J. S. Results of Reading. London, 1843. 8°. 419
Calef, R. Salem Witchcraft. Boston, 1828. 18°. 4623
Calhoun, J. C. Life, Speeches, &c. New York, 1843. 8°. . . 10964
Disquisition on Government, and Discourse on the Constitution and Government of the United States. Charleston, 1854. 8°. . . 10074
California. Debates in Const. Convention of. Washington, 1850. 8°. . 10435
Life in. A. Robinson. New York, 1846. 12°. 8889
Messages and Correspondence concerning. Washington, 1850. 8°. 10414
and Oregon. History of. R. Greenhow. Boston, 1845. 8°. . 7539
Texas, &c. Explorations in. J. R. Bartlett. N. Y. 1854. 2 v. 8°. 9376
What I saw in. E. Bryant. Philadelphia, 1848. 12°. . . . 9603
Californias, Travels in the. T. J. Farnham. New York, 1844. 8°. . 9484
Call to the Unconverted. R. Baxter. New York, 1839. 16°. . . 6230
Callcott, J. W. Musical Grammar. Boston, 1833. 16°. 10250
Callcott, Maria. History of Spain. London, 1828. 12°. . . . 7100
Callet, F. Logarithmes. Paris, 1795. 8°. 11666
Calmet, A. Dictionary of the Holy Bible. Ed. E. Robinson. Bost. 1832. 8°. 8795
Calvary, or Death of Christ, a Poem. R. Cumberland. Burling. 1795. 12°. 2380
Calvert, L. Life. G. W. Burnap. Boston, 1846. 12°. 8061
Calvin, J. Life. T. Beza. Tr. F. Sibson. Philadelphia, 1836. 12°. . . 8687
Institutes of the Christian Religion. Tr. J. Allen. Lond. 1838. 2 v. 8°. 5083
Calvinism Improved. J. Huntington. London, 1796. 8°. 5646
Cambacéres, J. J. R., Evenings with. L. L. Langon. Phil. 1838. 2 v. 12°. 8364
Cambridge, Conversations at. London, 1836. 12°. 3367
University Calendar for 1822. 12°. 3026
Camel Hunt, The. J. W. Fabens. Boston, 1851. 12°. 9821
Camilla, or a Picture of Youth. Miss F. Burney. Bost. 1797. 3 v. 12°. . 347

Camoëns, L. De. The Lusiad, an Epic Poem. Tr. Dublin, 1791. 2 v. 8°. 1862
Camp, G. S. Democracy. New York, 1841. 12°. 5912
Camp of Refuge, The. London, 1844. 2 v. 18°. 7476
Campaign of 1781 in the Carolinas. H. Lee. Philadelphia, 1824. 8°. . 7224
in Navarre, &c. C. F. Henningsen. Philadelphia, 1836. 12°. . 7422
Campaigns of the British Army at Washington and N. Orleans in 1814, 15.
London, 1836. 12°. 9831
Dragoon, to the Rocky Mountains. New York, 1836. 12°. . . 9807
of 1780 and 1781, Hist. of. B. Tarleton. London, 1787. 4°. . 11261
The same. Dublin, 1787. 8°. 6752
Campan, Mad. Memoirs of Maria Antoinette. Philadelphia, 1823. 8°. . 8535
Campbell, or the Scottish Probationer, a Novel. London, 1819. 2 v. 12°. 705
Campbell, A. and J. Walker. Debate on Baptism. Steubenville, 1820. 12°. 6492
Campbell, A. Voyage Round the World. New York, 1819. 12°. . . 9803
Campbell, D. Adventures in Overland Journey to India. N. Y. 1789. 12°. 9036
Campbell, G. Lectures on Ecclesiastical History. London, 1834. 8°. . 5031
Philosophy of Rhetoric. London, 1801. 2 v. 12°. . . . 10814
The same. Edinburgh, 1816. 2 v. 8°. 5064
Campbell, J. Lives of British Admirals to 1816. London, 1817. 8 v. 8°. 8554
Campbell, J. (Lord.) Lives of Chief Justices of England. Phil. 1851. 2 v. 8°. 7982
Lives of Atrocious Judges. Ed. R. Hildreth. N. Y. 1856. 12°. . 8638
Lives of the Lord Chancellors of Eng. to 1688. Lond. 1845. 3 v. 8°. 7878
Third series, from 1773 to 1838. London, 1845. 2 v. 8°. . . 7881
Campbell, J. W. Hist. of Virginia from Discovery to 1781. Phil. 1831. 12° 7442
Campbell, Mrs. M. Life of W. Hull. New York, 1848. 8°. . . . 7812
Campbell, T., Biographical Sketch of. W. Irving. New York, 1841. 12°. 2217
Frederick the Great, his Court and Times. London, 1844. 2 v. 8°. 8262
Life of F. Petrarch. Philadelphia, 1841. 8°. 7826
Life and Letters. W. Beattie. New York, 1850. 2 v. 12°. . . 7993
Poems and Memoir of. New York, 1850. 12°. 2438
Poems and Memoir of. vol. 2. Albany, 1810. 12°. 3046
S. Rogers and others. Poems. London, 1830. 8°. 1869
The same. Philadelphia, 1830. 1882
Campbell, W. British India, Decline of Hindooism and Progress of Christianity. London, 1839. 8°. 9476
Campbell, W. W. Annals of Tryon County, New York. N. Y. 1831. 8°. 11365
The same. New York, 1849. 12°. 11460
Memoir of Mrs. J. S. Grant. New York, 1844. 12°. 8385
Camperdown, or News from our Neighborhood. Philadelphia, 1836. 12°. 1467
Canada in 1837, 8. E. A. Theller. Philadelphia, 1841. 2 v. 12°. . . 6786
Backwoods of. London, 1846. 18°. 6886
Bubbles of. T. C. Haliburton. Philadelphia, 1839. 12°. . . 10807
Lower, Sketches of. J. Samson. New York, 1817. 12°. . . 9005
The same. 9035
Narrative of an Administration in. F. B. Head. London, 1839. 8°. 9115
Canadas, Hist., Statistics and Geography of. R. M. Martin. Lond. 1844. 12°. 5818
Canning, C. Life. R. Bell. New York, 1846. 12°. 7729
Memoirs. London, 1828. 2 v. 8°. 8644

Canning, C. Select Speeches. Philadelphia, 1835. 8°. 10658
Speeches and Life. R. Therry. London, 1836. 6 v. 8°. . . 10634
Canot, T. Twenty Yrs. of an African Slaver. Ed. B. Mayer. N.Y. 1854. 12°. 9791
Canterbury Tales, from Chaucer. Ed. J. Saunders. vol. 1. Lond. 1845. 16°. 7168
Capefigue, B. H. R. Diplomatists of Europe. Trans. Lond. 1845. 12°. 8396
Capital and Labor. C. Knight. London, 1845. 16°. 6885
Capital Punishment. G. B. Cheever. New York, 1842. 12°. . . . 6475
Cappadocia, History of. London, 1779. 8°. 7037
Captives, The, a Comedy. Plautus. Ed. J. Proudfit. N. Y. 1843. 16°. 3056
Carafas of Maddaloni. A. de Reumont. Trans. London, 1854. 12°. . 5180
Carew, T. Select Poems, with Life by E. Sanford. Phil. 1819. 16°. . 2119
Carey, Alice. Clovernook. New York, 1852. 12°. 562
Carey, H. C. Essay on the Rates of Wages. Philadelphia, 1835. 12°. . 10759
Carey, M. Miscellaneous Essays. Philadelphia, 1830. 8°. . . . 118
Carl Werner, and other Tales. W. G. Simms. New York, 1838. 2 v. 12°. 1543
Carlotina and the Sanfedesti. E. Farrenc. New York, 1853. 12°. . 560
Carlton, R. New Purchase. New York, 1843. 2 v. 12°. . . . 1290
Carlyle, T. Chartism. Boston, 1840. 12°. 863
The same. New York, 1848. 12°. 813
Critical and Miscellaneous Essays. Boston, 1838. 4 v. 12°. . . 844
The same. Boston, 1855. 8°. 26
German Romance, Specimens of. Boston, 1841. 2 v. 12°. . . 1214
Heroes and Hero-Worship. New York, 1841. 12°. . . . 848
The same. New York, 1841. 12°. 825
History of Frederick the Great. New York, 1859. 2 v. 12°. . 8655
Latter-Day Pamphlets. 1850. 12°. 812
Life of J. Sterling. Boston, 1852. 12°. 8002
Life of F. Schiller. London, 1825. 8°. 8158
The same. Boston, 1833. 12°. 8033
Past and Present. Boston, 1843. 12°. 11117
The same. Philadelphia, 1837. 12°. 247
The same. New York, 1848. 12°. 813
Carmichael, A. Life of J. G. Spurzheim. Boston, 1833. 12°. . . . 8682
Carpenter, W. W. Travels and Adventures in Mexico. N. Y. 1851. 12°. 9576
Carpenter, S. C. (Ed.) Select American Speeches. Phil. 1815. 3 v. 8°. . 10750
Carr, J. The Stranger in Ireland. New York, 1807. 12°. . . . 8915
Carrick, J. D. Life of Sir W. Wallace. London. 8°. 50
Carrel, A. Counter-Revolution in England, History of. London, 1846. 12°. 5492
Carter, Mrs. E. Letters to Mrs. Montagu. London, 1817. 3 v. 8°. . 435
Memoirs. M. Pennington. Boston, 1809. 8°. 8129
Carter, N. H. Letters from Europe. New York, 1827. 2 v. 8°. . . 9430
Carthaginians, History of the. London, 1779. 8°. 7042
Carver, J. Travels in North America. Philadelphia, 1796. 8°. . . 9214
Carver, John. Sketches of New England. New York, 1842. 12°. . . 9830
Cary, H. Civil War in England from 1646 to 1652. Lond. 1842. 2 v. 8°. 6967
Cary, H. F. Lives of Eng. Poets from S. Jonson to K. White. Lond. 1846. 12°. 8092
Memoir. H. Cary. London, 1847. 2 v. 12°. 8283
Translation and Notices of Early French Poets. London, 1846. 12°. 8093

Caspar Hauser, Account of. Boston, 1832. 16°. 7759
Cass, L. France, its King, Court, &c. New York, 1840. 18°. . . 7603
The same, with "Three Hours at St. Cloud." N. Y. 1841. 12°. 6805
Michigan, Hist. and Scientific Sketches of. Detroit, 1834. 12°. . 7427
Castilian, The. New York, 1829. 2 v. 12°. . . . . , . . 1406
Castle Dangerous. Sir W. Scott. Boston, 1845. 12°. 302
See also Scott, Sir W.
Castle of Otranto, The. H. Walpole. Philadelphia, 1840. 12°. . . 659
Castriot, G. Life. C. C. Moore. New York, 1850. 12°. . . . 8312
Catacombs of Rome. W. I. Kip. New York, 1859. 12°. . . . 6466
Catalogue of the Astor Library. New York, 1851. 8°. 9714
of Books on the Masonic Institution. Boston, 1852. 8°. . . 9711
of the Brothers' Library, Yale College. New Haven, 1851. 8°. . 9717
of the Free Public Library, New Bedford, Mass. N. B. 1858. 12°. 9709
de Livres Français. H. Bossange. Paris, 1845. 8°. . . . 8810
of the Library of the Amer. Antiq. Soc. in Worcester. 1837. 8°. . 9707
of the Library of Harvard University. Cambridge, 1830. 5 v. 8°. 9702
of the Library of the Young Men's Association, Alb. Alb. 1853. 8°. 9712
of the Young Men's Institute, Hartford. Hartford, 1844. 8°. . 9710
of the Linonian Library, Yale College. New Haven, 1846. 8°. . 9715
of the Mercantile Library, Boston. Boston, 1854. 8°. . . . 9717
of the Mercantile Library, New York. New York, 1837. 8°. . 9718
The same, revised. New York, 1850. 8°. 9708
Catalogues of Yale College. 1817–42. New Haven. 8°. . . . 9716
Catcott, A. Treatise on the Deluge. London, 1768. 8°. 5380
Catechism, Exposition of the. T. Vincent. New Haven, 1810. 12°. . 6610
Lectures on the. J. Abercrombie. Philadelphia, 1811. 8°. . . 5108
Catel, C. S. Treatise on Harmony. Boston, 1832. 12°. 4881
Catholic and Protestant Nations. N. Roussell. Boston, 1855. 8°. . . 5621
Church Controversy. W. C. Brownlee. New York, 1834. 8°. . 6427
Doctrines and Practices of. N. Wiseman. London, 1844. 12°. . 5675
Catlin, G. Manners, Customs, &c. of N. Amer. Indians. N. Y. 1841. 2 v. 8°. 9071
Notes of Travels in Europe. London, 1848. 2 v. 8°. . . . 9399
Catlin, J. Essays on Divine Truth. Hartford, 1818. 12°. . . . 4590
The same, with Questions. Middletown, 1826. 12°. . . 6551
Catullus. Carmina. Lipsiæ, 1843. 16°. 10853
Caubul, Account of the Kingdom of. M. Elphinstone. Lond. 1839. 2 v. 8°. 7590
Caucasus and Georgia, Letters from. London, 1823. 8°. 9435
Georgia and Persia, Travels in. R. Wilbraham. Lond. 1839. 8°. 9139
Western, Travels in. E. Spencer. London, 1838. 2 v. 8°. . . 9085
Caulincourt, A. A. L. de. Napoleon and his Times. Phil. 1838. 2 v. 12°. 8366
Caulkins, Miss F. M. History of New London, Ct. N. Lond. 1852. 8°. . 12049
History of Norwich, Ct. Norwich, 1845. 12°. 6768
Caunter, J. H. Poetry of the Pentateuch. London, 1839. 2 v. 8°. . 5027
Cave, W. Lives of the Apostles. London, 1834. 2 v. 12°. . . . 5777
Primitive Christianity. London, 1834. 2 v. 12°. 5785
Cavendish, T. and others. Lives and Voyages. New York, 1832. 16°. . 6615
The same. 8762
The same. New York, 1840. 12°. 5531

Cawthorne, J. Select Poems, with Life, by E. Sanford. Phil. 1819. 18°. . 2136
Caxton, W. Life. C. Knight. London, 1844. 16°. 7209
Caxtons, The. E. L. Bulwer. London, 1855. 12°. 554
Cecil, J. Memoirs of J. Newton. Philadelphia, 1839. 8°. . . . 5328
Cecil, Richard. Remains of. J. Pratt. Boston, 1833. 16°. . . . 6234
Cecil, R. (Earl of Salisbury.) Life. T. P. Courtenay. London, 1838. 12°. 9936
Cecil, W. (Lord Burleigh.) Life. London, 1832. 12°. 9932
Cecilia. Miss F. Burney. Boston, 1803. 3 v. 12°. 344
Celebrated Characters, Mem's of. A. De Lamartine. N. Y. 1854–6. 3 v. 12°. 8013
Celestial Scenery. T. Dick. New York, 1841. 12°. 5542
Cellini, B. Antobiography. London, 1828. 2 v. 16°. 7495
The same. 8431
Celtes, History of the. London, 1779. 8°. 7032
Celtic Manners. J. Logan. Boston, 1833. 8° 7351
Census Reports. See U. S. Public Documents.
Cerceau, Father. Life and Times of N. Rienzi. Phil. 1836. 12°. . . 8662
Cervantes, M. de. Don Quixote, Tr. C. Jarvis. Exeter, 1827. 4 v. 24°. 1733
The same. New York, 1855. 12°. 206
The same. Tr. C. Jarvis. Illust. Phil. 1852. 2 v. 8°. . 127
The same. New York, 1825. 3 v. 18°. 1765
Ceylon. Account of the Island of. R. Percival. London, 1805. 4°. . 11253
Chairolas, Prince of Paida. E. L. Bulwer. Phil. 1836. 12°. . . . 1240
Challenge of Barletta. M. D'Azeglio. Tr. New York, 1845. 12°. . 667
Chalmers, R. Biog. Dictionary of Eminent Scotsmen. Glasgow, 1835. 4 v. 8°. 8139
Chalmers, T. Application of Christianity to Affairs of Life. Hart. 1821. 12°. 6186
Christian Revelation. Authority of. Hartford, 1816. 16° . . 6237
Christian Rev. in Connection with Mod. Astronomy. N. Y. 1817. 8°. 5366
Lectures on the Romans. New York, 1844. 8°. 5588
The same. New York, 1843. 8°. 5016
Miscellanies. New York, 1847. 8°. 711
Nature Adapt. to Moral and Intell. Const. of Man. Phil. 1836. 8°. 6382
The same. Philadelphia, 1833. 12°. 6110
Polit. Econ. in Connection with Moral State of Soc. N. Y. 1832. 12°. 10797
Posthumous Works. Ed. W. Hanna. New York, 1851. 9 v. 12°. . 5762

Vol. 1–3. Daily Scripture Readings.
4, 5. Sabbath Scripture Readings.
6. Sermons.
7, 8. Institutes of Theology.
9. Lectures and Addresses.

Sermons. New York, 1848. 2 v. 8°. 5057
Works. Philadelphia, 1833. 8°. 5336
The same. Bridgeport, 1829. 3 v. 8°. 5382

Vol. 1. Evidence of Christianity ; Christian Revelation viewed in connection with Modern Astronomy ; Depravity of Human Nature.
2. Last concluded ; Application of Christianity to the Commercial and Ordinary Affairs of Life ; Charity Sermons.
3. Miscellaneous Sermons.

Chambers, R. Biog. Dict. of Eminent Scotsmen. Glasgow, 1835. 4 v. 8°. 8199
Cyclopædia of English Literature. Edinburgh, 1844. 2 v. 4°. . 8803
Hist. of Rebellions in Scotl'd, from 1638–1660. Edin. 1828. 2 v. 16°. 10007
in 1689 and 1715. Edinburgh, 1829. 16°. 10017
from 1745–1746. Edinburgh, 1827. 2 v. 16°. . . . 9998

Chambers' Miscellany. Ed. W. Chambers. Boston, 10 v. 12°. . . . 6161
Duplicate of vol. 1. 4283
Duplicates of vols. 8, 9 and 10. 1171
Papers for the People. Boston. 6 v. 12°. 1115
Chamier, F. Ben Brace. Philadelphia, 1836. 2 v. 12°. 1287
Champion, The. London, 1743. 2 v. 12°. 3012
Chancellors of England to 1688. Lives. J. Campbell. 3 v. 8°. . . 7878
Third series, from 1773–1838. London, 1847. 2 v. 8°. . . 7881
Channing, E. T. Life of W. Ellery. (Two copies.) Boston, 1836. 12°. . 8047
Channing, W. E. Discourses, &c. Boston, 1830. 8°. 6381
Emancipation. Boston, 1840. 12°. 11874
Essay on the Character of Napoleon. Boston, 1826. 8°. . . 6381
Slavery. Boston, 1835. 12°. 11197
Memoirs. Boston, 1848. 3 v. 12°. 5410
Works. Boston, 1841. 5 v. 8°. 6356

Vol. 1. Character and Writings of Milton—also of Fenelon; Life and Character of Napoleon; Moral Argument against Calvanism; National Literature; Remarks on Associations—also on Education; The Union.
2. Slavery; Abolitionists; Annexation of Texas to the United States; Catholicism; Creeds; Temperance; Self-culture.
3, 4. Sermons.
5. Letters on Slavery; Sermons and Lectures.

Chapin. A. B. Primitive Church. New Haven, 1842. 12°. 6125
Chapman, E. J. Notes on the New Testament. Canandaigua, 1819. 8°. . 6394
Chapman, N. Ed. Select Speeches, Forensic, &c. Philadel. 1808. 5 v. 8°. 10737
Duplicate of vol. 2. 11048
Character Essential to Success in Life. I. Taylor. Boston, 1820. 18°. 4943
Human, Book of. C. Bucke. London, 1837. 12°. 5805
Characteristics of Men, Manners, &c. Earl of Shaftesbury. 1749. 3 v. 18°. 4624
Charcoal Sketches. J. C. Neal. Philadelphia, 1838. 12°. 649
Charicles, or Private Life of Greeks. W. A. Becker. Tr. Lond. 1854. 8°. 11404
Charke, Mrs. Autobiography. London, 1830. 16°. 7486
The same. London, 1826. 16°. 7751
Charlemagne, or Church Delivered. L. Bonaparte. Phil. 1815. 2 v. 18°. 2752
History of. G. P. R. James. New York, 1833. 16°. 6613
The same. New York, 1841. 12°. 5876
Charles I. Diary of La. Willoughby relating to Reign of. N. Y. 1848. 12°. 8332
The same. New York, 1845. 12°. 9843
Court of. Lucy Aikin. Philadelphia, 1833. 2 v. 8°. . . . 8531
Life. W. Harris. London, 1814. 8°. 8154
Pourtraicture of. London, 1824. 12°. 7717
Charles II. Beauties of Court of. Mrs. A. Jameson. Phil 1839. 8°. 1897
Diary of the Times of. H. Sidney. London, 1843. 2 v. 8° . 7843
Life. W. Harris. London, 1814. 2 v. 8°. 8155
Memoirs. Count Grammont. Ed. Sir W. Scott, London, 1846. 12°. 11472
Charles V, History of the Reign of. W. Robertson. Albany, 1822. 3 v. 8°. 8184
The same. Ed. W. H. Prescott. Boston, 1857. 3 v. 8°. . 7821
Charles VIII of France, and Charles the Bold. History of. Philip de Comines. Trans. London, 1823. 2 v. 12°. 8268

Charles IX, Chronicles of the Times of. Tr. New York, 1830. 8°. . . 11389
Charles, XII of Sweden. F. M. A. de Voltaire. Tr. Otsego, 1811. 16°. 8465
The same. 11419
Histoire de. F. M. A. de Voltaire. Boston, 1823. 12°. . . . 8436
The same. New York, 1835. 16°. 8449
Charles Elwood. O. A. Brownson. Boston, 1840. 12°. 1643
Charles John, of Sweden. Memoirs. J. Philippart. Baltimore, 1815. 8°. 8565
Charles Lever, or the Man of the 19th Cent. W. Gresley. N. Y. 1843. 12°. 565
Charles O'Malley. C. Lever. Philadelphia, 1841. 8°. 46
Charles Tyrrell, or the Bitter Blood. G. P. R. James. N. Y. 1839. 2 v. 12°. 1527
The same. 1529
Charlotte Elizabeth. See Tonna, Mrs. C. E.
Charmed Sea, a Tale. Miss H. Martineau. Boston, 1832. 18°. . . 1699
Charnock, J. Naval Biography of Great Britain. Lond. 1794–8. 6 v. 8°. 8812
Chartism. T. Carlyle. Boston, 1840. 12°. 863
The same. New York, 1848. 12°. 813
Chastity, Lectures to Young Men on. S. Graham. Boston, 1847. 16°. . 6221
Chateaubriand, F. A. de. Beauties of Christianity. Tr. Phil. 1815. 8°. 5362
Congress of Verona. Tr. London, 1838. 2 v. 8°. . . . 7918
Martyrs, or Triumphs of Christian Religion. Tr. N. Y. 1812. 3 v. 12°. 6552
Recollection of Italy, England and America. Tr. Phil. 1816. 8°. 9158
Sketches of English Literature. Tr. London, 1836. 2 v. 8°. . 75
Travels in Greece, Palestine, Egypt, &c. Tr. N. Y. 1814. 8°. . 9468
Chatfield, C. Teutonic Antiquities. London, 1828. 8°. 11334
Chatfield, P. The Tin Trumpet. Philadelphia, 1836. 2 v. 12°. . . 1605
Chatham, Earl of. See Pitt, W.
Chatham and Mary Kay. H. Martineau. Hartford, 1845. 24°. . . 1680
Chatterton, T. Life. J. Davis. London. 16°. 7770
Poetical Works and Life. Cambridge, 1842. 2 v. 12°. . . . 8640
Select Poems and Life. Philadelphia, 1822. 18°. 2141
Chaucer, G. Canterbury Tales. Ed. J. Saunders. London, 1845. 16°. . 7168
Memoirs. J. Saunders. London, 1845. 16°. 7174
Poems, Select, with Life by E. Sanford. Philadelphia, 1819. 16°. 2118
Poems Modernized. London, 1841. 12°. 2050
Poetical Works, with Life by H. Nicolas. London, 1845. 6 v. 12°. 2036

Vol. 1. Memoir; Essay on the Language and Versification of Chaucer by T. Tyrwhitt; Introductory Discourses to the Canterbury Tales.
2, 3. Canterbury Tales.
4. The Romaunt of the Rose; Troilus and Creeside.
5. The Last Concluded; Legend of Good Women, Goodly Ballade of Chaucer; The Booke of the Dutchesse, or Death of Blanch; The Assembly of Foules.
6. Miscellaneous Pieces.

Cheetham, J. Life of T. Paine. London, 1817. 8°. 7898
Cheever, G. B. Hill of Difficulty and other Allegories. N. Y. 1849. 18°. 6362
(Editor) Journal of the Pilgrims at Plymouth, 1620. N. Y. 1849. 12°. 6794
Lectures on the Pilgrim's Progress. New York, 1845. 8°. . . 5061
The same. New York. 1849. 8°. 6363
Punishment by Death, its Authority & Expediency. N. Y. 1842. 12°. 6475
Wanderings in the Shadow of Mt. Blanc. New York, 1846. 12°. 9857

Cheever, G. B. Windings of the River of the Water of Life. N. Y. 1849. 8°. 6361
Cheever, H. T. Life in the Sandwich Islands. New York, 1851. 12°. . 8974
Chelsea Hospital. G. R. Gleig. London, 1838. 3 v. 12°. 1437
Chemical Affinity, Laws of. C. L. Berthollet. Tr. Baltimore, 1809. 12°. 6090
Chemistry, Animal. J. Liebig. Cambridge, 1842. 12°. 6051
Botany and Physiology. London, 1831. 8°. 5099
of Common Life. J. F. W. Johnston. New York, 1856. 2 v. 12°. 6082
Elements of. J. Black. Philadelphia, 1807. 3 v. 8°. 5975
Elements of. R. Kane. New York, 1843. 8°. 5950
Experimental. W. Henry. Philadelphia, 1822. 3 v. 8°. . . . 5979
First Principles of. B. Silliman, Jr. Phil. 1858. 12°. 6075
Geology, Agriculture, &c. J. F. W. Johnston. N. Y. 1847. 12°. . 6076
Lecture on. T. Cooper. Carlisle, 1812. 8°. 5974
Meteorology in Reference to Nat. Theol. W. Prout. Phil. 1834. 12°. 6483
The same. Philadelphia, 1836. 8°. 6382
Organic, its Applications to Agriculture and Physiology. J. Liebig. Cambridge, 1841. 12°. 6050
The same. New York. 1848. 12°. 6068
Theoretical and Practical. F. Accum. Phil. 1814. 2 v. 8°. . . 5965
Treatise on. M. Donovan. London, 1837. 12°. 9113
Chenevix, R. Essay on National Character. London, 1832. 2 v. 8°. . 10647
Chess, Book of. H. R. Agnel. New York, 1859. 12°. 1143
Chess-Player's Companion. H. Staunton. London, 1849. 12°. . . . 1161
Chess-Players. Engraved from a Drawing by M. Retzsch. 4°.
Chester, J. L. Greenwood Cemetery and other Poems. N. Y. 1843. 12°. 1940
Chesterfield, Earl of, (P. D. Stanhope,) Beauties of. Boston, 1828. 18°. . 4620
The same. Boston. 1831. 18°. 11150
Letters to his Son. vol. 3. New York, 1824. 18°. . . . 4949
The same. Boston, 1779. 2 v. 12°. 4873
The same. London, 1804. 4 v. 12°. 4918
Reflections on the Letters of. T. Hunter. London, 1777. 8°. . 432
Selections from the Letters of. Philadelphia, 1827. 18°. . . 4938
The same. Philadelphia, 1828. 18°. 11271
Works, with Memoirs. London, 1779. 4 v. 8°. 440
Cheveley, or the Man of Honor. Lady L. Bulwer. N. Y. 1839. 2 v. 12°. 1541
Chief Justices of England, Lives of. J. Lord Campbell. Phil. 1851. 2 v. 8°. 7982
Child, Mrs. L. M. Hobomok. Boston, 1824. 12°. 1653
Letters from New York. 1st and 2d series. N. Y. 1843. 2 v. 12°. 8966
Philothea. New York, 1836. 12°. 1570
(Editor,) The Oasis. Boston, 1834. 12°. 4894
Child of the Islands. Mrs. C. E. S. Norton. New York, 1846. 12°. . 5847
Chili, Tour in Southern. E. R. Smith. New York, 1855. 12°. . . . 9592
and La Plata, Travels in. J. Miers. London, 1826. 2 v. 8°. . . 9772
Peru and Mexico, Travels in, 1820–2. B. Hall. Phil. 1824. 2 v. 12°. 9034
The same. Edinburgh, 1827. 2 v. 16°. 9987
Chillingworth, W. Works. London, 1836. 8°. 10681
China, British Embassy to. A. Anderson. New York, 1795. 12°. . . 9044
Commercial Intercourse with. London, 1842. 12°. 5934

China, Description of. J. Conder. London, 1827. 16°. 9340
The same. 9669
Embassy from Great Britain to. G. Staunton. Dub. 1798. 2 v. 8°. 9211
and the English. New York, 1838. 16°. 11160
History of. London, 1781. 8°. 7053
and its Inhabitants. See Chinese, General Description of.
Residence in, from 1829–33. D. Abeel. New York, 1834. 12°. . 9804
Six Months in. Lord Jocelyn. London, 1841. 12°. . . . 9283
its State and Prospects. W. H. Medhurst. London, 1838. 8°. . 9446
Travels in. J. Barrow. Philadelphia, 1805. 8°. 9454
Voyages along the Coast of. C. Gutzlaff. New York, 1833. 12°. 9793
Visit to the Consular Cities of. G. Smith. New York, 1847. 12°. 9557
Chinese as they are. G. T. Lay. London, 1841. 8°. 9521
General Descriptron of the. J. F. Davis. N. Y. 1840. 2 v. 12°. . 5890
The same. London, 1840. 12°. 9284
The same, with a supplementary vol. Lond. 1845. 3 v. 16°. 7184
and Egyptians. C. de Pauw. Tr. London, 1795. 2 v. 8°. . . 11373
Empire, History of the. W. Winterbotham. London, 1795. 8°. . 6749
Empire, Journey through. M. Huc. New York, 1857. 2 v. 12°. 9805
Empire, Survey of. S. W. Williams. (2 cop.) N. Y. 1848. 2 v. 12°. 9585
Philosopher, Letters from London. London, 1782. 2 v. 12°. . . 8720
Chips from the Workshop. Poems. C. Ives. New Haven, 1843. 12°. . 2338
Chivalry, Ancient, Memoirs of. De St. Palaye. Tr. London, 1784. 8°. 7382
and the Crusades, History of. G. P. R. James. N. Y. 1831. 16°. 6625
The same. New York, 1840. 12°. 5524
The same. New York, 1831. 16°. 6643
History of. C. Mills. Philadelphia, 1826. 8°. 7228
and Romance, Letters on. R. Hurd. London, 1762. 12°. . . 4871
True Sense and Practice of. K. H. Digby. London, 1844. 12°. . 1174
Chorley, H. F. Life of Mrs. Hemans. London, 1842. 12°. . . . 8575
Sketches of a Sea-Port Town. Philadelphia, 1836. 2 v. 12°. . 1509
Choules, J. O. and T. Smith. History of Missions. Boston, 1842. 2 v. 4°. 4990
Christ, Divine Testimony Concerning. H. Grew. Hartford, 1824. 12°. 6120
Kingdom of. F. D. Maurice. New York, 1843. 8°. 5015
Kingdom of. R. Whately. New York, 1842. 12°. . . . 5696
Life of, A. Neander. New York, 1848, 8°. 6332
our Law. Caroline Fry. New York, 1842. 12°. . . . 5415
in Theology. H. Bushnell. Hartford, 1851. 12°. 5413
Christian Character, Essays on. G. Spring. New York, 1840. 12°. . 6123
Formation of the. H. Ware, Jr. Boston, 1831. 12°. . . . 6210
The same. 6212
Church. See Church.
Contemplated, The. W. Jay. New York, 1831. 16°. . . . 6238
The same. New York, 1831. 12°. 6549
Directory. R. Baxter. London, 1678. Folio. . . . 11243
Doctrine. J. Milton. Boston, 1825. 2 v. 8°. 5312
Education. T. Babington. Boston, 1819. 12°. 6550
Essays. S. E. Wilks. Boston, 1829. 12°. 6183

Christian Ethics. R. Wardlaw. New York, 1835. 12°. 5652
Instructed in the Ways of the Gospel and Church. J. A. Spencer. New York, 1844. 12°. 6525
Library. (vols. 1, 24–30 missing.) New York, 12° and 18°. . . 5223

Vol. 2. Practical View and Touchstone. W. Wilberforce.
3. Treatise on Religious Affections. J Edwards. Alarm to the Unconverted. J. Alleine.
4. The Pilgrim's Progress. J. Bunyan.
5. Saints' Rest. R. Baxter.
6. Call to the Unconverted. R. Baxter.
7. Life of Brainerd. J. Edwards.
8. Memoir of H. Martyn. J. Sargent.
9. History of Redemption. J. Edwards.
10. Persuasives to Early Piety. J. Pike. (Two copies.)
11. Guide for Young Disciples. J. Pike.
12. Memoir of Payson. A. Cummings.
13. Practical Thoughts. W. Nevins.
14. Evidences of Christianity. S. Jenyns and others.
15. Memoir of J. B. Taylor. J. and B. Rice.
16. Memoir of Buchanan. H. Pearson.
17. Elijah the Tishbite. F. Krummacher.
18. Essay on the Divine Authority of the New Testament. D. Bogue.
19. Bible Thoughts. H. Melvill.
20. Mammon or Covetousness. J Harris. Discourse on Meekness. M. Henry.
21. Treatise on Self-Knowledge. J. Mason. Counsels to Y'ng Men. J. Morrison.
22. Memoir of Pearce. A. Fuller. Memoir of Kilpin.
23. Memoir of Page. W. Hallock. Memoir of Hannah Hobbie. R. Armstrong.
31. Fountain of Life. J. Flavel.
32. Young Christian. J. Abbott.
33. Lives of Newton, Leighton, and Swartz; and Sermons to the Aged.

Christian life, Endeavors after the. J. Martineau. Boston, 1858. 12°. . 12170
Life in Early and Middle Ages. A. Neander. Tr. Lond. 1852. 12°. 5207
Ministry. Letters to those entering. W. Cogswell. Bost. 1837. 16°. 4934
Morals. Hannah More. New York, 1813. 16°. 6644
T. Browne. London, 1756. 16°. 7769
Observer, London. vols. 1–3, 12–18. Boston, 1802-20. 10 v. 8°. . 2160
Observer. American edition. vol. 1. New York, 1843. 8°. . 2170
Philosopher. T. Dick. Brookfield, 1828. 12°. 6101
Philosophy. V. Knox. London, 1835. 12°. 5792
Professor. J. A. James. New York, 1838. 16° 6579
Religion, Evidences of. S. S. Smith. Philadelphia, 1809. 12°. . 6157
Religion, Evidences and Doctrines of. O. Gregory. Lond. 1851. 12°. 5179
The same. New York, 1826. 2 v. 12°. 6473
Religion, Institutes of. J. Calvin. Tr. J. Allen. Lond. 1838. 2 v. 8° 5083
Religion, Survey of. T. Gisborne. New York, 1807. 12° . . 6531
Religion, Truth of the. Philadelphia, 1810. 12°. . . . 6512
Religion, Truth of the. A. Keith. New York, 1833. 12°. . . 5655
Religion, Truth of the. H. Grotius. Trans. London, 1777. 12°. 5628
The same. London, 1825. 12°. 6488
Retrospect and Register. R. Baird. New York, 1851. 12°. . . 5771
Review. vols. 6, 7. Roston, 1841, 2. 8°. 3232
Revelation, Authority of. T. Chalmers. Hartford, 1816. 16°. . 6237
Revelation, Discourses on. New York, 1817. 8°. 5366
Revelation, Evidences of. B. Porteus. Boston, 1814. 18°. . . 4616
Revelation, Evidences of. Beilby. New York, 1801. 12°. . . 3904
Revelation and Modern Astronomy. T. Chalmers. N. Y. 1817. 8°. 5366
Sects of all Denominations, History of. J. Evans. N. Y. 1844. 12°. 6147

Christian Spectator, (Monthly.) New Haven, 1819–1828. 10 v. 8°. . 2794
Spectator, (Quarterly.) vols. 1–10. New Haven, 1829–38. 8°. . 2804
Student. E. Bickersteth. Boston, 1830. 12°. 6158
Treasure. Providence, 1825. 12°. 6513
Christian's Vade Mecum. H. Cumming. Albany, 1819. 16°. . . 11296
Young, Advice to. New York, 1831. 18°. 4612
Great Interest. W. Guthrie. Andover, 1815. 12°. . . . 6533
Magazine. New York, 1806. 8°. 2246
Christianity, Ancient, and Doctrines of the Oxford Tracts. I. Taylor. Philadelphia, 1840. 12°. 6191
Application of, to Affairs of Life. T. Chalmers. Hartford, 1826. 12°. 6186
Apology for. R. Watson. Schenectady, 1796. 16°. . . . 4287
Beauties of. F. A. de Chateaubriand. Tr. Phil. 1815. 8°. . . 5362
Early Conflicts of. W. I. Kip. New York, 1850. 12°. . . . 6154
The same. New York, 1853. 12°. 6467
Evidences of. J. Addison. Philadelphia, 1805. 12°. . . . 6580
The same. London, 1753. 12°. 6606
Evidences of. J. J. Gurney. Boston, 1833. 16°. 6568
Evidences of. J. Morison. Boston, 1834. 16°. 6223
Evidences of. W. Paley. Philadelphia, 1825. 12°. . . . 6501
Evidences of. Various authors. New York. 16°. 5236
Evidences of. F. Wrangham. Edinburgh, 1828. 16°. . . . 10004
Dissertation on Rise and Progress of. R. Whately. Bost. 1853. 4°. 10035
History of. H. H. Milman. London, 1841. 3 v. 8°. . . . 5592
Introduction to. J. Sutcliffe. New York, 1814. 12°. . . . 6523
Lectures on. I. Taylor. New York, 1841. 12°. 6193
Practical View of. W. Wilberforce. Boston, 1799. 12°. . . 4579
Present state of. F. Shoberl. New York, 1828. 12°. . . . 6177
Primitive. W. Cave. London, 1834. 2 v. 12°. 5785
Primitive, Defence of. Hartford, 1816. 8°. 10705
The same. Hartford, 1816. 2 v. 8°. 10726
Reasonableness of. J. Locke. London, 1836. 12°. . . . 5798
The same. London, 1801. 8°. 6353
Relations to Poetry and Philosophy. Phil. 1847. 12°. . . . 6155
Christmas Holidays in Rome. W. I. Kip. New York, 1846. 12°. . . 8977
Stories. C. Dickens. Philadelphia. 8°. 70
Chronicle of the Cid. Tr. R. Southey. Lowell, 1846. 8°. . . . 11317
Chron. of the Canongate. W. Scott. 1st and 2d series. Phil. 1827. 4 v. 12°. 605
See also Scott, Sir W.
of Clovernook. D. Jerrold. London, 1846. 16°. 1629
of the Crusades. London, 1848. 12°. 5446
of Europe. J. Froissart. Trans. T. Johnes. Lond. 1839. 2 v. 4°. 7546
of Europe. E. de Monstrelet. Tr. T. Johnes. Lond. 1840. 2 v. 4°. 7544
of the Pilgrims. A. Young. (Two copies.) Boston, 1841. . . 6947
Chronology of History. H. Nicholas. London, 1838. 12°. . . . 9923
Chrysal, or the Adventures of a Guinea. London, 1796. 4 v. 12°. . . 362
Chrysostom, J. Life. A. Neander. Tr. J. C. Stapleton. Lond. 1845. 8°. 7905
Church, P. Philosophy of Benevolence. New York, 1836. 12°. . . 6465

Church, P. Religious Dissensions, Cause and Cure. N. Y., 1835. 12°. . 5748
Church, T. History of Philip's and other Indian Wars. Hartford. 8°. . 7273
Church, Antiquities of the. L. Coleman. Andover, 1841. 8°. . . 5024
Antiquities of the Anglo-Saxon. J. Lingard. Phil. 1848. 8°. . 5076
Book of the. R. Southey. Boston, 1825. 2 v. 8°. . . . 5367
in Brattle St., Boston, Hist. of. S. K. Lothrop. Bost. 1851. 12°. . 6506
in the Catacombs. C. Maitland. London, 1846. 8°. . . . 11332
Chronological Introduc. to Hist. of. S. F. Jarvis. N. Y. 1845. 8°. 5038
The same. 5039
Double Witness of the. W. I. Kip. New York, 1858. 12°. . 6478
of Eng. Discourses on Homilies of. A. Gordon. Lond. 1795. 2 v. 8°. 5377
of England, History of the. E. Rutledge. Middletown, 1825. 8°. 6376
of England, History of the. T. V. Short. Philadelphia, 1843. 8°. 5047
of England, Reformation of the. G. Burnet. Lond. 1825. 6 v. 16°. 6868
of England. Revenues of the. G. Coventry. London, 1830. 8°. 6428
First, Charlestown, Mass., Hist. of. W. I. Budington. Bost. 1845. 8°. 7627
History of the. E. Burton. New York, 1839. 12°. . . . 5687
History of the. G. Gregory. London, 1790. 2 v. 12°. . . 6547
History of the. J. Milner. Boston, 1809. 4 v. 8°. . . . 7311
History of the. A. Neander. Tr. J. Rose. London, 1842. 2 v. 8°. 5596
The same. Tr. J. Torrey. Boston, 1848. 3 v. 8°. . . 7574
History of the. H. Stebbing. London, 1833. 2 v. 12°. . . 9916
History of the. W. Palmer. New York, 1841. 12°. . . . 5732
The same. New York, 1844. 12°. 5685
History of the. A Poem. N. C. Brooks. Baltimore, 1841. 12°. . 2325
History of, to the Reformation. G. Waddington. Lond. 1833. 8°. 5095
History of Britain, to 1648. F. Fuller. London, 1837. 3 v. 8°. . 6973
Obligations of believers to. J. Harvey. New Haven, 1830. 12°. 6536
Planting and Training of the. A. Neander. Tr. Edin. 1842. 2 v. 12°. 5852
Presbyter., Catastrophe of the, in 1837. Z. Crocker. N. H. 1838. 12°. 6137
Presbyterian, of U. S., History of. C. Hodge. Phil. 1839. 8°. . 5585
Primitive. L. Coleman. Boston, 1844. 12°. 5723
Primitive, View of. A. B. Chapin. New Haven, 1842. 12°. . 6125
Principles, Results of. W. E. Gladstone. London, 1840. 8°. . 5032
Prot. Episc. in U. States, Memoirs of the. W. White. N. Y. 1836. 8°. 5369
of Rome, Lit. Policy of the. J. Mendham. London, 1830. 8°. . 5033
of Scotland, History of. W. M. Hetherington. N. Y. 1844. 8°. . 5054
and State, with Lay Sermons. S. T. Coleridge. London, 1839. 12° 11180
Churchill, C. Poems. London, 1776. 2 v. 8°. . . . . . . 1919.
Select Poems and Life. Philadelphia, 1819. 18°. 2139
Churchman Armed. W. Palmer and J. H. Hobart. N. Y. 1844. 12°. . 5685
Church Members, Manual for. L. Bacon. New Haven, 1833. 16°. . 6225
Churchyards, Chapters on. Caroline Southey. New York, 1842. 12°. . 4526
Cibber, C. Apology for his own Life. London, 1830. 16°. . . . 7480
The same. 7745
The same. London, 1750. 8°. 8261
Cicero, M. T. Opera. Lipsiæ, 1828. 10 v. 16°. 10587
De Oratore. New York, 1810. 8°. 11684

Cicero, M. T. De Republica. Boston, 1823. 12°. 10816
Letters. Tr. W. Melmoth. Dublin, 1753. 3 v. 12°. 4905
The same. (vol. 1 missing.) London, 1803. 3 v. 8°. . . 11685
Life. C. Middleton. Dublin, 1741. 2 v. 12°. 8606
The same. London, 1837. 8°. 8137
Orationes. Lipsiæ, 1828. 18°. 11272
Original and Translated. Ed. C. Anthon. 8°. 2689
Orations, &c. Translated. Duncan, Cockman and Melmoth. New York, 1840. 3 v. 12°. 5267
Libri Rhetorici. Paris, 1810. 12°. 4554
Tusculan Questions. Tr. G. A. Otis. Boston, 1839. 8°. . . . 6448
Cid, Chronicle of the. Tr. R. Southey. Lowell, 1846. 8°. 11317
The. G. Dennis. London, 1845. 16°. 7172
Cincinnati, Picture of. B. Drake. Cincinnati, 1815. 12°. 7128
Circassia; or, Tour to the Caucasus. G. L. Ditson. New York, 1850. 12°. 9256
Circassia, Krim-Tartary, &c., Travels in. E. Spencer. Lond. 1839. 4 v. 8°. 9083
Circumnavigation of the Globe. New York, 1840. 12°. 5541
Cities and Principal Towns of the World. London, 1830. 12°. . . . 9984
Citizen of the World, The. O. Goldsmith. Baltimore, 1829. 12°. . 3636
Civil Engineering. H. Mahan. New York, 1838. 8°. 11671
Civil Society, History of. A. Ferguson. Philadelphia, 1819. 8°. . . 753
Civiles Institutions. J. J. Rosseau. Paris, 1769. 2 v. 8°. . . . 10792
Civilization in Europe, Hist. of. F. Guizot. Tr. Oxford, 1838. 8°. . . 6719
The same, with a continuation. Tr. by W. Hazlitt. London, 1846. 3 v. 12°. 5499
Clan-Albin, a National Tale. London, 1815. 3 v. 12°. 654
Clara Howard. C. B. Brown. Boston, 1827. 12°. 1004
The same. 1430
Clarence. Miss C. M. Sedgwick. Philadelphia, 1830. 2 v. 12°. . . . 921
The same. London, 1830. 3 v. 12°. 1645
Clarendon, Earl of. Essays. Boston, 1820. 18°. 4631
Hist. of the Rebellion and Civil Wars in Eng. Oxford, 1827. 6 v. 8°. 6980
Life and Administration of. T. H. Lister. London, 1838. 3 v. 8°. 7902
Claret and Olives. A. B. Beach. New York, 1852. 12°. 1186
Clarissa Harlowe. S. Richardson. London, 1811. 8 v. 12°. . . . 934
Clark, J. A. Glimpses of the Old World. Philadelphia, 1840. 2 v. 12°. 9241
A Walk about Zion. Philadelphia, 1836. 12°. 5677
Clark, L. G. Knick-Knacks. New York, 1853. 12°. 1219
Clark, W. G. Literary Remains of. New York, 1844. 8°. 743
Clark. V. Rhyming Geography. Hartford, 1819. 12°. 2395
Clarke, A. Autobiography. New York, 1833. 12°. 8359
The same. 8400
Commentary on the Bible. vols. 1, 3–5. New York, 1840. 4°. . 4992
Works. London, 1736. 13 v. 8°. 6451

Vol.		Vol.	
1. 2.	Memoirs of the Wesley Family.	9.	Fleury's Israelites.
3, 4.	Sturm's Reflections.	10–12.	Detached Pieces.
5–8.	Sermons.	13.	Christian Missions.

Clarke, C. C. The Hundred Wonders of the World. N. H. 1821. 12°. . 8718

Clarke, E. D. Life and Remains. W. Otter. New York, 1827. 8°. . 8196
Travels in Europe, Asia, and Africa. Phil. 1811. 8°. 9494
Part 2d. New York, 1813. 12°. 8716
Part 2d, Section 2d. New York, 1813. 2 v. 12°. . . 9597
Clarke, Mrs. C. Concordance to Shakspeare. New York, 1846. 8°. 11680
Clarke, J. F. Hist. of the Campaign of 1812. New York, 1848. 8°. . 7812
Eleven Weeks in Europe. Boston, 1852. 12°. - 9639
Clarke, L. H. New York Convention, in 1821. Debates, &c. New York, 1821. 8°. 10657
Clarkson, T. Hist. of the Abol. of the Slave Trade. Lond. 1808. 2 v. 8°. 11059
The same. (vol. 1 missing.) New York, 1836. 3 v. 12°. . . 11142
Classical Learning, Commentaries on. D. H. Urquhart. London, 1803. 8°. 2694
Library. See Harper's.
Classical Literature, Lectures on. R. Ray. New York, 1826. 8°. . . 3288
Studies. B. Sears, B. B. Edwards, and C. C. Felton. Bost. 1843. 12°. 802
Classics, Dissertation on Reading the. H. Felton. London, 1753. 16°. . 3714
Claudius Ptolemæus. Geographia. Lipsiæ, 1843. 16°. 10349
Clausing, L. Life, or the Proscribed German Student. N. Y. 1836. 16°. 6224
Clavigero, D. F. S. History of Mexico. Philadelphia, 1804. 3 v. 8°. . 7210
Clavis Homerica. 12°. 1906
Clay, C. M. Writings and Memoir. Ed. H. Greeley. New York, 1848. 8°. 10967
Clay, H. Biography of. G. D. Prentice. Hartford, 1831. 12°. . . 8412
Life. E. Sargent. Auburn, 1852. 12°. 8628
Life and Speeches of. New York, 1843. 2 v. 8 v. . . . 10732
Life and Times. C. Colton. New York, 1846. 2 v. 8°. . . 7827
Cleopatra, History of. J. Abbot. New York, 1851. 12°. . . . 8073
Clerical Manners and Habits. S. Miller. New York, 1827. 12°. . . 4863
Cleveland, H. R. Life of H. Hudson. Boston, 1838. 12°. . . . 8052
Cliffton, W. Poems. New York, 1800. 16°. 3079
Clinton, De Witt. Life. J. Renwick. (Two copies.) N. Y. 1840. 12°. 5898
Clio, No. III. J. G. Percival. New York, 1827. 12°. 2019
Clockmaker; or Samuel Slick. T. C. Haliburton. Philadel. 1837. 12°. . 1470
Second series. Philadelphia, 1839. 12°. 1471
Cloney, T., Personal Narrative of. Dublin, 1832–8. 8°. 11359
Cloquet, J. Private Life of Lafayette. New York, 1836. 2 v. 12°. . 8310
Cloudesley. W. Godwin. New York, 1830. 2 v. 12°. 709
Clouds of Aristophanes. Ed. C. C. Felton. Cambridge, 1841. 8°. . 2220
Clovernook. A. Carey. New York, 1852. 12°. 562
Club, The, or a Gray Cap for a Green Head. J. Pinckle. London, 1834. 12°. 3365
Club-Book, The. New York, 1831. 12°. 321
The same. 2 v. 1272
Coast Survey Reports. See United States Public Documents.
Cobbett, W. Advice to Young Men. New York, 1831. 12°. . . . 4980
The same. 4988
Cottage Economy. New York, 1824. 8°. 11651
Grammar of the English Language. New York, 1846. 16°. . 4970
Hist. of Reformation in England and Ireland. N. Y. 1832. 2 v. 12°. 6582
Legacy to Parsons. New York, 1844. 16°. 6218

Cobbett, W. Life. Philadelphia, 1835. 12°. 8421
Paper against Gold, and Glory against Prosperity. London, 1815.
2 v. 8°. 10057
The same. New York, 1834. 12°. 11163
Porcupine's Works. A Faithful Picture of U. S. Lond. 1801. 12 v. 8°. 11023
Sermons. New York, 1846. 16°. 6216
Cochrane, G. Wanderings in Greece. London, 1837. 2 v. 8°. . . 9387
Cochrane, J. D. A Pedestr'n Journey through Russia. Edin. 1829. 2 v. 16°. 10012
Cochrane, T., (Lord.) Hist. of the Hoax and Trial of. N. Y. 1814. 12°. 11193
Cockburn, (Lord.) Life of Lord Jeffrey. Philadelphia, 1852. 2 v. 12°. . 8592
Cœlebs in Search of a Wife. Miss H. More. Philadelphia, 1810. 12°. . 1590
The same. New York, 1809. 2 v. 12°. 1586
Code Prussien. Paris, 1801. 5 v. 8°. 10781
Coffin, R. S. Boston Bard. Providence, 1826. 8°. 1892
Cogswell, W. Harbinger of the Millennium. Boston, 1833. 12°. . . 5665
Letters to Young Men Entering the Ministry. Boston, 1837. 12°. 4934
Cohen, M. M. Notices of Florida and the Campaigns. New York, 1836. 12° 7430
The same. 9264
Coins and Bullion, Manual of. J. R. Eckfeldt. Illust. Phil. 1842. 4°.
Coit, T. W. Puritanism. New York, 1835. 12°. 5775
The same. 6187
Coke, E. T. The Subaltern's Furlough. New York, 1833. 2 v. 12°. . 11413
Colbert, J. B. Life. G. P. R. James. Philadelphia, 1837. 2 v. 12°.. . 8362
Colburn, W. Key to Algebra. Boston, 1833. 12°. 3313
Colden, C. D. Five Indian Nations of Canada. London, 1750. 12°. . 6784
Life of R. Fulton. New York, 1817. 8°. 8202
The same. 8484
Cole, C. N. Life of S. Jenyns. Dublin, 1791. 2 v. 8°. 10770
Coleman, L. Antiquities of the Christian Church. Andover, 1841. 8°. . 5024
Primitive Church. Boston, 1844. 12°. 5723
Coleridge, H. N. Study of the Greek Poets. Philadelphia, 1831. 12°. . 3045
Coleridge, S. T. Aids to Reflection. Burlington, 1829. 8°. . . . 5350
The same. 6430
The same. New York, 1841. 12°. 6133
Biographia Literaria. Boston, 1834. 8°. 8499
Church and State, with Lay Sermons. London, 1839. 12°. . . 11180
Confessions of an Inquiring Spirit. Boston, 1841. 12°. . . 3338
The Friend, a Series of Essays. Burlington, 1831. 8°. . . . 52
Letters, Conversations, &c. New York, 1836. 12°. . . . 11190
Life. J. Gilman. vol. 1. London, 1838. 8°. 11267
Literary Remains. London, 1836. 4 v. 8°. 723
Poetical Works. Philadelphia, 1831. 8°. 1860
The same. London, 1840. 3 v. 12°. 2042
Statesman's Manual. Burlington, 1832. 12°. 11116
Table Talk. New York, 1835. 12°. 4890
and R. Southey. Reminiscences of. J. Cottle. N. Y. 1848. 12°. 8303
College Words and Customs. Hall. Cambridge, 1851. 12°. . . . 787
Collegiate System, Thoughts on the. F. Wayland. Boston, 1842. 12°. 4597

Collier, G. R. and C. MacCarthy. West African Sketches. Lond. 1824. 12°. 9249
Collier, J. P. Annals of the Stage, &c. (Two copies.) Lond. 1831. 3 v. 18°. 1109
Notes to Shakspeare's Plays. New York, 1853. 12°. 1145
Poetical Decameron. London, 1820. 2 v. 12°. 4546
Collins, L. Historical Sketches of Kentucky. Cincinnati, 1850. 8°. . 7595
Collins, W. Poetical Works. (Two copies.) Philadelphia, 1836. 8°. . 1858
The same, with Life by S. Johnson. Philadelphia, 1819. 18°. 2135
Colloquial Phrases for Conversation. A. Bolmar. (2 copies.) Phil. 1836. 16°. 4961
Collyer, W. B. Lectures on Scripture Facts. Boston, 1813. 8°. . . 5354
Colman Family. Memoirs. R. B. Peake. London, 1841. 2 v. 8°. . . 7872
Colman, G. Poetical Works. Philadelphia, 1822. 8°. 2114
Colman, H. European Life and Manners. Boston, 1850. 2 v. 12°. . 9582
Colman, L. Historical Geography of the Bible. Philadelphia, 1850. 12°. 3310
Colombia, Description of. J. Conder. London, 1825. 16°. . . . 9649
The same. 9672
Recollections of a Service in. London, 1828. 2 v. 8°. . . . 9480
Visit to. W. Duane. Philadelphia, 1826. 8°. 9436
Colonization and Christianity. W. Howitt. London, 1838. 8°. . . 5635
Society, Inquiry into Charac. & Tendency. W. Jay. N. Y. 1835. 12°. 11119
Colton, C. Four Years in Great Britain. New York, 1836. 12°. . . 8935
The same. New York, 1835. 2 v. 12°. 9623
Life and Times of H. Clay. New York, 1846. 2 v. 8°. . . . 7827
Religious State of the Country. New York, 1836. 12°. . . 5678
The same. 5679
Colton, C. C. Lacon. Bridgeport, 1828. 24°. . . . .
Colton, G. H. Tecumseh, a Poem. New York, 1842. 12°. . . . 2336
Colton, W. The Sea and the Sailor. New York, 1851. 12°. . . . 1147
Visit to Constantinople and Athens. New York, 1836. 12°. . . 9822
Columbia River, Adventures on the. R. Cox. New York, 1832. 8°. . 9091
The same. 9445
Columbiad, The. J. Barlow. Philadelphia, 1807. 4°. . . . . .
The same. Philadelphia, 1809. 2 v. 12°. 2323
Columbian Class Book. Ed. A. T. Lowe. Worcester, 1827. 12°. . . 3019
The same. 4845
Orator. Ed. C. Bingham. Boston, 1804. 12°. 4852
Columbus, C., First Voyages of. Tr. Boston, 1827. 8°. . . . 9501
Life and Voyages of. W. Irving. New York, 1828. 3 v. 8°. . 7933
The same. New York, 1831. 2 v. 8°. 7894
The same, revised. New York, 1851. 3 v. 12°. . . 532
Vision of. J. Barlow. Hartford, 1787. 12°. 1905
The same. 2430
Voyages of the Companions of. W. Irving. Philadelphia, 1831. 8°. 8222
Combe, A. Digestion and Dietetics. New York, 1836. 16°. . . . 4974
Physiology Applied to Health. New York, 1834. 16°. . . . 6271
The same. 8768
The same. New York, 1841. 12°. 5883
Constitution of Man. Boston, 1833. 12°. 4577
Notes on the United States in 1838–40. Philadelphia, 1841. 2 v. 12°. 9566

Coming Out. Misses J. and A. M. Porter. New York, 1828. 3 v. 12°. . 634
Commerce of America with Europe. J. P. Brissot. Tr. N. Y. 1795. 12°. 11179
Brit'sh, History of. G. L. Craik. London, 1844. 16°. 6880
History of. London. 8°. 5098
History of. A. Anderson. Dublin, 1790. 6 v. 8°. 10760
of the Prairies, or Journal of a Santa Fe Trader. J. Gregg. New York, 1844. 2 v. 12°. 8895
Reports on. See United States Public Documents.
&c. of the United States. T. Pitkin. New Haven, 1835. 8°. . 10731
The same. Hartford, 1816. 8°. 11051
Commercial Dictionary. J. R. McCulloch. Philadelphia, 1843. 8°. . 10930
Common Place Book. R. Southey. New York, 1849. 2 v. 8°. . . 30
Common Place Book of Prose. American Ed. G. B. Cheever. Bost. 1832. 12° 3355
The same. Boston, 1828. 12°. 4892
Common School Journal of Connecticut. Hartford, 1838, 9. 4°. . . . 11262
for 1838–42. H. Barnard. Hartford, 1842. 4°. 9701
Schools of Connecticut, Report for 1850. New Haven, 1850. 8°. . 10092
for 1853. Hartford, 1853. 8°. 10085
Schools of New York. Report for 1844. Albany, 1844. 8°. . 10102
for 1845. Albany, 1845. 8°. 10091
Schools. System of. S. S. Randall. Albany, 1844. 12°. . . 3397
Complete Angler. I. Walton and C. Cotton. London, 1836. 12°. . . 10154
Complexion of the Human Species. Smith. Boston, 1799. 12°. . . 3315
Composition, English, Aids to. R. G. Parker. Boston, 1844. 12°. . . 2997
English. Principles of. London, 1831. 12°. 3039
Comstock, J. L. History of the Greek Revolution. New York, 1828. . 7120
Outlines of Geology. (Three copies.) New York, 1837–8. 12°. 6077
Conant, Mrs. S. C. History of the English Bible Translation. New York, 1856. 12°. 5773
Condé, J. A. Dominions of the Arabs in Spain. London, 1854. 3 v. 12°. 5186
Condé, L. Life. (Lord) Mahon. New York, 1845. 12°. . . . 9848
The same. New York, 1848. 12°. . . . . . .
Conder, J. Modern Traveller. Popular Descriptions. London, 19 v. 16°

No. 9642. Brazil, Buenos Ayres.
9654. Greece.
9655. Egypt, Nubia, Abyssinia.
5656. America.
9657. Arabia, Burmah, Siam. Anam.
9658–60. Africa.
9661, 2. India.
9663–5. Italy.
9666. Mexico, Guatimala.
9667. Syria, Asia Minor.
9668. Palestine, Peru.
9669. Persia, China.
9670. Russia, Turkey.
9671. Spain, Portugal.
9672. Colombia.

The same. London, 1827. 20 v. 16°. 9337
Condorcet, J. History of Progress of Mind. Tr. Philadelphia, 1796. . 3971
Life of F. M. A. Voltaire. Tr. London, 1787. 8°. 7951
Confessional, History of the. J. H. Hopkins. New York, 1850. 12°. . . 477
Confessions and Crimes. Ed. H. Cannter. Philadelphia, 1836. 12°. . 1140
Confessions of Elderly Lady and Gent. Lady Blessington. Philadelphia, 1838. 2 v. 12°. 1465
of Fitz Boodle. W. M. Thackeray. New York, 1852. 12°. . . 958
of an Inquiring Spirit. S. T. Coleridge. Boston, 1841. 12°. . 3338

Confessions of an Old Maid. New York, 1828. 2 v. 12°. . . . 1344
of an Opium Eater. T. De Quincey. Boston, 1851. 12°. . . 892
of a Pretty Woman. Miss Pardoe. New York, 1851. 8°. . . 48
of a School Master. Andover, 1839. 12°. 4963
of St. Augustine. New York, 1844. 12°. 6141
The same. 6145
Confidence Man. H. Melville. New York, 1857. 12°. 1225
Conformity, a Tale. Mrs. C. E. Tonna. New York, 1842. 16°. . . 1707
Congregational Church of Belchertown, Mass., History of. M. Doolittle. New Haven, 1852. 12°. 6188
Order. Middletown, 1843. 16°. 6222
Congregationalism, History of. G. Punchard. Salem, 1841. 12°. . . 6140
The same. 6192
Congress of the U. States, History of. H. G. Wheeler. N. Y. 1848. 2 v. 8°. 7600
of the U. States, Abridg. of the Acts of. E. Ingersoll. Phil. 1825. 8°. 10065
See also United States Public Documents.
of Vienna. D. D. De Pradt. Tr. Philadelphia, 1816. 8°. . . 11052
Congressional Globe, for 1847–52. Washington. 16 v. 4°. . . . 10381
Congreve, W., and others. Dramatic Works. Ed. L. Hunt. Lond. 1840. 8°. 1794
Conic Sections, Spherical Geometry, &c. M. R. Dutton. N. H. 1824. 8°. 424
Coningsby, or the New Generation. B. D'Israeli. New York, 1845. 8°. 19
Connecticut Acad. of Arts and Sciences, Memoirs of. N. H. 1810. 8°. . 10077
Blue Laws of. Hartford, 1838. 12°. 11137
Common Schools. See Common Schools.
Forty Years Since, Sketch of. L. H. Sigourney. Hart. 1824. 12°. 1048
History of. S. Peters. New Haven, 1829. 12°. 6837
History of. T. Dwight, Jr. New York, 1840. 12°. . . . 5577
History of, from 1630 to 1713. B. Trumbull. Hartford, 1797. 8°. 7216
Poets of. C. W. Everest. Hartford, 1843. 8°. 1857
Part of, in the American Revolution. R. R. Hinman. Hart. 1842. 8°. 7252
Register, for 1854–5. Hartford. 2 v. 18°. 4607
Register, for 1857. Hartford. 18°. 4948
Report on the Geology of. J. G. Percival. New Haven, 1842. 8°. 5952
Retreat for the Insane, Seventh Report of. Hartford, 1831. 8°. . 10089
Statist. of Branches of Industry in. Ed. D. P. Tyler. Hart. 1846. 8°. 11667
System of the Laws of. Z. Swift. (2 copies.) Windham, 1795. 2 v. 8°. 10753
Connoisseur, The. B. Thornton and others. London, 1823. 2 v. 12°. . 3688
Conquest of Canaan, a Poem. T. Dwight. Hartford, 1785. 12°. . . 2370
The same. 2375
of Granada. W. Irving. New York, 1829. 2 v. 12°. . . . 6806
The same. New York, 1851. 12°. 537
Conscience, or the Bridal Night. J. Haynes. New York, 1821. 18°. . 3071
Cases of. S. Pike and S. Haywood. New York, 1808. 12°. . 6541
Consolations in Travel. H. Davy. Philadelphia, 1830. 16°. . . . 4285
Conspiracies of Europe in 15th and 16th Centuries. J. P. Lawson. Edinburgh, 1829. 2 v. 16°. 10018
Conspiracy against all the Religions and Governments of Europe by Free Masons, Illuminati, &c. J. Robison. New York, 1798. 8°. 6726

Conspiracy, Foreign, against the United States. S. F. B. Morse. New York, 1835. 18°. . . 11159

Constable's Miscellany of Original and Selected Publications. Edin. 1826–30. 36 v. 18°.

No. 9989. Adventures of British Seamen.
10012, 3. Cochrane's Jour. thro' Russia, &c.
10020. Conquest of Peru.
10018, 9. Conpiracies. J. P. Lawson.
9991. 2. Converts from Infidelity.
9993. 4 Embassy to the Birman Empire.
9986, 8. B. Hall's Voyages.
10002, 3. Illustrations of British History.
10014. Journey thro' Norway, Sweden, &c.
9990. Memoirs of Marchioness of La Rochejaquelein.
No. 10005. 6. Memorials of Late War.
10015, 6. The Ottoman Empire, History of.
9996. Perils and Captivity.
9997. Phenomena of Nature.
10004. The Pleiad. F. Wrangham.
10007. 8. Rebellions in Scotland, 1638–60
10017. Rebellions in Scotland, 1689 & 1715.
9998, 9. Rebellion in Scotland, 1745.
10009, 11. Revolutions in Europe. C. Koch.
10000, 1. Schiller's Thirty Years' War.
9995. Table-Talk, or Selec. from the Ana.

Constance de Castile. W. Sotheby. Boston, 1812. 16°. 3078
Constant, B. Philosophical Miscellanies. Tr. Boston, 1838. 8°. . . 769
Constantinople and Athens, Visit to. W. Colton. New York, 1836. 12°. 9822
History of. London, 1779. 8°. 7042
Residence at, during the Greek and Turkish Revolutions. R. Walsh. London, 1836. 2 v. 8°. 9394
Residence at, in year 1827. J. Brewer. New Haven, 1830. 12°. 9274
The same. 9279
Constitution, Federal. Debates on the, in the Virginia Convention of 1788. Richmond, 1805. 8°. 11081
Federal, Writings upon the. J. Marshall. Boston, 1839. 8°. . 10929
of Man. G. Combe. Boston, 1833. 12°. 4577
of the United States, Analysis of the Declaration of Independence, &c. (Two copies.) Ed. W. Hickey. Phil. 1847. 12°. . 11133
of the United States, Defense of the. J. Adams. Phil. 1797. 3 v. 8°. 10774
of the United States, New Views on. J. Taylor. Wash. 1823. 8°. 11049
Constitutional Convention, 1787, Secret Debates in. Albany, 1821. 8°. 10484
The same. Richmond, 1839. 12°. 9540
The same. 10811
Constitutions of the States and of the U. S. New York, 1813. 18°. . 11151
Consuelo. Madame Dudevant. Tr. F. G. Shaw. Boston, 1846. 2 v. 12°. 918
Contarini Fleming. B. D'Israeli. New York, 1832. 2 v. 12°. . . 1635
The same. Philadelphia, 1847. 8°. 5
Contemplations of the Saviour. S. G. Bulfinch. Boston, 1832. 12°. . 5664
Contest of the Twelve Nations, or a View of the different Bases of Human Character and Talent. Edinburgh, 1826. 8°. 742
Contracts, Essay on the Doctrine of. G. C. Verplanck. N. Y. 1825. 8°. 10054
Contrast. Regina M. Roche. New York, 1828. 2 v. 12°. . . . 969
Contrast between Good and Bad Men. G. Spring. N. Y. 1855. 2 v. 8°. 5086
Contributions of Q. Q. Jane Taylor. New York, 1826. 12°. . . . 3339
Conversation, Book of. Charleston, 1837. 16°. 4965
Conversations at Cambridge, England. London, 1836. 12°. . . . 3367
Convert's Guide to First Principles. I. Robords. New Haven, 1838. 12°. 5695
The same. 5711
Cooke, G. F. Life. W. Dunlap. New York, 1813. 2 v. 18°. . . . 8442
Cooke, G. W. History of Party from 1666 to 1832. Lond. 1836. 3 v. 8°. 7624

Cooke, G. W. Life of the Earl of Shaftesbury. London, 1836. 2 v. 8°. 7900
Cooke, P. Divine Law of Beneficence. 16°. 6215
Cooke, W. Memoirs of S. Foote. New York, 1806. 2 v. 12°. . . . 8390
The same. 8417
Cooksey, R. Lives of J. Somers and P. Hardwicke. Worcester, 1791. 4°. 7797
Cooley, J. W. American in Egypt, with Rambles through Arabia Petræa and the Holy Land. New York, 1842. 8°. 9369
Cooper, Sir A. Life. B. B. Cooper. London, 1843. 2 v. 8°. . . . 7914
Cooper, A. A. See Shaftesbury, Earl of.
Cooper, J. F. Afloat and Ashore. Philadelphia, 1844. 4 v. 12°. . . . 1537
Gleanings in Europe. Philadelphia, 1837. 2 v. 12°. 8946
The same. 9836
Homeward Bound. Philadelphia, 1838. 2 v. 12°. 1267
Last of the Mohicans. Philadelphia, 1826. 2 v. 12. 977
Mercedes of Castile. Philadelphia, 1841. 12°. 1263
The same. Philadelphia, 1840. 2 v. 12°. 1481
Naval History of the United States. Philadelphia, 1839. 2 v. 8°. 7630
Notions of the Americans. Philadelphia, 1828. 2 v. 12°. . . . 9271
Novels. Philadelphia, 1831. 22 v. 16°.

No. 350, 1. Water Witch.
352, 3. Wept of Wish Ton-Wish.
354, 5. Lionel Lincoln, or the Leaguer of Boston.
356, 7. Spy.
358, 9. Pilot.
No. 1033, 4. Pilot.
1027, 8. Bravo.
1029, 30. Pioneers.
1031, 2. Notions of the Americans.
1035, 6. Prairie.
1037, 8. Red Rover.

The same. Philadelphia, 1841. 11 v. 12°.

No. 1264. Deerslayer.
1262. Home as Found.
1261. Homeward Bound.
1263. Mercedes of Castile.
1259. Monikins.
1258. Notions of the Americans.
1254. Pilot.
1255. Prairie.
1260. Precaution.
1257. Water Witch.
1256. Wept of Wish-Ton-Wish.

Pathfinder. New York, 1851. 12°. 1232
The same. Philadelphia, 1841. 12°. 1576
Pilot. 2 v. 12°. 1627
Pioneers. Philadelphia, 1827. 2 v. 16°. 1719
Prairie. Philadelphia, 1827. 2 v. 12°. 632
Precaution. New York, 1820. 2 v. 12°. 952
Red Rover. 2 v. 12°. 1603
Review of the Court Martial of A. S. Mackenzie. N. Y. 1844. 8°. 10965
Satanstoe. New York, 1845. 12°. 1235
Sea Lions. New York, 1849. 12°. 1234
Sketches of Switzerland. Philadelphia, 1836. 2 v. 12°. . . 8948
Spy. New York, 1822. 2 v. 12°. 1667
Tales of a Traveler. New York, 1825. 2 v. 12°. 641
Two Admirals. New York, 1849. 12°. 1233
Water Witch. Philadelphia, 1831. 2 v. 12°. 1354
Wing-and-Wing. Philadelphia, 1842. 2 v. 12°. 965
Cooper, J. G. Poetical Works. Philadelphia, 1822. 18°. . . . 2140

Cooper, Rev. Mr. History of North America. Albany, 1815. 12°. . . 7443
The same. Lansingburgh, 1795. 12°. 11935
Cooper, S. Military Tactics. Philadelphia, 1836. 12°. 3347
Cooper, T. Lecture on Chemistry. Carlisle, 1812. 8°. . . , . 5974
Coote, C. History of Europe from 1763–1801. Philadelphia, 1811. 8°. . 11383
Copway, G. Traditional History of the Ojibway Nation. Bost. 1851. 12°. 7106
Corbet, R. Select Poems, with Life, by E. Sanford. Phil. 1849. 18°. . 2119
Corderius, M., Colloquies of. Original and Tr. Phil. 1818. 12°. . . 4846
Cordier, L. Essay on the Temperature of the Interior of the Earth. (Two copies.) Amherst, 1828. 12°. 6084
Corinneou, L' Italie. Mad. da Staël. Paris, 1836. 12°. 676
The same. Translated. New York, 1844. 8°. 20
The same. Philadelphia, 1836. 2 v. 12°. 674
Corinthians, I and II, Notes on. A. Barnes. New York, 1841. 2 v. 12°. 5727
Corn Law Rhymes. E. Elliott. London, 1833. 12°. 2258
Corn Laws, History of the. J. C. Platt. London, 1842. 12°. . . . 5929
Cornaro, L. Health and Long Life. Andover, 1824. 18°. . . . 4622
Corneille, P., and his Times. F. Guizot. New York, 1852. 12°. . . 8022
Œuvres Completes, Suivies des Œuvres de T. Corneille. Paris, 1838. 4 v. 12°. 1901
Cornelius, E. Memoir. B. B. Edwards. Boston, 1833. 12°. . . . 7723
Cornelius Nepos. De Vita Excellentium Imperatorum. Lipsiæ, 1843. 16°. 10861
The same, with English Notes. Boston, 1830. 12°. . . 3380
The same, with Translation. New York, 1806. 12°. . . 8466
Corner Stone, The. J. Abbott. Boston, 1834. 12°. 6159
Cornish, T. H. Historical Picture of Women. London, 1838. 12°. . 3902
Corse de Leon, or the Brigand. G. P. R. James. London, 1841. 3 v. 12°. 1281
Corsica, account of. J. Boswell. Glasgow, 1768. 8°. 9238
Cortes, H. Life. T. de Trueba. Edinburgh, 1829. 16°. 8457
Life. Boston, 1840. 16°. 7774
Despatches of. Trans. G. Folsom. (Two copies.) N. Y. 1843. 12°. 8629
Cottage Bible. Ed. W. Patton. Hartford, 1834. 2 v. 4°. . . . 4996
Cottages and Cottage Life. C. W. Elliott. New York, 1848. 8°. . 1073
Cottle, J. Reminis. of. S. T. Coleridge and R. Southey. N. Y. 1848. 12°. 8303
Cotton Manufacture, History of Rise and Progress. G. S. White. Philadelphia, 1836. 8°. 7857
Manufactures of Great Britain. A. Ure. London, 1836. 2 v. 12°. 2975
Cotton, N. Select Poems and Life, Philadelphia, 1822. 18°. . . . 2147
Counsels to the Young. E. Nott. (Two copies.) Philadelphia, 1832. 12° 4300
Count Julian. W. S. Landor. Lowell, 1831. 12°. . . . . : . 2223
Count Robert of Paris. W. Scott. Philadelphia, 1839. 8°. . . . 45
Countess and other Tales. Mrs. S. C. Hall and others. Phil. 1836. 12°. 244
Country Year-Book. W. Howitt. New York, 1850. 12°. 783
Course of Creation. J. Anderson. Cincinnati, 1851. 12°. . . . 6064
Course of Time, The. R. Pollok. Boston, 1828. 12°. 1963
Court Conspirator, The. M. E. Sue. New York, 1845. 8°. 49
Courtenay, T. P. Lives of British Statesmen. See British.
Memoirs of W. Temple. London, 1836. 2 v. 8°. . . . 7840

Courtship and Marriage, Letters on. 18°. 4940
Courtship of Miles Standish. H. W. Longfellow. Boston, 1859. 12°. . 1943
Cousin, V. Elements of Psychology. Tr. C. S. Henry. Hart. 1834. 8°. 6347
History of Philosophy. Tr. H. G. Linberg. Boston, 1832. 8°. 6373
The same, with 2d series. Tr. O. W. Wight. N. Y. 1857. 2 v. 8°. 6345
Report of Public Instruc. in Prussia. (2 cop.) Tr. N. Y. 1835. 12°. 4983
Philosophical Miscellanies. Tr. Boston, 1838. 8°. . . . 768
Cousin Marshall. Miss H. Martineau. Boston, 1833. 16°. . . . 10029
Coventry, G. Critical Enquiry regarding the Real Author of the Letters of Junius. London, 1825. 8°. 10730
Revenues of the Church of England. London, 1830. 8°. . . 6428
Cowell, J. Thirty Years among the Players. New York, 1844. 8°. . 9090
Cowley, A. Essays. Boston, 1820. 18°. 4633
Select Poems, with Life, by E. Sanford. Philadelphia, 1819. 16°. 2120
Cowper, W. Poems. Philadelphia, 1806. 3 v. 18°. 2743
Poems. Boston, 1833. 3 v. 12°. 2377
Poems. Amherst, 1808. 3 v. 16°. 2468
Poems. London, 1836. 2 v. 32°. 2792
Posthumous Poetry, with Life, by J. Johnson. N. Y. 1816. 18°. . 2757
Select Poems and Life. Philadelphia, 1822. 2 v. 18°. . . . 2148
Cox, F. A. Lectures on Book of Daniel. New York, 1836. 12°. . . 5692
Life of P. Melancthon. London, 1817. 8°. 8536
and J. Hoby. Baptists in America. New York, 1836. 12°. . 5393
The same. 5391
Cox, R. Adventures on the Columbia River. New York, 1832. 8°. . 9091
Cox, S. H. Quakerism not Christianity. Boston, 1833. 8°. . . . 5008
Coxe, A. C. Advent, a Mystery. New York, 1837. 12°. . . . 1945
The same. 1946
Athanasion, and other Poems. New York, 1842. 12°. . . . 2216
St. Jonathan: or, the Lay of a Scald. New York, 1838. 12°. . 2344
Coxe, W. History of the House of Austria. London, 1847. 3 v. 12°. . 5163
Memoir of the Duke of Marlborough. London, 1847. 3 v. 12°. . 5166
Memoirs of R. Walpole. London, 1800. 3 v. 8°. . . . 7958
Travels in Poland, Russia, Norway, Sweden and Denmark. London, 1802. 5 v. 8°. 9129
Travels in Switzerland. Basil, 1802. 3 v. 8°. 9257
Crabb, G. English Synonymes. New York, 1839. 8°. 1057
Crabbe, G. Life, Letters, Journey and New Poems, by his Son. Philadelphia, 1835. 2 v. 12°. 1955
Life of, by his Son. Cambridge, 1834. 8°. 7718
Poems. New York, 1808. 12°. 2285
Poetical Works, Life, Letters, &c. London, 1834. 8 v. 12°. . . 2268
Craftsman, The. C. D'Anvers. London, 1731. 16°. 4275
Craik, G. L. History of British Commerce. London, 1844. 3 v. 16°. . 6880
Hist. of Literature and Learn. in England. London, 1844. 6 v. 16°. 6895
The same. 7155
and others, Pictorial History of England to 1830. (vol. 6 missing.) London, 1841. 8 v. 4°. 7789

Craik, G. L. E. Spenser, and his Poetry. London, 1845. 3 v. 16°. . 6877
Cramp, J. M. Text Book of Popery. New York, 1831. 12°. 6185
The same. 6534
Cranmer, T. Life. London, 1831. 12°. 9932
Life and Times of. Mrs. H. Lee. Boston, 1841. 12°. 7458
Writings. London, 1830. 12°. 5656
Crawfurd, J. Jour. of an Embassy to Court of Ava. Lond. 1834. 2 v. 8°. 9136
Journal of an Embassy to the Courts of Siam and Cochin China.
London, 1830. 2 v. 8°. 9134
Crayon Miscellany. W. Irving. New York, 1851. 12°. 540
Creasy, E. S. Fifteen Decisive Battles of the World. New York, 1851. 12°. 7094
Creation, Course of. J. Anderson. Cincinnati, 1851. 12°. . . . 6064
Creation, a Philosophical Poem. R. Blackmore. Philadelphia, 1806. 12°. 2444
Crebillon, P. J. Œuvres. Paris, 1802. 3 v. 18°. 10894
Credulity and Superstition. R. Blakeman. New York, 1849. 12°. . 3927
Creed, an Exposition of the. J. Pearson. New York, 1844. 8°. . . 5310
Lord's Prayer, &c. R. Leighton. London, 1834. 12°. . . 5787
Creichton, J. Autobiography. London, 1830. 16°. . . . , . . 7755
The same. . . . . . , ... 7490
The same. 8433
Crichton, A. Converts from Infidelity. Edinburgh, 1827. 2 v. 16°. . 999
History of Arabia. New York, 1834. 2 v. 16°. 6239
and H. Wheaton. Hist. of Scandinavia. New York, 1841. 2 v. 12° 5910
Cricket on the Hearth. C. Dickens. New York, 1847. 8°. . . 97
Crimea, Turkey and Egypt, Travels in. J. Webster. Lond. 1830. 2 v. 8°. 9145
Crimes and Punishments, Essays on. C. B. Beccaria. Edin. 1788. 12°. . 3893
Criminal Trials, Remarkable. A. R. Feuerbach. Trans. Lady D. Gordon.
New York, 1846. 12°. 11195
Criticism, Elements of. H. H. Kames. vol. 2. Edin. 1769. 8°. . . 10806
Crocker, Z. Catastrophe of Presbyterian Church in 1837. N. H. 1838. 12°. 6137
Crockett, D. Exploits and Adventures in Texas. Philadelphia, 1836. 12°. 9287
Sketches and Eccentricities of. New York, 1833. 12°. . . . 1216
The same. 1340
Crockford's, or Life in the West. New York, 1828. 2 v. 12°. . . 984
The same. 1368
Crock of Gold, and other Tales. M. F. Tupper. New York, 1845. 12°. . 251
Crofton Boys, The. Miss H. Martineau. New York, 1851. 16°. . . 1679
Croly, G. Historical Sketches, Speeches, &c. London, 1842. 12°. . . 8549
Life and Times of George IV. New York, 1832. 18°. . . . 6275
The same. New York, 1840. 12°. 5517
The same. New York, 1831. 16°. 6274
Marston, or Memoirs of a Statesman. Philadelphia, 1845. 8°. . 22
Croly, G. Ten Thousand a Year. Philadelphia, 1841. 6 v. 12°. . . 1298
Cromwell, an Historical Novel. H. W. Herbert. N. Y. 1838. 2 v. 12°. . 1546
Cromwell, O. Life. London, 1747. 12°. 8377
Life. W. Harris. London, 1814. 8°. 8153
Life. M. Russell. New York, 1833. 2 v. 16°. 6258
The same. New York, 1841. 2 v. 12°. 5878

Cromwell, O. Life. R. Southey. New York, 1845. 16°. 7772
Life. J. Forster. London, 1838, 9. 2 v. 12°. 9927
A Vindication. J. H. M. D'Aubigne. New York, 1850. 12°. . 8624
Croppy, The, a Tale. J. Banim. Philadelphia, 1839. 2 v. 12°. . . 1314
Crowe, Catherine. Night Side of Nature. New York, 1850. 12°. . . 1150
Crowe, E. E. History of France. Philadelphia, 1835. 3 v. 12°. . . 5833
The same. London, 1831. 3 v. 12°. 9862
Lives of Eminent Foreign Statesmen. London, 1833. 12°. . . 9940
Croswell, W., Memoir. Rev. Harry Croswell. New York, 1854. 8°. . 7849
Cruikshank at Home. London, 1845. 2 v. 16°. 1624
Cruise of the Potomac, 1831–4. J. N. Reynolds. New York, 1835. 8°. . 9096
Crusades, Chronicles of the. London, 1848. 12°. 5446
History of the. C. Mills. Philadelphia, 1824. 8°. . . . 7227
Crusius, L. Lives of the Roman Poets. London, 1753. 2 v. 12°. . . 7450
Crustacea, Arachnides and Insecta. P. A. Latreille. Tr. N. Y. 1831. 2 v. 8°. 10130
Cuba. A. von Humboldt. Tr. New York, 1856. 12°. 8968
Cuba, and the Cubans. New York, 1850. 12°. 8689
Cudworth, R. Intellectual System of Universe. Andover, 1837. 2 v. 8°. 6308
Culprit Fay, and other Poems. J. R. Drake. New York, 1836. 8°. . 1854
Cumberland, R. Autobiography. New York, 1806. 8°. . . . 8547
Calvary. A Poem. Burlington, 1795. 12°. 2380
Cumming, H. Christian's Vade-Mecum. Albany, 1819. 16°. . . . 11296
Cumming, R. G. Hunter's Life in South Africa. N. Y. 1850. 2 v. 12°. . 9577
Cummings, A. Memoir of E. Payson. New York. 16°. 5234
The same. Boston, 1830. 18°. 8348
Life and Land of R. Burns. New York, 1841. 12°. . . . 8370
Life of W. Scott. Boston, 1832. 16°. 8462
Cunningham, A. Lives of Eminent Painters and Sculptors. New York,
1831. 5 v. 12°. 6253
The same. New York, 1840. 5 v. 12°. 5519
Cunningham, J. Select Poems and Life. Philadelphia, 1822. 18°. . . 2144
Cunningham, J. W. The Velvet Cushion. London, 1815. 12°. . . 1287
Cunningham, W. and J. Adams, Correspondence between. Bost. 1823. 8°. 10667
Curiosities of Literature. I. D'Israeli. London, 1823. 5 v. 12°. . . 849
Second series. London, 1824. 3 v. 8°. 148
First and Second series, with Curiosities of Amer. Literature.
Ed. R. W. Griswold. New York, 1844. 8°. . . . 36
Curran, J. C., and his Contem. Recollections of. C. Phillips. N. Y. 1818. 8° 8188
Currency and Banking, Treatise on. C. Raguet. Phil. 1839. 8°. . 10933
Currer Bell. See Brontë, C.
Currie, J. Memoirs. W. W. Currie. London, 1831. 2 v. 8°. . . 7909
Curtis, G. W. Lotus Eating. New York, 1856. 12°. 528
Howadji in Syria. New York, 1852. 12°. 8903
Potiphar Papers. New York, 1856. 12°. 527
Nile Notes of a Howadji. New York, 1851. 12°. 8902
Curtius, Rufus Q. De Rebus Gestis Alex. Magni. Lipsiæ. 1840. 16°. . 10612
Curzon, R. Visit to the Monasteries in the Levant. N. York, 1849. 12°. 9825
Cushing, C. Reminiscences of Spain. Boston, 1833. 2 v. 12°. . . 9247

Cushing, C. Review of late Revolution in France. Boston, 1833. 2 v. 12°. 7137
Cutter, C. Treatise on Anatomy and Physiology. Boston, 1846. 12°. . 3920
Cuvier, G., Baron. Rev. of the Surface of Globe. Tr. Phil. 1831. 12°. 6095
Memoirs. Mrs. R. Lee. New York, 1833. 12°. 8314
P. A. Latreille. The Animal Kingdom. Tr. N. Y. 1831. 4 v. 8°. 10128
Cyclopædia of Amer. Lit. E. A. & G. L. Duyckinck. N. Y. 1855. 2 v. 4°. 8796
Cyclopædia of Biography. Ed. F. L. Hawks. New York, 1856. 8°. . 8800
of Biblical Literature. J. Kitto. New York, 1846. 2 v. 8°. . 8807
of Eng. Literature. R. Chambers. Edinburgh, 1844. 2 v. 4° . 8803
of the Industry of all Nations. C. Knight. London, 1851. 8°. . 8832
of Useful Arts and Manufactures. C. Tomlinson. N. Y. 2 v. 8°. 8798
Cyril Thornton, Youth and Manhood of. T. Hamilton. N. Y. 1827. 2 v. 12°. 1404
Cyropædia, Xenophon. New York, 1841. 2 v. 12°. 5262
See also Xenophon.
Czar, his Court and People. J. S. Maxwell. New York, 1848. 12°. . 9808

D.

Dacre, Lady. Tales of the Peerage and Peasant. N. Y. 1835. 2 v. 12°. 1501
D'Aguesseau, H. Life. C. Butler. London, 1830. 8°. 8165
Dahlmann, Prof. Life of Herodotus. London, 1845. 12°. . . . 8254
Daily Words of the Brethren's Congregation. London, 1780. 12°. . . 6598
The same. 6599
Damascus and Palmyra. C. G. Addison. London, 1838. 2 v. 8°. . . 9407
Dampier, W. and others. Life and Voyages. New York, 1832. 16°. . 8762
The same. 6615
The same. New York, 1840. 12°. 5531
Dana, J. D. Manual of Mineralogy. New Haven, 1848. 12°. . . . 6086
Dana, Mrs. M. S. B. Parted Family and other Poems. N. Y. 1842. 12°. 2350
Dana, R. H. Poems and Prose Writings. New York, 1850. 2 v. 12°. . 1911
Dana, R. H., Jr. Two Years before the Mast. (2 copies.) N. Y. 1841. 12°. 5566
Danes, Ancient, Manners, Customs, &c. of the. Tr. Lond. 1770. 2 v. 8°. 11363
Danforth, J. N. Memoir of W. C. Walton. New York, 1837. 12°. . 8323
Daniel, G. Merrie England in Olden Time. London, 1842. 12°. . . 1137
Daniel, a Discourse on. Philadelphia, 1828. 8°. 6416
Lectures on Book of. F. A. Cox. New York, 1836. 12°. . . 5692
Dante, Alighieri. Divina Commedia. Tr. H. Boyd. Lond. 1802. 3 v. 8°. 1875
Illustrations of, by J. Flaxman. Folio. . . . .
Vision. Trans. H. Carey. New York, 1845. 12°. . . . 2453
D'Anville, J. B. B. Ancient Geography. Tr. New York, 1814. 2 v. 8°. 9215
D'Anvers, C. Craftsman. London, 1731. 7 v. 12°. 4275
Daphnis. S. Gessner. Tr. London, 1802. 12°. 4234
Da Ponte, L. L. History of the Florentine Republic. N. Y. 1833. 2 v. 12°. 7428
D'Arblay, Madame, Diary and Letters of. vol. 1. Philadelphia, 1842. 8°. 9731
Memoirs of. Mrs. H. Berkeley. New York, 1844. 12°. . . . 7454
Memoirs of C. Burney. Philadelphia, 1833. 8°. 8174
The same. 11333
See also Burney, Miss F.

Darby, W. Geographical Dictionary. Washington, 1843. 8°. . . . 8809
Travels through New York. New York, 1819. 8°. 9163
Dark Scenes of History. G. P. R. James. New York, 1850. 12°. . . 1217
Darley, O. C. Illustrations of Rip Van Winkle. New York, 1848. Folio.
Darnley. G. P. R. James. New York, 1834. 2 v. 12°. 1046
Darwin, C. Geol. and Nat. History of Various Countries. Lond. 1840. 8°. 10104
Voyage of a Naturalist round the World. New York, 1846. 2 v. 12°. 10202
Darwin, E. Life. Anna Seward. Philadelphia, 1804. 8°. . . . 11310
D'Aubigne, J. H. M. History of the Reformation in Germany, &c. New York, 1842. 4 v. 12°. 5681
The same. (vol. 1 missing.) New York, 1844. 4 v. 12°. . 6134
Oliver Cromwell, a Vindication. New York, 1850. 12°. . . 8624
Puseyism Examined. New York, 1843 16°. 6564
Daughters of Eng., their Position in Society. Mrs. S. Ellis. N. Y. 1843. 12° 4889
Daunou, M. The Court of Rome. Philadelphia, 1837. 12°. . . . 5686
Davenport, R. A. Hist. of the Bastile and its Captives. Lond. 1839. 16°. 7479
Narrative of Perils and Sufferings. London, 1840. 2 v. 12°. . 3360
Perilous Adventures. New York, 1846. 12°. 5211
David Copperfield. C. Dickens. New York. 2 v. 12°. . . . 201
Davidson, Margaret M. Poetical Remains and Life. Phil. 1841. 12°. . 2337
Davidson, Maria L., Life of. C. M. Sedgwick. Boston, 1837. 12°. . . 8049
Davie, W. R. Life. F. M. Hubbard. Boston, 1848. 12°. . . . 8067
Davies, C. Elements of Algebra. Baltimore, 1839. 12°. . . . 3933
Translation of Bourdon's Algebra. New York, 1845. 8°. . . 434
Davies, J. Select Poems with Life, by E. Sanford. Phil. 1819. 18°. . 2119
Davies, S. Sermons, with Essay on his Life and Time. A. Barnes. New York, 1842. 3 v. 12°. 5749
Davies, T. Criticisms on Shakspeare. London, 1785. 3 v. 12°. . . 841
Davis, C. A. Letters of Jack Downing. New York, 1834. 12°. . . 1226
Life and Writings of Jack Downing. Boston, 1834. 12°. . . 964
Davis, E. History of the Half Century. Boston, 1851. 12°. . . . 476
Davis, G. F. Memoir. Abigail L. Davis. Hartford, 1837. 12° . . 5647
Davis, H. Narrative of the Decline of Hamilton College. N. Y. 1830. 8°. 11688
Davis, J. Life of T. Chatterton. London. 16°. 7770
Davis, J. F. A General Description of the Chinese. N. Y. 1840. 2 v. 12°. 5890
The same. London, 1840. 12°. 9284
The same, with a supplementary vol. Lond. 1845. 4 v. 16°. 7184
Davis, M. L. Memoirs of A. Burr. New York, 1836. 2 v. 8°. . . 8495
Davis, Z. A. Freemason's Monitor. Philadelphia, 1843. 12°. . . 818
Davy, H. Consolations in Travel. Philadelphia, 1830. 18°. . . . 4285
Life. J. A. Paris. London, 1831. 2 v. 8°. 12089
Life and Collected Works. London, 1839, 40. 9 v. 8°. . . . 6004

Vol. 1. Life, by J. Davy.
2. Early Miscellaneous Papers.
3. Chemical and Philosophical Researches.
4. Elements of Chemical Philosophy.
5. Bakerian Lectures and Miscellanies.
6. Miscellanies and Researches on Safety Lamp.
7. Discourses and Elements of Agricultural Chemistry.
8. Elements of Agricultural Chemistry and Lectures.
9. Salmonia and Consolations of Travel.

Dawes, R. Geraldine and other Poems. New York, 1839. 12°. . . 1953
Day, J. Examination of Edwards on the Will. New Haven, 1841. 12°. 5702
Self-Determining Power of the Will. New Haven, 1838. 12°. . 6088
Day, Martha. Remains. New Haven, 1834. 12°. 2227
Day, S. Historical Collections of Pennsylvania. Phil. 1843. 8°. . . 7251
Day, T. and J. Murdock. Memoirs of Class of 1797, Yale College. New Haven, 1848. 8°. 12091
D'Azeglio, M. Challenge of Barletta. Tr. New York, 1845. 12°. . 667
Dead Sea, Expedition to. W. F. Lynch. Philadelphia, 1850. 8°. . . 9374
Death, Poem on. B. Porteus. Boston, 1814. 18°. 4616
Thoughts on. W. Dodd. London, 1773. 12°. 3903
Death's Doings. Compositions illustrating 30 designs, by R. Dagley. Boston, 1828. 2 v. 8°. 98
Decameron, or Ten Days' Entertainment. G. Boccaccio. Trans. London, 1822. 4 v. 24°. 1745
Decatur, S. Life and Character. S. P. Waldo. Hartford, 1821. 12°. . 8349
Life of. A. S. Mackenzie. Boston, 1846. 12°. 8063
Declaration of Independence, Signers of the. Lives. J. Sanderson. Philadelphia, 1827. 9 v. 8°. 11299
Deer, &c., Natural History of. W. Jardine. Edinburgh, 1835. 12°. . 10195
Deerslayer, or First War Path. J. F. Cooper. Philadelphia, 1841. 12°. 1264
De Félice, G. History of the Protestants of France. Tr. N. Y. 1851. 8°. 7265
De Foe, D. Novels and Miscellaneous Works. Edinburgh, 1810. 12 v. 16°. 322

Vol. 1-3. Life. Robinson Crusoe.
4, 5. Memoirs of a Cavalier.
6, 7. Life of Colonel Jack.
8, 9. Adventures of Captain Singleton.
10, 11. New Voyage round the World.
12. The Plague in London, in 1665.

Plague in London, with Religious Courtship. New York, 1857. 12°. 570
Plague in London, with Fire in London, Storm, &c. Lond. 1855. 12°. 5473
De Forest, J. W. History of the Indians of Conn. Hartford, 1851. 12°. 7367
Deformed, The. New York, 1835. 12°. 1252
Degerando, (Baron) J. M. Self Education. Tr. Boston, 1830. 8°. . 747
Deism, Cure of, or the Mediatorial Scheme by Jesus Christ. London, 1737. 2 v. 12°. 6441
Revealed. P. Skelton. London, 1751. 2 v. 12°. 6586
Deistical Writers of England, View of. J. Leland. Lond. 1757. 3 v. 8°. 5114
Deists, Short Method with. C. Leslie. London, 1723. 12°. . . . 4523
De Kay, J. E. Sketches of Turkey in 1831, 2. New York, 1833. 8°. . 9364
The same. 9443
Zoölogy of New York. Albany, 1842. 5 v. 4°. 13098
De Kock, C. P. Modern Cymon. Philadelphia, 1833. 2 v. 12°. . . 262
Delaware, or the Ruined Family. Philadelphia, 1833. 2 v. 12°. . . 1132
De Ligne, Prince, Letters and Reflections of. Philadelphia, 1809. 12°. . 3008
De Lisle, or The Sensitive Man. New York, 1828. 2 v. 12°. . . 628
De Lolme, L. Constitution of England, with Life. London, 1853. 12°. . 5185
De Louvois, Marquis. Life. G. P. R. James. Philadelphia, 1837. 12°. . 8363
Deluge, Doctrine of the. L. V. Harcourt. London, 1838. 2 v. 8°. . 5078

Deluge, Treatise on the. A. Catcott. London, 1768. 8°. 5380
Demerara. Illust. of Polit. Econ. Miss H. Martineau. Bost. 1832. 16°. 1674
The same. 10021
Demetrius, the Hero of the Don. A Poem. A. Eustaphieve. Bost. 1818. 12°. 2278
Democracy. G. S. Camp. New York, 1841. 12°. 5912
Democracy in America. See America.
Unveiled. T. G. Fessenden. New York, 1806. 2 v. 12°. . . . 1965
Democratic Review. vols. 1–31. Wash. and New York, 1838–52. 8°. . 4757
Demonology and Witchcraft, Letters on. W. Scott. (Two copies.) New York, 1830. 16°. 6269
The same. New York, 1839. 12°. 5513
Demosthenes. Opera. Lipsiæ, 1829. 3 v. 16° 10818
The same. Lipsiæ, 1812. 5 v. 18°. 10870
on the Crown. Review of Brougham's Trans. London, 1840. 12°. 3286
Orations. Tr. T. Leland. New York, 1832. 18°. 455
The same. New York, 1840. 2 v. 12°. 5263
Two copies of vol. 1. New York, 1834. 16°. . . . 8744
Select Orations. Ed. J. T. Champlin. Boston, 1848. 12°. . . 3002
Dendy, W. C. Philosophy of Mystery. New York, 1845. 12°. . . 4239
Denham, D., and others. Travels in Africa. Boston, 1826. 8°. . . 9460
Denham, J. Select Poems with life by E. Sanford. Phil. 1819. 16°. . 2120
Denmark, History of. London, 1782. 2 v. 8°. 7074
Sweden and Norway, Hist. of. S. A. Dunham. Lond. 1839, 40. 12°. 9865
Dennis, G. A Chronicle of the Cid. London, 1845. 16°. 7172
Denon, V. Trav. in Upper and Lower Egypt. Tr. N. Y. 1803. 2 v. 8°. 9495
Denton, D. Description of New York in 1670. New York, 1845. 8°. . 11318
De Pauw, C. Philosophical Dissertations on the Egyptians and Chinese. Trans. London, 1795. 2 v. 8°. 11373
Philosophical Dissert. on the Greeks. Tr. Lond. 1793. 2 v. 8°. 11375
De Quincy, Q. Imitation in the Fine Arts. London, 1837. 8°. . . 10133
Life of Raffaello. London, 1846. 12°. 5490
De Quincey, T. Autobiographic Sketches. Boston, 1855. 12°. . . 880
Biographical Essays. Boston, 1850. 12°. 893
Cæsars. Boston, 1851. 12°. 891
Confessions of an English Opium Eater. Boston, 1851. 12°. . 892
Essay on Poets. Boston, 1854. 12°. 887
Historical and Critical Essays. Boston, 1854. 2 v. 12°. . . 889
Letters to a Young Man. Boston, 1854. 12°. 888
Literary Reminiscences. Boston, 1851. 2 v. 12°. . . . 894
Narrative Papers. Boston, 1854. 2 v. 12°. 881
The Logic of Political Economy. London, 1844. 8°. . . . 10991
Philosophical Writers. Boston, 1854. 2 v. 12°. 885
Theological Essays. Boston, 1854. 2 v. 12°. 883
De Retz, Cardinal. Autobiography. Tr. Philadelphia, 1817. 3 v. 8°. . 8490
Life. G. P. R. James. Philadelphia, 1837. 12°. 8362
Dermoncourt, (Gen.) The Duchess of Berri in La Vendée. Lond. 1833. 8°. 7917
De Sacy, A. J. S. Principles of General Grammar. Tr. D. Fosdick, Jr. Andover, 1837. 12°. 4860

De Sévigné, Madame, and her Cotemporaries. Phil. 1842. 2 v. 12°. . 8616
De Staël, A. Letters on England. London, 1830. 8°. 9142
De Stael, Madame. Memoirs of Private Life of M. Necker. Lond. 1818. 8°. 7946
Corinne ou L'Italie. Paris, 1836. 12°. 676
The same. Trans. Philadelphia, 1836. 2 v. 12°. . . . 674
The same. New York, 1844. 8°. 20
Events of the French Revolution. Tr. New York, 1818. 2 v. 8°. 7315
Germany. London, 1814. 3 v. 8°. 9469
Influence of Literature on Society. Tr. Boston, 1813. 12°. . 4595
Reflections on Suicide. Tr. Philadelphia, 1816. 16°. . . 11294
Desultory Man, The. G. P. R. James. New York, 1836. 2 v. 12°. . 1490
De Tocqueville, A. Democracy in America. Tr. N. Y. 1838–40 2 v. 8°. 10061
The same. New York, 1845. 2 v. 8°. 10985
Old Regime and the Revolution. Tr. New York, 1856. 12°. . 7393
De Tott, (Baron.) Memoirs on Turks and Tartars. Tr. Dub. 1785. 3 v. 12°. 8382
De Vere, or the Man of Independence. R. P. Ward. N. Y. 1831. 2 v. 12°. 1025
Devereux. E. L. Bulwer. New York, 1829. 2 v. 12°. 1346
Devonshire Traditions. Mrs. Bray. London, 1838. 3 v. 8°. . . . 11415
Devout Life, Introduction to. Baltimore, 1816. 18°. 4613
Devout and Holy Life, Serious call to. W. Law. Andover, 1821. 12°. . 6532
Devotional and Practical Treatises. J. Hall. London, 1834. 12°. . . 5780
Dewar, D. Elements of Moral Philosophy, &c. London, 1826. 2 v. 8°. 6337
Observations on Character and Customs of the Irish. Lond. 1812. 8°. 9511
Dewey, O. Old World and New. New York, 1836. 2 v. 12°. . . 9832
DeWitt, J. Life. G. P. R. James. Philadelphia, 1837. 12°. . . 8363
Dial, The. Ed. R. W. Emerson. vol. 4. Boston, 1844. 8°. . . . 2247
Dialogues, Moral and Political, with Letters on Chivalry, &c. R. Hurd. London, 1765. 3 v. 16°. 3368
Diary, The. London, 1843. 12°. 5932
of a Désennuyée. Philadelphia, 1836. 12°. 1134
of an Invalid. H. Matthews. Philadelphia, 1836. 16°. . . 9315
Dibdin, C. Songs. London, 1841. 16°. 2034
Dibdin, T. F. Bibliomania. London, 1809. 8°. 425
Dick, J. Essay on the Inspiration of the Bible. Boston, 1811. 12°. . 6494
The same. 6495
Lectures on Theology. New York, 1846. 2 v. 8°. . . . 5048
Dick, T. Celestial Scenery. New York, 1841. 12°. 5542
Christian Philosopher. Brookfield, 1828. 12°. . . . 6101
Improvement of Society by Diffusing Knowledge. N. Y. 1833. 12°. 3391
The same. New York, 1840. 12°. 5875
Mental Illumination and Moral Improvement of Mankind. New York, 1836. 12°. 6190
Philosophy of Religion. Brookfield, 1829. 12°. 6102
The same. Brookfield, 1830. 12°. 6434
Philosophy of a Future State. New York, 1829. 12°. . . . 6103
Practical Astronomer. New York, 1846. 12°. 6093
Sidereal Heavens. New York, 1840. 12°. 5559
Dickens, C. Barnaby Rudge. 68
The same. New York, 1842. 12°. 658

Dickens, C. Battle of Life. New York, 1846. 8°. 97
Bleak House. Philadelphia. 8°. 72
Christmas Stories. Philadelphia. 8°. 70
Cricket on the Hearth. New York, 1847. 8°. 97
David Copperfield. New York. 2 v. 12°. 201
Dombey and Son. Philadelphia. 8°. 74
The same. New York, 1847. 8°. 97
(Editor.) Household Words. London, 1850–9. 8 v. 8°. . . . 2208
Home and Social Philosophy. First series. New York, 1852. 12°. 1188
Second series. New York, 1852. 12°. 1189
Little Dorrit. Philadelphia. 8°. 73
Martin Chuzzlewit. Philadelphia. 8°. 69
Memoirs of J. Grimaldi. London, 1838. 2 v. 12°. 8264
New Stories. Philadelphia. 8°. 71
Nicholas Nickleby. Philadelphia, 1839. 8°. 15
The same. Philadelphia. 8°. 67
Notes on America. New York, 1844. 8°. 9087
Oliver Twist. Philadelphia. 8°. 66
Pickwick Club. Philadelphia, 1837. 2 v. 12°. 1661
Sketches, By Boz. Philadelphia, 1839. 8°. 16
The same. 65
Dictionnaire Universel, D'Histoire Naturelle. Lyon, 1791. 15 v. 12°. . 8951
Dictionary of Arts, Manufactures and Mines. A. Ure. N. Y. 1843. 8°. 8811
Biographical. H. J. Rose. London, 1857. 12 v. 8°. 8834
of Dates. Ed. G. P. Putnam. New York, 1851–3. 12°. . . . 8885
of English Literature, and of British and American Authors. S. A. Allibone. Philadelphia, 1839. 2 v. 4°. 9673
of the English Language. 18°. 4939
Geographical. W. Darby. Washington, 1843. 8°. 8809
Geographical. R. M'Culloch. N. Y. 1847. 2 v. 8°. 8805
of Mechanical Science. A. Jamieson. London, 1832. 4°. . . 10918
Philosophical. See Philosophical.
Didactics, Social, Literary, and Political. R. Walsh. Phil. 1836. 2 v. 8° 2995
Digby, Sir K. Autobiography. London, 1827. 8°. 8159
Digby, K. H. Broadstone of Honor. London, 1844. 12°. 1174
Digestion and Dietetics. A. Combe. New York, 1836. 16°. . . . 4974
Gastric Juice, &c. Observations on. W. Beaumont. Bost. 1834. 8°. 401
Dillon, A. A Winter in Iceland and Lapland. London, 1840. 2 v. 12°. 9543
Dio Cassius. Historia Romana. Lipsiæ, 1829. 4 v. 16°. 10845
Diodorus Siculus. Bibliotheca Historica. Lipsiæ, 1829. 6 v. 16°. . . 10839
Diogenes Laertius. De Vitis Philosophorum. Lipsiæ, 1833. 16°. . . 10339
Dionysius Halicarnassensis. Opera. Lipsiæ, 1829. 3 v. 16°. . . . 10830
Diplomatic Correspondence of the American Revolution. Ed. J. Sparks. Boston, 1829. 12 v. 8°. 11035
Diplomatists of Europe. B. H. R. Capefigue. Tr. London, 1845. 12°. . 8396
Discoveries, Maritime and Inland. London, 1830. 3 v. 12°. . . . 9920
Diseases, Acute and Chronic. T. Sydenham. Philadelphia, 1809. 8°. . 9763
D'Israeli, B. Coningsby. New York, 1845. 8°. 19

D'Israeli, B. Contarini Fleming. New York, 1832. 2 v. 12°. . . . 1635
Henrietta Temple. Philadelphia, 1837. 2 v. 12°. 145
Novels, complete. Philadelphia, 1847. 8°. 5
Sybil. London. 1845. 8°. 10
Vivian Grey. Philadelphia, 1837. 2 v. 12°. 1665
The Young Duke. New York, 1831. 2 v. 12°. 1270
The same. 1021
D'Israeli, I. Amenities of Literature. London, 1841. 3 v. 8°. . . . 721
The same New York, 1845. 2 v. 12°. 512
Curiosities of Literature. London, 1823. 5 v. 12°. 849
Second series. London, 1824. 3 v. 8°. 148
First and second series. New York, 1844. 4°. 36
Genius of Judaism. London, 1833. 12°. 5634
Literary Character Illust. by the Hist. of Men of Gen. N. Y. 1818. 12° 3326
The same. London, 1822. 2 v. 12°. 1177
Quarrels of Authors. New York, 1814. 2 v. 12°. 4582
Dissenters, History of, from the Revolution to 1808. D. Bogue and J. Bennett. London, 1833. 8°. 5614
Distinguished Men of Modern Times, Lives of. New York, 1840. 2 v. 12°. 5896
Ditson, G. L. Circassia, or Tour to the Caucasus. New York, 1850. 12°. 9256
Diversions of Purley. J. H. Tooke. London, 1829. 2 v. 8°. . . . 1061
Divina Commedia, Dante Alighieri. London, 1802. 3 v. 8°. . . . 1875
Divine Efficiency, Doctrine of. E. D. Griffin. New York, 1833. 8°. . 5640
Legation of Moses. W. Warburton. London, 1742. 3 v. 8°. . 5637
Truth, Essays on. J. Catlin. Hartford, 1818. 12°. 4590
The same, with Questions. Middletown, 1826. 12°. . . 6551
Divinity, View of. M. Mather. Stamford, 1813. 12°. 6558
Dixon, W. H. Life of W. Penn. Philadelphia, 1851. 12°. . . . 7995
Dobney, H. H. Scripture Doctrine of Future Punishment. N. Y. 1850. 12°. 5690
Dobson, Mrs. L. Life of F. Petrarch. Philadelphia, 1817. 8°. . . . 8187
The same. Philadelphia, 1809. 2 v. 16°. 8426
Doctor, The. R. Southey. New York, 1836. 1531
Doctrine of Election. G. S. Faber. New York, 1840. 8°. 5064
Dodd, G. British Manufactures, Textile, Chemical, &c. Lond. 1846. 6 v. 16° 7466
Dodd, W. Reflections on Death. London, 1773. 12°. 3903
Thoughts in Prison. Boston, 1777. 12°. 6497
Doddridge, P. Lectures on Various Subjects. London, 1799. 2 v. 8°. . 5117
Life of J. Gardner. Exeter, 1795. 12°. 7776
Rise and Progress of Religion in the Soul. New York. 12°. . 6529
The same. 6539
Sermons to the Young. Boston, 1830. 18°. 4609
Works. London, 1804. 5 v. 8°. 5103
Dodington, G. B. Autobiography. London, 1828. 16°. 7501
Diary of. London, 1823. 8°. 10757
Dodsley, R. Poetical Works and Life. Philadelphia, 1822. 18°. . . 2138
Dollars and Cents. Amy Lothrop. New York, 1852. 2 v. 12°. . . 1279
Dombey and Son. C. Dickens. Philadelphia. 8°. 74
The same. New York, 1847. 8°. 97
Domestic Economy. M. Donovan. London, 1837. 2 v. 12°. . . . 9963

Domestic Recreation. Priscilla Wakefield. Philadelphia, 1805. 18°. . 4945

Donnegan, J. Greek Lexicon. 8°. 1066

Donne, J. Select Poems, with Life by E. Sanford. Phil. 1819. 16°. . 2119

H. Walton and others. Lives. J. Walton. N. York, 1846. 2 v. 12° 8705

Donovan, M. Domestic Economy. London, 1837. 2 v. 12°. . . . 9963

Treatise on Chemistry. London, 1837. 12°. 9913

Don Quixote, History and Adventures of. M. de Cervantes. Trans. Exeter, 1827. 4 v. 24°. 1733

The same. New York, 1825. 3 v. 18°. 1765

The same. New York, 1855. 12°. 206

The same. Tr. C. Jarvis. (Illustrated.) Phil. 1852. 2 v. 8° 127

Doolittle, M. Hist. of Cong. Church, Belchertown, Mass. N. Y. 1852. 12°. 6188

Doom of Devorgoil, The. Sir W. Scott. New York, 1830. 12°. . . 1424

Doomed, The. Philadelphia, 1834. 2 v. 12°. 311

Doré. New York, 1857. 12°. 9591

Doric Race, Hist. and Antiquities of. C. O. Müller. Tr. Lond. 1839. 2 v. 8° 6978

Douglas, J. Advancement of Society in Knowledge, &c. Hart. 1830. 12°. 6144

Errors Regarding Religion. New York, 1831. 12°. . . . 6432

Philosophy of the Mind. Edinburgh, 1839. 8°. 6320

Douglass, F. My Bondage and My Freedom. New York, 1855. 8°. . 8298

Dover, Lord. Life of Frederick II, King of Prussia. N. Y. 1839. 2 v. 12°. 5857

The same. New York, 1832. 2 v. 16°. 6632

Dowling, J. History of Romanism. New York, 1845. 8°. . . . 5010

Downes, J. The Mountain Decameron. London, 1836. 3 v. 12°. . . 1434

and F. Hunt. United States Almanac. Philadelphia, 1844. 12°. . 11876

Downing, A. J. Fruits and Fruit Trees. New York, 1849. 12°. . . 2978

Landscape Gardening and Rural Architecture. N. Y. 1849. 8°. . 10106

Drake, B. Life of Tecumseh and his Brother the Prophet. Cin. 1841. 12°. 8344

Drake, D. Statistical View of Cincinnati. Cincinnati, 1815. 12°. . . 7128

Drake, F., and others, Lives and Voyages of. New York, 1832. 16°. . 8762

The same. 6615

The same. New York, 1840. 12°. 5531

Drake, J. R. Culprit Fay and other Poems. New York, 1836. 8°. . 1854

Drake, N. Essays. London, 1805. 3 v. 12°. 4318

Literary Hours. London, 1804. 3 v. 8°. 151

Mornings in Spring. London, 1828. 2 v. 12°. 4235

Shakspeare and his Times. Paris, 1838. 8°. 51

Drake, S. G. Philip's and other Indian Wars. Exeter, 1834. 12°. . 6834

Drama, Defense of. New York, 1826. 18°. 4315

Drama of Exile and other Poems. E. B. Barrett. N. Y. 1845. 2 v. 12°. . 2013

Dramas, Sacred. Hannah More. London, 1782. 12°. 2269

Dramatic Art and Literature, Lectures on. A. W. von Schlegel. Tr. Phil. 1833. 8°. 32

The same. 94

The same. Tr. J. Black. London, 1846. 12°. 5194

Literature, Lectures on. W. Hazlitt. London, 1840. 12°. . . . 4588

Poets, Specimens of English. Ed. C. Lamb. New York, 1845. 12°. 9845

Scenes and other Poems. B. W. Proctor. Boston, 1857. 12°. . 1990

Dream, The, and other Poems. Mrs. C. E. S. Norton. N. Y. 1845. 12°. . 5846
of a Day and other Poems. J. G. Percival. N. Haven, 1843. 12°. 2400
Life. D. G. Mitchell. New York, 1851. 12°. 218
The same. 214
The same. New York, 1859. 12°. 207
Dreams and Reveries of a Quiet Man. T. S. Fay. N. Y. 1832. 2 v. 12°. 1381
Dred; Tale of Great Dismal Swamp. Mrs. Stowe. Bost. 1856. 2 v. 12°. 173
Drew, S. Essay on Resurrection of the Human Body. Brooklyn, 1811. 8°. 5121
Droz, J. Art of Being Happy. Tr. Boston, 1832. 12°. . . . 3392
Druids and Celtic Religion & Learning, Hist. of. J. Toland. Lond. 1790. 8°. 11336
Drummond, W. Origines, or Origin of Several Empires, States and Cities. London, 1824. 4 v. 8°. 7586
Poems. London, 1790. 18°. 2477
Drunkenness, Evils of Explained. P. H. Morris. New York, 1841. 12°. 11455
Drury, Anna H. Eastbury. New York, 1851. 12°. 561
Drury, R. Autobiography. London, 1831. 16°. 7484
The same. London, 1826. 16°. 7749
Dryden, J. Dramatic Works. London, 1725. 6 v. 12°. 3047
Life. W. Scott. Boston, 1829. 12°. 3934
Poetical Works, with Life by E. Sanford. Phil. 1819. 2 v. 18°. . 2125
Prose Works, with Life by E. Malone. London, 1800. 4 v. 8°. . 1888
Duane, W. Visit to Colombia. Philadelphia, 1826. 8°. 9436
Dubois, J. A. Description of the Character, Customs and Institutions of the People of India. Tr. Philadelphia, 1818. 2 v. 8°. . . . 9150
Ducas, T. Travels in Italy. Ed. C. Mills. London, 1822. 2 v. 8°. . 9461
Duchess De La Valliere, a Play. E. L. Bulwer. New York, 1836. 12°. . 2392
Correspondence. Tr. London, 1810. 2 v. 12°. 4529
Letters to H. Walpole and others. London, 1810. 4 v. 12°. . 3939
Dudevant, Mad. Consuelo. Tr. F. G. Shaw. Boston, 1846. 2 v. 12°. 918
Duelling, History of. J. G. Millingen. London, 1841. 2 v. 8°. . . 399
Duer, W. A. Life of Lord Stirling. New York, 1847. 8°. 7871
Duffield, G. Spiritual Life, or Regeneration. Carlisle, 1822. 8°. . . 5342
and A. Barnes. Discourses on the Sabbath. Phil. 1836. 16°. . 6231
Dufresny, Œuvres. Paris, 1811. 2 v. 18°. 10883
Duke Christian, or Tradition from Hartz. Jane Porter. Bost. 1824. 2 v. 12°. 1336
Dumas, A. Marguerite de Valois. New York, 1846. 8°. 11
Dumas, S. Travels in Egypt and Arabia Petræa. Tr. N. Y. 1839. 12°. 9563
Dumas, Count M. Memoirs of his own Time. Phil. 1839. 2 v. 12°. . 11393
Dumont, E. Recollections of H. G. R. Mirabeau. Tr. Phil. 1833. 8°. . 8538
Duncan, H. Sacred Philosophy of the Seasons. Boston, 1839. 4 v. 12°. . 6479
Duncan, J. Entomology. (vol. 1 missing.) Edin. 1835–7. 4 v. 12°. . 10181
Duncan, J. M. Travels through U. S. and Canada. N. Y. 1823. 2 v. 12°. 9029
Duncan, W. Elements of Logic. Albany, 1811. 12°. 3024
The same. Albany, 1804. 12°. 4981
Dunham, S. A. History of Denmark, Sweden and Norway. Lond. 1839–40. 3 v. 12°. 9865
History of Europe during the Middle Ages. Lond. 1833–4. 4 v. 12°. 9881
History of the Germanic Empire. London, 1834–5. 12°. . . 9868

Dunham, S. A. History of Poland. London, 1831. 12°. 9909
History of Spain and Portugal. London, 1832. 5 v. 12°. . . . 9874
The same. (vol. 3 missing.) Phil. 1835. 4 v. 12°. . . . 5829
Dunlap, W. Events that followed Bonaparte's Campaign in Russia. Hartford, 1814. 12°. 6824
History of the American Theatre. New York, 1832. 8°. . . 409
History of the Arts of Design in the United States. New York, 1834. 2 v. 8°. 10107
Life of G. F. Cooke. New York, 1813. 2 v. 18°. 8442
and H. L. Clarke. Life of Duke of Wellington. N. Y. 1814. 8°. . 8540
Dunlop, J. History of Fiction. Edinburgh, 1816. 3 v. 12°. 784
History of Roman Literature. Philadelphia, 1827. 2 v. 8°. . . 89
The same. 91
Memoirs of Spain, from 1621 to 1700. Edinburgh, 1834. 2 v. 8°. . 6675
Du Pan, J. M. Hist. of Destruction of the Helvetic Union. Bost. 1799. 12°. 7127
Duppa, R. Life of Michel Angelo. London, 1846. 12°. 5490
Durant, T. Memoirs of an Only Son. Andover, 1823. 12°. . . . 8330
Durbin, J. P. Observations in Europe. New York, 1844. 2 v. 12°. . 9535
Observations in the East. New York, 1845. 2 v. 12°. . . . 9579
Durfee, J. "What Cheer," or R. Williams in Banishment. Prov. 1840. 12°. 2341
Dutch in the Medway. London, 1845. 16°. 7474
Dutch Republic, Rise of the. J. L. Motley. New York, 1856. 3 v. 8°. . 7549
Dutton, M. R. Conic Sections, Spherical Geometry, &c. N. H. 1824. 8°. 424
Duty, or the White Cottage. Mrs. Roberts. London, 1815. 2 v. 18°. . 1683
Duyckinck, E. A. & G. L. Cyclopædia of Am. Literature. N. Y. 1845. 2 v. 4°. 8796
Dwight, E. W. Memoirs of H. Obookiah. New Haven, 1819. 18°. . . 8441
Dwight, H. E. Travels in the North of Germany. New York, 1829. 8°. 9448
Dwight, S. E. Life of D. Brainerd. New Haven, 1822. 8°. . . . 8513
Life of J. Edwards. New York, 1830. 8°. 7913
Dwight, Theodore. Character of T. Jefferson. Boston, 1839 12°. . . 8347
History of the Hartford Convention. New York, 1833. 8°. . . 10736
The same. 10766
Roman Republic, of 1849. New York, 1851. 12°. 6797
Dwight, Theodore, Jr. History of Connecticut. New York, 1842. 12°. . 5577
Dwight, Timothy. The Conquest of Canaan, a Poem. Hartford, 1785. 12°. 2370
The same. 2375
Life of. W. B. Sprague. Boston, 1845. 12°. 8056
Remarks on the Review of Inchiquin's Letters. Boston, 1815. 8°. 10082
Sermons. New Haven, 1828. 2 v. 8°. 5324
Theology Explained and Defended. Middletown, 1818. 5 v. 8°. . 5343
Travels in New England and New York. N. H. 1821. 4 v. 8°. . 9426
Dwight, Timo., Jr. Memoir. J. P. Thompson. New Haven, 1844. 12°. 7733
Dwyer, J. H. Essay on Elocution. Utica, 1829. 12°. 11878
Dyer, J. Poetical Works, with Life by S. Johnson. Phil. 1819. 18°. . 2131
Dying Thoughts. New York. 16°. 5227
The same. London, 1834. 12°. 5781
Dyspepsy Forestalled and Resisted. E. Hitchcock. Amherst, 1831. 8°. 3395
The same. Amherst, 1830. 4532

E.

Eagle Pass. Cora Montgomery. New York, 1852. 12°. 9001
Earl, G. W. Eastern Seas. London, 1837. 8°. 9393
Early Conflicts of Christianity. W. I. Kip. New York, 1853. 12°. . 6467
The same. New York, 1850. 12°. 6154
Earth. R. Mudie. London, 1835. 12°. 6105
and Man. A. Guyot. Boston, 1851. 12°. 6055
Remarkable Phenomena of the. W. M. Higgins. N. Y. 1840. 12°. 5888
Sacred Theory of the. T. Burnet. Glasgow, 1753. 12°. . . 6527
East, D. J. Western Africa, its Condition. London, 1844. 12°. . . 8699
East, Observations in the. J. P. Durbin. New York, 1845. 2 v. 12°. . 9579
Religion of the, with Impressions of Foreign Travel. J. Hawes. Hartford, 1845. 12°. 8973
Spirit of the, Illustrated by Journal of Travels. D. Urquhart. Philadelphia, 1839. 2 v. 12°. 9008
Travels in the. J. A. Spencer. New York, 1850. 8°. . . . 9389
East India Company, J. S. Buckingham's claims against. Lond. 1836. 8°. 10758
Co's Possessions, Hist. of. R. M. Martin. London, 1837. 2 v. 12°. 5814
Year Book for 1841. London, 1841. 12°. 4891
Eastbury. Anna H. Drury. New York, 1851. 12°. 561
Eastern Life, Present and Past. Harriet Martineau. Phil. 1848. 8°. . 9519
Seas, or Voyages in the Indian Archipelago. London, 1837. 8°. 9393
Seas, Voyages to. B. Hall. Edinburgh, 1826. 16°. 9986
Eastman, F. S. History of New York. New York, 1828. 12°. . . . 11468
Eaton, A. Botanical Grammar. Albany, 1828. 12°. 3325
Ecclesiastical Establishments in Europe. W. Graham. London, 1808. 12°. 3929
History, Eusebius Pamphilus. Tr. C. F. Cruse. Phil. 1840. 8°. 5075
History. W. Palmer. New York, 1841. 12°. 5732
The same. New York, 1844. 12°. 5685
The same. 6148
History. Socrates. Tr. London, 1844. 8°. 5063
History, Ancient and Modern. J. L. Mosheim. Tr. J. Murdock. New Haven, 1832. 3 v. 8°. 5080
The same. Tr. A. Maclaine. Philadelphia, 1797. 6 v. 8°. 6417
History of England. Bede. London, 1847. 12°. 5440
History, Epitome of. J. Marsh. New York, 1828. 12°. . . . 6178
History of First Three Centuries. J. L. Mosheim. Tr. London, 1813. 2 v. 8°. 5034
History, Lectures on. G. Campbell. London, 1834. 8°. . . . 5031
History of New England. C. Mather. Hartford, 1820. 2 v. 8°. 7222
History of U. States, Contributions to. F. L. Hawks. New York, 1836–39. 2 v. 8°. 5021
Duplicate of vol. 1. 5009
Polity. R. Hooker. London, 1821. 3 v. 8°. 5363
Reminiscences of the U. States. E. Waylen. New York, 1846. 8°. 7604
Echard, L. English Revolution in 1688. London, 1725. 12°. . . . 11445

Echard, L. History of England, with Oldmixon's Continuation, from B. C. 55 to A. D. 1727. London, 1707. Folio. 4 v. 11245
Echo, The, and other Poems. New York, 1807. 8°. 1883
Eckfeldt, J. R. Manual of Coins and Bullion. Philadelphia, 1842. 4°. .
Eclectic Magazine. vols. 1–46. New York, 1843–59. (Continued.) 8°. 4677
Eclectic Review, 1805–10. London. 11 v. 8°. 3561
Contributions to. J. Foster. London, 1844. 2 v. 8°. 715
Economy Cottage. W. Cobbett. New York, 1824. 8°. 11651
of Health. J. Johnson. New York, 1837. 16°. 4968
Public and Private. T. Sedgwick. New York, 1836. 3 v. . 10789
Edgar Huntly, or the Sleep Walker. C. B. Brown. Boston, 1827. 12°. 1005
The same. 1428
The same. Philadelphia, 1801. 3 v. 12°. 1292
Edgeworth, Miss M. The Absentee. Washington, 1812. 12°. . . 1650
Parent's Assistant. New York, 1836. 12°. 1148
Tales and Novels. New York, 1833. 12°. 200
Works. Boston, 1825. 13 v. 8°. 100
The same. New York, 1834. 10 v. 12°. 897

Vol. 1. Castle Rackrent. Essay on Irish Bulls. Essay on the Science of Self-Justification. Forester. Prussian Vase. Good Aunt.
2. Angelina. Good French Governess. Mlle. Panache. Knapsack. Lame Jervas. The Will. The Limerick Gloves, &c.
3. Murad the Unlucky. The Manufacturers. The Contrast, &c. Ennui. The Dun.
4. Manœuvering. Almeria. Vivian.
5. Absentee. Mad. de Fleury. Emilie de Coulanges. Modern Griselda.
6. Belinda.
7. Leonora. Letters. Patronage.
8. The Last Concluded. Comic Dramas.
9. Harrington. Thoughts on Bores. Ormond.
10. Helen.

and R. L. Practical Education. Boston, 1825. 8°. 100
Edgeworth, R. L. Essays on Professional Education. London, 1812. 8°. 2691
Edinburgh Annual Register. 1808–15. Edinburgh, 13 v. 8°. 3234
Encyclopædia, with Plates. New York and Philadelphia. 18 v. 4°. 8472
Monthly Review. vols. 1–5. Edinburgh, 1819–21. 8°. . . . 3813
Review. vols. 1–59. 1802–34. New York and Boston. 8°. 3754
The same. vols. 60–110. 1834–59. (Continued.) N. Y. 8°. 4012
Index to vols. 1–20. In the Rack.
Review. Selections from the. London, 1833. 4 v. 8°. . . . 4491
Education, American Annals of. Boston, 1831. 8°. . . . . .
of Daughters. (Bp.) F. Fenelon. Tr. Boston, 1820. 16°. . . 3979
Essays on. Milton and others. London, 1761. 8°. 1105
of Females. S. Smith. London, 1840. 8°. 375
Improvements in. J. Lancaster. New York, 1807. 12°. . . . 4851
Liberal, Essay on Acquiring a. V. Knox. Lond. 1785. 2 v. 16°. 3712
Loose Hints upon. Dublin, 1782. 12°. 3018
National, Chapters on. R. M. Macbrair. London, 1845. 8°. . 11694
Practical, Importance of. E. Everett. Boston, 1840. 12°. . . 3309
Professional, Essays on. R. L. Edgeworth. London, 1812. 8°. . 2691
Progressive. Mad. Necker de Saussure. Tr. Boston, 1835. 12°. . 2988

Educator, The. Prize Essays. London, 1839. 12°. 816
Edward, the Black Prince. Life. G. P. R. James. London, 1839. 2 v. 12°. 8402
Edward, D. B. History of Texas. Cincinnati, 1836. 12°. . , . 7122
Edwards, B. History of the West Indies. Dublin, 1793. 2 v. 8°. . 6763
Edwards, B. B. Biography of Self-taught Men. Boston, 1832. 12°. . 8336
Memoir of E. Cornelius. Boston, 1833. 12°. 7723
and E. A. Park. Select. from German Literature. And. 1839. 8°. 1070
Edwards, E. Memoirs of Libraries. London, 1859. 2 v. 8°. . . 9720
Edwards, J. Enquiry respecting the Freedom of the Will. Lond. 1775. 8°. 5622
The same. Reviewed by H. P. Tappan. 5699
History of Redemption. New York. 16°. 5230
Life of. S. Miller. (Two copies.) Boston, 1837. 12°. . . . 8050
Life. S. E. Dwight. New York, 1831. 8°. 7913
Life of D. Brainerd. New York. 16°. 5228
The same. 8447
Practical Sermons. Edinburgh, 1788. 8°. 5379
Treatise on Religious Affections. (Abridg.) New York. 16°. . 5224
Edwards, J. (Jr..) Review of Dr. Chauncy's "Salvation of all Men." New Haven, 1790. 18°. 5648
Edwards, Justin. Sabbath Manual. Philadelphia. 12°. 6114
Edwards, T. World's Laconics. New York, 1856. 12°. . . . 516
Edwards, W. H. Voyage up the Amazon. New York, 1847. 12°. . . 8933
Edwin the Fair. An Histor. Drama. H. Taylor. London, 1845. 16°. . 2089
Egan, P. Life in London. London, 1823. 8°. 4
Egypt American in. J. W. Cooley. New York, 1842. 8°. . . . 9369
Ancient and Modern. M. Russell. New York, 1841. 16°. . . 6627
and the Books of Moses. E. W. Hengstenberg. Tr. (Two copies.) Andover, 1843. 12°. 5697
and Arabia Petræa, Travels in. A. Dumas. Tr. N. Y. 1839. 12°. 9563
Arabia Petræa, and the Holy Land. Travels in. S. Olin. New York, 1845. vol. 2. 12°. . . . . . . , . . 9243
Arabia Petræa, &c., Incidents of Travel in. J. L. Stephens. New York, 1837. 2 v. 12°. 8711
Early History of. S. Sharpe. London, 1836. 8°. . . . 11263
Englishwoman in. Mrs. S. Poole. London, 1844. 3 v. 16°. . 7197
Expedition to, under Sir R. Abercromby. R. G. Wilson. Philadelphia, 1803. 8°. 7221
The same, abridged. London, 1803. 12°. 8735
History of. London, 1779. 8°. 7029
History of, to A. D. 640. S. Sharpe. London, 1846. 8°. . . 6988
History of British Expedition to. R. T. Wilson. Phil. 1803. 8°. . 7221
and its Monuments. F. L. Hawks. New York, 1850. 8°. . . 9375
and Nubia, Boat Life in. W. C. Prime. New York, 1857. 12°. . 9594
Nubia, and Abyssinia, Travels in. J. Conder. Lond. 1827. 2 v. 16°. 9337
The same. 9655
Nubia, Syria, and the Holy Land. C. L. Irby and J. Mangles. London, 1844. 12°. . . . . , . . 9286

Egypt and Palestine, Lectures on. J. S. Buckingham. N. York, 1838. 16°. 9320
Past and Present. J. P. Thompson. Boston, 1854. 12°. . . . 7421
and the Sources of the Nile. J. Bruce. Dublin, 1790. 6 v. 8°. . 9192
and Syria, Trav. in, 1783 to 1785. C. F. C. Volney. Dub. 1788. 8°. 9488
Turkey and Nubia, Travels in. R. R. Madden. Phil. 1830. 2 v. 18°. 9604
Upper and Lower, Travels in. V. Denon. Tr. N. Y. 1803. 2 v. 8°. 9495
Egyptians, Ancient, Manners and Customs of. J. G. Wilkinson. London, 1837. 6. v. 8°. 9116
Modern, Manners and Customs. E. W. Lane. Lond. 1836. 2 v. 12°. 5808
The same. London, 1846. 3 v. 16°. 7190
and Chinese. C. De Pauw. Tr. London, 1795. 2 v. 8°. . . . 11373
Eighteenth Century, History of. F. C. Schlosser. Tr. Lond. 1843. 6 v. 8°. 7296
Men and Women of. A. Houssaye. New York, 1852. 2 v. 12°. . 8299
Retrospect of. S. Miller. New York, 1803. 2 v. 8°. 6923
Eikōn Basilike. The Pourtraicture of his Sacred Majestie, Charles I. London, 1824. 12°. 7717
Eisdell, J. S. Treatise on the Industry of Nations. Lond. 1839. 2 v. 8°. 10668
Elder Sister. M. James. New York, 1855. 12°. 575
Eldon, Lord. (J. Scott.) Life. H. Twiss. Phil. 1844. 2 v. 8°. . . . 7850
Electricity, Experimental Researches in. M. Faraday. London, 1839. 8°. 5944
History of. J. Priestley. London 1767. 4°. 5962
Elegant Extracts in Poetry. London, 1801. 2 v. 8°. 1818
in Prose. Boston, 1826. 6 v. 18°. 2101
in Prose. 18°. 2697
in Verse. Boston, 1826. 6 v. 18°. 2107
Elephant, The, Viewed in Relation to Man. London, 1844. 16°. . . . 7178
The same. New York, 1844. 12°. 5249
Elia, Essays. C. Lamb. Second series. Philadelphia, 1828. 12°. . . 367
Elijah the Tishbite. F. W. Krummacher. Tr. New York. 16°. . . 5239
Elijah and Elisha, History of, a poem. Stamford, 1805. 16°. 2488
Eliot, J. Life. C. Francis. (Two copies.) Boston, 1836. 16°. . . 8045
Eliot, Sir J. Life. J. Forster. London, 1836. 12°. 9933
Eliot, S. Liberty of Rome. New York, 1849. 2 v. 8°. 7541
Elizabeth de Bruce. New York, 1837. 2 v. 12°. 956
Elizabeth, Queen, and her Times. T. Wright. London, 1838. 2 v. 8°. . 7876
Memoirs of the Court of. Lucy Aikin. Boston, 1821. 2 v. 8°. . 7635
Romantic Biog. of the Age of. W. C. Taylor. Phil. 1842. 2 v. 12°. 8611
and Mary Queen of Scots, History of. F. Von Raumer. London, 1836. 12°. 8594
Elkswatawa, or the Prophet of the West. New York, 1836. 2 v. 12°. . 1238
The same. 1241
Ella of Garveloch. Miss H. Martineau. Boston, 1832. 16°. 10022
Ellery, W. Life of E. T. Channing. (Two copies.) Boston, 1836. 12°. . 8047
Ellet, Elizabeth F. Women of the Amer. Revolution. N. Y. 1848. 3 v. 12°. 8632
Elliott, C. W. Cottages and Cottage Life. New York, 1848. 8°. . . . 1073
Elliott, C. W. Hist. of New England, from 986–1776. N. Y. 1857. 2 v. 8°. 7274
Elliott, E. Poetical Works. London, 1833. 2 v. 12°. 2258
The same. Edinburgh, 1840. 8°. 1799

Ellis, G. Specimens of Early English Poets. London, 1845. 3 v. 12°. . 2015
Ellis, G. E. Life of Anne Hutchinson. Boston, 1845. 12°. 8058
Life of J. Mason. Boston, 1844. 12°. 8055
Life of W. Penn. Boston, 1847. 12°. 8064
Ellis, Mrs. S. Daughters of England, their Position. N. Y. 1843. 12°. . 4889
Irish Girl and other Poems. New York, 1844. 12°. 1941
Pretension. Philadelphia, 1837. 2 v. 12°. 1564
Temper and Temperament. New York, 1846. 12°. 4559
Women of England. Philadelphia, 1839. 2 v. 12°. 4875
The same. New York, 1843. 12°. 8914
Works. New York, 1843. 3 v. 8°. . , ... 388
Ellis, W. Practical Farmer. London, 1759. 12°. 3301
History of Madagascar. London, 1838. 2 v. 8°. 6993
Polynesian Researches. London, 1831. 4 v. 12°. 9295
Ellmer Castle. Boston, 1833. 18°. 1703
Ellwood, T. Autobiography. London, 1830. 16°. 7755
The same. 7490
Elmes, J. Anecdotes, Relics, &c., of Arts & Artists. Lond. 1825. 3. v. 16°. 10246
Elocution, Book of. 12°. 4928
Cultivation of the Voice in. J. E. Murdoch. Boston, 1851. 12°. . 10157
Essay on. J. H. Dwyer. Utica, 1829. 12°. 11878
Exercises in. Ed. W. Enfield. Warrington, 1780. 12°. 3042
Grammar of. J. Barber. New Haven, 1830. 12°. 3332
Lectures on. T. Sheridan. Troy, 1803. 12°. 3025
The same. 3896
Eloisa, a Series of Orig. Letters. J. J. Rousseau. Tr. Lond, 1810. 3 v. 12°. 4539
Eloquence of the U. S. Ed. E. B. Williston. Middletown, 1827. 5 v. 8°. 10719
Principlence of. Abbe Maury. New York, 1848. 12°. 5258
Elphinstone, M. Account of the Kingdom of Caubul. Lond. 1839. 2 v. 8°. 7590
Elvira; a Tragedy. D. Mallet. London, 1778. 12°. 11887
Emancipation. W. E. Channing. Boston, 1840. 12°. 11874
Emerson, G. B. Duties of the Schoolmaster. (2 copies.) N. Y. 1844. 12°. 2993
Emerson, J. Life. R. Emerson. Boston, 1834. 12°. 8313
Emerson, R. W. English Traits. Boston, 1856. 12°. 1154
Essays. First series. Boston, 1850. 12°. 1155
Second series. Boston, 1844. 12°. 1156
The same. Boston, 1850. 12°. 1153
Poems. Boston, 1850. 12°. 1952
Representative Men. (Two copies.) Boston, 1850. 12°. . . 1151
Emilius and Sophia. J. J. Rousseau. Tr. London, 1783. 4 v. 12°. . 3964
Eminent Persons, Anecdotes of. London, 1797. 3 v. 8°. 7969
Emma; a Novel. Miss Austen. Philadelphia, 1838. 8°. 37
Emmeline, and other Pieces. Miss M. Brunton. New York, 1819. 12°. . 949
Emmett, R., Life. J. W. Burke. Philadelphia, 1852. 12°. . . . 7732
Emmet, T. A. Memoir. C. G. Haines. New York, 1829. 12°. . . 7782
The same. 8401
Emmons, E. Natural History. See New York.
Emmons, N. Sermons. Wrentham, 1800. 8°. 5389

›orıum of Arts and Sciences. Philadelphia, 1812–14. 4 v. 8°. . . 2966
yclopædia Americana. Philadelphia, 1830–33. 13 v. 8°. . . . 8818
of Antiquities. T. D. Fosbroke. London, 1843. 2 v. 8°. . . 8793
Britannica. vols. 1–16. (Continued.) Boston, 1853–9. 4°. . . 10035
or a Dictionary of Arts, Sciences, &c. Phil. 1798. 18 v. 4°. . . 8112
Supplement to the same. Philadelphia, 1803. 3 v. 4°. . 10923
See also Classified Index.
eld, W., (Ed.) Exercises in Elocution. Warrington, 1780. 12°. . 3042
History of Philosophy. Dublin, 1792. 2 v. 8°. 6400
land, American in. A. S. Mackenzie. New York, 1835. 2 v. 12°. . 8690
and America, Comparison between. New York, 1834. 8°. . . 9177
Bassompierre's Embassy to in 1626. Tr. London, 1819. 8°. . 9516
and the English. E. L. Bulwer. New York, 1833. 2 v. 12°. . 9031
Biographical Hist., from 827 to 1688. J. Granger. Lon. 1824. 6 v. 8°. 7940
The same continued to 1727. M. Noble. Lond. 1806. 3 v. 8°. 7383
Chief Justices of. See Chief Justices.
Chronicle of Kings of. William of Malmesbury. Tr. Lon. 1857. 12°. 5441
Civil War in, from 1646–52. H. Cary. London, 1842. 2 v. 8°. . 6967
Condition and Fate of. C. E. Lester. New York, 1843. 2 v. 12°. 8981
Conquest of, by the Normans. A. Thierry. Tr. London, 1841. 8°. 7254
The same. Tr. W. Hazlitt. London, 1847. 2 v. 12°. . . 5497
The same. Tr. W. Hazlitt. London, 1856. 2 v. 12°. . . 5448
Constitution of. J. L. De Lolme. London, 1853. 12°. . . . 5185
Constitution & Laws of, Lectures on. F. S. Sullivan. Dub. 1790. 8°. 10768
Counter Revolution in. A. Carrel. London, 1846. 12°. . . 5492
Court of, under the Stuarts. J. H. Jesse. London, 1840. 2 v. 8°. 8148
Continuation of the same. J. H. Jesse. Phil. 1840. 2 v. 8°. 8582
Ecclesiastical History of, Bede. London, 1847. 12°. . . . 5440
Fame and Glory of, Vindicated. London, 1842. 12°. . . . 9006
First Impressions of its People. Boston, 1851. 12°. . . . 6070
Foreigner's Opinion of. C. A. G. Gœde. Tr. Boston, 1822. 8°. . 9165
France, Spain, &c., Chronicles of. J. Froissart. Tr. T. Johnes. London. 1839. 2 v. 4°. . , ... 7546
France and Barbary, Travels in. M. M. Noah. New York, 1819. 8°. 9178
Glory and Shame of. C. E. Lester. (2 copies.) N. Y. 1842. 2 v. 12°. 8693
History of. London, 1783. 2 v. 8°. 7085
History of. London, 1788. 8°. 7126
History of, from B. C. 55 to A. D. 1727. L. Echard and J. Oldmixon. London, 1707. 4 v. Folio. 11245
History of. W. Godwin. London, 1824. 4 v. 8°. 7020
History of. O. Goldsmith. London, 1771. 4 v. 8°. . . . 11439
History of, from B. C. 55 to A. D. 1588. D. Hume. (vols 1 and 2 missing.) Boston, 1850. 6 v. 12°. 7115
The same. 8 v. 11431
The same, with a continuation to 1760, by T. Smollett. (vols. 1 and 4 missing.) London, 1825. 13 v. 8°. 7009
The same, abridged. Exeter, 1828. 2 v. 24°. 11269
The same. (vol. 1 missing.) London, 1810. 16 v. 16°. . 6851

England, History of, from B. C. 55 to A. D. 1821. D. Hume, T. Smollett, and J. R. Miller. Philadelphia, 1832–7. 4 v. 8°. . . . 6989
History of, to George III. I. Kimber. London, 1768. 8°. . . 7686
History of, from B. C. 55 to A. D. 1837. T. Keightley. (vol. 5 missing.) New York, 1840. 5 v. 12°. 5578
The same. Boston, 1840. 2 v. 8°. 6957
History of, from B. C. 55 to A. D. 1673. J. Lingard. London, 1823–5. 12 v. 8°. 6905
History of. T. B. Macaulay. vols. 1 and 2. New York, 1849. 8°. 7246
The same. vols. 3 and 4. New York, 1856. 12°. . . 7108
The same. New York, 1850. 8°. 7248
History of, from 1713 to 1748. Lord Mahon. Paris, 1841. 2 v. 8°. 7024
The same, with a continuation to 1763. Ed. H. Reed. New York, 1849. 2 v. 8°. 7238
History of, to 1588. J. Mackintosh. London, 1830–33. 3 v. 12°. . 5826
See also, Mackintosh, J.
History of during the Reign of George III. A continuation to Hume and Smollett. W. Jones. London, 1825. 3 v. 8°. . . . 7026
History of, from James I to the House of Hanover. Miss C. Macaulay. London, 1769. 5 v. 8°. 6720
History of, from the Earliest Time to 1603. S. Turner. Lond. 1839. 12 v. 8°. 7280
History of Rebellion and Civil Wars in. Earl of Clarendon. Oxford, 1827. 6 v. 8°. 6980
History of the Revolution in 1688. J. Mackintosh. Phil. 1835. 8°. 6685
The same. London, 1846. 8°. 6303
History of the Revolution in 1688. L. Echard. Lond. 1725. 12°. 11445
History of Party in, from 1666 to 1832. G. W. Cooke. London, 1836. 3 v. 8°. 7624
Holland, &c., Travels in. B. Silliman. Hartford, 1810. 2 v. 8°. . 9784
in 1835. F. Von Raumer. Tr. Philadelphia, 1836. 8°. . . . 9442
in the 19th Century, an Illustrated Itinerary of the County of Lancashire. London, 1842. 8°. 7788
Ireland and France, Tour in, by a German Prince. Tr. Phil. 1833. 8°. 9440
Laws of, Commentaries on. W. Blackstone. N. Y. 1845. 2 v. 8°. 10712
The same. London, 1783. 4 v. 8°. 10745
The same. vols. 3 and 4. Dublin, 1794. 12°. . . . 11185
Letters from. Don M. A. Espriella. Tr. London, 1808. 12°. . 8414
The same. 3 vols. 9307
Letters on. A. De Staël. London, 1830. 8°. 9142
Literature & Learning in, Hist. of. G. L. Craik. Lond. 1844. 6 v. 16°. 6895
The same. 7155
Naval History of. R. Southey. Philadelphia, 1835. 12°. . . . 7449
The same, with Lives of British Admirals to 1672. London, 1833–40. 5 v. 12°. 9927
Old, Sketch of. New York, 1822. 12°. 8717
Pictorial History of, to 1830. G. L. Craik and others. (vol. 6 missing.) London, 1841. 8 v. 4°. 7789

England, Political History of, in the 16th, 17th and 18th Centuries. F. Von Raumer. London, 1837. 2 v. 8°. 7620
Queen of, *vs.* D. O'Connell and others. Report. J. S. Armstrong. Dublin, 1844. 8°. 10653
Queens of. Agnes Strickland. Phil. 1843. 2 v. 12°. . . . 8292
Second series. vols. 2 and 3. Phil. 1843. 12°. . . . 8294
The same. 1st and 2d series. Phil. 1851. 12 v. in 6. 8°. . 7984
Remarks on the History of. Lord Bolingbroke. London. 8°. . 10778
Revenues of the Church of. G. Coventry. London, 1830. 8°. . 6428
Rural Life in. W. Howitt. London, 1840. 8°. 9449
Sports and Pastimes of. J. Strutt. London, 1834. 8°. . . . 21
Under Seven Administrations. A. Fonblanque. Lond. 1837. 3 v. 12°. 7112
Under the Reigns of Edward VI, and Mary. P. F. Tytler. London, 1839. 2 v. 8°. 6965
View of. F. A. Wendeborn. Tr. by the Author. Dub. 1791. 2 v. 12°. 8733
Views of. Maj. General Pillet. Tr. Boston, 1818. 16°. . . 9045
and Wales, Homes in. Catherine Sinclair. N. Y. 1838. 12°. . 9792
Worthies of. T. Fuller. London, 1840. 3 v. 8°. 7906
English and Scotch Poems. 18°. 2755
Annuals, Tales from. New York, 1835. 12°. 1249
Comic Writers, Lectures on. W. Hazlitt. London, 1819. 8°. . 87
Commonwealth during the Anglo-Saxon Period. F. Palgrave. London, 1832. 2 v. 4°. . . . , ... 11254
Composition, Principles of. D. Booth. London, 1831. 12°. . . 3039
Dramatic Poets, Specimens of. Ed. C. Lamb. N. Y. 1845. 12°. . 9845
Dramatic Poetry. J. P. Collier. London, 1831. 3 v. 12°. . . 1109
The same. 1112
Fashionables Abroad, a Novel. Boston, 1828. 2 v. 12°. . . 617
Government, Historical View of the. J. Millar. Dublin, 1789. 8°. 6901
Grammar. See Grammar.
History, Orig. Letters Illust. of. Ed. H. Ellis. Lond. 1825. 3 v. 12°. 7412
Second series. London, 1827. 4 v. 12°. 7415
Humorists of 18th Century. W. M. Thackeray. N. Y. 1854. 12°. 835
Literature, Cyclopædia of. R. Chambers. Edin. 1844. 2 v. 4°. . 8803
Literature. Lectures on. H. Reed. Philadelphia, 1855. 12°. . 522
Literature, Sketches of. F. A. de Chateaubriand. Lond. 1836. 2 v. 8°. 75
Past and Present. R. C. Trench. New York, 1855. 12°. . . 4516
Poets, Early, Specimens of. G. Ellis. London, 1845. 3 v. 12°. . 2015
Poets, Lives. R. Bell. London, 1839. 2 v. 12°. 9945
Poets, Lives, Johnson to K. White. H. F. Cary. Lond. 1846. 12°. 8092
Poets, Lives of. S. Johnson. London, 1831. 12°. 7780
Poets, Specimens of the. Ed. L. Hunt. New York, 1845. 12°. . 9844
Poetry, Ancient Reliques of. Ed. T. Percy. Phil. 1823. 3 v. 8°. . 1924
Poetry, History of. T. Warton. London, 1840. 8°. 712
Poetry, Lectures on. H. Neele. London, 1829. 12°. 864
The same. New York, 1829. 8°. 751
Poetry, Letters on. J. Aikin. New York, 1806. 12°. . . . 4929
Prose Literature, Origin of. W. Gray. Oxford, 1835. 8°. . . 749

English Prose Writers, Old, Library of. See Library.
Reader. Ed. L. Murray. New York, 1800. 12°. 4902
Reader, Sequel to. Ed. L. Murray. New York, 1800. 12°. . . 3035
Revolution, History of the. F. Guizot. Tr. Louise H. R. Coutier.
Oxford, 1838. 2 v. 8°. 6677
The same. 7302
The same. 7622
Rhythms, History of. E. Guest. London, 1838. 2 v. 8°. . . 733
Songs. J. Aikin. London, 1810. 12°. 2226
The same. London, 1816. 12°. 1916
Songs. B. W. Proctor. Boston, 1844. 12°. 2376
The same. Boston, 1851. 12°. 1948
Sonnets, Collection of. Ed. R. F. Housman. London, 1835. 12°. . 1949
Stage, View of the. W. Hazlitt. London, 1818. 8°. . . . 95
Surnames, Essays on. M. A. Lower. London, 1844. 12°. . . 459
Traits. R. W. Emerson. Boston, 1856. 12°. 1154
Universities. V. A. Huber. Tr. F. W. Newman. Lon. 1843. 3 v. 8°. 62
Woman in Egypt. Mrs. S. Poole. London, 1846. 3 v. 16°. . . 7197
Enoch, the Prophet, Book of. Tr. R. Laurence. Oxford, 1838. 8°. . . 5037
Ensenore, a Poem. P. H. Myers. New York, 1840. 8°. 1824
Entertaining Instructor, in French & Eng. Ed. J. Lockman. Lon. 1765. 12°. 3972
Enthusiasm, Natural History of. I. Taylor. Boston, 1830. 12°. . . 6472
Entick, J. History of the Late War, its Rise, &c. in Europe, Asia, Africa
and America. London, 1767. 5 v. 8°. 6744
Entomology. J. Duncan. (vol. 1 missing.) Edin. 1835–7. 4 v. 12°. . 10181
Eolopoesis, American Rejected Addresses. New York, 1855. 12°. . . 2005
Epea Ptereoenta. J. H. Tooke. London, 1829. 2 v. 8°. 1061
Episcopacy and Presbyterian Parity. G. S. Olds. Greenfield, 1815. 12°. 6528
Epitaphs, American, Collecton of. T. Alden. New York, 1814. 5 v. 16°. 10030
Ernest Maltravers. E. L. Bulwer. New York, 1837. 2 v. 12°. . . 660
Erasmus, D. Colloquia. Lipsiæ, 1829. 2 v. 16°. 10602
Colloquia Selecta. Neo Hantonia, 1809. 12°. 3363
Life. C. Butler. London, 1825. 8°. 8151
Life. J. Jortin. London, 1808. 3 v. 8°. 8246
Erie Canal, Geolog. Survey of District Adjoining. A. Eaton. Alb. 1824. 8°. 10080
Errata, or the Works of Will. Adams. J. Neal. N. Y. 1823. 2 v. 12°. . 1535
The same. 643
Errors, Vulgar, Exposition of. T. B. Redivivus. London, 1845. 12°. . 6608
Escalala, a Tale, S. B. Beach. Utica, 1824. 12°. 2286
Espriella, Don, M. A. Tr. Boston, 1808. 12°. 8414
The same. London, 1808. 3 v. 12°. 9307
Espy, J. P. Philosophy of Storms. Boston, 1841. 8°. 5946
Report to the U. S. Navy Dept. on Meteorology. Wash. 1850. 4°.
Essay on Man. A. Pope. London, 1786. 12°. 2389
See also Pope, A.
Essays Written in the Intervals of Business. London, 1843. 12°. . . 3900
Ethel Churchill. Miss L. E. Landon. Philadelphia, 1838. 2 v. 12°. . 1549
Ethel, or The Double Error. M. James. New York, 1855. 12°. . . 576

Ethical Philosophy, Progress of, during the 17th and 18th Centuries. J. Mackintosh. London, 1846. 8°. 6302
The same. Edinburgh, 1837. 8°. 6321
The same. Boston, 1853. 4°. 10035
Ethics, Introduc. to. T. Jouffroy. Tr. W. H. Channing. Bost. 1840. 2 v. 12°. 713
Rhetoric, &c., of Aristotle. Tr. T. Taylor. London, 1818. 8°. . 755
Political. F. Lieber. Boston. 1838. 2 v. 8°. 10063
Ethiopia, Highlands of. W. C. Harris. London, 1844. 8°. . . . 9473
Eton, W. Survey of the Turkish Empire. London, 1799. 8°. . . 9213
Etonian, The. vol. 2. London, 1823. 12°. 2287
Etruria, Ancient Sepulchres of. Mrs. H. Gray. London, 1841. 12°. . 9801
Ettrick Shepherd. See Hogg, J.
Euclid. Elements of Geometry. Ed. B. Simson. Philadelphia. 8°. . . 11682
Eugene Aram. E. L. Bulwer. Philadelphia, 1832. 2 v. 12°. . . . 1023
The same. New York, 1832. 2 v. 12°. 1274
Eugene of Savoy, Prince. Autobiography. London, 1830. 16°. . . 7752
The same. 7487
The same. New York, 1811. 16°. 7741
Euler, L. Letters on Natural Philosophy. New York, 1833. 2 v. 16°. . 6267
The same. New York, 1840. 2 v. 12°. 5871
The same. London, 1802. 2 v. 8°. 5971
Euripides. Tragedies. Tr. R. Potter. New York, 1834. 16°. . . 3074
The same. New York, 1841. 3 v. 12°. 5272
The same. (vol. 1 missing.) New York, 1834. 3 v. 16°. . 8752
The same. Selections from. Philadelphia, 1823. 18°. . 2117
Europe. London, 1842. 12°. 5933
Ancient History of. W. Russell. Philadelphia, 1801. 2 v. 8°. . 11384
after the Congress of Aix-La-Chapelle. D. D. De Pradt. Trans. G. A. Otis. Philadelphia, 1820. 8°. 9434
Art and Scenery in. Philadelphia, 1857. 8°. 468
Asia, Africa and America. Rise, &c. of the Late War in. J. Entick. London, 1767. 8°. 6744
Asia and Africa, Travels in. E. S. Clarke. Philadelphia, 1811. 8°. 9494
Part second. New York, 1813. 12°. 8716
Part second, section second. New York, 1815. 12°. . . 9597
Character of the Nations of. London, 1770. 2 v. 8°. . . 11448
during the Mid. Ages. H. Hallam. (vol. 1 mis'g.) Phil. 1821. 4 v. 8°. 7002
Supplemental Notes to the same. London, 1848. 8°. . . 6976
during the Mid. Ages, Hist. of. S. A. Dunham. Lond. 1833. 4 v. 12°. 9881
and the East, Travels in. V. Mott. New York, 1842. 8°. . . 9266
Eastern and the Emperor Nicholas. London, 1846. 3 v. 12°. . 9554
Ecclesiastical Establishments in. W. Graham. London, 1808. 12°. 3929
Eleven Weeks in. J. F. Clarke. Boston, 1852. 9639
Gleanings in. J. F. Cooper. Philadelphia, 1837. 2 v. 12°. . . 8946
The same. 9836
History of, from 1789 to 1815. A. Alison. London, 1835. 10 v. 8°. 7641
Second series, from 1815 to 1852. N. Y. 1855. 2 v. 8°. . 7255

Europe, History of Civilization in. F. Guizot. Tr. Oxford, 1838. 8°. . 6917
The same, with a continua'n. Tr. W. Hazlitt. Lond. 1846. 8°. 5499
Literature of, in the 15th, 16th and 17th Centuries. H. Hallam. London, 1837. 4 v. 8°. 113
Letters from. N. H. Carter. New York, 1827. 2 v. 8°. . . 9430
Modern, History of, to 1763. W. Russell. Lond. 1789. 5 v. 8°. . 11378
The same. Philadelphia, 1822. 6 v. 8°. 7304
The same, continued to 1802. C. Coors. Phil. 1811. 8°. . 11385
Northern, Visit to. R. Baird. New York, 1841. 2 v. 12°. . . 8918
The same. 8978
Observations in. J. P. Durbin. New York, 1844. 2 v. 12°. . . 9535
Past and Present. F. H. Ungewitter. New York, 1850. 12°. . 8886
Poets and Poetry of. H. Longfellow. Philadelphia, 1845. 8°. . 1806
Political Survey of. E. A. W. Zimmerman. Dublin, 1788. 8°. . 7687
Political System of. 1492 to 1821. A. H. L. Heeren. Tr. New York, 1828. 2 v. 8° 7319
Principal States of, History of the. S. Puffendorf. Continued by Martiniere. London, 1764. 2 v. 8°. 6765
Progress of Society in. 8°. 11357
Rambles in. Fanny W. Hall. New York, 1859. 2 v. 12°. . . 10142
Rambles in, in 1839. W. Gibson. Philadelphia, 1841. 12°. . . 9253
Remarkable Conspiracies of, in 15th and 16th Centuries. J. P. Samson. Edinburgh, 1829. 2 v. 16°. 10018
Revolutions in, History of the. C. W. Koch. Tr. A. Crichton. Hartford, 1832. 12°. 6795
The same. Edinburgh, 1828. 3 v. 12°. 10009
South of, Historical View of the Literature of. J. C. L. S. De Sismondi. Tr. T. Roscoe. New York, 1827. 2 v. 8°. . 82
The same. London, 1850. 2 v. 12°. 5125
Souvenirs of a Residence in, by a Lady of Virginia. Phil. 1842. 12°. 8897
State of, before and after the French Revolution. F. Gentz. Tr. T. C. Herries. London, 1804. 8°. 6725
Tourist in. New York, 1838. 12°. . . , ... 10141
Travels in. G. Catlin. London, 1848. 2 v. 8°. 9399
European Capitals, Sketches of. W. Ware. Boston, 1851. 12°. . . 8890
Colonies, Viewed in their condition, Social, Moral, &c. J. Howison. London, 1834. 3 v. 8°. 6679
Life and Manners. H. Colman. Boston, 1850. 2 v. 12°. . . 9582
Eusebius Pamphilus. Ecclesiastical Hist. Tr. C. F. Cruse. Phil. 1840. 8°. 5075
Eustace, J. C. Classical Tour through Italy, in 1802. Phil. 1816. 2 v. 8°. 9152
The same. London, 1841. 3 v. 12°. 9532
Eustaphieve, A. Demetrius, the hero of the Don, a Poem. Bost. 1818. 12°. 2278
Eutropius. Historical Romance. Lipsiæ, 1843. 16°. 10865
The same. Worcester, 1802. 12°. 11475
Evangeline. H. W. Longfellow. Boston, 1848. 12°. 2020
Evangiles de Toute L'Année. Paris, 1830. 18°. 4618
Evans, G. W. D. Classic and Connoisseur in Italy and Sicily. London, 1835. 3 v. 8°. 9112
Evans, J. History of all Christian Denominations. New York, 1844. 12°. 6147

Evans, N. Poems. Philadelphia, 1772. 8°. 2221
Evans, R. W. The Rectory of Valehead. Philadelphia, 1832. 12°. . 3358
Evans, T., and R. H. Old Ballads, Historical, &c. Lond. 1810. 4 v. 12°. 1978
Evarts, J. Life. E. C. Tracy. Boston, 1845. 8°. 7830
Evelina, or a Young Lady's Introduction to the World. Miss F. Burney.
New York, 1832. 2 v. 12°. 1577
Life of Mrs. Godolphin. New York, 1847. 12°. 8639
Evelyn, J. Memoirs. W. Bray. London, 1827. 5 v. 8°. , . . 7972
Life of Mrs. Godolphin. New York, 1847. 12°. 8639
Everest, C. W. Poets of Connecticut. Hartford, 1843. 8°. . . . 1857
Everett, A. H. General Survey of the Western Continent. Phil. 1827. 8°. 9766
Life of J. Warren. Boston, 1838. 12°. 8052
Life of P. Henry. Boston, 1844. 12°. 8053
Everett, E. Importance of Practical Education. Boston, 1840. 12°. . 3309
Life of J. Stark. Boston, 1834. 12°. 8068
Orations and Speeches. Boston, 1836. 8°. 10652
The same. 10960
The same. Second edition. Boston, 1850. 2 v. 8°. . . 10961
Every Day Book, The. W. Hone. vol. 3. London, 1838. 8°. . . 9722
Every Man his own Lawyer. New York, 1768. 8°. 11118
The same. Poughkeepsie, 1827. 12°. 3897
Ewbank, T. Hydraulics and Mechanics. New York, 1847. 8°. . . 5945
Life in Brazil. New York, 1856. 8°. 9367
Exmouth, Admiral Viscount. Life. E. Osler. London, 1835. 12°. . 8287
Exodus, Notes on. G. Bush. New York, 1841. 2 v. 12°. . . . 5743
Expedition of Orsua, and Crimes of Aguirre. R. Southey. Phil. 1821. 12°. 3906
Exploring Expedition to the Pacific and South Seas, Address on the. J.
N. Reynolds. New York, 1836. 8°. 428
Expedition, U. S., in 1838–42. C. Wilkes. Phil. 1845. 6 v. 8°. . 10628
Eye, Philosophy of the. J. Walker. London, 1837. 8°. 3285

F.

Fabens, J. W. Camel Hunt. Boston, 1851. 12°. 9821
Faber, G. S. Difficulties of Infidelity. Philadelphia, 1829. 12°. . . 5633
Difficulties of Romanism. Philadelphia, 1840. 12°. . . 6128
Doctrine of Election. New York, 1840. 8°. 5064
Faber, M. Sketches of the Internal State of France. Phil. 1812. 12°. 11470
Fable for Critics. J. R. Lowell. New York, 1848. 12°. 2347
Fables. J. La Fontaine. Tr. E. Wright. Boston, 1841. 8°. . . . 1074
Fables Amusantes. M. Perrin. New York, 1807. 12°. 1649
Fabliaux, or French Tales. P. J. B. Le Grand. Tr. G. L. Way. London, 1815. 3 v. 12°. 2002
Fábulas Literarias. D. T. de Iriarte. 16°. 2471
Færnus, G. Fabulæ. Lipsiæ, 1829. 16°. 10858
Faggot of French Sticks. F. B. Head. New York, 1852. 12°. . . 10146
Fairfield, S. L. Poems. New York, 1823. 16°. 3059
Fairy Queen. E. Spencer. Boston, 1839. 4 v. 8°. 1828
Observations on the. T. Warton. London, 1807. 2 v. 12°. . 1833

Fairy Queen, Exposition of the. J. S. Hart. New York, 1847. 8°. . 29
Falconer, W. Select Poems and Life. Philadelphia, 1819. 18°. . . 2139
The Shipwreck. A Poem. New York, 1800. 2495
The same. 2779
Fall of Jerusalem. A Dramatic Poem. H. H. Milman. N. Y. 1824. 16°. 2091
Falsehood and Truth. Mrs. C. E. Tonna. New York, 1841. 16°. . . 1705
Family Mansion, The. A Tale. Mrs. Taylor. Philadelphia, 1820. 18°. . 4605
Tourist. C. A. Goodrich. Hartford, 1848. 12°. 9176
Fanaticism. I. Taylor. New York, 1834. 12°. 3297
Fanning, E. Voyages to the South Seas, &c., with History of U. S. Exploring Expedition. New York, 1828. 12°. 8932
Voyages round the World. New York, 1833. 8°. 9095
Fanny and other Poems. F. G. Halleck. New York, 1839. 12°. . . 2339
Fanshawe, Lady A. Autobiography. London, 1830. 8°. . . . 8282
Faraday, M. Experimental Researches in Electricity. Lond. 1839. 8°. 5944
Farmer, The Practical. W. Ellis. London, 1759. 12°. 3301
Farmer's Boy, and other Rural Poems. R. Bloomfield. Lond. 1827. 12° 2027
Farmer's, Mechanic's, &c., Magazine. Mad. Le Prince de Beaumont. Tr. New York, 1812. 2 v. 16°. . . . . , ... 3088
Farmington, (Ct.) Hist. Discourse respecting. N. Porter. Hart. 1841. 8°. . 11326
The same . . . . , 11341
Farnham, Mrs. E. W. Life in Prairie Land. New York, 1846. 12°. . 4864
Farquhar, G. Dramatic Works. London, 1840. 8°. 1794
Farrar, J. Treatise on Astronomy. Cambridge, 1827. 8°. 5942
Farrenc, E. Carlotina and the Sanfedesti. New York, 1853. 12°. . . 560
Faroe Islands, History of. New York, 1841. 12°. 5907
Far West, The, or a Tour beyond the Mountains. New York, 1838. 2 v. 12°. 1474
Fashionable World Displayed. New York, 1806. 12°. 4913
Fast of St. Magdalen, a Romance. Miss A. M. Porter. Bost. 1819. 2 v. 12°. 1358
Fatalla Sayeghir, Narrative of. Tr. A. de Lamartine. Phil. 1836. 12°. . 1514
Father as he should be. Mrs. Hofland. Philadelphia, 1816. 2 v. 12°. . 1483
Faust. J. W. Von Goethe. Tr. J. Anster. London, 1835. 12°. . . 2332
The same. Tr. Anna Swanwick. London, 1850. 12°. . 5160
Fay, T. S. Dreams and Reveries of a Quiet Man. N. Y. 1832. 2 v. 18°. . 1381
Featherstonhaugh, G. W. Excur. through Slave States. N. Y. 1844. 8°. 9088
The same. 9097
Geological Report of the Country between the Missouri and Red Rivers. Washington, 1835. 8°. 5939
Feats on the Fiord. H. Martineau. London, 1844. 16°. 7175
Federalist, The. A. Hamilton and others. Hallowell, 1831. 8°. . , 10693
The same. New York, 1802. 2 v. 8°. 10772
Felinæ, Natural History of the. W. Jardine. Edinburgh, 1837. 12°. . 10194
Felton, H. A Dissertation on Reading the Classics. London, 1753. 16°. 3714
Female Education, Strictures on. Hannah More. Hartford, 1801. 12°. 3017
Female Sovereigns, Memoirs of. Mrs. A. Jameson. N. York, 1832. 2 v. 16°. 6260
The same. New York, 1840. 2 v. 12°. 5536
Fenelon, F. de S. de La M. Adventures of Telemachus. Tr. N. Y. 1820. 2 v. 18°. 1763

Fenelon. Life. M. L. F. de Bausset. Tr. London, 1810. 2 v. 8°. . . 7947
Life. C. Butler. Philadelphia, 1811. 12°. 8087
Lives of the Ancient Philosophers. Tr. New York, 1843. 12°. . 5914
R. Baxter and others. Preacher and Pastor. Andover, 1845. 12°. 811
Select. from Writings of, with Memoir. Mrs. Follen. Bost. 1841. 12°. 6142
The same. Boston, 1829. 12°. 6490
Treatise on the Education of Daughters. Tr. Boston, 1820. 16°. 3979
Fenn, J. (Editor) Paston Letters. London, 1849. 12°. 5442
Fennel, J. H. Natural History of Quadrupeds. London, 1843. 8°. . 10136
Ferdinand and Isabella, History of the Reign of. W. H. Prescott. Boston, 1838. 3 v. 8°. 7854
Fergus, H. History of the United States. (vol. 2.) London, 1832. 12°. 9861
Ferguson, A. Essay on the History of Civil Society. Phil. 1819. 8°. . 753
The same. 1106
History of the Roman Republic. London, 1829. 8°. 7005
The same, abridged. New York, 1836. 12°. 5502
Ferguson, J. Autobiography. London, 1830. 16°. 7750
The same. 7485
Introduction to Astronomy. Philadelphia, 1805. 12°. . . . 6097
Lectures on Philosophical Subjects. London, 1825. 8°. . . 5358
Ferme, C. Analysis of the Epistle to the Romans. Tr. Edin. 1850. 8°. 5088
Fessenden, T. G. Democracy Unveiled. New York, 1806. 2 v. 12°. . 1965
Terrible Tractoration, a Poetical Petition. London, 1803. 16°. . 2474
Festivals, Games and Amusements. H. Smith. New York, 1831. 16°. . 6618
Festus. A Poem. P. J. Bailey. Boston, 1845. 12°. 2275
Feuerbach, A. R. Remarkable Criminal Trials. Tr. N. York, 1846. 12°. 11195
Fichte, J. G. Memoir. W. Smith. Boston, 1846. 12°. 8011
Fiction, History of. J. Dunlop. Edinburgh, 1816. 3 v. 12°. . . 784
Fidler, I. Observations on the United States and Canada. N. Y. 1833. 12°. 9254
Field, G. Analogical Philosophy. London, 1839. 2 v. 8°. 739
Field, H. M. Irish Confederates and Rebellion of 1798. N. Y. 1851. 12°. 7419
Field Sports of United States. H. W. Herbert. New York, 1849. 8°. . 766
Fielding, or Society. R. P. Ward. Philadelphia, 1838. 12°. . . . 1332
Fielding, H. Joseph Andrews. London, 1792. 12°. 1128
Works. New York, 1813-16 12 v. 12°. 3594

Vol. 1-5. Life. Plays.
7, 8. Tom Jones.
10, 11. Amelia.
12. Life of Jonathan Wild. Causes of the Increase of Robbers.
13. A Journey from this World to the Next. A Voyage to Lisbon, and the True Patriot.
14. The Covent Garden Journal, Essays, &c.

Fifteen Decisive Battles of the World. E. S. Creasy. N. Y. 1851. 12°. 7094
Financial Report of United States. See U. S. Public Documents.
Finati, G. Life and Adventures. Tr. London, 1830. 2 v. 16°. . . . 8463
Findley, W. History of the Insurrection in Pennsylvania in 1794. Philadelphia, 1796. 8°. 6767
Fine Arts, Imitation in the, Essay on. Q. De Quincy. Tr. Lond. 1837. 8°. 10133

Fine Arts, History of. B. J. Lossing. New York, 1840. 12°. . . 5563
Finlayson, G. Mission to Siam and Memoir. T. S. Raffles. Lond. 1826. 8°. 9458
First Truths, and the Origin of our Opinions Explained. C. Buffier. Tr. London, 1780. 8°. 5386
Fish, F. W. Poems. New Haven, 1855. 16°. 2073
Fisher, A., J. Prior and others. Account of Voyages and Travels. London, 1820. 8 v. 8°. 9220
Fishes, Amphibious, and Reptiles, Natural History of. W. Swainson. London, 1838. 2 v. 12°. 9976
Fisk, B. F. Greek Exercises. Boston, 1838. 12°. 3381
Fisk, W. Life. J. Holdich. New York, 1842. 8°. 7868
Fiske, N. W. Memoir and Writings. Ed. H. Humphrey. Bost. 1850. 12°. 6152
Fitch, J., Life of. C. Whittlesey. Boston, 1845. 12°. 8058
Fitzgerald, E., (Lord.) Life and Death. T. Moore. N. Y. 1831. 2 v. 12°. 8099
Fitzosborne's Letters. W. Melmoth. London, 1807. 12°. . . . 4986
Five Years in an English University. C. A. Bristed. N. Y. 1852. 2 v. 12°. 823
Flag Ship, The, or a Voyage around the World. F. W. Taylor. New York, 1840. 2 v. 12°. 9809
Flatt, C. C. See T. C. Storr.
Flavel, J. The Fountain of Life. New York, 1841 12°. 5246
Flaxman, J. Illust. of Homer, Hesiod, Æschylus and Dante. 3 v. Folio.
Fleetwood, or the New Man of Feeling. W. Godwin. N. Y. 1805. 2 v. 18°. 1717
Fletcher, J. History of Poland. New York, 1831. 16°. . . . 6622
The same. New York, 1840. 12°. 5527
The same. New York, 1832. 16°. 8761
and F. Beaumont. See Beaumont, F.
Fleury, C. Manners of the Ancient Israelites. Tr. A. Clarke. London, 1836. 12°. 6459
Flint, T. Letters and Travels. 8°. 9482
Lectures on Natural History, Geology, &c. Boston, 1833. 12°. . 10153
Floral Biography. Mrs. C. E. Tonna. New York, 1840. 12°. . . 1202
Florence, History of. N. Machiavel. Tr. London, 1847. 8°. . . . 5128
Florentine Republic, Hist. of the. L. L. Da Ponte. N. Y. 1833. 2 v. 12°. 7428
Florian, J. P. C. Œuvres. Paris, 1810. 3 v. 18°. 11273
Guillaume Tell. Paris, 1805. 18°. 10903
Florida and the Campaigns, Notices of. M. M. Cohen. N. Y. 1836. 12°. 7430
The same. 9264
Conquest of, by H. De Soto. T. Irving. Philadelphia, 1835. 12°. 6790
Exiles of. J. R. Giddings. Columbus, 1858. 12°. . . . 10805
War, History of. J. T. Sprague. New York, 1848. 8°. . . 7268
and West Indies, Winter in. New York, 1839. 12°. . . . 8924
Floridas, Observations on the. C. Vignoles. New York, 1823. 8°. . 9365
Florus, L. A. Epitome Rerum Romanarum. Lipsiæ, 1827. 16°. . . 10832
Flower Garden. Mrs. C. E. Tonna. New York, 1840. 12°. . . . 1203
Fruit and Thorn Pieces. J. P. F. Richter. Tr. Bost. 1845. 2 v. 12°. 1659
of Innocence. Mrs. C. E. Tonna. New York, 1842. 16°. . . 1709
Flowers of History. Roger de Wendover. London, 1849. 2 v. 12°. . 5443
of Literature. W. Oxberry. London, 1821. 3 v. 12°. . . 860

Flowers of Wit. H. Keitt. Hartford, 1825. 16°. 4294
Flying Roll, The; or Free Grace Displayed. F. W. Krummacher. New York, 1841. 12°. 5706
Follen, C. Works, with Life. (vol. 4 missing.) Boston, 1841. 5 v. 12°. 5397

Vol. 1. Life.
2. Sermons.
Vol. 3. Lectures on Moral Philosophy.
5. Miscellaneous Writings.

Fonblanque, A. England under Seven Administr's. Lond. 1837. 3 v. 12°. 7112
Fool of Quality, The. H. Brooke. London, 1777. 3 v. 12°. . . . 694
Foote, H. S. Texas and the Texans. Philadelphia, 1841. 2 v. 12°. . . 10139
Foote, S. Memoirs. W. Cooke. New York, 1806. 2 v. 12°. . . 8390
The same. 8417
Dramatic Works. London, 1830. 3 v. 16°. 4312
Foote, W. H. Sketches of North Carolina. New York, 1846. 8°. . . 6952
Foot Prints of the Creator. H. Miller. Boston, 1850. 12°. . . . 6062
For Each and For All. Miss H. Martineau. Boston, 1833. 16°. . . 10023
Forbes, W. Acc't of the Life and Writings of J. Beattie. N. Y. 1807. 8°.. 8518
Ford, J. Dramatic Works. London, 1840. 8°. 1786
Ford, R. The Spaniards and their Country. New York, 1848. 12°. . 8898
Fordyce, D. A Dialogue on the Art of Preaching. London, 1755. 12°. 6607
Fordyce, J. Addresses to Young Men. Boston. 12°. 3021
Foreign Literature, Specimens of. Ed. G. Ripley. Bost. 1838. 12 v. 8°.

No. 768, 9. Philosophical Miscellanies of V. Cousin, T. Jouffroy and B. Constant. Trans. G. Ripley.
770. Select Minor Poems of Schiller and Goethe. Trans. J. S. Dwight and others.
771. The same.
772. Eckermann, J. P. Conversations with Goethe. Tr. Miss S. M. Fuller.
773, 4. Jouffroy, T. Introduction to Ethics. Tr. W. H. Channing.
775, 7. German Literature. W. Menzel. Tr. C. C. Felton.
778, 9. Theodore, or The Skeptic Converted. W. M. L. De Wette. Tr. J. F. Clarke.
780. Correspondence between Schiller and Goethe. Tr. G. H. Calvert.

Foreign Parts, Experiences in. D. Browne. Boston, 1857. 12°. . . 9829
Foreign Quarterly Review. vols. 11. 14–23, 26–30, 32–37. New York, 1833–46. 8°. 4043
Duplicates for 1834, 5. . . . . 3095, 3109
Review. vols. 1–5. London, 1828–30. 8°. 3556
Foreign Travel, Passages in. J. A. Jewett. Boston, 1848. 2 v. 12°. . 9797
Forest of Arden, a Tale. W. Gresley. New York, 1843. 12°. . . 566
Forest Life and Forest Trees. J. S. Springer. New York, 1851. 12°. . 9823
Forget-me-Not. Philadelphia, 1826. 18°. 4619
Forster, J. Statesmen of England, Lives of. New York, 1846. 8°. . 7825
Forsyth, J. Remarks on Antiq's, Arts and Letters of Italy. Bost. 1818. 8°. 9156
The same. 9444
Fortunes of Nigel, The. W. Scott. Boston, 1834. 12°. 273
See also Scott, Sir W.
Fosbroke, T. D. British Monachism, or Monks and Nuns of England. London, 1843. 8°. . . ; 5007
Encyclopædia of Antiquities. London, 1843. 2 v. 8°. . . . 8793

Fosbroke, T. D. Treatise on the Arts, &c., of the Greeks and Romans. London, 1833–5. 2 v. 12°. 9914
Foscarini, or the Patrician of Venice. New York, 1830. 2 v. 12°. . 971
Fossil Osteology, View of. H. Brougham. London, 1844. 18°. . . 7196
Foster, J. Appeal to the Young on Religion. New York. 12°. . . 5241
Contributions to the Eclectic Review. London, 1844. 2 v. 8°. . 715
Evils of Popular Ignorance. Boston, 1821. 12°. 3905
Importance of Religion. Boston, 1827. 12°. 6503
Lectures. London, 1853. 2 v. 12°. 5181
Life and Correspondence. J. E. Ryland. London, 1852. 2 v. 12°. 5183
The same. New York, 1846. 2 v. 12°. 8255
The same. New York, 1849. 12°. 8570
Living for Immortality. Boston, 1840. 12°. 6576
Obligations of the Married State. New York, 1845. 12°. . . 3362
Essay on the Spirit of Missions. Boston, 1833. 16°. . . . 6566
Foster-Brother, The. Edited by L. Hunt. New York, 1846. 8°. . . 6
Fouché, J. (Duke of Otranto.) Memoirs. Boston, 1825. 8°. . . 8534
Foundling of Belgrade. Tr. W. Jennings. New York, 1808. 12°. . . 369
Fountain and other Poems. W. C. Bryant. New York, 1842. 12°. . 2343
Fountain of Life, The. J. Flavel. New York, 1841. 12°. . . . 5246
Fouqué, F. de La M. Thiodolph, the Icelander. New York, 1848. 12°. 1197
The same. New York, 1845. 12°. 1612
Undine. New York, 1839. 12°. 1180
Four Ages of Life, The. Count P. de Segur. Tr. New York, 1826. 12°. 3353
Fourier, C., Doctrines of. P. Godwin. New York, 1844. 8°. . . 418
Four Sisters, The. Fredrika Bremer. Philadelphia. 12°. . . . 573
Fowler, O. S. and L. N. Phrenology Proved. New York, 1837. 12°. . 3336
Fowler, W. C. English Grammar. New York, 1851. 8°. . . . 11674
Fox, C. J. History of the Reign of James II. Philadelphia, 1808. 8°. . 6711
Memorials and Corresp. of. Lord J. Russell. Phil. 1853. 2 v. 12°. . 8006
Memoirs of the Latter Years of. J. B. Trotter. Phil. 1812. 8°. . 8250
Recollections of the Life of. 12°. 7459
Fox, H. W. Memoir. G. T. Fox. New York, 1851. 12°. 8637
Fox, J. Book of Martyrs, Revised and Improved by J. Malham. Philadelphia, 1830. 4°. 5004
Fragments from a Pastor's Study. G. Spring. New York, 1838. 12°. . 5709
Francaise, La Revue. vols. 1, 3. 1833–4. 8°. 11662
France in 1829–30. Lady S. Morgan. New York, 1817. 2 v. 12°. . 9048
The same. New York, 1830. 2 v. 12°. 7134
Prussia, Italy, &c., Traveler in. S. Laing. Philadelphia, 1846. 8°. 9414
Early Poetry of. Ed. Louisa S. Costello. London, 1835. 8°. . 1898
England, Spain, &c., Chronicles of. E. De Monstrelet. Tr. T. Johnes. London, 1840. 2 v. 4°. 7544
during the Reign of Napoleon. By Himself. Lond. 1823. 7 v. 8°. 7887
and the French Revolution. Tr. London, 1826. 4 v. 8°. . . 6998

Vol. 1, 2. Reign of Terror
3. Sufferings of the Royal Family.
4. Historical Sketch.

France, History of. London, 1836. 8°. 5100
History of. London, 1782. 3 v. 8° 7065
History of. Dublin, 1791. 2 v. 8°. 6753
History of. J. B. Bossuet. Tr. Edinburgh, 1762. 4 v. 12°. . . 7438
History of. E. E. Crowe. Philadelphia, 1835. 3 v. 12°. . . 5831
The same. London, 1830, 1. 3 v. 12°. 9862
History of. J. Michelet. Tr. G. H. Smith. vol. 1. N. Y. 1845. 8°. 11324
History of. A. Ranken. London, 1801–22. 9 v. 8°. . . . 7669
History of, from 1574 to 1610. N. W. Wraxall. Lond. 1814. 6 v. 8°. 7614
Idler in. Countess of Blessington. Philadelphia, 1841. 2 v. 12°. 9012
Its King, Court, &c. L. Cass. New York, 1840. 8°. . . . 7603
The same, with Three Hours at St. Cloud. N. Y. 1841. 12°. 6805
Lives of Eminent Lit. & Scientific Men of. Lond. 1838, 9. 3 v. 12°. 9948
Memoirs of the Court of, from 1643 to 1723. M. Anquetil. Trans. Edinburgh, 1791. 2 v. 8°. 8521
Modern Literature of. G. W. M. Reynolds. London, 1839. 2 v. 8°. 9236
Orators of. Timon. Tr. New York, 1849. 12°. . . . 8670
Politics of, in 1793–94. Helen M. Williams. London, 1795. 12°. . 6830
Residence in, during 1792–95. By an English Lady. Ed. J. Gifford. Elizabethtown, 1798. 8°. 9217
Restoration of Monarchy in. A. de Lamartine. Lond. 1854. 4 v. 12°. 5175
Review of the late Revol. in. C. Cushing. Boston, 1833. 2 v. 12°. 7137
Royal Family of, Secret Memoirs of the, during the Revolution. Philadelphia, 1826. 8°. 8533
Sketches of the Conspicuous Living Characters of. Trans. R. M. Walsh. Philadelphia, 1841. 12°. 8671
The same. 8666
Sketches of the Internal State of. M. Faber. Tr. Phil. 1812. 12°. 11470
Social, Literary and Political. E. L. Bulwer. N. Y. 1834. 2 v. 12°. 8944
Switzerland and Germany. Society in. J. Moore. London, 1783. 2 v. 8°. 11420
The same. Dublin, 1789. 2 v. 12°. 8731
Travels in. M. M. Noah. New York, 1819. 8°. 9178
Under Louis Philippe. L. Blanc. Tr. Philadelphia, 1848. 2 v. 8°. . 7362
Francia, J. G. B. de, Reign of. J. R. Rengger. Tr. Lond. 1827. 8°. . 6736
Francis I, Court and Reign of. Miss Pardoe. Phil. 1849. 2 v. 12°. . 7996
Life and Times of. J. Bacon. London, 1830. 2 v. 8°. . . . 7519
The same. 7521
Francis, C. Life of J. Eliot. (Two copies.) Boston, 1836. 12°. . . 8045
Life of S. Rale. Boston, 1845. 12°. 8059
Francis, G. H. Orators of the Age. New York, 1847. 12°. . . . 8704
Frankenstein. Mrs. M. W. Shelley. Philadelphia, 1833. 2 v. 12°. .. 669
Frank Forester. See Herbert, H. W.
Franklin, B. Autobiography. New York, 1825. 24°. 8423
The same, with Essays. New York, 1825. 24°. . . . 8424
The same, with Essays, &c. New York, 1840. 2 v. 12°. . 5552
The same. 4570
Familiar Letters and Miscellaneous Papers. Boston, 1833. 12°. . 3293

Franklin, B. Works, with Notes and Life. Ed. J. Sparks. (vols. 8 and 9 missing.) Boston, 1840. 10 v. 8°. 6282
Works and Life. Philadelphia, 1818. 6 v. 8°. 6029

No. 1. Memoir.
2. Historical Ruins of Pennsylvania.
3. Philosophical Papers.
4. American Politics. Political Economy. Ohio Settlement. Liberty of the Press and Moral Philosophy.
5. Secret Correspondence with Congress.
6. Private Correspondence.

Franklin, James. The Present State of Hayti. London, 1828. 12°. . 8976
Franklin, John. Expedition to the Polar Sea in 1819–22, and 1825–27. London, 1829. 4 v. 16°. 9333
Franklin Library. New York, 1835. 5 v. 12°. 1249

No. 1. Tales from English Annuals; Last Days of Pompeii, E. L. Bulwer; Bondman.
2. Tylney Hall, T. Hood; Three Nights in a Lifetime; Lost Election; Jacob Faithful, F. Maryatt; Magdalen and other Tales, J. S. Knowles.
3. Trials in Life; Real Life, from the Portfolio of a Chronicle; Peter Simple, F. Maryatt.
5. Brambletye House, H. Smith; Anne Grey; The Deformed; My Two Aunts.
8. Pacha of Many Tales, F. Maryatt; Tales; Transfusion, or the Unwalden, W. Godwin, Jr.

Franklin, Sir J., Grinnell Exped. in Search of. E. K. Kane. Phil. 1856. 8°. 9396
Second Expedition. Phil. 1857. 2 v. 8°. 9416
Frazer, J. B. History of Persia. New York, 1841. 12°. 5882
The same. New York, 1834. 16°. 6272
Mesopotamia and Assyria. New York, 1845. 12°. . . . 5209
The Persian Adventurer.. Philadelphia, 1831. 2 v. 12°. . . 253
Frederica Sophia Wilhelmina (Princess). Autobiog. Lond. 1828. 2 v. 16°. 7499
Frederick the Great, his Court & Times. T. Campbell. Lon. 1844. 2 v. 12°. 8262
History of. T. Carlyle. New York, 1859. 2 v. 12°. . . . 8655
Life. J. G. Zimmerman. Tr. Major Neuman. Dublin, 1792. 12°. 8074
Frederick II and his Times. F. Von Raumer. London, 1837. 8°. . . 8271
Life. Lord Dover. New York, 1839. 2 v. 12°. 5857
The same. New York, 1832. 2 v. 16°. 6632
Works. Tr. T. Holcraft. London, 1789. 13 v. 8°. 11064
Frederick III, Life and Times of. J. Tower. Dublin, 1787. 2 v. 8°. . 8573
Fredet, S. Ancient History, from 2247 to 1184, B. C. Balt. 1851. 12°. . 6785
Free Institutions, Nature and Tendency of. F. Grimke. N. Y. 1848. 8°. 10659
Freeman's Companion. Hartford, 1827. 8°. 2693
The same. 9765
Freemason's Monitor. Z. A. Davis. Philadelphia, 1843. 12°. . . . 818
Fremont, J. C. Memoir. J. Bigelow. New York, 1856. 12°. . . 8650
Report of Exploring Exped. to Rocky Mts., 1843, 44. Wash. 1845. 8°. 10453
See also United States Public Documents.
French Colloquial Phrases in. A. Bolmar. Phil. 1835. 16°. . . . 4961
The same. Philadelphia, 1836. 16°. 4962
French Conversation, Elements of. J. Perrin. New York, 1823. 16°. . 3978
French Gov't, Letter on the Genius and Disposition of. Boston, 1819. 8°. 11313

French Grammar. J. P. V. L. de Lévizac. New York, 1827. 12°. . . . 3040
Grammar. N. Wanostrocht. Boston, 1824. 12°. 3032
History, Stories from. W. Scott. Boston, 1845. 12°. 305
The same. Boston, 1834. 12°. 283
Homonyms. J. Martin. New York, 1807. 12°. 3010
Monarchy, Restora'n of. A. de Lamartine. Tr. Lond. 1855. 4 v. 12°. 5175
Poets, the Early, Trans. and Notices of. H. F. Cary. Lond. 1846. 12°. 8093
Revolution, Biograph. Mem. of. J. Adolphus. Lond. 1799. 2 v. 8°. 6709
Revolution, Consideration of Principal Events of. Madame de Staël. Trans. New York, 1818. 2 v. 8°. . . . . . .
Revolution, Defence of. J. Mackintosh. London, 1792. 8°. . . . [illegible]761
The same. London, 1846. . . . . [illegible]04
Revo., Diff. Opinions of Brit. Writers on. vols. 2 & 3. Lon. 1811. 8°. 7808
Revolution, from 1788–1815. A. Alison. London, 1835. 8°. . 7641
Revolution, Hist. of, 1789–1814. F. A. Mignet. Lond. 1846. 12°. 5493
The same. London, 1856. 12°. 5472
Revolution, Hist. of. L. A. Thiers. Tr. F. Shoberl. Phil. 1840. 3 v. 8°. 7527
Revo., Hist. of the Wars of, with Maps. E. Baines. Phil. 1835. 3 v. 8°. 7276
Revolution, Historical and Moral View of the. Mary Wollstonecraft. Philadelphia, 1795. 12°. 6836
Revolution, Lectures on the. W. Smyth. London, 1840. 3 v. 8°. 6928
The same. London, 1855. 2 v. 12°. 5190
Stage, Pictures During 50 Yrs. Ed. T. Hook. Lond. 1842. 2 v. 8°. 1135
Writers, Lives of. Mrs. M. W. Shelley & others. Phil. 1840. 2 v. 12°. 8613
Fresh Gleanings. D. G. Mitchell. New York, 1847. 12°. 217
The same. New York, 1859. 12°. 208
Frey, J. S. C. F. Narrative. New York, 1817. 16°. 8450
Friend; Series of Essays. S. T. Coleridge. Burlington, 1831. 8°. . . . 52
Friends in Council. A. Helps. Boston, 1849. 12°. 3330
Froissart, J., Chronicles of Eng. France, Spain, &c. Lond. 1839. 2 v. 4°. 7546
Frontenac, a Metrical Romance. A. B. Street. New York, 1841. 12°. . 2363
Frost, J. American Speaker. Philadelphia, 1836. 12°. 9858
British Poets, Falconer to Scott, &c. Phil. 1838. 8°. 1849
British Poets, Southey to Croly. Philadelphia, 1843. 8°. . . 1843
Fruits and Fruit Trees of America. A. J. Downing. N. Y. 1849. 12°. . 2978
Fruits of Leisure. New York, 1851. 12°. 1138
Fry, Caroline. Christ Our Law. New York, 1842. 12°. 5415
Fudge Doings. D. G. Mitchell. New York, 1859. 2 v. 12°. 209
Fudge Family in Paris. T. Moore. New York, 1818. 16°. 3080
Fuller, A. The Gospel its own Witness, &c. Clipstone, 1800. 8°. . . 6395
Memoirs of S. Pearce. New York, 1809. 12°. 5244
The same. New York. 16°. . . . .
Works; with Memoir by A. G. Fuller. London, 1852. 12°. . . 5196
Fuller, T. Church History of Britain. London, 1837. 3 v. 8°. . . . 6973
Worthies of England. Ed. P. A. Nuttall. London, 1840. 3 v. 8°. 7906
Fulton, R. Life. C. D. Colden. New York, 1817. 8°. 8202
The same. 8484
Life. J. Renwick. Boston, 1838. 12°. 8052

Fuseli, H. Life and Writings. J. Knowles. London, 1831. 3 v. 8°. . 372
Future Life, Doctrine of. C. F. Hudson. Boston, 1858. 12°. . . . 5719
Punishment, Lectures on. E. R. Tyler. Middletown, 1829. 12°. 6522
The same. 6530
The same. 6538
Punishment, Scripture Doctrine of. H. H. Dobney. N. Y. 1850. 12°. 5690

G.

Gaieties and Gravities. H. Smith. New York, 1852. 12°. . . . 4573
Galatians, Notes on. A. Barnes. New York, 1841. 12°. . . . 5728
Gallatin, A. Sketch of the Finances of the U. S. New York, 1796. 8°. 11088
Gallaudet, T. H. Christian Faith and Practice. New York, 1818. 8°. . 5349
Tribute to. H. Barnard. Hartford, 1852. 8°. 11311
Gallus, or Roman Scenes. W. A. Becker. Tr. F. Metcalfe. Lond. 1844. 8°. 11403
Galt, J. Autobiography. Philadelphia, 1833. 2 v. 12°. . . 8097
Diary of the Times of George IV. Philadelphia, 1839. 2 v. 12° 7097
Life and Studies of B. West. Philadelphia, 1816. 8°. . . . 8204
Life of Byron. New York, 1832. 16°. 6634
The same. New York, 1841. 12°. 5260
The same. New York, 1830. 16°. 6635
Life of Cardinal Wolsey. London, 1846. 12°. 5491
Lives of the Players. vol. 1. New York, 1831. 12°. . . . 8683
Mansie Wauch. New York, 1828. 12°. 988
Southennan, a Tale. New York, 1830. 2 v. 12°. 1121
Stanley Buxton. Philadelphia, 1833. 2 v. 12°. 1453
The Last of the Lairds. New York, 1827. 12°. 1396
Gambier, J. E. Guide to the Study of Moral Evidence. Bost. 1834. 16°. 6229
Gambling Unmasked. J. H. Green. Philadelphia, 1847. 12°. . . 3925
Gammell, W. Life of R. Williams. Boston, 1845. 12°. 8056
Life of S. Ward. Boston, 1846. 12°. 8061
Gardening, Modern, Observations on. Dublin, 1770. 12°. . . . 10171
Gardiner, J. Life. P. Doddridge. Exeter, 1795. 12°. 7776
Gardiner, W. Music of Nature. Boston, 1837. 8°. 10119
Gardner, A. K. Old Wine in New Bottles. New York, 1848. 12°. . 1142
Gardner, D. Treatise on International Law. Troy, 1844. 12°. . . 11132
Garland, H. Life of J. Randolph. New York, 1856. 2 v. 12°. . . 8620
Garland of Flowers. R. Walpole. New York, 1806. 12°. . . . 1962
The same. 2369
Garrick, D. Private Correspondence. London, 1831. 2 v. 4°. . . 11249
Gaskell, Mrs. E. C. Life of Charlotte Brontë. New York, 1857. 2 v. 12°. 8345
Gaston de Blondeville. Miss A. Radcliffe. Philadelphia, 1826. 3 v. 12°. 611
Gates, T. R. Life and Writings. Philadelphia, 1818. 12°. . . . 6602
Gaussen, S. R. L. Plenary Inspiration of the Bible. Trans. E. N. Kirk.
New York, 1842. 12°. 5710
Gay, J. Poetical Works, with Life by E. Sanford. Phil. 1819. 16°. . 2129
Gayane, C. Colonial History and Romance of Louisiana. N. Y. 1851. 8°. 7235
Gazetteer, Pocket, of the U. States. J. and R. C. Morse. N. H. 1826. 16°. 9322
The same. New Haven, 1828. 16°. 9326

Gazeteer, Pocket, Universal. Boston, 1832. 12°. 9303
Gebel Teir, or Mountain of Birds. Boston, 1829. 12°. 3298
Gebir. W. S. Landor. London, 1831. 18°. 2223
Geiyer, E. G. History of the Swedes. Tr. J. H. Turner. London. 8°. . 7236
Gellius, Aulus Noctes Atticæ. Lipsiæ, 1829. 16°. 10607
Genesis, Notes on. G. Bush. New York, 1840. 2 v. 12°. 5741
Geneva and France, Letters from. Boston, 1819. 2 v. 8°. 9181
Genius, an Essay on. A. Gerard. London, 1774. 8°. 6404
Infirmities of. R. R. Madden. Philadelphia, 1833. 2 v. 12°. . 4915
Powers of. J. B. Linn. Philadelphia, 1801. 12°. 11936
Genlis, Mad. S. F. de. Belisarius, a Romance. Philadelphia, 1810. 12°. . 1506
Memoirs of her own Life. N. York, 1825. 2 v. 8°. 8514
Moral Tales. Trans. New York, 1825. 12°. 1656
Genoa, History of. London, 1782. 8°. 7071
Gentleman's Magazine, The, 1731–1834. London. 154 v. 8°. . . 3402
Index to vols. 1–88. 5 vols. In the Rack.
Gentleman of the Old School, The. G. P. R. James. N. Y. 1839. 2 v. 12°. 233
Gentz, F. State of Europe, before and after the French Revolution. Tr. J. C. Herries. London, 1804. 8°. 6725
Geographical Dictionary. W. Darby. Washington, 1843. 8°. . . 8809
Dictionary. J. R. M'Culloch. New York, 1847. 2 v. 8°. . . 8805
View of the World. J. Goldsmith. New York, 1826. 12°. . 9016
Geographie, Leeons de. New York, 1813. 16°. 4959
Geography, Ancient, for Students. S. Butler. New York, 1821. 12°. . 3374
of the Bible. L. Coleman. Philadelphia, 1850. 12°. 3310
Encyclopædia of. H. Murray. Philadelphia, 1837. 3 v. 8°. . 10915
and History, Summary of. A. Adams. London, 1802. 8°. . . 6769
Physical. See Physical.
in Rhymes. V. Clark. Hartford, 1819. 12°. 2395
Universal. C. Malte-Brun. Philadelphia, 1827. 6 v. 8°. . . 9077
Universal. J. Morse. Boston, 1812. 2 v. 8°. 9124
The same. Charlestown, 1819. 2 v. 9166
Geological Manual. H. T. De La Beche. Philadelphia, 1832. 8°. . . 5986
Report of the Country between the Missouri and Red Rivers. G. W. Featherstonhaugh. Washington, 1835. 8°. 5939
Survey of Ohio. W. W. Mather. Columbus, 1838. 8°. . . 6002
Survey of New York. Albany, 1838, 9. 3 v. 8°. 5957
Survey of Wisconsin, &c. D. D. Owen. Phil. 1852. 2 v. 4°. . 13115
Geologists and Naturalists, Transactions of the American Association of, 1840–2. Boston, 1843. 8°. 5960
Geology of the Bass Rock. H. Miller. New York, 1851. 12°. . . . 6104
Certainties of. W. S. Gibson. London, 1840. 8°. 5940
of Connecticut, Report on the. J. G. Percival. N. Haven, 1842. 8°. 5952
Elementary. E. Hitchcock. New York, 1841. 12°. 6073
The same. New York, 1856. 12°. 6056
Elements of. C. A. Lee. New York. 12°. 5254
Introduction to. R. Bakewell. London, 1829. 8°. 5955
Lectures on. J. R. Smith. London, 1839. 8°. 5941

Geology, Outlines of. J. L. Comstock. (Three copies.) N. Y. 1837–8. 12°. 6077
Outlines of. J. Renwick. New York, 1838. 12°. . . . 6089
Primary Treatise on. H. S. Boase. London, 1834. 8°. . . . 5943
Principles of. C. Lyell. Philadelphia, 1837. 2 v. 8°. . . . 5947
The same. 5953
Religion of. E. Hitchcock. Boston, 1851. 12°. 6058
Scriptural. G. Young. London, 1840. 8°. 5973
Treatise on. J. Phillips. London, 1837–9. 2 v. 12°. . . . 9981
Wonders of. G. A. Mantell. London, 1839. 12°. . . . 6098
and Astronomy, First Lessons in. H. L. Smith. Cleve. 1848. 12°. 6071
and Chemistry, Applied to Agri. J. F. W. Johnston. N. Y. 1847. 12°. 6076
and Mineral., in Ref. to Nat. Theol. W. Buckland. Phil. 1837. 2 v. 8°. 6387
The same. 6389
and Nat. Hist. of Various Countries. C. Darwin. Lond. 1840. 8°. 10104
Geometry, Elements of. Euclid. Ed. R. Simson. Philadelphia. 8°. . 11682
Plain, Solid and Spherical. London, 1830. 8°. 5097
Practical, and Mensuration. J. Bonnycastle. London, 1806. 12°. 4560
and Trig., Ele. of. A. M. Legendre. Tr. D. Brewster. N. Y. 1828. 8°. 9730
George II, Memoirs of the Reign of. Lord J. Hervey. Phil. 1848. 2 v. 12°. 7110
George III, Annals of the Reign of. J. Aikin. London, 1816. 2 v. 8°. . 7931
Memoirs of the Reign of. H. Walpole. Phil. 1845. 2 v. 8°. . 7535
Memoirs of the Reign of, to 1793. W. Belsham. Dub. 1796. 2 v. 8°. 8224
Men of Letters & Sci. of the Time of. H. Brougham. Phil. 1845. 12°. 8631
Second series. Philadelphia, 1846. 12°. 8010
Statesmen of the Time of. Lord Brougham. Phil. 1839. 2 v. 12°. 8497
The same. 8601
Second series. Philadelphia, 1839. 2 v. 12°. . . . 8327
Third series. London, 1845. 2 v. 16°. 7204
George IV, Diary Illustrating Times of. Ed. J. Galt. Phil. 1839. 2 v. 12°. 7097
Life and Times of. G. Croly. (Two copies.) N. Y. 1831. 16°. . 6274
The same. New York, 1840. 16°. 5517
Georgia Scenes, Characters, &c. A. B. Longstreet. New York, 1843. 12°. 1609
Georgian Era, The, or Memoirs of Eminent Persons of Great Britain. London, 1833. 4 v. 12°. 7408
Gerald and other Poems. J. W. Marston. London, 1842. 12°. . . 2346
Geraldine, Athenia of Damascus. R. Dawes. New York, 1839. 12°. . 1953
Geral-Milco. A. R. M. Payne. New York, 1852. 12°. 8989
Gerard, A. Essay on Genius. London, 1774. 8°. 6404
German Empire, History of the. London, 1782. 3 v. 8°. 7071
Experiences. W. Howitt. London, 1844. 12°. 8725
Grammar. See Grammar.
Language, Introduc. to the Study of. T. Bokum. Phil. 1832. 12°. 3384
Literature. W. Menzel. Tr. Boston, 1840. 3 v. 12°. . . 509
The same. Boston, 1838. 3 v. 8°. 775
Lit. Selections from. B. B. Edwards and E. A. Park. And. 1839. 8°. 1070
Novelists. Tr. T. Roscoe. London, 1826. 4 v. 12°. . . . 1123
Poetry, Historic Survey of, with Translations. W. Taylor. London, 1830. 3 v. 8°. 1850

German Prose Writers, Fragments from. Tr. Sarah Austin. Lon. 1830. 8°. 508
The same. 817
Pulpit, a Selection of Sermons. Tr. R. Baker. London, 1829. 8°. 5030
Romance, Specimens of. T. Carlyle. Boston, 1841. 2 v. 12°. . 1214
University Education. W. C. Perry. London, 1845. 12°. . . 2984
Germanic Empire, History of the. S. A. Dunham. London, 1790. 12°. . 9868
Political Constitution of the. J. S. Pütter. Tr. Lond. 1790. 3 v. 8°. 6703
The same. 7229
Germany. Madame De Staël. Tr. London, 1814. 3 v. 8°. . . . 9469
in 1831. J. Strang. New York, 1836. 12°. 9610
France and Switzerland, Society in. J. Moore. London, 1783. 12°. 8731
History of. F. Kohlrausch. Tr. J. D. Haas. N. Y. 1845. 8°. . 7266
History of. W. Menzel. Tr. G. Horrocks. London, 1848. 3 v. 12°. 5147
The same. London, 1852. 3 v. 12°. . . . , . . 5427
Modern Polite Literature in. H. Heine. Tr. Boston, 1836. . . 4897
Poetry of. Original and Tr. A. Baskerville. Phil. 1856. 12°. . 1938
Prose Writers of. F. H. Hedge. Philadelphia, 1849. 8°. . . 27
and the Revolution. Prof. J. Goerres. Tr. J. Black. Lond. 1820. 8°. 11328
Tour in, in 1820–22. J. Russell. Boston, 1825. 8°. . . . 9463
Travels in the North of. H. E. Dwight. New York, 1829. 8°. . 9448
its Universities, Theology, &c, P. Schaff. Philadelphia, 1857. 12°. 6131
Gerry, E. Life. J. T. Austin. Boston, 1828. 8°. 7921
Gessner, S. Death of Abel. Tr. London, 1802. 12°. 11286
Works. Tr. London, 1802. 3 v. 12°. 4232
Gesta Romanorum, Select Tales from. New York, 1845. 12°. . . 232
Gibbon, E. Autobiography. London, 1830. 2 v. 16°. 7493
Essay on Literature. Dublin, 1788. 12°. 4569
Hist. of Decline and Fall of the Roman Empire. Dub. 1789, 6 v. 8°. 7693
The same. New York, 1835. 4 v. 8°. 7322
The same, with Notes by H. H. Milman. Lond. 1841. 4 v 8°. 6691
The same. New York, 1851. 6 v. 12°. 7699
The same, abridged. Ed. W. Smith. New York, 1857. 12°. 7394
Miscellaneous Works. Dublin, 1796. 3 v. 8°. 444

Vol. 1. Memoirs of Life and Writings, and Letters.
2. Letters and *Extraits du Journal.*
3. The last concluded: *Recueil de mes Observations*, &c.; Outlines of the History of the World; Observations on the Sixth Book of the Æneid; Vindication of some Passages in Hist. of Rome and Antiquities of the House of Brunswick.

The same. London, 1837. 393
The same. 746
Gibson, W. Rambles in Europe in 1839. Philadelphia, 1841. 12°. . 9253
Gibson, W. S. Certainties of Geology. London, 1840. 8°. . . . 5940
Giddings, J. R. Exiles of Florida. Columbus, 1850. 12°. . . . 10805
Gifford, W. Autobiography. London, 1830. 16°. 7755
The same. 7490
Baviad and Mæviad. New York, 1800. 16°. 2490
Gil Blas, Aventures de. A. R. Le Sage. Paris, 1826. 4 v. 18°. . . 11279
Gilbart, J. W. History of Banking in America. London, 1837. 8°. . 10495

Gilbart, J. W. Treatise on Banking. London, 1836. 8°. 10060
Giles, H. Christian Thoughts on Life. Boston, 1851. 12°. 876
Illustrations of Genius. Boston, 1854. 12°. 879
Lectures and Essays. Boston, 1851. 2 v. 12°. 877
Giles, W. B. (Editor.) Political Miscellanies. Richmond, 1827. 8°. . 10661
Gilfillan, G. Bards of the Bible. New York, 1851. 12°. . . . 5406
Gillespie, W. M. Philosophy of Mathematics. New York, 1857. 8°. . 1067
Gillies, J. History of Ancient Greece. Dublin, 1786. 3 v. 8°. . . 7688
Memoirs of Whitfield. London, 1772. 8°. 8539
The same. Middletown, 1838. 8°. 5348
Gilliss, J. M. Astronomical Expedition. See U. S. Public Documents.
Gillman, J. Life of S. T. Coleridge. London, 1838. 8° 11267
Gilly, W. S. Memoirs of F. Neff. Philadelphia, 1832. 12°. . , . 7771
Gilman, Mrs. C. Poetry of Traveling in the U. States. N. Y. 1838. 12°. 9285
Giovanni Sbogarro, a Venetian Tale. Tr. New York, 1820. 12°. . . 1585
Gipsy, The. G. P. R. James. New York, 1836. 12°. 1042
The same. 1387
Gipsies of Spain. G. Borrow. London, 1841. 2 v. 12°. 11410
Girard, S. Biography. S. Simpson. Philadelphia, 1832. 12°. . . 8416
Girault, A. N. Vie de George Washington. Philadelphia, 1835. 16°. . 8452
Girondists, The, History of. A. de Lamartine. Tr. N. Y. 1848. 3 v. 12°. 7705
The same. London, 1848. 3 v. 12°. 5177
Gisborne. T. Principles of Moral Philos. Investigated. Lond. 1798. 8°. 6408
Sermons. London, 1804. 2 v. 8°. 5598
Survey of the Christian Religion. New York, 1807. 12°. . . 6531
Gladstone, T. H. Englishman in Kansas. New York, 1857. 12°. . . 8991
Gladstone, W. E. The State in its Rela. to the Church. Lon. 1841. 2 v. 8°. 10664
Church Principles, Considered in their Results. London, 1840. 8°. 5032
Glances at Life. C. Webbe. London, 1836. 12°. 1464
Glaucus, or the Wonders of the Shore. C. Kingsley. Boston, 1855. 12°. 10172
Gleig, G. R. Biog. of Brit. Military Commanders. Lond. 1831. 3 v. 12°. 9924
Chelsea Hospital and its Traditions. London, 1838. 3 v. 12°. . 1437
History of the Bible. New York, 1833. 2 v. 16°. 6247
The same. New York, 1830. 2 v. 12°. 6249
The same. New York, 1841. 2 v. 12°. 5514
The Only Daughter. London, 1839. 3 v. 12°. 1459
Glenarvon, a Tale. Philadelphia, 1817. 2 v. 12°. 1400
Glimpses at the Past. Mrs. C. E. Tonna. New York, 1841. 16°. . . 1706
The same. 1711
Glossology, The Nature of Language. C. Kraitsir. New York, 1852. 12°. 3932
Glover, R. Select Poems and Life. Philadelphia, 1822. 18°. 2145
Gneisenau, Gen. Life of Marshal Blücher. London, 1815. 8°. 7952
Goats, Deer and Sheep, Nat. History of. W. Jardine. Edin. 1835, 6. 12°. 10196
Goddard. T. H. Hist. of Banks of Europe and America. Lond. 1836. 8°. 10662
Godman, J. D. American Natural History. Phil. 1831. 3 v. 8°. . . 10167
Godolphin, E. L. Bulwer. New York, 1848. 2 v. 12°. 1486
Godolphin, Mrs. Life. J. Evelyn. New York, 1847. 12°. 8639
Godwin, Mrs. M. W. Memoirs. Philadelphia, 1804. 12°. 8379
Godwin, P. Doctrines of Fourierism. New York, 1844. 8°. 418

Godwin, P. Handbook of Universal Biography. New York, 1852. 12°. 8884
Political Essays. New York, 1856. 12°. 857
Godwin, W. Cloudesley, a Tale. New York, 1830. 2 v. 12°. . . . 709
Fleetwood, or The New Man of Feeling. New York, 1805. 2 v. 18°. 1717
History of the Commonwealth of England. Lond. 1824. 4 v. 8°. . 7020
Lives of the Necromancers. New York, 1835. 12°. . . . 8673
Mandeville. Philadelphia, 1818. 2 v. 12°. 656
St. Leon. Alexandria, 1801. 2 v. 18°. 1700
Transfusion, or The Orphans of Unwalden. New York, 1835. 12°. 1253
Gœde, C. A. G. Foreigner's Opinion of England. Tr. Boston, 1822. 8°. 9165
Goerres, Prof. J. Germany and the Revolu. Tr. J. Black. Lon. 1820. 8°. 11328
Goethe, J. W. Von. Autobiography. New York, 1824. 8°. . . . 11337
The same, with Travels. London, 1848, 9. 2 v. 8°. . . 5158
Characteristics of. Tr. Sarah Austin. London, 1833. 3 v. 12°. . 4549
The same. Philadelphia, 1841. 2 v. 12°. 4544
Conversations with J. P. Eckermann. Tr. Boston, 1838. 8°. . 772
Correspondence with a Child. Lowell, 1841. 2 v. 12°. . . . 4524
Dramatic Works. London, 1850. 12°. 5160
Faustus. Tr. J. Anster. London, 1835. 12°. 2332
Goetz of Berlichengen, with the Iron Hand. Tr. N. Y. 1814. 18°. 2735
Novels and Tales. Tr. London, 1854. 12°. 5423
Sämmtliche Werke. Stuttgart, 1840. 20 v. 16°. 10312
Sorrows of Werter. Tr. W. Render. Boston, 1824. 18°. . . 1681
Wilhelm Meister's Apprenticeship. Boston, 1828. 3 v. 18°. . . 1723
and Schiller, Corres. between. Tr. G. H. Calvert. N. Y. 1845. 12°. 780
and Schiller, Select Minor Poems of. Tr. Boston, 1839. 12°. . 770
The same. 771
Gold Mines of the Gila. C. W. Webber. New York, 1849. 12°. . . 9011
Golden Age of American Oratory. E. G. Parker. Boston, 1857. 12°. . 486
Dagon. New York, 1856. 12°. 9638
Legend. H. W. Longfellow. Boston, 1852. 12°. . . . 1989
Violet. Miss L. E. Landon. Philadelphia, 1827. 12°. . . 2498
Goldoni, C. Autobiography. London, 1828. 2 v. 16°. 7502
Goldsmith, J. Geographical View of the World. New York, 1826. 12°. 9016
The same. Boston, 1828. 12° 9277
Manners, Customs and Curiosities of Nations. vol. 1. Phil. 1810. 12°. 9270
Goldsmith, O. Essays and the Bee. Boston, 1820. 18°. . . . 4629
Essays and Criticisms. London, 1798. 2 v. 12°. 4593
History of Animated Nature. Philadelphia, 1825. 5 v. 8°. . . 10111
History of England. London, 1771. 4 v. 8°. 11439
Life. W. Irving. New York, 1840. 2 v. 12°. 5894
The same, New York, 1851. 12°. 536
Life. J. Prior. London, 1837. 2 v. 8°. 8175
Ministre de Wakefield. Boston, 1831. 12°. 1532
Miscellaneous Works and Life. Baltimore, 1809. 5 v. 12°. . . 3635

Vol. 1. Life; Vicar of Wakefield.
2. Citizen of the World.
3. The same concluded; The Bee.
4. Present State of Polite Learning; Essays; Life of T. Parnell; Life of Lord Bolingbroke.
Vol. 5. Deserted Village; Comedies; Miscellanies.

Goldsmith, O. Miscel. Works and Life. Ed. W. Irving. Phil. 1834. 8°. . 1861
The same. vols 3 and 4. Edinburgh, 1836. 12°. . . 4847
Natural History. Abridged. Philadelphia, 1829. 12°. . . 10204
Roman History. 12°. 11443
The same. Abridged. Hartford, 1831. 12°. . . . 7119
Select Poems with Life, by T. Campbell. Philadelphia, 1822. 18°. 2142
Vicar of Wakefield. Walpole, 1809. 12°. 1732
Good, J. M. The Book of Nature. New York, 1827. 8°. . . . 423
Memoirs of the Life, Writings, &c. of. O. Gregory. Bost. 1829. 12°. 7726
Goodman, G. Court of James I. London, 1839. 2 v. 8°. . . . 6672
Goodrich, Chauncey A. Greek Grammar. Hartford, 1833. 12°. . . 4869
The same. Hartford, 1838. 12°. 4859
Goodrich, Charles A. History of the U. S. Bellows Falls, 1828. 12°. . 6867
Family Tourist. Hartford, 1848. 12°. 9176
History of America to the Present. Hartford, 1851. 8°. . . 7597
Lives of the Signers of the Dec. of Independ. Hartford, 1848. 12°. 8596
Pictorial View of Religions. Hartford, 1851. 8°. . . . 5631
Goodrich, C. N. Universal Traveler. Hartford, 1820. 12°. . . . 9228
Goodrich, C. R. and others. Progress of Science and Mechanism. Illustrated from New York Exhibition. N. Y. 1853, 4. 4°. .
Goodrich, S. G. Hist. of all Nations. Illustrated. N. Y. 1857. 2 v. 4°.
Recollections of a Lifetime. New York, 1856. 2 v. 12°. . . 809
Sketches from a Student's Window. Boston, 1841. 12°. . . 2981
Gordon, A. Discourses on the Homilies of the Church of England. London, 1795. 2 v. 8°. 5377
Lives of Pope Alexander VI, and Cæsar Borgia. Folio. Lond. 1729. 11244
Gordon, T. F. History of Pennsylvania. Philadelphia, 1829. 8°. . . 11362
State Gazetteer of New York. New York. 8°. 9123
Gordon, W. History of American Revolution. London, 1788. 4 v. 8°. 7665
Gore, Mrs. C. F. Polish Tales. London, 1833. 3 v. 12°. . . . 1417
Gorton, S., Life of. J. M. Mackie. Boston, 1845. 12°. 8057
Gospel its own Witness. A. Fuller. Clipstone, 1800. 8°. . . . 6395
Mystery of Sanctification. W. Marshall. New York, 1811. 12°. . 6504
Tragedy, an Epic Poem. T. Brockway. Worcester, 1795. 12° . 2051
Gospels, The, Notes on. A. Barnes. New York, 1841. 2 v. 12°. . . 5735
and Acts, Veracity of the. J. J. Blunt. Boston, 1829. 12°. . . 6121
Gould, Hannah F. Poems. Boston, 1835. 12°. 2447
Gouraud, F. F. Phreno-Mnemotechny, or Art of Memory N. Y. 1845. 8°. 1072
Government, Discourses on. A. Sidney. New York, 1805. 3 v. 8°. . 10644
Disquisition on. J. Calhoun. Charleston, 1851. 8°. . . . 10074
Science of. A. W. Young. Rochester, 1843. 12°. . . . 11191
Gower, J. Select Poems with Life, by E. Sanford. Phil. 1819. 16°. . 2118
Græca Majora. Ed. A. Dalzel. Boston, 1837. 2 v. 8°. . . . 11656
Gradus ad Parnassum. A. J. Valpy. London, 1838. 12°. . . . 2986
Graham's Magazine. vols. 19, 20. Philadelphia, 1841. 8°. . . . 3110
Graham, Catharine M. Immutability of Moral Truth. London, 1783. 8°. 6407
Graham, Mrs. J. Life and Writings. New York, 1819. 12°. . . 7739
The same. New York, 1819. 12°. 7722

Graham, S. Lectures to Young Men on Chastity. Boston, 1847. 16°. 6221
Graham, W. Review of the Ecclesiastical Establishments of Europe. London, 1808. 12°. 3929
Grahame, J. History of the U. States, till 1688. London, 1833. 2 v. 8°. 6953
Grainger, J. Select Poems and Life. Philadelphia, 1822. 18°. . . . 3139
Grammar, English. W. Cobbett. New York, 1846. 16°. 4970
English. W. C. Fowler. New York, 1851. 8°. 11674
English. S. Kirkham. Rochester, 1835. 12°. 4922
The same. Baltimore, 1834. 12°. 3317
English. L. Murray. New York, 1819. 8°. 11687
English, Exercises in. Hartford, 1829. 12°. 4858
English and Hebrew. S. Johnson. London, 1771. 8°. . . 11696
English, Introduction to. R. Lowth. Philadelphia, 1775. 12°. . 4904
The same. 4985
French. A. Bolmar. Philadelphia, 1839. 12°. 3400
French. J. P. V. L. De Levizac. New York, 1827. 12°. . . 3040
French. N. Wanostrocht. Boston, 1824. 12°. 3032
French-English. D. Mackintosh. Boston, 1797. 8°. . . . 11654
General Principles of. A. J. S. De Sacy. Tr. Andover, 1837. 12°. 4860
German. G. J. Adler. New York, 1846. 12°. 2980
Greek. London, 1763. 16°. 3977
Greek. C. Anthon. New York, 1838. 12°. 3388
Greek. P. Buttmann. Tr. Boston, 1831. 8°. 2690
Greek. C. A. Goodrich. Hartford, 1833. 12°. 4869
The same. Hartford, 1838. 12°. 4859
Greek. Moor. Tr. P. Bullions. New York, 1831. 12°. . . 3346
Greek. R. Kühner. Tr. Andover, 1847. 12°. 2987
Greek. E. A. Sophocles. Hartford, 1853. 12°. 12210
Latin. See A. Adams.
Latin. E. A. Andrews and S. Stoddard. Boston, 1844. 12°. . . 3387
Latin. J. Ross. Philadelphia, 1829. 12°. 3390
Latin, Introduction to. London, 1776. 16°. 4960
Schools. London, 1842. 12° 5930
Universal, or "Hermes." J. Harris. London, 1806. 8°. . . 10076
Grammont, Count. Memoires. A. Hamilton. London, 1783. 4°. . . 11264
The same. Tr. Philadelphia, 1836. 8°. 11312
Memoirs of the Court of Charles II. Ed. W. Scott. Lond. 1846. 12°. 11472
Granby, a Novel. New York, 1826. 2 v. 12°. 1377
Granada, Conquest of. W. Irving. Philadelphia, 1829. 2 v. 12°. . . 6806
The same. New York, 1851. 12°. 537
Grandfather, The, a Novel. Ellen Pickering. New York, 1845. 8°. . 8
Granger, J. Biograph. Hist. of Eng. from 827 to 1688. Lon. 1824. 6 v. 8°. 7940
Grant, A. Nestorians, or the Lost Tribes. New York, 1841. 12°. . . 7104
The same. New York, 1841. 12°. 6798
Grant, Mrs. A. Memoir and Correspon. P. Grant. Lond. 1844. 3 v. 12°. 8608
Memoirs of an American Lady. New York, 1809. 12°. . . . 8679
Grant, Mrs. J. S. Memoir. W. W. Campbell. New York, 1844. 12°. . 8385
Grant, R. Metropolitan Pulpit. New York, 1839. 12°. . . . 5705

Grant, R. Paris and its People. London, 1844. 2 v. 12°. 9538
Random Recollections of the House of Commons. Phil. 1836. 12°. 8663
Sketches of London. Philadelphia, 1839. 2 v. 12°. 9838
The Great Metropolis. New York, 1837. 2. v. 12°. 1243
Granville, G. Select Poems, with Life by E. Sanford. Phil. 1819. 18°. . 2130
Grattan, H. Life and Times. H. Grattan. London, 1839. 5 v. 8°. . 7860
Speeches. New York, 1813. 8°. 10769
The same. 11082
Grattan, T. C. Agnes de Mansfeldt. Philadelphia, 1836. 2 v. 12°. . 962
High-Ways and By-Ways. Second series. Phil. 1825. 2 v. 12°. . 1599
Third series. Philadelphia, 1827. 2 v. 12°. 1588
History of the Netherlands. London, 1833. 12°. 9983
The same. Philadelphia, 1831. 12°. 5836
History of Switzerland. Philadelphia, 1832. 12°. 5838
Traits of Travel. New York, 1829. 2 v. 12°. 9052
Graves, Mrs. A. J. Woman in America. New York, 1843. 12°. . . 5216
Gray, A. Botanical Text Book. New York, 1845. 12°. 6065
Gray, Mrs. H. Sepulchres of Ancient Etruria. London, 1841. 12°. . 9801
Gray, T. Letters. Boston. 1820. 24°. 4630
Poems. London, 1777. 16°. 2716
Poetical Works. (Two copies.) London, 1836. 8°. 1858
Select Poems, with Life by S. Johnson. Phil. 1822. 18°. . . 2141
Gray, W. Origin of English Prose Literature. Oxford, 1835. 8°. . 749
Gray's Inn Journal, The. London, 1756. 2 v. 12°. 4268
Great Awakening in time of Edwards & Whitfield. J. Tracy. Bost. 1842. 8°. 5026
Great Britain, Cotton Manufactures of. A. Ure. London, 1836. 2 v. 12°. 2975
Four Years in. C. Colton. New York, 1836. 12°. 8935
The same. New York, 1835. 2 v. 12°. 9623
France, and Belgium, Tour in, in 1835. H. Humphrey. Amherst, 1838. 2 v. 12°. 9003
The same. New York, 1838. 2 v. 12°. 9037
History of. R. Henry. London, 1788. 12 v. 8°. 7333
Illustrations of the History of. R. Thompson. Edin. 1828. 2 v, 16°. 10002
and Ireland, Lives of Eminent Literary and Scientific Men of. vol. 2. London, 1837. 12°. 9947
and Ireland, Sketches of Soci. in. C. S. Stewart. Phil. 1834. 2 v. 12°. 8986
The same. 9050
Journal of a Residence in. Jehangeer Nowrojee and Hirjeebhoy Merwanjee, of Bombay. London, 1841. 12°. 9240
Memoirs of Literary Ladies of. G. Ballard. Oxford, 1752. 4°. . 7807
Popular Antiquities of. J. Brand. London, 1841. 3 v. 12°. . . 1183
The same. London, 1848. 3 v. 12°. 5437
Tour in 1810–11. New York, 1815. 2 v. 8°. 9154
Textile Manufactures of. G. Dodd. London, 1844. 16°. . . 7466
Treaties of, with other Powers. London, 1790. 2 v. 8°. . . 11062
Great Cities, Dangers of. J. Todd. Boston, 1841. 16°. 4971
The same. 6570
Commission, The. J. Harris. Boston, 1842. 12°. 5654

Great Events by Great Historians. Ed. F. Lieber. Boston, 1840. 12°. . 11457
Men, Lectures on. London, 1856. 12°. 815
Metropolis, The. R. Grant. New York, 1837. 2 v. 12°. . . 1243
Question, The. H. Boardman. Philadelphia, 1858. 12°. . . 6132
Grecian Wreath of Victory, The. New York, 1824. 18°. . . . 4944
Greece, Ancient, Essays on the Institutions of. H. D. Hill. Lond. 1823. 12°. 3899
Ancient, History of. J. Gillies. Dublin, 1786. 3 v. 8°. . . 7688
Ancient, History of. W. Robertson. Edinburgh, 1821. 8°. . . 6760
Anct. Politics of. A. H. L. Heeren. Tr. G. Bancroft. Boston, 1824. 8°. 7321
Antiquities of. J. Potter. New York, 1825. 8°. 11347
and Constantinople, Visit to, in 1827–8. H. A. V. Post. N. Y. 1830. 8°. 9451
Description of. J. Conder. London, 1826. 2 v. 16°. . . . 9640
The same. 9654
Description of. Pausanias. Tr. London, 1794. 3 v. 8°. . . 6739
History of. London, 1829. 8°. 5093
History of. G. Grote. New York, 1857. 12 v. 12°. . . . 7396
The same. (vols. 1–4.) London, 1846. 8°. . . . 7292
History of. W. Mitford. (vol. 1 missing.) Boston, 1823. 8 v. 8°. 6695
History of. C. Thirlwall. (vol. 6 missing.) Lond. 1835–44. 8 v. 12°. 9888
The same. New York, 1848. 2 v. 8°. 7278
in 1823–4. Letters, &c., on Greek Rev. L. Stanhope. Phil. 1825. 8°. 7006
of the Greeks. G. A. Perdicaris. New York, 1845. 2 v. 12°. . 8892
Letters from. E. Blaquiere. London, 1828. 8°. 9459
Letters on. M. Savary. Tr. Dublin, 1788. 8°. 6743
Modern, History of. Boston, 1827. 8°. 7637
Modern, Residence in. H. M. Baird. New York, 1856. 12°. . 9584
Palestine, Egypt, &c., Travels in. F. A. de Chateaubriand. New York, 1814. 8°. 9468
Political Antiquities of. C. F. Hermann. Tr. Oxford, 1836. 8°. . 10966
Travels in, by Anacharsis the Younger. J. J. Barthélemi. Tr. London, 1791. 7 v. 8°. 9198
Turkey, &c., Tour through, 1818–19. P. E. Laurent. Lond. 1822. 8°. 9472
and Turkey, Travels in. G. Temple. London, 1836. 2 v. 12°. . 9522
Turkey, Russia, &c., Travels in. J. L. Stephens. N. Y. 1841. 2 v. 12°. 8908
The same. New York, 1845. 2 v. 12°. 8906
The same. New York, 1838. 2 v. 12°. 9621
Wanderings in. G. Cochrane. London, 1837. 2 v. 8°. . . 9387
Greek Anthology, Collections from. R. Bland and others. Lond. 1813. 8°. 1879
Exercises. B. F. Fisk. Boston, 1838. 12°. 3381
Exercises. E. A. Sophocles. Hartford, 1841. 12°. . . . 4535
Idioms. F. Viger. Trans. and Abridged. J. Seager. Lond. 1828. 8°. 10084
Islands, Argos, Attica, History of the. London, 1779. 3 v. 8°. . 7033
Islands, and the Peloponnesus, Observations upon, in 1829. R. Anderson. Boston, 1830. 12°. 8988
Lexicon. Boston, 1829. 8°. 1063
Lexicon. J. Donnegan. 8°. 1066
Lexicon. B. Hedericus. London, 1727. 4°. 1055
Paradigm. Method of Teaching. D. F. Thierich. N. Y. 1830. 8°. 11673
Poets, Study of the. H. N. Coleridge. Philadelphia, 1831. 12°. . 3045

Greek Prosody. P. Wilson. New York, 1811. 12°. 3030
Reader. 12°. 4883
Reader. Colton. 8°. 11653
Reader. New York, 1844. 12°. . . . .
Revolution, History of the. J. L. Comstock. New York, 1828. 12°. 7120
Historical Sketch of. S. G. Howe. New York, 1828. 8°. . . 6796
The same. 7099
Greeks, Ancient, Charicles, or Private Life of the. W. A. Becker. Tr. London, 1844. 8°. 11404
Polit'l Antiq. of. W. Wachsmuth. Tr. E. Woolrych. Ox. 1837. 2 v. 8°. 6933
Philosoph. Dissert. on. C. De Pauw. Tr. London, 1793. 2 v. 8°. 11375
Ancient Manners of the. J. A. St. John. London, 1844. 3 v. 8°. . 7358
Romans, Treat. on Arts, &c., of. T. Fosbroke. Lond. 1833–5. 2 v. 12°. 9914
Theatre of the. London. 8°. 10078
Greeley, H. Hints towards Reform. New York, 1850. 12°. . . . 797
American Laborer. New York, 1843. 8°. 10928
Green, C. and S. Y. Wells. Millennial Church. Albany, 1823. 12°. . 6182
Green, J. H. Gambling Unmasked. Philadelphia, 1847. 12°. . . . 3925
Green, M. Political Works, with Life, by E. Sanford. Phil. 1819. 18°. . 2130
Green, N. Life. G. W. Green. Boston, 1846. 12°. 8062
Green, T. J. Journal of Texian Expedition against Mier. N. Y. 1845. 8°. 9371
Greene, A. G. Recollections of the Jersey Prison Ship. Prov. 1829. 12°. 4580
Greenhow, R. N. W. Coast of North America. New York, 1840. 8°. . 11319
History of Oregon and California. Boston, 1845. 8°. . . . 7539
Greenland, Iceland and Faroe Islands, History of. New York, 1841. 12°. 5907
Greenleaf, M. Statistical View of the State of Maine. Boston, 1816. 8°. 9767
Greenwood Cemetery, and other Poems. J. L. Chester. N. Y. 1840. 12°. 1940
Gregg, J. Commerce of the Prairies, or Journal of a Santa Fe Trader. New York, 1844. 2 v. 12°. 8895
Grégoire, H. Intellectual Faculties of Negroes. Trans. Brooklyn, 1810. 12°. 1107
Gregory, G. History of the Christian Church. London, 1790. 2 v. 12°. . 6547
Gregory, O. Astronomy. Cambridge, 1801. 8°. 6003
Letters on the Evidences, &c., of Chris. Relig. N. Y. 1826. 2 v. 12°. 6473
The same. London, 1851. 12°. 5179
Memoirs of the Life, Writings, &c., of J. M. Good. Bost. 1829. 12°. 7726
Greppo, J. G. H. Essay on the Hieroglyphic System of Champollion. Tr. I. Stuart. Boston, 1830. 12°. 859
Gresham, T. Life. London, 1845. 16°. 7208
Gresley, W. Chas. Lever, or the Man of the 19th Century. N. Y. 1843. 12°. 565
Forest of Arden. New York, 1843. 12°. 566
Siege of Lichfield, a Tale. New York, 1843. 12°. 567
Grew, H. Divine Testimony concerning Christ. Hartford, 1824. 12°. . 6120
Greylock, G. Taghconic. Boston, 1852. 12°. 11880
Greyslaer. C. F. Hoffman. New York, 1840. 2 v. 12°. 1497
Griffin, Edward D. Doctrine of Divine Efficiency. New York, 1833. 8°. 5640
Sermons, with Memoir. W. B. Sprague. New York, 1839. 2 v. 8°. 5059
Griffin, Edm'd D. Remains, with Memoir. J. Mc Vickar. N. Y. 1831. 2v. 8°. 9474
The same. 9477

Griffin, G. Tales of My Neighborhood. Philadelphia, 1836. 2 v. 12°. . 264
Griffith Abbey, or Memoirs of Eugenia. Mrs. C. Matthews. N. Y. 1808. 12°. 1584
Grimaldi, J. Memoirs. C. Dickens. London, 1838. 2 v. 12°. . . . 8264
Grimes, J. S. Phrenology. Buffalo, 1839. 12°. 3373
Grimke, F. Nature and Tendency of Free Institutions. N. Y. 1848. 8°. 10659
Grimke, T. S. Reflections on Science, Literature, &c. N. H. 1831. 12°. 3372
Grimm, F. M., and D. Diderot. Historical and Literary Memoirs and Anecdotes. London, 1814. 2 v. 8°. 7953
Grimshaw, W. Hist of the United States to 1821. Phil. 1830. 12°. . 7433
Grimshawe, T. S. Life and Works of W. Cowper. N. Y. 1849. 8°. . 1800
Memoirs of L. Richmond. New York, 1829. 12°. 7725
Grindrod, R. B. Bacchus, Prize Essay. New York, 1840. 12°. . . 514
Griscom, J. H. Animal Mechanism and Physiology. N. Y. 1840. 12°. . 5543
Griswold, R. W. Curiosities of American Literature. N. Y. 1844. 8°. . 36
Female Poets of America. Philadelphia, 1849. 8°. 1789
Poets and Poetry of America. Philadelphia, 1842. 8°. 1787
Prose Writers of America. Illustrated. Philadelphia, 1847. 8°. . 28
Grote, G. History of Greece. New York, 1857. 12 v. 12°. 7396
The same. vols. 1–4. London, 1846. 8°. 7292
Grotius, H. Life. C. Butler. London, 1826. 8°. 8160
Truth of the Christian Religion. Tr. J. Clarke. Lond. 1825. 12°. 6488
The same. London, 1777. 8°. 5628
Grund, F. J. Amer. in their Relations, Moral, Social, &c. Bost. 1837. 12°. 2999
Guatemala, Journey to. G. W. Montgomery. New York, 1839. 8°. . 9149
and Mexico, Travels in. J. Conder. London, 1825. 2 v. 16°. . 9645
The same. 9666
Guardian, The. J. Addison, and R. Steele. London, 1823. 3 v. 12°. . 3676
Guest, E. History of English Rhythms. London, 1838. 2 v. 8°. . . 733
Guiana, Voyages to. Sir W. Raleigh. Edinburgh, 1820. 8°. . . . 7634
Guide to the Conscientious. R. Philip. New York, 1834. 16°. . . 6565
to an Irish Gentleman. M. O'Sullivan. Philadelphia, 1833. 12°. 6581
to the Thoughtful. R. Phillip. Boston, 1835. 12°. . . . 6577
for Young Disciples. J. G. Pike. New York. 16°. 5233
Guizot, F. Corneille and his Times. New York, 1852. 12°. 8022
Essay on the Character of Washington. Tr. Boston, 1840. 16°. . 4585
History of Civilization in Europe. Tr. Oxford, 1838. 8°. . . 6719
The same, with continuation. Tr. W. Hazlitt. Lon. 1846. 12°. 5499
Hist. of the Eng. Revolu. Tr. Louise H. Courtier. Ox. 1838. 2 v. 8°. 6677
The same. 7302
The same. 7622
Representative Government in Europe. Tr. London, 1852. 12°. . 5133
Memoirs of G. Monk. Tr. J. S. Wortley. London, 1838. 8°. . 7916
Gulliver's Travels. J. Swift. Edinburgh, 1803. 12°. 338
Gummere, J. Surveying and Plane Trigonometry. Phil. 1825. 8°. . 2688
Gunpowder, Experiments on. Washington, 1845. 8°. 11670
Gurley, R. R. Life and Eloquence of S. Larned. New York, 1844. 12°. 8680
Life of J. Ashmun. Washington, 1835. 8°. . . . . . , 7899
The same. 8138

Gurney, J. J. Evidence of Christianity. Boston, 1833. 16°. . . . 6568
Gurowski, A. G. de. America and Europe. New York, 1857. 12°. . . 7392
Gustavus Adolphus, History of. W. Harte. London, 1807. 2 v. 8°. . 7523
Guthrie, W. Christian's Great Interest. Andover, 1815. 12°. . . 6533
Gutzlaff, C. Voyages along the Coast of China. New York, 1833. 12°. . 9793
Guy Mannering. W. Scott. Philadelphia, 1826. 2 v. 12°. . . . 579
The same. Boston, 1820. 8°. 1090
The same. Boston, 1835. 12°. 286
Guy Rivers. W. G. Simms. New York, 1834. 2 v. 12°. . . . 1506
Guyon, Madame de la M. Life. T. C. Upham. N. Y. 1847. 2 v. 12°. . 8580
Life of, with a Short Method of Prayer. Baltimore, 1812. 18°. . 4610
Guyot, A. Earth and Man. Boston, 1851. 12°. 6055
Gypsies of Spain, Account of the. G. Borrow. London, 1841. 2 v. 12°. 11410

H.

H—— Family. Miss F. Bremer. New York, 1844. 8°. 13
Hadad, a Dramatic Poem. J. A. Hillhouse. New York, 1825. 12°. . 1894
The same. 1922
Hahn-Hahn, Ida, Countess. Travels in Turkey, Egypt, &c. Lond. 3 v. 12°. 9545
Haines, C. G. Memoir of T. A. Emmet. New York, 1829. 12°. . . 7782
The same. 8401
Hayti, Notes on. C. Mackenzie. London, 1830. 2. v. 12°. . . . 8994
Present State of. J. Franklin. London, 1828. 12°. . . . 8976
Hajji Baba, of Ispahan, in England. J. Morier. N. York, 1828. 2 v. 12°. 622
Hale, M. Advice to his Grandchildren. Boston, 1817. 12°. . . . 4989
Life. G. Burnet. London, 1820. 16°. 7775
Hale, Mrs. S. J. Traits of American Life. Philadelphia, 1835. 12°. . 9635
Hale, S. History of the United States to 1817. N. Y. 1841. 2 v. 12°. . 5892
Half-Century, History of. E. Davis. Boston, 1851. 12°. . . . 476
Half-Hours with the Best Authors. C. Knight. N. York, 1848. 4 v. 12°. 790
Haliburton, T. C. Bubbles of Canada. Philadelphia, 1839. 12°. . . 10807
History of Nova Scotia. Halifax. 2 v. 8°. 6921
Rule and Misrule of the English in America. New York, 1851. 12°. 7093
The same. 11418
Sayings and Doings of Samuel Slick. Philadelphia, 1837. 12°. . 1470
Second series. Philadelphia, 1839. 12°. . . . 1471
Hallam, H. Europe during the Middle Ages. (vol. 1 missing.) Philadelphia, 1821. 4 v. 8°. 7002
Supplemental Notes to the same. London, 1848. 8°. . . . 6976
Literature of Europe, in 15th–17th Centuries. Lond. 1837. 4 v. 8°. 113
Hallam, R. A. Lectures on Morning Prayer. Philadelphia, 1856. 12°. . 5402
Sermons. Philadelphia, 1856. 12°. 5403
Hall, B. Fragments of Voyages and Travels. Philadelphia, 1831. 2 v. 12°. 9305
Patch Work. Philadelphia, 1841. 2 v. 12° 9795
Skimmings, or a Winter at Schloss Hainfeld. Phil. 1836. 12°. . 9800
Travels in Chili, Peru and Mexico, in 1820–2. Phil. 1824. 2 v. 12°. 9034
The same. Edinburgh, 1826. 2 v. 16°. 9987

Hall, B. Travels in N. America, In 1827, 8. Philadelphia, 1829. 2 v. 12°. 9280
Voyage to Loo-Choo, Eastern Seas, &c. Edinburgh, 1826. 16°. . 9986
Hall, E. Exposition of Baptism. New York, 1840. 16°. . . . 6226
The Puritans and their Principles. New York, 1846. 8°. . . 5020
Hall, James. Border Tales. Philadelphia, 1835. 12°. 688
Legends of the West. Philadelphia, 1833. 12°. 1634
Life of T. Posey. Boston, 1846. 12°. . . . . . . , 8061
Memoir of W. H. Harrison. Philadelphia, 1836. 16°. . . . 7768
Notes on the Soil, Climate, &c., of the West. States. Phil. 1833. 12°. 8927
Sketches of the West. Philadelphia, 1835. 2 v. 12°. . . . 9046
The Wilderness and War Path. New York, 1846. 12°. . . 243
Hall, James. Natural History. See New York.
Hall, Joseph. Devotional and Practical Treatises. London, 1834. 12°. . 5780
Select Poems, with Life by E. Sanford. Philadelphia, 1819. 16°. . 2119
Hall, R. Miscellan. Works, with Life. Ed. O. Gregory. Lond. 1846. 12°. 5136
Works, with Life. New York, 1830. 2 v. 8°. 6379
The same. Ed. O. Gregory. New York, 1833. 3 v. 8°. . 5371

Vol. 1. Sermons and Charges.
2. Political and Miscellaneous Tracts; Articles from the Eclectic Review; Miscellaneous Pieces.
3. Life by O. Gregory; His Character as a Preacher by J. Forster; Notes of Sermons; Letters; Sermons.

Hall, Mrs. S. C. Uncle Horace. Philadelphia, 1838. 2 v. 12°. . . 1420
The same. 1422
Hall, S. R. Lectures on School Keeping. Boston, 1830. 12°. . . 4591
Halleck, F. G. Fanny, a Poem. Boston, 1824. 8°. 2339
Poetical Works. Illust. New York, 1850. 8°. 1864
(Ed.) Selections from the British Poets. New York, 1841. 2 v. 12°. 5575
Hallock, W. A. Memoir of H. Page. New York, 1835. 12°. . . 7779
The same. New York. 16°. 5245
Halsted, Miss C. A. Life of Richard III. Philadelphia, 1844. 8°. . . 8147
Halyburton, T. Memoirs. Princeton, 1833. 12°. 8341
Hampden in the 19th Century. London, 1834. 2 v. 8°. . . . 407
Hampden, J. Life. J. Forster. London, 1837. 18°. 9934
Hamilton, A. Life. J. C. Hamilton. New York, 1840. 2 v. 8°. . . 7810
Duplicate of vol. 1. New York, 1834. 8°. . . . 8502
and J. Jay, Lives of. New York, 1841. 12°. 5905
and others. Federalist. Hallowell, 1831. 8°. 10693
The same. New York, 1802. 2 v. 8°. 10772
Works. Edited by J. C. Hamilton. New York, 1851. 7 v. 8°. . 11004

Vol. 1. Correspondence.
2 Political Miscellanies.
3. Papers as Secretary of the Treasury.
4. Cabinet Papers.
Vol. 5. Cabinet Papers; Military Papers; Correspondence.
6. Corres. and Political Papers.
7. Polit. and Law Papers; Index.

Hamilton, Antoine. Memoires de Grammont. London, 1783. 4°. . 11264
The same. Tr. Philadelphia, 1836. 8°. 11312
Hamilton, C. Hist. of the Afgans of Hindostan. London, 1787. 8°. . 6762
Hamilton, Elizabeth. Letters. Salem, 1821. 2 v. 12°. 6114

Hamilton, Lady E. Memoirs, with Anec. of Lord Nelson. Lon. 1835, 12°. 8257
Hamilton, T. Annals of Peninsular Campaign. Phil. 1831. 3 v. 12°. . 6803
The same. 9524
Men and Manners in America. Philadelphia, 1833. 2 v. 12°. . 8940
Youth and Manhood of Cyril Thornton. N. Y. 1827. 2 v. 12°. . 1404
Hamilton College, Narrative of the Decline of. H. Davis. N. Y. 1830. 8°. 11688
Hamlets, The, a Tale. Miss H. Martineau. Boston, 1836. 16°. . . 10027
Hammond, J. D. Hist. of the Political Parties of N. Y. Alb. 1842. 2 v. 8°. 6961
Hampden, J., his Party and Times, Memorials of. Lord Nugent. London, 1832. 2 v. 8°. 8166
Hancock, T. Principles of Peace Exemplified. Phil. 1829. 12°. . . 4954
Hand, its Mechanism, &c., Evincing Design. C. Bell. Phil. 1833. 12°. . 6484
Handbook of Games. Ed. H. G. Bohn. London, 1850. 12°. . . . 1160
of Hydropathy. J. Shew. New York, 1844. 12°. . . . 4521
for Readers. A. Porter. New York, 1845. 12°. 5215
Handy Andy, a Tale of Irish Life. S. Lover. New York, 1843. 8°. . . 14
Hanway, J. Earliest Accounts of the Caspian Trade. Travels in Russia, &c. The Persian Revolutions. London, 1762. 2 v. 4°. . 10921
Happiness, Christian Piety, &c., Essays on. J. M'Laurin. Phil. 1836. 12°. 6493
a Tale for the Grave and Gay. Philadelphia, 1822. 2 v. 18°. . 1726
Harcourt, L. V. Doctrine of the Deluge. London, 1838. 2 v. 8°. . . 5078
Harcourts, The. Part III. New York, 1837. 16°. 11152
Hardenberg, F. von. Henry of Ofterdingen, a Romance. Tr. Camb. 1842. 12°. 1218
Hardwicke, Earl of. Life. R. Cooksey. Worcester, 1791. 4°. . . 7797
Hare, A. W. Sermons to a Country Congregation. New York, 1839. 8°. 5308
Harmony, Treatise on. C. S. Catel. Boston, 1832. 12°. 4881
Harper's Classical Library. New York, 1836–47. 32 v. 12°.

No. 5261. Æschylus, translated by R. Potter.
5262. Xenophon, translated by M. A. Cooper.
5263. Demosthenes, translated by T. Leland.
5264. Sallust, translated by W. Rose.
5265, 6. Cæsar, translated by W. Duncan.
5267, 8. Cicero, translated by Duncan and others.
5269, 70. Virgil, translated by Dryden and others.
5271. Sophocles, translated by T. Francklin.
5272–4. Euripides, translated by R. Potter.
5275, 6. Horace, translated by P. Francis. Phædrus, translated by C. Smart.
5277, 8. Ovid, translated by Dryden and others.
5279, 80. Thucydides, translated by W. Smith.
5281–5. Livy, translated by G. Baker.
5286–8. Herodotus, translated by W. Beloe.
5289–91. Homer, translated by A. Pope.
5293. Pindar, trans. by C. A. Wheelwright, and Anacreon by T. Bourne.

Harper's Family Library. New York, 1830–44. 18°.

5540. Abercrombie, J. Inquiries concerning the Intellectual Powers.
5874. Abercrombie, J. Philosophy of the Moral Feelings.
5261. Æschylus. Ed. by R. Potter.
5251, 2. American Courage and Enterprise.
5221. Bacon F. (Lord.) Essays; and J. Locke, on the Conduct of the Understanding.
5532. Barrow, J. Description of Pitcairn's Island, and Account of the Mutiny of the ship Bounty.
6616. The same.
5881. Barrow, J. Life of Peter the Great.
5212–5. Belknap, J. American Biography, Ed. by F. M. Hubbard.

Harper's Family Library, *continued.*

5525, 6. Bell, H. G. Life of Mary Queen of Scots.
6637. The same.
5558. Birds, Natural History of.
5866. Brewster, D. Letters on Natural Magic.
6617. The same.
5906. Brewster, D. Lives of Galileo, Tycho Brahe, and Kepler.
5528. Brewster, D. Life of Sir Isaac Newton.
6619. The same.
5573. Bryant, W. C. Selections from American Poets.
5574. The same.
5917. Bucke, C. Beauties, Harmonies, and Sublimities of Nature.
5909. Bucke, C. Ruins of Ancient Cities.
5530. Buonaparte, Court and Camp of.
6621. The same.
5512. Bush, G. Life of Mohammed.
6614. The same.
5912, Camp, G. S. Democracy.
5541. Circumnavigation of the Globe.
6271. The same.
5883. Combe, A. Principles of Physiology applied to Health and Education.
6239–40. Crichton, A. History of Arabia.
5910, 11. Crichton, A., and H. Wheaton. History of Denmark, Norway and Sweden.
5517. Croly. G. Life of George IV.
6274. The same.
6275. The same.
5519–23. Cunningham, A. Lives of British Painters, Sculptors, and Architects.
6253–7. The same.
5566. Dana, R. H., Jr. Two Years Before the Mast.
5567. The same.
5568. The same.
5211. Davenport, R. A. Perilous Adventures, or Narratives of Peril and Suffering.
5890, 1. Davis, J. F. The Chinese.
5875· Dick, T. On the Improvement of Society by the Diffusion of Knowledge.
5542. Dick, T. Celestial Scenery.
5559. Dick, T. The Sidereal Heavens.
5857, 8. Dover, (Lord.) Life of Frederick the Great of Prussia.
6632, 3. The same.
5531. Drake, Cavendish, and Dampier, Lives and Voyages of.
6615. The same.
5577. Dwight, T., Jr. History of Connecticut.
5249. Elephant, Natural History of the.
5871, 2. Euler, L. Letters on Nat. Philosophy. Ed. by D. Brewster and J. Griscom.
6267, 8. The same.
5914. Fenelon, F. de S. de L. Lives of the Ancient Philosophers.
5502. Ferguson, A. History of Roman Republic.
5527. Fletcher, J History of Poland.
6622. The same.
5253. The same.
5545. Florian, M. The Moors of Spain.
5253–7. The same.
5552, 3. Franklin. B. Life of Himself, and Select Writings.
5882. Fraser, J. B. History of Persia.
6272. The same.
5209. Fraser, J. B. Mesopotamia and Assyria.
5260. Galt, J. Life of Byron.
6634. The same.
6635. The same.
5514, 5. Gleig, G. R. History of the Bible.
6247, 8. The same.
6249, 50. The same.
5894, 5. Goldsmith, O. Selections from his Writings; with Life, by W. Irving.
5216. Graves, Mrs. A. J. Woman in America; her Moral and Intellectual Condition.
5543. Griscom, J. H. Animal Mechanism and Physiology.
5892, 3. Hale, S. History of the United States.
5575, 6. Halleck, F. G. Selections from the British Poets.
5921, 2, Hazen, E. Popular Technology; or Professions and Trades.
5904. Head, F. B. Life and Travels of Bruce.
5915, 6. Henry, C. S. Translated. History of Philosophy.
5888. Higgins, W. M. The Earth; its Physical Condition and Phenomena.
5907. Iceland, Greenland, and the Faroe Islands, History of.
5510, 1. Insects, Natural History of.
6636. The same.
5876. James, G. P. R. History of Charlemagne.
6613. The same.
5524. James, G. P. R. History of Chivalry and the Crusades.

Harper's Family Library, *continued.*

6625. The same.
6643. The same.
5536, 7. Jameson, Anna. Memoirs of Female Sovereigns.
6260, 1. The same.
5908. Japanese, Manners and Customs of the.
5571, 2. Johnson, S. Life of, with Selections from his Works.
5578–82. Keightley, T History of England.
5538, 9. Lander, R. and J. Travels in Africa, and Discovery of Source of the Niger.
6628, 9. The same.
5913. Lanman, J H. History of Michigan.
5254. Lee, C. A. Geology and Mineralogy.
5516. Leslie, J., and others. Discov. and Adventure in the Polar Seas & Regions.
6273. The same.
5926, 7. Lewis, M., and W. Clarke. Travels West of the Mississippi. Ed. by A Mc-Vickar.
5918. Lieber, F. Essays on Property and Labor.
Locke, J. See Bacon, F.
5506, 7. Lockhart, J. G. Life of Napoleon Bonaparte.
6630, 1. The same.
6639, 40. The same.
5563. Lossing, J. B. History of the Fine Arts.
5901, 2. Mackenzie, A. S. Life of Oliver Hazard Perry.
6241–3. Massinger, P. Plays.
6623. Memes, J. S. Memoirs of the Empress Josepine.
6624. The same.
5219. Michelet, J. Elements of Modern History. Ed. by A. Potter.
5503–5. Milman, H. H. History of the Jews.
6244–6. The same.
5880. Montgomery, J. Lectures on Poetry, Literature, &c.
5873. Mudie, R. Popular Guide to the Observation of Nature.
5518. Murray, H., and others. Discovery and Adventure in Africa.
6611. The same.
5561, 2. Murray, H., and others. History of British America.
5863, 5. Murray, H., and others. Account of British India.
6264–6. The same.
5556, 7. Paley, Wm. Nat. Theology, with Notes by H. Lord Brougham, and C. Bell.
5565. Park, Mungo, Writings, Life, and Travels of.
5569, 70. Parry, W. E. Three Voyages for the Discovery of a North-West Passage.
5885, 6. Paulding, J. K. Life of George Washington.
5928. Polo Marco, Travels of.
5250. The same.
5215. Potter, A. Hand-book for Readers and Students.
5258. Potter, A. Maury's Principles of Eloquence.
5257. Potter, A. Political Economy, &c.
5255. Potter, A. The Advantages of Science.
5554, 5. Pursuit of Knowledge Under Difficulties.
5564. Quadrupeds, Natural History of.
5898, 9. Renwick, J. Life of Dewitt Clinton.
5259. Renwick, J. Lives of John Jay and Alexander Hamilton.
5905. The same.
5256. Renwick, J. Familiar Illustrations of Mechanics.
5259. Robertson, W. M. History of America.
5875, 9. Russell, M. Life of Oliver Cromwell.
6258, 9. The same.
5884. Russell, M History of the Barbary States.
6627. Russell, M. History of Egypt.
5877. Russell, M. History of Nubia and Abysinia.
6626. The same.
5529. Russell, M. History of Palestine.
6620. The same.
5[illegible]10. Russell, M. History of Polynesia.
5513. Scott, W. Letters on Demonology and Witchcraft.
6269, 70. The same.
5889. Sforzosi, L. History of Italy. Translated by N. Greene.
5859, 60. Smedley, E. Sketches from Venetian History.
6618. Smith. H. Festivals, Games and Amusements.
5508. Southey, R, Life of Horatio Lord Nelson.
6612. The same.
5923, 5. Spalding, W. Italy and the Italian Islands.
5854–7. St. John, J. A. Lives of Celebrated Travelers.
6276–8. The same.
5217, 8. Stone, W. L. Border Wars of the Revolu., embracing Life of Joseph Brant.
5867, 8. Taylor, W. C. History of Ireland. With Additions by W. Sampson.
6[illegible]62, 3. The same,
5861, 2. Thatcher, B. B. Indian Biography.
6641, 2. The same.

Harper's Family Library, *continued.*

5887. Ticknor, C. Philosophy of Living.
6251. 2. The same.
5533-5. Turner, S. Sacred History of the World.
5546-51. Tytler, A. F Universal History to 1700; continued to 1820, by E Nares.
5869. Tytler, P. F. Hist. of Discovery on the more Northern Coasts of America.
5560. Upham, T. C. Outlines of Imperfect or Disordered Mental Action.
5220. Voyages Round the World.
5919. White, G. Natural History of Selborne.
5509. Williams, J. Life of Alexander the Great.
5920. Wrangler, F. Expedition to the Polar Sea.

Harper's New Month. Mag. vols. 1–18. (continued.) N. Y. 1850–59. 8°. 3715
Harris, James. "Hermes," or Universal Grammar. London, 1806. 8°. 10076
Harris, John. The Great Commission, &c. Boston, 1842. 12°. . . . 5654
Mammon. New York, 1841. 16°. 5242
The same. 6227
Pre-Adamite Earth. Boston, 1850. 12°. 6060
Harris, T. W. Treatise on New England Insects injurious to Vegetation. Cambridge, 1842. 8°. 10103
Harris, W. Lives of James I, Cromwell, and Charles I. and II. London, 1814. 5 v. 8°. 8152
Harris, W. C. Highlands of Ethiopia. London, 1844. 8°. . . . 9473
Harrison, W. H. Memoir. J. Hall. Philadelphia, 1836. 16°. . . 7768
Harry Franco, Adventures of. C. Briggs. New York, 1839. 2 v. 12°. . 1499
Hart, J. S. Essay on Life and Writings of E. Spenser. N. York, 1847. 8°. 29
Harte, W. History of Gustavus Adolphus. London, 1807. 2 v. 8°. . 7523
Select Poems and Life. Philadelphia, 1812. 18°. 2141
Hartford Convention, History of. T. Dwight. New York, 1833. 8°. . 10736
The same. 10766
Letters in Defence of. H. G. Otis. Boston, 1824. 8°. . . . 10094
Hartley, D. Observ. on Man, his Frame, Duty, &c. London, 1834. 8°. . 6341
Harvard Library, Catalogue of. Cambridge, 1830. 5 v. 8°. . . . 9702
Magazine. vols. 1–5. (continued.) Cambridge, 1855. 8°. . . 12095
University, History of. B. Peirce. Cambridge, 1833. 8°. . . 11335
University, History of. J. Quincy. Cambridge, 1840. 2 v. 8°. . 7552
Harvey, J. Oblig. of Believers to the Church. New Haven, 1830. 12°. 6536
Hastings, W., History of the Trial of. London, 1796. 8°. . . . 11093
Hatfield, E. F. Universalism as it is. New York, 1841. 12°. . . 6129
Hausset, Madame du. Private Memoirs of. New York, 1827. 12°. . 8080
Hawes, J. Lectures to Young Men. Hartford, 1828. 12°. . . . 6117
The same. Hartford, 1829. 16°. 4298
The same. 6555
Religion of the East, with Imp. of For. Travel. Hart. 1845. 12°. 8973
Hawker, R. Poor Man's Morning Portion. New York, 1819. 12°. . 6508
Hawkesworth, J. and others. The Adventurer. London, 1823. 3 v. 12°. 3683
The same. London, 1756. 3 v. 12°. 11932
Hawkins, E. Sermons on Attaining Christian Truth. Oxford, 1840. 8°. 5036
Hawkins, Sir J., & C. Barry. Hist of Music. (Condensed.) Ed. T. Busby. London, 1819. 2 v. 8°. 10120
Hawks of Hawk Hollow, The. R. M. Bird. Philadelphia, 1835. 2 v. 12°. 1504

Hawks, F. L. Contributions to Ecclesiastical History of United States. New York, 1836–39. 2 v. 8°. 5021
The same. vol. 1. 5009
Monuments of Egypt. Illustrated. New York, 1850. 8°. . . 9375
Narrative of Perry's Expedition to Japan, &c. New York, 1857. 8°. 9386
Hawthorne, N. House of Seven Gables. Boston, 1851. 12°. . . 1246
Scarlet Letter. Boston, 1850. 12°. 1248
Snow-Image, and other Twice-Told Tales. Boston, 1852. 12° . 1247
Twice-Told Tales. Boston, 1842. 2 v. 12°. 1374
Haydn, F. J. Life. L. A. C. Bombet. Tr. R. Brewin. Boston, 1839. 16°. 8043
Haydon, B. R., and W. Hazlitt. Painting and Fine Arts. Edin. 1838. 12°. 10164
Hayley, W. Life of J. Milton. Dublin, 1797. 8°. 8226
Triumphs of Temper. A Poem. Kennebunk, 1804. 12°. . . 11883
Haynes, J. Conscience. A Tragedy. New York, 1821. 16°. . . 3071
Hays, Miss M. Biog., or Memoirs of Cel. Females. Lond. 1803. 6 v. 12°. . 8404
Hayti. See Haiti.
Hazen, E. Trades and Professions. New York, 1842. 2 v. 12°. . . 5921
Hazlewood Hall, a Village Drama. R. Bloomfield. London, 1823. 12°. 2029
Hazlitt, W. British Eloquence. Brooklyn, 1810. 2 v. 8°. . . . 11057
Conversations of J. Northcote. London, 1830. 8°. . . . 767
Criticisms on Art. London, 1843. 2 v. 12°. 10179
Dramatic Literature of the Age of Elizabeth. London, 1840. 12°. 4588
Lectures on the English Comic Writers. London, 1819. 8°. . 88
Life of Napoleon. New York, 1849. 3 v. 12°. 8652
Literary Remains. New York, 1836. 8°. 87
and B. R. Haydon. Painting and the Fine Arts. Edin. 1838. 12°. 10164
Sketches and Essays. London, 1839. 12°. 4589
Spirit of the Age. New York, 1844. 12°. 4515
Table-Talk. New York, 1847. 2 v. 12°. 9840
and others. Imitations of Celebrated Authors. London, 1844. 8°. 467
View of the English Stage. London, 1818. 8°. 95
Head, F. B. Bubbles from the Brunnen of Nassau. N. Y. 1846. 12°. . 9846
Faggot of French Sticks. Paris in 1851. New York, 1852. 12°. . 10146
Life and Adventures of J. Bruce. New York, 1841. 12°. . . 5904
Narrative of his Administration in Canada. London, 1839. 8°. . 9115
Headley, J. T. Alps and the Rhine. New York, 1846. 12°. . . . 9854
Letters from Italy. New York, 1846. 12°. . . . . . , 9599
Napoleon and his Marshals. New York, 1846. 2 v. 12°. . . 8301
Sacred Mountains. New York, 1851. 12°. 3894
Sacred Scenes and Characters. New York, 1851. 12°. . . . 3895
Washington and his Generals. New York, 1847. 2 v. 12°. . . 8648
Heads of the People, or Portraits of the English. D. Jerrold and others. Philadelphia, 1841. 8°. 47
Health, Economy of. J. Johnson. New York, 1837. 16°. . . . 4968
Influence of Mental Cultivation upon. A. Brigham. Hart. 1832. 12°. 3287
The same. 4886
The same. Boston, 1833. 12°. 3924
The same. 4877

Health, Journal of. Philadelphia, 1830. 2 v. 8°. 11660
and Longevity, Effects of the Arts, Trades, &c., on. C. T. Thackrah. Philadelphia, 1831. 16°. 4621
and Long Life. L. Cornaro. Andover 1824. 18°. . . . 4622
Heart, The. M. F. Tupper. New York, 1845. 12°. 251
of Mid-Lothian. Sir W. Scott. Boston, 1834. 12°. . . . 271
See also Scott, Sir W.
Heat, Treatise on. D. Lardner. London, 1833. 12°. 9960
Heathen Gods and Heroes, Hist. Account of. King. London, 1761. 12°. 4903
Heavens, The. R. Mudie. London, 1835. 12°. 6108
Mechanism of. Mrs. M. Somerville. Philadelphia, 1832. 16°. . 4604
Heber, R. Life. By his Widow. New York, 1830. 2 v. 8°. . . . 7852
Life of J. Taylor. London, 1824. 2 v. 12°. 7715
Journey through Upper India. Philadelphia, 1829. 2 v. 12°. . 8992
Palestine and other Poems. Philadelphia, 1828. 16°. . . . 2082
Poems. Hingham, 1830. 16°. 3087
Sermons Preached in England. New York, 1829. 8°. . . . 5331
Hebrew Lexicon, S. Pike. Cambridge, 1811. 8°. 10079
Hebrews, Notes on. A. Barnes. New York, 1843. 12°. 5729
Hebrides, Tour to the, by J. Boswell and S. Johnson. Phil. 1810. 8°. . 9171
Hedericus, B. Lexicon Graecum. London, 1727. 4°. 1055
Hedge, F. H. Prose Writers of Germany. Philadelphia, 1849. 8°. . . 27
Hedge, L. Elements of Logic. Cooperstown, 1846. 12°. 4594
Heeren, A. H. L. History of the States of Antiquity. Tr. Ox. 1833. 8°. 7361
The same. Tr. G. Bancroft. New York, 1828. 8°. . . 7320
Political System of Europe, 1492–1821. Tr. G. Bancroft. N. York, 1829. 2 v. 8°. 7319
Politics of Ancient Greece. Tr. G. Bancroft. Boston, 1826. 8°. . 7321
Politics and Trade of the Ancient Nations of Africa. Tr. Oxford, 1832, 3. 2 v. 8°. 10686
Politics and Trade of the Ancient Nations of Asia. Tr. Oxford, 1833. 3 v. 8°. 10683
Heine, H. Letters on Polite Literature in Germany. Tr. G. W. Haven. Boston, 1836. 16°. 4897
Heir of Wast-Wayland. Mary Howitt. New York, 1851. 12°. . . . 549
Heiress of the De Veres. Mrs. Marsh. New York, 1845. 8°. 48
Helen Fleetwood. Mrs. C. E. Tonna. New York, 1841. 12°. 1208
Hellenes, History of the Manners of the Ancient Greeks. J. A. St. John. London, 1844. 3 v. 8°. 7358
Helm, Miss E. Instructive Rambles in London. New York, 1814. 12°. . 9278
Helon's Pilgrimage to Jerusalem. F. Strauss. Tr. Boston, 1835. 12°. . 8916
Helps, A. Friends in Council. Boston, 1849. 12°. 3330
Helvetic Union, Hist. of Destruction of. J. M. Du Pan. Bost. 1799. 12°. 7127
Hemans, Mrs. F. Life. H. Chorley. London, 1842. 12°. . . . 8575
Poems. Boston, 1827. 2 v. 8°. 1880
Poetical Works. Philadelphia, 1836. 8°. 1837
Henderson, E. Residence in Iceland, in 1814, 15. Boston, 1831. 12°. . 8714
Henderson, J. Observ. on the Colonies of N. S. Wales. Calcutta, 1832. 8°. 9786

Hengstenberg, E. W. Egypt and the Book of Moses. Tr. R. D. C. Robbins. (Two copies.) Andover, 1843. 12°. 5697
Henningsen, C. F. Twelve Months' Campaign in Navarre. Phil. '36. 12°. 7422
Henriade. Voltaire, F. M. A. de. Paris, 1829. 16°. 2076
Henrietta Temple. B. D'Israeli. Philadelphia, 1837. 2 v. 12°. . . 145
The same. Philadelphia, 1847. 8°. 5
Henry II. Life. G. Lyttleton. London, 1769. 6 v. 8°. . . . 8541
Henry IV. Life. G. P. R. James. New York, 1850. 2 v. 12°. . . 8584
Henry VIII, Court of. Mrs. A. T. Thomson. London, 1826. 2 v. 8°. . 7517
Henry the Great, Memoirs of, and of the Court of France, during his Reign. London, 1824. 2 v. 8°. 7961
Henry, J. J. Acct. of Campaign against Quebec, 1775. Lancas. 1812. 12°. 6835
Henry, M. Exposition of Old and New Testament. N. Y. 1831. 6 v. 8°. 5301
The same. Philadelphia, 1833. 6 v. 8°. 5295
Memoirs. J. B. Williams. Boston, 1830. 12°. 7724
Henry, P. Life. A. H. Everett. Boston, 1844. 12°. 8053
Life. W. Wirt. Ithaca, 1850. 8°. 7920
The same. Philadelphia, 1817. 8°. 7508
The same. New York, 1835. 8°. 8599
Henry, R. History of Great Britain. London, 1788. 12 v. 8°. . . 7333
Henry, W. Experimental Chemistry. Philadelphia, 1822. 3 v. 8°. . 5979
Henry of Guise. G. P. R. James. New York, 1839. 2 v. 12°. . . 1468
Henry Milner. Parts 1–3. Mrs. Sherwood. New York, 1833. 12°. . 184
Fourth part. 198
Henry of Ofterdingen, a Romance. F. von Hardenberg, (Novalis.) Tr. Cambridge, 1842. 12°. 1218
Henslow, J. S. Physiological and Descriptive Botany. Lond. 1836. 12°. 9985
Herbert, C. Italy and Italian Literature. London, 1835. 12°. . . 492
Herbert, E., (Lord.) Autobiography. London, 1830. 18°. 7752
The same. 7487
The same. 8434
Herbert, G. Temple and other Poems. London, 1838. 12°. . . . 2035
Herbert, H. W. Field Sports of the United States. New York, 1849. 8°. 766
Cromwell, an Historical Novel. New York, 1838. 2 v. 12°. . . 1546
Herbert Wendall, a Tale of the Revolution. N. Y. 1835. 2 v. 12°. . . 1472
Herma, J. Spirits of Odin, or a Father's Curse. N. Y. 1826. 2 v. 12°. 1392
Hermeneutics, Legal and Political. F. Lieber. Boston, 1839. 12°. . . 10796
Hermann, C. F. Political Antiquities of Greece. Tr. Oxford, 1836. 8°. 10966
Herndon, W. M. Explor. of Valley of the Amazon. Wash. 1853. 2 v. 8°. 10452
Herodianus, Historiæ Romanæ. Lipsiæ, 1829. 16°. 10343
Herodotus, Dissertation on the Geog. of. B. G. Niebuhr. Tr. Ox. 1830. 8°. 11327
Historiæ. Lipsiæ, 1829. 2 v. 16°. 10849
The same. Tr. W. Beloe. (vol. 3 mis'g.) Lon. 1791. 4 v. 8°. 11405
The same. New York, 1841. 3 v. 12°. 5286
The same. vol. 3. New York, 1836. 16°. 8756
The same. Tr. H. Cary. (3 copies.) London, 1850. 12°. . 5434
The same. Tr. I. Littlebury. London, 1738. 2 v. 12°. . 7425
Life. Dahlmann. Tr. London, 1845. 12°. 8254

Herodotus. Summary and Index of. Ed. G. Long. London, 1829. 12°. 5433
Heroes, Hero Worship and the Heroic in Hist. T. Carlyle. N. Y. 1841. 12°. 848
The same. New York, 1841. 12°. 825
Heroines of Sacred History. Mrs. Steele. New York, 1842. 16°. . . 6219
Herschel, J. F. W. Discourse on Nat. Philosophy. London, 1835. 12°. . 9954
The same. Philadelphia, 1835. 12°. 5842
Treatise on Astronomy. London, 1838. 12°. 9957
Hervey, J., (Lord.) Meditations and Contemplations. N. Y. 1824. 16°. 4600
The same. 4606
The same. New York, 1822. 12°. 6510
Defence of Theron and Aspasio. London, 1760. 12°. . . . 6588
Memoirs of the Reign of George II. Philadelphia, 1848. 2 v. 12°. 7110
Hesiodus. Carmina. Lipsiæ, 1829. 16°. 10356
Illustrations of, by Flaxman. Folio. . . . .
Hess, J. G. Life of U. Zwingle. Tr. Lucy Aikin. London, 1812. 12°. . 8306
Hetherington, W. M. History of the Church of Scotland. N. Y. 1844. 8°. 5054
History of the Westminster Assembly of Divines. N. Y. 1843. 12°. 5671
Hewitt, Mary E. Songs of our Land, and other Poems. Bost. 1846. 12°. 2352
Hiawatha, Song of. H. W. Longfellow. Boston, 1856. 12°. . . 1987
Hieroglyphic System of Champollion, Essay on. J. G. H. Greppo. Trans. I. Stuart. Boston, 1830. 12°. 859
Higgins, W. M. Physical Condition and Remarkable Phenomena of the Earth. New York, 1840. 12°. 5888
High-Ways and By-Ways. T. C. Grattan. 2d series. Phil. 1825. 2 v. 12°. 1599
Third series. Philadelphia, 1827. 2 v. 12°. . . . 1588
Hildreth, R. History of the United States. New York, 1849. 6 v. 8°. . 7259
(Editor.) Lives of Atrocious Judges. New York, 1856. 12°. . 8638
Hillard, G. S. Life of Capt. J. Smith. Boston, 1834. 12°. . . . 8069
Hill, G. Poems. Boston, 1839. 8°. 1823
Hill, H. D. Essays on the Institutions of Ancient Greece. Lond. 1823. 12°. 3899
Hill, R. Life. W. S. Porter. Boston, 1835. 16°. 7767
Life. E. Sidney. New York, 1834. 12°. 8368
Hill of Difficulty and other Allegories. G. B. Cheever. N. York, 1849. 8°. 6362
Hill and Valley, a Tale. Miss H. Martineau. Boston, 1832. 16°. . 10026
Hill and Valley, or Hours in England and Wales. Catherine Sinclair. New York, 1838. 12°. 9792
Hillhouse, J. A. Dramas, Discourses, and other Pieces. Bost. 1839. 2 v. 12°. 1957
Hadad, a Dramatic Poem. New York, 1825. 12°. . . . 1894
The same. 1922
Percy's Masque, a Drama. New York, 1820. 12°. . . . 2458
Hills of the Shatemuc. Anna Warner. New York, 1857. 12°. . . 1224
Himalaya Mountains, Tour among. W. Lloyd and A. Gerard. London, 1840. 2 v. 8°. 9127
Hindoos, Hist., Lit. and Relig. of the. W. Ward. Hartford, 1824. 12°. . 7124
Hindoostan, Institutions, Lit. &c. of. T. Maurice. Lond. 1800. 7 v. 8°. 11366
Scenes and Characteristics of. Emma Roberts. Phil. 1836. 2 v. 12°. 9265
Hindu Philosopher, Shahcoolen, Letters of. Boston, 1802. 12°. . . 8715
Theatre, Specimens of. Tr. H. H. Wilson. London, 1835. 2 v. 8°. 1826

Hinman, R. R. The Part of Conn. in the War of the Rev. Hart. 1842. 8°. 6752
Hinton, J. B. and others. History of the United States. Boston, 1831. 4°.
Hints to my Countrymen, by an American. New York, 1826. 12°. . 1141
Hints toward Reforms. H. Greeley. New York, 1850. 12°. . . . 797
Historic Doubts on the Life and Reign of Richard III. H. Walpole. London, 1768. 4°. 11266
Historical Discourse. J. L. Kingsley. New Haven, 1838. 8°. . . 6684
Essays. T. de Quincey. Boston, 1854. 2 v. 12°. . . . 889
Memoirs of His Own Times. N. W. Wraxall. Lond. 1836. 4 v. 8°. 7610
Parallels. Boston, 1831. 12°. 6205
The same, with Additions. London, 1846. 3 v. 16°. . . 7463
Proof, Process of. I. Taylor. London. 1828. 8°. 5074
Sketches, Speeches and Characters. G. Croly. London, 1842. 12°. 8549
History, Ancient. C. Rollin. London, 1800. 10 v. 12°. . . . 6838
See also Rollin, C.
Ancient, from 2247 to 1184, B. C. P. Fredet. Baltimore, 1851. 12°. 6785
Ancient, Lectures on. G. Niebuhr. Tr. Phil. 1835. 3 v. 8°. . 7364
Ancient, Manual of. A. H. L. Heeren. Tr. Oxford, 1833. 8°. . 7361
The same. Tr. G. Bancroft. New York, 1828. 8°. . . 7320
Ancient, Universal. J. Swinton and others. Lond. 1779. 18 v. 8°. 7029

Vol. 1. The Flood, Egypt, Moab, Midians, Canaan, Syrians.
2, 3. Phœnicians and Jews.
3. Assyrians, Babylonians, Phrygians.
4. Medes, Persians, Celts, Lydians.
5. Heroic Times, Sicyon, Argos, Attica, Athens.
6. Thebes, Achaia, Ætolia, Epirus, Ionia, Syracuse.
7. Syracuse, Rhodes, Greek Islands, Cyprus, Macedonia.
8. Macedonia, Seleucidæ in Syria, Armenians.
Vol. 9. Cappadocia, Pergamus, Parthians, Persians.
9, 14. Roman History.
14, 15. Constantinopolitan Empire, Carthaginians, Numidians, Mauritanians.
15, 16. Ethiopians, Germans, Britain, Hunns, Goths.
17. Vandals, Franks, Tartars and Moguls, Indians, Chinese.
18. Etruscans, Index.

Ancient and Modern, Lectures on. J. C. Abraham. Eton, 1845. 8°. 6713
Ancient and Modern, J. E. Worcester. Boston, 1852. 12°. . . 11454
Beauties of. London, 1785. 2 v. 12°. 11465
Chronology of. H. Nicolas. London, 1838. 12°. 9923
Compend of. S. Whelpley. New York, 1814. 8°. . . . 6735
Family Book of. J. Olney and J. W. Barber. (Two cop.) N. H. 8°. 7564
General, Elements of. Abbé C. F. X. Millot. Trans. Worcester, 1789. 5 v. 8°. 6727
and General Policy, Lectures on. J. Priestly. Phil. 1803. 2 v. 8°. 6737
Modern. P. Fredet. Baltimore, 1850. 12°. 7102
Modern. J. Michelet. New York, 1843. 12°. 5219
Modern. Lectures on. T. Arnold. Ed. H. Reed. N. Y. 1845. 12°. 6793
The same. London, 1843. 8°. 6995
Modern, Lectures on. W. Smyth. Cambridge, 1841. 2 v. 8°. . 7331
The same. London, 1854. 2 v. 12°. 5192
Modern, Student's Manual of. W. C. Taylor. London, 1841. 12°. 7091

History, Modern Universal. Copied from Original Authors. vols. 1–42. London, 1780–4. 8°. 7047

Vol. 1–3. Mohammed, Arabs, and Turks.
3–5. Seljuks, Moguls and Tartars.
5. Persia.
6. Hither Peninsula of India.
7. E. Tartary, China, Morea, Japan.
7–10. E. Indies, Othman Empire, Jews.
11–15. Africa.
12. African Islands, Abyssinia, Adel, &c.
15. Malta.
16–21. Spain, Portugal, Navarre, France.

Vol. 22–5. Italy, Venice, Naples, Genoa.
25–7. German Empire.
27–30. Holland, Denmark, Sweden.
30–2. Poland, Prussia, Russia.
32. Swiss, Geneva, Bohemia.
33–4. Mecklenburg, Tuscan States, Milan, Savoy.
34–6. America.
36–8. Conclusion of Mod. History.
39–42. England, Scotland, Ireland.

Outlines of. T. Keightley. Philadelphia, 1837. 12°. 9859
The same. 5837
Philosophy of. F. von Schlegel. Tr. J. B. Robertson. New York, 1841. 2 v 12°. 819
The same. London, 1848. 12°. 5127
The same. London, 1835. 2 v. 8°. 11343
Sketches of Univer., Sac. and Profane. F. Butler. Hart. 1819. 12°. 7129
The same. Hartford, 1818. 12°. 7130
Universal M. Bossuet. Tr. Edinburgh, 1762. 8°. . . . 11348
Universal. S. G. Goodrich. Illust. New York, 1857. 2 v. 4°. .
Universal. J. Von Müller. Tr. London, 1818. 3 v. 8°. . . 7369
Universal. F. M. Voltaire. Tr. Edinburgh, 1777. 4 v. 12°. . 7144
Use and Study of. W. T. McCullagh. Dublin, 1842. 8°. . . 12050
Hitchcock, D. Poetical Dictionary. Lenox, 1808. 12°. 2500
Hitchcock, E. Dyspepsy, Forestalled and Resisted. Amherst, 1831. 8°. 3395
The same. Amherst, 1830. 12°. 4532
Elementary Geology. New York, 1841. 12°. 6073
The same. New York, 1856. 12°. 6056
Religion of Geology. Boston, 1851. 12°. 6058
Religious Truth Illustrated from Science. Boston, 1857. 12°. . 6069
Hoadley, C. J. Records of the New Haven Colony, from 1638 to 1649. Hartford, 1857. 8°. 7240
from 1653 to 1665. Hartford, 1858. 8°. 7241
Hoary Head. J. Abbott. Boston, 1838. 18°. 1695
Hobart, J. H. (Bp.) Apology for Apostolic Order. New York, 1844. 12°. 5685
Works, with Memoirs. W. Berrian. New York, 1833. 3 v. 8°. . 5111
Hobart, N. Life of E. Swedenborg. Boston, 1845. 12°. 8044
Hobbes, T. English Works. (vol. 2 missing.) London, 1839, 40. 6 v. 8°. 6310
Hobomok, a Tale of Early Times. Mrs. S. M. Child. Boston, 1824. 12°. 1653
Hochelaga, or Eng. in the New World. E. Warburton. N. Y. 1846. 12°. 9618
Hodge, A., Trial of, for Murder of his Slave Prosper. Middlet'n, 1812. 12° 11885
Hodge, C. History of Presbyter. Church of U. S. Philadelphia, 1839. 8°. 5585
Hodgson, A. Remarks during a Journey through North America, in 1819 and 1821. New York, 1822. 8°. 9726
Hodgson, R. Life of B. Porteus. New York, 1811. 13° 8076
Hoffman, C. F. Greyslaer. New York, 1840. 2 v. 12°. . . . 1497
Life of J. Liesler. Boston, 1844. 12°. 8055

Hofland, Mrs. A Father as he should be, a Novel. Phil. 1816. 2 v. 12°. 1483
Hogg, J. Familiar Anecdotes of Scott, and Life, by S. D. Bloodgood. New York, 1834. 12°. 8329
The same. 8468
Poetical Works. New York, 1825. 2 v. 18°. 2765
Queen's Wake. New York, 1818. 18°. 2746
Songs. New York, 1832. 12°. 2270
The Brownie of Bodsbeck, and other Tales. New York, 1818. 12°. 925
Wars of Montrose. Phil. 1836. 2 v. 12°. 1447
Holberg, L. Autobiography. Trans. London, 1827. 16°. 7491
Holdich, J. Life of W. Fisk. New York, 1842. 8°. 7868
Holidays Abroad. Mrs. Kirkland. New York, 1849. 2 v. 12°. . . . 8910
Holland, Government of. L. Bonaparte. Trans. London, 1820. 3 v. 8°. 7662
History of. London, 1782. 2 v. 8°. 7073
Holland, J. Life and Ministry of J. Summerfield. New York, 1830. 8°. 8157
Present State of Manufactures in Metals. London, 1833–7. 3 v. 12°. 9966
Holland, Lady. Memoir of S. Smith. New York, 1855. 2 v. 12°. . 7998
Holland, W. M. Life and Polit. Opinions of M. Van Buren. Hart. 1835. 8°. 8290
The same. 8337
Hollister, G. H. Mount Hope, a Romance. New York, 1851. 12°. . . 558
Holmes, A. Life of E. Stiles. Boston, 1798. 12°. 8605
Annals of America from 1492 to 1826. Camb. 1829. 2 v. 8°. . 6986
Holmes, E. Life of J. C. W. A. Mozart. New York, 1846. 12°. . . 8415
Holmes, J. The Art of Rhetoric. London, 1755. 8°. 3296
Holmes, O. W. Astræa. Boston, 1850. 12°. 2330
Poems. Boston, 1836. 12°. 2333
Holstein, H. L. V. D. Memoirs of S. Bolivar. Boston, 1829. 8°. . . 8221
Holthaus, P. D. Wanderings of a Tailor. Tr. W. Howitt. Lond. 1844. 12°. 8724
Holy Land, Pilgrimage to. A. De Lamartine. Tr. Phil. 1835. 2 v. 12°. 8942
Holy Life, Great Examplar of. J. Taylor. London, 1835. 3 v. 12°. . 5795
Holy Living and Dying. J. Taylor. London, 1850. 12°. . . . 5447
Holy Spirit, Divinity and Operations of. London, 1835. 12°. . . 5790
Home, or Family Cares and Joys. F. Bremer. New York, 1843. 8°. . 8
See also Bremer, Fredrika.
Education. I. Taylor. New York, 1838. 12°. 3295
as Found. J. F. Cooper. Philadelphia, 1841. 12°. . . . 1262
Missionary. A. Peters. vol. 1. New York, 1829. 8°. . . 2245
Scenes and Heart Studies. G. Aguilar. New York, 1853. 12°. . 1200
the School and the Church. vol. 1. Philadelphia, 1850. . . 2248
and Social Philosophy. C. Dickens. New York, 1852. 2 v. 12°. 1188
Homerica Clavis. 12°. 1906
Homerus. Ilias. Lipsiæ, 1839. 16°. 10335
The same. New York, 1830. 16°. 11295
The same. Græce et Latine. Ed. S. Clarke. New York, 1826. 2 v. 8°. 1877
The same, in French. 2 v. 11486
The same. Tr. A. Pope. Baltimore, 1812. 24°. . . . 2727
The same. New York, 1812. 2 v. 18°. 2728

Homerus. Ilias. 1797. 2 v. 18°. 2714
The same. New York, 1825. 2 v. 24°. 2790
The same. Philadelphia, 1822. 2 v. 18°. 2152
The same. Tr. W. Cowper. Philadelphia, 1838. 2 v. 16°. 2079
The same. Tr. W. Munford. Boston, 1846. 2 v. 8°. . . 1821
Illustrations of, by J. Flaxman. Folio.
and Odyssea. Tr. A. Pope. New York, 1840. 3 v. 12°. . . 5289
Duplicate of vol. 2. New York, 1836. 16°. . . . 8757
Odyssea. Lipsiæ, 1839. 16°. 10336
The same. Tr. W. Cowper. London, 1854. 2 v. 12°. . 5471
The same. New York, 1830. 8°. 1927
The same. Tr. A. Pope. Philadelphia, 1822. 18°. . . 2154
Homer, W. B. Memoir and Writings. E. A. Park. Andover, 1842. 12°. 5390
Homes Abroad, a Tale. Harriet Martineau. Boston, 1833. 18°. . . 1673
The same. 1675
Homeward Bound. J. F. Cooper. Philadelphia, 1838. 2 v. 12°. . . 1267
The same. Philadelphia, 1841. 12°. 1261
Homonyms, French. J. Martin. New York, 1807. 12°. . . . 3010
Hone, W. Every-Day Book. vol. 3. London, 1838. 8°. . . . 9722
The Year-Book of Recreation and Information. London, 1833. 8°. 9723
Honeywood, St. J. Poems. New York, 1801. 12°. 2499
Honor O'Hara, a Tale. Anna M. Porter. New York, 1827. 2 v. 12°. . 1594
Hood, T. Hood's Own, with Comic Illustrations. New York, 1852. 12°. 1671
Tylney Hall. New York, 1835. 12°. 1250
Up the Rhine. New York, 1852. 12°. 1191
Second series. 1192
Whimsicalities. New York, 1852. 12°. 1193
Hook, T. Births, Deaths, and Marriages. Paris, 1839. 8°. . . . 11683
Pascal Bruno. Philadelphia, 1839. 12°. 1573
Hooke, N. Roman History. London, 1825. 3 v. 8°. 6732
The same. London, 1766. 11 v. 8°. . . . . , . 7651
Hooker, E. W. Memoir of Mrs. S. L. Smith. Boston, 1839. 12°. . . 8357
Hooker, R. Works, with Life. I. Walton. London, 1821. 3 v. 8°. . 5363
Hooker, W. Lessons from Medical Delusions. New York, 1850. 12°. . . 3308
Physician and Patient. New York, 1849. 12°. 3004
Hooper, J. Writings. London. 12°. 5659
Hooper, Lucy. Poetical Remains, with Mem. J. Kesee. N. Y. 1845. 12°. 1933
Hope Leslie. Miss C. M. Sedgewick. New York, 1827. 2 v. 12°. . . 1651
Hope, T. Anastasius. New York, 1832. 2 v. 12°. 1019
Hopkins, J. H. History of the Confessional. N. Y. 1850. 12°. . . 477
Hopkins, S. Reminiscences. W. Patten. New York, 1843. 16°. . . 8458
Hopkins, W. Treatise on Trigonometry, Calculus, Alg. &c. Lon. 1833. 8°. 5096
Hopkinson, F. Misscellaneous Essays and Writings. Phil. 1792. 3 v. 8°. 462
Horace in London, or Imitation of the Odes of Horace. Bost. 1813. 16°. 1694
Horatius, Q. F. Opera. Vinaria, 1821. 12°. 2501
Opera. Delphin. Ed. Philadelphia, 1826. 8°. 1887
The same. Philadelphia, 1804. 8°. 1887
The same. Tr. P. Francis. New York, 1840. 2 v. 12°. . 5275

Horatius, Q. F. Opera. Duplicate of vol. 2. New York, 1835. 16°. . 8774
Horne, G. Letters on Infidelity. Oxford, 1784. 12°. 6213
Commentary on the Book of Psalms. New York, 1814. 8°. . . 5357
The same, with Memoir by W. Jones. Lond. 1836. 3 v. 12°. 5800
Horne, M. Letters on Missions. Andover, 1815. 18°. 4611
Horne, R. H. New Spirit of the Age. New York, 1844. 12°. . . . 8369
Horne, T. H. Introduction to the Study of the Bible. N. Y. 1833. 12°. 6153
The same. Boston, 1827. 12°. 6118
Horner, F. Memoir and Corresp. L. Horner. Abridged. Edin. 1849. 12°. 8356
Horry, P. Life of Francis Marion. Philadelphia, 1831. 12°. . . . 8388
Horse. History of. W. C. L. Martin. London, 1845. 16°. . . . 6894
Treatise on. W. Youatt. London, 1842. 12°. 5937
Horse Shoe Robinson. J. P. Kennedy. Philadelphia, 1836. 2 v. 12°. . 1617
Horsley, S. Sermons. Philadelphia, 1816. 8°. 6393
Horton, R. G. Life of J. Buchanan. New York, 1856. 12°. . . , 8651
Hot Corn; Life Scenes in New York. S. Robinson. N. Y. 1854. 12°. . 574
House I Live in, or the Human Body. W. A. Alcott. Boston, 1837. 12°. 4893
House of Commons, Random Recollections of. R. Grant. Phil. 1836. 12°. 8663
House of Seven Gables. N. Hawthorne. Boston, 1851. 12°. . . 1248
Household Words. Ed. C. Dickens. London, 1850–9. 8 v. 8°. . . 2208
Housekeeper, Recollections of a. Mrs. C. Packard. N. Y. 1838. 18°. . 4975
Houssaye, A. Men and Women of the 18th Century. N. Y. 1852. 2 v. 12°. 8299
Philosophers and Actresses. New York, 1852. 2 v. 12°. . . 506
Houston, Mrs. Texas and the Gulf of Mexico. Philadelphia, 1845. 16°. 9324
Houston, S. Life. Illustrated. (Two copies.) New York, 1855. 12°. . 8342
How, T. Y. Letters to S. Miller on Christian Ministry. Utica, 1808. 8°. 6429
How to Observe. Harriet Martineau. New York, 1838. 12°. . . . 4887
Howadji, Nile, Notes of a. G. W. Curtis. New York, 1851. 12°. . . 8902
in Syria. G. W. Curtis. New York, 1852. 12°. 8903
Howard, E. Memoirs of Sir S. Smith. London, 1839. 2 v. 8°. . . 8143
Outward Bound. New York, 1839. 2 v. 12°. 1265
Howard, H. Select Poems, with Life. Philadelphia, 1819. 18°. . . 2118
Howard, H. R. Life and Adventures of V. A. Stewart. N. Y. 1836. 12°. 8334
Howe, Admiral R. Life. J. Barrow. London, 1838. 8°. . . . 7897
Howe, H. Historical Collections of Virginia. Charleston, 1845. 8°. . 7250
Historical Collections of Ohio. Cincinnati, 1850. 8°. . . . 7606
Howe, J. Theol. Treatises, with a Memoir. T. Taylor. Lond. 1835. 12°. 5793
Works, with Life. E. Calamy. New York, 1838. 2 v. 4°. . . 5005
Howe, S. G. Historical Sketches of the Greek Revolution. N. Y. 1828. 8°. 6796
The same. 7099
Howison, J. The European Colonies viewed in their Condition, Social, Moral, &c. London, 1834. 2 v. 8°. 6679
Howison, R. R. Hist. of Virginia to the Present Time. Phil. 1846. 2 v. 8°. 7592
Howitt, Mary. Ballads, and other Poems. New York, 1848. 12°. . . 2351
Birds and Flowers. Boston, 1839. 18°. 2374
Heir of Wast-Wayland. New York, 1851. 12°. 549
Strive and Thrive. Boston, 1840. 18°. 1714
Wood Leighton, or a Year in the Country. Phil. 1837. 12°. . 1210

Howitt, R. Impressions of Australia Felix. London, 1845. 12°. . . . 9028
Howitt, W. Colonization and Christianity. London, 1838. 8°. . . . 5635
Country Year-Book. New York, 1850. 12°. 783
German Experiences. London, 1844. 12°. 8725
History of Priestcraft in all Ages. London, 1853. 12°. . . 5666
The same. London, 1845. 12°. 6184
Homes of Poets. New York, 1847. 2 v. 12°. 9558
Land, Labor, and Gold. (Australia.) Boston, 1855. 2 v. 12°. . 9636
Rural Life in England. London, 1840. 8°. 9449
Traditions of the Most Ancient Times. London, 1839. 2 v. 12°. . 6775
Visits to Remark. Places, Old Halls, Battle Fields, &c. Phil. '41. 12°. 9564
Hubbard, F. M. Life of W. R. Davie. Boston, 1848. 12°. . . . 8067
Huber, F. Natural History of Bees. London, 1841. 12°. . . . 10156
Huber, V. A. Eng. Universities. Tr. F. W. Newman. Lon. 1843. 3 v. 8°. 62
Huc, M. Journey to Tartary, China, &c., 1844–6. Tr. N. Y. '52. 2 v. 12°. 9024
The same. Tr. W. Hazlitt. London, 1856. 12°. . . 8894
Journey through the Chinese Empire. New York, 1857. 2 v. 12°. 9805
Hudibras. S. Butler. Edinburgh, 1799. 18°. 2486
See also Butler, S.
Hudson, C. F. Doctrines of Future Life. Boston, 1858. 12°. . . . 5719
Hudson, H., Life of. H. R. Cleveland. Boston, 1838. 12°. . . . 8052
Hudson, H. N. Lectures on Shakspeare. New York, 1848. 2 v. 12°. . 807
Hudson River and Vicinity, Letters about, 1835, 6. F. Hunt. New York,
1836. 16°. 9311
Hughes, T. S. Life of T. Sherlock, Notes on Sermons, &c. Lon. 1830. 12°. 5752
Hugo, V. The Rhine. Tr. New York, 1845. 12°. 9842
The Slave King. Philadelphia, 1833. 12°. 1642
Hugenot, The. G. P. R. James. New York, 1839. 2 v. 12°. . . . 1521
The same. 1620
Hugenots, History of the, 1598–1838. W. S. Browning. Lond. 1839. 8°. 5589
in France and America. Mrs. H. Lee. Cambridge, 1843. 2 v. 12°. 6180
Hull, W. Defense of Himself. Boston, 1814. 12°. 10788
Life. Mrs. M. Campbell. New York, 1848. 8°. 7812
Mem. of the Campaign of the N. W. Army in 1812. Bost. 1824. 8°. 11308
Hulsean Lectures. R. C. Trench. Philadelphia, 1856. 12°. . . . 6468
Human Character, Book of. C. Birch. London, 1834. 12°. . . . 5805
Nature, Dignity of. J. Burgh. 8°. 3289
Nature, Discourses on. T. Boston. Air, 1797. 12°. . . . 6609
Responsibility, Limitations of. F. Wayland. Boston, 1838. 12°. . 6111
Humboldt, A. von. Ancient Inhabitants of Amer. Lond. 1814. 2 v. 8°. 9507
Cuba. Tr. New York, 1856. 12°. 8968
Political Essay on New Spain. Tr. New York, 1811. 2 v. 8°. . 9189
Travels to the Equinoctial Regions of the New Continent, 1799–1804.
Tr. Philadelphia, 1815. 8°. 9169
Travels and Researches. W. Macgillivray. New York, 1840. 12°. 5870
Views of Nature. London, 1850. 12°. 5487
Hume, D. Autobiography. London, 1826. 16°. 7481
The same. London, 1829. 16°. 7746

Hume, D. Essays and Treatises. Edinburgh, 1800. 8°. 124
History of England. See England.
Life and Correspondence. J. H. Burton. Edin. 1846. 2 v. 8°. . 7869
Philosophical Essays, with Life. T. Ewell. George. 1817. 2 v. 8°. 122
Philosophical Works. Edinburgh, 1826. 4 v. 8°. 6333

Vol. 1. Life; Letter from Adam Smith to Wm. Strachan; Controversy between Hume and Rousseau; Scotticisms; The Understanding.
2. The Passions; Morals.
3. Essays, Moral, Political, and Literary.
4. An Inquiry concerning the Understanding; An Inquiry concerning Morals; Appendix; The Natural History of Religion; Additional Essays.

Humor and Pathos. G. R. W. Baxter. London, 1842. 12°. . . . 1127
Humphrey, H. Letters to a Son in the Ministry. Boston, 1843. 12°. . 4861
The same. New York, 1842. 12°. 6469
Miscellaneous Discourses and Reviews. Amherst, 1834. 12°. . 831
The same. 4586
Tour in Europe, 1835. Amherst, 1838. 2 v. 12°. 9003
The same. New York, 1838. 2 v. 12°. 9037
Humphrey Clinker. T. Smollett. London, 1808. 12°. 1376
Humphreys, D. Letters con'g the Serpent of the Ocean. N. Y. 1817. 12°. 11881
Miscellaneous Works. New York, 1790. 8°. 1917
Hungary, History of. Life of L. Kossuth. London, 1854. 12°. . . 5432
in 1851. C. L. Brace. New York, 1852. 12°. 7103
Revolution in. W. H. Stiles. New York, 1852. 8°. . . . 9412
and Transylvania, Condition of. J. Paget. London, 1839. 2 v. 8°. 6654
Hunt, F. Letters about the Hudson River. New York, 1836. 18°. . . 9311
Hunt, J., and others. The Reflector, a Col. of Essays. Lon. 1810. 2 v. 8°. 2971
Hunt, L. (Ed.) Beaumont and Fletcher. Selections. Lond. 1855. 12°. . 5169
Book for a Corner. New York, 1852. 12°. 1187
Byron and some of his Contemporaries. London, 1828. 2 v. 8°. . 8145
(Editor.) Imagination and Fancy. New York, 1845. 12°. . . 2410
The same. 9844
Indicator. New York, 1845. 12°. 523
Italian Poets, Stories from and Notices of. New York, 1846. 12°. 1170
The same. 9850
Men, Women and Books. New York, 1847. 2 v. 12°. . . . 474
Poetical Works. London, 1832. 8°. 1841
Poetry of Science. Boston, 1850. 18°. 6059
Hunter, H. Sacred Biog., or Hist. of the Patriarchs. Bost. 1794. 3 v. 8°. 8528
Hunter, J. D. Manners and Cust. of Several Indian Tribes. Phil. 1823. 8°. 9157
Hunter, T. Reflections on Chesterfield's Letters. London, 1777. 8°. . 432
Huntingdon, Countess of. Life and Times. London, 1844. 2 v. 8°. . 7836
Huntington, F. D. Sermons for the People. Boston, 1856. 12°. . . 5720
Huntington, J. Calvinism Improved. London, 1796. 8°. . . . 5646
Hurd, Bishop, R. Letters on Chivalry and Romance. Lond. 1762. 12°. 4871
Moral and Political Dialogues. London, 1761. 3 v. 12°. . . 3368

Hurd. Bishop R. Works. London, 1811. 8 v. 8°. 6294

Vol. 1. Critical Notes.
2. Critical Dissertations.
Vol. 3-4. Moral and Political Dialogues.
5-8. Theological Works.

Hurdis, J. Lectures on Poetry. Oxford, 1797. 4°. 1803
Huskisson, W. Speeches, with Memoir. London, 1831. 3 v. 8°. . . 10640
Hutcheson, F. Intro. to Moral Philosophy. Tr. Glasgow, 1772. 2 v. 16°. 4295
Hutchinson, Anne, Life of. G. E. Ellis. Boston, 1845. 12°. . . . 8058
Hutchinson, Lucy. Life of Col. J. Hutchinson. London, 1808. 4°. . . 7796
The same, with Siege of Lathom House. London, 1846. 12°. 5134
Hutchinson, T. History of Mass., from 1620–1750. Salem, 1795. 2 v. 8°. 6755
Hutton, Catharine. Oakwood Hall. Philadelphia, 1819. 2 v. 12°. . 319
Hutton's "Book of Nature Laid Open." J. L. Blake. Boston, 1833. 12°. 6100
Hydropathy, Hand-Book of. J. Shew. New York, 1844. 12°. . . 4521
Hydraulics, &c. T. Ewbank. New York, 1847. 8°. 5945
Hydrostatics and Pneumatics, Treatise on. D. Lardner. Lond. 1836. 12°. 9961
The same. Philadelphia, 1832. 12°. 5841
Hieroglyphics, Sys. of Champollion. J. G. H. Greppo. Tr. Bost. 1830. 12°. 859
Hyperion, a Romance. H. W. Longfellow. Boston, 1853. 12°. . . 1245

I.

Iamblichus. Life of Pythagoras. Tr. T. Taylor. London, 1818. 8°. . 8164
Iceland and Lapland, a Winter in. A. Dillon. London, 1840. 2 v. 12°. . 9543
Greenland and the Faroe Islands, Hist. &c., of. N. Y. 1841. 12°. . 5907
Journey to. I. Pfeiffer. Tr. New York, 1852. 12°. 9000
Letters on. J. Banks and others. London, 1780. 8°. . . . 9455
Residence in, in 1814, 15. E. Henderson. Boston, 1831. 12°. . 8714
Icelandic Poetry. Trans. Bristol, 1797. 8°. 1867
Ida May. Mary Langdon. Boston, 1855. 12°. 1175
Idler, The. S. Johnson. London, 1823. 12°. 3682
Ignorance, Popular, Evils of. Boston, 1821. 12°. 3905
Iliad. See Homerus.
Illuminism, Existence and Danger of. S. Payson. Charleston, 1802. 12°. 6507
Illustrations of Genius. H. Giles. Boston, 1854. 12°. 879
Illustrious Men, Biography of. T. B. Macaulay. Boston, 1857. 12°. . 830
Imaginary Conversations. W. S. Landor. London, 1826. 3 v. 8°. . . 77
Second series. London, 1829. 2 v. 8°. 80
Imagination, Pleasures of, a Poem. M. Akenside. New York, 1819. 16°. 3058
Imagination and Fancy. Ed. L. Hunt. New York, 1845. 12°. . . . 2410
The same. 9844
Imitation of Christ. T. A Kempis. New York, 1846. 12°. 5670
Imitations of Celebrated Authors. W. Hazlitt and others. Lond. 1844. 8°. 467
Imlay, G. Topography of the West Territory of N. Amer. Lond. 1792. 8°. 9489
Immola, a Tragedy. 1835. 12°. 2414
Immortality, a Poem. P. Robinson. New York, 1846. 12°. . . 2365
Inchbald, Mrs. (Editress.) British Theatre. London. 9 v. 16°. . . 2459
Mourning Ring. New York, 1821. 12°. 1348

Inchiquin, the Jesuit's, Letters. C. J. Ingersoll. New York, 1810. 8°. . 9485
Remarks on the Review of. T. Dwight. Boston, 1815. 8°. . 10082
Incognito, or Sins and Peccadilloes. T. D. Trueba. N. Y. 1831. 2 v. 12°. 257
Independent Whig, The, or a Defence of Prim. Christianity. Hart. 1816. 8°. 10705
The same. Hartford, 1816. 2 v. 8°. 10726
India, Ancient and Modern, Account of. D. O. Allen. Boston, 1856. 8°. 7543
Ancient, Historical Disquisition on. W. Robertson. Dub. 1791. 8°. 9490
British, Decline of Hindooism, and Prog. of Christ'y., with Remarks on Manners, Customs, &c. W. Campbell. Lond. 1839. 8°. . 9476
British, Hist. and Destiny of. H. Murray, etc. N. Y. 1840. 3 v. 12°. 5863
The same. New York, 1833. 3 v. 16°. 6264
British, History of. London, 1781. 8°. 7052
British, History of. J. Mills. London, 1826. 6 v. 8°. . . . 7345
China, and Japan, a Visit to. B. Taylor. New York, 1855. 12°. 9562
Description of. J. Conder. London. 2 v. 16°. 9661
Letters from, in 1828–31. V. Jacquemont. Tr. Lond. 1835. 2 v. 12°. 9291
People of, Description of. J. A. Dubois. Tr. Phil. 1818. 2 v. 8°. 9150
Present Polit cal State of. A. F. Tytler. London, 1815. 2 v. 8°. . 9512
Upper, Journey Through. R. Heber. Philadelphia, 1829. 2 v. 12°. 8992
Indicator. L. Hunt. New York, 1845. 12°. 523
Indian Biography. B. B. Thatcher. New York, 1832. 2 v. 16°. . . 6641
The same. New York, 1840. 2 v. 12°. 5861
Nations of Canada, The Five, Hist. of. C. Colden. Lond. 1750. 12°. 6784
Sketches. J. T. Irving, Jr. Philadelphia, 1835. 2 v. 12°. . . 9817
Tribes, Several, Manners and Cus. of. J. D. Hunter. Phil. 1823. 8°. 9157
Wars, Philip's War, &c. S. G. Drake. Exeter, 1834. 12°. . . 6834
Wars, with Philip's War. T. Church. Hartford. 8°. . . . 7273
Wars of the United States. W. V. Moore. Philadelphia, 1840. 12°. 6788
Indians, N. Amer., Manners. Cust., &c., of. G. Catlin. N. Y. 1841. 2 v. 8°. 9071
North American, Mental Characteristics, &c., of. H. R. Schoolcraft. New York, 1839. 2 v. 12°. 10137
North American, History of. Buffalo, 1851. 8°. 9409
of Connecticut, Hist. of the. J. W. DeForest. Hartford, 1851. 12°. 7367
of the United States, Tour among in 1820. J. Morse. N. H. 1822. 8°. 10056
Speeches on the Bill for the Removal of. Boston, 1830. 12°. . 11122
Indies, West, Emancipation in. J. A. Thome and J. H. Kimball. (Two copies.) New York, 1838. 12°. 8969
East and West, History of European Settlements in. W. T. Raynal. Tr. Edinburgh, 1782. 6 v. 12°. 7139
East, History of. London, 1781. 4 v. 8°. 7053
East, History of. R. M. Martin. London, 1837. 16°. . . . 5816
West, Chronological History of. T. Southey. Lond. 1827. 3 v. 8°. 6681
West, History of. B. Edwards. Dublin, 1793. 2 v. 8°. . . 6763
West, History of. R. M. Martin. London, 1836. 2 v. 12°. . . . 5817
West and Florida, Winter in. New York, 1839. 12°. . . 8824
Inductive Sciences, Philosophy of. W. Whewell. London, 1840. 2 v. 8°. 410
History of. W. Whewell. London, 1837. 3 v. 8°. . . . 412
Industry of All Nations, Encyclopædia of. C. Knight. London, 1851. 8°. 8832

Industry of Nations, Treatise on. J. S. Eisdell. London, 1839. 2 v. 8°. 10668
Infidel, The, or Fall of Mexico. R. M. Bird. Philadelphia, 1835. 2 v. 12°. 1525
The same. 1533
Infidelity, Converts from. A. Crichton. Edinburgh, 1827. 2 v. 16°. . 9991
Difficulties of. G. S. Faber. Philadelphia, 1829. 12°. . . 5633
Infidelity, Letters on. G. Horne. Oxford, 1784. 12°. 6213
Refuted. C. Babbage. Philadelphia, 1841. 8°. 6386
Sermons on. A. Thompson. New York, 1833. 16°. 6572
Ingersoll, C. J. History of the Second War between the United States and Great Britain. vol. 1. Philadelphia, 1845. 8°. . . 7538
Inchiquin, the Jesuit's Letters. New York, 1810. 8°. 9485
Ingersoll, E. Abridgment of the Acts of Congress. Philadelphia, 1825. 8°. 10065
Inglis, H. D. Spain in 1830. London, 1831. 2 v. 8°. 9093
Travels in Norway, Sweden and Denmark. Edinburgh, 1829. 16°. 10014
South-West. New York, 1835. 2 v. 12°. . . . , . . 9625
Innisfoyle, Abbey, a Tale. D. I. Moriarty. London, 1840. 12°. . . 1492
Inquisicion de Espana, Historia Critica de la. J. A. Llorente. (Abridged.) Ed. R. Buron. Paris, 1823. 2 v. 16° 6849
Inquisition, dealings with. G. Achilli. New York, 1851. 12°. . . 5404
of Spain, Hist. of. J. A. Llorente. Tr. Abridg. Lond. 1826. 8°. 6716
Imprisonment in the Dungeons of, at Madrid. Don Juan Von Hulen. New York, 1828. 8°. 9418
Insane, Report of Connecticut Retreat for the. Hartford, 1831. 8°. . 10089
Insect Architecture. J. Rennie. London, 1845. 2 v. 16°. 7176
The same. Boston, 1830. 16°. 6198
Miscellanies. Boston, 1832. 12°. 6206
Transformations. Boston, 1831. 12°. 6200
Insects, Modern Classifications of. J. O. Westwood. London, 1839. 8°. 10134
Natural History of. New York, 1830. 16°. 6636
The same. New York, 1831. 16°. 8759
The same, with second series. New York, 1840. 2 v. 12°. 5510
of New England, Treatise on the. T. W. Harris. Camb. 1842. 8°. 10103
Instinct, Dialogues on. H. Brougham. London, 1844. 16°. 7196
Instruction, Manual of. W. Russell. Boston, 1826. 12°. 4536
Insubordination and other Tales. T. S. Arthur. Philadelphia, 1844. 8°. . 18
Intellectual and Active Powers of Man. T. Reid. London, 1827. 8°. . 6371
The same. vol. 1. Philadelphia, 1793. 8°. 6405
Powers, Inquiries concerning the. J. Abercrombie. N. Y. 1841. 18°. 5540
Qualities, Transmission of. New York, 1844. 12°. 3354
System of the Universe. R. Cudworth. Andover, 1837. 2 v. 8°. 6308
Intemperance, Prize Essay on. R. B. Grindrod. New York, 1840. 12°. 514
Six Sermons on. L. Beecher. Boston, 1830. 16°. 4288
Intemperate, Plea for the. D. M. Reese. New York, 1814. 18°. . . 4964
Intermarriage. A. Walker. New York, 1839. 12°. 3376
Interior, or Hidden Life. T. C. Upham. Boston, 1845. 12°. 5416
Inventions and Discov., Hist. of. J. Beckmann. Tr. Lond. 1817. 4 v. 8°. 762
The same. London, 1846. 2 v. 12°. 5161
Ion, a Tragedy. T. N. Talfourd. New York, 1837. 12°. 2058

I Promessi Sposi. Trans. Washington, 1834. 8°. 23
Irby, C. L. and J. Mangles. Travels in Egypt, Nubia, Syria and the Holy Land. London, 1844. 12°. 9286
Ireland, a Tale. Miss H. Martineau. Boston, 1833. 16°. . . . 10025
Description of. J. G. Kohl. New York, 1844. 8°. . . . 9090
History of. London, 1784. 8°. 7088
History of. Abbé MacGeoghegan. Trans. New York. 4°. . 7806
History of. T. Moore. London, 1836–40. 3 v. 12°. . . . 9910
History of. W. C. Taylor. New York, 1833. 2 v. 16°. . . 6262
The same. New York, 1841. 2 v. 12°. 5867
Legends and Stories of. S. Lover. First and second series. London, 1837. 2 v. 16°. 1640
Repeal of the Union. R. L. Shiel. London, 1845. 8°. . . 10711
Social, Political, and Religious. G. de Beaumont. Ed. W. C. Taylor. London, 1839. 2 v. 12°. 9552
State of, in 1797. T. L. O'Beirne. London, 1799. 8°. . . . 5351
The Stranger in. J. Carr. New York, 1807. 8°. . . . 8915
Trials in, for High Treason. Baltimore, 1804. 8°. . . . 10767
Views of, Moral, Polit. and Relig. J. O'Driscol. Lond. 1823. 2 v. 8°. 9509
Worthies of. R. Ryan. London, 1821. 2 v. 8°. 8168
Iriarte, D. T. de Fabulas. Literarias. 16°. 2471
Irish, Confederates, and the Rebell. of 1798. H. M. Field. N. Y. 1851. 12°. 7419
Observations on the Character, Customs, &c. of the. D. Dewar. London, 1812. 8°. 9511
Eloquence, Spec. of, with Biog. Notices. C. Phillips. N. Y. 1820. 8°. 10718
Girl and other Poems. Mrs. S. Ellis. New York, 1844. 12°. . 1941
Rebellion in 1798. Cambridge. 12°. 7445
Irishmen, The United. Their Lives and Times. R. R. Madden. Philadelphia, 1842. 2 v. 12°. 8664
Third series. Dublin, 1846. 3 v. 8°. 7990
Iron Horse and Yankee Land. D. March. Hartford, 1840. 12°. . . 2218
Iroquois, Notes on. H. R. Schoolcraft. Albany, 1847. 8°. . . . 9372
Irving, D. Lives of Scotish Writers. Edinburgh, 1839. 2 v. 12°. . . 8252
The same. 8627
Irving, Edward. Orations. New York, 1825. 8°. 6431
Orations, Lectures, and Sermons. New York, 1825. 8°. . . 10483
Irving, J. T. Indian Sketches. Philadelphia, 1835. 2 v. 12°. . . . 9817
Irving, T. Conquest of Florida, by H. De Soto. Phil. 1835. 12°. . . 6790
Irving, W. Adventures of Capt. Bonneville. New York, 1851. 12°. . 539
The Alhambra. Philadelphia, 1832. 2 v. 12°. 991
The same. New York, 1851. 12°. 542
Astoria. Philadelphia, 1836. 2 v. 8°. 9187
The same. New York, 1851. 12°. 535
Bracebridge Hall. New York, 1822. 2 v. 12°. 923
The same. New York, 1850. 12°. 538
Conquest of Granada. New York, 1829. 2 v. 12°. 6806
The same. New York, 1851. 12°. 537
Crayon Miscellany. New York, 1851. 12°. 540

Irving, W. Knickerbocker's History of New York. N. Y. 1826. 2 v. 12. 1164
The same. New York, 1851. 12°. 544
The same. Philadelphia, 1835. 12°. 545
The same. Philadelphia, 1819. 2 v. 12°. 7131
Life and Voyages of Columbus. New York, 1831. 2 v. 8°. . . 7894
The same. New York, 1838. 3 v. 8°. 7933
The same, revised. New York, 1851. 3 v. 12°. . . . 532
Life of O. Goldsmith, with Select Writings. N. Y. 1840. 2 v. 12°. 5894
The same. New York, 1851. 12°. 536
Life of Washington. New York, 1856–9. 5 v. 12°. . . . 8657
Mahomet and his Successors. New York, 1859. 2 v. 12°. . . 529
Rocky Mountains, or Scenes in the Far West. Phil. 1837. 2 v. 12°. 8983
The Sketch Book. New York, 1819. 8°. 1163
The same. New York, 1851. 12°. 541
Tales of a Traveller. New York, 1825. 2 v. 12°. 1166
The same. New York, 1851. 12°. 531
Voyages of the Companions of Columbus. Phil. 1831. 8°. . . 8222
Wolfert's Roost. New York, 1855. 12°. 543
and J. K. Paulding. Salmagundi. New York, 1835. 2 v. 12°. . 1304
Second series. 2 v. 1306
Isaeus. Orationes. Lipsiæ, 1829. 16°. 10348
Isaiah, New Translation, with Notes. R. Lowth. London, 1833. 8°. . 5110
Notes on, with New Translation. A. Barnes. Bost. 1840. 3 v. 8°. 5017
Island, The. Byron, G. G. (Lord.) New York, 1823. 16°. . . . 3083
Isocrates. Orationes et Epistolæ. Lipsiæ, 1829. 16°. 10334
Panegyrics of, in Greek and Latin. Glasguae, 1778. 12°. . . 4856
Israel, the Land of. A. Keith. New York, 1844. 12°. 9537
Israel Potter, his Fifty Years' Exile. H. Melville. N. Y. 1855. 12°. . 1149
Israelites, Ancient, Manners of. C. Fleury. Tr. A. Clarke. Lon. 1836. 12°. 6459
Italian Novelists, Selected and Translated. T. Roscoe. Lon. 1836. 3 v. 12°. 1324
Painters. Mrs. A. Jameson. London, 1845. 2 v. 16°. . . . 6892
Poets, Stories from the, and Notices of. L. Hunt. N. Y. 1846. 12°. 9850
The same. 1170
Poets, Lives of the. H. Stebbings. London, 1831. 3 v. 12°. . 8707
Republics, History of the. J. C. L. DeSismondi. Lond. 1832. 12°. 9887
The same. Philadelphia, 1832. 12°. 5839
Italy. Lady S. Morgan. New York, 1821. 2 v. 8°. 9161
Antiquities, Arts and Letters of. J. Forsyth. Boston, 1818. 8°. . 9444
The same. 9156
Compendious History of. Philadelphia, 1839. 12°. 5889
Classical Tour through, in 1802. J. C. Eustace. Phil. 1816 2 v. 8°. 9152
The same. London, 1841. 3 v. 12°. 9532
Description of. J. Conder. London, 1839. 3 v. 16°. . . . 9663
England and America, Recollections of. Philadelphia, 1816. 8°. . 9158
History of. G. Procter. London, 1844. 8°. 7540
History of the Reformation in. T. M'Crie. London, 1833. 8°. . 5591
Idler in. Countess of Blessington. Paris, 1839. 8°. . . . 9453
and its Inhabitants, Observations on. Tr. T. Nugent. Lon. 1769. 8°. 9787

Italy and the Italian Islands, Hist. of. W. Spalding. N. Y. 1842. 3 v. 12°. 5923
and Italian Literature. C. Herbert. London, 1835. 12°. . . . 492
and the Italians. F. Von Raumer. London, 1840. 2 v. 12°. . . 9548
Journal of a Tour in, in 1821, by an American. N. Y. 1824. 8°. . 9170
Letters from. J. T. Headley. New York, 1846. 9599
Literary History of. F. V. Barbacovi. Tr. Edin. 1835. 12°. . 4882
Lives of Eminent Literary and Scientific Men of. Mrs. M. W. Shelley and others. Philadelphia, 1841. 2 v. 12°. 8004
Painting in, Hist. of. A. L. Lanzi. Tr. T. Roscoe. Lon. 1828. 6 v. 8°. 10122
The same. London, 1847. 3 v. 12°. 5122
a Poem. S. Rogers. Philadelphia, 1828. 18°. 2703
Remarks on Several Parts of, in 1701–3. J. Addison. Lon. 1705. 8°. 9820
and Sicily, Classic and Connoisseur in. G. W. D. Evans. London, 1835. 3 v. 8°. 9112
Spain and Portugal, Sketches of. W. Beckford. Phil. 1834. 2 v. 12°. 9293
Spain and Portugal, Lives of Eminent Literary and Scientific Men of. London, 1835–7. 3 v. 12°. 9951
and Switzerland, Tour Through. E. Griffin. N. Y. 1831. 2 v. 8°. 9474
The same. 9477
Travels in. T. Ducas. Ed. C. Mills. London, 1822. 2 v. 8°. . 9461
Venice, &c., History of. London, 1782. 4 v. 8°. 7068
View of Society and Manners in. J. Moore. Lond. 1783. 2 v. 8°. 9218

Ivanhoe. Sir W. Scott. Hartford, 1822. 8°. 1085
See also Sir W. Scott.

Ives, C. Poems. New Haven, 1843. 12°. 2338

Izard, R. Correspondence and Memoir. New York, 1844. 12°. . . 11141

J.

Jack Downing's Letters. C. A. Davis. New York, 1834. 12°. . . 1226
Life and Writings. C. A. Davis. Boston, 1834. 12°. . . . 964

Jack Ketch, Autobiography of. Philadelphia, 1835. 12°. . . . 684

Jacob Faithful. F. Marryatt. Philadelphia, 1834. 3 v. 12°. . . . 1327
The same. New York, 1835. 12°. 1250

Jacob Wrestling with the Angel. G. D. Krummacher. Tr. N. Y. 1841. 12°. 5745

Jacobs, F., and F. W. Döring. Latin Reader. New York, 1831. 12°. . 4850

Jackson, A. Memoirs. S. P. Waldo. Hartford, 1819. 12°. . . . 8091
The same. Hartford, 1818. 12°. 8397

Jacquemont, V. Letters from India in 1828–31. Tr. Lond. 1835. 2 v. 12°. 9291

Jacquerie, The. G. P. R. James. New York, 1842. 12°. 1398

Jahangueir, Emperor. Autobiography of. Tr. D. Price. Lond. 1829. 4°. 11259

Jahn, J. Biblical Archæology. Tr. T. C. Upham. New York, 1832. 8°. 5077

Jamaica in 1850. J. Bigelow. New York, 1851. 12°. 7434
Island of, Tour through, in 1823. C. R. Williams. Lond. 1827. 8°. 9102
its Past and Present State. J. M. Phillipo. Phil. 1843. 8°. . . 9419

James I, Court of. G. Goodman. London, 1839. 2 v. 8°. . . . 6672
Life. W. Harris. London, 1814. 8°. 8152

James II, History of the Reign of. C. J. Fox. Philadelphia, 1808. 8°. . 6911

James, G. P. R. Blanche of Navarre, a Play. New York, 1839. 12°. . 2409
Dark Scenes of History. New York, 1850. 12°. 1217
History of Charlemagne. New York, 1833. 16°. 6613
The same. New York, 1841. 12°. 5876
History of Chivalry. New York, 1840. 12°. 5524
The same. New York, 1831. 16°. 6625
The same. 6643
Life of Edward, the Black Prince. London, 1839. 2 v. 12°. . . 8402
Life of Henry IV. New York, 1850. 2 v. 12°. 8584
Life of Richard Cœur de Lion. New York, 1842. 2 v. 12°. . . 8675
The same. . . . . , . . 8677
The same. London, 1854. 2 v. 12°. 5199
Life and Times of Louis XIV. London, 1851. 2 v. 12°. 5197
Lives of De Retz, Colbert, DeWitt, and Marquis De Louvois. Philadelphia, 1837. 2 v. 12°. 8362
Lives of Eminent Foreign Statesmen. London, 1833–8. 4 v. 16°. 9941
Memoirs of Celebrated Women. Philadelphia, 1839. 2 v. 12°. . 8325
Novels. New York and London, 1839–48. 34 v. 8°. and 12°.

No. 1566, 7. Ancient Regime.
9. Arabella Stuart.
995, 6. Attila.
1527, 8. Charles Tyrrell. Two copies.
1280–2. Corse De Leon, or the Brigand.
1046, 7. Darnley.
1490, 1. The Desultory Man.
232, 3. Gentlemen of the Old School.
1042. Gipsy.
1387. The same.
1468, 9. Henry of Guise.
No. 1521. Huguenots.
1620. The same.
1398. The Jacquerie.
1009. John Marston Hall.
1579–80. The King's High Ways.
1015 6. Mary of Burgundy.
1044, 5. Philip Augustus.
1041, 2. Richelieu.
1479, 80. The same.
49. Whim and Its Consequences.

James, J. A. Anxious Enquirer after Salvation. New York, 1834. 16°. . 6574
Christian Professor. New York, 1838. 12°. 6579
Young Man's Friend. New York, 1852. 12°. 3892
James, J. Sketches of Trav. in Sicily, Italy, and France. Alb. 1820. 12°. 9027
James, M. Elder Sister. New York, 1855. 12°. 575
Ethel, or the Double Error. New York, 1855. 12°. 576
James, W. Military Occurrences of the Late War between Great Britain and the United States. London, 1818. 8°. 11345
Jameson, Mrs. A. Beauties of the Court of Charles II. Phil. 1839. 8°. . 1897
Characteristics of Women. New York, 1833. 12°. 4230
Italian Painters. London, 1845. 2 v. 16°. 6892
Mem's of Celebrated Female Sovereigns. N. York, 1832. 2 v. 16°. 6260
The same. New York, 1840. 2 v. 12°. 5536
Memoirs and Essays Illustrative of Arts, &c. New York, 1846. 12°. 829
Romance of Biography. London, 1837. 2 v. 12°. 8646
Jameson, Mrs. A. Visits and Sketches at Home and Abroad. New York, 1834. 2 v. 12°. 1445
Winter Studies and Sum. Ramb. in Canada. N. Y. 1839. 2 v. 12°. 8925
The same. 8996
Jameson, L. and others. Discov. and Advent. in Africa. N. Y. 1840. 12°. 5518
The same. New York, 1831. 16°. 6611
Jamieson, A. Grammar of Rhetoric. New Haven, 1835. 12°. . . . 3343

Jamieson, A. Grammar of Logic. 12°. 4927
Dictionary of Mechanical Science. 10918
Jane Bouverie. Catharine Sinclair. New York, 1851. 12°. . . . 252
Jane Eyre. Miss C. Brontë. New York, 1857. 12°. 177
Jane Talbot. C. B. Brown. Boston, 1827. 2 v. 12°. 1003
The same. 1429
Janin, J. American in Paris during the Winter. Tr. N. York, 1844. 8°. 9423
Japan, History of. London, 1781. 8°. 7053
and China Seas, Expedition to, by M. C. Perry. F. L. Hawks. New York, 1857. 8°. 9386
Japanese, Manners and Customs of the. P. F. von Siebold. Translated. London, 1841. 12°. 9235
The same. New York, 1841. 12°. 5908
Japhet in Search of a Father. F. Marryatt. Philadelphia, 1835. 2 v. 12°. 1519
Jardine, W. Ornithology and Mammalia. See Naturalists' Library.
Jarves, J. J. History of the Sandwich Islands. Boston, 1843. 8°. . 6963
Jarvis, S. F. Chronological Introduction to the History of the Church. (Two copies.) New York, 1845. 8°. 5038
Two Discourses on Prophecy. New York, 1843. 12°. . . . 5746
Jasher, Book of. Tr. New York, 1840. 8°. 5311
Java, History of. T. S. Raffles. London, 1830. 2 v. 8°. . . . 6996
Plates to the same. London, 1844. 4°. . . . . .
Jay, J., and A. Hamilton. Lives. New York, 1841. 12°. . . . 5905
Life. W. Jay. New York, 1833. 2 v. 8°. 7936
Jay, W. Character of the American Colonization and Anti-Slavery Societies. New York, 1835. 12°. 11119
The Christian contemplated. New York, 1831. 16°. . . . 6238
The same. New York, 1831. 12°. 6549
Jeames' Diary. W. M. Thackeray. New York, 1853. 12°. . . . 960
Jean Paul. See Richter, J. P. F.
Jebb, J. Correspond. with A. Knox. Ed. C. Forster. Phil. 1835. 2 v. 8°. 33
Jefferson, T., Character of. T. Dwight. Boston, 1839. 12°. 8347
Life. G. Tucker. Philadelphia, 1837. 2 v. 8°. 8503
Manual of Parliamentary Practice. Philadelphia, 1843. 16°. . 11161
Jefferson, T. Memoir, Correspondence and Miscellanies. Ed. T. J. Randolph. Boston, 1830. 4 v. 8°. 11083
Observations on the Writings of. H. Lee. New York, 1832. 8°. 10682
Jefferson, T. Notes on the State of Virginia. Philadelphia, 1794. 8°. . 3294
Jeffrey, F. Essays. London, 1844. 4 v. 8°. 717
Jeffrey, Lord. Life and Corresp. Lord Cockburn. Phil. 1852. 2 v. 12°. 8592
Jeffreys, Judge G. Memoirs. H. W. Woolrych. London, 1827. 8°. . 11315
Jeffreys, Judge G. Memoirs. Philadelphia, 1852. 12° 8003
Jehangeer Nowrogee. Residence in Great Britain. London, 1841. 12°. 9240
Jenkins, J. S. Life of S. Wright. Auburn, 1850. 12°. 8618
Jenkins, W. Ohio Gazetteer and Traveler's Guide. Columbus, 1837. 12°. 8980
Jenner, E. Life. J. Baron. London, 1838. 2 v. 8°. 7525
Jenyns, S. Works with Life. C. N. Cole. Dublin, 1791. 2 v. 8°. . 10770
Select Poems, and Life. Philadelphia, 1822. 18°. 2144

Jerningham, Mr. Poems. London, 1767. 12°. 2434
Jerrold, D. Chronicles of Clovernook. London, 1846. 16°. . . . 1629
Men of Character. New York. 12°. 1181
Punch's Complete Letter Writer. London, 1845. 12°. . . . 1213
Specimens of Wit of. Boston, 1858. 12°. 1195
Jerusalem, Cairo, and Damascus, Excursions to. G. Jones. N. Y. 1836. 12°. 9630
Delivered. T. Tasso. Tr. E. Fairfax. London, 1844. 2 v. 16°. . 7170
See also Tasso, T.
Fall of, a Dramatic Poem. H. H. Milman. New York, 1820. 16°. 2091
Jersey Prison Ship, Recollect. of. A. G. Greene. Providence, 1829. 12°. 4580
Jesse, (Capt.) Life of G. Brummell. Philadelphia, 1844. 8°. . . . 8190
Jesse, J. H. Memoirs of the Court of England under the Stuarts. London, 1840. 2 v. 8°. 8148
Continuation of the same. Phil. 1840. 2 v. 8°. . . . 8582
Jesuit Juggling, Forty Jesuit Frauds Detected and Disclosed. R. Baxter. (Two copies.) New York, 1835. 12°. 6444
Jesuits at Rome, Mornings among the. M. H. Seymour. N. Y. 1849. 12°. 5730
A Year among. A. Steinmetz. New York, 1846. 12°. . . 5810
History of the. A. Steinmetz. Philadelphia, 1848. 2 v. 8°. . 55119
Missions in North America. W. I. Kipp. New York, 1848. 12°. . 6476
Secret Instructions of the. Princeton, 1831. 16°. . . . 6228
Travels of, into Various Parts of the World. J. Lockman. London, 1762. 2 v. 8°. 8882
Jewett, I. A. Passages in Foreign Travel. Boston, 1838. 2 v. 12°. . . 9797
Jewitt, J. R. Narrative of his Own Adventures and Sufferings. Middletown, 1815. 12°. 9300
Jewsbury, Miss M. J. The Three Histories. Boston, 1831. 12°. . . 926
Jews, Ancient History of the. London, 1779. 2 v. 8°. 7030
Modern History of the. London, 1781. 8°. 7056
History of the. H. H. Milman. New York, 1830. 3 v. 16°. . 6244
The same. New York, 1840. 3 v. 12°. 5503
Joanna of Naples. Miss L. J. Park. Boston, 1838. 12°. . . . 1397
Jocelyn, Lord. Six months in China. London, 1841. 12°. . . . 9283
John Marston Hall. G. P. R. James. New York, 1834. 2 v. 12°. . . 1009
John of Gaunt, Duke of Lancaster, Adventures of. J. White. Dublin. 1790. 2 v. 16°. 7777
Johnson, A. B. Treatise on Language. New York, 1836. 8°. . . 750
Johnson, C. History of the Pirates. Norwich, 1814. 12° 8374
The same. 8376
Johnson, J. Economy of Health. New York, 1837. 16°. . . . 4968
Johnson, S. English and Hebrew Grammar. London, 1771. 8°. . . 11696
Lives of the English Poets. London, 1831. 12°. 7780
Life and Writings. W. P. Page. New York, 1841. 12°. . . 5571
Life. J. Boswell. Boston, 1824. 5 v. 12°. 8082
Life of J. Dyer. Philadelphia, 1819. 18°. 2131
Life and Select Poems. Philadelphia, 1822. 18°. 2143
The same. New York, 1837. 2 v. 8°. 7532
Lives. See British Poets.

Johnson, S. Lives and Works of the Poets of Great Britain and Ireland, with Criticisms. Dublin, 1804. 8 v. 8°. 1778
Sermons. Boston, 1821. 18°. 4634
The Idler. London, 1823. 12°. 3682
The Rambler. London, 1791. 4 v. 12°. 4923
The same. London, 1823. 3 v. 12°. 3679
Works. (vol. 2 missing.) Dublin, 1793. 5 v. 8°. 6045
Duplicate of vol. 1. 3710
The same. London, 1816. 11 v. 12°. 3653

Vol. 1. Life and Poems.
2. Philological Tracts.
3. (Missing.)
4–6. The Rambler.
Vol. 7. The Idler.
8. Miscellaneous Essays, &c.
9–11. The Lives of the English Poets.
12. Lives of Eminent Persons.

Johnsoniana, Anecdotes and Sayings of S. Johnson. Ed. J. W. Croker. Philadelphia, 1842. 12°. 2998
Johnston, J. F. W. Agricultural Chemistry and Geology. N. Y. 1847. 12°. 6076
Chemistry of Common Life. New York, 1856. 2 v. 12°. . . . 6082
Jones, G. Excursions to Cairo, Jerusalem, Damascus, &c. N. Y. 1836. 12°. 9630
Sketches of Naval Life. New Haven, 1829. 2 v. 12°. . . . 9275
Jones, J. P., Life and Character of. J. H. Sherburne. Wash. 1825. 8°. . 8234
Life and Correspondence. New York, 1830. 8°. 8195
Life. A. S. Mackenzie. New York, 1846. 2 v. 12°. 7730
Jones, Sir W. Life, Writings and Corres. Lord Teigmouth. Phil. 1805. 8°. 8201
Poetical Works, with Life. London, 1810. 2 v. 16°. . . . 2472
and others. Select Poems and Life. Philadelphia, 1827. 18°. . 2147
Jones, W. Biographical Sketches of the Reform Ministers of England. London, 1832. 8°. 10170
Hist. of Eng. during the Reign of George III. Lond. 1825. 3 v. 8°. 7026
Jones, Rev. W. Figurative Lang. of the Holy Scriptures. Phil. 1818. 8°. 5332
Letters from a Tutor to his Pupil. New York, 1832. 24°. . . 4641
Catholic Doctrine of a Trinity. Philadelphia, 1838. 12°. . . 6594
Jonson, Ben. Works of. London, 1716. 12°. 2368
Jortin, J. Life of Erasmus. London, 1808. 3 v. 8°. 8246
Joseph Andrews. H. Fielding. London, 1792. 12°. 1128
Josephine, History of. J. S. C. Abbott. New York, 1851. 12°. . . 8389
Conf. Corres. with Napoleon. Ed. J. S. C. Abbott. N. Y. 1856. 12°. 4520
Memoirs. M'lle M. A. Le Normand. Tr. Phil. 1848. 2 v. 12°. . 8008
Memoirs. J. S. Memes. (Two copies.) New York, 1832. 16°. . 6623
Josephus, F. Works. Tr. R. L'Estrange. Amer. 1774. 3 v. 8°. . . 6770
The same. Tr. W. Whiston. Philadelphia, 1841. 2 v. 8°. . 6938
Jouffroy, T. Intro. to Ethics. Tr. W. H. Channing. Bost. 1838. 2 v. 12°. 773
Philosophical Miscellanies. Tr. G. Ripley. Boston, 1840. 2 v. 12°. 768
Judah's Lion. Mrs. C. E. Tonna. New York, 1843. 12°. . . . 1207
Judaism, The Genius of. I. D'Israeli. London, 1833. 12°. . . . 5634
Judæa Capta. Mrs. C. E. Tonna. New York, 1845. 18°. . . . 7478
Judd, S. J. Philo, an Evangeliad. Boston, 1850. 12°. 2340
Judges, Atrocious, Lives. J. Lord Campbell. Ed. R. Hildreth. New York, 1856. 12°. 8638

Judicature in Parliaments. J. Selden. London. 12°. 11184
Judiciary, Debates on the, in the Senate of the U. States. Phil. 1802. 8°. 10517
Judson, E. Memoir. E. P. Barrows, Jr. Boston, 1852. 12°. . . . 8335
Julian, or Scenes in Judea. W. Ware. New York, 1841. 2 v. 12°. . 1322
Junius, Critical Inquiry regarding. G. Coventry. London, 1825. °8. . 10730
Essay on, and Letters of. J. Wade. London, 1850. 2 v. 12°. . 5430
Letters of. Philadelphia, 1813. 2 v. 8°. 10728
The same. New York, 1821. 2 v. 12°. 11120
Posthumous Works, Inquiry respecting the Author, and Life of J. H. Tooke. New York, 1829. 8°. 10749
Justina, or the Will, a Domestic Story. New York, 1823. 12°. . . 1380
Justinus. Historiæ Philippicæ. Lipsiæ, 1829. 16°. 10850
The same. 11287
Juvenal, D. J. Satiræ. Lipsiæ, 1829. 16°. 10864
The same. Trans. C. Badham. New York, 1837. 12°. . 5292
The same. Trans. W. Gifford. Phil. 1803. 2 v. 8°. . . 1852
The same. London, 1806. 8°. 1928
New Translation of the Third Satire, with Notes. N. Y. 1806. 12°. 2288

K.

Kaloolah, or Journeyings of the Djébel Kumri. W. S. Mayo. N. Y. 1849. 12°. 8888
Kames, H. H., (Lord.) Elements of Criticism. vol. 2. Edin. 1769. 8°. . 10806
Sketches of the History of Man. Edinburgh, 1813. 3 v. 8°. . . 420
The same. Dublin, 1779. 2 v. 8°. 11691
Kamschatka, Travels in. London, 1790. 2 v. 8°. 9770
Kane, E. K. Grinnell Expedi. in Search of Sir J. Franklin. Phil. 1856. 8°. 9396
Second Expedition. Philadelphia, 1857. 2 v. 8°. . . . 9416
Kane, R. Elements of Chemistry. New York, 1843. 8°. 5950
Kansas, Englishmen in. T. H. Gladstone. New York, 1857. 12°. . . 8991
Kant, I. Metaphysical Works. Tr. J. Richardson. London, 1836. 8°. . 6344
Kavanagh, a Tale. H. W. Longfellow. Boston, 1849. 12°. . . . 1616
Kean, E. Life. B. W. Proctor. New York, 1835. 12°. . . . 8316
The same. 8331
Keats, J., Life and Letters of. R. M. Milnes. New York, 1848. 12°. . 8320
Poetical Works. New York, 1846. 12°. 1792
Keese, J., (Editor.) Poets of America. (Two copies.) N. Y. 1849. 12°. 2328
Keightley, T. Hist. of Eng. to 1837. (vol. 5 mis'g.) N. Y. 1840. 5 v. 12°. 5578
The same. Boston, 1840. 2 v. 8°. 6957
History of the Roman Empire. Boston, 1841. 8°. 7272
Mythology of Greece and Italy. London, 1838. 8°. . . . 7602
Outlines of History. Philadelphia, 1831. 12°. 9859
The same. 5837
Keith, A. Evidence of Prophecy. New York. 16°. 5240
The Land of Israel. New York, 1844. 12°. 9537
Truth of the Christian Religion. New York, 1833. 12°. . . 5655
Kellogg, E. Labor and other Capital. New York, 1849. 8°. . . . 10059

Kelly, M. Autobiog. and Reminiscences of the Stage. N. Y. 1826. 8°. . 8488
Kelly, W. K. History of Russia. London, 1854. 2 v. 12°. 5201
Kemble, J. P. Life. J. Boaden. Philadelphia, 1825. 8°. 8183
The same. 8189
Kempis, T. A. Imitàtion of Christ. New York, 1846. 12°. 5670
Kendall, E. A. Travels through the Northern States, in 1807, 8. New York, 1809. 3 v. 12°. 9527
Kendall, G. W. Sante Fé Expedition. New York, 1844. 2 v. 12°. . . 8936
Kenilworth. W. Scott. Boston, 1829. 8°. 1097
See also Scott, Sir W.
Kennedy, J. Conversations with Lord Byron. Philadelphia, 1833. 12°. 3382
Kennedy, J. P. Horse-Shoe Robinson. Philadelphia, 1836. 2 v. 12°. . 1617
Memoirs of W. Wirt. Philadelphia, 1850. 2 v. 8°. 7858
Rob of the Bowl. Philadelphia, 1838. 2 v. 12°. 1523
The same. 1555
The Swallow-Barn. Philadelphia, 1832. 2 v. 12°. 230
The same. 240
The same. 255
Kennett, B. Antiquities of Rome. London, 1763. 8°. 9205
The same. Philadelphia, 1822. 8°. 7233
Kent, J. Commentaries on American Law. New York, 1840. 4 v. 8°. . 10714
Course of English Reading. New York, 1853. 12°. 4867
Kentucky, Historical Sketch of. L. Collins. Cincinnati, 1850. 8°. . . 7595
Keppell, H. Expedition of H. S. M. Dido to Borneo. N. Y. 1846. 12°. . 8985
Kett, H. Elements of General Knowledge. Philadelphia, 1805. 2 v. 12°. 3393
Flowers of Wit. Hartford, 1825. 16°. 4294
Kettell, S. (Editor.) Specimens of Amer. Poetry. Boston, 1819. 3 v. 12°. 2402
Kidd, J. Adap. of Nature to the Phys. Condition of Man. Phil. 1833. 12°. 6486
Kidder, D. P. Residence and Travels in Brazil. Phil. 1845. 2 v. 8°. . 9517
Kilbourn, J. Ohio Gazetteer. Columbus, 1821. 12°. 9301
Kilpin. S. Memoir. New York. 16°. 5244
Kimber, I. History of England to George III. London, 1768. 8°. . . 7686
King, J. A. Twenty-four Years in the Argentine Republic. N. Y. 1846. 12°. 6792
King, Lord. Life and Correspondence of J. Locke. London, 1830. 2 v. 8°. 7949
King, W. Literary and Political Anecdotes. Boston, 1819. 12°. . . 11697
King's Own, The. F. Marryatt. Philadelphia, 1834. 2 v. 12°. . . 1581
The same. New York, 1836. 12°. 1295
King's Highway. G. P. R. James. New York, 1836. 2 v. 12°. . . 1579
Kingdom of Christ. F. D. Maurice. New York, 1843. 8°. . . . 5015
R. Whately. New York, 1842. 12°. 5696
Kingsley, C. Alton Locke. New York, 1856. 12. 1222
Amyas Leigh, Voyages and Adventures of. Boston, 1857. 12°. . 1220
Glaucus, or the Wonders of the Show. Boston, 1855. 12°. . . 10172
Poems. Boston, 1856. 12°. 1999
Two Years Ago. Boston, 1837. 12°. 1221
Yeast, a Problem. New York, 1851. 12°. 1223
Kingsley, J. L. Historical Discourse delivered at New Haven, April 25, 1838. New Haven, 1838. 8°. 6684

Kingsley, J. L. Life of E. Stiles. Boston, 1845. 12°. 8058
Kip, W. I. Catacombs of Rome. New York, 1859. 12°. 6466
Christmas Holydays in Rome. New York, 1846. 12°. 8977
Double Witness of the Church. New York, 1858. 12°. 6478
Early Conflicts of Christianity. New York, 1850. 12°. 6154
The same. New York, 1853. 12°. 6467
Early Jesuit Mission in North America. New York, 1848. 12°. 6476
History, Object, &c., of the Season of Lent. New York, 1859. 12°. 6477
Recantation. New York, 1846. 12°. 6603
Kirby, W. Power, Wis., &c. of God, Manifested in Animals. Phil. 1836. 8°. 6385
The same. vol. 1. London, 1852. 12°. 5488
Kirk, E. N. Sermons. New York, 1841. 12°. 6194
Kirkham, S. English Grammar. Rochester, 1835. 12°. 4922
The same. Baltimore, 1834. 12°. 3317
Holidays Abroad. New York, 1849. 2 v. 12°. 8910
New Home—Who'll Follow. New York, 1839. 12°. 1593
Western Clearings. New York, 1846. 12°. 9856
Kirkland, S. Life. S. K. Lothrop. Boston, 1848. 12°. 8067
Kissam, W. I. The Oxonians. New York, 1830. 2 v. 12°. 1356
Kitto, J. Cyclopædia of Biblical Literature. New York, 1846. 2 v. 8°. 8807
Scripture Lands. London, 1850. 12°. 5477
The Lost Senses. Deafness. London, 1845. 16°. 7195
Second series. Blindness. London, 1845. 16°. 6883
Klopstock, F. G. and Margaret. Memoirs. Tr. Bath, 1809. 12°. 7721
Klopstock, Odes of. Tr. W. Nind. London, 1848. 12°. 2260
Knapp, S. L. Advice in the Pursuits of Literature. New York, 1832. 12°. 4914
Bachelors. New York, 1836. 12°. 1227
Biographical Sketches of Statesmen, &c. Boston, 1821. 8°. 8537
Knickerbocker, The. vols. 1–53. (continued.) N. Y. 1832–59. 8°. 4384
Knickerbocker's History of New York. W. Irving. N. Y. 1826. 2 v. 12°. 1164
See also Irving, W.
Knick-Knacks. L. G. Clarke. New York, 1853. 12°. 1219
Knight, C. Capital and Labor, with Results of Machinery. Lon. 1845. 16°. 6885
Cyclopædia of the Industry of All Nations. London, 1851. 8°. 8832
Half Hours with the Best Authors. New York, 1848. 4 v. 12°. 790
Life of. W. Caxton. London, 1844. 16°. 7209
Pictorial London. London, 1841. 6 v. 4°. 7800
Volume of Varieties. London, 1844. 16°. 7173
Knight, H. C. Poems. Boston, 1821. 2 v. 16°. 2077
Knight, R. P. Principles of Taste. London, 1805. 8°. 2686
Knight, W. Orien. Outlines, Tour thro' Greece, Turkey, &c. Lon. 1839. 12°. 8726
Knighton, Sir W. Memoirs. Lady Knighton. Philadelphia, 1838. 8°. 8150
Knights of Malta, Achievements of. A. Sutherland. Phil. 12°. 4522
Knorring, Baroness. Peasant and his Landlord. Tr. N. Y. 1848. 12°. 1237
Knowledge, Elements of. N. Webster. Hartford, 1812. 12°. 3364
The same. New Haven, 1806. 12°. 4932
General, Elements of. H. Kett. Phil. 1805. 2 v. 12°. 3393
Human, Principles of. 8°. 11695

Knowles, J. Life and Writings of H. Fuseli. London, 1831. 3 v. 8°. . 372
Knowles, J. D. Memoir of R. Williams. Boston, 1834. 12°. 8358
Knowles, J. S. Dramatic Works. London, 1841. 3 v. 12°. 1907
The Love-Chase, a Comedy. New York, 1838. 18°. 2393
Select Works. Boston, 1833. 16°. 2482
Knox, A. Corres. with J. Jebb. Ed. C. Forster. Phil. 1835. 2 v. 12°. . 33
Knox, J. History of the Reformation in Scotland. Glasgow, 1832. 8°. . 5587
Life, with Reformation in Scotland, &c. T. M'Crie. N. Y. 1819. 8°. 8486
Writings. London. 12°. 5658
Knox, V. Christian Philosophy. London, 1835. 12°. 5792
Essays. London, 1823. 3 v. 12°. 3697
Treatise on acquiring a Liberal Education. Lond. 1785. 2 v. 16°. 3712
Winter Evenings. London, 1823. 3 v. 12°. 3700
Koch, C. W. Revolutions of Europe. Tr. A. Crichton. Hart. 1832. 12°. 6795
The same. Edinburgh, 1828. 3 v. 16°. 10009
Kohl, J. G. Description of Ireland. New York, 1844. 8°. 9090
Russia and the Russians in 1842. Philadelphia, 1843. 8°. . . . 9421
Kohlrausch, F. History of Germany. Tr. J. D. Haas. N. Y. 1845. 8°. . 7266
Koningsmarke. J. K. Paulding. New York, 1834. 2 v. 12°. 1810
The same. New York, 1823. 2 v. 12°. 975
Koran, The. Tr. G. Sale. Bath, 1795. 2 v. 8°. 5629
Körner, C. T. Life, with Select Poems, Tales, &c. Tr. G. F. Richardson. London, 1827. 2 v. 12°. 8354
Kossuth, L. Life, and Revolutions of Hungary. London, 1854. 12°. . 5432
Kotzebue, A. von. Autobiography. London, 1830. 2 v. 16°. . . . 7488
The same. London, 1830. 2 v. 16°. 7753
The same. 3 v. 8429
Kraitsir, C. Glossology. Nature of Language. New York, 1852. 12°. . 3932
Krebs, J. P. Guide for Writing Latin. Tr. S. H. Taylor. And. 1843. 12°. 10791
Krummacher, F. W. Elijah, the Tishbite. Tr. New York, 1848. 16°. . 5239
The Flying Roll, or Free Grace Displayed. Tr. N. Y. 1841. 12°. . 5706
Solomon and the Shulamite. New York, 1841. 12°. 5745
Krummacher, G. D. Jacob Wrestling with the Angel. Tr. N. Y. 1841. 12°. 5745
Kühner, R. Elementary Greek Grammar. Tr. Andover 1847. 12°. . 2987
Kuzzilbash, The, a Tale of Khorasan. New York, 1828. 2 v. 12°. . . 1362

L.

LaBaume, E. Napoleon's Campaign in Russia. Tr. Phil. 1815. 8°. . 9493
The same. Hartford, 1816. 8°. 9498
Labor, and other Capital. E. Kellogg. New York, 1849. 8°. . . 10059
and Property, Essays on. F. Lieber. New York, 1841. 12°. . 5918
Lackington, J. Autobiography. London, 1830. 16°. 7497
Confessions of. London, 1804. 12°. 4909
Laconics, or the Best Words of the Best Authors. Phil. 1829. 3 v. 16°. . 3091
World's, or Best Thoughts, &c. T. Edwards. New York, 1856. 12°. 516
Ladd, J. B. Lit. Remains, with Life. W. B. Chittenden. N. Y. 1832. 12°. 2229
The same. 2348

Ladies of England, Literary, Memoirs of. G. Ballard. Oxford, 1752. 8°. 7807
Lady, An American, Memoirs of. Mrs. Grant. New York, 1856. 12°. . 8679
of the Manor. Mrs. M. M. Sherwood. New York, 1837. 4 v. 12°. 192
The same. Bridgeport, 1828. 7 v. 18°. 1768
Lafayette, G. M. Memoirs. B. Sarrans. London, 1832. 2 v. 8°. . . 8170
Memoirs, Correspondence, &c. vol. 1. New York, 1827. 8°. . 9733
Private Life of. J. Cloquet. New York, 1836. 2 v. 12°. . . 8310
LaFontaine, J., Fables of. Tr. E. Wright. Boston, 1841. 8°. . . 1074
Laing, S. Tour in Sweden. London, 1839. 8°. 9143
Residence in Norway, in 1834–6. London, 1837. 8°. . . . 9122
Travels in France, Prussia, Switzerland, &c. Phil. 1846. 8°. . 9414
Lake Ngami. C. J. Andersson. New York, 1856. 12°. 9593
Superior, Physical Character, &c., of. L. Agassiz, and J. E. Cabot. Boston, 1850. 8°. 5956
See also United States Public Documents.
Lalla Rookh. T. Moore. London, 1844. 2 v. 16°. 2254
The same. New York, 1849. 12°. 2022
Lamartine, A. de. History of the Girondists. London, 1848. 3 v. 12°. . 5172
The same. New York, 1848. 3 v. 12°. 7705
Lamb, C. Letters, with Life. T. N. Talfourd. London, 1837. 2 v. 12°. 490
Memoirs of Celebrated Characters. New York, 1854. 3 v. 12°. . 8013
Pilgrimage to the Holy Land. Tr. Philadelphia, 1835. 2 v. 12°. 8942
Poems, with Life. Philadelphia, 1830. 8°. 1882
The same. London, 1830. 8°. 1869
Poetical Works. London, 1836. 12°. 2446
Prose Works. London, 1836. 3 v. 12°. 487
(Edited.) Specimens of Eng. Dramatic Poets. N. Y. 1846. 12°. . 9845
Restoration of Monarchy in France. Tr. Lond. 1859. 4 v. 12°. . 5175
Lambert, E. R. Hist. of the Colony of New Haven. N. H. 1838. 12°. . 7423
The same. 11452
Lambeth and the Vatican, or Anecdotes of the Church of Rome and the Reformed Churches. London, 1825. 3 v. 16°. 6591
Lancashire, Traditions of. J. Roby. (vol. 1 miss.) Lond. 1843. 3 v. 12°. 11399
Lancaster, J. Improvements in Education. New York, 1807. 12°. . . 4851
Land, Labor and Gold. W. Howitt. Boston, 1855. 2 v. 12°. 9636
Lander, R. and J. Journal of Exped. up the Niger. N. Y. 1832. 2 v. 16°. 6628
Travels in Africa. New York, 1841. 2 v. 12°. 5538
Landon, Miss L. E. Ethel Churchill. Philadelphia, 1838. 2 v. 12°. . 1549
The Golden Violet, and other Poems. Philadelphia, 1827. 12°. . 2498
Literary Remains, with Life. L. Blanchard. Phil. 1841. 2 v. 12°. 3943
Poetical Works. Philadelphia, 1838. 8°. 1798
The Troubadour. Philadelphia, 1825. 12°. 2416
Landor, W. S. Citation and Examination of W. Shakspeare for Deer Stealing. London, 1834. 12°. 827
Gebir, Count Julian, and other Poems. London, 1831. 12°. . . 2223
Imaginary Convers. of Lit. Men and Statesmen. Lond. 1826. 3 v. 8°. 77
Second series. London, 1829. 2 v. 8°. 80

Landor, W. S. Pericles and Aspasia. Philadelphia, 1839. 2 v. 12°. . 161
The same. 163
Lands, Classical and Sacred. Lord Nugent. London, 1846. 2 v. 16°. . 7193
Landscape Gardening and Rural Arch. A. J. Downing. N. Y. 1844. 8°. 10106
Lane, B. I. Mysteries of Tobacco, New York, 1846. 12°. . . . 4596
Responses on the Use of Tobacco. New York, 1844. 12°. . . 3303
Lane, E. W. The Modern Egyptians. London, 1836. 2 v. 12°. . . 5808
The same. London, 1846. 3 v. 16°. 7190
Langdon, Mary. Ida May. Boston, 1855. 12°. 1175
Langhorne, J. Select Poems and Life. Philadelphia, 1822. 18°. . . 2142
Solyman and Almena. E. Windsor, 1799. 12°. 2439
Langon, L. L. Evenings with Prince Cambacérès. Phil. 1836. 2 v. 12°. 8364
Langsdorff, G. H. von. Voyages and Travels. Carlisle, 1817. 8°. . . 9168
Language, Glossology, Nature of. C. Kraitsir. New York, 1852. 12°. . 3932
Treatise on. A. B. Johnson. New York, 1836. 8°. . . . 750
Lanman, J. H. History of Michigan. New York, 1839. 8°. . . . 7244
The same. New York, 1841. 12°. 5913
Lanzi, A. L. Hist. of Painting in Italy. Tr. T. Roscoe. Lon. 1828. 6 v. 8°. 10122
The same. London, 1847. 3 v. 12°. 5122
L'Ardeche, L. de. Hist. of Napoleon Bonaparte. Tr. N. Y. 1842. 2 v. 8°. 8135
Lardner, D. and H. Kater. Treatise on Arithmetic. London, 1836. 12°. 9956
Treatise on Heat. London, 1833. 12°. 9960
Treatise on Hydrostatics and Pneumatics. London, 1836. 12°. . 9961
The same. Philadelphia, 1832. 12°. 5841
Treatise on Mechanics. Philadelphia, 1833. 12°. 5840
The same. London, 1837. 12°. 9958
Treatise on the Steam Engine. Philadelphia, 1836. 8°. . . . 404
The same, revised. London, 1840. 8°. 6325
and others. The Cabinet Cyclopædia. Lond. 1830–41. 129 v. 12°.

Arts and Manufactures.

No. 9963, 4. Domestic Economy. M. Donovan.
9966–8. Manufactures in Metal. J. Holland.
9969. Manufacture of Porcelain and Glass. G. R. Porter.
9965. Manufacture of Silk. G. R. Porter.

Biography.

9924–6. British Military Commanders. G. R. Gleig.
9932–8. British Statesmen. J. Forster and others.
9945, 6. British Poets. R. Bell.
9940–4. Foreign Statesmen. E. E. Crowe.
9947. Literary and Scientific Men of Great Britain and Ireland.
9948, 9. Literary and Scientific Men of France.
9951–3. Literary and Scientific Men of Italy.
9927–31. Naval History of England. R. Southey.

Geography.

9984. Cities and Principal Towns.
9920–4. Maritime and Inland Discovery. W. D. Cooley.

History.

9914, 15. Arts, &c., of the Greeks and Romans. T. Fosbroke
9916, 17. Christian Church. H. Stebbing.
9923. Chronology of History. H. Nicolas.
9865–7. Denmark, Sweden and Norway. S. A. Dunham.
9898–907. England. J. Mackintosh
9881–4. Europe during the Middle Ages.
9862–4. France. E. E. Crowe.

Lardner, D. and others. The Cabinet Cyclopædia, *continued.*

Germanic Empire. S. A. Dunham.
9888-95. Greece. C. Thirlwall.
9887. Italian Republics. J. C. L. de Sismondi.
9910-12. Ireland. T. Moore.
9983. Netherlands. T. C. Grattan.
9859. Outlines of History. T. Keightley.
9909. Poland.
9918, 19. Reformation. H. Stebbing.
9885, 6. Rome.
9871-3. Russia. R. Bell.
9879, 80. Scotland. W. Scott.
9874-8. Spain and Portugal. S. A. Dunham.
9908. Switzerland.
9861. The United States. H. Fergus.

Natural History.

9975. Animals in Menageries. W. Swainson.
9973, 4. Birds. W. Swainson.
9913. Chemistry. M. Donovan.
9985. Descriptive and Physiological Botany. J. S. Henslow.
9970. Discourse on Study of Natural History. W. Swainson.
9976, 7. Fishes, Amphibians and Reptiles. W. Swainson.
9971. Geography and Classification of Animals. W. Swainson.
9981, 2. Geology. J. Phillips.
9979. Habits and Instincts of Animals. W. Swainson.
Insects. W. Swainson and W. Shackard.
9978. Malacology. W. Swainson.
9972. Quadrupeds. W. Swainson.
9980. Taxidermy and Bibliography. W. Swainson.

Natural Philosophy.

9956. Arithmetic. D. Lardner.
9957. Astronomy. J. F. W. Herschel.
9954. Discourse on Study of Nat. Philosophy. J. F. W. Herschel.
5962. Essay on Probabilities. A. De Morgan.
9960. Heat. D. Lardner.
9955. History of Natural Philosophy. B. Powell.
9961. Hydrostatics and Pneumatics. D. Lardner.
9958. Mechanics. H. Kater and D. Lardner.
9959. Optics. D. Brewster.

Larned, S., Life and Eloquence of. R. R. Gurley. New York, 1844. 12°. 8680
Las Cases, Count de. Journal of the Private Life of Napoleon, at St. Helena. London, 1823. 8 v. 8°. 6660
Last Days of Pompeii. E. L. Bulwer. London, 1854. 12°. 553
The same. New York, 1835. 12°. 927
The same. New York, 1835. 12°. 1249
Last of the Barons. E. L. Bulwer. New York, 1843. 8°. 1083
Last of the Lairds. J. Galt. New York, 1827. 12°. 1396
Last of the Mohicans. J. F. Cooper. Philadelphia, 1826. 2 v. 12°. . 977
Latham, R. G. Man and his Migrations. New York, 1852. 12°. . . 6160
Lathy, T. P. Memoirs of the Court of Louis XIV. Lond. 1819. 3 v. 8. 7955
Latimer, H. Select Sermons and Letters. London. 12°. 5662
Latin Dictionary. N. Ainsworth. Philadelphia, 1825. 8°. 1056
Dictionary. J. Mair. New York, 1809. 12°. 3331
Exercises. E. A. Andrews. Boston, 1839. 12°. 3928
Grammar. See Grammar.
Guide for Writing. J. P. Krebs. Tr. S. H. Taylor. And. 1843. 8°. 10791
Reader. F. Jacobs and F. W. Döring. New York, 1831. 12°. . 4850
Tutor. F. P. Leverett. Boston, 1838. 12°. 3345
La Tour, S. de. Lives of Scipio and Epaminondas. Tr. R. Parry. London, 1787. 2 v. 8°. 8259

Latreille, P. A. Crustacea, Arachnides & Insecta. Tr. N. Y. 1831. 2 v. 8°. 10130
Latrobe, C. J. Rambles in Mexico. New York, 1836. 12°. 9819
The Rambler in America. New York, 1835. 2 v. 12°. 9631
Latter-Day Pamphlets. T. Carlyle. 1850. 12°. 812
Laud, W. Life and Times. J. P. Lawson. Lond. 1829. 2 v. 8°. . . 7927
Laurent, P. E. Tour through Greece, Italy, &c. London, 1822. 2 v. 8°. 9472
Lavater, J. C. Essay on Physiognomy. London. 12°. 3337
Lavater, The Pocket. Tr. New Haven, 1829. 24°. 4640
The same. Hartford. 18°. 4942
Lavengro; the Scholar, the Gipsy, the Priest. G. Borrow. N. Y. 1851. 12°. 547
The same. 548
Law, International, Treatise on. D. Gardner. Troy, 1844. 12°. . . 11132
Lectures on. J. Wilson. Philadelphia, 1804. 3 v. 8°. . . . 11020
Nat. and Polit. Princi. of. J. J. Burlamaqui. Tr. Dub. 1776. 2 v. 12°. 11177
Law, W. A Serious Call to a Devout and Holy Life. Andover, 1821. 12°. 6532
Lawrence, A., Diary and Corres. of. W. B. Lawrence. Boston, 1856. 12°. 9756
Lawrence, J. Biography. New Brunswick, 1813. 24°. 8428
Lawrence, W. Lectures on Physiology, &c. Salem, 1828. 8°. . . 752
Lawyer, Every Man his Own. Poughkeepsie, 1827. 12°. 3897
Lawyers, Statesmen, &c, Biog. Sketches of. S. L. Knapp. Bost. 1821. 8°. 8537
Lawson, J. P. Life and Times of Archbishop W. Laud. Lond. 1829. 2 v. 8°. 7927
Remarkable Conspiracies in Europe, in the 15th and 16th Centuries.
Edinburgh, 1829. 2 v. 16°. 10018
Layard, A. H. Nineveh and its Remains. New York, 1849. 2 v. 8°. . 9384
Lay, G. T. Chinese as they are. Moral, Social and Literary Character.
London, 1841. 8°. 9521
Lay of a Scald, The, or St. Jonathan. A. C. Coxe. New York, 1838. 12°. 2344
of the Last Minstrel. W. Scott. New York, 1811. 7 v. 18°. . 2720
of the Scotch Fiddle. New York, 1813. 18°. 2772
Lays of My Home. J. G. Whittier. Boston, 1843. 12°. 2448
Leavitt, J. Memoir, by his Sister. New Haven, 1822. 12°. . . . 8435
The same. 8461
Le Bas, C. W. Life of J. Wiclif. New York, 1832. 16°. 8740
Ledyard, J. Life. J. Sparks. Cambridge, 1828. 8°. 8249
The same. Boston, 1847. 12°. 8066
Lee, A. Life. R. H. Lee. Boston, 1829. 2 v. 8°. 7813
Lee, C. Life. Dublin, 1792. 8°. 8227
Life. J. Sparks. Boston, 1846. 12°. 8060
Lee, C. A. Elements of Geology. New York. 12°. 5254
Lee, Eliza. Life of J. P. F. Richter. Boston, 1842. 2 v. 12°. . . 8088
Lee, Eliza B. Memoirs of J. and J. S. Buckminster. Boston, 1757. 12°. 8572
Lee, H. Campaign of 1781 in the Carolinas. Philadelphia, 1824. 8°. . 7224
Mem. of the War in Southern Dep't of the U. S. Phil. 1812. 2 v. 8°. 7219
Observations on the Writings of T. Jefferson. N. Y. 1832. 8°. . 10682
Lee, Mrs. H. Huguenots in France and America. Camb. 1843. 2 v. 12°. 6180
Life and Times of T. Cranmer. Boston, 1841. 12°. . . . 7458
Life and Times of M. Luther. Boston, 1841. 12°. 8387
Sketches of the Old Painters. (Two copies,) Boston, 1841. 12°. 10199

Lee, Mrs. R. Memoirs of G. Cuvier. New York, 1833. 12°. . . . 8314
Lefanan, Miss A. Memoirs of Mrs. F. Sheridan. London, 1824. 8°. . . 8258
Legaré, H. S. Writings, with Life of. New York, 1846. 2 v. 8°. . . 6292
Legend of Montrose. Boston, 1845. 12°. 291
The same. Philadelphia, 1826. 3 v. 12°. 589
The same. Boston, 1820. 8°. 1095
The same. Hartford, 1822. 8°. 1087
Legend of Reading Abbey. London, 1845. 2 v. 16°. 7476
Legendary, The. Ed. N. P. Willis. Boston, 1828. 2 v. 12°. . . . 1352
Legendre, A. M. Ele. of Geom. and Trig. Tr. D. Brewster. N. Y. 1828. 8°. 9730
Legends of the West. J. Hall. Philadelphia, 1833. 12°. 1634
Leggett, W., Political Writings of. New York, 1840. 2 v. 12°. . . 10794
Legislation, Principles of. J. Bentham. Bost. 1830. 2 v. 8°. . . . 11139
Le Grand, T. P. B. Fabliaux, or French Tales. Tr. G. L. Way. London, 1815. 3 v. 12°. 2002
Leighton, R. Expositions of the Creed, Lord's Prayer, &c. Lon. 1834. 12°. 5787
Works, with Life. Edinburgh, 1840. 8°. 5029
Leila, or Siege of Grenada. E. L. Bulwer. New York, 1838. 12°. . . 1545
Leisler, J. Life of C. F. Hoffman. Boston, 1844. 12°. 8055
Leland, J. Life. New York. 12°. 5248
View of Deistical Writers of England. London, 1757. 3 v. 8°. . 5114
Leland, T. Life and Reign of Philip of Macedon. Lond. 1820. 2 v. 8°. . 7864
Lempriere, J. Universal Biography. New York, 1810. 2 v. 8°. . . 8851
The same, with additions by E. Lord. New York, 1825. 8°. 8854
Lempriere, W. A Tour through Northern Africa. London, 1793. 8°. . 9450
Lent, History, Object, and Observance of. W. I. Kip. N. Y. 1859 12°. 6477
Sermons for. Ed. R. Cattermore. London, 1834. 12°. . . 5788
Leo X, Life and Pontificate of. W. Roscoe. Phil. 1805, 6. 4 v. 8°. . 8205
The same. London, 1846. 2 v. 12°. 5137
LeSage, A. R. Bachelor of Salamanca. Tr. Phil. 1854. 2 v. 12°. . 360
Aventuras de Gil Blas. Exeter, 1828. 18°. 11279
Leslie, C. Short Method with the Deists. London, 1723. 12°. . . 4523
Leslie, Sir J., and others. Discoveries in Polar Seas. N. Y. 1840. 12°. . 5516
The same. New York, 1831. 16°. 6273
Leslie, J. Progress of Mathematical and Physical Science during the 18th Century. Boston, 1853. 4°. 10035
Leslie, Miss E. Pencil Sketches. Phil. 1833. 2 v. 697
Lester, C. E. Condition and Fate of England. N. York, 1843. 2 v. 12°. 8981
Glory and Shame of England. (Two copies.) N. Y. 1842. 2 v. 12°. 8693
and A. Foster. Life and Voyages of Americus Vespucius. New York, 1846. 8°. 7829
Letters from Abroad. Miss C. M. Sedgwick. New York, 1841. 2 v. 12°. 8697
from a Father to his Sons in College. Philadelphia, 1843. 12°. . 4879
from the South. J. K. Paulding. New York, 1835. 2 v. 12°. . 1308
from the South and West. A. Singleton. Boston, 1824. 8°. . 9782
of a Traveler. W. C. Bryant. New York, 1850. 12°. . . . 9799
on Practical Subjects. By a Clergyman. Hartford, 1822. 18°. . 4947
to a Son in the Ministry. H. Humphrey. Boston, 1843. 12°. . 4861
to a Young Lady. J. Bennett. New York, 1830. 24°. . . 11283

Letters to a Young Man. T. De Quincey. Boston, 1854. 12°. . . . 888
Lettres sur des Sciences. London, 1777. 12°. . . . . , . . 3299
Levant, Tour in. W. Turner. London, 1820. 3 v. 8°. 9502
Lever, C. Charles O'Malley. Philadelphia, 1841. 8°. 46
Leverett, F. P. Latin Tutor. Boston, 1830. 12°. 3345
Levizac, J. P. V. L. de. Elements of French Grammar. N. Y. 1827. 12°. 3040
Lewis, G. H. Biographical History of Philosophy. (vol. 1 missing.) London, 1845. 4 v. 16°. 7180
Lewis XI of France, History of. Philip de Comines. Trans. London, 1823. 2 v. 12°. 8268
Lewis, M. and W. Clarke. Expedition to the Sources of the Missouri, &c., in 1804–6. New York, 1842. 2 v. 12°. 5926
The same. Philadelphia, 1809. 12°. 9615
Lewis, M. G. Life and Correspondence. London, 1839. 2 v. 8°. . . 8510
Tales of Wonder. Poems. New York, 1801. 12°. . . . 368
Lewis, T. Plato against the Atheists. New York, 1845. 12°. . . 2977
Leybourn, T. Mathematical Repository. vol. 1. London, 1806. 8°. . 2698
L'Homond, C. F. Viri Illustres Urbis Romæ. New York, 1828. 18°. . 4952
Libraries, Memoirs of, and Hand-book of Library Economy. E. Edwards. London, 1859. 2 v. 8°. 9720
Library of Entertaining Knowledge. Boston, 1830–32. 15 v. 12°. . 6195

Vol. 1. The Menageries.
2. Vegetable Substances; Trees, Fruits.
3. The Pursuit of Knowledge under Difficulties.
4. Insect Architecture.
5. The New Zealanders.
6. Insect Transformations.
7. The Menageries.
Vol. 8. The Pursuit of Knowledge under Difficul'ies.
9. The Architecture of Birds.
10. Paris and its Historical Scenes.
11. Historical Parallels.
12. Insect Miscellanies.
13. Pompeii.
14. Paris and its Historical Scenes.
15. Vegetable Substances; Food.

Library of Old English Prose Writers. Cambridge, 1831. 6 v. 12°. . 4561
Library of Useful Knowledge. London, 1829–37. 10 v. 8°. . . . 5090

No. 5097. Algebraical Geometry. S. Waud.
5098. American Rev., History of.
5099. Animal Mechanics. C Bell.
5098. Art of Brewing. D. Booth.
5096. Arithmetic and Algebra.
5099 Botany. J. Lindley.
5096. Calculus. A. De Morgan.
5099. Chemistry.
5095. Church, Hist. of. G. Waddington.
5098. Commerce, Treatise on. J. R McCulloch.
5097. Geometry
5093. Greece, History of.
5098. Iron Manufacture of. Needham.
5096. Mathematics, Study of.
5090-2. Natural Philosophy.
5098. Novum Organon, Bacon's Account of.
5099. Physiology, Vegetable and Animal. P. M. Roget.
5098. Probability, Essay on.
5094. Spain and Portugal, History of. M. M. Bask.
5096. Trigonometry. W. Hopkins.

Library of Select Novels. New York, 1834. 19 v. 12°.

No. 1009–10. John Marston Hall. G. P. R. James.
1011, 2. Smuggler. J. Banim.
1013, 4. Tales of Glauber Spar
1017, 8. Westward Ho. J. K. Paulding.
No. 1019–20. Anastasius. T Hope.
1021, 2. Young Duke. B. D'Israeli.
1023, 4. Eugene Aram. E. L. Bulwer.
1025, 6. De Vere. R. P. Ward.

Lieber, F. Essays on Labor and Property. New York, 1841. 12°. . 5918
Legal and Political Hermeneutics. Boston, 1839. 12°. . . . 10796

Lieber, F. Political Ethics. Boston, 1838. 2 v. 8°. 10063
Reminiscences of G. B. Niebuhr. Philadelphia, 1835. 12°. . . 8333
The same. 8361
The Stranger in America, or Letters to a Friend in Germany. Philadelphia, 1835. 8°. 9420
Liebig, J. Animal Chemistry. Cambridge, 1842. 12°. 6051
The same. New York, 1848. 12°. 6068
Organic Chemistry, applied to Agricul. and Phys. Camb. 1841. 8°. 6050
Life, Christian Thoughts on. H. Giles. Boston, 1851. 12°. . . . 876
of Col. Jack. D. De Foe. Edinburgh, 1810. 2 v. 16°. . . 327
in Earnest. C. B. Smith. New Haven, 1848. 12°. . . . 3398
Four Ages of. Count P. De Segur. New York, 1826. 12°. . . 3353
Human, View of. F. Petrarch. Tr. London, 1797. 8°. . . 1104
in the New World. C. Seatsfield. Tr. New York. 8°. . . 9172
Life Thoughts. H. W. Beecher. Boston, 1858. 12°. 5722
Life in the Wilds. Miss H. Martineau. Boston, 1833. 18°. . . . 1678
Lighton, W. B. Autobiography. Concord, 1838. 18°. 8446
Lights and Shadows of Scottish Life. J. Wilson. Philadelphia. 16°. . 5973
Lillo, G. Dramatic Works. London, 1810. 12°. 11982
Lilly, W. Autobiography. London, 1829. 16°. 7481
The same. 7746
Lincoln, B., Life of. F. Bowen. Boston, 1847. 12°. 8065
Lincoln, W. History of Worcester, Mass. Worcester, 1837. 8°. . . 7558
Lingard, J. History of England, from B. C. 55 to A. D. 1673. London, 1823–5. 12 v. 8°. 6905
Linn, J. B. Powers of Genius. Philadelphia, 1801. 12°. . . . 11936
Antiquities of the Anglo-Saxon Church. Philadelphia, 1848. 8°. . 5076
Lionel Lincoln. J. F. Cooper. Philadelphia, 1831. 2 v. 16°. . . . 354
Lionel Wakefield. Philadelphia, 1837. 2 v. 12°. 1228
Lister, T. H. Life and Admin. of Earl of Clarendon. Lond. 1838. 3 v. 8°. 7902
Literati. E. A. Poe. New York, 1850. 12°. 505
The same. New York, 1857. 12°. 508
Literary Character, The. I. D'Israeli. New York, 1818. 12°. . . . 3326
The same. London, 1822. 2 v. 12°. 1177
Extracts, from Eng. and other works. J. Poynder. Lond. 2 v. 8°. 85
Gem, or Legend and Lyrics.s Boston, 1827. 18°. 4951
and Historical Miscellanies. G. Bancroft. New York, 1855. 8°. . 35
Hours. N. Drake. London, 1804. 3 v. 8°. 151
Recollections. R. Warner. London, 1830. 2 v. 8°. . . . 731
Reminiscences. T. De Quincey. Boston, 1851. 2 v. 12°. . . 894
World. Ed. C. E. Hoffman. New York, 1847. 2 v. 8°. . . 3096
Literature, Advice in the Pursuits of. S. L. Knapp. New York, 1832. 12°. 4914
Amenities of. I. D'Israeli. New York, 1845. 2 v. 12°. . . 512
American, Guide to. N. Trübner. London, 1859. 8°. . . 8833
Ancient and Modern, Hist. of. F. Schlegel. Tr. Phil. 1818. 8°. 453
Anecdotes of. W. Beloe. London, 1807. 6 v. 8°. 447
Characteristics of. H. T. Tuckerman. Philadelphia, 1849. 12°. . 806
Curiosities of. See Curiosities.

Literature, Cyclopædia of American. E. A. and J. L. Duyckinck. New York, 1855. 2 v. 4°. 8796
Cyclopædia of English. R. Chambers. Edin. 1844. 2 v. 4°. . 8803
and Ethics, Essays in. C. White. Boston, 1853. 8°. . . . 456
History of, Lectures on. F. von Schlegel. Tr. Phil. 1818. 8°. . 453
Influence of, upon Society. Mad. De Stael. Tr. Bost. 1813. 12°. 4595
and Poetry, Lectures on. J. Montgomery. New York, 1840. 12°. 5880
The same. New York, 1833. 16°. 8767
Pursuits of, a Satirical Poem. Philadelphia, 1800. 8°. . . 93
of Slavic Nations. Talvi. New York, 1850. 12°. . . . 828
Study of. E. Gibbon. Dublin, 1788. 12°. 4569
Little Dorrit. C. Dickens. Philadelphia. 8°. 73
Little Frenchman, and his Water Lots. G. P. Morris. Phil. 1839. 12°. 1176
Savage. F. Marryat. New York, 1849. 12°. 550
The same. 1286
Littleton, G., (Lord.) Letters. Philadelphia, 1821. 24°. . . . 4937
The same. 4955
Select Poems, with Life, by S. Johnson. Philadelphia, 1822. 18°. 2143
Liverpool, Earl of, Mem's of the Public Life and Admin. of. Lond 1827. 8°. 8199
Living Beings, Lectures on. C. Matteucci. Tr. Philadelphia, 1848. 12°. 788
for Immortality. J. Foster. Boston, 1840. 12°. 6576
Livingston, V. Remarks on Oxford Theology. New York, 1841. 12°. . 6571
Livingston, W. Memoirs. T. Sedgwick, Jr. New York, 1833. 2 v. 8°. 7922
The same. 8130
Livius, T. Historiæ. Lipsiæ, 1829. 3 v. 16°. 10357
The same. Tr. G. Baker. New York, 1841. 5 v. 12°. . 5281
The same. Boston, 1823. 6 v. 8°. 11351
Historiarum libri priores quinque. Utica, 1821. 12°. . . . 11467
The same. 11477
Llorente, J. A. History of the Spanish Inquisition. Trans. and abridged. London, 1826. 8°. 6716
Historia Critica de la Inquisicion de Espana. Abridged. R. Buron. Paris, 1823. 2 v. 16°. 6849
Lloyd, W. and A. Gerard. Tour among the Himalaya Mountains. London, 1840. 2 v. 8°. 9127
Locke, J. Life and Corespondence. Lord King. London, 1830. 2 v. 8°. 7949
Reasonableness of Christianity. London, 1836. 12°. . . . 5798
Treatise on the Understanding. Boston, 1828. 18°. . . . 4614
The same. New York, 1823. 18°. 4637
The same. New York, 1845. 12°. 5221
Two Treatises of Government. London, 1772. 8°. 11087
Works. London, 1753–1801. 8 v. 8°. 6348
Lockhart, J. G. History of Napoleon. New York, 1840. 2 v. 12°. . 5506
The same. New York, 1830. 2 v. 16°. 6630
The same. New York, 1833. 2 v. 16°. 6639
Life of R. Burns. New York, 1831. 18°. 8438
Memoirs of the Life of W. Scott. Boston, 1837, 8. 7 v. 12°. . . 8036
and others Peter's Letters to his Kinsfolk. New York, 1820. 8°. 9725

Lockhart, J. G. Valerius, a Roman Story. Boston, 1821. 2 v. 12°. 701
Lockman, J. Travels of the Jesuits into Various Parts of the World. London, 1762. 2 v. 8°. 8882
Lodge, E. Brit. History, Biography, &c. Illust. London, 1838. 3 v. 8°. 7581
Portraits of Illustrious Personages of G. Brit. Lond. 1849. 8 v. 12°. 5478
Logan, a Family History. Philadelphia, 1822. 2 v. 12°. 1411
Logan, James. The Scottish Gaël. Boston, 1833. 8°. 7351
Logan, John. Sermons. Boston, 1804. 8°. 5385
Logarithms. F. Callet. Paris, 1795. 8°. 11666
Logic, Elements of. W. Duncan. Albany, 1811. 12°. 3024
The same. Albany, 1804. 12°. 4981
Elements of. L. Hedge. Cooperstown, 1846. 12°. 4594
Elements of. I. Watts. London, 1792. 8°. 454
The same. Boston, 1819. 12°. 3028
System of. J. S. Mills. New York, 1848. 8°. 396
Lomène, L. de. Beaumarchais and his Times. Tr. New York, 1857. 12°. 7395
London Art Journal for 1853–58. 4°. . . . .
Instructive Rambles in. Elizabeth Helm. New York. 1814. 12°. 9278
Life in. P. Egan. London, 1823. 8°. 4
Night's Entertainments. L. Ritchie. Phil. 1830. 2 v. 12°. . . 1129
Pictorially Illustrated. C. Knight. London, 1841. 6 v. 4°. . . 7800
Quarterly Review. vols. 52–103. (continued.) N. Y. 1834–59. 8°. 4326
Residences at the Court of, in 1817–25. R. Rush. Phil. 1845. 8°. 9164
The same, continued to 1825. (Two copies,) Phil. 1845. 8°. 9382
Sketches of. R. Grant. Philadelphia, 1839. 2 v. 12°. . . . 9838
Stage, The, a Collection of Tragedies, Comedies, &c. Lond. 3 v. 8°. 1929
Times, Essays from. New York, 1852. 12°. 4574
Second series. New York, 1852. 12°. 4576
and Westminster Review. vols. 25–33. New York, 1836–40. 8°. 4354
What I Saw in. D. W. Bartlett. Auburn, 1852. 12°. . . . 8891
Long, G. Grammar Schools. London, 1842. 18°. 5930
Long, S. H. Expedi. to the Rocky Mts. in 1819, 20. Phil. 1823. 2 v. 8°. 9432
Long Look Ahead. A. S. Roe. New York, 1856. 12°. 12209
Longfellow, H. W. Courtship of Miles Standish. Boston, 1859. 12°. . 1943
Evangeline. Boston, 1848. 12°. 2020
Golden Legend. Boston, 1852. 12°. 1989
Hyperion. Boston, 1853. 12°. 1245
Kavanagh, a Tale. Boston, 1849. 12°. 1616
Outre-Mer. New York, 1835. 2 v. 12°. 1607
Poems. Boston, 1853. 2 v. 12°. 1988
Poets and Poetry of Europe. Philadelphia, 1845. 8°. . . . 1806
Song of Hiawatha. Boston, 1856. 12°. 1987
Voices of the Night. Cambridge, 1840. 12°. 2373
Longinus. De Sublimitate. New York, 1812. 8°. 2692
Longitude Tables. Margett. London, 1790. 4° 11988
Longstreet. A. B. Georgia Scenes, Characters, &c. New York, 1843. 12°. 1609
Loom and Lugger, The, a Tale. Harriet Martineau. Bost. 1833. 2 v. 18°. 1692
Loomis, E. Recent Progress of Astronomy. New York, 1850. 12°. . 5998

Lord Nial, a Romance, with the Wizard's Grave, &c. J. M. M. New York, 1834. 12°. 1960
Lord's Prayer, Lectures on. W. R. Williams. Boston, 1851. 12°. . . 5703
Prayer, Creed and Commandments, Expositions of. R. Leighton. London, 1834. 12°. 5787
Lorenz, F. Life of Alcuin. Tr. Jane M. Slee. London, 1837. 12°. . 7734
Lorenzo de Medici. Life. W. Roscoe. London, 1847. 12°. . . . 5135
Lorette, History of. Louise G. Bourne. New York, 1834. 18°. . . 1691
Lorgnette, or Studies about Town. D. G. Mitchell. N. Y. 1851. 2 v. 12°. 219
The same. New York, 1859. 2 v. 12°. 211
Los Gringos. Lieut. Wise. New York, 1849. 12°. 8920
The same. New York, 1850. 12°. 8921
Lossing, B. J. History of the Fine Arts. New York, 1840. 12°. . . 5563
Pictorial Field-Book of the Revolution. N. Y. 1859. 2 v. 8°. . 11986
Lost Senses. Blindness. J. Kitto. London, 1845. 16°. 6883
Deafness. London, 1845. 16°. 7195
Lothrop, Amy. Dollars and Cents. New York, 1852. 2 v. 12°. . . 1279
Lothrop, S. K. Hist. of the Church in Brattle St., Bost. Bost. 1851. 12°. . 6506
Life of S. Kirkland. Boston, 1848. 12°. 8067
Lotus Eating. G. W. Curtis. New York, 1856. 12°. 528
Louis, Prince of Condé. Life. Lord Mahon. New York, 1848. 12°. . 8371
Louis XIII, History of the Reign of. M. LeVassor. Tr. Lond. 1700. 8°. 11453
Louis XIV, The Age of. F. M. A. de Voltaire. Tr. Lond. 1752. 2 v. 8°. 11408
and the Court of France, in the 17th Century. Miss Pardoe. New York, 1848. 2 v. 8586
Life and Times of. G. P. R. James. London, 1851. 2 v. 12°. . 5197
Memoirs of the Court of. T. P. Lathy. London, 1819. 3 v. 8°. . 7955
Memoirs of the Court of France during the Reign of. M. Anquetil. Tr. Edinburgh, 1791. 2 v. 8°. 8521
Louis XVI, Memoirs of the Reign of. J. L. Soulavie. Tr. London, 1802. 6 v. 8°. 8235
Political and Confidential Correspondence of. Tr. Helen M. Williams. London, 1803. 3 v. 8°. 11016
Private Mem's of. A. F. A. de Moleville. Tr. Lond. 1797. 3 v. 8°. 7966
Louis XVIII, Private Memoirs of the Court of. By a Lady. London, 1830. 2 v. 8°. 7584
Louis Philippe. Life and Times. G. N. Wright. London. 8°. . . 7842
Louisiana, Colonial History and Romance of. C. Gayarre. N. Y. 1851. 8°. 7235
History of. B. Marbois. Tr. Philadelphia, 1830. 2 v. 8°. . . 7225
Lounger, The. London, 1823. 2 v. 18°. 3692
The same. New York, 1789. 2 v. 12°. 4273
Love, C. Sermons. London, 1653. 12°. 11875
Love, Conjugal and Scortatory. E. Swedenborg. Boston, 1840. 8°. . 5012
Love-Chase, The, a Comedy. J. S. Knowles. New York, 1838. 18°. . 2393
Lovell, J. E. Ed. United States Speaker. Charleston, 1837. 12°. . . 3320
The same. (Two copies.) New Haven, 1833. 12°. . . 3321
Loves of the Angels. T. Moore. London, 1844. 12°. 2256
The same. New York, 1823. 16°. 3077

Lovejoy, E. P. Memoir. J. C. and O. Lovejoy. New York, 1838. 12°. . 8422
Lover, S. Handy Andy, a Tale of Irish Life. New York, 1843. 8°. . 14
Legends and Stories of Ireland. London, 1837. 2 v. 16°. . . 1640
Lovzinski, Baron de. Autobiography. Hartford, 1800. 18°. . . . 8425
Lowell, J. R. Conversations on some of the Old Poets. Camb. 1845. 12°. 4581
Fable for Critics. New York, 1848. 12°. 2347
Poems. Cambridge, 1844. 12°. 2455
The same. Boston, 1849. 2 v. 12°. 1997
Lower, M. A. Essays on English Surnames. London, 1844. 12°. . . 459
Lowman, M. Paraphrase and Notes on the Revelation of St. John. London, 1773. 8°. 5370
Lowrie, W. M. Memoirs. New York, 1849. 8°. 7847
Lowth, R. Introduction to English Grammar. Philadelphia, 1775. 12°. 4904
The same. 4985
Life of. W. Wykeham. London, 1758. 12°. 8625
New Translation of Isaiah, with Notes. London, 1833. 8°. . . 5110
Lucanus, M. A. Pharsalia. Lipsiæ, 1834. 16°. 10614
Lucianus. Opera. Lipsiæ, 1829. 16°. 10821
Select Dialogues, with Latin Trans. E. Murphy. Phil. 1804. 12°. 3319
The same. 3327
Complete Works. Tr. T. Francklin. London, 1781. 4 v. 8°. . 6025
Luck of Barry Lyndon. W. M. Thackeray. New York, 1853. 12°. . 959
The same. 2 v. 1632
Lucretius Carus, T. De Rerum Natura. Lipsiæ, 1833. 16°. . . . 10611
Lusiad, The, an Epic Poem. L. De Camoëns. Tr. W. J. Mickle. Dublin, 1791. 2 v. 8°. 1862
Luther, M. Life. A. Bower. Philadelphia, 1824. 8°. 11309
Life and Times. Mrs. H. Lee. Boston, 1841. 12°. 8387
Life. M. Meuren. Tr. New York, 1848. 8°. 7848
Deeds, and Opin. of. J. F. W. Tischer. Tr. J. Kortz. Hud. 1818. 12°. 7727
J. Michelet. Tr. G. H. Smith. New York, 1846. 12°. . . . 8672
Table Talk of. Tr. W. Hazlitt. London, 1848. 12°. . . . 5489
Lydians, History of. London, 1779. 8°. 7032
Lyell, C. Principles of Geology. Philadelphia, 1837. 2 v. 8°. . . 5947
The same. 5953
Second Visit to the United States. New York, 1850. 2 v. 12°. . 8912
Travels in North America. New York, 1845. 12°. . . . 9255
Lying in all its Branches Illustrated. Mrs. A. Opie. Hartford, 1827. 12°. 6489
The same. Boston, 1827. 12°. 917
Lynch, W. F. Expedition to the Dead Sea. Philadelphia, 1850. 8°. . 9374
Lyon, G. F. Journal and Residence in Mexico. London, 1828. 12°. . 9239
Lyric Poems. I. Watts. Boston, 1790. 16°. 2454
Lysias. Orationes. Lipsiæ, 1829. 16°. 10344
Lyttleton, G. (Lord.) Life of Henry II. London, 1769. 6 v. 8°. . . 8541

M.

Macaulay, Catharine. Hist. of Eng. from 1603 to 1660. Lon. 1769. 5 v. 8°. 6720
Macaulay, T. B. Biographical and Historical Sketches. N. Y. 1857. 12°. 834

Macaulay, T. B. Critical and Miscellaneous Essays. Phil. 1842. 4 v. 12°. 869
The same. vols. 2 and 3. 873
History of England. vols. 1 and 2. New York, 1849. 8°. . 7246
The same. New York, 1850. 8°. 7248
The same. vols. 3 and 4. New York, 1856. 12°. . . 7108
New Biographies of Illustrious Men. Boston, 1857. 12°. . . 830
Speeches. New York, 1853. 2 v. 12°. 11135
Macbriar, R. M. Chapters on National Education. London, 1845. 8°. . 11694
M'Crie, T. Hist. of the Reform'n in Italy and Spain. Ed. 1829-33. 2 v. 8°. 5590
The same. Edinburgh, 1827-9. 2 v. 8°. 7329
Life of J. Knox, with Reformation in Scotland, &c. N. Y. 1833. 8°. 8486
McCullagh, W. T. The Use and Study of History. Dublin, 1842. 8°. . 12050
McCulloch, J. R. Commercial Dictionary. Philadelphia, 1843. 2 v. 8°. 10930
Geographical Dictionary. New York, 1847. 2 v. 8°. 8805
McFarlane, C. The Romance of Travel. vol. 1. London, 1846. 16°. . 7188
Lives of Banditti and Robbers of All Nations. Phil. 1833. 12°. . 8078
The same. Philadelphia, 1839. 2 v. 12°. 8685
McFingal. J. Trumbull. Boston, 1799. 16°. 3067
M'Gavin, W. The Protestant. Essays. Hartford, 1833. 2 v. 8°. . . 5601
Mac-Geoghegan. History of Ireland. Tr. New York. 4°. 7806
Macgillivray, W. Travels and Res. of A. von Humboldt. N. Y. 1840. 12°. 5870
MacGregor, J. Progress of America. London, 1847. 2 v. 8°. . . . 7798
M'Guire, E. C. Religious Opin. and Char. of G. Washington. N. Y. '36. 12°. 6130
Machiavelli, N. Works of. Tr. London, 1720. 4°. 11251
History of Florence and other Works. London, 1847. 12°. . . 5128
M'Ilvaine, C. P. Oxford Divinity. Philadelphia, 1841. 8°. 5011
McHarg, C. Life of M. de Talleyrand. New York, 1837. 12°. . . . 8643
Mackay, C. Voices from the Mts. and from the Crowd. Bost. 1853. 12°. 1985
Mackenzie, A. S. The American in England. New York, 1835. 2 v. 12°. 8690
Life of S. Decatur. Boston, 1846. 12°. 8063
Life of Paul Jones. New York, 1846. 2 v. 12°. 7730
Life of O. H. Perry. New York, 1841. 2 v. 12°. 5900
The same. New York, 1841. 2 v. 12°. 5901
Review of the Naval Court Martial of. J. F. Cooper. N. Y. 1844. 8°. 10965
Spain Revisited. New York, 1836. 2 v. 12°. 9572
A Year in Spain. New York, 1836. 3 v. 12°. 8899
Mackenzie, C. Notes on Haiti. London, 1830. 2 v. 12°. . . . 8994
Mackenzie, H. Works. (vol. 1 missing.) Glasgow, 1820. 3 v. 24°. . 1737

2. The Man of the World.
3. Julia De Roubigne; Papers from the Minor.

Mackie, J. M. Life of S. Gorton. Boston, 1845. 12°. 8057
Life of Tai-Ping-Wang. New York, 1857. 12°. 8667
Mackintosh, D. French-English Grammar. Boston, 1797. 8°. . . 11654
Mackintosh, J. Defence of the French Revolution. London, 1792. 8°. . 6761
History of England to 1588. London, 1833. 3 v. 12°. . . . 5826
The same. 6827
The same. (vol. 3 missing.) 6825

Mackintosh, J. History of England, with a continuation to 1760, by W. Wallace and others. London, 1836. 10 v. 12°. . . . 9898
History of the Revolution in England in 1688. Phil. 1835. 8°. . 6685
Memoirs. R. J. Mackintosh. London, 1836. 2 v. 8°. . . . 8181
The same. Philadelphia, 1835. 2 v. 12°. 8296
Progress of Ethical Philosophy. Boston, 1853. 4°. . . . 10035
The same. Edinburgh, 1837. 8°. 6321
Works. London, 1846. 3 v. 8°. 6302

1. Progress of Ethical Philosophy; Philosophical Genius of Bacon and Locke; Law of Nature and Nations; Life of Sir Thomas Moore; Authorship of Icon Basilikê; Affairs of Holland.
2. English Revolution of 1688; Partition of Poland; Administration and Fall of Struensee; Case of Donna Maria of Portugal; Charles First, Marquis Cornwallis; Character of George Canning; Preface to a Reprint of the Edinburgh Review of 1755; Writings of Machiavelli; Lives of Milton's Nephews; Review of Roger's Poems; Madame de Stael's Germany. Discourse at the Literary Society of Bombay.
3. Defence of the French Revolution; State of France in 1815; Right of Parliamentary Suffrage; Defence of Jean Peltier; Charge to Grand Jury of Bombay; Speeches.

M'Laurin, J. Essays on Happiness, Christian Piety, &c. Phil. 1836. 12°. 6493
Macneill, H. Select Poems and Life. Philadelphia, 1822. 18°. . . 2151
Macnish, R. Philosophy of Sleep. New York, 1834. 12°. . . . 4884
Tales, Essays, and Sketches. London, 1844. 2 v. 8°. . . . 1168
M'Roy, Annals of the Family of. Mrs. Blackford. New York, 1837. 12°. 8288
Macedonia, History of. London, 1779. 2 v. 8°. 7035
Madagascar, History of. W. Ellis. London, 1838. 2 v. 8°. . . . 6993
Madden, R. R. Infirmities of Genius. Philadelphia, 1833. 12°. . . 4915
Life and Corres. of Countess of Blessington. New York, 1856. 12°. 8020
Lives and Times of the United Irishmen. Phil. 1842. 2 v. 12°. . 8664
Third series. Dublin, 1846. 3 v. 8°. 7990
Mussulman. London, 1830. 2 v. 12°. 1360
Travels in Egypt, Nubia, and Turkey. Phil. 1830. 2 v. 18°. . . 9604
Madeline. Mrs. A. Opie. Boston, 1827. 12°. 907
Madison, J. Political Papers. Washington, 1840. 3 v. 8°. . . . 10467
Madrid in 1835. New York, 1836. 8°. 9144
Magee, W. Atonement and Sacrifice. New York, 1839. 2 v. 8°. . . 5050
Magic, Natural, Letters on. D. Brewster. New York, 1832. 16°. . . 4956
The same. 5866
The same. 6617
Philosophy of. E. Salverte. Tr. New York, 1847. 2 v. 12°. . 3333
Maginn, W. Shakspeare Papers. New York, 1856. 12°. . . . 526
Magoon, E. Living Orators in America. New York, 1849. 12°. . . 8669
Orators of American Revolution. New York, 1848. 12°. . . 8668
Mahan, D. H. Elements of Civil Engineering. New York, 1838. 8°. . 11671
Mahomet and his Successors. W. Irving. New York, 1859. 2 v. 12°. . 529
See also Mohammed.
Mahon, Lord. History of England from 1713–1748. Paris, 1841. 2 v. 8°. 7024
The same, with a continuation to 1763. Ed. H. Reed. New York, 1849. 2 v. 8°. 7238

Mahon, Lord. Hist. of the War of the Succession in Spain. Lond. 1836. 8°. 6674
Life of Belisarius. Philadelphia, 1832. 12°. 8411
Life of Louis, Prince of Condé. New York, 1845. 12°. . . . 8371
Maiden and Married Life of Mary Powell. New York, 1852. 12°. . . 8727
Maine, History of the District of. J. Sullivan. Boston, 1795. 8°. . . 6757
Statistical View of. M. Greenleaf. Boston, 1816. 8°. . . . 9767
Maitland, F. L. The Church in the Catacombs. London, 1846. 8°. . 11332
Surrender of Bonaparte. Boston, 1826. 12°. 11412
Mair, J. Latin Dictionary. New York, 1809. 12°. 3331
Malcolm, H. Sketches of Persia, &c. London, 1828. 2 v. 12°. . . 9574
Travels in South Eastern Asia. Boston, 1839. 2 v. 12°. . . 9568
Malibran, M. G. Memoirs. Countess de Merlin. Phil. 1840. 2 v. 12°. . 8317
Mallet, D. Elvira, a Tragedy. London, 1778. 12°. 11887
Poetical Works, with Life by S. Johnson. Phil. 1822. 18°. . . 2138
Malta, History of. London, 1782. 8°. 7062
Knights of. A. Sutherland. Philadelphia, 1846. 12°. . . . 4522
Maltby, J. Elements of War. Boston, 1813. 12°. 3344
Malte-Brun, C. Universal Geography. Philadelphia, 1827. 6 v. 8°. . 9077
Malthus, T. R. Essay on Population. Georegtown, 1809. 2 v. 8°. . . 10518
Mammalia, Natural History of. See Naturalist's Library.
Mammon, or Covetousness the Sin of the Church. J. Harris. N. Y. 16°. 5242
The same. 6227
Man About Town. C. Webbe. London, 1838. 2 v. 12°. 143
Man, Adapt. of Nature to his Phys. Condition. J. Kidd. Phil. 1833. 12°. 6486
Constitution of. A. Combe. Boston, 1833. 12°. 4577
and His Migrations. R. G. Latham. New York. 1852. 12°. . 6160
and his Motives. G. Moore. New York, 1843. 6496
Natural Laws of. J. G. Spurzheim. Boston, 1832. 16°. . . . 6569
Observ. on his Frame, Duty, &c. D. Hartley. Lond. 1834. 8°. . 6341
Sketches of the History of. Lord Kames. Edin. 1813. 3 v. 8°. . 420
The same. Dublin, 1779. 2 v. 8°. 11691
of the World, The. H. Mackenzie. Glasgow, 1820. 24°. . . 1737
Manchester Strike. Miss H. Martineau. Boston, 1838. 16°. . . . 10024
Mandeville. W. Godwin. Philadelphia, 1818. 2 v. 12°. 656
Mangles, J., and C. L. Irby. Trav. in Egypt, Nubia, &c. Lond. 1844. 12°. 9286
Mankind, Moral Improvement, &c., of. T. Dick. New York, 1836. 12°. . 5190
Physical History of. J. C. Prichard. London, 1836. 2 v. 8°. . 405
The same. London, 1842. 4 v. 8°. 735
Manly Piety. R. Philip. New York, 1833. 12°. 6590
The same. New York, 1834. 12°. 6573
Mann, H. Letters and Speeches on Slavery. Boston, 1853. 12°. . . 11144
Thoughts for a Young Man. Boston, 1850. 12°. 4979
Mansfield Park. Miss J. Austen. Philadelphia, 1832. 2 v. 12°. . . 1515
The same. Philadelphia, 1838. 8°. 37
Mansie Wauch, Life of. J. Galt. New York, 1828. 12°. . . . 988
Mantell, G. Wonders of Geology. London, 1839. 12°. 6098
Manufact., British, Chem., Textile, &c. G. Dodd. Lond. 1844. 6 v. 16°. 7466
Manzoni, A. I Promessi Sposi, or the Betrothed. Tr. Wash. 1834. 8°. 23

Marbois, B. History of Louisiana. Tr. Philadelphia, 1830. 8°. . . 7225
March, D. Yankee Land and the Iron Horse. Hartford, 1840. 12°. . 2218
Marchmont Papers. London, 1831. 3 v. 8°. 6686
Marco Polo, Travels of. H. Murray. New York, 1845. 12°. . . . 5250
The same. New York, 1845. 12°. 5928
Marcy, G. B. Explor. of the Red River, in 1852. Wash. 1854. 2 v. 8°. 10430
Margaret Ravenscroft. J. A. St. John. Philadelphia, 1836. 2 v. 12°. . 1296
Margaret Smith's Journal, 1678-9. Boston, 1849. 12°. 3919
Margett, G. Longitude Tables. London, 1790. 4°. 11988
Margravine of Anspach. Autobiography. London, 1826. 2 v. 8°. . . 7964
of Bareith. Autobiography. London, 1828. 2 v. 16°. . . 7499
Marguerite de Valois. A. Dumas. New York, 1846. 8°. . . . 11
Maria Antoinette. Memoirs. J. Weber. Tr R. C. Dallas and others. London, 1805. 3 v. 8°. 7815
Memoirs of the Private Life of. Mad. Campan. Phil. 1823. 8°. . 8535
Mariendorpt. Anna M. Porter. Boston, 1821. 2 v. 12°. 1637
Marigny, Abbe De. History of the Arabians. Tr. Lond. 1758. 4 v. 8°. 6777
Mariner's Chronicle. New Haven, 1834. 12°. 6789
Marion, F. Life. P. Horry and L. M. Weems. Philadelphia, 1831. 12°. 8388
W. G. Simms. New York, 1844. 12°. 8305
Marlborough, Duke of, Memoirs of. London, 1847. 3 v. 12°. . . . 5166
Sarah, Duch. of. Mems. Mrs. A. T. Thomson. Lond. 1829. 2 v. 8°. 7866
Marmion. W. Scott. Philadelphia, 1808. 2 v. 12°. 1388
Marmontel, J. F. Autobiography. London, 1830. 2 v. 16°. . . . 7747
The same. London, 1829. 16°. 7482
The same. Philadelphia, 1807. 2 v. 12°. . . . . , 7455
Moral Tales. London, 1800. 2 v. 12°. 1654
Marquesas, Life in the. H. Melville. New York, 1846. 12°. . . . 9855
Marquette, Father, Life of. J. Sparks. Boston, 1838. 12°. . . . 8052
Marriage, Adultery, &c., Essay on. R. Polwhele. London, 1823. 12°. . 3926
and Courtship, Letters on. 18°. 4940
Married State, its Obligations, &c. J. Foster. New York, 1845. 12°. . 3362
Marryatt, F. Diary in America. Philadelphia, 1839. 12°. . . . 9007
Second series. Philadelphia, 1840. 12°. 9815
Jacob Faithful. Philadelphia, 1834. 3 v. 12°. 1327
The same. New York, 1835. 12°. 1250
Japhet in Search of a Father. Philadelphia, 1835. 2 v. 12°. . 1519
The King's Own. Philadelphia, 1834. 2 v. 12°. 1581
The same. New York, 1836. 12°. 1295
Little Savage. New York, 1849. 12°. 550
The same. 1286
Masterman Ready. New York. 3 v. 18°. 1686
Newton Forster. Philadelphia, 1833. 2 v. 12°. 1613
Pacha of Many Tales. Philadelphia, 1834. 2 v. 12°. . . . 1385
The same. New York, 1835. 12°. 1253
Peter Simple. Philadelphia, 1835. 2 v. 12°. 707
The same. . , ... 1251
Phantom-Ship. Philadelphia, 1839. 2 v. 12°. 1560

Marryatt, F. Pirate and Three Cutters. New York, 1836. 2 v. 12°. . 670
The same. Philadelphia, 1836. 12°. 672
The same. 954
The same. 1399
Snarleyyou, or the Dog Fiend. Philadelphia, 1837. 12°. . . 237
Marsh, Mrs. Mordaunt Hall. New York, 1851. 8°. 48
Mount Sorel. New York, 1851. 8°. 48
Marsh, James. Memoir and Remains. Boston, 1843. 8°. . . . 6305
Marsh, John. Epitome of Ecclesiastical History. New York, 1828. 12°. 6178
Marshall, J. History of American Colonies. Philadelphia, 1824. 8°. . 7226
Life of George Washington. Philadelphia, 1804. 5 v. 8°. . . 8216
The same, with an Atlas. Philadelphia, 1833. 3 v. 8°. . 7514
Writings upon the Federal Constitution. Boston, 1839. 8°. . 10929
Marshall, W. Gospel Mystery of Sanctification. New York, 1811. 12°. . 6504
Marston, J. W. Gerald and other Poems. London, 1842. 12°. . . 2346
Marston, or the Memoirs of a Statesman. G. Croly. Phil. 1845. 8°. . 22
Marten, H. Life. J. Forster. London, 1838. 12°. 9935
Martialis, M. V. Epigrammata. Lipsiæ, 1829. 16°. 10613
Martin Chuzzlewit. C. Dickens. Philadelphia. 8°. 69
Martin, W. C. L. History of the Horse. London, 1845. 16°. . . 6894
Martin, J. Account of the Tonga Islands. Boston, 1820. 8°. . . . 8831
French Homonyms. New York, 1807. 12°. 3010
Martin, R. M. British Colonial Library. London, 1837–43. 16°. . . 5818

Vol. 1. The Canadas.
2. Austral-Asia.
3. Southern Africa.
4. West Indies.
5. The same.
Vol. 6. Nova Scotia.
7. Mediterranean Possessions.
8. 9. East Indies.
10. Possessions in the Indian and Atlantic Oceans.

Eastern Life. Philadelphia, 1848. 8°. 9519
Martineau, M ss H. Crofton Boys. New York, 1856. 16°. . . . 1679
Feats on the Fiord. London, 1844. 16°. 7175
The Hamlets, a Tale. Boston, 1836. 16°. 10027
How to Observe. New York, 1838. 12°. 4887
Miscellanies. Boston, 1836. 2 v. 12°. 798
Retrospect of Western Travel. New York, 1838. 2 v. 12°. . . 9601
Society in America. New York, 1837. 2 v. 8°. 9611
Sowers not Reapers. Hartford, 1845. 18°. 1680
Illustrations of Political Economy. Boston, 1833. 13 v. 18°.

No. 10028. Brooke and Brooke Farm.
1699. The Charmed Sea.
10029. Cousin Marshall.
1674. Demerara.
10021. The same.
10022. Ella of Garveloch.
10023. For Each and All.
10026. Hill and Valley.
No. 1673. Homes Abroad.
10025. Ireland.
1678. Life in the Wilds.
1692. Loom and Lugger.
10024. Manchester Strike.
1676. Weal and Woe in Garveloch.
1677. The same.

Martineau, J. Endeavors after the Christian Life. Boston, 1858. 12°. . 12170
Martyn, H. Journal and Letters. Ed. S. Wilberforce. N. Y. 1851. 12°. 5731

Martyn, H. Memoir. J. Sargent. Boston, 1820. 8°. 8231
The same. Abridged. New York. 18°. 5229
Martyr of Antioch, a Dramatic Poem. H. H. Milman. Lond. 1840. 18°. 2031
Wife, a Domestic Romance. New York, 1844. 8°. . . . 1103
Martyrs, Book of. J. Fox. Ed. J. Malham. Philadelphia, 1830. 4°. . 5004
or Triumphs of Christian Religion. Tr. F. A. de Chateaubriand. New York, 1812. 3 v. 12°. 6552
of Science, Lives of. D. Brewster. New York, 1841. 12°. . . 5906
Mary of Burgundy. G. P. R. James. New York, 1833. 2 v. 12°. . . 1015
Queen of Scots. Life. H. G. Bell. New York, 1840. 2 v. 12°. . 5525
The same. New York, 1831. 2 v. 16°. 6637
and Elizabeth, History of. F. Von Raumer. London, 1836. 12°. . 8594
Mason, E. P. Life and Writings. D. Olmsted. New York, 1842. 12°. . 8307
The same. 8635
Mason, J., Life of. G. E. Ellis. Boston, 1844. 12°. 8055
Treatise on Self Knowledge. New York. 16°. 5243
The same. London, 1784. 12°. 11930
Mason, J. M. Writings. Ed. E. Mason. New York, 1833. 4 v. 8°. . 5609
Mason, W. A Spiritual Treasury. vol. 2. New York, 1803. 8°. . . 6377
Masonic Institution, Catalogue of Books on. Boston, 1852. 12°. . . 9711
Masonry and Anti-Masonry, Letters on. W. L. Stone. N. Y. 1832. 8°. . 9760
Speculative, Opinions on. J. C. Odiorne. Boston, 1830. 12°. . 4543
Massachusetts Bay, Chron. of the Colony of. A. Young. Bost. 1846. 8°. 7271
Bay, Hist. of, from 1748. G. R. Minot. Boston, 1798. 2 v. 8°. . 7372
Historical Collections of. J. W. Barber. Washington, 1841. 8°. . 6690
History of D. Shay's Rebellion in. G. R. Minot. Bost. 1810. 8°. 6927
History of, from 1775–89. A. Bradford. Boston, 1825. 8°. . 11329
History of, from 1620–1750. T. Hutchinson. Salem, 1795. 2 v. 8°. 6755
Journal of the Settlement. J. Winthrop. Hartford, 1798. 8°. . 10804
Scenery of. Illustrated. Northampton, 1842. 4°. . . . .
Massey, G. Poems and Ballads. New York, 1854. 12°. . . . 2355
Massillon, J. B. Sermons, with Life. Tr. W. Dickson. Dun. 1803. 3 v. 12°. 6542
Massinger, P. Dramatic Works. London, 1840. 8°. 1786
Plays. New York, 1831. 3 v. 16°. 6241
Masterman Ready, or the Wreck of the Pacific. F. Marryatt. N. Y. 3 v. 18°. 1686
Mathematical Repository. T. Leybourn. vol. 1. London, 1806. 8°. . 2698
Study, Advantages of. J. R. Young. London, 1846. 12°. . . 3307
Mathematics, Philosophy of. W. M. Gillespie. New York, 1851. 8°. . 1067
and Physical Science, Progress of. J. Playfair. Boston, 1853. 4°. 10035
and Physical Science, Progress of, during 18th Century. J. Leslie. Boston, 1853. 4°. 10035
Mather, C., Life of. W. B. O. Peabody. (Two copies.) Bost. 1836. 12°. 8047
Magnalia Christi Americana. Hartford, 1820. 2 v. 8°. . . . 7222
Mather, M. View of Divinity. Stamford, 1813. 12°. 6558
Mather, W. W. Geological Survey of Ohio. Columbus, 1838. 8°. . . 6002
and others. Geology of New York. Albany, 1843. 3 v. 4°. . 13107
Mathew, T. Memoir. J. Bermingham. New York, 1841. 12°. . . 11455
Mathews, Cornelius. Various Writings. New York, 1843. 8°. . . 9732

Mathews, Charles. Memoirs. Mrs. C. Mathews. Phil. 1839. 2 v. 12°. . 8578
The same, continued. Philadelphia, 1839. 2 v. 12°. . . 8603
Mathews, Mrs. C. Griffith Abbey, or Memoirs of Eugenia. N. Y. 1808. 12°. 1584
Matter and Spirit. Disquisitions on. J. Priestly. Birming. 1782. 2 v. 8°. 6397
Matteucci, C. Lectures on Living Beings. Phil. 1848. 12°. . . . 788
Matthews, H. Diary of an Invalid. Paris, 1836. 16°. 9315
Matthias and his Impostures. W. L. Stone. New York, 1835. 16°. . 6575
Maturin, E. Montezuma. the Last of the Aztecs. N. Y. 1845. 2 v. 12°. . 1318
Maturin, R. C. Melmoth, the Wanderer. New York, 1835. 2 v. 12°. . 1571
Maud and other Poems. A. Tennyson. Boston, 1855. 12°. . . . 1950
Maundevile, Sir J. Voiage and Travaile. London, 1839. 8°. . . . 9456
Maurice, F. D. Kingdom of Christ. New York, 1843. 8°. . . . 5015
Maurice, T. Institutions, Litera., &c., of Hindostan. Lond. 1800. 7 v. 8°. 11366
Maury, Abbe. Principles of Eloquence. New York, 1848. 12°. . . 5258
Maury, M. F. Physical Geography of the Sea. New York, 1856. 8°. . 5951
Maxwell, J. S. The Czar, his Court and People. New York, 1848. 12°. 9808
May, T. E. The Imperial Parliament. London, 1842. 12°. . . . 5931
May-Day with the Muses. R. Bloomfield. London, 1822. 12°. . . 2029
Mayer, B. History of Mexico. Hartford, 1851. 8°. 7253
Mexico as it was and is. New York, 1844. 8°. 6977
(Editor.) Twenty Years of an African Slaver. N. Y. 1854. 12°. 9791
Mayflower, or Sketches of Scenes and Characters among the Descendants of the Pilgrims. Mrs. H. B. Stowe. New York, 1843. 16°. .
Mayo, R. Origin, Operations, &c., of the Treasury Department and its Various Fiscal Bureaus. Washington, 1847. 4°. . . . 13114
Mayo, W. S. Berber, a Tale of Morocco. New York, 1850. 12°. . . 250
Kaloolah, or Journeyings to Djébel Kumri. New York, 1849. 12°. 8888
Mayor of Wind-Gap. J. Banim. Philadelphia, 1835. 12°. . . . 261
The same. (Two copies.) New York, 1835. 12°. . . 1316
Mechanical Science, Dictionary of. A. Jamieson. London, 1832. 4°. . 10918
Mechanics, Illustrations of. H. Moseley. New York, 1844. 12°. . . 5256
Treatise on. D. Lardner and H. Kater. Philadelphia, 1833. 12°. 5840
The same. London, 1837. 12°. 9958
Elements of. J. Renwick. Philadelphia, 1832. 8°. . . . 11668
Mechanism of the Heavens. Mrs. M. Somerville. Philadelphia, 1832. 16°. 4604
of Nature, Philosophy of. New York, 1852. 8°. 394
Medea. L. A. Seneca. Cambridge, 1834. 16°. 3072
Medes, History of. London, 1779. 8°. 7032
Medhurst, W. H. China, its State and Prospects. London, 1838. 8°. . 9446
Medical Delusions. W. Hooker. New York, 1850. 12°. 3308
Medici, De L. Life. W. Roscoe. Philadelphia, 1803. 3 v. 8°. . . 8242
The same. London, 1847. 12°. 5135
Medwin, T. Conversations with Byron. Baltimore, 1825. 12°. . . 4853
See also Byron.
Meikle, J. Meditations on Various Subjects, with Life. N. Y. 1832. 16°. 9323
Solitude Sweetened, or Religious Meditations. N. Y. 1811. 12°. . 1964
Meinhold, W. Amber-Witch, or Trial for Witchcraft. Tr. N. Y. 1845. 12°. 1596
Melancholy, Anatomy of. R. Burton. London, 1826. 2 v. 8°. . . 119

Melancthon, P. Life. F. A. Cox. London, 1817. 8°. 8536
Melangés Litteraires. Paris, 1827. 2 v. 12°. 11488
Melanie, and other Poems. N. P. Willis. New York, 1837. 12°. . . 2411
Melish, J. Geographical Description of the United States. N. Y. 1826. 8°. 9191
Mellen, G. W. F. Argu. on Unconstitutionality of Slavery. Bost. 1841. 12°. 11138
Melmoth, the Wanderer. R. C. Maturin. New York, 1835. 2 v. 12°. . 1571
Melmoth, W. Fitzosborne's Letters. London, 1807. 12°. 4986
Melvill, H. Thoughts on the Bible. New York. 16°. 5241
Melville, A. Commentary on the Epistle to the Romans. Edin. 1850. 8°. 5088
Melville, H. Confidence Man. New York, 1857. 12°. 1225
Israel Potter, his Fifty Years' Exile. New York, 1855. 12°. . . 1149
Moby-Dick, or the Whale. New York, 1851. 12°. 557
Omoo, Adventures in the South Seas. New York, 1847. 12°. . 556
Piazza Tales. New York, 1856. 12°. 1269
Redburn, his First Voyage. New York, 1849. 12°. . . . 555
Typee, or Life in the Marquesas. New York, 1846. 12°. . . 9855
White-Jacket, or the World in a Man-of-War. N. York, 1850. 12°. 546
Memes, J. S. Hist. of Sculpture, Painting and Architec. Bost. 1831. 12°. 10148
The same. 10155
Memoirs of the Empress Josephine. New York, 1832. 18°. . . 6623
The same. 6624
Memoirs of a Cavalier. D. DeFoe. Edinburgh, 1810. 2 v. 16°. . . 325
from 1754–58. Earl of Waldegrave. Philadelphia, 1822. 12°. . 7133
of Literature from 1725–42. Ed. M. De La Roche. Lond. 35 v. 8°. 3250
of an Only Son. T. Durant. Andover, 1823. 12°. . . . 8330
of a Working Man. London, 1844. 16°. 7200
Memory, Art of. F. Gouraud. New York, 1845. 8°. 1072
Men of Character. D. Jerrold. New York. 12°. 1181
Men, Women, and Books. L. Hunt. New York, 1847. 2 v. 12°. . . 474
Menageries, The. Boston, 1830. 12°. 6195
The same. vol. 2. Boston, 1832. 12°. 6201
Mendham, J. Literary Policy of the Church of Rome. Lond. 1830. 8°. . 5033
Mennais, F. de la. Words of a Believer. Tr. New York, 1834. 16°. . 6217
Mendon Association, History of. M. Blake. Boston, 1853. 12°. . . 6124
Men's Wives. W. M. Thackeray. New York, 1853. 12°. 958
Mental Action, Imperfect and Disordered. T. C. Upham. N. Y. 1841. 12°. 5560
Discipline, &c. H. F. Burder. New York, 1830. 12°. . . . 4241
Menzel, W. German Literature. Tr. C. C. Felton. Bost. 1840. 3 v. 12°. 509
The same. Boston, 1838. 3 v. 8°. 775
History of Germany. Tr. Mrs. G. Horrocks. Lond. 1848. 3 v. 12°. 5147
The same. London, 1852. 3 v. 12°. 5427
Mephistophiles in England. New York, 1835. 2 v. 12°. 1320
Mercedes of Castile. J. F. Cooper. Philadelphia, 1841. 12°. . . . 1263
The same. Philadelphia, 1840. 2 v. 12°. 1481
Merchant's Clerk and other Tales. S. Warren. New York, 1836. 12°. . 647
The same. 1622
Mercy Seat, The. G. Spring. New York, 1850. 12°. 5774

Meredith, or Mystery of the Meschianza. Philadelphia, 1831. 12°. . . 1462
Merlin, M. de, (Countess.) Mem. of M. G. Malibran. Tr. Phil. 1846. 2 v. 12°. 8317
Merrie England in the Olden Time. G. Daniel. London, 1842. 12°. . 1137
Merry, R. Pains of Memory. New York, 1820. 12°. . . . . .
Mesmerism, Facts in. C. H. Townshend. New York, 1848. 12°. . . 3305
Mesopotamia and Assyria. J. B. Fraser. New York, 1845. 12°. . . 5209
Messages, Presidents', from Washington to Harrison. N. York, 1841. 12°.
See also Public Documents.
Metals, Improvement and Present State of Manufacture in. J. Holland.
London, 1833, 4. 3 v. 16°. 9966
Metastasio Piètro, Opere di. Mantova, 1816. 7 v. 16°. 11198
Meteorology, Elements of. J. Brocklesby. New York, 1849. 12°. . . 6081
Report on, to the U. S. Navy Dept. J. P. Espy. Wash. 1850. 4°.
See also U. S. Public Documents.
Methodism, Rise and Progress of. J. Young. New Haven, 1830. 12°. . 6502
Metro-English, Elements of. R. Roe. London, 1801. 8°. . . . 10165
Metropolitan Magazine. vol. 1–13. New York, 1836–41. 8°. . . . 3112
Pulpit. London. R. Grant. New York, 1839. 12°. . . . 5705
Meurer, M. Life of M. Luther. New York, 1848. 8°. 7848
Mexican Revolution, Memoirs of the. W. D. Robinson. Phil. 1820. 8°. 9447
Mexico, Adventures and Travels in. W. W. Carpenter. N. Y. 1851. 12°. 9576
as it was and is. B Mayer. New York, 1844. 8°. 6977
and Guatimala, Description of. J. Conder. London, 1825. 2 v. 16°. 9644
The same. 9666
History of. B. Mayer. Hartford, 1851. 8°. 7253
History of. H. G. Ward. London, 1829. 2 v. 8°. 9100
History of. F. S. Clavigero. Tr. C. Cullen. Phil. 1804. 3 v. 8°. . 7210
History of the Conquest of. W. H. Prescott. N. Y. 1843. 3 v. 8°. 6949
in 1842. New York, 1842. 16°. 9319
Journal of Residence and Tour in. G. F. Lyon. Lond. 1828. 12°. 9239
Life in. Madame C. de La Barca. Boston, 1843. 2 v. 12°. . . 9244
Rambler in. C. J. Latrobe. New York, 1836. 12°. . . . 9819
Recollections of. W. Thompson. New York, 1836. 12°. . . 9262
and the Rocky Mts. Adventures in. G. F. Ruxton. N. Y. 1848. 12°. 9827
and the U. S., Mexican Hist. of War between. Tr. N. Y. 1850. 12°. 7096
Mexique, Histoire de la Conqueste du. A. de Solis. Tr. Paris, 1714. 2 v. 12°. 11482
Michael Armstrong, Life and Adven. of. Mrs. Trollope. N. Y. 1840. 2 v. 12°. 1553
Michelet, J. History of France. Tr. vol. 1. New York, 1845. 8°. . 11324
History of the Roman Republic. Tr. W. Hazlitt. Lond. 1847. 12°. 5494
Life of M. Luther. Tr. G. H. Smith. New York, 1846. 12°. . 8672
Modern History. Tr. A. Potter. New York, 1843. 12°. . . 5219
Priests, Women and Families. Tr. London, 1846. 12°. . . 896
Michican, History of. J. H. Lanman. New York, 1839. 8°. . . . 7244
The same. New York, 1841. 12°. 5913
Hist. and Scien. Sketches of. L. Cass and others. Detroit, 1834. 12°. 7427
Mickle, W. J. Life and Poems. Philadelphia, 1823. 18°. . . . 2146
Microcosm. vol. 3. New Haven, 1837. 8°. 2244
Microscope, The. vol. 1. New Haven, 1820. 8°. 11655

Middle Ages, Europe during the. See Europe.
Literary History of the. London, 1846. 12°. 5496
Secret Societies of. London, 1846, 12°. 11480
Middle Kingdom, or China. S. W. Williams. New York, 1848. 2 v. 12°. 9585
The same. 2 v. 9587
Middleton, C. Life of M. T. Cicero. London, 1837. 8°. 8137
Midians, History of the. London, 1779. 8°. 7029
Miers, J. Travels in Chili and La Plata. London, 1836. 2 v. 8°. . . 9772
Mignet, F. A. Hist. of French Revolution, 1789–1814. Lond. 1846. 12°. 5493
The same. London, 1856. 12°. 5472
Milburn, W. H. Rifle, Axe, and Saddle-Bags. New York, 1857. 12°. . 205
Military Commanders, British, Biog. of. G. R. Gleig. Lon. 1831, 2. 3 v. 12°. 9924
Discipline, English. Abridgement. London, 1685. 16°. . . 11162
Journal during the Revolution. J. G. Simcoe. N. Y. 1844. 8°. . 7578
Maxims of Napoleon. Tr. J. Akerly. New York, 1845. 12°. . 3922
Sketch Book. New York, 1827. 2 v. 12°. . . . . , . 1364
Tactics. S. Cooper. Philadelphia, 1836. 12°. 3347
Mill, J. History of British India. London, 1826. 6 v. 8°. . . . 7345
Phenomena of the Human Mind. London, 1829. 2 v. 8°. . . 6318
Principles of Political Economy. Boston, 1848. 2 v. 8°. . . 10926
System of Logic. New York, 1848. 8°. 396
Millar, J. Historical View of the English Government. Dub. 1789. 8°. 6901
Millennial Church. (Shakers.) C. Green and S. Y. Wells. Alb. 1823. 12°. 6182
Millennium, Harbinger of the. W. Cogswell. Boston, 1833. 12°. . . 5665
Treatise on. G. Bush. New York, 1832. 12°. 6498
Miller, J. R. History of England. See England.
Miller, H. First Impressions of England and its People. Bost. 1851. 12°. 6073
Footprints of the Creator. Boston, 1850. 12°. 6062
Geology of the Bass Rock. New York, 1851. 12°. 6104
Old Red Sandstone. Boston, 1851. 12°. 6063
Scenes and Legends of North Scotland. Cincinnati, 1851. 12°. . 6061
Testimony of the Rocks. Boston, 1857. 12°. 6052
Miller, L. W. Exile to Van Dieman's Land. Fredonia, 1842. 12°. . 9230
Miller, S. Letters on Clerical Manners and Habits. New York, 1827. 12°. . 4863
Letters from a Father to his Sons in College. Phil. 1843. 12°. . 4879
Life of J. Edwards. (Two copies.) Boston, 1837. 12°. . . 8050
Retrospect of 18th Century. New York, 1803. 2 v. 8°. . . 6923
Miller, T. Rural Sketches. Philadelphia, 1842. 12°. 235
Millengen, J. G. History of Duelling. London, 1841. 2 v. 8°. . . 399
Millot, Abbé C. F. X. Elem'ts of Gen. Hist. Tr. Worc. 1789. 5 v. 8°. 6727
Mills, C. History of Chivalry. Philadelphia, 1825. 8°. . . . 7228
History of the Crusades. Philadelphia, 1824. 8°. . . . 7227
History of Mohammedanism. London, 1818. 8°. 6327
Mills, S. J. Memoirs. G. Spring. New York, 1820. 8°. . . . 8251
The same. Boston, 1829. 18°. 8440
Milman, H. H. (Editor.) Gibbon's Rome. See Gibbon, E.
Fall of Jerusalem, a Dramatic Poem. New York, 1820. 16°. . 2091
History of Christianity. London, 1841. 3 v. 8°. 5592

Milman, H. H. History of the Jews. New York, 1830. 3 v. 16°. . . 6244
The same. New York, 1849. 3 v. 5503
Nala and Damayanti, and other Poems. Oxford, 1835. 4°. . . 1802
Poetical Works. London, 1840. 3 v. 12°. 2031
Milne, W. Life Illustrated by Biographical Annals of Asiatic Missions. R. Philip. New York, 1840. 12°. 8012
Milnes, R. M. Life and Literary Remains of J. Keats. N. York, 1848. 12°. 8320
Poems of Many Years. Boston, 1846. 12°. 2280
Milns, W. The Well-Bred Scholar, or Essays for Improving the Taste, &c. London, 1794. 8°. 11689
Milner, J. History of the Church. Boston, 1809. 4 v. 8°. . . . 7311
Milton, J. Life. W. Hayley. Dublin, 1797. 8°. 8226
Life and Poems. E. Sanford. Philadelphia, 1819. 2 v. 16°. . 2121
Paradise Lost. Boston, 1833. 12°. 2388
The same. Philadelphia, 1809. 12°. 2773
Paradise Regained. London, 1753. 2 v. 16°. 2719
Poetical Works. Boston, 1839. 2 v. 8°. 1814
The same. Philadelphia, 1836. 8°. 1858
The same. Philadelphia, 1842. 8°. 1859
Prose and Poetical Works. London, 1846. 8°. 1801
Prose Works. Ed. J. A. St. John. London, 1848. 3 v. 12°. . 5151

Vol. 1. Defence of the People of England; Second Defence. Eikonoklastes.
2. Tenure of Kings and Magistrates; Areopagitica; Tracts on the Commonwealth; Observations on Ormond's Peace; Letters of State; Manifesto of Lord Protector; Notes on Dr. Griffith's Sermon; Reformation in England; Prelatical Episcopacy; The Reason of Church Government urged against Prelacy; True Religion, Heresy, Schism, and Toleration; Civil Power in Ecclesiastical Causes.
3. Likeliest Means to Remove Hirelings out of the Church; Animadversions upon the Remonstrant's Defence against Smectymnuus; Apology for Smectymnuus; Doctrine and Discipline of Divorce; Judgment of Martin Bucer concerning Divorce; Tetrachordon; Colasterion; Education; Declaration for John III, King of Poland; Familiar Letters.

Selections from Prose Works. Boston, 1826. 2 v. 12°. 4237
Treatise on Christian Doctrine. Boston, 1825. 2 v. 8°. . . 5312
and others. Essays on Education. London, 1761. 8°. . . 1105
Mind amongst Spindles, from the Lowell Offering. London, 1845. 16°. . 7162
Body in Relation to. G. Moore. New York, 1848. 12°. . . 4240
Diseases of. B. Rush. Philadelphia, 1818. 8°. 2696
Human, Essay on. Edward, Earl of Clarendon. Lond. 1815. 16°. 4304
Human, Philosophy of the. T. Brown. Hollowell, 1829. 2 v. 8°. 6374
Human, Youth's Book on the. C. Pearl. Portland, 1847. 12°. . 4223
Improvement of. I. Watts. New Brunswick, 1813. 8°. . . 6343
The same. Boston, 1826. 16°. 4598
Philosophy of the. J. Douglas. Edinburgh, 1839. 8°. . . 6320
Progress of the. Condorcet. Tr. Philadelphia, 1796. . . 3971
Phenomena of the. J. Mill. London, 1829. 2 v. 8°. . . . 6318
Mineral Kingdom, The. London, 1842. 12°. 5938
Mineralogy, Manual of. J. D. Dana. New Haven, 1848. 12°. . . 6086
Treatise on. C. U. Shepard. New Haven, 1835. 2 v. 12°. . . 5999

Mineralogy, Treatise on. C. U. Shepard. New Haven, 1832. 12°. 6001
See also Geology.
Miner, C. History of Wyoming. Philadelphia, 1845. 8°. 6940
Minnesota, Explorations of, in 1849. J. Pope. Washington, 1850. 8°. 10422
Minot, G. R. D. Shay's Rebellion in Massachusetts. Boston, 1810. 8°. 6927
History of Massachusetts Bay from 1748. Boston, 1798. 2 v. 8°. 7372
Ministre de Wakefield. Boston, 1831. 12°. 1532
Minstrel and other Poems. J. Beattie. New York, 1802. 16°. 2481
The same. Philadelphia, 1787. 16°. 2478
Minstrelsy, Ancient and Modern. W. Motherwell. Boston, 1846. 2 v. 12°. 2066
of the Scottish Border. W. Scott. London, 1839. 8°. 1842
Minute Philosopher. G. Berkeley. London, 1797. 16°. 6433
Mirabeau, H. G. Autobiography. Tr. London, 1835. 4 v. 8°. 7883
Mirabeau, a Life History. J. S. Smith. Philadelphia, 1848. 12°. 8622
Recollections. E. Dumont. Tr. Philadelphia, 1833. 8°. 8538
The Secret History of the Court of Berlin. Tr. Dublin, 1789. 8°. 6742
Miracles of our Lord, Notes on. R. C. Trench. New York, 1856. 8°. 5055
Miriam, or the Power of Truth. Philadelphia, 1833. 12°. 1728
Mirror, The. Philadelphia, 1793. 2 v. 12°. 2493
The same. London, 1823. 2 v. 12°. 3690
The same. London, 1786. 3 v. 12°. 4270
Library. New York, 1840. 3 v. 4°. 1075
Miscellaneous Addresses, &c. New Haven, 1788. 12°. 3315
Miscellanies. Boston, 1821. 18°. 1144
or Talisman. G. C. Verplanck, W. C. Bryant, and R. C. Sands.
New York, 1833. 3 v. 16°. 4289
Miserrimus. J. K. Paulding. New York, 1833. 12°. 3359
Missionaries after the Apostolic School. E. Irving. New York, 1825. 8°. 6431
Missionary Enterprises in South Sea Islands. J. Williams. N. Y. 1837. 8°. 9183
The same. 9184
Herald. vols. 15–20 and 24–47. Boston, 1819–51. 8°. 2503
Missions. A. Clarke. London, 1836. 8°. 6463
Discourses on. C. Buchanan. Boston, 1811. 8°. 9173
Letters on. M. Horne. Andover, 1815. 18°. 4611
Letters on, W. Swan. Boston, 1831. 12°. 6585
Origin and Hist. of. J. O. Choules and T. Smith. Bost. 1842. 2 v. 4°. 4990
Sketch of. M. Winslow. Andover, 1819. 12°. 6500
Spirit of. J. Foster. Boston, 1833. 16°. 6566
Mississippi, Expedi. to Source of, in 1832. H. R. Schoolcraft. N. Y. 1834. 8°. 9439
Travels to Sources of. in 1820. H. R. Schoolcraft. Alb. 1821. 8°. 9476
Travels West of the. S. Bell. Boston, 1830. 16°. 9321
Missouri Lead Mines. H. R. Schoolcraft. New York, 1819. 8°. 5984
and Arkansas, Natural Hist. of. H. R. Schoolcraft. N. Y. 1819. 8°. 5984
Illinois, &c., Sketches of. J. M. Peck. Boston, 1831. 16°. 9328
Mitchel, O. M. Planetary and Stellar Worlds. New York, 1851. 12°. 6080
Mitchell, D. G. Battle Summer. New York, 1850. 12°. 216
The same. New York, 1859. 12°. 213
Dream Life. New York, 1851. 12°. 218

Mitchell, D. G. Dream Life. New York, 1851. 12°. . . . 214
The same. New York, 1859. 12°. 207
Fresh Gleanings in Europe. New York, 1847. 12°. . . . 217
The same. New York, 1859. 12°. 208
Fudge Doings. New York, 1859. 2 v. 12°. 209
Lorgnette, or Studies of the Town. New York, 1851. 2 v. 12°. . 219
The same. New Yor,k 1859. 2 v. 12°. 211
Reveries of a Bachelor. New York, 1851. 12°. 215
The same. New York, 1859. 12°. 213½
Mitchell, J. Tour through Belgium, Holland, &c. London, 1816. 8°. . 9769
Mitchell, T. L. Australian Expedition. London, 1839. 2 v. 8°. . . 9437
Mitford, Mary R. Our Village. New York, 1828. 4 v. 12°. . . . 221
Mitford, W. History of Greece. (vol. 1 missing.) Boston, 1823. 8 v. 8°. 6695
Moby-Dick, or the Whale. H. Melville. New York, 1851. 12°. . . 557
Modern Accomplishments. Catharine Sinclair. New York, 1836. 12°. . 4242
The same, concluded. New York, 1837. 12°. . . . 3918
Cymon. P. De Kock. Philadelphia, 1833. 2 v. 12°. . . . 262
History. See History.
Painters. J. Ruskin. New York, 1847–56. 3 v. 12°. . . . 10161
Philosophy. J. Murdock. Hartford, 1842. 16°. 4301
Traveller. See Conder, J.
Moffat, R. Missionary Labors in Southern Africa. New York, 1843. 12°. 8938
Mogul Empire, Trav. in. F. Bernier. Tr. I. Brock. Lond. 1826. 2 v. 8°. 9486
Moguls and Tartars, History of. London, 1780. 2 v. 8°. . . . 7050
Mohammed, Life of. New York, 1841. 12°. 5512
See also Mahomet.
The same. New York, 1830. 16°. 6614
Moleville, A. F. B. de. Private Memoirs of Louis XVI. Trans. London, 1797. 3 v. 8°. 7966
Life of, and History of Arabs and Turks. 3 v. 7047
Molière, J. B. P. Œuvres. Paris, 1813. 8 v. 18°. 10875
Monachism, British. J. D. Fosbroke. London, 1843. 8°. . . . 5007
Monasteries, Excursion to the. W. Beckford. Philadelphia, 1835. 12°. 9617
in the Levant, a Visit to. R. Curzon. New York, 1849. 12°. . 9825
Monastery. W. Scott. Boston, 1834. 12°. 270
See also Scott, Sir W.
Monikins. J. F. Cooper. Philadelphia, 1841. 12°. 1259
Monitor for an Apprentice. I. Watts and others. Boston, 1808. 12°. . 3907
Monk, G. Life. W. Webster. Dublin, 1724. 12°. 8315
Memoir. F. Guizot. Tr. J. S. Wortley. London, 1838. 8°. . 7916
Monkeys, Natural History of. W. Jardine. Edinburgh, 1833. 12°. . 10193
Monroe, J. Conduct of the U. S. Executive in Foreign Affairs. Philadelphia, 1797. 8°. 10401
Monroe, J. Tour of, through the Northern and East. States. S. L. Waldo. Hartford, 1820. 12°. . . . . , 9010
The same. Hartford, 1818. 12°. 8738
Monsalratge, R. Life. R. Baird. New York, 1845. 16°. . . . 8460

Monstrelet, E. De. Chronicles of England, France, Spain, &c. Trans. T. Johnes. London, 1840. 2 v. 4°. 7544
Montagu, E. W. Reflections on Ancient Republics. Phil. 1806. 12°. . 3901
Montagu, Mary W. Letters on the East. London, 1777. 12°. . . 4901
Works, Correspondence, &c. London, 1803. 4 v. 16°. . . 4322
The same. Philadelphia, 1837. 2 v. 8°. 9727
Montaigne, M. de. Essays. Tr. London, 1759. 3 v. 8°. . . . 456
Montesquieu, C. de. Persian Letters. Tr. Floyd. Lond. 1762. 2 v. 12°. 4910
The same. Tr. J. Ozell. London, 1730. 3 v. 12°. . . 4898
De l'Esprit des Lois. Paris, 1817. 5 v. 12°. 10897
The same. Tr. Edinburgh, 1768. 2 v. 12°. . . . 11182
Works. Tr. London, 1777. 4 v. 8°. 10513

Vol. 1. Eulogium on President Montesquieu, by D'Lambert; The Spirit of Laws.
2. The Last concluded.
3. Grandeur and Declension of the Roman Empire; A Dialogue between Sylla and Eucrates; Persian Letters; Three Letters to De Bruant.
4. Familiar Letters; An Oration; An Essay on Taste; The Pleasures of the Soul; The Temple of Gnidus; Cupid Distressed; Lysimachus; An Analysis and Defence of the Spirit of Laws; an Index to the Spirit of Laws, to the Article on the Roman Empire, and to the Persian Empire.

Montezuma, the Last of the Aztecs. E. Maturin. N. Y. 1845. 2 v. 12°. 1318
Montgomery, Cora. Eagle Pass. New York, 1852. 12°. . . . 9001
Montgomery, G. W. Journey to Guatemala. New York, 1839. 8°. . 9149
Montgomery, J. Lectures on Literature, Poetry, &c. N. Y. 1840. 12°. 5880
The same. New York, 1833. 16°. 8767
Poetical Works. Boston, 1825. 4 v. 16°. 2085
The same. London, 1830. 8°. 1869
The same. Philadelphia, 1830. 8°. 1882
Prose by a Poet. Philadelphia, 1824. 16°. 4601
West Indies and other Poems. Boston, 1810. 18°. 2754
Montgomery, R. Life. J. Armstrong. Boston, 1834. 12°. . . . 8068
Monthly Review. (New series.) vols. 1–20. London, 1826–32. 8°. . 2590
Old series. vol. 35. 1801. 2242
Montrose, Earl of. (J. Graham.) Life and Times. M. Napier. Ed. 1840. 12°. 8615
Moor, Dr. Greek Grammar. Tr. and Ed. P. Bullions. N. Y. 1831. 12°. 3346
Moore, C. C. Life of G. Castriot. New York, 1850. 12°. . . . 8312
Moore, E. Select Poems, with Life. Philadelphia, 1819. 18°. . . 2135
Moore, G. The Body in Relation to Mind. New York, 1848. 12°. . . 4240
Man and his Motives. New York, 1848. 12°. 6496
Power of the Soul over the Body. New York, 1847. 12°. . . 6173
Moore, H. Life of Ethan Allen. Plattsburgh, 1834. 12°. . . . 7781
The same. 8378
Moore, J. View of Manners in France, Switzerland and Germany. London, 1783. 2 v. 8°. 9218
The same. Dublin, 1789. 2 v. 12°. 8731
View of Society and Manners in Italy. London, 1783. 2 v. 8°. . 11420
Moore, T. Fudge Family in Paris. New York, 1818. 16°. . . . 3080
History of Ireland. London, 1836–40. 3 v. 12°. 9910
Lalla Rookh. New York, 1849. 12°. 2022

Moore, T. Life and Death of Lord E. Fitzgerald. N. Y. 1831. 2 v. 12°. 8099
Life of R. B. Sheridan. Philadelphia, 1826. 2 v. 12°. . . . 8351
The same. 8372
Life, Letters, and Journal of Byron. New York, 1830. 2 v. 8°. . 8191
Loves of the Angels. New York, 1823. 16°. 3077
Melodies, Songs, &c. New York, 1821. 16°. 3076
Memoirs, Journal, &c. Lord J. Russell. New York, 1857. 2 v. 8°. 7834
(Translator.) Odes of Anacreon. New York, 1805. 12°. . . . 2712
Poetical Works. London, 1844. 9 v. 12°. 2249

Vol. 1. Odes of Anacreon; Juvenile Poems.
2. Juvenile Poems; Poems Relating to America.
3. Corruption and Intolerance; The Sceptic; Twopenny Post-Bag; Satirical and Humorous Poems; Irish Melodies.
4. Irish Melodies; National Airs; Sacred Songs; The Summer Fete.
5. Evenings in Greece; Ballads, Songs, and Miscellaneous Poems.
6. Lalla Rookh.
7. The same concluded; Political and Satirical Poems: The Fudge Family in Paris; Fables for the Holy Alliance; Rhymes on the Road; Miscellaneous Poems.
8. The Loves of the Angels; Miscellaneous Poems; Satirical and Humorous Poems.
9. Satirical and Humorous Poems; The Fudges in England; Songs from M. P., or the Blue Stocking; Miscellaneous Poems.

The same. New York, 1825. 6 v. 18°. 2759
Tom Cribb's Memorial to Congress. New York, 1819. 16°. . . 3073
Works. New York, 1825. 18°. . . . .

Vol. 1. Memoir; Lalla Rookh.
2. Epistles, Odes and other Poems.
3. Melodies; Sacred Songs; National Airs.
4. Odes of Anacreon; Miscellaneous Poems.
5. The Fudge Family in Paris; Miscellaneous Pieces; The Twopenny Post-Bag; Trifles.
6. The Loves of the Angels; Dublin Mail; A Packet of Poems.

and W. Scott, Beauties of. Ed. B. F. French. Phil. 1827. 8°. . 2075
Moore, W. V. Indian Wars of the United States. Phil. 1840. 8°. . . 6788
Moors in Spain, History of. J. Bourke. London, 1811. 4°. . . . 11257
History of. J. P. C. Florian. Tr. New York, 1841. 12°. . . 5253
Moraes, F. de. Palmerin of Eng. Tr. R. Southey. Lond. 1807. 4 v. 16°. 8453
Moral and Active Powers, Philosophy of. D. Stewart. Bost. 1828. 2 v. 8°. 6339
The same. Cambridge, 1829. 4542
Evidence, Guide to the Study of. J. E. Gambier. Bost. 1834. 16°. 6229
Feelings, Philosophy of. J. Abercrombie. New York, 1840. 12°. 5874
The same. New York, 1833. 16°. 8765
Influence of Great Cities. J. Todd. Northampton, 1841. 12°. . 6570
The same. 4971
Philosophy. C. Follen. Boston, 1841. 12°. 5399
Philosophy, Elements of. J. Adams. New York, 1837. 8°. . . 6306
Philosophy, Elements of. D. Dewar. London, 1836. 2 v. 8°. . 6337
Philosophy, Introduc. to. F. Hutcheson. Tr. Glas. 1772. 2 v. 16°. 4295
Philosophy, Investigation of Principles of. T. Gisborne. Lon. 1798. 8°. 6408
Philosophy, Sketches of. S. Smith. New York, 1850. 12°. . . 6413
Philosophy, Treatise on. L. A. Sawyer. New York, 1845. 12°. . 6189

Moral Reformer and Teacher on the Human Constitution. W. A. Alcott. Boston, 1835. 12°. 3014
Science, Elements of. J. Beattie. vol. 1. Dublin, 1787. 8°. . 6409
Science, Elements of. F. Wayland. New York, 1835. 8°. . . 6396
Sentiments, Theory of. A. Smith. London, 1777. 8°. . . . 6406
The same. London, 1792. 2 v. 8°. 12130
The same. Ed. D. Stewart. London, 1853. 12°. . . . 5189
Tales. J. F. Marmontel. Tr. London, 1800. 2 v. 12°. . . 1654
Tales. Madame de Genlis. Tr. New York, 1825. 12°. . . 1656
Truth, Immutability of. Cath. M. Graham. London, 1783. 8°. . 6407
Morale en Action. Paris, 1829. 12°. 4917
Mordaunt Hall. Mrs. Marsh. New York, 1851. 8°. 48
More, Hannah. Christian Morals. New York, 1813. 16°. . . . 6644
Cœlebs in Search of a Wife. Philadelphia, 1810. 12°. . . . 1590
The same. New York, 1809. 2 v. 12°. 1586
Female Education. Hartford, 1801. 12°. 3017
Memoirs. W. Roberts. New York, 1835. 2 v. 12°. . . . 8266
Practical Piety. Boston, 1811. 2 v. 16°. 6235
Sacred Dramas. London, 1782 12°. 2269
Works. Boston, 1827. 2 v. 8°. 391

Vol. 1. Tales; Epitaphs; Ballads and Hymns; Bible Rhymes; Sacred Dramas; Allegories; Manners of the Great; An Estimate of Religion; Strictures on Female Education: Practical Piety.
2. Hints for forming the Character of a Princess; Christian Morals; Character and Writings of St. Paul; Cœlebs in Search of a Wife; Foreign and Domestic Sketches; Reflections on Prayer; Spirit of Prayer.

More, Sir T. Life. London, 1831. 12°. 9932
Moreau, V. Life and Campaigns. Tr. New York, 1806. 12°. . . 8079
Memoirs. J. Phillipart. Philadelphia, 1816. 8°. 8203
Morell, J. D. Philosophy of Religion. New York, 1849. 12°. . . . 5740
Speculative Philosophy of Europe. New York, 1848. 8°. . . 6323
Morgan, A. de. Essay on Probabilities. London, 1838. 12°. . . . 9962
Morgan, Lady S. Dramatic Scenes from Real Life. New York, 1833. 12°. 822
France. New York, 1817. 2 v. 12°. 9048
France in 1829, 30. New York, 1830. 2 v. 12°. 7134
Italy. New York, 1821. 2 v. 8°. 9161
Morgan, T. C., and Lady S. Book without a Name. N. Y. 1841. 2 v. 12°. 1449
Morier, J. Adventures of Hajji Baba in England. N. Y. 1828. 2 v. 12°. 622
Moriarty, D. I. Innisfoyle Abbey. London, 1840. 3 v. 12°. . . . 1492
Morison, J. Evidences of Christianity. Boston, 1834. 16°. . . . 6223
Mormonism in all Ages. J. B. Turner. New York, 1842. 12°. . . 5668
Morning Prayer, Lectures on the. R. A. Hallam. Phil. 1856. 12°. . 5402
Mornings among the Jesuits at Rome. H. Seymour. New York, 1849. 12°. 5730
The same. 8688
Mornings in Spring. N. Drake. London, 1828. 2 v. 12°. . . . 4235
Morocco, Egypt, Turkey, &c. Ali Bey. Philadelphia, 1816. 2 v. 8°. . 9505
Morocco, Tour to. W. Lempriere. London, 1793. 8°. 9450

Morrell, B. Voyages and Discoveries in the South Sea, Pacific Ocean, &c. New York, 1832. 8°. 9778
Morris, G. Life and Writings. J. Sparks. Boston, 1832. 3 v. 8°. . . 10649
Morris, G. P. The Little Frenchman and his Water Lots. Phil. 1839. 12°. 1176
Morris, P. H. Evils of Drunkenness Explained. New York, 1841. 12°. 11455
Morrison, R. Memoirs. Mrs. Morrison. London, 1839. 2 v. 8°. . . 8133
Morse, J. American Universal Geography. Charlestown, 1819. 2 v. 8°. 9166
The same. Boston, 1812. 2 v. 8°. 9124
Tour among the Indians of the U. S. in 1820. New Haven, 1822. 8°. 10056
and R. C. Traveller's Guide, or Pocket Gazetteer. N. H. 1826. 16°. 9322
The same. New Haven, 1823. 16°. 9326
Morse, S. F. B. Foreign Conspiracy against the U. States. N. Y. 1835. 8°. 11159
Moscheles, I. Life of Beethoven. London, 1841. 2 v. 12°. . . . 8272
Moschus, Bion, and Theocritus. Idyls. Tr. M. J. Chapman. Lon. 1836. 12°. 1915
Moseley, H. Illustrations of Mechanics. New York, 1844. 12°. . . 5256
Mosheim, J. L. Ancient and Modern Ecclesiastical Hist. Tr. J. Murdock. New Haven, 1832. 3 v. 8°. 5080
The same. Tr. A. Maclaine. Philadelphia, 1797. 6 v. 8°. . 6417
The Christians before Constantine the Great. Tr. R. S. Vidal. London, 1813. 2 v. 8°. 5034
Mother's Recompense. Grace Aguilar. New York, 1851. 12°. . . 1199
The same. New York, 1851. 8°. 48
Motherwell, W. Minstrelsy, Ancient and Modern. Boston, 1846. 12°. . 2066
Poems, Narrative and Lyrical. Boston, 1841. 12°. . . . 2456
Posthumous Poems. Boston, 1851. 1954
Motley, J. L. Rise of the Dutch Republic. New York, 1856. 3 v. 8°. . 7549
Mott, V. Travels in Europe and the East. New York, 1842. 8°. . . 9366
Motteville, Mad. de. Mem. of Anne of Austria. Tr. Lond. 1726. 5 v. 12°. 7783
Mount Blanc, Wanderings in Shadow of. G. B. Cheever. N. Y. 1846. 12°. 9857
Mount Hope, a Romance. G. H. Hollister. New York, 1851. 12°. . . 558
Mount Sorel, or Heiress of the De Veres. Mrs. Marsh. N. Y. 1851. 8°. 48
Mountain Decameron, The. J. Downes. London, 1836. 3 v. 12°. . . 1434
Mourning Ring. Mrs. Inchbald. New York, 1821. 12°. 1348
Mouse Trap, and other Poems. New York. 12°. 2379
Mozart. J. C. W. T. Life. L. A. C. Bombet. Tr. Boston, 1839. 12°. . 8043
Life. E. Holmes. New York, 1845. 12°. 8415
Mudie, R. Earth, Air, Sea and Heavens. London, 1835. 4 v. 12°. . . 6105
Guide to the Study of Nature. New York, 1833. 16°. . . . 4292
The same. 8764
The same. New York, 1839. 12°. 5873
Muhammedanism, History of. C. Mills. London, 1818. 8°. . . . 6327
Müller, C. O. Hist. and Antiq. of the Doric Race. Tr. Lond. 1839. 2 v. 8°. 6978
Müller, J. von. Universal History. Tr. London, 1818. 3 v. 8°. . . 7369
Murdoch, J. E. Cultivation of the Voice in Elocution. Boston, 1851. 12°. 10157
Murdock, J. Modern Philosophy. Hartford, 1842. 16°. 4301
Murphy, A., (Translator.) Tacitus' Works. See Tacitus, C.
Murray, C. A. Travels in N. America, in 1834, 5. N. Y. 1839. 2 v. 12°. 9834
Murray, H. Discoveries and Travels in Africa. Edin. 1818. 2 v. 8°. . 9110

Murray, H. Discoveries and Travels in Asia. Edinburgh, 1820. 3 v. 8°. 9107
Encyclopædia of Geography. Philadelphia, 1837. 3 v. 8°. . . 10915
History of British America. Edinburgh, 1840. 3 v. 12°. . . 5849
The same, abridged. New York, 1840. 2 v. 12°. . . 5561
Hist. of Discoveries and Travels in N. America. Lond. 1839. 2 v. 8°. 6959
Travels of Marco Polo. New York, 1845. 12°. 5250
The same. New York, 1845. 12°. 5928
and others. History of British India. New York, 1840. 3 v. 12°. 5863
The same. New York, 1833. 3 v. 16°. 6264
Murray, J. Autobiography. Albany, 1843. 12°. 7710
Murray, L. Autobiography. York, 1827. 8°. 8161
English Grammar. New York, 1819. 8°. 11687
Museum of Foreign Lit. and Sci. vols. 1, 3, 4, 5, 13–19. Phil. 1826–31, &c. 3221
or Literary and Historical Register. vols. 1–3. Lond. 1746, 7. 8°. 3247
Criticum, or Cambridge Classical Researches. Camb. 1826. 2 v. 8°. 415
Music, History of, Condensed from the Works of T. Hawkins and C. Burney.
T. Busby. London, 1819. 2 v. 8°. 10120
of Nature. W. Gardiner. Boston, 1837. 8°. 10119
Our Church. N. P. Willis. New York, 1856. 12°. . . . 10147
Physiology of, or Music Explained. London, 1845. 16°. . . 3711
Rudimental Lessons in. J. F. Warner. New York, 1845. 16°. . 10252
Musical Biography, or Sketches of Emi. Musical Characters. Bost. 1825. 8°. 10110
Cyclopædia. W. S. Porter. Boston, 1834. 16°. 10249
The same. 10251
Grammar, in Four Parts. A. Callcott. Boston, 1833. 16°. . . 10250
Harmony, Treatise on. C. S. Catel. Boston, 1832. 12°. . . 4881
Mussulman. R. R. Madden. London, 1830. 2 v. 12°. 1360
Mussulmans, Biblical Legends of. G. Weil. Tr. New York, 1846. 12°. 6175
My Aunt Pontypool. Philadelphia, 1836. 2 v. 12°. 259
My Bondage and My Freedom. F. Douglass. New York, 1855. 8°. . 8298
My Cousin Nicholas. R. H. D. Barnham. London, 1848 2 v. 12°. . 1457
My Novel, or Var. in English Life. E. L. Bulwer. Lond. 1855. 2 v. 12°. 551
My Prisons. Silvio Pellico. Tr. S. Roscoe. (Two cop.) N. Y. 1833. 12°. 1284
The same, with additions. Cambridge, 1836. 2 v. 12°. . 8729
My Uncle Hobson and I. Pascal Jones. New York, 1845. 12°. . . 204
Myers, F. Lectures on Great Men. London, 1856. 12°. . . . 815
Myers, P. H. Ensenore, a Poem. New York, 1840. 8°. 1824
Mystery, Philosophy of. W. C. Dendy. New York, 1845. 12°. . . 4239
Mystic, The, and other Poems. P. J. Bailey. Boston, 1856. 12°. . . 1995
Mythology of Ancient Greece and Italy. J. Keightley. Lond. 1838. 8°. 7602
Elements of. Philadelphia, 1830. 16°. 4599

N.

Nala and Damayanti, and other Poems. H. H. Milman. Oxford, 1835. 4°. 1802
Napier, E. Wild Sports in Europe, Asia, Africa. London, 1840. 2 v. 12°. 794
Napier, M. Life and Times of J. Graham, Earl of Montrose. Edinburgh, 1840. 12°. 8615

Napier, W. F. P. History of the Peninsular War, with Maps. Philadelphia, 1842. 5 v. 8°. 7559
Naples, History of. London, 1782. 8°. 7070
under Spanish Dominion. A. de Reumont. London, 1854. 12°. . 5180
Napoleon. See Bonaparte.
Narrative Papers. T. De Quincey. Boston, 1854. 2 v. 12°. . . . 881
National Calendar, for 1831. Ed. P. Forge. Washington, 1831. 12°. . 4556
Character, an Essay on. R. Chenevix. London, 1832. 2 v. 8°. . 10647
Industry, Addresses on. Philadelphia, 1820. 12°. 11879
Preceptor. Ed. J. Olney. New York, 1839. 12°. 3399
The same. Hartford, 1837. 12°. 3311
Pride. 12°. 3015
Natural History. G. L. L. Buffon. (vol. 1 miss.) Bost. 1831. 5 v. 16°. 10241
The same, abridged. Dublin, 1791. 8°. 10166
O. Goldsmith. Philadelphia, 1825. 5 v. 8°. 10111
The same, abridged. Philadelphia, 1829. 12°. . . . 10204
C. Plinius. Lipsiæ, 1830. 5 v. 16°. 10360
The same, abridged. London, 1829. 12°. 10201
American. J. D. Godman. Philadelphia, 1831. 3 v. 8°. . . 10167
of Birds. New York, 1840. 12°. 5558
Dictionnaire Universel. de Lyons, 1791. 15 v. 12°. . . . 8951
Discourse on the Study of. W. Swainson. London, 1834. 12°. . 9970
Lectures on. T. Flint. Boston, 1833. 12°. 10153
of Man. W. F. Van Amringe. New York, 1848. 8°. 6322
of New York. See New York.
Philosophy of. W. Smellie. Philadelphia, 1791. 8°. . . . 10109
The same, with an Introduc. by J. Ware. Bost. 1832. 8°. . 10132
The same. Boston, 1838. 12°. 10149
Philosophy of, Elementary. J. G. Burkhard. London, 1804. 12°. 10174
of Quadrupeds. New York, 1840. 12°. 5564
of Quadrupeds. J. H. Fennel. London, 1843. 8°. . . . 10136
of Society. W. C. Taylor. New York, 1841. 2 v. 12°. . . 3930
Natural Philosophy. W. Nicholson. London, 1790. 2 v. 8°. . . 5963
D. Olmsted. New Haven, 1830. 2 v. 8°. 5989
The same. New Haven, 1840. 8°. 5987
Compendium of. D. Olmsted. New Haven, 1833. 8°. . . . 5978
Conversations on. J. L. Blake. Hartford, 1823. 12°. . . . 6094
Discourse on Study of. J. F. W. Herschel. London, 1835. 12°. . 9954
The same. Philadelphia, 1835. 12°. 5842
with Discourse on Science. London, 1829. 3 v. 8°. . . . 5090
History of. B. Powell. London, 1837. 12°. 9955
Letters on. L. Euler. Tr. H. Hunter. New York, 1833. 2 v. 16°. 6267
The same. New York, 1840. 2 v. 12°. 5871
The same. London, 1802. 2 v. 8°. 5971
Lectures on. G. Adams. London, 1799. 4 v. 8°. 5967
Plates to illustrate the Lectures. London, 1793. 4 v. 16°. . . 5994
Natural Religion, Principles of. J. Wilkins. London, 1678. 12°. . . 6515
Natural Theology. W. Paley. Philadelphia, 1802. 8°. 5626

Natural Theology. Illustrated. Boston, 1850. 12°. 6446
The same. New York, 1830. 2 v. 12°. 5556
Discourses on. H. Brougham. Philadelphia, 1835. 12°. . . . 6143
Naturalist, Journal of. 16°. 10245
Voage of, Round the World. C. Darwin. N. Y. 1846. 2 v. 12°. 10202
Naturalist's Library, The. Ed. Sir W. Jardine. Edin. 1835–7. 18 v. 12°.

No. 10181. Beetles. J. Duncan.
10190. 1. Birds of Africa. W. Swainson.
10192. British Birds. W. Jardine.
10182. British Butterflies. J. Duncan.
10183. British Moths. J Duncan.
10195. Deer, &c. W. Jardine.
10197. Elephants. W. Jardine.
10194. Felinæ. W. Jardine.
10186. Gallinaceous Birds. W. Jardine.
No. 10187. Game Birds. W. Jardine.
10196. Goats, Sheep, &c. W. Jardine.
10184. 5. Humming Birds. W. Jardine.
10193. Monkeys. W. Jardine.
10189. Parrots. P. Selby.
10188. Pigeons. P. Selby.
10198. Whales. R. Hamilton.

Nature Adapted to Moral Constitu. of Man. T. Chalmers. Phil. 1836. 8°. 6382
Adapted to Physical Condition of Man. Phil. 1833. 12°. . . . 6486
Beauties and Sublimities of. C. Bucke. London, 1837. 3 v. 8°. . 759
The same, abridged. New York, 1842. 12°. 5917
Hutton's Book of. Ed. J. L. Blake. Boston, 1833. 12°. . . . 6100
Light of. A. Tucker. London, 1807. 8°. 6399
Marvellous Works of. C. C. Reiche. Phil. 1791. 12°. 6595
Popular Guide to the Observation of. R. Mudie. N. Y. 1839. 12°. 5873
The same. New York, 1833. 16°. 4292
The same. 8764
Religion of, Delineated. W. Wollaston. London, 1750. 8°. . . . 5641
Remarkable Phenomena of. H. G. Bell. Edinburgh, 1827. 16°. . 9997
Studies of. J. H. B. de St. Pierre. Tr. H. Hunter. Worcester, 1797.
3 v. 8°. 2700
The same, abridged. Philadelphia, 1836. 8°. 3304
Selections from the same. Tr. London, 1799. 8°. . . . 3291
The same. 3300
and the Supernatural. H. Bushnell. New York, 1859. 8°. . . 5085
Views of. A. von Humboldt. London, 1850. 12°. 5487
Naval Battles, American. Boston, 1837. 8°. 11446
Biography of G. Britain, 1660–1798. J. Charnock. Lon. 1794. 6 v. 8°. 8812
Heroes, American. S. P. Waldo. Hartford, 1823. 8°. 8493
History, British, to 1816. J. Cambell and others. Lon. 1817. 8 v. 8°. 8554
History of England, Early. R. Southey. Phil. 1835. 12°. . . 7449
The same. 11478
The same, with Lives of British Admirals to 1672. London,
1833–40. 5 v. 12°. 9927
History of G. Britain, 1783–1836. E. P. Brenton. Lon. 1837. 2 v. 8°. 7269
History of the United States. J. F. Cooper. Phil. 1839. 2 v. 8°. 7639
Life, Sketches of. G. Jones. New York, 1829. 2 v. 8°. . . . 9275
Navarre, History of. London, 1782. 8°. 7065
Navarre, &c., Twelve Months' Camp. in. C. F. Henningsen. Phil. 1836. 12°. 7422
Navigation, an Epitome of the Art of. J. Atkinson. London, 1762. 12°. 4878
Navigator, Practical, &c. N. Bowditch. New York, 1817. 8°. . . 1054

Navigators, Lives and Voyages of the Early. New York, 1840. 12°. . 5531
Navy of the U. S., Uniform and Dress of. Illustrated. Phil. 1852. 4°. .
Neal, D. History of the Puritans. Portsmouth, 1816. 5 v. 8°. . . 5337
The same. New York, 1844. 2 v. 8°. 7556
Neal, J. Errata, or the Works of Will Adams. New York, 1823. 2 v. 12°. 1535
The same. 643
Rachel Dyer. Boston, 1828. 12°. 920
Neal, J. C. Charcoal Sketches. Philadelphia, 1838. 12°. 649
Neander, A. Christian Life in Early Ages. Tr. J. E. Ryland. Lon. 1852. 12°. 5207
Hist. of Christian Relig. and Church. Tr. H. Rose. Lon. 1842. 2 v. 8°. 5596
The same. Tr. J. Torrey. Boston, 1848. 3 v. 8°. . . 7574
Life of Christ. New York, 1848. 8°. 6332
Life and Times of St. Bernard. Tr. Matilda Wrench. Lon. 1843. 12°. 7735
Life of St. Chrysostom. Tr. J. C. Stapleton. London, 1845. 8°. . 7905
Planting and Training of the Church. Tr. J. E. Ryland. Edinburgh, 1842. 2 v. 12°. . . . . , ... 5852
Necker, J. Miscellanies. Tr. London, 1818. 8°. 7946
Memoirs of the Private Life of. Mad. de Staël. Tr. Lond. 1818. 8°. 7946
Necker de Saussure, Mad. Progressive Education. Tr. Bost. 1835. 12°. 2988
Necromancers, Lives of. W. Godwin. New York, 1835. 12°. . . . 8673
Neele, H. Literary Remains. London, 1829. 12°. 864
The same. New York, 1829. 8°. 751
Romance of History. England. Philadelphia, 1828. 2 v. 12°. . 313
Neff, F. Memoir. W. S. Gilly. Philadelphia, 1832. 12°. . . . 7771
Negroes, Intellectual Faculties of. H. Grégoire. Tr. Brooklyn, 1810. 12°. 1107
Neighbors, The. Miss F. Bremer. Tr. London, 1852. 12°. . . . 5206
The same. New York, 1844. 8°. 13
Nelson, H. Life. R. Southey. Hartford, 1814. 12°. 8381
The same. New York, 1847. 12°. 5508
The same. New York, 1830. 16°. 6612
Nervous System, Functions of. J. A. Smith. New York, 1840. 12°. . 2989
Nestorians, or the Lost Tribes. A. Grant. New York, 1841. 12°. . . 6798
The same. 7104
Netherlands, Annals of Troubles in. Tr. & Ed. B. Romans. Hart. 1778. 12°. 7437
History of. T. C. Grattan. Philadelphia, 1831. 12°. . . . 5836
The same. London, 1833. 12°. 9983
History of Revolution in. F. Schiller. Tr. N. Y. 1847. 2 v. 12°. 5154
The same. 11469
Nettleton, A. Memoir. B. Tyler. Hartford, 1845. 12°. . . . 8623
Nevins, W. Memoir and Select Remains. New York, 1836. 12°. . . 8304
Practical Thoughts. New York. 16°. . . . . , . . 5235
New England, Northener in. J. T. Smith. . , ... 7107
History, from 986–1776. C. W. Elliott. New York, 1857. 2 v. 8°. 7274
and her Institutions. Boston, 1835. 12°. 7121
Legends of. J. G. Whittier. Hartford, 1831. 12°. . . . 651
The same. 2330
Magazine. vols. 1–7. Boston, 1831–7. 8°. 2942
and New York, Travels in. T. Dwight. N. Haven, 1821. 4 v. 8°. 9426

New England, Sketches of. J. Carver. New York, 1842. 12. . . . 9830
Supernaturalism of. London, 1847. 12°. 814
New Englander, The. vols. 1–17, (continued) 1843–59. 4469
New Hampshire, History of. J. Belknap. Boston, 1792. 3 v. 8°. . . 6781
New Haven City Directory. Ed. J. H. Benham. New Haven, 1846. 12°. 4857
The same, for 1847–8. New Haven. 12°. 4557
Colony of. History. E. R. Lambert. New Haven, 1838. 12°. . 7423
The same. 11452
Colony, Historical Discourses on. L. Bacon. New Haven, 1839. . 7638
Colony, Records of 1638–49. C. J. Hoadly. Hartford, 1857. 8°. 7240
from 1653–65. Hartford, 1858. 8°. 7241
Two Hundredth Anniversary of. J. L. Kingsley. N. H. 1838. 8°. 6684
New Home—Who'll Follow? Mrs. C. M. Kirkland. N. Y. 1839. 12°. . 1593
New Jersey, Historical Collections of. J. W. Barber and H. Howe. New York, 1844. 8°. 6689
New Jerusalem, &c. E. Swedenborg. Trans. Philadelphia, 1815. 12°. 11877
New London, Conn., History of. Miss F. M. Caulkins. N. L. 1852. 8°. 12049
New Netherland, History of. E. B. O'Callaghan. N. Y. 1848. 2 v. 8°. 7242
New Pastoral. T. B. Read. Phil. 1855. 12°. 1993
New Purchase. R. Carlton. New York, 1843. 2 v. 12°. . . . 1290
New South Wales, Observations on the Colonies of. J. Henderson. Calcutta, 1832. 8°. . , ... 9786
New Spirit of the Age. R. H. Horne. New York, 1844. 12°. . . 8369
New Testament. New York, 1829. 16°. 11937
Divine Authority of. D. Bogue. New York. 18°. . . . 5240
Notes on Passages in. E. J. Chapman. Canandaigua, 1819. 8°. . 6394
New Stories. C. Dickens. Philadelphia. 8°. 71
New Voyage around the World. D. De Foe. Edin. 1810. 2 v. 16°. . 231
New York, Analysis of the Rules of the Legislature of. Alb. 1856. 16°. 11153
Annual Register. E. Williams. New York, 1836. 12°. . . 11884
Book of Poetry. New York, 1837. 8°. 1825
Border Warfare of. W. W. Campbell. New York, 1849. 12°. . 11460
The same. New York, 1831. 8°. 11365
Common Schools of. See Common Schools.
Code of Procedure of. Albany, 1849. 8°. 10101
Documentary Hist. of. E. B. O'Callaghan. Albany, 1849–51. 4 v. 8°. 10455
Exhibition of Art, Science, &c., Illustrations from. B. Silliman, Jr., C. R. Goodrich, and others. N. Y. 1854. 2 v. 4°. . .
Governor's Speeches. 1777–1824. New York, 1825. 8°. . . 11061
Glance at, embracing its Gov't, Theatres, &c. N. Y. 1837. 16°. . 9327
History of its Polit. Parties. J. D. Hammond. Alb. 1842. 2 v. 8°. 6961
History of. F. S. Eastman. New York, 1828. 12°. . . . 11468
in 1670. D. Denton. New York, 1845. 8°. . . . . , . 11318
Knickerbocker's History of. W. Irving. N. Y. 1826. 2 v. 12°. . 1164
See also Irving. W.
Letters from. Mrs. L. M. Child. First and second series New York, 1843. 2 v. 12°. 8967

New York, Natural History of. Albany, 1842–47. 15 v. 4°. 13098

Vol. 1–5. Part First. Zoölogy, by James E. De Kay.
6, 7. Part Second. Botany, by J. Torrey.
8. Part Third. Mineralogy, by L. C. Beck.
9–12. Part Fourth. Geology, by W. W. Mather, E. Emmons, L. Vanuxem, and J. Hall.
13, 14. Part Fifth. Agriculture, by E. Emmons.
15. Part Sixth. Palæontology, by J. Hall.

Natural History of, Third Report of the Regents of the University on the Cabinet of. Albany, 1853. 8°. . . . . .
Picture of, or Traveler's Guide. New York, 1807. 16°. . . 9325
Proceed. of the State Conven. of. L. H. Clarke. N. Y. 1821. 8°. 10657
Reports of the Geological Survey of. Albany, 1838, 9. 3 v. 8°. . 5957
Review. vols. 1–10. New York, 1837–42. 8°. 4090
State Gazetteer. T. F. Gordon. New York. 8°. 9123
State Register. R. S. Skinner. New York, 1831. 18°. . . 4941
State Society for the Promotion of Useful Arts, Transactions of. vol. 2. Albany, 1807. 8°. 11665
The same. vols. 1 and 4. Albany, 1801. 8°. 11675
State Agricultural Soc., Transactions of. vols. 7–9. Alb. 1848. 8°. 10464
Travels through. W. Darby. New York, 1819. 8°. 9163
University of, Reports of the Regents of, from 1838–49. Albany, 1838–49. 8 v. 8°. 10093

Newcomes. W. M. Thackeray. New York, 1855. 8°. 1
Newell, C. History of the Revolution in Texas. New York, 1838. 12°. 7123
Newman, S. P. Practical System of Rhetoric. Andover, 1836. 12°. . 4862
Newton, I. Life. D. Brewster. New York, 1840. 12°. . . . 5528
The same. New York, 1833. 16°. 6619
Newton, J. Autobiography. New York. 12°. 5248
Works, with Memoir. J. Cecil. Philadelphia, 1839. 2 v. 8°. . 5328
Newton, T. Dissertations on the Prophecies. London, 1771. 3 v. 12°. 5649
Newton Forster. F. Marryatt. Philadelphia, 1833. 2 v. 12°. . . 1613
New Zealanders. Boston, 1830. 12°. 6199
Ney, M. (Marshal.) Memoirs. Philadelphia, 1834. 8°. 7925
Nicaragua, its People, Scenery, &c. E. G. Squier. New York, 1856. 8°. 9373
The same. New York, 1852. 2 v. 8°. 9410
Nice, Council of, Historical View of. O. Boyle. Philadelphia, 1840. 8°. 5075
Nicholas Nickleby. C. Dickens. Philadelphia, 1839. 8°. . . . 15
The same. Philadelphia. 8°. 67
Nicholson, W. Natural Philosophy. London, 1790. 3 v. 8°. . . 5963
Nicol, J. Essay on Scripture Sacrifices. London, 1823. 8°. . . . 5603
Nicolas, H. Chronology of History. London, 1838. 12°. . . . 9923
Nicolay, C. G. Oregon and its Inhabitants. London, 1846. 16°. . . 7183
Niebuhr, B. G. History of Rome. Tr. Philadelphia, 1835. 2 v. 8°. . 6971
Dissertation on the Geography of Herodotus. Oxford, 1830. 8°. 11327
Lectures on Ancient History. Philadelphia, 1852. 3 v. 8°. . . 7364
Life and Letters. Bunsen. New York, 1852. 12°. . . . 8571
Reminiscences. F. Lieber. Philadelphia, 1835. 12°. 8333
The same. 8361

Niger, Journal of Expedit. to. R. and J. Lander. N. Y. 1832. 2 v. 16°. 6628
Night and Morning. E. L. Bulwer. New York, 1841. 2 v. 12°. . . . 1557
Side of Nature. Catharine Crowe. New York, 1850. 12°. . . . 1150
Thoughts. E. Young. Hartford, 1830. 16°. 2069
See also Young, E.
Nile Notes of a Howadji. G. W. Curtis. New York, 1851. 12°. . . . 8902
Niles, H. History of American Revolution. Baltimore, 1822. 8°. . . . 7548
Ed. Weekly Register. vols. 1–35. Baltimore, 1811–35. 8°. . 4642
Index to vols. 1–12. In the rack.
Nineveh and its Remains. A. H. Layard. New York, 1839. 2 v. 8°. . 9384
Noah and his Times. J. M. Olmstead. Boston, 1854. 12°. 485
Noah, M. M. Travels in England, France, Spain and Barbary States, in 1813, &c. New York, 1819. 8°. 9178
Noble, M. Granger's Biographical History of England, continued to 1727. London, 1806. 3 v. 8°. 1783
Noble, S. Appeal in Behalf of New Jerusalem Church. Bost. 1845. 12°. 5642
Noctes Ambrosianæ. J. Wilson. Philadelphia, 1843. 4 v. 12°. . . . 865
The same. New York, 1857. 5 v. 12°. 493
No Fiction. A. Reed. New York, 1835. 12°. 1548
The same. Boston, 1821. 18°. 1689
Reviewed, with an Autobiography of its Hero. F. Barnett. Boston, 1823. 2 v. 16°. 8444
Normal Schools, &c. H. Barnard. Hartford, 1851. 8°. 10090
Norman, B. M. Rambles in Yucatan. New York, 1853. 8°. 9106
Norman Conquest. A. Thierry. Tr. London, 1841. 8°. 7254
The same. Tr. W. Hazlitt. London, 1847. 2 v. 12°. . 5497
The same. 1856. 5448
Normand, M'lle M. A. Memoirs of Josephine. Tr. Phil. 1848. 2 v. 12°. 8008
Norse-Folk, a Visit to Norway and Sweden. C. L. Brace. N. Y. 1857. 12°. 8939
North American Review, from vol. 1–87. (Contin.) Bost. 1815–59. 8°. 4100
Index to vols. 1–20. In the Rack.
North British Review. vols. 1–24. (Continued.) N. Y. 1846–58. 8°. . 4059
North Briton, The. Dublin, 1764. 12°. 4244
North Carolina, Sketches of. W. H. Foote. New York, 1846. 8°. . 6952
North Pole, Possibility of Approaching it Asserted. D. Barrington. New York, 1818. 8°. 10081
North, F., D. and J. Lives. R. North. London, 1826. 3 v. 8°. . . . 8566
Northanger, Abbey. Miss J. Austen. Philadelphia, 1832. 12°. . . . 37
The same. Philadelphia, 1833. 2 v. 12°. 928
The same. 1451
Northcote, J., Conversations of. W. Hazlitt. London, 1830. 8°. . . . 767
Memoirs of J. Reynolds. Philadelphia, 1817. 8°. 8197
Northmen in N. England. J. T. Smith. Boston, 1839. 12°. 7107
Northmore, T. Washington, or Liberty Restored, a Poem. Balt. 1809. 12°. 11882
Northwest, Notes on the. J. A. Bradford. London, 1846. 12°. . . . 805
Territory, Early Settlement of. J. Burnet. New York, 1847. 8°. . 7237
Norton, Mrs. C. E. S. Child of the Islands. New York, 1846. 12°. . 5847
Dream, and other Poems. New York, 1845. 12°. 5846

Norton, Mrs. C. E. S. Poems. Boston, 1833. 12°. 2065
Norton, J. P. Elements of Agriculture. Albany, 1850. 12°. 3001
Norway, Journal of a Residence in, in 1834–6. S. Laing. Lond. 1837. 8°. 9122
and Sweden, Visit to. C. L. Brace. New York, 1857. 12°. . 8939
Sweden and Denmark. H. D. Inglis. Edinburgh, 1829. 16°. . 10014
Norwich, Conn., History of. Miss F. M. Caulkins. Norwich, 1845. 12°. 6768
Notes of a Professional Life. W. Fergusson. London, 1846. 8°. . . 9729
Not so Bad as we Seem, a Comedy. E. L. Bulwer. New York, 1851. 16°. 340
Notions of the Americans. J. F. Cooper. Philadelphia, 1833. 2 v. 16°. . 1031
See also Cooper, J. F.
Nott, E. Miscellaneous Works. Schenectady, 1810. 8°. . . . 11664
Counsels to the Young. New York, 1841. 16°. 4300
Nourmahal, an Oriental Romance. M. J. Quin. London, 1838. 3 v. 12°. 1431
Nova Scotia, Newfoundland, &c., Hist. of. R. M. Martin. Lond. 1837. 12°. 5822
History of. T. C. Haliburton. Halifax. 2 v. 8°. 6931
Novelists, German. Tr. T. Roscoe. London, 1826. 4 v. 12°. . . . 1123
Novum Organum. F. Bacon. Tr. London, 1842. 2 v. 16°. . . . 4977
Now and Then. S. Warren. New York, 1848. 12°. 1485
Nubia and Abyssinia, History of. M. Russell. New York, 1833. 16°. . 6626
The same. 8766
The same. New York, 1840. 12°. 5877
Popular Description of. J. Conder. London, 1827. 18°. . . 9337
The same. 9655
Nugent, Lord. Memorials of J. Hampden, his Party and Times. London, 1832. 8°. 8166
Lands, Classical and Sacred. London, 1846. 2 v. 16°. . . 7193
Nuttall, T. Travels in Arkansas. Philadelphia, 1821. 8°. . . . 9783
Nuts to Crack. Philadelphia, 1835. 12°. 1139

O.

Oakfield. W. D. Arnold. (Two copies.) Boston, 1855. 12°. . . . 571
Oakwood Hall. Catharine Hutton. Philadelphia, 1819. 2 v. 12°. . . 319
Oasis. Ed. Mrs. L. M. Child. Boston, 1834. 12°. 4894
O'Beirne, T. L. Sermons on the State of Ireland, in 1797. Lond. 1799. 8°. 5351
Oberon. C. M. Wieland. Trans. W. Sotheby. London, 1826. 12°. . 2054
Obligations of the World to the Bible. G. Spring. New York, 1839. 8°. 5586
Obookiah, H. Memoirs. E. W. Dwight. New Haven, 1819. 12°. . . 8441
Observer, The. London, 1823. 3 v. 12°. 3694
O'Callaghan, E. B. History of New Netherlands. N. Y. 1848. 2 v. 8°. . 7242
Documentary History of New York. Albany, 1849–51. 4 v. 8°. . 10455
Occidente, Maria del. Zóphiël. Boston, 1834. 12°. 2435
Occult Sciences. E. Smedley and others. London, 1855. 12°. . . 6072
Ockley, S. The History of the Saracens. Cambridge, 1757. 2 v. 8°. . 11429
O'Connell, D. and others, the Queen *vs.* Report. J. S. Armstrong. Dublin, 1844. 8°. 10653
Odes upon Cash, Corn, Catholics, and other Matters. Phil. 1828. 12°. . 2018
Odd Whims and Miscellanies. H. Repton. London, 1804. 12°. . . 955

Odiorne, T. Progress of Refinement, &c. Boston, 1792. 16°. . . . 2479
Odiorne, J. C. Opinions on Speculative Masonry. Boston, 1830. 12°. . 4543
O'Driscol, J. Views of Ireland. London, 1823. 2 v. 8°. 9509
O'Haloran, J. C. Life of St. Patrick. Philadelphia, 1813. 12°. . . 8674
Odyssea. See Homerus.
Oglethorpe, J. Life of. W. B. O. Peabody. Boston, 1844. 12°. . . 8054
Ohio Gazetteer. J. Kilbourn. Columbus, 1821. 12°. 9301
Gazetteer and Traveller's Guide. W. Jenkins. Colum. 1837. 12°. 8980
Geological Survey of. W. W. Mather. Columbus, 1838. 8°. . 6002
Historical Collections of. H. Howe. Cincinnati, 1850. 8°. . . 7606
Ojibway Nation, Traditional History of. G. Copway. Bost. 1851. 12°. . 7106
Old Bachelor in the Old Scottish Village. T. Aird. Lond. 1845. 12°. . 1648
Old Ballads, Historical, &c. T. and B. H. Evans. Lond. 1810. 4 v. 12°. 1978
Old Humphrey's Addresses. New York, 1841. 12°. 832
Observations. New York, 1841. 12°. 833
Old Mortality. W. Scott. Boston, 1820. 12°. 1093
See also Scott, Sir W.
Old Painters, Sketches of. Mrs. H. Lee. (Two copies.) Bost. 1841. 12°. 10199
Old Plays, Collection of. Ed. R. Dodsley. London, 1825–7. 11 v. 8°. . 2228
Old Portraits and Modern Sketches. J. G. Whittier. Boston, 1850. 12°. 875
Old Red Sandstone. (Illust.) H. Miller. Boston, 1851. 12°. . . 6063
Old Regime and the Revolution. A. De Tocqueville. Tr. N. Y. 1856. 12°. 7393
Old Wine in New Bottles. A. J. Gardner. New York, 1848. 12°. . . 1142
Old World, Glimpses of. J. A. Clarke. Philadelphia, 1840. 2 v. 12°. . 9241
Letters from. New York, 1840. 2 v. 12°. 8922
and the New. O. Dewey. New York, 1836. 2 v. 12°. . . . 9832
Old and New Testament Connected. H. Prideaux. Balt. 1833. 2 v. 8°. . 6329
Oldbuck, J. See Wethington, L.
Oldmixon, J. History of England. See England.
Olds, G. S. Sermons on Episcopacy and Presby. Parity. Green. 1815. 12°. 6528
Olin, S. Travels in Egypt, Arabia Petræa and the Holy Land. vol. 2.
New York, 1844. 12°. , ... 9243
Olive Branch Answered. New York, 1816. 12°. 11189
Oliver, Isabella. Poems. Carlisle, 1805. 12°. 2449
Oliver Twist. C. Dickens. Philadelphia, 1839. 18°. 648
The same. Philadelphia. 8°. 66
Ollapodiana. W. G. Clark. New York, 1844. 8°. 743
Ollendorff's Method of German. G. J. Adler. New York, 1846. 12°. . 2980
Olmsted, D. Compendium of Natural Philosophy. New Haven, 1833. 8°. 5978
Introduction to Astronomy. New York, 1839. 8°. 5985
Life and Writings of E. P. Mason. New York, 1842. 12°. . . 8307
The same. 8635
Natural Philosophy. New Haven, 1840. 2 v. 8°. 5987
The same. New Haven, 1838. 2 v. 8°. 5989
Olmsted, F. A. Incidents of a Whaling Voyage. New York, 1841. 12°. 9816
Olmsted, F. L. Journey through Texas. New York, 1857. 12°. . . 8971
Seaboard Slave States, Journey through. New York, 1856. 12°. 8972
Olmstead, J. M. Noah and his Times. Boston, 1854. 12°. . . . 485

Olney, J., and J. W. Barber. Family Book of History. New Haven, 8°. 7564
The same. 7565
O'Meara, B. E. Napoleon in Exile. Boston, 1823. 2 v. 12°. . . . 7452
Omoo; Adventures in the South Seas. H. Melville. N. Y. 1847. 12°. . 556
Onderdonk, B. T. Trial of. New York, 1845. 8°. 10660
Onderdonk, H., Jr. Revolutionary Incid. of Queen's Co. N. Y. 1846. 12°. 7420
Onéota, or Characteris. of Amer. Indians. H. R. Schoolcraft. N. Y. 1845. 8°. 9483
Only Daughter, The. G. R. Gleig. London, 1839. 3 v. 12°. . . . 1459
Opie, Amelia. Illustrations of Lying. Hartford, 1827. 12°. . . . 6489
Works. Boston, 1827. 11 v. 12°. 907

Vol. 1. Madeline.
2. Adeline Mowbray.
3. Black Velvet Pelisse. Death Bed. Unfashionable Wife and Unfashionable Husband. Robber. Mother and Son. Love and Duty.
4. Soldier's Return. Brother and Sister. Revenge. Uncle and Nephew. Murder will out. Orphan.
5. Lady Anne and Lady Jane. Austin and his Wife. Mysterious Stranger. Appearance is against her.
6. Valentine's Eve.
7. Mrs. Arlington. White Lies. Henry Woodville.
8. Young Man of the World. Tale of Trials. Odd Tempered Man. Ruffian Boy. Welcome Home.
9, 10. Temper, or Domestics Scenes.
11, 12. Father and Daughter. Illustrations of Lying.

Opinions, Essays on the Formation of. Philadelphia, 1831. 12°. . . . 4555
Optics. D. Brewster. London, 1835. 12°. 9959
The same, with Notes. Philadelphia, 1833. 12°. . . 6087
Optimist. H. T. Tuckerman. New York, 1850. 12°. 826
Orations, Elegant. 12°. 11165
Orator's Text Book. Ed. D. Macleod. Washington, 1830. 12°. . . 4916
Orators of the Age. G. H. Francis. New York, 1847. 12°. . . . 8704
in America, Living. E. L. Magoon. New York, 1849. 12°. . . 8669
of American Revolution. E. L. Magoon. New York, 1848. 12°. . 8668
of France. Timon. Tr. New York, 1849. 12°. 8670
Oratory, Lectures on. J. Ward. London, 1759. 2 v. 12°. . . . 2982
Oregon and California, History of. R. Greenhow. Boston, 1845. 8°. . 7539
History and Discovery of. T. Twiss. New York, 1846. 12°. . 7092
and its Inhabitants. C. G. Nicolay. London, 1846. 16°. . . 7183
O'Reilly, H. Sketches of Rochester. Rochester, 1838. 12°. . . . 7095
Oriental Customs, or Illust's of Scripture. S. Burder. Phil. 1807. 2 v. 8°. 9464
Outlines, or Tour in Turkey, Greece, &c. W. Knight. Lon. 1839. 12°. 8726
Origines, or Origin of Empires, States, &c. W. Drummond. London, 1824. 4 v. 8°. 7586
Orlando Furioso. L. Ariosto. Tr. J. Hoole. London, 1783. 5 v. 8°. . 1870
Orlando Innamorato, The. Tr. W. S. Rose. Edinburgh, 1823. 12°. . 1914
Orleans, House of. Memoirs of. W. C. Taylor. London, 1850. 2 v. 12°. 8000
Orme, W. Mem's and Select Remains of J. Urquhart. Bost. 1828. 2 v. 16°. 7757
Ormond, or the Secret Witness. C. B. Brown. Boston, 1827. 12°. . 1002
The same. 1430
Ornithology, Amer. A. Wilson and C. L. Bonaparte. Edin, 1831. 4 v. 12°. 10175
See also Naturalist's Library.

Orphans of Unwalden. W. Godwin. New York, 1835. 12°. 1253
Orpheus, Musaeus, et Callimachus. Lipsiæ, 1839. 16°. 10345
Osborn, L. Poems. Boston, 1823. 12°. 2012
Osborn, S. Leaves from an Arctic Journal. New York, 1852. 2 v. 12°. 9002
Osborne, T. (Earl of Danby.) Life. T. P. Courtenay. London, 1838. 12°. 9936
Osgood, Mrs. F. S. Poems. New York, 1846. 12°. 2023
Osler, E. Life of Admiral Viscount Exmouth. London, 1835. 12°. . 8287
Osma and Almeria. Regina M. Roche. New York, 1810. 12°. . . . 979
Ossoli, Margaret F., Memoirs of. Boston, 1852. 2 v. 12°. 8018
Osterwald, J. F. Compendium of Christian Theology. Hart. 1788. 12°. 2985
O'Sullivan, M. Guide to an Irish Gentleman. Philadelphia, 1833. 12°. 6581
Oswald, J. Appeal in behalf of Religion. London, 1768. 2 v. 8°. . . 6414
Othman Empire, History of. London, 1781. 18°. 7056
Othuriel and other Poems. T. Aird. Edinburgh, 1840. 8°. 1835
Otis, H. G. Letters in Defence of Hartford Convention. Bost. 1824. 8°. 11094
Otis, J. Life. F. Bowen. Boston, 1844. 12°. 8054
Life. W. Tudor. Boston, 1823. 8°. 8194
Ottoman Empire, History of. E. Upham. Edinburgh, 1829. 2 v. 16°. . 10015
Otway, T. Select Poems, with Life by E. Sanford. Phil. 1819. 18°. . 2124
Our First Mother. New York, 1852. 12°. 6524
Our Village. Mary R. Mitford. New York, 1828. 4 v. 12°. 221
The same. 3 v. 1006
Outre-Mer. H. W. Longfellow. New York, 1835. 2 v. 12°. 1607
Outward Bound. E. Howard. New York, 1839. 2 v. 12°. 1265
Ovidius Naso, Publius. Metamorphoses. London, 1812. 16°. . . 2717
Opera. Lipsiæ, 1829. 3 v. 16°. 10599
The same. Tr. Dryden, Pope and others. N. Y. 1836. 2 v. 16°. 8754
The same. New York, 1838. 2 v. 12°. 5277
Tristia. Tr. F. Arden. New York, 1821. 8°. 1791
Owen, D. D. Geological Survey of Wisconsin, &c. Phil. 1852. 2 v. 4°. 13115
Owen, J. The Fashionable World Displayed. New York, 1806. 12°. . 4913
History of the British and Foreign Society. New York, 1817. 8°. 6423
Owen R. New View of Society, or Formation of Charac. N. Y. 1825. 12°. 6487
Owen, W. F. W. Voyages to Explore Coasts of Africa, Arabia, and Madagascar. New York, 1833. 2 v. 12°. 9251
Owenson, Miss. Wild Irish Girl. New York, 1807. 12°. 366
The same. 673
Oxberry, W. Flowers of Literature, or Encyclopædia of Anecdote. London, 1821. 3 v. 12°. 860
Oxford Divinity. C. P. M'Ilvaine. Philadelphia, 1841. 8°. 5011
Prize Essays. Oxford, 1836. 4 v. 12°. 837
Prize Poems. Oxford, 1828. 12°. 2492
Sausage, The. London, 1815. 8°. 1816
Theology. V. Livingston. New York, 1841. 12°. 6571
University Calendar. 1824. 12°. 3027
Views of, Illustrated. Oxford, 1831. 4°. . . . . . .
Oxonians, a Glance at Society. W. I. Kissam. N. Y. 1830. 2 v. 12°. . 1356

P.

Pacha of Many Tales. F. Marryatt. Philadelphia, 1834. 2 v. 12°. . . 1385
The same. New York, 1835. 12°. 1253
Pachydermes. W. Jardine. Edinburgh, 1836. 12°. 10197
Pacific, Cruise in. Porter. New York, 1822. 2 v. 8°. 9499
The same. New York, 1815. 8°. 9452
Three Years in the. W. S. W. Ruschenberger. Phil. 1834. 8°. . 9424
Packard, Mrs. C. Recollections of a Housekeeper. New York, 1838. 16°. 4975
Paddock, J. Shipwreck of the Oswego on Barbary Coast. N. Y. 1818. 8°. 9479
Page, H. Memoir. W. A. Hallock. New York. 12°. 7779
The same. New York. 16°. 5245
Paget, J. Hungary and Transylvania, Condition of. Lond. 1839. 2 v. 8°. 6654
Paine, M. Soul and Instinct. New York, 1849. 12°. 6138
Paine, T. Life. J. Cheetham. London, 1817. 8°. 7898
Painters, Italian. Mrs. A. Jameson. London, 1845. 2 v. 16°. . . 6892
Modern. J. Ruskin. New York, 1847–56. 3 v. 12°. 10161
the Old, Sketches of. Mrs. H. Lee. (Two copies.) Bost. 1841. 12°. 10199
and Sculptors. Lives. A. Cunningham. N. Y. 1831. 5 v. 12°. . 6253
The same. New York, 1840. 5 v. 12°. 5519
Sculptors and Architects. Lives. G. Vasari. Lond. 1850. 5 v. 12°. 5139
Painting, Lectures on. J. Barry, J. Opie, and H. Fuseli. Lond. 1848. 12. 5486
Paintings and Architecture. Lectures on. J. Ruskin. N. Y. 1856. 12°. 10160
and the Fine Arts. B. R. Haydon, and W. Hazlitt. Edin. 1838. 12°. 10164
in Italy, History of. A. L. Lanzi. Trans. Lond. 1828. 6 v. 8°. . 10122
The same. London, 1847. 3 v. 12°. 5122
The same. Abridg. G. W. D. Evans. London, 1835. 8°. . 9112
Sculpture and Architec., Hist. of. J. S. Memes. Bost. 1831. 12°. 10148
The same. 10155
Palæmon's Creed Reviewed. D. Wilson. London, 1762. 2 v. 12°. . 6596
Palestine, Biblical Researches in. E. Robinson. Boston, 1841. 3 v. 8°. 9074
The same, with Maps. Boston, 1856. 4 v. 8°. . . . 9378
Description of. J. Conder. London. 16°. 9652
The same. 9668
Early Travels in. Ed. T. Wright. London, 1847. 12°. . . 5445
History of. M. Russell. New York, 1832. 16°. 6620
The same. New York, 1840. 12°. 5529
and Lebanon, three Weeks in. London, 1824. 12°. . . . 9023
and other Poems. R. Heber. Phil. 1828. 16°. 2082
Paley, W. Evidences of Christianity. Phil. 1825. 16°. 6501
Natural Theology. New York, 1840. 2 v. 12°. 5556
The same. 5626
Works. Philadelphia, 1831. 8°. 5109
The same. (vol. 3 missing.) New York, 1824. 4 v. 16°. . . 6649

Vol. 1. Evidences of Christianity. | Vol. 4. Horae Paulinae.
2. Moral and Political Philosophy. | 5. Sermons.

Palfrey, W. Life. J. G. Palfrey. Boston, 1845. 12°. 8059

Palgrave, F. English Commonwealth during the Anglo-Saxon Period. London, 1832. 2 v. 4°. 11254
History of the Anglo-Saxons. London, 1837. 16°. 8760
Palingenius Stellati, M. Zodiacus Vitae. Lipsiæ, 1832. 12°. . . . 10851
Palmyra, Letters from. W. Ware. Boston, 1837. 2 v. 12°. . . . 9039
Palmer, W. Church History. New York, 1841. 12°. 5732
The same. New York, 1844. 12°. 5685
The same. 6148
Palmerin of England. F. De Moraes. Tr. R. Southey. Lond. 1807. 4 v. 16°. 8453
Pamela, or Virtue Rewarded. S. Richardson. London, 1811. 4 v. 12°. . 930
Pamphlets on Various Subjects. (Bound.) 17 v.

No. 9734. Assemblee Générale de la Sociéte Biblique Protestante de Paris.
9735. Ninth Annual Report of New York Deaf and Dumb Institution.
9736. Smithsonian Reports of Public Libraries.
9737. Orations and Discourses.
9738. Life of Roger M. Sherman and College Addresses.
9739. Annual Reports of American and Foreign Anti-Slavery Society.
9740. Public Speeches.
9741. Reports of Anti-Slavery Societies.
9742. Reports and Sermons.
9743. College and Public Addresses.
9744. Whitman's Letters.
9745. Statistics of County of Middlesex, Conn., and Constitutions of Bible Societies.
9746. Reports and Addresses.
9747. Phi Beta Kappa Orations and Poems.
9748. J. D. Dana's Miscellanies.

Panorama and other Poems. Boston, 1856. 12°. 1996
Pantheon, The. A. Locke. London, 1726. 12°. 4933
Paper against Gold, and Glory against Prosperity. W. Cobbett. London, 1815. 2 v. 8°. 10057
The same. New York, 1834. 12°. 11163
Parables of our Lord. Notes on. R. C. Trench. N. Y. 1859. 8°. . . 5056
Paracelsus. R. Browning. London, 1835. 12°. 2396
Paradise Lost. J. Milton. Boston, 1833. 12°. 2388
Paradise Regained. J. Milton. London, 1753. 2 v. 16°. 2718
See also Milton, J.
Paraguay, in the Reign of J. G. R. de Francia. J. R. Rengger. Trans. London, 1827. 8°. 6736
Francia's Reign in. J. P. and W. P. Robertson. Phil. 1839. 2 v. 12°. 1551
Pardoe, Miss. Court and Reign of Francis I. Phil. 1849. 2 v. 12°. . 7996
Confessions of a Pretty Woman. New York, 1851. 8°. 48
Louis XIV, and Court of France. New York, 1847. 2 v. 12°. . 8586
Traits and Traditions of Portugal. Phil. 1834. 2 v. 12°. . . 9288
Parent's Assistant. Maria Edgeworth. New York, 1836. 12°. . . 1148
Paris, J. A. Life of H. Davy. London, 1831. 2 v. 8°. 12089
Paris, American in, during the Winter. J. Janin. New York, 1844. 8°. 9423
and its People. J. Grant. London, 1844. 2 v. 12°. 9538
and its Historical Scenes. Boston, 1831. 12°. 6204
The same. vol. 2. Boston, 1832. 12°. 6208
and the Parisians. Mrs. F. Trollope. New York, 1836. 8°. . 9148
in 1851. F. B. Head. New York, 1852. 12°. 10146

Paris Sketch Book. W. M. Thackeray. New York, 1852. 2 v. 12°. . 1630
Park, E. A. Memoir and Writings of W. B. Homer. And. 1842. 12°. . 5390
(Editor.) The Preacher and Pastor. Andover, 1845. 12°. . . 811
Park, Miss L. J. Joanna of Naples. Boston, 1838. 12°. . . . 1397
Park, M. Journal of Travels in Africa. Philadelphia, 1800. 8°. . . 9129
Life. New York, 1840. 12°. 5565
Life and Travels. Edinburgh, 1835. 12°. 8077
Parker, A. A. A Trip to Texas and the West. Concord, 1835. 12°. . 9824
Parker, E. G. Golden Age of American Oratory. Boston, 1857. 12°. . 486
Parker, J. Lectures on Universalism. New York, 1841. 12°. . . 6146
Parker, R. G. Aids to English Composition. Boston, 1844. 12°. . . 2997
Parker, S. Tour Beyond the Rocky Mountains. Ithaca, 1838. 12°. . 8950
The same. (Two copies.) 9811
Parkman, F., Jr. History of the Conspiracy of Pontiac. Bost. 1851. 8°. 7267
Parkyns, M. Life in Abyssinia. New York, 1854. 2 v. 12°. . . . 9560
Parliament, the Imperial. J. E. May. London, 1842. 8°. . . . 5931
Parliamentary Diary, from 1656–9. T. Bunton. London, 1828. 4 v. 8°. 10694
Practice, Manual of. Philadelphia, 1840. 16°. 11161
Register, 1774–9. London, 1775. 14 v. 8°. 11095
Reports, from 1794–8. W. Woodfall. London, 1794–8. 17 v. 8°. 10496
Parnell, T. Poetical Works and Life. Edinburgh, 1778. 2 v. 12°. . . 2774
Parr, S. Works. Ed. J. Johnstone. London, 1828. 8 v. 8°. . . 5066
Parricide. Philadelphia, 1836. 2 v. 12°. 1372
Parrot, F. Journey to Ararat. Tr. W. D. Cooley. New York, 1846. 12°. 9600
Parrots, Treatise on. P. J. Selby. Edinburgh, 1836. 12°. 10189
Parry, W. E. Journal of 2d Voyage to find N. W. Passage. N. Y. 1824. 8°. 9425
Journal of Three Voyages. London, 1835. 4 v. 16°. . . . 9329
The same. New York, 1840. 2 v. 12°. 5569
Parson, T. Essays. Boston, 1845. 12°. 480
Parsons, Legacy to. W. Cobbett. New York, 1844. 16°. . . . 6218
Parted Family and other Poems. Mary S. B. Dana. N. Y. 1842. 12°. . 2350
Parthians, History of. London, 1779. 8°. 7037
Party, History of, from 1666 to 1832. G. W. Cooke. Lond. 1836. 3 v. 8°. 7624
Pascal, B. Pensées. Paris, 1832. 16°. 6648
Provincial Letters. Tr. New York, 1828. 12°. 6491
Thoughts on Religion. Tr. E. Craig. Amherst, 1829. 12°. . . 6112
Pascal Bruno. S. Hooke. Philadelphia, 1839. 12°. 1573
Passing Thoughts. Mrs. C. E. Tonna. New York, 1841. 18°. . . . 1708
Past and Present. T. Carlyle. Boston, 1843. 12°. 11117
The same. Philadelphia, 1837. 12°. 247
The same, with Chartism. New York, 1848. 12°. . . . 813
Paston Letters. Ed. J. Fenn. London, 1849. 12°. 5442
Pastor, Fragments from the Study of. G. Spring. New York, 1838. 12°. 5709
Pastor's Sketches. I. S. Spencer. New York, 1851. 12°. . . . 6557
Patch Work. B. Hall. Philadelphia, 1841. 2 v. 12°. 9795
Patent Office Reports. See U. S. Public Documents.
Pathfinder. J. F. Cooper. Philadelphia, 1841. 12°. 1576
The same. New York, 1851. 12°. 1232

Patmos and the Seven Churches of Asia. J. Brewer. Bridgeport, 1851. 8°. 5089
Paton, A. A. Servia, or Residence in Belgrade. London, 1845. 12°. . 9231
Patronage. Miss M. Edgeworth. New York, 1834. 2 v. 12°. . . 903
Patten, W. Reminiscences of S. Hopkins. New York, 1843. 16°. . . 8458
Paul Clifford. E. L. Bulwer. New York, 1830. 2 v. 12°. 1330
The same. 1342
The same. 1775
Paul Fane. N. P. Willis. New York, 1857. 12°. 203
Paulding, J. K. Koningsmarke. New York, 1834. 2 v. 12°. . . . 1310
The same. New York, 1823. 2 v. 12°. 975
Letters from the South. New York, 1817. 2 v. 12°. . . . 9606
The same. New York, 1835. 2 v. 12°. 1308
Life of G. Washington. New York, 1835. 2 v. 16°. . . . 8771
The same. New York, 1840. 2 v. 12°. 5885
Miserrimus. New York, 1833. 12°. 3359
Slavery in the United States. New York, 1836. 12°. . . . 11157
Westward Ho. New York, 1832. 2 v. 12°. 1017
and W. Irving. Salmagundi. First Series. N. Y. 1835. 2 v. 12°. 1304
Second series. New York, 1835. 2 v. 12°. 1306
Paul's Letters to his Kinsfolk. W. Scott. Edinburgh, 1817. 8°. . . 9210
The same. Boston, 1829. 12°. 3938
Pausanias. Græciæ Descriptio. Lipsiæ, 1829. 2 v. 16°. . . . 10823
The same. Tr. London, 1795. 3 v. 8°. 6739
Paxton, J. Introduction to the Study of Anatomy. Bost. 1840. 2 v. 8°. 1068
Payne, A. R. M. Residence in a Brazilian Valley. New York, 1852. 12°. 8989
Payson, E. Memoir. A. Cummings. New York. 16°. 5234
The same. Boston, 1830. 16°. 8348
Payson, S. Proofs of the Existence and Danger of Illuminism. Charleston, 1802. 12°. 6507
Peabody, G., Dinner given by, to Americans connected with the World's Fair at London. London, 1851. 8°. 12132
Peabody, W. B. O. Life of A. Wilson. Boston, 1834. 12°. 8069
Life of D. Brainerd. (Two copies.) Boston, 1837. 12°. . . 8050
Life of C. Mather. (Two copies.) Boston, 1836, 12°. . . . 8047
Life of J. Oglethorpe. Boston, 1844. 12°. 8054
Life of I. Putnam. Boston, 1837. 12°. 8049
Life of J. Sullivan. Boston, 1844. 12°. 8055
Peace, Principles of, Exemplified. T. Hancock. Philadelphia, 1829. 12°. 4954
Society Addresses. E. B. Perkins, L. Bacon, and others. Brooklyn, 1828. 8°. 2974
and War, Essays on. Portland, 1827. 16°. 4286
The same. Exeter, 1827. 16°. 4293
Peake, R. B. Memoirs of the Colman Family. London, 1841. 2 v. 8°. 7872
Pearce, S. Memoir. A. Fuller. New York. 16°. 5244
The same. Newark, 1809. 12°. 8413
Pearl, C. Youth's Book on the Mind. Portland, 1847. 12°. . . . 4223
Pearson, H. Memoir of C. Buchanan. New York, 1841. 16°. . . 5238
The same. Boston, 1818. 12°. 8034

Pearson, H. Memoir of C. F. Swartz. New York, 1835. 12°. . . . 8619
Pearson, J. Exposition of the Creed. New York, 1844. 8°. . . . 5310
Peasant and his Landlord. Baroness Knorring. Tr. N. York, 1848. 12°. 1237
Peck, J. M. Guide for Emigrants. Boston, 1831. 16°. 9328
Life of D. Boone. Boston, 1847. 12°. 8065
Peel, Sir R. Memoirs. London, 1842. 2 v. 12°. 8590
Peel, Sir R., and Duke of Wellington. Lives. New York, 1852. 12° . 8392
Pekin, Residence at the Court of. Father Ripa. Tr. N. Y. 1846. 12°. 9842
Pierce, B. History of Harvard University. Cambridge, 1833. 8°. . 11335
Pellet, Major General. Views of England. Tr. Boston, 1818. 12°. . 9045
Peloponnesian War, Hist. of. Thucydides. Tr. W. Smith. Phil. 1836. 8°. 7555
The same. New York, 1839. 2 v. 12°. 5279
Pencil Sketches. Miss E. Leslie. Philadelphia, 1833. 12°. . . . 697
Second series. (Two copies.) Philadelphia, 1835. 12°. . 698
Pencillings by the Way. N. P. Willis. New York, 1836. 2 v. 12°. . 8998
Pendennis, History of. W. M. Thackeray. New York, 1850. 2 v. 8°. . 2
Peninsular Campaigns, Annals of. T. Hamilton. Phil. 1831. 3 v. 12°. . 6803
The same. 9524
War. R. Southey. (vols. 5, 6 missing.) London, 1828. 6 v. 8°. 6656
War, Memorials of. Edinburgh, 1828. 2 v. 16°. 10006
War, Hist. of, with Maps. W. F. P. Napier. Phil. 1842. 5 v. 8°. 7559
Penitentiary System in the United States. G. de Beaumont and A. de Tocqueville. Tr. F. Lieber. Philadelphia, 1833. 8°. . 10068
Pen Owen. New York, 1822. 2 v. 12°. 682
Penn, W. Life. G. E. Ellis. Boston, 1847. 12°. 8064
Life. W. H. Dixon. Philadelphia, 1851. 12°. 7995
Select Works, with a Life of the Author. London, 1825. 3 v. 8°. . 6042
Pennington, M. Life of Mrs. E. Carter. Boston, 1809. 8°. . . . 8129
Pennsylvania, Historical Collections of. S. Day. Phil. 1843. 8°. . . 7251
History of. T. F. Gordon. Philadelphia, 1829. 8°. . . . 11362
History of, with Life of W. Penn. R. Proud. Phil. 1797. 2 v. 8°. 6714
History of Insurrection in. W. Findley. Philadelphia, 1796. 8°. 6767
Review of the Constitution of, &c. London, 1759. 8°. . . . 10808
Penny Cyclopædia. London, 1833–43. 26 v. 4°. 9675
Magazine. London, 1832–41. 4°. 3098
Pentateuch, Poetry of. J. H. Caunter. London, 1839. 2 v. 8°. . . 5027
Pepys, S. Memoirs. R. Braybrooke. London, 1828. 5 v. 8°. . . 7977
Percival, J. G. Clio, No. III. New York, 1827. 12°. 2019
Dream of a Day, and other Poems. New Haven, 1843. 12°. . . 2400
Poems. New York, 1823. 8°. 1932
Report on the Geology of Connecticut. New Haven, 1842. 8°. . 5952
Percival, R. Account of the Island of Ceylon. London, 1805. 4°. . 11253
Percy Mallory. Philadelphia, 1824. 2 v. 12°. 1402
Percy's Masque, a Drama. J. A. Hillhouse. New York, 1820. 12°. . . 2458

Percy, S. and R. Percy Anecdotes. London, 1823. 20 v. 16°. . . . 3992

Vol. 1. Humanity and Eloquence.	Vol. 11. Beneficence and Exile.
2. Youth and George III.	12. War and Pastime.
3. Enterprise and Captivity.	13. Patriotism and Commerce.
4. Science and Heroism.	14. Stage, Crimes and Punishments.
5. Justice and Instinct.	15. Traveling and Literature.
6. Humor and Imagination.	16. Woman and Honor.
7. Fidelity and Fine Arts.	17. Fashion and Music.
8. Hospitality and the Bar.	18. Senate and Ingenuity.
9. Genius and Shipwreck.	19. Eccentricity and Integrity.
10. Pulpit and Industry.	20. Conviviality and Domestic Life.

Percy, T. (Editor.) Reliques of Ancient English Poetry. Phil. 1823. 8°. 1924
Perdicaris, G. A. Greece of the Greeks. New York, 1845. 2 v. 12°. . 8892
Peregrine Pickle. T. Smollet. New York, 1816. 4 v. 16°. . . . 1751
Perfection, Spiritual, Unfolded and Enforced. W. Bates. Lond. 1834. 16°. 5779
Pergamus, History of. London, 1779. 8°. 7037
Pericles and Aspasia. W. S. Landor. Philadelphia, 1839. 2 v. 12°. . 161
The same. 163
Perilous Adventures. R. A. Davenport. New York, 1846. 12°. . . 5211
Perils and Captivity. Edinburgh, 1827. 16°. 9996
Perils and Sufferings, Narrat. of. R. A. Davenport. Lond. 1840. 2 v. 12°. 3360
Perkins, J. H. Life and Writings. Ed. W. H. Channing. Bost. 1851. 2 v. 8°. 800
Perkins, J. Residence of Eight Years in Persia. Andover, 1843. 8°. . 9073
Perkins, G. W. Sermons, with a Memoir. New York, 1859. 12°. . 5733
Perkins, S. Historical Sketches of the United States. N. Y. 1830. 12°. 8031
Hist. of the late War between U. S. and G. Brit. N. H. 1825. 8°. 6902
Perrin J. Fables Amusantes. New York, 1807. 12°. 1649
Elements of French and English Conversation. N. Y. 1823. 16°. 3978
Perry, O. H. Life. A. S. Mackenzie. New York, 1841. 2 v. 12°. . 5900
The same. New York, 1841. 2 v. 12°. 5902
Perry, M. C. Expedition to Japan and China Seas. F. L. Hawks. New York, 1857. 8°. 9386
Perry, W. C. German University Education. London, 1845. 12°. . 2984
Persecuted Family. R. Pollok. Boston, 1829. 16°. . . . . , 6560
Persia, Description of. J. Conder. London, 1827. 2 v. 16°. . . 9339
The same. 9669
History of. J. B. Fraser. New York, 1834. 16°. 6272
The same. New York, 1841. 12°. 5882
History of. J. Hanway. London, 1762. 2 v. 4°. . . . 10921
The same. London, 1781. 8°. 7051
Residence in, among the Nestorians. J. Perkins. And. 1843. 8°. 9073
Sketches of. Philadelphia, 1828. 12°. 9616
Sketches of. H. Malcom. London, 1828. 2 v. 12°. . . . 9574
Turkey, &c., Trav. in. A. and R. and T. Sherley. Lond. 1825. 12°. 8713
Persian Adventurer. J. B. Fraser. Philadelphia, 1831. 2 v. 12°. . . 253
Letters. C. de Montesquieu. Tr. J. Flloyd. Lond. 1762. 2 v. 12°. 4910
The same. Tr. J. Ozell. London, 1730. 3 v. 12°. . . 4898
Persians, History of. London, 1799. 8°. 7032
Persius Flaccus, A. Satiræ. Tr. W. Drummond. New York, 1837. 12°. 5292
The same. Tr. W. Gifford. London, 1821. 8°. 1868

Persius Flaccus, A. Satiræ. Tr. W. Gifford. Philadelphia, 1822. 18°. . 2114
Personal Recollections. Mrs. C. E. Tonna. New York, 1843. 12°. . 1205
The same. 1206
Persuasion. Miss J. Austen. Philadelphia, 1838. 8°. 37
The same. Philadelphia, 1832. 2 v. 12°. 1440
Persuasives to Early Piety. J. G. Pike. New York. 12°. 5231
The same. 5232
Peru, Conquest of, by the Spaniards. T. de Trueba. Edin. 1830. 16°. . 10020
Description of. J. Conder. London. 16°. 9668
History of the Conquest of. W. H. Prescott. N. Y. 1848. 2 v. 8°. 7257
Travels in. J. J. von Tschudi. New York, 1847. 12°. . . . 9853
Peruvian Antiq. M. E. Rivero, and J. J. von Tschudi. Tr. N. Y. 1853. 8°. 9147
Petavius, D. Rationarium Temporum. Paris, 1652. 16°. 11291
Peter, W. (Editor.) Poets and Poetry of the Ancients. Phil. 1848. 8°. . 1788
Peter Simple. F. Marryatt. New York, 1835. 2 v. 12°. 707
Peter the Great, Anecdotes of. Mr. Stæhlin. Dublin, 1789. 12°. . . 8467
Life. J. Barrow. New York, 1841. 12°. 5881
Peter Pindar, Works of. J. Wolcott. 8°. 2360
Peter's Letters to his Kinsfolk. J. G. Lockhart and others. N. Y. 1820. 8°. 9725
Peters, S. History of Connecticut. New Haven. 1829. 12°. . . . 6837
Petit Jack, a System of French Instruction. London, 1833. 12°. . . 3038
Petrarch, F. Life. T. Campbell. Philadelphia, 1841. 8°. 7826
Life. Mrs. S. Dobson. Philadelphia, 1817. 8°. 8187
The same. Philadelphia, 1809. 2 v. 16°. 8426
View of Human Life. Tr. London, 1797. 8°. 1104
Pettengell, A. Manual of Astronomy. New Haven, 1826. 16°. . . 4284
Peveril of the Peak. W Scott. Boston, 1845. 12°. 294
See also Scott, Sir W.
Peyrouse, J. G. F. de la. Journal of a Voyage Round the World. Boston, 1801. 12°. 9302
Pezron, P. Antiquities of Nations, Rise and Fall of States, &c. Tr. London, 1809. 16°. 11298
Pfeiffer, Ida. Second Journey Round the World. New York, 1856. 12°. 9590
Journey to Iceland, &c. Tr. New York, 1852. 12°. 9000
Phædon, Dialogue on the Immortality of the Soul, with a Life of Plato. Tr. Mad. Dacier. New York, 1833. 12°. 6443
Phædrus. Fabulæ. Lipsiæ, 1843. 16°. 10863
The same. Lipsiæ, 1829. 10858
The same. Tr. C. Smart. New York, 1840. 12°. . . . 5276
Phalaris, Themistocles, Socrates, and Euripides, Dissertations on the Epistles of. R. Bentley. (Two copies.) London, 1836. 2 v. 8°. . 378
Phantom Ship, The. F. Marryatt. Philadelphia, 1839. 2 v. 12°. . . 1560
Phantasmion. New York, 1839. 2 v. 12°. 1488
Phelps, A. A. Slavery and its Remedy. Boston, 1834. 18°. . . . 11155
Phelps, Mrs. A. H. Botany for Beginners. New York, 1841. 16°. . . 4553
Phenix, a Collection of Old and Rare Fragments. New York, 1835. 12°. 4537
Philadelphia, Annals of. J. F. Watson. Philadelphia, 1830. 8°. . . 7317
Book. Philadelphia, 1836. 12°. 840

Philip and his Garden. Mrs. C. E. Tonna. New York, 1842. 16°. . . 1704
Philip Augustus. G. P. R. James. New York, 1831. 3 v. 12°. . . 1044
Philip De Comines. History of Lewis XI and Charles VIII of France, and of Charles the Bold. London, 1823. 2 v. 12°. 8268
Philip of Macedon, History of. T. Leland. London, 1820. 2 v. 8°. . 7864
Philip, R. Guide to the Thoughtful. Boston, 1835. 16°. . . . 6577
Guide to the Conscientious. New York, 1834. 16°. . . . 6565
Life and Times of J. Bunyan. New York, 1839. 12°. . . . 8291
Life of W. Milne, with Annals of Asiatic Missions. N. Y. 1840. 12°. 8012
Manly Piety. New York, 1834. 16°. 6573
The same. New York, 1833. 12°. 6590
Philip II, of Spain, History of. R. Watson. London, 1779. 3 v. 8°. . 8228
History of the Reign of. W. H. Prescott. Boston, 1855–8. 3 v. 8°. 7818
Philip Van Artevelde. H. Taylor. Boston, 1825. 2 v. 12°. . . . 2484
Philippart, J. Memoirs of Charles John of Sweden. Baltimore, 1815. 8°. 8565
Life of V. Moreau. Philadelphia, 1816. 8°. 8203
Napoleon's Campaign in Germany, &c. London, 1814. 2 v. 8°. . 9514
Phillippo, J. M. Jamaica, its Past and Present State. Phil. 1843. 8°. . 9419
Phillips, C. Public Speeches, &c. Rochester, 1823. 12°. . . . 11181
Recollections of J. P. Curran and his Cotemporaries. N Y. 1818. 8°. 8188
Specimens of Irish Eloquence, with Biog. Notices. N. Y. 1820. 8°. 10718
Phillips, J. Treatise on Geology. London, 1837–9. 2 v. 12°. . . 9981
Philo, an Evangeliad. S. Judd, Jr. Boston, 1850. 12°. . . . 2340
Philosophers, Ancient, Lives of. F. de Fenelon. Tr. N. Y. 1814. 12°. . 5914
and Actresses. A. Houssaye. New York, 1852. 2 v. 12°. . . 506
Philosophical Dictionary. F. M. A. De Voltaire. Tr. Lon. 1824. 6 v. 12°. 9017
The same. London, 1765. 8°. 5617
Essays. D. Stewart. Philadelphia, 1811. 8°. 6342
Essays on Various Subjects. I. Watts. London, 1773. 12°. . . 6057
Miscellanies. V. Cousin, T. Jouffroy and others. Tr. G. Ripley. Boston, 1838. 8°. 768
Writers. T. De Quincey. Boston, 1854. 2 v. 12°. 885
Philosophy of Active and Moral Powers. D. Stewart. Bost. 1828. 2 v. 8°. 6339
The same. Cambridge, 1849. 12°. 4542
Analogical, Outlines of. G. Field. London, 1839. 2 v. 8°. . . 739
Ancient, History of. H. Ritter. Tr. Oxford, 1838. 3 v. 8°. . . 6315
Biographical History of. G. H. Lewes. (vol. 1 missing.) London, 1843. 4 v. 16°. 7180
of Europe, Speculative. J. D. Morell. New York, 1848. 8°. . 6323
of the Future State. T. Dick. New York, 1829. 12°. . . . 6103
of History. F. von Schlegel. Tr. London, 1848. 2 v. 12°. . . 819
See also Schlegel, F. von.
History of. Tr. C. S. Henry. New York, 1841. 2 v. 12°. . . 5915
History of. W. Enfield. Dublin, 1792. 2 v. 8°. 6400
History of. W. E. Tennemann. Tr. A. Johnson. Oxford, 1832. 8°. 6372
of the Human Mind. T. Brown. Hallowell, 1829. 2 v. 8°. . . 6374
of the Inductive Sciences. W. Whewell, London, 1840. 2 v. 8°. 410
Introduction to the History of. See Cousin, V.

Philosophy of Living. C. Ticknor. New York, 1836. 12°. 4957
The same. New York, 1841. 12°. 5887
of Magic. E. Salverte. Tr. New York, 1847. 2 v. 12°. . . 3333
of the Mechanics of Nature. Z. Allen. New York, 1852. 8°. . 394
Metaphysics and Ethics, Progress of. D. Stewart. Bost. 1853. 4°. 10035
of the Mind. J. Douglas. Edinburgh, 1839. 8°. 6320
Modern. See Modern.
Moral. See Moral.
Natural. See Natural.
of Natural History. Elementary. J. G. Buckhard. Lon. 1804. 12°. 10174
of Natural History. W. Smellie. Philadelphia, 1791. 8°. . . 10109
The same, with an Introduc. by J. Ware. Boston, 1832. 8°. 10132
The same. Boston, 1838. 12°. 10149
of the Plan of Salvation. New York, 1842. 12°. 5739
The same. Boston, 1856. 12°. 5422
of Religion. T. Dick. Brookfield, 1839. 12°. 6102
The same. Brookfield, 1830. 6434
of Religion. J. D. Morell. New York, 1849. 12°. . . . 5740
of Rhetoric. G. Campbell. Edinburgh, 1816. 2 v. 8°. . . . 1064
The same. London, 1801. 2 v. 8°. 10816
Speculative, Essays on. F. Bowen. Boston, 1842. 12°. . . 789
Youth's Manual of. Geneva, 1826. 18°. 4602
Philothea. Mrs. L. M. Child. New York, 1836. 12°. 1570
Philpot, J. Examinations and Letters. London. 12°. 5657
Phips, Sir W., Life of. F. Bowen. Boston, 1827. 12°. 8049
Phonecians, History of. London, 1779. 2 v. 8°. 7030
Phonographic Reader. S. P. Andrews and A. F. Boyle. N. Y. 1850. 12°. 4872
Phraseologia Generalis. W. Robertson. Cambridge, 1693. 12°. . . 3342
Phrases and Words Peculiar to the U. S. J. Pickering. Boston, 1816. 8°. 10083
Phrenology. J. S. Grimes. Buffalo, 1839. 12°. 3373
or Doct. of Mental Phenom. J. G. Spurzheim. Bost. 1832. 2 v. 8°. 1059
in Connection with Physiognomy. J. G. Spurzheim. Bost. 1836. 8°. 1058
Examined. T. Sewall. Washington, 1837. 8°. 11678
Proved. O. S. and L. N. Fowler and S. Kirkham. N. Y. 1837. 12°. 3336
Phreno-Mnemotechny, or Art of Memory. F. F. Gouraud. N. Y. 1845. 8°. 1072
Phrygians, History of the. London, 1779. 8°. 7031
Physical Geography. M. Somerville. Philadelphia, 1848. 12°. . . 9581
Geography, Curiosities of. W. Wittich. 2d series. Lon. 1846. 16°. 7189
Geography of the Sea. M. F. Maury. New York, 1856. 8°. . 5951
History of Man. J. C. Prichard. London, 1836. 2 v. 8. . . 405
The same. London, 1841. 8°. 735
Sciences, Connection of. Mrs. M. Somerville. N. York, 1846. 12°. 6092
Theory of Another Life. I. Taylor. New York, 1836. 12°. . . 6511
Physician and Patient. W. Hooker. New York, 1849. 12°. . . . 3004
Physics, Elements of. N. Arnott. Philadelphia, 1831. 2 v. 8°. . . 5982
Physiognomy, Essay on. J. C. Lavater. London. 12°. 3387
Outlines of. J. W. Redfield. New York, 1849. 8°. . . . 11652
Physiology. See Phrenology.

Physiology and Anatomy. C. Cutter. Boston, 1846. 12°. 3920
Chemistry and Botany. London, 1831. 8°. 5099
of Music, or Music Explained. London, 1845. 16°. . . . 3711
Outlines of. P. M. Roget. Philadelphia, 1839. 8°. 1071
Principles of, applied to Health. A. Combe. N. Y. 1841. 12°. . 5883
The same. New York, 1834. 16°. 6271
The same. 8768
in Reference to Natural Theology. Philadelphia, 1836. 2 v. 8°. . 6383
Zoölogy, &c., Lectures on. W. Lawrence. Salem, 1828. 8°. . 752
Piazza Tales. H. Melville. 1856. 12°. 1269
Pickering, Ellen. Secret Foe. London, 1841. 3 v. 12°. 167
The Grandfather. New York, 1843. 8°. 8
Pickering, J. Words and Phrases Peculiar to the U. S. Boston, 1816. 8°. 10083
The same. 11677
Pickwick Papers. C. Dickens. Philadelphia, 1837. 2 v. 12°. . . 1661
Pic-Nics, or Legends and Stories of Ireland. Phil. 1837. 2 v. 12°. . . 1455
Pictorial Book of Ballads. Ed. J. S. Moore. London, 1847. 2 v. 8°. . 1844
Picturesque, Essays on. U. Price. London, 1810. 3 v. 8°. . . . 158
Pierpont, J. Airs of Palestine, and other Poems. Boston, 1840. 18°. . 2401
Pierre, J. H. B. St. Botanical Harmony. Tr. Worcester, 1797. 8°. . 5993
Studies of Nature. Tr. H. Hunter. Worcester, 1797. 3 v. 8°. . 2700
The same, abridged. Philadelphia, 1836. 8°. . . . 3304
Selections from the same. Tr. London, 1799. 8°. . . 3291
The same. 3300
Pigeons, Treatise on. P. J. Selby. Edinburgh, 1835. 2 v. 16°. . . 10188
Pignotti, J. History of Tuscany. Tr. J. Browning. Lond. 1826. 4 v. 8°. 6668
Pigott, G. A Manual of Scandinavian Mythology. London, 1829. 12°. . 11461
Pike, A. Prose Sketches and Poems. Boston, 1834. 12°. . . . 2024
Pike, J. G. Guide for Young Disciples. New York. 16°. . . . 5233
Persuasives to Early Piety. New York. 16°. 5231
Pike, S. Hebrew Lexicon. Cambridge, 1811. 2 v. 8°. 10079
and S. Hayward. Religious Cases of Conscience. Lond. 1808. 12°. 6541
Pike, Z. M., Life of. H. Whiting. Boston, 1845. 12°. 8057
Pilgrim Fathers, Chronicles of the. A. Young. Boston, 1844. 8°. . . 6948
The same. Boston, 1841. 8°. 6947
Good Intent, Progress of the. New York, 1802. 12°. . . . 6589
The same. 6526
Pilgrim's Progress. J. Bunyan. Hartford, 1826. 8°. 5375
The same. Exeter, 1829. 2 v. 16°. 6646
The same. New York. 16°. 5225
Lectures on the. G. B. Cheever, New York, 1845. 8°. . . 5061
The same. New York, 1849. 8°. 6363
Pilgrims at Plymouth in 1620, Journal of. Ed. G. B. Cheever. New York, 1844. 12°. 6794
of the Rhine. E. L. Bulwer, New York, 1824. 12°. 687
The same. 1503
Pilot, The. J. F. Cooper, Philadelphia, 1833. 2 v. 12°. . . . 1033
The same, Philadelphia, 1831. 2 v. 16°. 358

Pilot, The. J. F. Cooper. Philadelphia, 1841. 12°. 1254
The same. 2 v. 1627
Pindar. Carmina. Lipsiæ, 1829. 16°. 10346
The same. Trans. C. A. Wheelwright. N. Y. 1837. 12°. . 5293
Pindar, Peter, Works of. J. Wolcott. 8°. 2360
Pinkerton, R. The Past and Present State of Russia. Lond. 1833. 8°. . 9363
Pinkney, W. Life and Writings, Account of. H. Wheaton. N. Y. 1826. 8°. 8198
The same. (Two copies.) Boston, 1836. 12°. 8047
Pioneers. J. F. Cooper. Philadelphia, 1831. 2 v. 16°. 1029
The same. Philadelphia, 1827. 2 v. 16°. 1719
Piozziana, or Recollections of the late Mrs. H. L. Piozzi. Lond. 1833. 12°. 8308
Pirate, The. W. Scott. Boston, 1834. 12°. 272
See also Scott, Sir W.
Pirate and Three Cutters. F. Marryatt. Philadelphia, 1836. 2 v. 12°. . 670
See also Maryatt, F.
Pirates, Atrocities of. A. Smith. New York, 1824. 12°. . . . 11288
History of. C. Johnson. Norwich, 1814. 12°. 8374
The same. 8376
Pitcairn's Island and its Inhabitants. J. Barrow. N. Y. 1832. 16°. . 6616
The same. New York, 1840. 12°. 5532
Pitkin, T. Political and Civil History of the U. S. N. H. 1828. 2 v. 8°. 7326
Statistics of the Commerce, &c., of the U. S. N. H. 1835. 8°. . 10731
The same. Hartford, 1816. 8°. 11051
Pitt, C. Poems, with Life, by S. Johnson. Phil. 1819. 18°. . . . 2133
Correspondence of. London, 1838. 2 v. 8°. 10698
Pitt, W., (Earl of Chatham.) Anecdotes of, with his Speeches in Parliament. Dublin, 1792. 2 v. 8°. 8519
The same. 8550
Letters to his Nephew. New York, 1804. 12°. 3371
Pitt, W. Memoirs. Philadelphia, 1806. 12°. 7742
Speeches in the House of Commons. London, 1806. 4 v. 8°. . 11077
Pizarro, a Tragedy. 8°. 1817
Pizarro, F. Life. Boston, 1840. 16°. 7774
Plague in London. D. DeFoe. Edinburgh, 1810. 16°. 333
The same. New York, 1857. 12°. 570
The same. London, 1855. 12°. 5473
Plain Sermons, by Contribut. to "Tracts for the Times." N. Y. 1841. 2 v. 12°. 5712
Speaker, Opinions on Books, &c. W. Hazlitt. Lond. 1826. 2 v. 8°. 402
Planché. J. R. British. London, 1846. 12°. 3011
Planetary and Stellar Worlds. O. M. Mitchell. New York, 1851. 12°. . 6080
Plantagenets, The Last of the. New York, 1829. 2 v. 12°. . . . 950
Plato against the Atheists. T. Lewis. New York, 1845. 12°. . . 2977
on the Immortality of the Soul. New York, 1833. 12°. . . 6443
Opera. Lipsiæ, 1829. 4 v. 16°. 10553
Platt, J. Universal Biography. London, 1825. 5 v. 8°. 8846
Platt, J. C. History of the Corn Laws. London, 1842. 12°. . . . 5929
Plautus. Comediæ, &c. Lipsiæ, 1842. 2 v. 16°. 10597
Captives, The. Ed. J. Proudfit. New York, 1843. 16°. . . 3056

Players, Lives of the. J. Galt. Boston, 1831. 12°. 8683
Thirty Years among the. J. Kohl. New York, 1844. 8°. . . 9090
Plays. 2 v. 12°. 2496
Plays. London, 1702. 2 v. 12°. 11888
Living. Boston, 1831. 10 v. 24°. 2780
Old, Select Collection of. Ed. R. Dodsley. Lond. 1825–7. 11 v. 8°. 2228
Playfair, J. Progress of Matter and Phys. Science. Boston, 1853. 4°. . 10035
Pleasant Memo's of Pleasant Lands. Mrs. L. H. Sigourney. Bost. 1842. 16°. 1157
Pleasures of Memory, and other Poems. S. Rogers. N. Y. 1824. 16°. . 2084
of Religion, and other Poems. New York, 1820. 16°. . . . 2090
Plinius, C. Historia Naturalis. Lipsiæ, 1829, 30. 5 v. 16°. . . . 10360
The same, abridged. London, 1829. 12°. 10201
Plinius, C., the Younger. Epistolæ. Lipsiæ, 1829. 16°. 10369
The same. Trans. W. Melmoth. London, 1786. 2 v. 8°. . 429
Plutarch, British, or Lives of Emin't British Charac. Lond. 1791. 8 v. 12°. 8104
Modern British. W. C. Taylor. London, 1846. 12°. . . . 8030
Moralia. Lipsiæ, 1829. 6 v. 16°. 10571
Selections from. Ed. and Trans. G. Long. London, 1846. 3 v. 16°. 7460
Vitæ Parallelæ. Lipsiæ, 1829. 5 v. 16°. 10577
The same. Tr. J. and W. Langhorne. Phil. 1834. 4 v. 12°. 7711
The same. Ithaca, 1838. 8°. 8193
The same. (vols 4 and 6.) London, 1774. 11484
Plymouth, History of. J. Thatcher. Boston, 1835. 12°. 6802
Pocket Magazine. London, 1829, 30. 3 v. 12°. 3706
Poe, E. A. The Literati. New York, 1850. 12°. 505
E. A. Works. New York, 1857. 4 v. 12°. 501

Vol. 1. Sketch of Edgar A. Poe, by J. R. Lowell; his death, by N. P. Willis; Tales.
2. The Raven, and other Poems; Eureka; Rationale of Verse, and other Prose Articles.
3. The Literati.
4. Narrative of a Gordon Pym; Miscellanies.

Poems by Amelia. New York, 1847. 12°. 1937
of Many Years. R. M. Milnes. Boston, 1846. 12°. 2280
of the Orient. B. Taylor. Boston, 1855. 12°. 2000
and Prose Sketches. A. Pike. Boston, 1834. 12°. 2024
Poésie de Boileau-Despréaux. London, 1809. 12°. 2366
Poetical Decameron. J. P. Collier. London, 1820. 2 v. 12°. . . . 4546
Dictionary. D. Hitchcock. Lenox, 1808. 12°. 2500
Quotations. J. F. Addington. Philadelphia, 1829. 4 v. 12°. . 2007
Poetry, American, Essays on. S. Brown. New Haven, 1818. 12°. . . 3915
American, Selections from. Ed. S. Kettell. Boston, 1829. 12°. . 2402
of the East. R. Alger. Boston, 1856. 12°. 1939
English, History of. T. Warton. London, 1840. 8°. . . . 712
English, Lectures on. H. Neele. London, 1829. 12°. 864
The same. Boston, 1850. 12°. 751
English, Letters on. J. Aikin. New York, 1806. 12°. . . . 4929
of Germany, Original and Trans. A. Baskerville. Phil. 1856. 12°. 1938

Poetry and Literature, Lectures on. J. Montgomery. N. Y. 1840. 12°. . 5880
and Music, Essays on. J. Beattie. London, 1779. 8°. . . . 154
of the Pentateuch. J. H. Caunter. London, 1839. 2 v. 8°. . . 5027
Sacred, of the 17th Century. Ed. R. W. Cattermole. Lond. 1855. 12°. 5794
The same. vol. 2. London, 1836. 12°. 5799
of Science. R. Hunt. Boston, 1850. 12°. 6059
Sources of the Pleasures of. J. Hurdis. London, 1797. 4°. . 1803
of Travelling in the U. States. Mrs. C. Gilman. N. Y. 1838. 12°. 9285
Poet's Tribute. W. B. Tappan. Boston, 1840. 12°. 2052
Poets of America, Illustrated. Ed. J. Keese. New York, 1842. 12°. . 2328
The same. 2329
of America, Female. R. W. Griswold. Philadelphia, 1849. 8°. . 1789
American, Beauties of the. Ed. Roach. London, 1784. 12°. . 3054
American, Selections from. Ed. W. C. Bryant. N. Y. 1841. 12°. 5573
The same. 5574
British. See British Poets.
English. Lives. R. Bell. London, 1839. 2 v. 12°. . . . 9945
English, Lives of. S. Johnson. London, 1831. 12°. . . . 7780
English, Lives of, Johnson to White. H. F. Cary. Lond. 1846. 12°. 8092
English, Dramatic, Specimens of. Ed. C. Lamb. N. Y. 1845. 12°. 9845
English, Specimens of. Ed. L. Hunt. New York, 1845. 12°. . 9844
The same. 2410
English, and other writers, Essays on the. T. De Quincey. Boston, 1854. 12°. 887
Early French. Lives. H. F. Cary. London, 1846. 12°. . . 8093
Italian, Lives of the. H. Stebbings. London, 1831. 3 v. 12°. . 8707
Italian, Stories from and Notices of. L. Hunt. N. Y. 1846. 12°. . 1170
The same. 9850
Old, Conversations on. J. R. Lowell. Cambridge, 1845. 12°. . 4581
and Poetry of America. R. W. Griswold. Phil. 1842. 8°. . . 1787
and Poetry of the Ancients. W. Peter. Philadelphia, 1848. 8°. . 1788
and Poetry of Europe. H. Longfellow. Philadelphia, 1845. 8°. . 1806
Roman, Lives of the. L. Crusius. London, 1753. 2 v. 12°. . . 7450
Thoughts on. H. T. Tuckerman. New York, 1846. 12°. . . 5848
Uneducated, Lives of. R. Southey. London, 1836. 8°. . . 8281
Poland, History of. Dublin, 1795. 8°. 11377
History of. London, 1783. 2 v. 8°. 7076
History of. S. A. Dunham. London. 1831. 12°. 9909
History of. J. Fletcher. New York, 1831. 16°. 6622
The same. New York, 1840. 12°. 5527
The same. New York, 1832. 16°. 8761
History of the Revolution in. New York, 1833. 8°. 6964
Russia, &c., Travels in. W. Coxe. London, 1832. 5 v. 8°. . . . 9129
Polar Sea. Expedition to the, in 1820–3. F. Wrangell. N. Y. 1841. 12°. 5920
Exped. to the, in 1819–22 & 1825–27. J. Franklin. Lon. 1829. 4 v. 16°. 9333
Polar Seas, Discoveries in. Sir J. Leslie and others. N. Y. 1831. 16°. . 6273
The same. New York, 1840. 12°. 5516
Police Reports, New York, 1828, 9. J. B. Skillman. N. Y. 1830. 8°. . 10656

Polish Tales. Mrs. C. F. Gore. London, 1833. 3 v. 12°. 1417
Political Class Book. W. Sullivan. Boston, 1831. 12°. 11196
Disquisitions. J. Burgh. (vol. 1 missing.) Phil. 1775. 3 v. 8°. . 10809
Economy. A. Potter. New York, 1841. 12°. 5257
Economy. J. B. Say. Tr. Boston, 1824. 8°. 10724
Economy in connection with Moral State of Society. T. Chalmers. New York, 1832. 12°. 10797
Economy, Elements of. F. Wayland. New York, 1837. 8°. . 10692
Economy, Illustrations of. See Martineau, Miss H.
Economy, Principles of. J. S. Mill. Boston, 1848. 2 v. 8°. . . 10926
Economy, Principles of. H. Vethake. Philadelphia, 1838. 8°. . 10932
Economy, The Logic of. T. De Quincey. London, 1844. 8°. . 10991
Essays. P. Godwin. New York, 1856. 12°. 857
Essays. P. Webster. Philadelphia, 1791. 8°. 11113
Legacies. G. Washington. New York, 1800. 12°. 4935
Mirror, a Review of Jacksonism. New York, 1835. 12°. . . 11164
Miscellanies. Ed. W. B. Giles. Richmond, 1827. 8°. . . . 10661
Philosophy. H. Lord Brougham. London, 1844. 3 v. 8°. . . 10708
Pollok, R. Course of Time. Boston, 1828. 12°. 1963
Persecuted Family. Boston, 1829. 16°. 6560
Polwhele, R. Essay on Marriage, Adultery, &c. London, 1823. 12°. . 3926
Traditions and Recollections, &c. London, 1826. 2 v. 8°. . . 8562
Polybius. Historiæ. Lipsiæ, 1836. 2 v. 16°. 10567
Polynesia, History of. M. Russell. New York, 1845. 12°. 5210
Polynesian Researches. W. Ellis. London, 1831. 4 v. 12°. . . . 9295
Pomeroy, J. L. Sermons. Northampton, 1826. 12°. 6174
Pomfret, J. Select Poems, with Life by E. Sanford. Phil. 1819. 16°. . 2124
Pompeii. Boston, 1833. 12°. 6207
The same. 9629
Pomponius, M. De Situ Orbis. Lipsiæ, 1831. 16°. 10860
Pontiac, Hist. of the Conspiracy of. F. Parkman, Jr. Boston, 1851. 8°. 7267
Poole, Mrs. S. Englishwoman in Egypt London, 1845. 16°. . . . 7197
Poole, W. F. Index to Periodical Literature. In the Rack.
Poor Man's Morning Portion. R. Hawker. New York, 1819. 12°. . 6508
Pope, A. Essay on Man. London, 1786. 12°. 2389
The same. Hartford, 1824. 16°. 2092
The same. 3057
The same. Hartford, 1832. 16°. 3070
Letters. London, 1770. 12°. 3366
Poetical Works, with Life by S. Johnson. Philadelphia, 1839. 8°. 1836
The same. Philadelphia, 1819. 2 v. 18°. 2132
Poetical Works, with Life. London, 1787. 4 v. 24°. 2768

Vol. 1. Life: Recommendatory Poems; Pastorals; Messiah; Windsor Forest; Rape of the Lock; Sappho to Phaon; Eloisa to Abelard; Miscellanies; The Temple of Fame; January and May.
2. Essay on Man; Letter to Mr. Racine, and Reply; Universal Prayer; Essay on Criticism; Moral Essays; The Wife of Bath; Thebais of Statius.
3. Fable of Dryope; Vertumnus and Pomona; Imitations of English Poets and of Horace; Satires; Epistles; Miscellanies; Epitaphs.
4. Testimonies of Authors; Prefaces; Advertisements; Parallel of Characters; The Dunciad.

Pope, A. Works, with Notes and Life. S. Johnson. Lon. 1812. 8 v. 12°. 3645

Vol. 1. Life; Panegyrical Poems; Pastorals; Messiah; Windsor Forest; Odes; Essay on Criticism.
2. Rape of the Lock; Sappho to Phaon; Eloisa to Abelard; Translations and Imitations; Imitations of English Poets; Miscellanies; Epitaphs; Letter to a Lord.
3. Essay on Man; Universal Prayer; Moral Essays; Satires and Epistles; Imitations of Horace; on receiving a Standish and Two Pens; Fragment of a Satire.
4. The Dunciad, with Advertisements, &c.; Guardians.
5. Memoirs of Martinus Scriblerus; Writings of Scriblerus; Memoirs of P. P., Clerk of this Parish; Poet Laureate; Norris on the Frenzy of J. Dennis; Poisoning of E. Curll; A Key to the Lock; Miscellaneous Thoughts; Plan of an Epic Poem; Preface to the Iliad; Postscript to the Odyssey; Preface and Catalogue of the Surreptitious Edition.
6–8. Letters to and from Friends.

Essay on Genius and Writings of. J. Warton. Lond. 1806. 2 v. 8°. 156
Pope, J. Exploration of Minnesota, in 1849. Washington, 1850. 8°. . 10422
Pope, Sir T. Life. Warton. 8°. 8512
Pope Alexander VI, and Cæsar Borgia. Lives. Folio London, 1729. . 11244
Popery, History of. New York, 1836. 12°. 6127
Text Book of. J. M. Cramp. New York, 1831. 12°. . . . 6185
The same. 6534
Pope's Supremacy, Treatise on the. J. Barrow. New York, 1844. 8°. . 5316
Popes of Rome, History of. L. Ranke. Tr. Mrs. S. Austin. London, 1841. 3 v. 8°. 7352
The same. Trans. E. Foster. London, 1847. 3 v. 12°. . 5144
Popish Plot. History of. London, 1680. 12°. 6601
Population, Essay on. T. R. Malthus. Georgetown, 1809. 2 v. 8°. . 10518
Porcelain and Glass, Manufacture of. G. R. Porter. London, 1832. 12°. 9969
The same. Philadelphia, 1834. 12°. 5843
Porson, R. Adversaria. London, 1812. 8°. 397
Tracts, and Miscellaneous Criticisms of. London, 1815. 8°. . . 398
Porter, A. Handbook for Readers. New York, 1845. 12°. . . . 5215
Porter, G. R. Manufacture of Porcelain and Glass. Phil. 1834. 12°. . 5843
The same. London, 1832. 12°. 9969
Treatise on Silk Manufacture. Philadelphia, 1832. 12°. . . 5844
The same. London, 1831. 12°. 9965
Porter, Miss A. M. Fast of St. Magdalen. Boston, 1819. 2 v. 12°. . 1358
Honor O'Hara. New York, 1827. 2 v. 12°. 1594
Mariendorpt. Boston, 1821. 2 v. 12°. 1637
The Recluse of Norway. New York, 1815. 2 v. 12°. . . . 1394
Porter, D. Journal of a Cruise in the Pacific, in 1812. Phil. 1815. 8°. . 9452
The same. New York, 1822. 2 v. 9499
Porter, E. Principles of Rhetorical Delivery. Andover, 1827. 12°. . 3031
The same. 3036
Rhetorical Reader. Andover, 1832. 12°. 3324
The same. New York, 1835. 12°. 4868
Porter, Miss J. Bannockburn. Philadelphia, 1822. 2 v. 12°. . . 1409
Duke Christian. Boston, 1824. 2 v. 12°. 1336
Scottish Chiefs. New York, 1857. 12°. 524
Thaddeus of Warsaw. Philadelphia, 1817. 3 v. 12°. . . . 1729
The same. New York, 1858. 12°. 525

Porter, Miss J., and A. M. Coming Out. New York, 1828. 3 v. 12°. . 634
Porter, N. Historical Discourse on Farmington. Hartford, 1841. 8°. . 11326
The same. 11341
Porter, R. K. Travels in Russia and Sweden, 1805–8. Phil. 1809. 8°. . 9180
Porter, W. S. Life of R. Hill. Boston, 1835. 16°. 7767
Musical Encyclopædia. Boston, 1834. 16°. 10249
The same. 10251
Porteus, B. Evidences of Revel'n, and Poem on Death. Bost. 1814. 18°. 4616
Life. R. Hodgson. New York, 1811. 12°. 8076
Port Folio, Literary. Philadelphia, 1830. 4°. 11681
a Popular Magazine. Philadelphia, 1813. 6 v. 8°. 2949
Portico, a Review. vol. 4. 1817. 8°. 2240
Portugal, Civil War in. London, 1836. 12°. 6801
History of. London, 1783. 8°. 7064
Révolutions de. M. L. de Vertot. Paris, 1816. 18°. . . . 10902
Traits and Traditions of. Miss J. Pardoe. Philadelphia. 2 v. 12°. 9288
and Spain. See Spain.
Portuguese Literature. F. Bouterwek. Tr. London, 1823. 2 v. 8°. . 729
Posey, T . Life of J. Hall. Boston, 1846. 12°. 8061
Post, H. A. V. Visit to Greece and Constan'ple, 1827, 8. N. Y. 1830. 8°. 9451
Posthumous Papers, Facetious and Fanciful. New York, 1828. 12°. . 1583
Post Office, The, History and Statistics of. London, 1842. 12°. . 5936
Potiphar Papers. G. W. Curtis. New York, 1856. 12°. 527
Potomac, Frigate, Voyage of the, around the Globe. J. N. Reynolds,
New York, 1835. 8°. 9096
Potter, A. Political Economy. New York, 1841. 12°. 5257
School, The, its Objects, Relations, &c. New York, 1842. 12°. . 2993
The same. New York, 1842. 12°. 2994
Potter, J. Antiquities of Greece. New York, 1825. 8°. 11347
Powell, Mary, Maiden and Married Life of. New York, 1852. 12°. . . 8727
Powell, P. History of Natural Philosophy. London, 1851. 12°. . . 9555
Power, T. Impressions of America. Philadelphia, 1836. 2 v. 12°. . 10144
Power, Wisdom, &c., of God, manifested in Animals. W. Kirby. Philadelphia, 1836. 8°. 6385
The same. vol. 1. London, 1852. 12°. 5488
Powhattan, a Metrical Romance. S. Smith. New York, 1841. 12°. . 2361
Poynder, J. Literary Extracts, &c. London, 1844. 2 v. 8°. 85
Practical Farmer. W. Ellis. London, 1759. 12°. 3301
Piety. Hannah More. Boston, 1811. 2 v. 16°. 6235
Reader. M. R. Bartlett. New York, 1822. 12°. 3041
Thoughts. W. Nevins. New York. 16°. 5235
Pradt, D. D. de. The Congress of Vienna. Tr. Philadelphia, 1816. 8°. 11052
Europe after the Congress of Aix-La-Chapelle. Tr. G. A. Otis. Philadelphia, 1820. 8°. 9434
Praed, W. M. Poetical Works. Ed. R. W. Griswold. N. York, 1844. 12°. 2006
Prairie, The. J. F. Cooper. Philadelphia, 1833. 2 v. 16°. . . . 1035
The same. Philadelphia, 1841. 12°. 1255
The same. Philadelphia, 1827. 2 v. 12°. 632

Prairie du Chien, Tour to, in 1829. C. Atwater. Columbus, 1831. 12°. . 9304
Prairie Land, Life in. Mrs. E. W. Farnham. New York, 1846. 12°. . 4864
Pratt, J. Remains of R. Cecil. Boston, 1833. 16°. 6234
Prayer, Bible History of. C. A. Goodrich. Hartford, 1848. 12°. . . 5645
Short Method of. Baltimore, 1812. 18°. 4610
Preacher and Pastor, The. F. de Fenelon and others. Ed. E. A. Park. Andover, 1845. 12°. 811
Preaching, Art of. D. Fordyce. London, 1755. 12°. 6607
and Hearing, Aids to. T. H. Skinner. New York, 1839. 12°. , 2992
Pre-Adamite Earth. J. Harris. Boston, 1850. 12°. 6060
Preble, E., Life of. L. Sabine. Boston, 1847. 12°. 8064
Precaution, J. F. Cooper. Philadelphia, 1841. 12°. 1260
The same. New York, 1820. 2.v. 12°. 952
Preceptor, The, for the Instruction of Youth. London, 1763. 12°. . . 2695
The same. 3003
National. Ed. J. Olney. Hartford, 1837. 12°. 3311
The same. New York, 1839. 12° 3399
Prelude, or Growth of a Poet's Mind. W. Wordsworth. N. Y. 1850. 12°. 2001
Prentice, G. D. Biography of H. Clay. Hartford, 1831. 12°. . . 8412
Presbyterian Church. See Church.
Prescott, W. H. Biographical and Critical Miscellanies. N. Y. 1845. 8°. 56
The same. Boston, 1855. 8°. 57
History of the Conquest of Mexico. New York, 1843. 3 v. 8°. . 6949
History of the Conquest of Peru. New York, 1848. 2 v. 8°. . 7257
History of Reign of Ferdinand and Isabella. Bost. 1838. 3 v. 8°. 7854
History of the Reign of Philip II. Boston, 1855–8. 3 v. 8°. . 7818
Life of C. B. Brown. Boston, 1834. 12°. 8068
(Ed.) History of Charles V, by W. Robertson. Bost. 1857. 3 v. 8°. 7821
President's Daughters. Miss F. Bremer. New York, 1844. 8°. . . 12
The same. London, 1853. 12°. 5205
Presidents' Messages from Washington to Harrison, with a Memoir of W. H. Harrison. New York, 1841. 8°. 10700
Messages and Executive Documents. See U. S. Public Documents.
Pretension. Miss S. Stickney, (Mrs. S. Ellis.) Phil. 1837. 2 v. 12°. . 1564
Price, R. Sermons. London, 1787. 12°. 5616
Price, U. Essays on the Picturesque. London, 1810. 3 v. 8°. . . 158
Prichard, J. C. Physical History of Mankind. London, 1836. 2 v. 8°. 405
The same. London, 1841. 4 v. 8°. 735
Treatise on Insanity, &c. London, 1835. 8°. . . . .
Pride and Prejudice. Miss Austen. Phil. 1838. 8°. 37
Prideaux, H. Connec. of Old and New Testament. Balt. 1833. 2 v. 8°. 6328
Priestcraft, History of. W. Howitt. London, 1833. 12°. . . . 5666
The same. London, 1845. 12°. 6184
Priestly, J. Disquisitions on Matter and Spirit. Birming. 1782. 2 v. 8°. 6397
History of Electricity. London, 1767. 4°. 5962
Lectures on History and General Policy. Phil. 1803. 2 v. 8°. . 6737
Priesthood, Book of the, An Argument. T. Stratten. N. Y. 1831. 12°. . 6436
Priests, Women, and Families. J. Michelet. Tr. London, 1846. 12°. . 896

Prime, W. C. Boat-Life in Egypt and Nubia. New York, 1857. 12°. . 9594
Princeton Theological Essays. (1st and 2d series.) New York, 1846. 2 v. 8°. 5013
Principalities and Powers. Mrs. C. E. Tonna. New York, 1842. 12°. . 1204
Printing, History of. I. Thomas. Worcester, 1810. 2 v. 8°. 744
Prior, J. Life of E. Burke. Philadelphia, 1825. 8°. 8241
Life of O. Goldsmith. London, 1837. 2 v. 8°. 8175
Prior, M. Poems, with Life by E. Sanford. Phil. 1819. 16°. . . . 2128
Prison Discipline Society, Annual Report of. Boston, 1832. 8°. . . 11360
Thoughts in. W. Dodd. Boston, 1777. 12°. 6497
Prisons and Prisoners. J. Adshead. London, 1845. 8°. 10666
Prisoner of State, Memoirs of. A. Andryane. Tr. Lond. 1842. 2 v. 8°. 8285
Probabilities, Essay on. A. de Morgan. London, 1838. 12°. . . . 9962
Probus, or Rome in the 3d Century. W. Ware. N. York, 1838. 2 v. 12°. 9613
Procter, G. History of Italy. London, 1844. 8°. 7540
Proctor, B. W. Dramatic Scenes, and other Poems. Boston, 1857. 12°. 1990
English Songs, and other Poems. Boston, 1844. 12°. . . . 2376
The same. Boston, 1851. 12°. 1948
Life of E. Kean. New York, 1835. 12°. 8316
The same. 8331
Professor. Miss C. Brontë. New York, 1857. 12°. 180
Progress of Refinement, and other Poems. Boston, 1792. 16°. . . . 2479
of Dullness. J. Trumbull. Boston, 1794. 16°. 3084
Promessi Sposi, or the Betrothed. A. Manzoni. Tr. Wash. 1834. 8°. . 23
Prometheus Bound, and other Poems. Mrs. Browning. N. Y. 1851. 12°. 1947
The same. New York, 1858. 12°. 1982
Propertius. Carmina. Lipsiæ, 1843. 16°. 10853
Prophecies. T. Newton. London, 1771. 3 v. 12°. 5649
Prophecy, Evidence of. A. Keith. New York. 16°. 5240
Hints on. M. Stuart. Andover. 1842. 12°. 6435
Two Discourses on. S. F. Jarvis. New York, 1843. 12°. . . 5746
Prophesying, Liberty of. Jeremy Taylor. London, 1834. 12°. . . 5776
Prose, by a Poet. J. Montgomery. Philadelphia, 1824. 16°. . . 4601
Prose Sketches and Poems. A. Pike. Boston, 1834. 12°. . . . 2024
Prose Writers of America. Illust. R. W. Griswold. Phil. 1847. 8°. . 28
of Germany. Illust. F. H. Hedge. Philadelphia, 1849. 8°. . 27
Protestant, The, Essays. W. M'Gavin. Hartford, 1833. 2 v. 8°. . . 5601
The, a Tale of Queen Mary's Reign. New York, 1829. 2 v. 12°. . 993
and Catholic Nations Compared. N. Roussell. Boston, 1855. 12°. 5621
Protestantism and Catholicity of Europe. J. Balmes. Balt. 1851. 8°. . 5046
Protestants of France, History of. G. De Félice. Tr. N. York, 1851. 8°. 7265
Proud, R. History of Pennsyl., with Life of W. Penn. Phil. 1797. 2 v. 8°. 6714
Prout, W. Chemistry, Meteorology in Ref. to Nat. Theol. Phil. 1834. 12°. 6483
Proverbial Philosophy. M. F. Tupper. New York, 1846. 12°. . . 9852
The same. New York, 1848. 12°. 1951
Proverbes Dramatiques. Boston, 1830. 12°. 2222
Proverbs, Lessons in. R. C. Trench. New York, 1855. 12°. . . . 4519
National, in Five Languages. Caroline Ward. London, 1842. 16°. 3060
Spanish, Dictionary of. Tr. London, 1823. 12°. . . . 3306

Prussia, History of. London, 1783. 8°. 7077
Public Instruction in. V. Cousin. Tr. Sarah Austen. N. Y. 1835. 12°. 4983
The same. New York, 1834. 12°. 4984
Prussian Code. Paris, 1801. 5 v. 8°. 10781
Psalms, Commentary on. G. Horne. London, 1836. 3 v. 12°. . . 5800
The same. New York, 1814. 8°. 5357
Translated and Explained. J. A. Alexander. N. Y. 1851. 3 v. 12°. 5394
Psychology, a View of the Human Soul. F. A. Rauch. N. Y. 1840. 8°. 6307
Elements of. V. Cousin. Tr. C. S. Henry. Hartford, 1834. 8°. . 6347
Public Characters, Sketches of. H. Lord Brougham. Phil. 1839. 2 v. 12°. 8701
Public Economy of Athens. A. Bœckh. Tr. London, 1842. 8°. . . 7605
Puckler-Muskau, Prince. Tutti Frutti. Tr. New York, 1834. 12°. . 1513
Puckle, J. The Club, or a Gray Cap for a Green Head. Lond. 1834. 16°. 3365
Puffendorf, S. Introduction to the History of Europe. Lon. 1764. 2 v. 8°. 6765
Pulaski, Count, Life of. J. Sparks. Boston, 1845. 12°. 8056
Pulpit, American, Annals of. W. B. Sprague. New York, 1857. 5 v. 8°. 5040
British. W. Suddards. vol. 2. Philadelphia, 1839. 8°. . . 5595
German, a Selection of Sermons. Tr. R. Baker. Lond. 1829. 8°. 5030
Power of the. G. Spring. New York, 1859. 12°. . . . 5418
Punchard, G. History of Congregationalism. Salem, 1841. 12°. . . 6140
The same. 6192
Punch's Complete Letter Writer. D. Jerrold. London, 1845. 12°. . . 1213
Punch's Prize Novelists. W. M. Thackeray. New York, 1853. 12°. . 961
Puritan, The. L. Withington. (Jonathan Oldbuck.) Bost. 1836. 2 v. 16°. 4316
The same. 4571
Puritanism. T. W. Coit. New York, 1845. 12°. 5775
The same. 6187
Puritans, History of the. D. Neal. New York, 1844. 2 v. 8°. . . 7556
The same. Portsmouth, 1816. 5 v. 8°. 5337
The, and their Principles. E. Hall. New York, 1856. 8°. . . 5020
Pursuit of Knowledge under Difficulties. New York, 1840. 2 v. 12°. . 5554
The same. London, 1832. 2 v. 12°. 5806
The same. Boston, 1830. 12°. 6197
The same. vol. 2. Boston, 1832. 12°. 6202
The same. London, 1845. 3 v. 16°. 7163
Pursuits of Literature, a Satirical Poem. Philadelphia, 1800. 8°. . . 93
Puseyism Exam'ned. J. H. M. D'Aubigne. New York, 1843. 16°. . 6564
Putnam, G. P. American Facts. London, 1845. 12°. 10813
Dictionary of Dates. New York, 1851. 12°. 8885
Putnam, I., Life of. O. W. B. Peabody. Boston, 1837. 12°. . . . 8049
Putnam's Monthly Magazine. vols. 1–10. New York, 1853–57. 8°. . 3738
Pütter, J. S. Polit. Constitu. of Germanic Emp. Tr. Lon. 1790. 3 v. 8°. 6703
The same. 7229
Pym, J. Life. J. Forster. London, 1837. 12°. 9934
Pythagoras. Life. Iamblichus. Tr. T. Taylor. London, 1818. 8°. . 8164

Q.

Quadrupeds, Natural History of. J. H. Fennel. London, 1843. 8°. . 10136
The same. New York, 1840. 12°. 5564
Natural Hist. and Classification of. W. Swainson. Lond. 1835. 12°. 9972
Quakerism not Christianity. S. H. Cox. Boston, 1833. 8°. 5008
Quakers, History of. W. Sewell. New York, 1844. 8°. . . . 7534
Quarrels of Authors. I. D'Israeli. New York, 1815. 2 v. 12°. . . 4582
Quarterly Observer, American. vols. 1–3. Boston, 1833, 4. 8°. . . 3818
Register, American. vols. 2–8. Andover, 1830–6. 8°. . . 2583
Review. vols. 1–51. London, 1809–34. 8°. 2814
Review. Index to vols. 21–39, in the Rack.
Review, Papers from. New York, 1852. 12°. 4575
Review, American. vols. 1–20. Philadelphia, 1827–36. 8°. . . 4493
Quebec, Campaign against, in 1775. J. J. Henry. Lancaster, 1812. 12°. 6835
Queechy. Anna Warner. New York, 1852. 12°. 1276
Queen's Wake. J. Hogg. New York, 1818. 18°. 2746
Queen's County, Revolu. Incidents of. H. Onderdonk, Jr. N. Y. 1846. 12°. 7420
Queens of England. Agnes Strickland. Philadelphia, 1843. 2 v. 12°. . 8292
Second series. vols. 2, 3. Phil. 1843. 12°. . . . 8294
The same, complete. Philadelphia, 1851. 6 v. 8°. . . 7984
of Scotland. Agnes Strickland. New York, 1851–5. 7 v. 12°. . 8023
Quentin Durward. W. Scott. . Boston, 1845. 12°. 295
See also Scott, Sir W.
Quevedo, F. de, Visions of. Philadelphia, 1832. 12°. 1626
Quin, M. J. Nourmahal, and Oriental Romance. London, 1838. 3 v. 12°. 1431
Quincy, J. History of Harvard University. Cambridge, 1840. 2 v. 8°. . 7552
Quincy, J., Jr. Memoir. J. Quincy. Boston, 1825. 8°. . . . 8223
Quintilianus, M. F. De Institutione Oratoria. Lipsiæ, 1829. 16°. . . 10366

R.

Rachel Dyer. J. Neal. Portland, 1828. 12°. 920
Racine, J., and the French Drama. Mad. Blaz de Bury. Lond. 1845. 16°. 6884
Racine, J. Œuvres. Paris, 1827. 5 v. 18°. 2741
The same. Paris, 1817. 5 v. 18°. 10889
The same. Paris, 1838. 2 v. 12°. 2990
Radcliffe, Anne. St. Alban's Abbey. Philadelphia, 1826. 3 v. 12°. . 611
Raffaello. Life. Q. de Quincy. London, 1846. 12°. 5490
Raffles, T. Memoirs of T. Spencer. Hartford, 1815. 12°. 8075
The same. 8090
Raffles, T. S. History of Java. London, 1830. 2 v. 8°. 6996
Plates to the same. London, 1844. 4°.
Life and Correspondence. Mrs. Raffles. London, 1835. 2 v. 8°. . 7838
Memoir of G. Finlayson. London, 1826. 8°. 9458
Raguet, C. Treatise on Currency and Banking. Phil. 1839. 8°. . . 10933
Raikes, T. The City of the Czar. London, 1838. 8°. 9104

Railroads, a Practical Treatise on. N. Wood. Philadelphia, 1832. 8°. . 6024
Rale, S. Life. C. Francis. Boston, 1845. 12°. 8059
Raleigh, Sir W. History of the World. Edinburgh, 1820. 6 v. 8°. . 7629
Memoirs. Mrs. A. T. Thomson. Philadelphia, 1831. 12°. . . 9860
Voyages to Guiana. Edinburgh, 1820. 8°. 7634
Rambler, The. S. Johnson. London, 1823. 3 v. 12°. 3679
See also Johnson, S.
Rambles by Rivers. J. Thorne. (Two copies.) London, 1844. 16°. . 7472
Ramsay, A. Poems and Life. Philadelphia, 1822. 18°. . . . 2138
Tea Table Miscellany. Berwick, 1793. 2 v. 12°. . . . 2451
Ramsay, D. History of the American Revolution. Phil. 1789. 2 v. 8°. 11391
History of South Carolina, from 1670–1808. Charles. 1809. 2 v. 12°. 6758
History of the United States, continued by S. S. Smith and others. Philadelphia, 1818. 3 v. 8°. . . . . , . . 6706
Rand, A. Sermons. Portland, 1825. 12°. 6535
Randall, S. S. Common School System of New York. Albany, 1844. 12°. 3397
Randolph, J. Letters to a Young Relative. Philadelphia, 1834. 8°. . 370
Life. H. A. Garland. New York, 1851. 2 v. 12°. . . . 8620
Random Shots and Southern Breezes. L. F. Tasistro. N. Y. 1842. 2 v. 12°. 1230
Ranke, L. Hist. of Popes of Rome. Tr. Mrs. S. Austin. Lon. 1840. 3 v. 8°. 7352
The same. Tr. E. Foster. London, 1847. 3 v. 12°. . . 5144
Hist. of Servia and the Insurrection in Bosnia. Tr. Lond. 1853. 12°. 5208
Ranken, A. History of France. London, 1801–22. 9 v. 8°. . . . 7669
Rankin, J. Letters on American Slavery. Boston, 1833. 18°. . . 11158
Rantoul, R., Jr. Memoirs and Writings. Ed. L. Hamilton. Bost. 1854. 8°. 10990
Rapp, J. Autobiography and Memoirs of Napoleon. London, 1823. 8°. 7875
Rauch, F. Psychology, a View of the Human Soul. N. Y. 1840. 8°. . 6307
Raumer, F. Von. America and American People. Tr. N. Y. 1846. 8°. . 9105
England in 1835. Tr. Philadelphia, 1836. 8°. 9442
Polit. Hist. of Eng., in 16th–18th Centuries. Tr. Lon. 1837. 2 v. 8°. 7620
Frederick II and His Times. Tr. London, 1807. 8°. . . . 8271
History of Elizabeth, and Mary, Queen of Scots. Lond. 1836. 12°. 8594
History of the 16th, 17th Centuries. Tr. London, 1835. 2 v. 12°. 11401
Italy and the Italians. Tr. London, 1840. 2 v. 12°. . . . 9548
Ray, R. Lecture on Classical Literature. New York, 1826. 8°. . . 3288
Ray, W., Poems and Life of. Auburn, 1821. 12°. 4321
Raynal, W. T. European Settlements in the East and West Indies. (vol. 1 missing.) Tr. Edinburgh, 1782. 6 v. 12°. . . 7139
Read, H. Memoirs of Babajee, the Converted Brahmun. N. Y. 1836. 12°. 5693
Read, T. B. New Pastoral. Philadelphia, 1855. 12°. 1993
Sylvia, and other Poems. Boston, 1857. 12°. 1994
Reading, Exercises in. Ed. J. Barber. Boston, 1828. 12°. . . . 4552
Course of English. J. Kent. New York, 1853. 12°. . . . 4867
Recantation. W. I. Kip. New York, 1846. 12°. 6603
Recluse of Norway. Miss A. M. Porter. New York, 1815. 2 v. 12°. . 1394
Recollections of a Lifetime. S. G. Goodrich. New York, 1856. 2 v. 8°. 809
of the Peninsula. Philadelphia, 1824. 12°. 9596
of a Housekeeper. Mrs. C. Packard. New York, 1838. 16°. . 4975

Rectory of Valehead. R. W. Evans. Philadelphia, 1832. 12°. . . . 3358
Redburn, His First Voyage. H. Melville. New York, 1849. 12°. . . 555
Reedmption, History of. J. Edwards. New York. 16°. 5230
Redivivus, T. B. Exposition of Vulgar Errors. London, 1845. 12°. . 6608
Redfield, J. W. Outlines of Physiognomy. New York, 1849. 8°. . . 11652
Redfield, W. C. Whirlwind Storms, with Replies to Dr. Hare. New York, 1842. 8°. 5949
Redgauntlet. W. Scott. Boston, 1834. 12°. 275
See also Scott, Sir W.
Red River, Exploration of, in 1852. R. B. Marcy. Wash. 1854. 2 v. 8°. 10430
Red Jacket, Life and Times of. W. L. Stone. New York, 1841. 8°. . 7824
Red Rover. J. F. Cooper. Philadelphia, 1833. 2 v. 12°. . . . 1037
The same. 1603
Reed, A. No Fiction. New York, 1835. 12°. 1548
The same. Boston, 1821. 18°. 1689
and J. Matheson. Visit to the American Churches. New York, 1835. 2 v. 12°. 8904
Reed, H. Lectures on Eng. History and Tragic Poetry. Phil. 1856. 12°. 7324
Lectures on English Literature. Philadelphia, 1855. 12°. . . 522
Reed, J. Life. H. Reed. Boston, 1846. 12°. 8060
Life and Correspondence. W. B. Reed. Philadelphia, 1847. 2 v. 8°. 7831
Reed, Miss R. T. Six Months in a Convent. Boston, 1835. 16°. . . 6563
Rees, A., and others. The Cyclopædia. Philadelphia. 41 v. 4°. . . 8783
Reese, D. M. Plea for the Intemperate. New York, 1814. 18°. . . 4964
Reflector, The. J. Hunt and others. London, 1810. 2 v. 18°. . . 2971
Reflections on the Works of God. C. C. Sturm. Tr. Lond. 1826. 8°. . 5381
The same. Hudson, 1814. 2 v. 12°. 6171
The same. Tr. A. Clarke. London, 1836. 2 v. 12°. . . 6453
Reform Ministers of England, Biog. Sketches of. London, 1832. 8°. . 10170
Reform, Philosophy of. C. B. Smith. New York, 1846. 12°. . . 6471
Reformation, Anti-Papal Spirit of. G. Rossetti. Tr. Lond. 1834. 2 v. 12°. 5643
in the Church of Eng., Hist. of. G. Burnet. Lon. 1825. 6 v. 16°. 6868
in Eng. and Ireland, Hist. of the. W. Cobbett. N. Y. 1832. 2 v. 12°. 6582
Essay on the Spirit of. C. Villers. Philadelphia, 1833. 12°. . 6116
The same. London, 1805. 8°. 5388
in Germany, Hist. of. J. H. M. D'Aubigne. N. Y. 1842. 4 v. 12°. 5681
The same. (vol. 1 missing.) New York, 1844. 3 v. 12°. . 6134
History of the. H. Stebbing. London, 1836. 2 v. 12°. . . 9918
in Italy and Spain, Hist. of. T. M'Crie. Edin. 1829–33. 2 v. 8°. 5590
The same. Edinburgh, 1827–9. 2 v. 8°. 7329
in Scotland, History of. J. Knox. Glasgow, 1832. 8°. . . 5587
Reformed Pastor. R. Baxter. 1766. 12°. 6516
Reformers. See British Reformers.
Refugee in America. Mrs. F. Trollope. New York, 1833. 2 v. 12°. . 692
Regeneration, or Spiritual Life. C. Backus. Hartford, 1810. 12°. . 6600
or Spiritnal Life. G. Duffield. Carlisle, 1822. 8°. . . . 5342
Rehoboth, Mass., History of. L. Bliss, Jr. Boston, 1836. 8°. . . . 7310
Reiche, C. C. Works of Nature. Philadelphia, 1791. 12°. . . . 6595

Reid, T. Essay on Intellect. and Active Powers of Man. Lond. 1827. 8°. 6371
The same. vol. 1. Philadelphia, 1793. 8°. 6405
Reid, W. Law of Storms. London, 1838. 8°. 5961
Reign of Terror. French History. London, 1826. 2 v. 8°. 6998
Reinhard, F. V., Mem's and Confess. of. Tr. O. A. Taylor. Bost. 1832. 12°. 5673
The same. 8419
Rejected Addresses, American. New York, 1855. 12°. 12005
Religion, Analogy of, to Nature. J. Butler. Boston, 1809. 8°. . . 5387
See also Butler, J.
and a Christian Life. W. Beveridge. Lond. 1834. 2 v. 16°. . 5783
Appeal to the Young on. J. Foster. New York. 12°. . . 5241
Errors Regarding. J. Douglas. New York, 1831. 12°. . . 6432
Importance of. J. Foster. Boston, 1827. 12°. 6503
Philosophy of. T. Dick. Brookfield, 1829. 12°. 6102
The same. Brookfield, 1830. 12°. 6434
Philosophy of. J. D. Morell. New York, 1849. 12°. . . . 5740
Religious Denom's of the U. S., Hist. of. Ed. D. J. Rupp. Phil. 1844. 8°. 5052
Affections, Treatise on. J. Edwards. New York. 16°. . . 5224
Courtship. D. De Foe. New York, 1857. 12°. 570
Dissensions, their Cause and Cure. P. Church. N. Y. 1838. 12°. . 5748
Experience. C. Buck. Boston, 1810. 12°. 6109
Liberty, History of. B. Brook. London, 1820. 2 v. 8°. . . 5355
Magazine. vol. 2. Boston, 1835. 8°. 2243
Philosopher. Tr. J. Chamberlayne. London, 1745. 3 v. 12°. 6437
Progress. W. R. Williams. Boston, 1850. 12°. 5414
State of the Country. C. Colton. (Two copies.) N. Y. 1836. 12°. 5678
System, View of the Prevailing. W. Wilberforce. N. York. 16°. 5223
Religions, Pictorial View of. Charles A. Goodrich. Hartford, 1851. 8°. 5631
Rengger, J. R. Reign of De Francia in Paraguay. Tr. Lond. 1827. 8°. 6736
Rennie, J. Insect Architecture. London, 1845. 2 v. 16°. . . . 7176
Renwick, J. The Elements of Mechanics. Philadelphia, 1832. 8°. . 11668
Life of DeWitt Clinton. (Two copies.) New York, 1840. 12°. . 5898
Life of D. Rittenhouse. Boston, 1837. 12°. 8049
Life of R. Fulton. Boston, 1838. 12°. 8052
Life of Count Rumford. Boston, 1845. 12°. 8057
Lives of J. Jay and A. Hamilton. New York, 1840. 18°. . . 5905
Outlines of Geology. New York, 1838. 12° 6089
The Steam Engine. New York, 1830. 8°. 6023
Represent. Gov't. in Europe, Hist. of. M. Guizot. Tr. Lond. 1852. 12°. 5133
Men. R. W. Emerson. (Two copies.) Boston, 1850. 12°. . . 1151
Repton, H. Odd Whims and Miscellanies. London, 1804. 12°. . . 955
Republics, Ancient, Reflections on. E. W. Montagu. Phil. 1806. 12°. . 3901
Resurrection, Sermons on the. J. Barrow, and others. Lond. 1835. 12°. 5789
Sermons on. S. Horsely. Philadelphia, 1816. 18°. . . . 6393
of the Human Body, Essay on. S. Drew. Brooklyn, 1811. 8°. . 5121
Results of Reading. J. S. Caldwell. London, 1843. 8°. . . . 419
Retreat, The, or Sketches from Nature. New York, 1821. 12°. . . 1379
Retrospect, The, or Review of Providential Mercies. Boston, 1822. 12°. 6557

Retrospect of Western Travel. Miss H. Martineau. N. Y. 1838. 2 v. 12°. 9601
Retrospective Review. vols. 1–14. London, 1820–6. 8°. 4193
Retzsch, M. The Chess Players, a Drawing. 4°.
Illustrations of Shakspeare. Folio. New York, 1849.
Reumont, A. de. Carafas of Maddaloni. London, 1854. 12°. . . 5180
Revelation of Nature, a Poem. New York. 16°. 2489
Notes on. A. Barnes. New York, 1852. 12°. 5737
Consistency of. P. N. Shuttleworth. New York, 1847. 16°. . 6220
Paraphrase and Notes on. M. Lowman. London, 1773. 8°. . . 5370
Reveries of a Bachelor. D. Mitchell. New York, 1851. 12°. . . . 215
The same. New York, 1859. 12°. 213½
Revivals, Sermons on. A. Barnes. New York, 1841. 12°. . . . 6211
Revolution, American. See American.
Revolutionary Orders of Gen. Washington. H. Whiting. N. Y. 1844. 8°. 10654
Revolutions of the Surface of the Globe. G. Cuvier. Phil. 1831. 12°. . 6095
Reynard, the Fox, and his Son Reynardine. London, 1844. 16°. . . 1043
Reynolds, F. Life and Times. Philadelphia, 1826. 8°. . . . 8487
The same. vol. 1. 11307
Reynolds, G. W. M. Modern Literature of France. Lond. 1839. 2 v. 8°. 9236
Reynolds, J. Lit. Works and Mem. Ed. H. W. Beechey. Lon. 1835. 2 v. 12°. 7736
The same. London, 1852. 2 v. 12°. 5170
Varieties on Art and Memoirs by J. Northcote. Phil. 1817. 8°. . 8197
Reynolds, J. N. Explor. Expedi. to Pacific and South Seas. N. Y. 1836. 8°. 428
Voyage of the Potomac round the Globe, in 1831–4. N. Y. 1835. 8°. 9096
Rhetoric, Art of. J. Holmes. London, 1755. 8°. 3296
and Belles Letters, Lectures on. H. Blair. New York, 1815. 8°. 748
Elements of. R. Whately. Boston, 1841. 12°. 3401
The same. New York. 16°. 4973
Ethics and Politics. Aristotle. Tr. T. Taylor. Lond. 1818. 2 v. 8°. 755
Grammar of. A. Jamieson. New Haven, 1835. 12°. . . . 3343
Philosophy of. G. Campbell. London, 1801. 2 v. 8°. . . . 10814
The same. Edinburgh, 1816. 2 v. 8°. 1064
Practical System of. S. P. Newman. Andover, 1836. 12°. . . 4862
Rhetorical Delivery, &c., Analysis of. E. Porter. Andover, 1827. 12°. . 3031
The same. 3036
Reader. E. Porter. Andover, 1832. 12°. 3324
The same. New York, 1835. 12°. 4868
Rhetorici Libri. M. T. Cicero. Paris, 1810. 12°. 4554
Rhine, The. V. Hugo. New York, 1845. 12°. 9842
Industry of the. T. C. Banfield. London, 1846. 16°. 7179
Rhode Island Historical Soci., Collections of. E. R. Potter, W. R. Staples,
and others. vols. 2–5. Providence, 1835–43. 8°. . . 11320
Institute of Instruction, Journal of. H. Barnard. Prov. 1846. 8°. 10088
Rhymes on Art. M. A. Shee. Philadelphia, 1815. 12°. 2445
Rhymes and Recollections of a Weaver. W. Thom. Lond. 1845. 8°. . 1913
of Travel. B. Taylor. New York, 1849. 12°. 2356
Ribault, J. Life. J. Sparks. Boston, 1845. 12°. 8059
Rice, E. L. Origin and Development of Eng. Language. Cincin. 1846. 12°. 515

Rice, J. H. and B. H. Memoir of J. B. Taylor. New York, 1835. 12°. . 8626
The same. New York. 16°. 5237
The same. 7762
Richard Cœur-de-Lion. Life and Times. W. E. Aytoun. Lond. 1840. 16°. 8769
Life and Times. G. P. R. James. New York, 1842. 12°. . . 8675
The same. 8677
The same. London, 1854. 2 v. 12°. 5199
Richard III. Life. Miss C. A. Halsted. Philadelphia, 1844. 8°. . . 8147
Richardson, G. F. Sketches in Prose and Verse. 2d series. Lon. 1838. 12°. 2979
Richardson, Major. Wacousta, or the Prophecy. Phil. 1833. 2 v. 18°. . 1712
Richardson, S. Works, with Life. Ed. E. Mangin. Lond. 1811. 19 v. 12°. 930

Vols. 1-4. Pamela, or Virtue Rewarded.
5-12. History of Clarissa Harlowe.
13-19. History of Sir Charles Grandison.

Richelieu. G. P. R. James. 2 v. 12°. 1041
The same. New York, 1835. 2 v. 12°. 1479
Richmond, L. Memoirs. T. S. Grimshawe. New York, 1829. 12°. . 7725
Richter, J. P. F. Autobiog., with Mem. Eliza Lee. Bost. 1842. 2 v. 12°. 8088
Flower, Fruit & Thorn Pieces. 1st & 2d series. Tr. Bost. '45. 2 v. 12°. 1659
Rider, Miss J. C., Account of. L. W. Belden. Springfield, 1834. 18°. . 8439
Ridley, N., Treatises and Letters of. London. 12°. 5657
Riedesel, Madame De. Letters on Amer. Revolution. Tr. N. Y. 1827. 8°. 11398
Rienzi, N. Life and Times. Father Cerceau. Phil. 1836. 12°. . . 8662
Rienzi, the Last of the Tribunes. E. L. Bulwer. Phil. 1836. 2 v. 12°. . 1338
The same. New York, 1836. 12°. 666
Rifle, Axe, and Saddle-Bags. W. H. Milburn. New York, 1857. 12°. . 205
Rip Van Winkle, Illustrations of, by O. C. Darley. N. Y. 1848. Folio. .
Ripa, Father. Residence at the Court of Pekin. Tr. N. Y. 1846. 12°. 9842
Rise of the Dutch Republic. J. L. Motley. New York, 1856. 3 v. 8°. . 7549
Rise of Iskander. B. D'Israeli. Philadelphia, 1847. 8°. 5
Rise and Progress of Religion in the Soul. P. Doddridge. N. Y. 12°. . 6529
The same. 6539
Ritchie, L. London Nights' Entertainments. Phil. 1833. 2 v. 12°. . 1129
Rittenhouse, D. Life. J. Renwick. Boston, 1837. 12°. 8049
Ritter, C., and others. Asia, History, Geography, &c., of. Lon. 1842. 12°. 5935
Ritter, H. History of Ancient Philosophy. Tr. Oxford, 1838. 3 v. 16°. 6315
Rivals of Acadia. New York, 1827. 12°. 1341
of Este, and other Poems. J. G. and Miss Brooks. N. Y. 1829. 12°. 2284
Rob of the Bowl. J. P. Kennedy. Philadelphia, 1838. 2 v. 12°. . . 1523
Rob Roy. W. Scott. Boston, 1845. 12°. 288
See also Scott, Sir W.
Robber, The. E. L. Bulwer. New York, 1838. 2 v. 12°. . . . 997
Robbins, A. Loss of the Brig Commerce on Coast of Africa. Roch. 1818. 12°. 8736
The same. 9026
Roberts, Emma. Scenes and Charac. of Hindostan. Phil. 1836. 2 v. 12°. 9265
Roberts, Mrs. Duty, or the White Cottage. London, 1815. 2 v. 18°. . 1683
Roberts, W. Memoirs of Hannah More. New York, 1835. 2 v. 12°. . 8266
Robertson, D. Reports of the Trials of A. Burr. Phil. 1808. 2 v. 8°. . 10734

Robertson, F. W. Lectures and Addresses. Boston, 1859. 12°. . . . 469
Sermons. First, Second and Third series. 1859. 3 v. 12°. . . . 5407
Robertson, J. P. & W. P. Francia's Reign in Paraguay. Phil. 1829. 2 v. 12°. 1551
Robertson, W. An Historical Disquisition on India. Dublin, 1791. 8°. . 9490
History of America. Philadelphia, 1821, 2. 2 v. 8°. . . 7007
The same. Dublin, 1777. 2 v. 8°. 7691
The same, abridged. New York, 1848. 12°. . . . 5259
History of Ancient Greece. Edinburgh, 1821. 8°. . . . 6760
History of the Reign of Charles V. Albany, 1822. 3 v. 8°. . . 8184
The same. Ed. W. H. Prescott. Boston, 1857. 3 v. 8°. . 7821
Hist. of Scotl'd in Reigns of Mary and James VI. Dub. 1766. 2 v. 12°. 11450
The same. Philadelphia, 1811. 2 v. 8°. 6717
Life and Writings. D. Stewart. London, 1802. 8°. . . . 8548
Phraseologia Generalis. Cambridge, 1693. 12°. 3342
Robin Day. R. M. Bird. Philadelphia, 1839. 2 v. 12°. . . . 1495
The same. 1601
Robinson, A. Life in California. New York, 1846. 12°. . . . 8889
Robinson, E. Biblical Researches in Palestine. Boston, 1841. 3 v. 8°. . 9074
The same, with Maps. Boston, 1856. 4 v. 8°. . . . 9378
Revision of A. Calmet's Dictionary of the Bible. Boston, 1832. 8°. 8795
Robinson, Mrs. M. Autobiography. London, 1826. 16°. . . . 7751
The same. London, 1830. 16°. 7486
Robinson, P. Immortality, a Poem. New York, 1846. 12°. . . . 2365
Robinson, S. Hot Corn. New York, 1854. 12°. 574
Robinson, W. D. Memoirs of the Mexican Revolution. Phil. 1820. 8°. . 9447
Robinson Crusoe. D. De Foe. Edinburgh, 1810. 3 v. 16°. . . . 322
Robison, J. Conspiracy against all the Religions and Governments of Europe by the Free Masons, &c. New York, 1798. 8°. . . 6726
Robords, I. Convert's Guide to First Principles. New Haven, 1838. 12°. 5695
The same. 5711
Roby, J. Traditions of Lancashire. (vol. 1 mis'g.) Lond. 1843. 3 v. 12°. 11399
Roche, Regina M. Contrast. New York, 1828. 2 v. 12°. . . . 969
Osma and Almeria. New York, 1810. 12°. 979
Rochefoucault, L. de La. Travels in the U. States. Lond. 1799. 2 v. 4°. 10919
Rochejaquelein, Marchioness de La. Memoirs. Tr. Edin. 1827. 16°. . 9990
Rochester, J., Earl of, (J. Wilmot.) Life. G. Burnet. Lond. 1820. 16°. 7775
Select Poems, with Life by E. Sanford. Phil. 1819. 16°. . . 2124
Rochester, Sketches of. H. O'Reilly. Rochester, 1838. 12°. . . . 7095
Rocky Mountains, or Scenes in the Far West. W. Irving. Philadelphia, 1837. 2 v. 12° 8983
Dragoon Campaigns to the. New York, 1836. 12°. . . . 9807
Expedition to the, in 1819, 20. S. H. Long. Phil. 1823. 2 v. 8°. 9432
Exploring Expedition to, 1842–44. J. C. Fremont. Wash. 1845. 8°. 10453
Lewis and Clarke's Expedition to. New York, 1842. 2 v. 12°. . 5926
Tour Beyond. S. Parker. Ithaca, 1838. 12°. 8950
Roderick, the Last of the Goths, a Poem. R. Southey. Phil. 1815. 18°, 2756
Roe, A. S. Long Look Ahead. New York, 1856. 12°. 12209
Roe, R. Elements of English Metre. London, 1801. 8°. . . . 10165

Roger de Wendover. Flowers of History. Trans. Lond. 1849. 2 v. 12°. 5443
Rogers, Eliza. Lives of the XII Cæsars. London, 1811. 5 v. 8°. . . 7377
Rogers, S. Italy, a Poem. Philadelphia, 1828. 18°. 2703
Pleasures of Memory, and other Poems. New York, 1824. 16°. . 2084
Poems. London, 1834. 12°. 1900
Table-Talk. London, 1856. 8°. 466
White and others. Poems. London, 1830. 8°. 1869
The same. Philadelphia, 1830. 8°. 1882
Roget, P. M. Outlines of Physiology. Philadelphia, 1839. 8°. . . 1071
Physiology Applied to Natural Theology. Phil. 1836. 2 v. 8°. . 6383
Rokitansky, C. Treatise on Pathological Anatomy. New York, 1845. 8°. 11672
Rollin, C. Ancient History. Tr. London, 1800. 10 v. 12°. . . . 6838
The same. (vol. 5 missing.) Hartford, 1836. 8 v. 12°. . 7148
The same. London, 1768. 7 v. 8°. 11422
History of the Arts and Sciences of the Antients. Tr. London, 1767. 3 v. 8°. 10116
Method of Studying the Belles Lettres. Tr. Lond. 1759. 12°. . 4908
Roman Antiquities. A. Adams. (Two copies.) New York, 1833. 8°. . 11339
Commonwealth, History of. T. Arnold. New York, 1846. 8°. . 7245
Empire, Decline and Fall of. E. Gibbon. Dublin, 1789. 6 v. 8°. 7693
See also Gibbon, E.
Empire, History of. T. Keightley. Boston, 1841. 8°. . . . 7272
Empire, Overthrow of. W. C. Taylor. London, 1836. 12°. . . 7105
History. London, 1779. 6 v. 8°. 7037
History. O. Goldsmith. 12°. 11443
The same, abridged. Hartford, 1831. 12°. 7119
History. N. Hooke. London, 1825. 3 v. 8°. *6732
The same. London, 1766. 11 v. 8°. 7651
See also Florus, Herodianus, and other Latin Authors.
Literature, History of. J. Dunlop. Philadelphia, 1827. 2 v. 8°. . 89
The same. 91
Nights, or Tombs of the Scipios. A. Verri. Tr. N. Y. 1825. 2 v. 12°. 986
Poets, Lives of. L. Crusius. London, 1753. 2 v. 12°. . . . 7450
Republic, History of. A. Ferguson, London, 1829. 8°. . . 7005
The same, abridged. New York, 1836. 12°. . . . 5502
Republic, Hist. of. J. Michelet. Tr. W. Hazlitt. Lond. 1847. 12°. . 5494
Republic of 1849. T. Dwight. New York, 1851. 12°. . . 6797
Republic, Revolutions in. London, 1770. 2 v. 8°. . . . 6773
Romance of Biography. Mrs. A. Jameson. London, 1837. 2 v. 12°. . 8646
of History. England. H. Neele. Philadelphia, 1828. 2 v. 12°. . 313
of History Spain. T. De Trueba. New York 1830. 2 v. 12°. . 225
of Travel. N. P. Willis. New York, 1840. 12°. 1664
of Travel. C. Mac Farlane. vol. 1. London, 1846. 16° . . 7188
Romanism, Difficulties of. G. S. Faber. Philadelphia, 1840. 12°. . . 6128
History of. J. Dowling. New York, 1845. 8°. 5010
Lectures on. J. F. Berg. Philadelphia, 1840. 12°. . . . 5715
Mysteries of. C. Sparry. New York, 1847. 8°. 5359
Romans, Institutions and Domestic Manners of. London, 1826. 12°. . 7136

Romans, Paul's Epistle to, Notes on. A. Barnes. New York, 1841. 12°. 5726
Paul's Epistle to, Analysis of. C. Ferme. Edinburgh, 1850. 8°. . 5088
Commentary on. A. Melville. Edinburgh, 1850. 8°. . . . 5088
Lectures on. T. Chalmers. New York, 1844. 8°. 5588
The same. New York, 1843. 5016
Romans, B. Troubles in the Netherlands Hartford, 1778. 12°. . . 7437
Rome, Antiquities of. B. Kennett. Philadelphia, 1822. 8°. . . . 7233
The same. London, 1763. 8°. 9205
Antiquities, and other Curiosities of. E. Burton. London, 1828. 2 v. 12°. 9530
Church of, Literary Policy of the. J. Mendham. Lond. 1830. 8°. 5033
Civil Wars of. Selections from Lives of Plutarch. Tr. London, 1844. 3 v. 16°. 7460
Court of. M. Daunou. Tr. Philadelphia, 1837. 12°. . . . 5686
History of. J. Adams. Dublin, 1792. 2 v. 8°. . . . 7678
History of. T. Arnold. London, 1840. 3 v. 8°. 7355
History of. London, 1836. 2 v. 12°. 9885
History of. G. B. Niebuhr. Tr. Philadelphia, 1835. 2 v. 8°. . 6971
in the 19th Century. Miss Waldie. New York, 1827. 2 v. 12°. . 9608
in the 19th Century. Charlotte A. Eaton. London, 1852. 2 v. 12°. 5475
Letters from, in the 3d Century. W. Ware. N. Y. 1838. 2 v. 12°. 9613
Liberty of. S. Eliot. New York, 1849. 2 v. 8°. 7541
and Naples, a Journey to. H. Sass. New York, 1818. 8°. . . 9789
Romilly, S. Autobiography and Correspondence. Lond. 1840. 3 v. 8°. 8177
The same. London, 1841. 2 v. 12°. 7737
Rosamond, or Captivity of a Female under Popish Priests. N. Y. 1836. 12°. 5674
Roscoe, W. Life. H. Roscoe. Boston, 1833. 2 v. 8°. 8274
Life of Lorenzo D. Medici. Philadelphia, 1803. 3 v. 8°. . . 8242
The same. London, 1847. 12°. 5135
Life and Pontificate of Leo X. Philadelphia, 1805, 6. 4 v. 8°. . 8205
The same. London, 1846. 2 v. 12°. 5137
Roscommon, Earl of., (W. Dillon.) Poems, with Life, by E. Sanford. Philadelphia, 1819. 16°. 2124
Rose, H. J. Biographical Dictionary. London, 1857. 12 v. 8°. . . 8834
Rose Douglas, Autobiography of a Minister's Daughter. N. Y. 1851. 12°. 564
Ross, J. Second Voyage in search of a N. West Passage. Phil. 1835. 8°. 9441
The same in French. Bruxelles, 1835. 3 v. 12°. . . 9316
Latin Grammar. Philadelphia, 1829. 12°. 3390
Roussetti, G. Anti-Papal Spirit of the Reformation. Tr. Lond. 1834. 12°. 5391
Rotteck, C. von. General Hist. of World, from earliest times to 1831. Trans. and continued to 1840. F. Jones. Phil. 1840, 1. 4 v. 8°. . 6943
Rousseau, J. J., Confessions of, with Letters. Tr. London, 1783. 5 v. 12°. 3955
Eloisa, a series of Original Letters. Tr. London, 1810. 3 v. 12°. 4539
Emilius and Sophia. Tr. London, 1783. 4 v. 12°. . . . 3964
Institutions Civiles. Paris, 1769. 2 v. 8°. 10792
Miscellaneous Works. Tr. London, 1767. 4 v. 12°. . . . 3960
Œuvres. Paris, 1817. 4 v. 18°. 10866
Treatise on the Social Compact. 12°. 11192

Rousseau and Voltaire against the Atheists. New York, 1845. 12°. . 5672
The same. 5676
Roussell, N. Catholic and Protestant Nations Compared. Bost. 1855. 8°. 5621
Rowcroft, C. The Bush Ranger of Van Dieman's Land. N. Y. 1846. 8°. 7
Rowe, Mrs. E., Letters of. London. 8°. 9759
Roxobel. Mrs. M. M. Sherwood. New York, 1832. 3 v. 12°. . . 1696
Royal, Mrs. A. The Tennessean. New Haven, 1827. 12°. . . . 1351
Royal Convent, a Tragedy. London, 1776. 12°. 2502
Rule and Misrule of the Eng. in Amer. T. C. Haliburton. N. Y. 1851. 12°. 7093
The same. 11418
Rugby School Sermons. T. Arnold. New York, 1846. 12°. . . . 6604
The same. 6605
Rumford, B., (Count.) Essays Polit., Economical, &c. Bost. 1798. 2 v. 8°. 125
Life of. J. Renwick. Boston, 1845. 12°. 8057
Rural Sketches. T. Miller. Philadelphia, 1842. 12°. 235
Rural Hours. New York, 1850. 12°. 1146
Tales, Ballads and Songs. R. Bloomfield. London, 1826. 18°. . 2027
Ruschenberger, W. S. W. Three Years in the Pacific. Phil. 1834. 8°. . 9424
A Voyage Round the World in 1835–7. Philadelphia, 1834. 8°. . 9422
Rush, B. On Diseases of the Mind. Philadelphia, 1818. 8°. . . . 2696
Rush, J. On the Human Voice. Philadelphia, 1833. 8°. 754
Rush, R. A Residence at the Court of London in 1817–19. Phil. 1833. 8°. 9164
The same, continued to 1825. (Two copies.) Phil. 1845. 8°. 9382
Ruskin, J. Lectures on Architecture and Painting. New York, 1856. 12°. 10160
Modern Painters. New York, 1847–56. 3 v. 12°. 10161
Seven Lamps of Architecture. New York, 1849. 12°. . . 10159
Russell, J. Tour in Germany, 1820–22. Boston, 1825. 8°. 9463
Russell, J., Lord. Memoirs, Journal of T. Moore. N. Y. 1857. 2 v. 8°. 7834
Memorials and Correspondence of C. J. Fox. Phil. 1853. 2 v. 12°. 8006
Russell, M. Ancient and Modern Egypt. New York, 1831. 16°. . . 6627
History of Nubia and Abyssinia. New York, 1840. 12°. . . 5877
The same. New York, 1833. 16°. 6626
The same. 8766
History of the Barbary States. New York, 1835. 12°. . . 5884
The same. New York, 1835. 16°. 8770
History of Palestine. New York, 1832. 16°. 6620
The same. New York, 1840. 12°. 5529
History of Polynesia. New York, 1845. 12°. 5210
Life of O. Cromwell. New York, 1833. 2 v. 16°. . . . 6258
The same. New York, 1841. 2 v. 12°. 5878
Russell, Lady R., Letters of. London, 1809. 8°. 9757
The same. Boston, 1820. 18°. 4632
The same, with additions. Philadelphia, 1854. 12°. . . 4538
Russell, W. History of Ancient Europe. Philadelphia, 1801. 2 v. 8°. . 11384
History of Modern Europe to 1763. London, 1789. 5 v. 8°. . 11378
The same. Philadelphia, 1822. 6 v. 8°. 7304
Russell, Wm. Manual of Mutual Instruction. Boston, 1826. 12°. . . 4536
Russell, W., Lord. Life. Lord J. Russell. London, 1820. 2 v. 8°. . . 8162

Russia, Campaign in, Narrative of the. E. Labaume. Tr. Hart. 1816. 8°. . 9498
The same. Philadelphia, 1815. 9493
Description of. J. Conder. London, 1825. 16°. 9653
The same. 9670
History of. London, 1783. 2 v. 8°. 7077
History of, R. Bell. London, 1836. 12°. 9871
History of. W. K. Kelly. London, 1854. 2 v. 8°. . . . 5201
Miscellaneous Observations on. R. Pinkerton. Lond. 1833. 8°. . 9363
A Pedestrian Journey thro'. J. D. Cochrane. Edin. 1829. 2 v. 16°. 10012
and the Russians, in 1842. J. G. Kohl. Philadelphia, 1843. 8°. . 9421
Travelling Sketches of. R. K. Porter. Philadelphia, 1809. 8°. . 9180
Travels in. See Coxe, W.
Travels in, Persian Revolu., &c. J. Hanway. Lond. 1762. 2 v. 4°. 10921
Russian Empire, in Reign of Cath. II. W. Tooke. London, 1800. 3 v. 8°. 7386
Poets, Specimens of. Tr. J. Bowring. Boston, 1822. 12°. . . 2289
The same. 2279
The same, with Second Part. London, 1821. 2 v. 12°. . 2436
Russie, Histoire de la Guerre de. Sarrazin. Paris, 1815. 8°. . . . 11447
Rupp, I. D. (Ed.) History of all Religious Denominations of the United States. Philadelphia, 1844. 8°. 5052
Rutledge, E. History of the Church of England. Middletown, 1825. 8°. 6376
Ruxton, G. F. Adventures in Mexico and the Rocky Mts. N. Y. 1848. 12°. 9827
Ryan, J. Grammar of Astronomy. New York, 1825. 12°. . . . 6096
Ryan, R. Worthies of Ireland. London, 1821. 2 v. 8°. . . . 8168
Rybrent de Cruce. New York, 1829. 2 v. 12°. 1511
Ryland, J. E. Life and Correspondence of J. Foster. N. Y. 1846. 2 v. 12°. 8255
The same. London, 1852. 2 v. 12°. 5183

S.

Sabbath, Book for the. J. B. Waterbury. New York, 1840. 12°. . . 5669
Discourses on. G. Duffield and A. Barnes. Phil. 1836. 16°. . . 6231
Manual. J. Edwards. Philadelphia. 12°. 6214
Remarks on the Different Opinions concerning the. R. Burnside. Schenectady, 1827. 12°. 6545
Sabine, L. Life of E. Preble. Boston, 1847. 12°. 8064
Amer. Loyalists to the British Crown in the Revolu. Bost. 1857. 8°. 7833
Sacramental Meditations and Advice. J. Willison. Hartford, 1815. 16°. 6645
Sacred Biography. H. Hunter. Boston, 1794. 3 v. 8°. 8528
Classics, Library of. (vols. 7, 8 & 27 mis'g.) Lon. 1834, 5. 27 v. 12°. 5776
Dramas. Hannah More. London, 1782. 12°. 2269
History of the World. See Turner, S.
Mountains. J. T. Headley. New York, 1851. 12°. 3894
Scenes and Characters. J. T. Headley. New York, 1851. 12°. . 3895
Songs and National Airs. T. Moore. New York, 1821. 18°. . 2761
St. Alban's Abbey. Anne Radcliffe. Phil. 1826. 2 v. 12°. . . . 613
St. Augustine, Confessions of. New York, 1844. 12°. 6141
The same. 6145

St. Bernard, Life and Times of. A. Neander. Tr. M. Wrench. Lon. 1843. 12°. 7735
St. Cloud, Secret History of the Court and Cabinet. Lond. 1806. 3 v. 12°. 7446
The same. 8101
St. Domingo, History of the Island of. New York, 1824. 8°. . . . 7328
St. John, J. A. Hellenes, or History of the Manners of the Ancient Greeks.
London, 1844. 3 v. 8°. 7358
St. John, James A. Lives of Celebrated Travellers. N. Y 1832. 3 v. 16°. 6276
The same. New York, 1841. 3 v. 12°. 5854
Margaret Ravenscroft. Philadelphia, 1836. 2 v. 12°. . . . 1296
St. John, J. H. Letters from an American Farmer. Phil. 1783. 12°. . 8737
St. Jonathan, or the Lay of a Scald. A. C. Coxe. New York, 1838. 12°. 2344
St. Leon. W. Godwin. Alexandria, 1801. 2 v. 18°. 1700
St. Patrick. Life and Acts. J. C. O'Haloran. Phil. 1823. 12°. . . 8674
St. Palaye de. Memoirs of Ancient Chivalry. Tr. London, 1784. 8°. . 7382
St. Petersburgh, a Visit to, in 1829, 30. S. Raikes. London, 1838. 8°. . 9104
St. Pierre, J. H. B. de. Studies of Nature. Phil. 1836. 8°. . . . 3304
St. Ronan's Well. W. Scott. Philadelphia, 1827. 2 v. 12°. . . . 599
See also Scott, Sir W.
St. Valentine's Day. W. Scott. Boston, 1845. 12°. 301
See also Scott, Sir W.
Saints' Rest. R. Baxter. New York. 12°. 5226
The same, abridged. Ed. B. Fawcett. Phil. 1831. 16°. . . 6232
Sale, Lady. Journals of Disasters in Affghanistan, 1841, 2. Lon. 1843. 12°. 9788
Salem Belle, a Tale of 1692. Boston, 1842. 18°. 337
Witchcraft. R. Calef. Boston, 1828. 18°. 4623
Salle, R. de la, Life of. J. Sparks. Boston, 1844. 12°. 8053
Sallustius, C. C. Bella Catilinaria et Jugurthini. New York, 1808. 12°. 11479
The same. Ed. E. A. Andrews. New Haven, 1841. 12°. . 11456
The same. New York, 1830. 12°. 11464
Opera. Lipsiæ, 1840. 16°. 10859
The same. Tr. W. Rose. New York, 1837. 12°. . . . 5264
Salmagundi. J. K. Paulding and W. Irving. New York, 1835. 2 v. 12°. 1304
The same. Second series. 2 v. 12°. 1306
Salvation of All Men, Chauncey's, Reviewed. J. Edwards, Jr. N. H. 1790. 8°. 5648
Philosophy of the Plan of. New York, 1843. 12°. . . . 5739
The same. Boston, 1856. 12°. 5422
The Way of. A. Barnes. New York, 1836. 12°. . . . 5707
Salvation by Grace, Essays on. J. Witherspoon. Lond. 1765. 3 v. 12°. 5811
Salverte, E. Philosophy of Magic. Tr. New York, 1847. 2 v. 12°. . 3333
Samuel Slick, Sayings and Doings of. T. C. Haliburton. Phil. 1837. 12°. 1470
The same. Second series. Phil. 1839. 12°. . . . 1471
Samor, Lord of the Bright City, a Poem. H. H. Milman. Lon. 1840. 16°. 2032
Sansom, J. Sketches of Lower Canada. New York, 1817. 12°. . . . 9005
The same. 9033
Sampson, W. Autobiography. London, 1832. 16°. 7744
The same. 8595
Sand, G. See Dudevant, Mad.

Sanderson, J. Lives of Signers of Dec. of Independence. Phil. 1827. 9 v. 8°. 11299
Sands, R. C. Writings of, in Prose and Verse. New York, 1835. 2 v. 8°. 6290
and others. Miscellanies. New York, 1833. 18°. 4289
Sandwich Islands, History of the. J. J. Jarves. Boston, 1843. 8°. . . . 6963
History of the. H. Bingham. New York, 1847. 8°. 9368
Journal of a Residence in. C. S. Stewart. New York, 1828. 12°. 9269
The same. 9794
Life in. H. T. Cheever. New York, 1851. 12°. 8974
Sanford, E. Lives. See British Poets.
Santa Fé Expedition. G. W. Kendall. New York, 1844. 2 v. 12°. . 8936
Santo Sebastiano, or the Young Protector. Boston, 1832. 3 v. 12°. . . 1442
Saracens, History of. S. Ockley. Cambridge, 1757. 2 v. 8°. 11429
Lands of the. B. Taylor. New York, 1855. 12°. . . . 9014
Saratoga. Boston, 1824. 2 v. 12°. 652
Sardanapalus. Lord Byron. New York, 1822. 16°. 2081
Sargent, E., (Ed.) Expedition in Search of Franklin. Bost. 1857. 12°. . 9595
Life of H. Clay. Auburn, 1852. 12°. 8628
Sargent, J. Life of T. T. Thomason. New York, 1833. 12°. . . . 8324
Memoir of H. Martyn. Boston, 1820. 8°. 8231
The same, abridged. New York. 16°. 4229
Sarrans, B. Memoirs of Lafayette. London, 1832. 2 v. 8°. . . . 8170
Sarrazin. History de la Guerre de Russie et d'Allemagne. Paris, 1815. 8° . 11447
Sass, H. Journey to Rome and Naples. New York, 1818. 8°. . . 9789
Satanstoe. J. F. Cooper. New York, 1845. 12°. 1235
Saturday Evening. I. Taylor. Boston, 1832. 12°. 310
Saunders, J. Memoirs of G. Chaucer. London, 1812. 16°. . . . 7174
Saurin, J. Sermons. Tr. R. Robinson and others. Princeton, 1827. 2 v. 8°. 5314
Savage, M. W. Bachelor of the Albany. New York, 1848. 12°. . . 1568
Savage, R. Life and Poems. S. Johnson. Phil. 1819. 16°. . . . 2131
Savary, M. Letters on Greece. Tr. Dublin, 1788. 8°. 6743
Sawyer, L A. Moral Philosophy. New York, 1845. 12°. . . . 6189
Saxe, J. G. Poems. Boston, 1851. 12°. 1992
Say, J. B. Political Economy. Boston, 1824. 8°. 10724
Sayers, E. Fruit Garden Companion. Boston, 1838. 12°. . . . 3016
Scandinavia, Ancient and Modern. A. Crichton and H. Wheaton. New York, 1841. 2 v. 12°. 5910
Scandinavian Mythology. G. Pigott. London, 1829. 12°. . . . 11461
Scarlet Letter, a Romance. N. Hawthorne. Boston, 1850. 12°. . . 1248
Scenes and Legends of North of Scotland. H. Miller. Cin. 1851. 12°. . 6061
Skepticism, Lectures on. L. Beecher. Cincinnati, 1835. 12°. . . . 6122
Schaff, P. Universities, Theology, &c., of Germany. Phil. 1857. 12°. . 6131
Schiller, F. von Æsthetic Lettters, Essays, &c. Boston, 1845. 16°. . 1162
Don Carlos, and other Dramas. London, 1847. 12°. 5156
Early Dramas and Ghost-Seer. Tr. London, 1849. 12°. . . 5157
Historical Dramas. Tr. London, 1847. 12°. 5155
History of the Thirty Years' War. Tr. New York, 1846. 12°. . 7431
The same, with Revolt in Netherlands, &c. Tr. London, 1846. 2 v. 12°. 5154
Revolt of Netherlands, Siege of Antwerp, &c. Tr. N. Y. 1847. 12°. 11469

Schiller, F. von. Historical Works. Edinburgh, 1828. 2 v. 16°. . . 10000
Life, and Examination of Works of. T. Carlyle. Lond. 1825. 8°. . 8158
Life, and Examination of Works of. C. Follen. Boston, 1833. 12°. 8033
Poems and Ballads of. Tr. E. L. Bulwer. New York, 1844. 12°. . 2364
Sämmtliche Werke. Stuttgart, 1838. 12°. 10300
The same. 11698
Select Minor Poems of.* Tr. Boston, 1839. 12°. 770
The same. 771
Wallenstein's Camp. Tr. G. Moir. Boston, 1831. 12°. . . 2021
and Goethe. Correspondence of. Tr. New York, 1845. 12°. . 780
Schlegel, A. W. von. Lectures on Dramatic Art and Literature. Trans.
Philadelphia, 1833. 8°. 32
The same. 94
The same. Tr. J. Bleek. London, 1846. 12°. . . . 5194
Schlegel, F. von. Æsthetic Miscellaneous Works. Tr. Lond. 1849. 12°. 5195
History of Literature. Tr. Philadelphia, 1818. 8°. . . . 453
Philosophy of History. Tr. with Memoir. N. York, 1841. 2 v. 12°. 819
The same. London, 1848. 12°. 5127
The same. London, 1835. 2 v. 8°. 11343
Schlosser, F. C. History of the 18th Century. Tr. Lond. 1843. 6 v. 8°. 7296
Scholar Armed against the Errors of the Time. London, 1800. 2 v. 8°. 6425
The Well-bred. Essays on Taste, &c. W. Milns. Lond. 1794. 8°. 11689
Schoolcraft, H. R. Algic Researches, &c., of N. American Indians. New
York, 1839. 2 v. 22°. 10137
Historical and Scientific Sketches of Michigan. Detroit, 1834. 12°. 7427
History of the American Indians. Buffalo, 1851. 8°. . . . 9409
Natural Hist. of the West, and Lead Mines of Mo. N. Y. 1819. 8°. 5984
Notes on the Iroquois. Albany, 1847. 8°. 9372
Oneota, or the Red Race of America. New York, 1845. 8°. . . 9483
Tour to Itasca Lake, in 1832. New York, 1834. 8°. . . . 9439
Travels to the Sources of the Mississippi, in 1820. Alb. 1821. 8°. . 9776
School Days at Rugby. Boston, 1859. 12°. 1194
School Keeping, Lectures on. S. R. Hall. Boston, 1830. 12°. . . . 4591
of Fashion. New York, 1829. 2 v. 12°. 967
and Schoolmaster. A. Potter and G. B. Emerson. N. Y. 1842. 12°. 2944
The same. New York, 1844. 12°. 2993
Schoolmaster, Confessions of a. Andover, 1839. 12°. 4963
Schools, Common. See Schools.
Public Report for 1845. H. Barnard. Providence, 1846. 8°. . 10086
Science and Mechanism, Progress of, illustrated from New York Exhibition,
1853, 4. C. R. Goodrich and others. New York, 1854. 4°.
Moral Elements of. vol. 1. J. Beattie. Dublin, 1787. 8°. . . 6409
Poetry of. R. Hunt. Boston, 1850. 12°. 6059
Religious Truth illustrated from. E. Hitchcock. Bost. 1857. 12°. 6069
Reports of the British Association for Advancement of. London,
1835. 11 v. 8°. 10670
and Revealed Religion, Lectures on. N. Wiseman. And. 1837. 8°.
and Literature, Discourses on the Objects, &c., of. N. Y. 12.°. . 5255

Science, Literature, &c., Reflections on. T. S. Grimke. N. H. 1831. 12°. 3372
Sciences, Lettres sur L'Origine des. London, 1777. 12°. 3299
Scientific Discovery, Annals of. Ed. D. A. Wells and G. Bliss. Bost. 1850, 1.
2 v. 12°. 6066
Scipio Africanus. S. de La Tour. Tr. London, 1787. 2 v. 8°. . . . 8259
Scotland, History of. London, 1784. 8°. 7087
History of. G. Buchanan. London, 1836. 2 v. 8°. 6941
History of. W. Scott. Philadelphia, 1835. 2 v. 12°. 5824
The same. Philadelphia, 1830. 2 v. 12°. 6822
The same. London, 1835. 2 v. 12°. 9879
History of the Church of. W. M. Hetherington. N. Y. 1844. 8°. 5054
Hist. of the Rebel. in, 1689–1715. R. Chambers. Edin. 1829. 16°. 10017
Hist. of the Rebel. in, 1638–60. R. Chambers. Edin. 1828. 2 v. 16°. 10007
History of the Rebel. in, 1745, 6. R. Chambers. Edin. 1827. 2 v. 16°. 9998
History of the Reformation in. J. Knox. Glasgow, 1832. 8°. . 5587
Queens of. Agnes Strickland. New York, 1851–5. 7 v. 12°. . 8023
in Reigns of Mary and James VI. W. Robertson. Dub. 1766. 2 v. 12°. 11450
The same. Philadelphia, 1811. 2 v. 8°. 6717
Scenes and Legends of North of. H. Miller. Cincin. 1851. 12°. . 6061
and the Scotch. Miss C. Sinclair. New York, 1840. 12°. . . 9261
Summer in. J. Abbott. New York, 1848. 12°. 9246
Scotsmen, Biog. Dictionary of Eminent. R. Chalmers. Glas. 1835. 4 v. 8°. 8139
Scott, J. Select Poems and Life. Philadelphia, 1822. 18°. . . . 2144
Scott, J. M. The Blue Lights, a Poem. New York, 1817. 24°. . . 2778
Scott, Mrs. J. H. Poems and Memoir. Boston, 1843. 16°. . . . 2483
Scott, T., (Editor.) Bible, with Notes and Observations. Bost. 1830. 6 v. 4°. 4998
Force of Truth, a Narrative. New York, 1825. 16°. . . . 4603
Life of. J. Scott. Boston, 1822. 12°. 8035
Scott, Sir W. The Abbot. Hartford, 1821. 8°. 1086
Account of Life and Works of. A. Cunningham. Bost. 1832. 16°. 8462
Anne of Geierstein. Philadelphia, 1829. 2 v. 12°. 624
The same. 626
Antiquary. Hartford, 1821. 8°. 1084
Ballads and Lyric Poems. Boston, 1807. 12°. 2011
Beauties of. Philadelphia, 1827. 12°. 2075
Black Dwarf. New York, 1817. 12°. 315
Bride of Lammermoor. Hartford, 1824. 8°. 1087
The same, illustrated. New York, 1850. 4°. . . . 11985
Castle Dangerous. (Two copies.) New York, 1832. 12°. . . 1610
Count Robert of Paris. (Two copies.) New York, 1832. 12°. . 1610
Chronicles of the Canongate. Philadelphia, 1827. 2 v. 12°. . . 703
Doom of Devorgoil. New York, 1830. 12°. 1424
Familiar Anecdotes of. J. Hogg. New York, 1834. 12°. . . 8329
The same. 8468
Guy Mannering. Philadelphia, 1823. 2 v. 12°. 645
History of Scotland. Philadelphia, 1835. 2 v. 12°. . . . 5824
The same. Philadelphia, 1830. 2 v. 12°. 6822
The same. London, 1835. 2 v. 12°. 9879

Scott, Sir W. Ivanhoe. Hartford, 1821. 8°. 1085
The same. Boston, 1834. 12°. 176
The same. Philadelphia, 1835. 12°. 1182
Kenilworth. New York, 1821. 2 v. 16°. 1715
The same. Hartford, 1821. 8°. 1086
Lay of the Last Minstrel, and other Poems. N. Y. 1811. 7 v. 18°. 2720
Lay of the Scotch Fiddle. New York, 1813. 18°. 2772
Legend of Montrose. Hartford, 1827. 8°. 1087
Letters on Demonology and Witchcraft. New York, 1830. 16°. . 6269
The same. New York, 1832. 16°. 6270
The same. New York, 1839. 12°. 5513
Life. G. Allan. Philadelphia, 1835. 8°. 8128
Life of Napoleon. New London, 1834. 3 v. 8°. 8212
The same. Philadelphia, 1827. 3 v. 8°. 7511
Marmion. Philadelphia, 1808. 2 v. 12°. 1388
Memoirs of the Life of. J. G. Lockhart. Boston, 1837, 8. 7 v. 12°. 8036
Minstrelsy of the Scottish Border. London, 1839. 8°. 1842
Miscellanies, Essays, &c. Philadelphia, 1841. 3 v. 12°. . . 482
Monastery. Hartford, 1821. 8°. 1085
Old Mortality. Philadelphia, 1834. 12°. 1592
The same. New York, 1817. 2 v. 12°. 315
Paul's Letters to his Kinsfolk. Edinburgh, 1817. 8°. 9210
Peveril of the Peak. New York, 1823. 2 v. 12°. 1370
Pirate. Hartford, 1822. 8°. 1088
Poems. 18°. 2734
Poems, Ballads, &c. Baltimore, 1813. 18°. 2758
Prose Works. Boston, 1829. 5 v. 12°. 3934

Vol. 1. Life of J. Dryden.
2. Life of J. Swift.
3. Biog. Notices of Eminent Novelists.
Vol. 4. Biographical Memoirs.
5. Paul's Letters to his Kinsfolk.

Redgauntlet. 12°. 679
The same. Exeter, 1824. 2 v. 24°. 1748
Rob Roy. Hartford, 1821. 8°. 1084
St. Ronan's Well. Philadelphia, 1824. 2 v. 12°. 677
The same. 1415
St. Valentine's Day. New York, 1828. 2 v. 12°. 662
The same. 664
Search after Happiness, and other Poems. Philadelphia, 1820. 12°. 3068
The same. 3082
Tales of the Crusaders. Boston, 1825. 2 v. 12°. 680
Tales of a Grandfather. First & second series. Phil. 1829. 4 v. 18°. 1759
Third series. Philadelphia, 1830. 2 v. 18°. 1721
Waverley Novels. (vols. 1, 2 missing.) Philadelphia, 1839. 5 v. 8°. 43

Vol. 3. Kenilworth; Pirate; Fortunes of Nigel; Peveril of the Peak; Quentin Durward.
4. St. Ronan's Well; Redgauntlet; Betrothed; Talisman; Woodstock.
5. Highland Widow; Two Drovers; My Aunt Margaret's Mirror; Tapestried Chamber; The Laird's Jock; Fair Maid of Perth; Anne of Geierstein; Count Robert of Paris; Castle Dangerous; The Surgeon's Daughter; Glossary.

Scott, Sir W. Waverley Novels. (vols. 2, 4–8, 10, 14, 16, 18, 23, missing.) Boston, 1834. 27 v. 12°. 268

Vol. 1. Waverley.
3. Antiquary.
9. Monastery.
11. Heart of Mid-Lothian.
12. Pirate.
13. Fortunes of Nigel.
15. Quentin Durward.
17. Redgauntlet.
19. Woodstock.
20. Chronicles of the C nongate. First series. Highland Widow; Two Drovers; Surgeon's Daughter; My Aunt Margaret's Mirror; Tapestried Chamber; Laird's Jock.
21. Chronicles of the Canongate. Second series. St. Valentine's Day.
22. Anne of Geierstein.
24. Castle Dangerous.
24–26. Stories from Scottish History. } Tales of a Grandfather.
27. Stories from French History. }

The same. (vols. 8–11, 22, 23, miss.) Bost. 1845. 27 v. 12°. 285

Vol. 1. Waverley.
2. Guy Mannering.
3. Antiquary.
4. Rob Roy.
5. Black Dwarf. }
6. Heart of Mid-Lothian. } Tales of My Landlord
7. Bride of Lammermoor, and Legend of Montrose. }
12. Pirate.
13. Fortunes of Nigel.
14. Peveril of the Peak.
15. Quentin Durward.
16. St. Ronan's Well.
17. Redgauntlet.
18. Betrothed, and Talisman. (Tales of the Crusaders.)
19. Woodstock.
20. Chronicles of the Canongate. First series.
21. Chronicles of the Canongate. Second series.
24. Castle Dangerous.
24–26. Stories from Scottish History. } Tales of a Grandfather.
27. Stories from French History. }

The same. (vol. 9 missing.) Philadelphia, 1826. 48 v. 12°. 577

Vol. 1, 2. Waverley.
3, 4. Guy Mannering.
5, 6. Antiquary.
7, 8. Rob Roy.
10, 11. Old Mortality. }
13, 14. Heart of Mid-Lothian. } Tales of My Landlord.
15. Bride of Lammermoor. }
15–17. Legend of Montrose. }
18, 19. Monastery.
20, 21. Abbot.
30–32. Peveril of the Peak.
3,5 36. St. Ronan's Well.
37, 38. Redgauntlet.
41, 42. Woodstock.
43–46. Chronicles of the Canongate. First and Second series.
47, 48. Anne of Geierstein.

The same. Boston, 1820. 14 v. 8°. . . . . . .

No. 1089. Waverley.
1090. Guy Mannering.
1091. Antiquary.
1092. Rob Roy.

Scott, Sir W. Waverley Novels.

No. 1093-5. Black Dwarf; Old Mortality; Heart of Mid-Lothian; Bride of Lammermoor; Legend of Montrose. } Tales of My Landlord.
1096. Abbot.
1097. Kenilworth.
1098. Pirate.
1099. Fortunes of Nigel.
1100. Quentin Durward.
1101. St. Ronan's Well.
1102. Redgauntlet.

Waverley. Boston, 1821. 18°. 1682
Woodstock. Boston, 1839. 12°. 284
The same. New York, 1826. 2 v. 12°. 248
The same. 973
Scottish Border Minstrelsy. W. Scott. London, 1839. 8°. 1842
Chiefs. Miss J. Porter. New York, 1857. 12°. 524
Fiddle, the Lay of the. W. Scott. New York, 1813. 18°. . . 2772
Gael. J. Logan. Boston, 1833. 8°. 7351
The same. 8627
History, Stories from. See Scott, Sir W.
Life, Lights and Shadows of. J. Wilson. Phil. 12°. 3973
Poets, Lives of, with Portraits. London, 1821. 4 v. 18°. . . 2730
Writers, Lives of. D. Irving. Edinburgh, 1839. 2 v. 12°. . . 8252
The same. 8627
Scout, or Black Riders of Congaree. W. G. Simms. N. Y. 1854. 12°. . 568
Scrap Table, The. Boston, 1830. 12°. 1463
Scripture Facts, Lectures on. W. B. Collyer. Boston, 1813. 8°. . . 5354
Figurative Language of. W. Jones. Philadelphia, 1818. 8°. . 5332
The same. 9764
Guide. Philadelphia, 1838. 16°. 6561
History. Illust. J. Watts. Ed. R. C. Shimeall. Phil. 1831. 12°. 6156
Lands. J. Kitto. London, 1850. 12°. 5477
Illustrated from Oriental Customs. S. Burder. Phil. 1807. 8°. . 9465
Readings, Daily. T. Chalmers. New York, 1851. 3 v. 12°. . . 5762
Readings, Sabbath. T. Chalmers. New York, 1848. 3 v. 12°. . 5765
Sacrifices, Nature and Design of. J. Nicol. London, 1813. 8°. . 5603
Scriptures, Essay on the Inspiration of the. J. Dick. Boston, 1811. 12°. 6494
The same. 6495
Sculpture, Painting and Architecture. J. S. Memes. Bost. 1831. 12°. . 10148
The same. 10155
Sea, Physical Geography of. M. F. Maury. New York, 1856. 8°. . . 5951
Sea. R. Mudie. London, 1835. 12°. 6107
Lions, or the Lost Sealers. J. F. Cooper. New York, 1849. 12°. 1234
and the Sailor. Notes on France and Italy. W. Colton. New York, 1851. 12°. 1147
Seaborn, A. Symzonia, a Voyage of Discovery. New York, 1820. 12°. 9267
Seabury, S. Sermons. Hudson, 1815. 2 v. 8°. 5101
Search after Happiness, and other Poems. W. Scott. Phil. 1820. 12°. . 3068
The same. 3069

Sears, B., and others. Ancient Lit. and Art, Essays on. Boston, 1849. 12°. 470
Classical Studies. Boston, 1843. 12°. 802
Sears, Reuben. Ballston and Saratoga, a Poem. Ballston, 1819. 16°. . 3069
Sears, Robert. History of the Bible. (Two copies.) N. Y. 1844, 5. 8°. 7598
Seasons, The. J. Thompson. Glasgow, 1792. 12°. 2433
Seasons, Sacred Philosophy of the. H. Duncan. Baltimore, 1839. 4 v. 12°. 6479
Seatsfield, C. Life in the New World. Trans. New York. 8°. . . . 9172
Life in Texas, or Cabin Book. Trans. New York, 1844. 8°. . 9089
Secret Foe. Miss E. Pickering. London, 1841. 3 v. 12°. . . . 167
Passions, The. R. F. Williams. London, 1844. 3 v. 12°. . . 131
Societies of the Middle Ages. London, 1846. 12°. 11480
Sedgwick, Miss C. M. Clarence. Philadelphia, 1830. 2 v. 12°. . . 921
The same. London, 1830. 3 v. 12°. 1645
Hope Leslie. New York, 1827. 2 v. 12°. 1651
Letters from Abroad. New York, 1841. 2 v. 12°. . . . 8697
Life of Maria L. Davidson. Boston, 1837. 12°. 8049
Tales and Sketches. 12°. 1663
Sedgwick, T., Jr. Life of W. Livingston. New York, 1833. 2 v. 8°. . 7922
The same. 8130
Public and Private Economy. New York, 1838, 9. 3 v. 12°. . 10789
Segur, Count P. de. The Four Ages of Life. Tr. N. Y. 1826. 12°. . 3353
Napoleon's Expedition to Russia in 1812. Tr. Phil. 1825. 2 v. 12°. 7435
Selborne, Natural History of. G. White. New York, 1842. 12°. . . 5919
The same. Ed. E. Jesse. London, 1851. 12°. 5474
Selby, P. J. Treatise on Parrots. Edinburgh, 1836. 12°. 10189
Treatise on Pigeons. Edinburgh, 1835. 12°. 10188
Selden, J. Judicature in Parliament. London. 12°. 11184
Selectæ e Profanis Scriptoribus Historiæ. (Two copies.) Phil. 1819. 12°. 11462
The same. 11473
Select Poems. Stanford, 1805. 12°. 2488
Sentences from Eminent Divines and others. London, 1768. 12°. 6578
Speeches. Ed. N. Chapman. Philadelphia, 1808. 5 v. 8°. . . 10737
Speeches. J. Sergeant. Philadelphia, 1832. 8°. 10992
Speeches, American. Ed. S. C. Carpenter. Phil. 1815. 3 v. 8°. . 10750
Self-Education. Le Baron Degerando. Boston, 1830. 8°. 747
Selections from Taylor, Latimer, Milton and others. Ed. B. Montague.
New York, 1845. 12°. 9843
Self-Cultivation Recommended. I. Taylor. Boston, 1820. 18°. . . 4615
Self-Knowledge, Treatise on. J. Mason. New York. 12°. 5243
The same. London, 1784. 12°. 11930
Self-Taught Men, Biography of. B. B. Edwards. Boston, 1832. 12°. . 8336
Seljuks, History of. London, 1780. 8°. 7049
Semmes, R. Service Afloat and Ashore. Cincinnati, 1851. 8°. . . . 9520
Seneca, L. A. Medea. Cambridge, 1834. 16°. 3072
Opera. Lipsiæ, 1829. 3 v. 16°. 10583
Tragœdiæ. Lipsiæ, 1829. 16°. 10586
Sense and Sensibility, a Romance. Miss J. Austen. Phil. 1833. 2 v. 12°. 1517
The same. 1838. 8°. 8°. 37

Sergeant, J. Select Speeches. Philadelphia, 1832. 8°. 10992
Sermons for the New Life. H. Bushnell. New York, 1859. 12°. . . 5734
for the People. F. D. Huntington. Boston, 1856. 12°. . . 5720
Servia, or a Residence in Belgrade, 1843, 4. A. A. Paton. Lond. 1845. 12°. 9231
Servia, History of. L. Ranke. Trans. London, 1853. 12°. . . . 5208
Service Afloat and Ashore during Mexican War. Cincinnati, 1851. 8°. . 9520
Seven Lamps of Architecture. J. Ruskin. New York, 1849. 12°. . . 10159
Sewall, T. Phrenology examined in Two Lectures. Washington, 1837. 8°. 11678
Seward, Miss A. Letters of, from 1784–1807. London, 1811. 6 v. 12°. . 4224
Life of E. Darwin. Philadelphia, 1804. 8°. 11310
Seward, W. H. Life of J. Q. Adams. Auburn, 1840. 12°. . . 8017
Works. Ed. G. E. Baker. New York, 1853. 3 v. 8°. . . 10982

Vol. 1. Biographical Memoir; Speeches in New York Senate; Speeches in United States Senate; Forensic Arguments.
2. Notes on New York; State Papers; Official Correspondence; Pardon Papers.
3. Orations and Discourses; Occasional Speeches and Addresses; Executive Speeches: Political Writings; General Correspondence; Letters from Europe; Speeches in the U. S. Senate.

Sewel, W. History of the Quakers. New York, 1844. 8°. . . . 7534
Sexagenarian. W. Beloe. London, 1818. 2 v. 8°. 757
Seymour, H. Mornings among the Jesuits at Rome. N. Y. 1849. 12°. . 5730
The same. 8688
Shabby Genteel Story. W. M. Thackeray. New York, 1852. 12°. . 11892
Shaftesbury, Earl of. A. A. Cooper. Characteristics of Men, Manners, Opinions and Times. 1749. 3 v. 18°. 4624
Life. G. W. Cooke. London, 1836. 2 v. 8°. 7900
Shahcoolan, a Hindu. Letters from Philadelphia. Bost. 1802. 12°. . 8715
Shakers, History of the. C. Green and S. Y. Wells. Albany, 1823. 12°. 6182
Shakspeare, W., Beauties of. Ed. W. Dodd. Phil. 1830. 16°. . . 3081
Concordance to. Mrs. Mary C. Clarke. New York, 1846. 8°. . 11680
Criticisms on. T. Davies. London, 1783. 3 v. 12°. . . . 841
Dramatic Works and Life of. Boston, 1839. 7 v. 8°. . . . 1807
The same. London, 1809. 11 v. 12°. 2417
The same. (vol. 1 missing.) Boston, 1810. 9 vols. 12°. . 1970
The same. (vols. 5, 6, 7, 8, miss.) N. Y. 1821. 10 v. 12°. 3629
The same. New York, 1830. 9 vols. 12°. 2056
The same. Hartford, 1830. 8°. 1838
The same. London, 1798. 8 v. 16°. 2704
and his Friends. R. F. Williams. London, 1844. 3 v. 8°. . . 134
The same. Paris, 1838. 8°. 129
Illustrations of Dramatic Works of. M. Retzsch. Folio. N. Y. 1849.
Lectures on. H. N. Hudson. New York, 1848. 2 v. 12°. . . 807
Notes to Plays of. J. P. Collier. New York, 1853. 12°. . . 1145
Papers. W. Maginn. New York, 1856. 12°. 526
and his Times. N. Drake. Paris, 1838. 8°. 51
Trial of, for Deer Stealing. W. S. Landor. London, 1834. 12°. . 827
Youth of. R. F. Williams London, 1844. 3 v. 8°. . . . 137

Shaler, W. Sketches of Algiers. Boston, 1826. 8°. 9126
Sharp, G. Life. C. Stuart. New York, 1836. 12°. 8420
Sharpe, S. Early History of Egypt. London, 1836. 8°. . . . 11263
History of Egypt to A. D. 640. London, 1846. 8°. . . . 6988
Shaw, C. Life and Select Poems. Philadelphia, 1822. 18°. . . . 2143
Shays' Rebellion in Massachusetts, 1786. G. R. Minot. Boston, 1810. 8°. 6927
Shee, M. A. Rhymes on Art. Philadelphia, 1815. 12°. . . . 2445
Sheep, Natural History of. W. Jardine. Edinburgh, 1835. 16°. . . 10196
Shelley, Mrs. M. W. Frankenstein. Philadelphia, 1833. 2 v. 12°. . . 668
and others. Lives of Eminent French Writers. Phil. 1840. 2 v. 12°. 8613
Lives of Emi. Lit. and Scientific Men of Italy. Phil. 1841. 2 v. 12°. 8004
Shelley, P. B. Essays and Letters from Abroad. Phil. 1840. 2 v. 8°. . 438
Shells and Shell-Fish, Treatise on. W. Swainson. London, 1840. 12°. . 9978
Shenstone, W. Essays on Men and Manners. Boston, 1820. 18°. . . 4633
Poetical Works of, with Life by E. Sanford. Phil. 1819. 18°. . 2136
Shepard, C. W. Treatise on Mineralogy. New Haven, 1835. 2 v. 12°. . 5999
The same. New Haven, 1832. 12°. 6001
Shepherd, W. Life of P. Bracciolini. Liverpool, 1802. 8°. . . . 11252
Sherburne, A. Autobiography. Providence, 1831. 12°. . . . 7728
The same. 8032
Sherburne, J. H. Life and Character of J. P. Jones. Wash. 1825. 8°. . 8234
Sherer, M. Memoirs of the Duke of Wellington. Phil. 1833. 2 v. 12°. . 8394
Sheridan, Mrs. F. Memoirs. Miss A. Lefanu. London, 1824. 8°. . . 8258
Sheridan, R. B. Dramatic Works, with Life. London, 1848. 12°. . . 5150
Life. T. Moore. Philadelphia, 1826. 2 v. 12°. 8351
The same. 8372
Speeches of, and Sketch of his Life. London, 1842. 3 v. 8°. . 10987
Sheridan, T. Lectures on Elocution. Troy, 1803. 12°. 3025
The same. 3896
Sherley, A. B., and T. Travels in Persia, Russia, &c. Lond. 1825. 12°. 8713
Sherlock, T., Sermons of, with Life. T. S. Hughes. Lond. 1830. 5 v. 12°. 5752
Sherman, H. Slavery in the United States. Hartford, 1858. 12°. . . 11188
Sherwood, Mrs. M. M. The Lady of the Manor. Bridgeport, 1828. 7 v. 18°. 1768
Roxobel. New York, 1822. 3 v. 12°. 1696
Works of. New York, 1836. 15 v. 12°. 184

Vol. 1. Henry Milner, Parts 1-3.
2. Fairchild Family; Orphans of Normandy; The Latter Days.
3. Little Henry and his Bearer; Lucy and her Dhaye; Memoirs of Sergeant Dale; Susan Gray, &c.
4. Indian Pilgrim; Clara Stephens, &c.
5. Infant's Progress; Flowers of the Forest; Juliana Oakley; Ermina; Emancipation.
6. Governess; Little Momiere: Stranger at Home; Pere La Chaise; English Mary; My Uncle Timothy.
7. Nun; Intimate Friends; My Aunt Kate; Emeline, &c.
8. Victoria; Arzoomund; Birth-day Present; Errand Boy, &c.
9-12. Lady of the Manor.
13 Mail Coach; My Three Uncles; Old Lady's Complaint, &c.
14. Monk of Cimies; Rosary; Roman Baths, &c.
15. Henry Milner. Part 4.

Shetland and Shetlanders. Miss C. Sinclair. New York, 1840. 12°. . 9260
Shew, J. Hand-Book of Hydropathy. New York, 1840. 12°. . . 4521

Sheil, R. L. Memoir and Speeches. Ed. T. McNevin. London, 1845. 8°. 10711
Shimeall, R. C. Age of the World, and Signs of the Times. New York, 1842. 12°. 3312
(Ed.) Scripture History. I. Watts. Philadelphia, 1851. 12°. . 6156
Shipp, J. Autobiography. vol. 2. New York, 1829. 12°. 8469
Shippey, J. Poetry and Prose on Subjects Moral, Political and Religious. New York, 1841. 12°. 1936
Shipwreck, The, a Poem. W. Falconer. New York, 1800. 18°. . . 2495
The same. 2779
Shirley, a Tale. Miss Charlotte Brontë. New York, 1857. 12°. . . 179
Shoberl, F. Present State of Christianity. New York, 1828. 12°. . 6177
Short, T. V. History of the Church of England. Philadelphia, 1834. 8°. 5047
Shuttleworth, P. N. Consistency of Revelation. New York, 1847. 16°. 6220
Siam, Mission to. G. Finlayson. London, 1826. 8°. 9458
Birmah and Anan, a Popular Descrip. of. J. Conder. Lond. 1826. 16°. 9646
The same. 9657
and Cochin China, Embassy to. J. Crawfurd. Lon. 1830. 2 v. 8°. 9134
and Muscat, Embassy to, in 1835–7. W. S. W. Ruschenberger. Philadelphia, 1838. 8°. 9422
Siamese Twins. E. L. Bulwer. New York, 1831. 12°. 1910
Sicily, a Pilgrimage. H. T. Tuckerman. New York, 1852. 12°. . . 1190
Italy, &c., Travels in. J. Jarves. Albany, 1820. 12°. . . . 9072
and Malta, a Tour Through. P. Brydone. New York, 1813. 12°. 9273
Sidereal Heavens, The. T. Dick. New York, 1840. 12°. . . . 5559
The same. New York, 1840. 16°. 8775
Sidney, A. Discourses on Government, with Life. N. Y. 1805. 3 v. 8°. 10644
Sidney, E. Life of R. Hill. New York, 1834. 12°. 8368
Sidney, H. Diary of the Times of Charles II. London, 1843. 2 v. 8°. . 7843
Sidney, P., Life and Times of. Boston, 1859. 12°. 8642
Life and Writings. T. Zouch. York, 1809. 4°. 11260
Siebold, P. F. von. Manners and Customs of the Japanese. Tr. London, 1841. 12°. 9235
The same. New York, 1841. 12°. 5908
Siege of Baltimore. A. Umphraville. Baltimore, 1817. 12°. . . . 11891
of Lichfield. W. Gresley. New York, 1843. 12°. 567
Signers of the Declaration of Independence. Lives. C. A. Goodrich. Hartford, 1848. 12°. 8596
See also Declaration.
Sigourney, Mrs. L. H. Pleas. Memories of Pleas. Lands. Bost. 1842. 16°. 1157
Traits of the Aborigines of America. Cambridge, 1832. 12°. . 2282
Zinzendorff and other Poems. 1835. 12°. 2327
Silliman, A. E. Gallop among American Scenery. New York, 1843. 12°. 9290
Silliman, B. Journal of a Tour to Quebec. New York, 1820. 12°. . . 9263
Travels in England, &c. Hartford, 1810. 2 v. 8°. 9784
Silliman, B., Jr. First Principles of Chemistry. Phil. 1858. 12°. . . 6075
First Principles of Natural Philosophy. Philadelphia, 1859. 12° . 6074
and others. World of Art and Industry. Illustrated from New York Exhibition, 1853, 4. New York, 1854. 4°. . . . .

Silius Italicus. Punica. Lipsiæ, 1834. 16°. 10610
Silk Manufacture, Treatise on. G. R. Porter. London, 1831. 12°. . 9965
The same. Philadelphia, 1812. 12°. 5844
Silvio Pellico. My Prisons. Tr. T. Roscoe. (Two copies.) N. Y. 1833. 12°. 1284
The same, with Additions. Cambridge, 1836. 2 v. 12°. . 8729
Simcoe, J. G. Military Journal during Am. Rev. New York, 1844. 8°. . 7578
Simms, W. G. Carl Werner, and other Tales. New York, 1838. 2 v. 12°. 1543
Guy Rivers. New York, 1834. 2 v. 12°. 1507
Life of F. Marion. New York, 1844. 12°. 8305
Life of Capt. John Smith. New York, 1846. 12°. 8338
Scout, or Black Riders of Congaree. New York, 1854. 12°. . . 568
Southern Passages and Pictures. New York, 1839. 12°. . . 2326
The same. 2415
Views and Reviews of American Hist., Lit., &c. N. Y. 1845. 12°. 854
Woodcraft, or Hawks about the Dovecote. New York, 1854. 12°. 569
Yemassee, a Romance of Carolina. New York, 1835. 2 v. 12°. . . 685
Simond, L. Tour and Residence in Switzerland. Bost. 1822. 2 v. 8°. . 9174
Simple Flower, and other Tales. Mrs. C. E. Tonna. N. Y. 1842. 16°. . 1710
Simpson, S. Biography of S. Girard. Philadelphia, 1832. 12°. . . 8416
Simpson, T. Treatise on Algebra. London, 1782. 8°. 3290
Sinclair, Sir J., Correspondence of. London, 1831. 2 v. 8°. . . . 9761
Sinclair, Miss C. Hill and Valley, or Hours in England and Wales. New York, 1838. 12°. 9792
Jane Bouverie, or Prosperity and Adversity. New York, 1851. 12°. 252
Modern Accomplishments. New York, 1836. 12°. 4242
The same, concluded. New York, 1837. 12°. 3918
Scotland and the Scotch. New York, 1840. 12°. 9261
Shetland and Shetlanders. New York, 1840. 12°. 9260
Singleton, A. Letters from the South and West. Boston, 1824. 8°. . 9782
Sinless Child, The, and other Poems. Mrs. E. O. Smith. N. Y. 1843. 12°. 2372
Sir Charles Grandison. S. Richardson. London, 1811. 7 v. 12°. . . 942
Sir Thomas More, or Colloquies on Society. R. Southey. London, 1831. 2 v. 8°. 727
Sismondi, J. C. De. History of the Crusades against the Albigenses. Tr. Boston, 1833. 12°. 6505
The same. 6833
History of the Italian Republics. London, 1832. 12°. . . . 9887
The same. Philadelphia, 1832. 12°. 5839
Literature of the South of Europe. Tr. N. Y. 1827. 2 v. 8°. . 82
The same. London, 1850. 2 v. 12°. 5125
Six Months in a Convent. Miss R. T. Reed. Boston, 1835. 16°. . . 6563
Supplement to. Boston, 1835. 16°. 6567
Skelton, J. Select Poems, with Life, by E. Sanford. Phil. 1819. 16°. . 2118
Skelton, P. Deism Revealed. London, 1751. 2 v. 12°. 6586
Sketch Book, The. W. Irving. New York, 1825. 12°. 1163
The same. New York, 1851. 12°. 541
Sketches by "Boz." C. Dickens. Philadelphia. 8°. 65
The same. Philadelphia, 1839. 8°. 16

Sketches, Poetical. N. P. Willis. Boston, 1827. 8°. 1923
in Prose and Verse. G. F. Richardson. Second series. London, 1838. 12°. 2979
of a Sea-Port Town. H. F. Chorley. Phil. 1836. 2 v. 12°. . . 1509
from a Student's Window. S. C. Coodrich. Bost. 1841. 12°. . 2981
Skillman, J. B. New York Police Reports, 1828, 9. New York, 1830. 8°.. 10656
Skinner, R. S. New York Annual Register. New York, 1831. 18°. . 4941
Skinner, T. H. Aids to Preaching and Hearing. New York, 1839. 12°. . 2992
Religion of the Bible. New York, 1839. 12°. 5704
Slater, S. Memoir. G. S. White. Philade'phia, 1836. 8°. . . . 7857
Slave King, The. V. Hugo. Philadelphia, 1833. 12°. 1642
States, Excursion through the. G. W. Featherstonhaugh. New York, 1844. 8°. 9088
The same. 9097
States, Seaboard, Jour. through. F. L. Olmsted. N. Y. 1856. 12°. 8972
Trade, African. T. F. Buxton. New York, 1840. 12°. . . . 11147
Trade, Hist. of the Abolition of. T. Clarkson. Lond. 1808. 2 v. 8°. 11059
The same. (vol. 1 missing.) New York, 1836. 3 v. 12°. . 11142
Slaver, Twenty Years of an African. T. Canot. Ed. B. Mayer. New York, 1853. 12°. 9791
Slavery. W. E. Channing. Boston, 1835. 12°. 11197
American, Facts and Arguments on. Le Roy Sunderland. New York, 1837. 16°. 6562
American, Letters on. J. Rankin. Boston, 1833. 18°. . . 11158
Letters and Speeches on. H. Mann. Boston, 1853. 12°. . . 11144
Occasional Essays on. L. Bacon. New York, 1846. 12°. . . 5421
Picture of. G. Bourne. Middletown, 1834. 16°. 11156
and its Remedy, Lectures on. A. A. Phelps. Boston, 1834. 18°. . 11155
Scriptural Views of. A. Barnes. Philadelphia, 1846. 12. . . 5417
Sketch of the Laws Relating to. G. M. Stroud. Phil. 1827. 8°. 10052
and the Slave Trade in the United States. (Two copies.) E. A. Andrews. Boston, 1836. 12°. 11166
Testimony of God Against. Le Roy Sunderland. Bost. 1836. 12°. 6584
Unconstitutionality of. G. W. F. Mellen. Boston, 1841. 12°. . 11938
in the United States. H. Sherman. Hartford, 1858. 12°. . . 11188
in the United States. J. K. Paulding. New York, 1836. 12°. . 11157
Anti, Records, 1835–37. New York, 1838. 3 v. 12°. . . . 11128
Anti, Society, Report of the American. New York, 1834. 8°. . 10053
Slavic Nations, Literature of. Talvi. New York, 1850. 12°. . . . 828
Sleep, Philosophy of. R. Macnish. New York, 1834. 12°. . . . 4884
Smart, C. Select Poems and Life. Philadelphia, 1822. 18°. . . . 2142
Smedley, E. Sketches of Venetian History. New York, 1840. 2 v. 12°. 5859
and others. Occult Sciences. London, 1855. 12°. . . . 6072
Smellie, W. Philosophy of Natural History. Philadelphia, 1791. 8°. . 10109
The same, with an Introduction by J. Ware. Bost. 1832. 8°. 10132
The same. Boston, 1838. 12°. 10149
Smith, Aaron. Atrocities of the Pirates. New York, 1824. 16°. . . 11289
Smith, Adam. Theology of Moral Sentiments. London, 1777. 8°. . . 6406

Smith, Adam. Theology of Moral Sentiments. London, 1792. 2 v. 8°. . 12131
The same, with Life. Ed. D. Stewart. London, 1853. 12°. 5189
Wealth of Nations. Dublin, 1785. 2 v. 8°. 11109
Smith, C. B. Life in Earnest. New Haven, 1840. 12°. 3398
Philosophy of Reform. New York, 1846. 12°. 6471
Smith, Miss E. Prose and Verse, with Life. H. M. Bowdler. Bur. 1811. 12°. 8380
Smith, Mrs. E. O. The Sinless Child, and other Poems. N. Y. 1843. 12°. 2372
Smith, E. R. Araucanians. New York, 1855. 12°. 9592
Smith, G. Visit to the Consular Cities of China, 1844–6. N. Y. 1847. 12°. 9557
Smith, Horace. Arthur Arundel. New York, 1844. 8°. 17
Brambletye House. Boston, 1826. 3 v. 12°. 306
The same. New York, 1835. 12°. 229
The same. 1252
Gaieties and Gravities. New York, 1852. 12°. 4573
Zillah. New York, 1829. 2 v. 12°. 615
and James. Poems. Ed. E. Sargent. 1918
Smith, Horatio. Festivals, Games and Amusements. N. York, 1831. 16°. 6618
Smith, H. L. First Lessons in Astronomy and Geology. Cleve. 1848. 12°. 6071
Smith, Captain John. Life. G. S. Hilliard. Boston, 1834. 12°. . . 8069
Life. W. G. Simms. New York, 1846. 12°. 8338
Smith, J. A. Nervous System *vs.* Phrenology, &c. New York, 1840. 12°. 2989
Smith, J. P. Scripture and Geology. London, 1839. 8°. 5941
Smith, J. S. Mirabeau, a Life History. Philadelphia, 1848. 12°. . . 8622
Smith, J. T. Northmen in New England, 10th Century. Bost. 1819. 12°. 7107
Smith, Mrs. S. L., Memoir. E. W. Hooker. Boston, 1839. 12°. . . 8357
Smith, Seba. Powhatan, a Metrical Romance. New York, 1841. 12°. . 2361
Smith, Sydney. Miscellanies. vol. 3. Philadelphia, 1844. 12°. . . 4531
Memoirs of. Lady Holland. New York, 1855. 2 v. 12°. . . 7998
Sermons. Philadelphia, 1846. 12°. 5420
Sketches of Moral Philosophy. New York, 1850. 12°. 6413
Works. London, 1840. 3 v. 8°. 375

Vol. 1–3. Miscellanies Originally Published in the Edinburgh Review.
3. Speeches; Letters; Sermons.

Smith, S. S. Evidences of the Christian Religion. Phil. 1809. 12°. . 6157
Smith, Sir Sidney. Memoirs of. E. Howard. London, 1839. 2 v. 8°. . 8143
Smith, T. and J. C. Choules. History of Missions. Boston, 1842. 2 v. 4°. 4990
Smith, W. Memoir of J. G. Fichte. Boston, 1846. 12°. 8011
Smollett, T. Humphrey Clinker. London, 1808. 12°. 1376
Peregrine Pickle. New York, 1816. 4 v. 16°. 1751
Select Poems, with Life. Philadelphia, 1822. 18°. 2145
and D. Hume. See Hume, D.
Smuggler, The. J. Banim. New York, 1832. 2 v. 12°. 1011
Smyth, T. Unity of the Human Races. New York, 1850. 12°. . . . 5721
Smyth, W. Lectures on the French Revolution. London, 1840. 3 v. 8°. 6928
The same. London, 1855. 2 v. 12°. 5190
Lectures on Modern History. Cambridge, 1841. 2 v. 8°. . . . 7331
The same. London, 1852. 2 v. 12°. 5192

Snarleyyow, or the Dog Fiend. F. Marryatt. Phil. 1827. 12°. . . . 247
Snodgrass, J. J. Narrative of the Burmese War. London, 1827. 8°. . 7232
Snow-Image, and other Twice-Told Tales. N. Hawthorne. Bost. 1852. 12°. 1247
Social Compact, Treatise on. J. J. Rousseau. 12°. 11192
Destiny of Man. A. Brisbane. Philadelphia, 1840. 12°. . . 11148
The same. 3302
Society, Advancement of, in Knowledge, &c. J. Douglas. Hart. 1830. 12°. 6144
Essay upon Natural History of. W. C. Taylor. N. Y. 1841. 2 v. 12°. 3930
Essay on the History of Civil. Philadelphia, 1819. 8°. 753
Improvement of. T. Dick. New York, 1833. 12°. . . . 3391
The same. New York, 1840. 12°. 5875
New View of. R. Owen. New York, 1825. 12°. 6487
Socrates. Ecclesiastical History. Tr. London, 1844. 8°. . . . 5063
Solitude, Influence on Mind and Heart. J. G. Zimmermann. Lon. 1797. 8°. 431
Sweetened, or Religious Meditations. J. Meikle. N. Y. 1811. 12°. 1964
Solis, A. de. History of the Conquest of Mexico. Tr. Paris, 1714. 2 v. 12°. 11482
Solomon and the Shulamite. F. W. Krummacher. New York, 1841. 12°. 5745
Solyman and Almena. J. Langhorne. E. Windsor, 1799. 12°. . . 2439
Somers, J. Lord, Life and Character. R. Cooksey. Worcester, 1791. 4°. 7797
Somerville, Mrs. M. Connection of Physical Sciences. N. Y. 1846. 12°. 6092
Discourse on the Mechanism of the Heavens. Phil. 1832. 16°. . 4604
Physical Geography. Philadelphia, 1848. 12°. 9581
Somerville, W. Select Poems, with Life by E. Sanford. Phil. 1819. 16°. 2130
Song Writing, with English Songs. J. Aikin. London, 1816. 12°. . . 1916
The same. London, 1810. 12°. 2226
Songs of our Land. Mary E. Hewitt. Boston, 1846. 12°. . . . 2352
Sophocles. Antigone. Ed. T. D. Woolsey. Cambridge, 1835. 8°. . . 2219
Tragedies. Tr. T. Francklin. New York, 1840. 12°. . . . 5271
The same. New York, 1834. 16°. 8751
The same. Selections from. Philadelphia, 1828. 18°. . 2117
The same. Tr. R. Potter. Oxford, 1819. 8°. . . . 1866
Sophocles, E. A. Greek Exercises. Hartford, 1841. 12°. . . . 4535
Greek Grammar. Hartford, 1853. 12°. 12210
Sordello. R. Browning. London, 1840. 12°. 2399
Sorrows of Werter. J. W. von Goethe. Tr. W. Render. Bost. 1824. 18°. 1681
Sotheby, W. Constance de Castile, a Poem. Boston, 1812. 16°. . . 3078
Soul and Body. Philadelphia, 1824. 2 v. 12°. 637
and Instinct. M. Paine. New York, 1849. 12°. 6138
Enquiry into the Nature of. R. Baxter. London, 1745. 2 v. 8°. . 6411
Appendix to the preceding. R. Baxter. Lond. 1750. 12°. 5667
Plato on the Immortality of the. New York, 1833. 12°. . . 6443
Power of, over the Body. G. Moore. New York, 1847. 12°. . 6173
Soulavie, J. L. Memoirs of Reign of Louis XVI. Tr. Lond. 1802. 6 v. 8°. 8235
South America. See America.
Carolina, Hist. of, 1670–1808. D. Ramsay. Charleston, 1809. 2 v. 8°. 6758
South, Letters from, in 1816. J. K. Paulding. New York, 1817. 2 v. 12°. 9606
Pacific, &c., Voyages to. E. Fanning. New York, 1838. 12°. . 8932
Sea, Voyages and Discoveries in, 1822–31. B. Morrell. N. Y. 1832. 8°. 9778

South Sea Islands, Visit to. D. Tyerman & G. Bennet. Bost. 1832. 3 v. 12°. 9041
Seas, a Visit to, 1829, 30. C. S. Stewart. Phil. 1834. 2 v. 12°. . 8986
See also Stewart, C. S.
and West, Letters from. A. Singleton. Boston, 1824. 8°. . . . 9782
South-West, The. New York, 1835. 2 v. 12°. 9625
South, R. Discourses. Boston, 1827. 8°. 6326
Southennan. J. Galt. New York, 1830. 2 v. 12°. 1121
Southern Literary Messenger, vols. 7, 8, 9, 11. Richmond, 1841–5. 8°. . 2155
Ocean, Adventures of British Seamen. Edinburgh, 1827. 16°. . 9989
Passages and Pictures. W. G. Simms. New York, 1839. 12°. . 2326
The same. 2415
Review. vols. 1–8. Charleston, 1828. 8°. 2955
Southey, Caroline. Chapters on Churchyards. New York, 1842. 12°. . 4526
Southey, R. Biog. of British Naval Commanders. Lond. 1833–40. 16°. . 9927
Book of the Church. Boston, 1825. 2 v. 8°. 5367
(Ed.) British Poets, from Chaucer to Johnson. Lond. 1831. 8°. . 1893
Chronicle of the Cid. Tr. Lowell, 1846. 8°. 11317
Common-Place Book. New York, 1849. 2 v. 8°. 30
The Doctor. New York, 1836. 12°. 1531
Expedition of Orsua, and the Crimes of Aguirre. Phil. 1821. 12°. 3906
Letters from Spain and Portugal. London, 1808. 2 v. 16°. . . 9312
Life and Correspondence. C. C. Southey. New York, 1851. 8°. 8132
Life of H. Nelson. Hartford, 1814. 12°. 8381
The same. New York, 1841. 5508
The same. New York, 1830. 16°. 6612
Life of O. Cromwell. New York, 1845. 16°. 7772
Life of J. Wesley, and History of the Rise and Progress of Methodism. New York, 1820. 2 v. 8°. 8516
Lives of Uneducated Poets. London, 1836. 8°. 8281
Moral and Political Essays. London, 1832. 16°. 4302
Naval History of England. Philadelphia, 1835. 12°. . . . 7449
The same. 11478
The same, with Lives of British Admirals to 1672. London, 1833–40. 5 v. 12°. 9927
Palmerin of England. Trans. 6 v. 6656
Peninsular War. (vols. 5, 6, missing.) London, 1838. 8°. . . 7559
Poetical Works. New York, 1842. 8°. 1797
Roderick, the Last of the Goths. Philadelphia, 1815. 18°. . . 2756
and S. T. Coleridge, Reminiscences of. G. Cottle. N. Y. 1848. 12°. 8303
Sir Thomas More, or Colloquies on Society. Lond. 1831. 2 v. 8°. 727
A Tale of the Paraguay, a Poem. Boston, 1827. 16°. . . . 3085
Thalaba, or the Destroyer. Boston, 1812. 2 v. 16°. . . . 3063
Southey, T. Chronological History of the West Indies. London, 1827. 3 v. 8°. 6681
Southgate, H. Syrian (Jacobite) Church of Mesopotamia. N. Y. 1844. 12°. 5747
Tour through Armenia, Mesopotamia, &c. N. Y. 1840. 2 v. 12°. 9627
The same. 9570
Souvenirs of a Residence in Europe, by a Lady of Va. Phil. 1842. 12°. 8897

Sowers not Reapers. Miss H. Martineau. Hartford, 1845. 18°. . . . 1680
Spain, Ancient, Poetry and Romances of. Tr. J. Bowring. Lond. 1824. 12°. 2224
The Arabs in. London, 1840. 2 v. 12°. 7682
Dominion of the Arabs in. J. A. Condé. London, 1854. 3 v. 12°. 5186
History of. London, 1782. 8°. 7062
History of. Maria Callcott. London, 1827. 2 v. 12°. 7100
History of the Reformation in. T. M'Crie. Edin. 1829. 8°. . 5590
History of the Reformation in, and Italy. 2 v. 8°. 5590
in 1830. H. D. Inglis. London, 1831. 2 v. 8°. 9093
Journey through, 1786, 87. J. Townsend. London, 1791. 3 v. 8°. 9232
Memoirs of, from 1621 to 1700. J. Dunlop. Edin. 1834. 2 v. 8°. 6675
Moors in. T. Bourke. London, 1811. 4°. 11257
Reminiscences of its People, History, &c. C. Cushing. Boston, 1833. 2 v. 12°. 9247
Revisited. A. S. Mackenzie. New York, 1836. 2 v. 12°. . . . 9572
Scenes and Adventures in, in 1835–40. Philadelphia, 1846. 12°. . 9310
Travels in. M. M. Noah. New York, 1819. 8°. 9178
Travels through, 1775, 76. H. Swinburne. Dublin, 1769. 8°. . 9497
War of the Succession in. Hist. of. Lord Mahon. Lond. 1836. 8°. 6674
a Year in. A. S. Mackenzie. New York, 1836. 3 v. 12°. . . 8899
and Portugal, History of. S. A. Dunham. London, 1832. 5 v. 12°. 9874
The same. (vol. 3 missing.) Philadelphia, 1835. 4 v. 12°. 5829
History of. London, 1782. 6 v. 8°. 7062
History of, from B. C. 1000 to A. D. 1814. London, 1833. 8°. . 5094
Letters from. R. Southey. London, 1808. 2 v. 16°. . . . 9312
Popular Description of. J. Conder. London, 1826. 2 v. 16°. . 9341
The same. 9671
Sketches of. W. Beckford. Philadelphia, 1834. 2 v. 12°. . . 9293
Spalding, W. Hist. of Italy and the Ital. Islands. N. Y. 1842. 3 v. 12°. 5923
Spaniards and their Country. R. Ford. New York, 1848. 12°. . . 8898
Spanish Ballads. Tr. J. G. Lockhart. New York, 1842. 8°. . . . 1921
Daughter, The. G. Butt. Boston, 1824. 2 v. 18°. . . . 1757
Literature, History of. F. Bouterwek. Tr. London, 1847. 12°. 5495
The same with Portuguese Literature. Lond. 1823. 2 v. 8°. 729
Literature, History of. G. Ticknor. New York, 1849. 3 v. 8°. . 53
Proverbs, Dictionary of. Tr. London, 1823. 12°. 3306
Sparks, J. (Ed.) Library of American Biography. First and second series. vols. 1–4. Boston, 1834, 5. 12°. 8068
The same. vols. 5–25. Boston, 1836–48. 12°. 8045

Vol. 1. Stark, John, by E. Everett.
Brown, Charles B., by W. H. Prescott.
Montgomery, R., by J. Armstrong.
Allen, Ethan, by J. Sparks.
2. Wilson, Alex., by W. B. O. Peabody.
Smith, Capt. John, by G. S. Hillard.
3. Arnold, Benedict, by J. Sparks.
4. Wayne, Anthony, by J. Armstrong.
Vane, Sir Henry, by C. W. Upham.
5. Eliot, John, by C. Francis.
6. Pinkney, Wm., by H. Wheaton.
Ellery, William, by E. T. Channing.
Mather, Cotton, by W. B. O. Peabody.

Vol. 7. Phips, Sir Wm., by F. Bowen.
Putnam, Israel, by O. W. B. Peabody.
Davidson, L. Maria, by C. M. Sedgwick.
Rittenhouse, David, by J. Renwick.
8. Edwards, Jonathan, by S. Miller.
Brainerd, David, by W. B. O. Peabody.
9. Steuben, Baron, by F. Bowen.
Cabot, Sebastian, by C. Hayward, Jr.
Eaton, Wm., by C. C. Felton.
10. Fulton, Robert, by J. Renwick.
Hudson, Henry, by H. R. Cleveland.
Warren, Joseph, by A. H. Everett.
Marquette, by J. Sparks.

Sparks, J. (Ed.) Library of American Biography, (continued.)

Vol. 11. Salle, R. de la, by J. Sparks.
Henry, Patrick, by A. H. Everett.
12. Otis, James, by F. Bowen.
Oglethorpe, James, by W. B. O. Peabody
13. Sullivan, John, by O. W. B. Peabody.
Leisler, Jacob, by C. F. Hoffman.
Bacon, Nathaniel, by W. Ware.
Mason, John, by G. E. Ellis.
14. Williams, Roger, by W. Gammell.
Dwight, Timothy, by W. B. Sprague.
Pulaski, Count, by J. Sparks.
15. Rumford, Count, by J. Renwick.
Pike, Z. M., by H. Whiting.
Gorton, Samuel, by J. M. Mackie.
16. Stiles, Ezra, by J. L. Kingsley.
Fitch, John, by C. Whittlesey.
Hutchinson, Anne, by G. E. Ellis.

Vol. 17. Ribault, John, by J. Sparks.
Rale, Sebastian, by C. Francis.
Palfrey, Wm., by J. G. Palfrey.
18. Lee, Charles, by J Sparks.
Reed, Joseph, by H. Reed.
19. Calvert, Leonard, by G. W. Burnap.
Ward, Samuel, by W. Gammell.
Posey, Thomas, by J. Hall.
20. Greene, Nathaniel, by G. W. Greene.
21. Decatur, Stephen, by A. S. Mackenzie.
22. Preble, Edward, by L Sabine.
Penn, William, by G. E. Ellis.
23. Boone, Daniel, by J. M. Peck.
Lincoln, Benjamin, by F. Bowen.
24. Ledyard, John, by J Sparks.
25. Davie, W. R., by F. M. Hubbard.
Kirkland, Samuel, by S. K. Lothrop.

Diplomatic Corresp. of the Amer. Revol. Boston, 1829. 12 v. 8°. . 11035
Life of J. Ledyard. Cambridge, 1828. 8°. 8249
Life and Writings of B. Franklin. See Franklin, B.
Life and Writings of G. Morris. Boston, 1832. 3 v. 8°. . . . 10649
Life of G. Washington. Boston, 1839. 8°. 7554
See also Washington, G.
Trinitarian and Unitarian Doctrines Compared. Boston, 1823. 8°. 5360
Sparry, C. Mysteries of Romanism. New York, 1847. 8°. 5359
Speaking, Art of. London, 1794. 8°. 3292
Speaker, American. Ed. J. Frost. Philadelphia, 1836. 12°. 9858
Specimens of American Poets. S. Kettell. Boston, 1829. 3 v. 12°. . 2402
of Wit. D. Jerrold. Boston, 1858. 12°. 1181
Spectator, The. J. Addison and others. New York, 1810. 9 v. 12°. . 3579
See also Addison, J.
Speculator, The. (Two copies.) Dublin, 1791. 12°. 4266
Speculative Philosophy, Essays on. F. Bowen. Boston, 1842. 12°. . 789
Spencer, E. Travels in Circassia, Krim-Tartary, &c. Lond. 1839. 2 v. 8°. 9083
Travels in Western Caucasus, &c. London, 1838. 2 v. 8°. . . 9085
Tutti Frutti. New York, 1834. 12°. 1513
Spencer, J. A. Christian Instructed in the Ways of the Gospel and Church. New York, 1844. 12°. 6525
Travels in Egypt and the Holy Land. New York, 1850. 8°. . . 9389
Spencer, J. S. Pastor's Sketches. New York, 1851. 12°. 6470
Spencer, T., Memoirs of the Life and Ministry of. T. Raffles. Hartford, 1815. 12°. 8075
The same. 8090
Spenser, E. Essay on Life and Writings of. J. S. Hart. N. Y. 1847. 8°. 29
Poetical Works, with an Introduction. Boston, 1839. 5 v. 8°. . . 1828
and his Poetry. G. L. Craik. London, 1835. 3 v. 16°. . . . 6877
Spirit of the Age. W. Hazlitt. New York, 1849. 12°. 4515
the, of Laws. C. de Montesquieu. Tr. Edin. 1768. 2 v. 12°. . 11182
Spirits of Odin, or a Father's Curse. J. Herma. New York, 1826. 2 v. 12°. 1392
Spiritual Christianity. I. Taylor. New York, 1841. 12°. 6193
Despotism. I. Taylor. New York, 1835. 12°. 5653
The same. 6440

Spiritual Perfection, Unfolded and Enforced. W. Bates. Lond. 1834. 12°. 5779
Treasury. W. Mason. vol. 2. New York, 1803. 8°. . . . 6377
Spix, J. B. von, and C. F. P. von Martius. Trav. in Brazil. Lon. 1824. 8°. 9466
Splendid Village. E. Elliot. London, 1833. 12°. 2258
Sportsman in France. F. Tolfrey. London, 1841. 2 v. 12°. . . . 9550
Sprague, C., Writings of. New York, 1841. 8°. 1777
The same. Boston, 1850. 12°. 1944
Sprague, J. T. History of the Florida War. New York, 1848. 8°. . . 7268
Sprague, W. B. Lectures to Young People. New York, 1831. 12°. . 3916
Life of T. Dwight. Boston, 1845. 12°. 8056
Annals of the American Pulpit. New York, 1857. 5 v. 8°. . . 5040
Spring, G. Bethel Flag. New York, 1848. 12°. 5419
Contrast between Good and Bad Men. New York, 1855. 2 v. 8°. 5086
Essays on Christian Character. New York, 1840. 12°. . . . 6123
Fragments from a Pastor's Study. New York, 1838. 12°. . . 5709
Memoir of S. J. Mills. Boston, 1829. 18°. 8440
The same. New York, 1820. 8°. 8251
Mercy Seat. New York, 1850. 12°. 5774
Obligations of the World to the Bible. New York, 1839. 8°. . 5586
The same. New York, 1844. 12°. 5691
Power of the Pulpit. New York, 1849. 12°. 5418
Springer, J. S. Forest Life and Forest Trees. New York, 1851. 12°. . 9823
Spurzheim, J. G. Life. A. Carmichael. Boston, 1833. 12°. . . 8682
Natural Laws of Man. Boston, 1832. 16°. 6569
Objections to the Doctrines of, Examined. Boston, 1833. 12°. . 4888
Phrenology, or Doctrine of Mental Phenomena. Bost. 1832. 2 v. 8°. 1056
Phrenology in connection with Physiognomy. Boston, 1836. 8°. . 1059
Spy, The. J. F. Cooper. New York, 1822. 2 v. 12°. 1667
The same. Philadelphia, 1831. 2 v. 12°. 356
Unmasked. H. L. Barnum. New York, 1828. 8°. . . . 8569
Squier, E. G. Nicaragua, its People, Scenery, &c. N. Y. 1852. 2 v. 8°. 9410
The same. New York, 1856. 8°. 9373
Stable and Table Talk. Philadelphia, 1845. 12°. 796
Stack, R. Lectures on the Acts of the Apostles. Annapolis, 1815. 8°. . 6391
Staehlin, Mr. Anecdotes of Peter the Great. Dublin, 1789. 12°. . . 8467
Staël, Mad. de. Corinne, ou L'Italie. Paris, 1836. 12°. 676
The same. Tr. New York, 1844. 8°. 20
The same. Philadelphia, 1836. 2 v. 12°. 674
Stage, British, Biography of. New York, 1824. 12°. 8398
Character and Influence of. J. Styles. London, 1807. 12°. . . 4568
English, Annals of. J. P. Collier. London, 1831. 3 v 12°. . . 1109
The same. 1112
Nature and Effects of. J. Witherspoon. New York, 1812. 12°. . 4578
Standard Library Cyclopædia. London, 1848. 4 v. 12°. . . . 5129
Stanhope, L. Greece in 1823, 4. Letters, &c., on the Revolu. Phil. 1825. 8°. 7006
Stanhope, S. S. The Bandit's Bride. 1831. 3 v. 18°. 334
Stanley, or Recollections of a Man of the World. Phil. 1838. 2 v. 12°. . 1562
Stanley, A. P. Life and Correspondence of T. Arnold. N. Y. 1845. 12°. 8391

Stanley, Buxton, or the Schoolfellows. J. Galt. Phil. 1833. 2 v. 12°. . 1453

Stansbury, H. Exploration of Great Salt Lake Valley, with Maps. (Two copies.) Philadelphia, 1852. 2 v. 8°. 9401

Star Papers. H. W. Beecher. New York, 1855. 12°. 5772

Star of Seville, a Drama. Mrs. F. Butler. New York, 1837. 12°. . . 2391

Stark, J. Life. E. Everett. Boston, 1834. 12°. 8068

State and Church, Essay on. W. E. Gladstone. London, 1841. 2 v. 8°. 10664

States and Empires, Rise and Fall of. R. Pezron. London, 1809. 16°. . 11298

Statesman, The. H. Taylor. London, 1836. 16°. 1644

Statesman's Manual. S. T. Coleridge. Burlington, 1832. 12°. . . 11116

Statesmen, Eminent British. J. Forster and others. Lond. 1836. 7 v. 12°. 9932

See also Forster, J.

Eminent Foreign. E. E. Crowe and G. P. R. James. Lond. 1833–8. 5 v. 12°. 9940

Vol. 1. Cardinal Amboise; Ximenes; Leo the Tenth; Cardinal Granvelle; Barneveldt; Sully; Duke of Lerma; Duke of Ossuno; Lorenzo Di Medici. } E. E. Crowe.

2. Armaud Jean Du Plessis; Cardinal De Richelieu; Axel; Count Oxensteirn; Gaspar De Guzman; Count Olivarez; Duke of San Lucar; Julius; Cardinal Mazarin.
3. Jean Francois Paul de Gondi; Jean Baptiste Colbert; John De Witt; Francois Michel Le Tellier.
4. Louis De Haro; Cardinal Alberoni; John William; Duke of Ripperda.
5. Andrew Hercules; Philip Louis; Sebastian Joseph; Joseph Monino; Stephen Francis; James Necker. } G. P. R. James.

of the Time of George III. See George III.

Staunton, G. Embassy to China. Dublin, 1798. 2 v. 8°. . . . 9211

Staunton, H. Chess-Player's Companion. London, 1849. 12°. . . 1161

Steam Engine Explained and Illustrated. D. Lardner. Phil. 1836. 8°. . 404

The same, revised. London, 1840. 8°. 6325

Treatise on the. J. Renwick. Philadelphia, 1830. 8°. . . 6023

Stebbings, H. History of the Christian Church. London, 1833. 2 v. 12°. 9916

History of the Reformation. London, 1836. 2 v. 12°. . . . 9918

Lives of the Italian Poets. London, 1831. 3 v. 12°. . . . 8707

Steedman, A. Wanderings and Adventures in S. Africa. Lon. 1835. 2 v. 8°. 9405

Steele, Mrs. Heroines of Sacred History. New York, 1842. 16°. . . 6219

Steele, A. Life of W. Brewster. Philadelphia, 1857. 8°. . . . 7874

Steinmetz, A. History of the Jesuits. Philadelphia, 1848. 2 v. 8°. . 5119

A Year among the Jesuits. New York, 1846. 12°. . . . 5810

Stephen, J. Critical and Miscellaneous Essays. Phil. 1846. 8°. . . 24

Stephens, A. Memoirs of J. H. Tooke. London, 1813. 2 v. 8°. . . 8232

Stephens, J. L. Inci. of Travel in Greece, Turkey, &c. N. Y. 1841. 2 v. 12°. 8908

The same. New York, 1845. 2 v. 12°. 8906

The same. New York, 1838. 2 v. 12°. 9621

Incidents of Travel in Yucatan. New York, 1843. 2 v. 8°. . . 9774

Incidents of Travel in Yucatan, Central America, and Chiapas. New York, 1841. 2 v. 8°. 9779

Travels in Egypt, Arabia Petræa, &c. New York, 1837. 2 v. 12°. 8711

Sterling, J. Poetical Works. Philadelphia, 1842. 12°. 2225

Sterne, J. Letters and Sermons. Dublin, 1780. 3 v. 12°. 3968
Works. New York, 1813. 6 v. 12°. 3588

Vols. 1, 2. Life and Opinions of Tristram Shandy.
3. Sentimental Journey through France and Italy; History of a good warm Watch Coat.
4. 5. Sermons.
6. Letters; The Koran.

Stewart, C. S. Residence in the Sandwich Islands. N. Y. 1828. 12°. . 9269
The same. 9794
Sketches of Society in G. Britain and Ireland. Phil, 1834. 2 v. 12°. 8986
The same. 9050
Visit to the South Seas, 1829, 30. New York, 1833. 2 v. 12°. . 9249
The same. Philadelphia, 1834. 2 v. 12°. 8986
The same. New York, 1831. 2 v. 12°. 9633
The same. vol. 1. 9802
Stewart, D. Dissertation on the Progress of Philosophy. Bost. 1853. 4°. 10035
Life and Writings of W. Robertson. London, 1802. 8°. . . 8548
Philosophical Essays. Philadelphia, 1811. 8°. 6342
Philosophy of Active and Moral Powers of Man. Bost. 1828. 2 v. 8°. 6339
The same. Cambridge, 1849. 12°. 4542
Works. Cambridge, 1829. 7 v. 8°. 6364

Vols. 1, 2. Elements of the Philosophy of the Human Mind.
3. The same concluded; Outlines of Moral Philosophy.
4. Preliminary Dissertation; Philosophical Essays.
5. Philosophy of the Active and Moral Powers of Man.
6. Progress of Metaphysical, Ethical, and Political Philosophy.
7. Account of the Life and Writings of Adam Smith; of Dr. Robertson; of Dr. Reid; Tracts Relative to the Election of Professor Leslie.

Stewart. V. A. Adventures in Capturing J. A. Murrell. H. R. Howard. New York, 1836. 12°. 8334
Stickney, Miss S. See Ellis, Mrs. S.
Stiles, E. Life. A. Holmes. Boston, 1798. 12°. 8605
Life. J. L. Kingsley. Boston, 1845. 12°. 8058
Stiles, W. H. Austria in 1848, 9. New York, 1852. 2 v. 8°. . . 9412
Stilling, H. Autobiography. New York, 1846. 8°. 6
Stirling, Earl of. (W. Alexander.) Life. W. A. Duer. N. Y. 1847. 8°. 7871
Select Poems, with Life by E. Sanford. Philadelphia, 1819. 16°. 2119
Stirling, J. Life. T. Carlyle. Boston, 1852. 12°. 8002
Stobæus, J. Florilegium. Lipsiæ, 1838. 3 v. 16°. 10836
Stoicheia tou Politikou Dikaiou. Smyrna, 1835. 2 v. 12°. . . . 11145
Stone, W. L. Border Wars of the Am. Revolution. N. Y. 1845. 2 v. 12°. 5217
History of Wyoming. New York, 1841. 12°. 2217
Life of J. Brant. New York, 1838. 2 v. 8°. 7938
Life and Times of Red Jacket. New York, 1841. 8°. . . . 7824
Letters on Masonry and Anti-Masonry. New York, 1832. 8°. . 9760
Matthias and his Impostures. New York, 1835. 16°. . . . 6575
Tales and Sketches. New York, 1834. 2 v. 12°. 1383
Uncas and Miantonomoh. Historical Discourses. (Two copies.) N. York, 1842. 16°. 7760
Up and Downs in Life of a Distressed Gentleman. N. Y. 1836. 12°. 1615

Stones of Venice. J. Ruskin. New York, 1851. 8°. 10105
Stories from the Italian Poets. New York, 1846. 12°. 1170
Storm, The. D. De Foe. London, 1855. 12°. 5473
Storms, Law of. W. Reid. London, 1838. 8°. 5961
Philosophy of. J. P. Espy. Boston, 1841. 8°. 5946
Storr, T. C., and C. C. Flatt. Biblical Theology. Tr. And. 1826. 2 v. 8°. 5352
Stowe, Mrs. H. B. Dred, Tale of Great Dismal Swamp. Bost. 1856. 2 v. 12°. 173
Uncle Tom's Cabin. Boston, 1852. 2 v. 12°. 171
Strabo. Res Geographicæ. Lipsiæ, 1829. 3 v. 16°. 10833
Strafford, Earl of, (T. Wentworth,) Life. J. Forster. London, 1836. 12°. 9933
Strang, J. Germany in 1831. New York, 1836. 12°. 9610
Stratten. Book of the Priesthood. New York, 1831. 12°. . . . 6436
Stratton Hill, a Tale of the Civil wars. New York, 1829. 2 v. 12°. . 1349
Strauss, F. Helon's Pilgrimage to Jerusalem. Tr. Boston, 1835. 12°. . 8916
Street, A. B. Frontenac, a Metrical Romance. New York, 1849. 12°. . 2363
Poetical Works. New York, 1846. 8°. 1839
Strickland, Agnes. Queens of England. See England.
Queens of Scotland. New York, 1851–5. 7 v. 12°. 8023
Strong, N. Astronomy Improved. New Haven, 1784. 12°. 4558
Sermons. Hartford, 1800. vol. 2. 8°. 5623
Strive and Thrive. Miss M. Howitt. Boston, 1840. 18°. . . . 1714
Stroud, G. M. Sketch of Laws relating to Slavery. Phil. 1827. 8°. . 10052
Strutt, J. Sports and Pastimes of England. London, 1834. 8°. . . 21
Stuart, C. Life of G. Sharp. New York, 1836. 12°. 8420
Stuart, I. W. Life of J. Trumbull. Boston, 1859. 8°. 11316
Stuart, J. Three Years in North America. New York, 1833. 2 v. 12°. . 9813
Stuart, M. Hints on Prophecy. Andover, 1842. 12°. 6435
Student, Young, Letters to a. Boston, 1832. 12°. 4966
The same. 4987
Student's Gibbon. Hist. of Roman Empire, abridged. N. Y. 1847. 12°. 7394
Manual. J. Todd. Northampton, 1835. 12°. 3020
Manual of Modern History. W. C. Taylor. London, 1841. 12°. . 7091
Window, Sketches from a. S. G. Goodrich. Boston, 1841. 12°. . 2981
Sturm, C. C. Reflections on the Works of God. Tr. London, 1826. 18°. 5381
The same. Hudson, 1814. 2 v. 12°. 6171
The same. Tr. A. Clarke. London, 1836. 2 v. 12°. . . 6453
Sturt, C. Two Expeditions into Australia, 1828–31. Lond. 1834. 2 v. 8°. 9397
Styles, J. Character and Influence of the Stage. London, 1807. 12°. . 4568
Life of D. Brainerd. Boston, 1821. 12°. 7457
Styria, Lower, Winter in. B. Hall. Philadelphia, 1836. 12°. . . . 9800
Subaltern in America. Philadelphia, 1833. 12°. 4231
Subaltern's Furlough. E. T. Coke. New York, 1833. 2 v. 12°. . . 11413
Suddards, W. British Pulpit. Philadelphia, 1839. vol. 2. 8°. . . 5595
Sué, E. Count Conspirator. New York, 1845. 8° 49
The Wandering Jew. New York, 1846. 2 v. 8°. 41
Suede, de, Historie des Révolutions. 2 v. 18°. 11205
Suetonius, C. Opera. Lipsiæ, 1829. 16° 10605
Lives of the First XII Cæsars, Tr. A. Thomson. Lond. 1796. 8°. 8564

Suicide, Reflections on. Madame de Staël. Tr. Phil. 1816. 16°. . . 11294
Sullivan, F. S. Lectures on the Constitution and Laws of England. Dublin, 1790. 8°. 10768
Sullivan, James. History of the District of Maine. Boston, 1795. 8°. . 6757
Sullivan, John. Life. O. W. B. Peabody. Boston, 1844. 12°. . . 8055
Sullivan, W. Political Class Book. Boston, 1831. 12°. . . . 11196
Sully, M. de B. Memoirs. Tr. Philadelphia, 1817. 5 v. 8°. . . . 8523
Summerfield, J. Life and Ministry. J. Holland. New York, 1830. 8°. . 8157
Sermons. New York, 1842. 8°. 5025
Sumner, C. Orations and Speeches. (Two copies.) Boston, 1850. 12°. . 11123
Sunderland, La Roy. Anti-Slavery Manual. New York, 1837. 16°. . 6562
Testimony of God against Slavery. Boston, 1836. 16°. . . 6584
Supernaturalism of New England. London, 1847. 12°. 814
Superstition and Credulity. B. Blakeman. New York, 1849. 12°. . . 3927
Superville, Daniel de. Le Vrai Communiant. Nismes, 1817. 16°. . . 4972
Surveying and Plane Trigonometry. J. Gummere. Phil. 1825. 8°. . 2688
Sutcliffe, J. An Introduction to Christianity. New York, 1814. 12°. . 6523
Sutherland, A. The Knights of Malta. Philadelphia, 1846. 12°. . . 4522
Swain, C. Poems. Boston, 1857. 12°. 3086
Swainson, W. Animals in Menageries. London, 1838. 12°. . . . 9975
Birds of Africa. Edinburgh, 1833. 2 v. 12°. 10190
Discourse on the Study of Natural History. London, 1834. 12°. . 9970
Geography and Classification of Animals. London, 1835. 12°. . 9971
Habits and Instincts of Animals. London, 1840. 12°. . . . 9979
Natural Hist. and Classification of Birds. London, 1836. 2 v. 12°. 9973
Natural History and Classification of Quadrupeds. Lond. 1835. 12°. 9972
Nat. Hist. of Fishes, Amphibious and Reptiles. Lon. 1838. 2 v. 16°. 9976
Shells and Shell-Fish. London, 1840. 12°. 9678
Taxidermy and Bibliography, Treatise on. London, 1840. 12°. . 9980
Swallow Barn. J. P. Kennedy. Philadelphia, 1832. 2 v. 12°. . . 230
The same. 240
The same. 255
Swan, W. Letters on Missions. Preface by W. Orme. Bost. 1831. 12°. 6585
Swartz, C. F. Life. New York. 12°. 5248
Memoirs. H. Pearson. New York, 1835. 12°. 8619
Sweden, History of. London, 1783. 2 v. 8°. 7075
Hist. of the Revolution in. Abbé de Vertot. Tr. Lond. 1711. 12°. 11458
Tour in. S. Laing. London, 1838. 8°. 9143
Travels in. See Coxe, W.
Traveling Sketches of. R. K. Porter. Phil. 1809. 8°. 9180
Norway and Denmark, Travels in. H. D. Inglis. Edin. 1829. 16°. 10014
Swedenborg, E. Conjugial Love and Scortatory Love. Tr. Bost. 1840. 8°. 5012
Doctrine of the New Jerusalem. Tr. Philadelphia, 1815. 12°. . 11877
Life. N. Hobart. Boston, 1845. 12°. 8044
Swedes, History of the. F. G. Geijer. Tr. J. H. Turner. London. 8°. . 7236
Swift, D. Life, Writings and Character of J. Swift. London, [1755. 8°. 8270
Swift, J. Gulliver's Travels. Edinburgh, 1803. 12°. 338
Memoirs. W. Scott. Boston, 1829. 12°. 3935

Swift, J. Works. (vols. 1, 7, missing.) Edinburgh, 1768. 10 v. 12°. . 3945
The same. New York, 1812. 3 v. 12°. . . . . .

Vols. 1 and 2. Life; Contests and Dissensions in Athens and Rome.
3. A Tale of a Tub; History of Martin; a Project; Battle of the Books; Mechanical Operation of the Spirit; Critical Essay on the Mind; Meditation upon a Broomstick; Thoughts on Free Thinking; Preface to Temple's Memoirs; Sentiments of a Church of England Man.

Swift, Z. A System of the Laws of Connecticut. (Two copies.) Windham, 1795. 2 v. 8°. 10753
Swiftiana. London, 1804. 2 v. 16°. 4310
Swinburne, H. Travels through Spain in 1775, 76. Dublin, 1769. 8°. . 9497
Swinton, J., and others. Ancient Universal History. See History.
Switzerland, History of. T. C. Grattan. London, 1832. 12°. . . 9908
The same. Philadelphia, 1832. 12°. 5838
Jour. of a Tour and Residence in. L. Simond. Bost. 1822. 2 v. 8°. 9174
Sketches of. J. F. Cooper. Philadelphia, 1836. 2 v. 12°. . . 8948
Travels in. W. Coxe. Basil, 1802. 3 v. 8°. 9257
France and Germany, Society in. See France.
Sybil. B. D'Israeli. London, 1845. 8°. 10
Sydenham, T. Works on Acute and Chronic Diseases. Ed. B. Rush. Philadelphia, 1809. 8°. 9763
Sydney, A. Life. G. Van Santvoord. New York, 1851. 12°. . . 8636
Sydney, H., (Earl of Romney.) Diary of Times of Charles II. London, 1843. 2 v. 8°. 7843
Sylvia, and other Poems. T. B. Read. Philadelphia, 1857. 12°. . . 1994
Symes, N. Embassy to Ava in 1795. Ed. H. G. Bell. Edin. 1827. 2 v. 16°. 9993
Symzonia, A Voyage of Discovery. A. Seaborn. New York, 1820. 12°. 9267
Synonymes. G. Crabb. New York, 1839. 8°. 1057
François. M. C. Abbe Girard. Rouen, 1783. 2 v. 12°. . . . 3006
of the New Testament. R. C. Trench. New York, 1855. 12°. . 4517
Syria, Howadji in. G. W. Curtis. New York, 1852. 12°. . . . 8903
and Asia Minor, Description of. J. Conder. London. 2 v. 16°. . 9647
The same. London, 1824. 16°. 9667
Nubia, &c., Travels in. C. L. Irby and J. Mangles. Lond. 1844. 12°. 9286
Syrian, (Jacobite,) Church in Mesopotamia. H. Southgate. N. Y. 1844. 12°. 5747
Syrians, History of the. London, 1779. 8°. 7029

T.

Table Talk. S. T. Coleridge. New York, 1835. 12°. 4890
W. Hazlitt. New York, 1847. 2 v. 12°. 9840
M. Luther. Tr. W. Hazlitt. London, 1848. 12°. 5489
S. Rogers. London, 1856. 8°. 466
Book of. London, 1836. 2 v. 12°. 5803
or, Selections from the Ana. Edinburgh, 1827. 16°. 9995
Tablet, The. New Haven, 1831. 18°. 1702
Tacitus, C. C. Opera. Lipsiæ, 1829. 16°. 10582

Tacitus, C. C. Works. Tr. A. Murphy. Philadelphia, 1840. 8°. . . . 6702
The same. Philadelphia, 1842. 8°. 6956
The same. (vols. 1 and 2 missing.) Dublin, 1794. 4 v. 8°. 6750
The same. Philadelphia, 1844. 8°. 6955
The same. London, 1830. 2 v. 16°. 8749
Taghconic. G. Greylock. Boston, 1852. 12°. 11880
Tai-Ping-Wang. Life. J. M. Mackie. New York, 1857. 12°. . . . 8667
Tale of Paraguay. R. Southey. Boston, 1827. 16°. 3085
Tales. H. Zschökke. Tr. P. Godwin. New York, 1845. 12°. . . 9849
of the Border. J. Hall. Philadelphia, 1835. 12°. 688
of the Borders and of Scotland. J. M. Wilson. N. Y. 1848. 5 v. 8°. 1078
of the Crusaders. W. Scott. Boston, 1845. 12°. 298
The same. Philadelphia, 1839. 8°. 44
The same. Boston, 1825. 2 v. 12°. 680
Essays and Sketches. R. Macnish. London, 1844. 2 v. 8°. . . 1168
from the Gesta Romanorum. New York, 1845. 12°. 232
of Glauber-Spa. New York, 1832. 2 v. 12°. 1013
of the Good Woman. New York, 1829. 12°. 1408
of a Grandfather. See Scott, Sir W.
of the Hall, a Poem. G. Crabbe. London, 1835. 2 v. 12°. . . 2267
of Great St. Bernard. New York, 1829. 2 v. 12°. 982
of My Neighborhood. G. Griffin. Philadelphia, 1836. 2 v. 12°. . 264
of the Peerage and Peasantry. Lady Dacre. N. Y. 1835. 2 v. 12°. 1501
of the Puritans. Miss D. Bacon. New Haven, 1831. 12°. . . 651
and Sketches. Miss C. M. Sedgwick. 12°. 1663
and Sketches. W. L. Stone. New York, 1834. 2 v. 12°. . . 1383
and Sketches, Hist. and Domestic. Mrs. D. Clarke. Lond. 1838. 8°. 96
of a Traveller. W. Irving. New York, 1825. 2 v. 12°. . . 1166
The same. New York, 1851. 531
The same. New York, 1825. 2 v. 12°. 641
of the West. New York, 1828. 2 v. 12°. 630
of Wonder. Poems. M. G. Lewis. New York, 1801. 12°. . . 368
for Youth. Philadelphia, 1848. 16°. 1685
Talfourd, T. N. The Athenian Captive. New York, 1838. 12°. . . 2334
Critical and Miscellaneous Essays. Philadelphia, 1846. 8°. . . 24
The same. Philadelphia, 1842. 12°. 481
Tragedies. New York, 1837. 12°. 2053
Vacation Rambles. London, 1845. 12°. 9790
Talleyrand, M. de. Life. London, 1834. 2 v. 8°. 8172
Life. C. K. McHarg. New York, 1857. 12°. 8643
Tamerlain, History of. Tr. London, 1723. 2 v. 12°. 8095
Tappan, H. P. Doctrine of the Will, from Consciousness. N. Y. 1840. 12°. 5700
Doctrine of the Will applied to Moral Agency. N. Y. 1841. 12°. 5701
Review of Edwards on the Freedom of the Will. N. Y. 1839. 12°. 5699
Tappan, W. B. Poems. Boston, 1840. 12°. 2052
Poems. Philadelphia, 1836. 16°. 2480
Tarleton, B. Campaigns in South of N. America, 1780, 1. Lond. 1787. 4°. 11261
The same. Dublin, 1787. 8°. 6752

Tartary, China, &c., Journey to, in 1844–6. M. Huc. N. Y. 1852. 2 v. 12°. 9024
The same. Tr. W. Hazlitt. London, 1856. 12°. . . . 8894
Tartars, History of. London, 1780. 2 v. 8°. 7050
Tasistro, L. F. Random Shots and Southern Breezes. N. Y. 1842. 2 v. 12°. 1230
Task, The. W. Cowper. Albany, 1810. 12°. 2394
The same. Philadelphia, 1787. 12°. 3055
The same. Boston, 1833. 16°. 3065
Tasso, T. Jerusalem Delivered. Tr. E. Fairfax. London, 1844. 2 v. 16°. 7170
The same. New York, 1846. 12°. 9851
The same. Tr. J. Hoole. Dublin, 1788. 2 v. 12°. . . 2428
The same. Tr. J. H. Hunt. Philadelphia, 1822. 2 v. 16°. . 2115
The same. Tr., with Life, J. H. Wiffen. Lond. 1830. 2 v. 12°. 2457
Tassoni, A. Memoirs. S. Walker. London, 1815. 12°. 7720
Taste, Essays on. A. Alison. Dublin, 1790. 8°. 2699
Inquiry into the Principles of. R. P. Knight. London, 1687. 8°. 2686
Morals, &c., Essays on. G. Tucker. Georgetown. 12°. . . 1108
Tatler, The. Addison, Steele, and others. London, 1823. 4 v. 12°. . 3664
Taylor, B. India, China and Japan. New York, 1855. 12°. 9562
Journey to Central Africa. New York, 1856. 12°. . . . 8887
Lands of the Saracen. New York, 1854. 12°. 9014
Poems of the Orient. Boston, 1855. 12°. 2000
Rhymes of Travel, Ballads and Poems. New York, 1849. 12°. . 2356
Views A-Foot, or Europe seen with Knapsack. N. Y. 1856. 12°. . 9015
Taylor, F. W. The Flag Ship, or Voyage round the World. New York, 1840. 2 v. 12°. 9809
Taylor, H. Edwin the Fair and Isaac Comnenus. London, 1845. 16°. . 2089
Philip Van Artevelde. Boston, 1835. 2 v. 12°. 2484
The Statesman. London, 1836. 16°. 1644
Taylor, I. Advice to to the Teens. Boston, 1820. 18°. 4950
Ancient Christianity and the Doctrines of the Oxford Tracts. Philadelphia, 1840. 8°. 6191
Character Essential to Success in Life. Boston, 1820. 18°. . . 4943
Elements of Thought. London, 1842. 12°. 4587
The same. New York, 1851. 12°. 6410
Fanaticism. New York, 1834. 12°. 3297
Home Education. New York, 1838. 12°. 3295
Natural History of Enthusiasm. Boston, 1830. 12°. . . . 6472
Process of Historical Proof. London, 1828. 8°. 5074
Saturday Evening. Boston, 1832. 12°. 310
Self-Cultivation Recommended. Boston, 1820. 18°. . . . 4615
Spiritual Christianity. New York, 1841. 12°. 6193
Spiritual Despotism. New York, 1835. 12°. 5653
The same. 6440
Taylor, Mrs. I. The Family Mansion, a Tale. Philadelphia, 1820. 18°. . 4605
Taylor, Jane. Contributions of Q. Q. New York, 1826. 12°. . . . 3339
Taylor, Jeremy. Discourses on Various Subjects. Boston, 1816. 3 v. 8°. 5333
Great Examplar of Sanctity and Holy Life. Lond. 1834. 3 v. 12°. 5795
Holy Living and Dying. London, 1850. 12°. 5447

Taylor, Jeremy. Liberty of Prophesying. London, 1834. 12°. . . . 5776
Life. R. Heber. London, 1824. 2 v. 12°. 7715
Works. London, 1836. 3 v. 8°. 6279
Taylor, John. Records of My Life. New York, 1833. 8°. . . . 8200
Taylor, John, (of Va.) New Views on the Constitution of the United States. Washington, 1823. 8°. 11049
Taylor, J. B. Memoir. J. H. and B. H. Rice. New York, 1835. 12°. . 8626
The same. New York. 16°. 5237
The same. 7762
Taylor, T. Memoir of J. Howe. London, 1835. 12°. 5793
Taylor, W. Historic Survey of German Poetry. London, 1830. 3 v. 8°. 1850
Taylor, W. C. Essay on the Nat. Hist. of Society. N. Y. 1841. 2 v 12°. 3930
History of Ireland. New York, 1833. 2 v. 16°. 6262
The same. New York, 1841. 2 v. 12°. 5867
Memoirs of the House of Orleans. London, 1850. 2 v. 12°. . . 8000
Modern British Plutarch. London, 1846. 12°. 8030
Overthrow of the Roman Empire. London, 1836. 8°. . . . 7105
Romantic Biography of the Age of Elizabeth. Phil. 1842. 2 v. 12°. 8611
Student's Manual of Modern History. London, 1841. 12°. . . 7091
Taylor, Z., and his Generals. Lives. Philadelphia, 1847. 12°. . . . 8094
The same. Hartford, 1848. 12°. 8703
Taxidermy and Bibliography. W. Swainson. London, 1840. 12°. . . 9980
Tea Table Miscellany. A. Ramsay. Berwick, 1793. 2 v. 12°. . . 2451
Teacher, The. J. Abbott. Boston, 1834. 12°. 3921
Technology, Elements of. J. Bigelow. Boston, 1831. 8°. . . . 5991
Tecumseh, a Poem. G. H. Colton. New York, 1842. 12°. . . . 2336
and his Brother. Life. B. Drake. Cincinnati, 1841. 12°. . . 8344
Teeth, Structure and Diseases of. H. and J. Burdell. N. York, 1838. 8°. 11669
Teignmouth, Lord. Life, Writings, &c., of Sir W. Jones. Phil. 1805. 8°. 8201
Télémaque, Les Adventures de. Paris. 2 v. 18°. 10887
Telemachus, Adventures of. S. de la Fénélon. Tr. N. Y. 1820. 2 v. 18°. 1763
Tell, Guillaume. M. de Florian. Paris, 1805. 18°. 10903
Temper, or Domestic Scenes. Mrs. A. Opie. Boston, 1827. 3 v. 12°. . 915
Triumphs of, a Poem. W. Hayley. Kennebunk, 1804. 12°. . . 11883
and Temperament. Mrs. S. Ellis. New York, 1846. 12°. . . 4559
Temperature of the Interior of the Earth, Essay on. L. Cordier. Tr. (Two copies.) Amherst, 1828. 12°. 6084
The same. 6085
Temple, G. Travels in Greece and Turkey. London, 1836. 2 v. 12°. . 9522
Temple, Sir W. Memoirs. T. P. Courtenay. London, 1836. 2 v. 8°. . 7840
Works. London, 1814. 4 v. 8°. 10491

Vol. 1. Life; Essay on the Original and Nature of Government; Observations upon the United Provinces of the Netherlands; Letters on the Transactions in Christendom from 1665–72.
2. Letters; Survey of the Constitutions and Interests of the Empires of Sweden, Denmark, &c.; Letter to the Duke of Ormond; Memoirs of Events in Christendom, from 1672 to the Author's Retirement.
3. Essays and Miscellaneous Pieces; Poems and Translations.
4. Letters to the King, Prince of Orange, &c.

Temple, The, and other Poems. G. Herbert. London, 1838. 12°. . . 2035
Ten Thousand a Year. S. Warren, M. D. Philadelphia, 1841. 6 v. 12°. . 1298
Tenant of Wildfell Hall. Miss E. Brontë. New York, 1857. 12°. . . 182
The same. New York, 1848. 12°. 183
Tennemann, W. G. Hist. of Philosophy. Tr. A. Johnson. Ox. 1832. 18°. 6372
Tennent, J. E. Belgium. London, 1841. 2 v. 12°. 9541
Tennessean, The. Mrs. A. Royal. New Haven, 1827. 12°. . . . 1351
Tennyson, A. Poems. Boston, 1848. 2 v. 12°. 2276
Terentius, P. Comœdiæ. Lipsiæ, 1843. 16°. 10606
Select Comedies. Tr. G. Colman. Philadelphia, 1822. 18°. . . 2114
Terrible Tractoration. London, 1803. 16°. 2474
Terry, A. R. Travels in South America, in 1832. Hartford, 1834. 12°. . 9282
Testimony of the Rocks. H. Miller. Boston, 1857. 12°. 6052
Teutonic Antiquities. C. Chatfield. London, 1828. 8°. 11334
Texas, Exploits in. D. Crockett. Philadelphia, 1830. 12°. . . . 9287
History of. D. B. Edward. Cincinnati, 1836. 12°. 7122
History of the Revolution in. C. Newell. New York, 1838. 12°. 7123
Journey through. F. L. Olmsted. New York, 1857. 12°. . . 8971
New Mexico, &c., Explor. in. J. R. Bartlett. N. Y. 1854. 2 v. 8°. 9376
See also United States Public Documents.
and the Gulf of Mexico. Mrs. Houston. Philadelphia, 1845. 16°. 9324
and Mex. Sketches and Life in. C. Seatsfield. Tr. N. Y. 1844. 8°. 9089
and the Texans. H. S. Foote. Philadelphia, 1841. 2 v. 12°. . 10139
and the West, a Trip to. A. A. Parker. Concord, 1835. 12°. . 9824
Texian Expedition against Mier. T. J. Green. New York, 1845. 8°. . 9371
Textile Manufactures of Great Britain. G. Dodd. London, 1844. 16°. . 7466
Thacher, J. Military Journal during the American Revolution, from 1775 to 1783. Boston, 1823. 8°. 9781
Thackeray, F. Britain under the Roman Emperor. Lond. 1843. 2 v. 8°. 6969
Thackeray, W. M. Ballads. Boston, 1856. 12°. 1986
Book of Snobs. New York, 1853. 12°. 961
Confessions of Fitz-Boodle. New York, 1853. 12°. . . . 958
English Humorists of the 18th Century. New York, 1854. 12°. . 835
History of Pendennis. New York, 1850. 2 v. 8°. 2
Jeames' Diary. New York, 1853. 12°. 960
Journey from Cornhill to Grand Cairo. New York, 1846. 12°. . 9846
Luck of Barry Lyndon. New York, 1853. 12°. 959
The same. 2 v. 1632
Men's Wives. New York, 1853. 12°. 958
Newcomes. New York, 1855. 8°. 1
Paris Sketch Book. New York, 1852. 2 v. 12°. 1630
Punch's Prize Novelists. New York, 1853. 12°. 961
Shabby Genteel Story, and other Tales. New York, 1852. 12°. . 11892
Yellow-Plush Papers. New York, 1853. 12°. 960
Thackrah, C. T. Effects of the Arts, &c., on Health and Longevity. Philadelphia, 1831. 18°. 4621
Thaddeus of Warsaw. Miss J. Porter. Philadelphia, 1817. 3 v. 12°. . 1729

Thaddeus of Warsaw. New York, 1858. 12°. 525
Thalaba, or the Destroyer. R. Southey. Boston, 1812. 2 v. 18°. . . 3063
Thatcher, B. B. Indian Biography. New York, 1832. 2 v. 16°. . . 6641
The same. New York, 1840. 2 v. 12°. 5861
Thatcher, J. History of Plymouth and the Aborigines. Boston, 1835. 12°. 6802
Theatre, American, History of the. W. Dunlop. N. York, 1832. 8°. . 409
Character and Influence of. J. Styles. London, 1807. 12°. . . 4568
of the Greeks. London. 8°. 10078
Nature and Effects of. J. Witherspoon and others. New York, 1812. 2 v. 12°. 4578
Theism, Treatise on. F. Wharton. Philadelphia, 1859. 12°. . . . 6464
Theller, E. A. Canada in 1837, 8. Philadelphia, 1841. 12°. . . . 6786
Thelwall, J. Life. Mrs. Thelwall. vol. 1. London, 1837. 8°. . . 7924
Theocritus, Bion et Moschus. Opera. Lipsiæ, 1843. 16°. . . . 10353
Idyls. Tr. M. J. Chapman. London, 1836. 12°. 1915
Theological Dictionary. C. Buck. Philadelphia, 1824. 8°. . . . 5327
Essays, from the Princeton Review. New York, 1846. 8°. . . 5013
Second series. New York, 1847. 8°. 5014
Essays. T. De Quincey. Boston, 1854. 2 v. 12°. 885
Theology, Compendium of. J. F. Osterwald. Tr. Hartford, 1788. 8°. . 2985
Explained and Defended. T. Dwight. Middletown, 1818. 5 v. 8°. 5343
Institutes of. T. Chalmers. New York, 1849. 2 v. 12°. . . 5768
Lectures on. J. Dick. New York, 1846. 2 v. 8°. 5048
Views in. L. Beecher. Cincinnati, 1836. 12°. 5708
See also Divine Truth and Divinity.
Theophrastus, Epictetus et Cebes. Lipsiæ, 1829. 16°. 10355
Theron and Aspasia, Defence of. London, 1760. 12°. 6588
Letters on. London, 1768. 2 v. 8°. 5624
Reviewed and Examined. D. Wilson. London, 1762. 12°. . . 6596
Therry, R. Life and Speeches of G. Canning. London, 1836. 6 v. 8°. . 10634
Thierry, A. Conquest of Eng. by the Normans. Tr. Lond. 1856. 2 v. 12°. 5448
The same. London, 1847. 2 v. 12°. 5497
The same. London, 1841. 8°. 7254
Thiers, M. A. Hist. of French Rev. Tr. F. Shoberl. Phil. 1840. 3 v. 8°. 7527
Thiersch, D. F. Method of Teaching the Greek Paradigm. N. Y. 1830. 8°. 11673
Things New and Old. Sermons. Portland, 1845. 8°. 5615
Thiodolph The Icelander. F. De La M. Fouqué. Tr. N. Y. 1843. 12°. 1179
The same. New York, 1845. 12°. 1612
Thirlwall, C. Hist. of Greece. (vol. 6 miss.) Lond. 1835–44. 8 v. 12°. 9888
The same. New York, 1848. 2 v. 8°. 7278
Thirty Years' Corresp. between J. Jebb and A. Knox. Phil. 1835. 2 v. 8°. 33
View of U. S. Government. T. H. Benton. N. Y. 1854. 2 v. 8°. . 10934
War in Germany. F. Schiller. Tr. New York, 1846. 12°. . . 7431
The same. London, 1846. 12°. 5154
Thirty-Nine Articles of the Church of England, Exposition of the. G. Burnet. Ed. J. R. Page. New York, 1845. 8°. 5309
Thom, W. Rhymes and Recollections of a Weaver. London, 1845. 8°. 1913
Thomas, E. S. Reminiscences of Sixty-Five Years, from 1775 to 1840, and Autobiography. Hartford, 1840. 2 v. 12°. . . . 8597

Thomas, E. S. Recollections of Sixty-Five Years, from 1775 to 1840, and Autobiography. Hartford, 1840. 2 v. 12°. 11395
Thomas, I. History of Printing. Worcester, 1810. 2 v. 8°. 744
Thomason, T. T. Life. J. Sargeant. New York, 1833. 12°. 8324
Thome, J. A. and J. H. Kimball. Emancipation in the West Indies. (Two copies.) New York, 1838. 12°. 8969
Thompson. A. Sermons on Infidelity. New York, 1833. 16°. . . . 6572
Thompson, J. P. Egypt, Past and Present. Boston, 1854. 12°. . . . 7421
Memoir of T. Dwight. New Haven, 1844. 12°. 7733
Thompson, W. Recollections of Mexico. New York, 1846. 12°. . . . 9262
Thompson, W. Poems. Philadelphia, 1822. 18°. 2140
Thompson, Z. History of Vermont. Burlington, 1842. 8°. 7596
Thomson, Mrs. A. T. Memoirs of the Court of Henry VIII. London, 1826. 2 v. 8°. 7517
Memoirs of the Duchess of Marlborough. London, 1829. 2 v. 8°. 7866
Memoirs of Sir W. Raleigh. Philadelphia, 1831. 12°. 9860
Thomson, J. Poetical Works, with Life by E. Sanford. Phil. 1831. 18°. 2134
The same. London. 2 v. 12°. 2397
The Seasons, with Life. Glasgow, 1792. 12°. 2433
and W. Cowper. Works. Philadelphia, 1831. 8°. 1855
Thomson, J. B. Higher Arithmetic. New York, 1848. 12°. 3335
Thomson, R. Illust. of the History of G. Britain. Edin. 1828. 2 v. 16°. 10002
Thorburn, G. Forty Years in America. Boston, 1834. 12°. 8710
Thoresby, R. Diary and Correspondence. London, 1830. 4 v. 8°. . 8505
Thorne, J. Rambles by Rivers. (Two copies.) London, 1844. 16°. . 7472
Thornton and others. Connoisseur. London, 1823. 2 v. 12°. 3689
Thought, Elements of. I. Taylor. New York, 1851. 12°. 6410
The same. London. 1842. 12°. 4587
Thoughts on Habit and Discipline. London, 1844. 16°. 4584
for a Young Man. H. Mann. Boston, 1850. 16°. 4979
Three Courses and a Dessert. Illust. by G. Cruikshank. Lond. 1850. 12°. 5476
Histories, The. Miss M. J. Jewsbury. Boston, 1831. 12°. . . 926
Milanese, The, a Tragedy. 1835. 12°. 2414
Nights in a Lifetime. New York, 1835. 12°. 1250
Spaniards. G. Walker. New York, 1827. 2 v. 18°. 4638
Wise Men of Gotham. New York, 1826. 12°. 1639
Thucydides. Peloponnesian War. Tr. W. Smith. N. York, 1839. 2 v. 12°. 5279
The same. Philadelphia, 1836. 8°. 7555
Tibullus. Carmina. Lipsiæ, 1843. 16°. 10853
Tickell, T., Works with Life, by E. Sanford. Philadelphia, 1819. 16°. . 2130
Ticknor, C. Philosophy of Living. New York, 1836. 12°. 4957
The same. New York, 1841. 12°. 5887
Ticknor, G. History of Spanish Literature. New York, 1849. 3 v. 8°. 53
Tillotson, J. Works. vols. 3–7, 9, 10. Edinburgh, 1759. 12°. . . 6514
Timon. Orators of France. Tr. New York, 1849. 12°. 8670
Tindal, W., Works of, with Life. London. 12°. 5663
Tin Trumpet. P. Chatfield. Philadelphia, 1836. 2 v. 12°. 1605
Tischer, J. F. W. Life, Deeds, and Opinions of M. Luther. Tr. J. Kortz. Hudson, 1818. 12°. 7727

Tobacco, Mysteries of. B. I. Lane. New York, 1846. 12°. . . . 4596
Responses on the use of. B. I. Lane. New York, 1846. 12°. . 3303
Todd, J. Dangers of Great Cities. Northampton, 1841. 16°. . . . 4971
The same. 6570
The Student's Manual. Northampton, 1835. 12°. 3020
Toland, J. History of the Celtic Religion, Druids, &c. London, 1790. 8°. 11336
Tolfrey, F. The Sportsman in France. London, 1845. 2 v. 12°. . . 9550
Tom Brown's School Days at Rugby. Boston, 1859. 12°. . . . 1194
Tom Cribb's Memorial to Congress. T. Moore. New York, 1819. 16°. . 3073
Tomlinson, C. Cyclopædia of Useful Arts and Manufactures. N. Y. 2 v. 8°. 8798
Tom Jones. H. Fielding New York, 1815. 3 v. 12°. 3599
Tonga Islands, Account of. J. Martin. Boston, 1820. 8°. . . . 8831
Tone, T. W. Autobiography. London, 1831. 16°. 7498
Tonna, Mrs. C. E. Conformity, a Tale. New York, 1842. 16°. . . 1707
Falsehood and Truth. New York, 1841. 16°. 1705
Floral Biography. New York, 1840. 12°. 1202
Flower Garden. New York, 1840. 12°. 1203
Flower of Innocence. New York, 1842. 16°. 1709
Glimpses at the Past. New York, 1841. 16°. 1706
The same. 1711
Helen Fleetwood. New York, 1841. 12°. 1208
Judæa Capta. New York, 1845. 16°. 7478
Judah's Lion. New York, 1843. 12°. 1207
Passing Thoughts. New York, 1841. 16°. 1708
Peep into Number Ninety. New York, 1841. 12°. . . . 1209
Personal Recollections. (Two copies.) New York, 1843. 12°. . 1205
Philip and his Gardener. New York, 1842. 16°. 1704
Principalities and Powers in Heavenly Places. N. Y. 1842. 12°. . 1204
Simple Flower, and other Tales. New York, 1842. 16° . . 1710
Tooke, A. The Pantheon. London, 1726. 12°. 4933
Tooke, J. H. Diversions of Purley. London, 1829. 2 v. 8°. . . . 1061
Memoirs. A. Stephens. London, 1813. 2 v. 8°. 8232
Tooke, W. View of the Russian Empire in Reign of Catherine II. London, 1800. 3 v. 8°. 7386
Topsail-sheet Blocks, or Naval Foundling. London, 1838. 2 v. 12°. . 165
Torrey, J. Botany of New York. Albany, 1843. 2 v. 4°. . . . 13103
Tourist in Europe. New York, 1838. 12°. 10141
Tower, J. Life and Times of Frederick III, King of Russia. Dublin, 1789. 2 v. 8°. 8573
Tower of London, History of. J. Bayley. London, 1830. 8°. . . . 7437
Town, S. Analysis of Derivative Words. New York, 1836. 12°. . . 3314
Townsend, J. Journey through Spain, in 1786, 7. Lond. 1791. 3 v. 8°. 9232
Townshend, C. H. Facts in Mesmerism. New York, 1848. 12°. . . . 3305
Tract Society, American, Proceedings for first Ten Years, Boston. 12°. . 6537
Tracts for the Times. New York, 1839. 5 v. 8°. 5604
Tracy, E. C. Life of J. Evarts. Boston, 1845. 8°. 7830
Tracy, J. Great Awakening in the Time of Edwards and Whitefield. Boston, 1842. 8°. 5026

Trades and Professions. E. Hazen. New York, 1842. 2 v. 12°. . . 5921
Traditions of Devonshire. Mrs. A. E. Bray. London, 1838. 3 v. 8°. . 11415
of Lancashire. J. Roby. (vol. 1 missing.) London, 1843. 12°. 11399
of the most Ancient Times. W. Howitt. London, 1839. 2 v. 12°. 6775
and Recollections, Domestic, &c. R. Polwhele. Lond. 1826. 2 v. 8°. 8562
Traits of Travel. T. C. Grattan. New York, 1829. 2 v. 12°. . . . 9052
Transfusion, or Orphans of Unwalden. W. Godwin. N. Y. 1835. 12°. . 1253
Translation, Essay on. A. F. Tytler. London, 1791. 8°. . . . 155
Travel, Foreign, Uses of. London, 1762. 12°. 4871
Traveler, Letters of a. W. C. Bryant. New York, 1850. 12°. . . 9799
Traveler's Song. Anglo-Saxon Poem. Ed. J. M. Kemble. Lond, 1835. 12°. 2025
Travelers, Lives of Celebrated. J. A. St. John. N. York, 1841. 3 v. 12°. 5854
The same. New York, 1832. 3 v. 16°. 6276
Treaties, Debates on the Powers of Congress with Respect to. Philadelphia, 1796. 2 v. 8°. 10520
British, with other Powers. London, 1790. 2 v. 8°. . . . 11062
Tremaine. R. P. Ward. Philadelphia, 1825. 3 v. 12°. 619
Trench, R. C. English, Past and Present. New York, 1855. 12°. . . 4516
Hulsean Lectures. Philadelphia, 1856. 12°. 6468
Lessons in Proverbs. New York, 1855. 12°. 4519
Notes on the Miracles of our Lord. New York, 1856. 8°. . . 5055
Notes on the Parables of our Lord. New York, 1859. 8°. . . 5056
Poems. New York, 1856. 12°. 2354
Study of Words. New York, 1855. 12°. 4518
Synonyms of the New Testament. New York, 1855. 12°. . . 4517
Trenck, F. Autobiography. 8°. 433
The same. Boston, 1828. 18°. 8437
Treves, a Pilgrimage to. C. E. Anthon. New York, 1845. 12°. . . 8692
Trials and Cases of Jurisprudence, Celebrated. London, 1825. 6 v. 8°. . 10798
in Ireland, for High Treason. Baltimore, 1804. 8°. . . . 10767
of Life. New York, 1829. 2 v. 12°. 1597
Reports of Remarkable. London, 1844. 12°. 11127
Triangle, The. S. Whelpley. New York, 1832. 8°. 5600
Trigonometry, Calculus, &c., Elements of. W. Hopkins. Lond. 1833. 8°. 5096
Trinitarian and Unitarian Doctrines Compared. J. Sparks. Bost. 1822. 8°. 5360
Trinity, Catholic Doctrines of. W. Jones. Philadelphia, 1838. 12°. . 6594
Tristia, Ovid. Tr. F. Arden. New York, 1821. 8°. 1791
Tristram Shandy. L. Sterne. New York, 1813. 2 v. 12°. . . . 3588
Triumphs of Temper, a Poem. W. Hayley. Kennebunk, 1804. 12°. 11883
Trollope, Mrs. F. Belgium and Western Germany, in 1833. Phil. 1834. 8°. 9103
Domestic Manners of the Americans. (Two copies.) N. Y. 1832. 8°. 9491
Adventures of Michael Armstrong. New York, 1840. 2 v. 12°. . 1553
Paris and the Parisians. New York, 1836. 8°. 9148
The Refugee in America. New York, 1833. 2 v. 12°. . . . 692
Trollopiad, The. New York, 1837. 12°. 2345
Trotter, J. B. Memoirs of the Latter Years of C. J. Fox. Phil. 1812. 8°. 8250
Troubadour, The. L. E. Landon. Philadelphia, 1825. 12°. . . . 2416
Trübner, N. Guide to American Literature. London, 1859. 8°. . . 8833

Tryphiodorus. De Rebus Trojanis. Lipsiæ, 1829. 16°. 10342
Trueba, T. de. Incognito, Sins and Peccadilloes. N. Y. 1831. 2 v. 12°. 257
Life of H. Cortes. Edinburgh, 1829. 16°. 8457
Conquest of Peru by the Spaniards. Edinburgh, 1830. 16°. . . 10020
Romance of Spanish History. Philadelphia, 1820. 2 v. 12°. . 225
Trumbull, B. Hist. of Connecticut, from 1630 to 1713. Hart. 1797. 8°. 7216
Trumbull, J. McFingal. Boston, 1799. 16°. 3067
Progress of Dulness. Boston, 1794. 16°. 3084
Life. I. W. Stuart. Boston, 1859. 8°. 11316
Poetical Works. (Two copies.) Hartford, 1820. 8°. . . . 1895
Trumbull, J., (Col.) Autobiography, Reminiscences, &c. N. H. 1841. 8°. 7577
Truth, Force of, a Narrative. T. Scott. New York, 1825. 16°. . . 4603
Immutability of. Catharine M. Graham. London, 1783. 8°. . 6407
Knowledge, &c., Essays on. Philadelphia, 1831. 16°. . . . 4282
Moral Nature, and Immutability of., Essay on. J. Beattie. Dublin, 1773. 16°. 4321
Tryon County, Annals of. W. W. Campbell. New York, 1831. 8°. . . 11365
The same. New York, 1849. 12°. 11460
Tschudi, von, J. J. Travels in Peru. New York, 1846. 12°. . . . 9853
and M. E. Rivero. Peruvian Antiquities. Tr. N. York, 1853. 8°. 9147
Tucker, A. Light of Nature. London, 1807. 8°. 6399
Tucker, G. Essays on Taste, Morals, &c. Georgetown, 1822. 12°. . . 1108
Life of T. Jefferson. Philadelphia, 1837. 2 v. 8°. 8503
Progress of the U. S. in Population and Wealth. N. Y. 1843. 8°. 10691
Theory of Money and Banks. Boston, 1839. 12°. 10812
Tuckerman, H. T. Artist-Life. New York, 1847. 12°. 10152
Biographical and Critical Essays. Boston, 1857. 8°. . . . 121
Characteristics of Literature. Philadelphia, 1849. 12°. . . 806
The Optimist. New York, 1850. 12°. 826
Poems. Boston, 1851. 12°. 1991
Sicily, a Pilgrimage. New York, 1852. 12°. 1190
Thoughts on the Poets. New York, 1846. 12°. 5848
Tudor, W. Life of J. Otis. Boston, 1823. 8°. 8194
Tupper, M. F. Poetical Works. Boston, 1850. 12°. 2367
Proverbial Philosophy. New York, 1846. 12°. 9852
The same. New York, 1848. 12°. 1951
The Twins, the Heart, and the Crock of Gold. N. York, 1845. 12°. 251
Turkey, Egypt and Nubia, Trav. in. R. R. Madden. Phil. 1830. 2 v. 12°. 9604
Egypt, &c. Countess Hahn-Hahn. London. 3 v. 12°.. . . 9545
Turkey, Egypt, &c., Travels in. J. Webster. London, 1830. 2 v. 8°. . 9145
and Russia, Description of. J. Conder. London, 1827. 16°. . . 9651
The same. 9670
Sketches of, in 1831, 2. J. E. De Kay. New York, 1833. 8°. . . 9364
The same. 9443
Turkish Empire, Survey of. W. Eaton. London, 1799. 8°. 9213
Evening Entertainments. Tr. J. P. Brown. N. Y. 1850. 12°. . 1236
Spy at Paris. London, 1753. 12°. 11169
Turks, History of. London, 1780. 2 v. 8°. 7048

Turks and Tartars, Memoirs of. M De Tott. Tr. Dublin, 1785. 3 v. 12°. 8382
Turnbull, P. E. Travels in Austria. London, 1840. 2 v. 8°. 9140
Turner, J. B. Mormonism in all Ages. New York, 1842. 12°. . . . 5668
Turner, S. History of the Anglo-Saxons. Philadelphia, 1841. 2 v. 8°. . 7579
Hist. of Eng. from the earliest Period to 1603. Lond. 1839. 12 v. 8°. 7280
Sacred History of the World. New York, 1839. 3 v. 16°. . . . 5533
The same. 6874
The same. vols. 1 and 2. New York, 1833. 18°. . . . 6251
Turner, W. Tour in the Levant. London, 1820. 3 v. 8°. 9502
Tuscan States, History of. London, 1783. 8°. 7079
Tuscany, History of. L. Pignotti. Tr. J. Browning. Lond. 1826. 4 v. 8°. 6668
Tusculan Questions. M. T. Cicero. Tr. G. A. Otis. Boston, 1839. 8°. . 6448
Tutti Frutti. Prince Pückler Muskau. Tr. E. Spencer. N. Y. 1834. 12°. 1513
Twelve Nations, The Contest of the. Edinburgh, 1820. 8°. 742
Twice-Told Tales. N. Hawthorne. Boston, 1842. 2 v. 12°. . . . 1374
Twins, The. M. F. Tupper. New York, 1845. 12°. 251
Twiss, H. Life of Lord Eldon. Philadelphia, 1844. 2 v. 8°. 7850
Twiss, T. History and Discovery of Oregon. New York, 1846. 12°. . 7092
Two Admirals; a Tale. J. F. Cooper. New York, 1849. 12°. . . 1233
Two Families. New York, 1852. 12°. 563
Two Mentors, The. London, 1783. 2 v. 12°. 342
Two Years Ago. C. Kingsley. Boston, 1857. 12°. 1221
Two Years and a Half in the Navy, 1829–31. E. C. Wines. Philadelphia, 1832. 2 v. 12°. 9619
Two Years before the Mast. R. H. Dana. (Two copies.) N. Y. 1841. 12°. 5566
Tyerman, D., and G. Bennet. Voyages and Travels. Bost. 1832. 3 v. 12°. 9041
Tyler, B. Memoir of A. Nettleton. Hartford, 1845. 12°. 8623
Tyler, E. R. Lectures on Future Punishment. Middletown, 1829. 12°. 6522
The same. 6530
The same. 6538
Tyler, R. Ahasuerus, a Poem. New York, 1842. 12°. 2349
Tylney Hall. T. Hood. New York, 1835. 12°. 1250
Tyng, S. H. Memoir of G. T. Bedell. Philadelphia, 1836. 12°. . . . 8309
The same. 8681
Typee, or Life in the Marquesas. H. Melville. New York, 1846. 12°. . 9855
Tytler, A. F. Present Political State of India. London, 1815. 2 v. 8°. . 9512
and E. Nares. Universal History from the Creation to 1820. New York, 1840. 6 v. 12°. 5546
Essay on Translation. London, 1791. 8°. 155
Tytler, P. F. England under Edward VI and Mary. London, 1839. 2 v. 8°. 6965

U.

Umphraville, A. Siege of Baltimore, and other Poems. Balt. 1817. 12°. 11891
Uncas and Miantonomoh. Historical Discourse. W. L. Stone. (Two copies.) New York, 1842. 16°. 7760
Uncle Horace, a Novel. Mrs. S. C. Hall. Philadelphia, 1838. 2 v. 12°. 1420
The same. 1422

Undine. F. de la M. Fouque. New York, 1839. 12°. 1180
Uncle Tom's Cabin. Mrs. H. B. Stowe. Boston, 1852. 2 v. 12° . . 170
Underhill, U. Life. Hartford, 1816. 18°. 8448
Understanding, Treatise on. J. Locke. Boston, 1828. 18°. . . . 4614
See also Locke, J.
Unitarian and Trinitarian Doctrines Compared. J. Sparks. Bost. 1823. 8°. 5360
Ungewitter, F. H. Europe, Past and Present. New York, 1850. 12°. . 8886
United Brethren, History of Missions of the, to 1817. London, 1827. 8°. . 6392
United Irishmen, their Lives and Times. R. R. Madden. Phil. 1842. 2 v. 12°. 8664
Third series. Dublin, 1846. 3 v. 8°. 7990
United States Almanac. J. Downes and F. Hunt. vol. 2. Phil. 1844. 12°. 11876
Appeal respecting. R. Walsh, Jr. Philadelphia, 1819. 8°. . . 6712
The same. 10981
Army of. See Army.
and Canada, Observations on. J. Fidler. New York, 1833. 12°. 9254
and Canada, Trav. in. J. M. Duncan. New York, 1823. 2 v. 12°. 9029
Commerce of. T. Pitkin. New Haven, 1835. 8°. . . . 10731
Conduct of Executive of, in For. Affairs. J. Monroe. Phil. 1797. 8°. 10401
Congress of the, History of. H. G. Wheeler. N. Y. 1848. 2 v. 8°. 7600
Constitution, of, Analysis of Declara. of Independ., &c. W. Hickey.
(Two copies.) Philadelphia, 1847. 12°. 11133
Consti. and Gov. of, Discourse on. J. Calhoun. Charleston, 1854. 8°. 10074
Constitutions of the several States of. New York, 1813. 16°. . 11151
Contrib. to Ecclesi. Hist. of. F. L. Hawks. N. Y. 1836–39. 2 v. 8°. 5021
The same. vol 1. 5009
Constitution, Debates on. See Constitutional Convention.
Diplomacy of the. Boston, 1826. 8°. 11050
Eloquence of the. Ed. E. B. Williston. Middletown, 1827. 5 v. 8°. 10719
The same. 11011
Exploring Expedition in 1838–42. C. Wilkes. Phil. 1845. 6 v. 8°. 10628
Faithful Picture of. W. Cobbett. London, 1801. 12 v. 8°. . . 11023
Finances of the. A. Gallatin. New York, 1796. 8°. 11088
Foreign Conspiracy against the. S. F. B. Morse. N. Y. 1835. 18°. 11159
Geographical Description of. J. Melish. New York, 1826. 8°. . 9191
Historical Sketches from 1815–30. S. Perkins. N. Y. 1830. 12°. . 8031
History of, from 1492. G. Bancroft. Boston, 1841–58. 7 v. 8°. . 7566
History of. F. Butler. Hartford, 1821. 3 v. 8°. 7374
History of. H. Fergus. vol. 2. London, 1832. 12°. . . . 9861
History of. C. A. Goodrich. Bellows Falls, 1828. 16°. . . 6867
History of, till 1688. J. Graham. London, 1833. 2 v. 8°. . . 6953
History of. W. Grimshaw. Philadelphia, 1830. 12°. . . . 7433
History of, to 1817. S. Hale. New York, 1841. 2 v. 12°. . . 5892
History of. R. Hildreth. New York, 1849–56. 6 v. 8°. . . 7259
History of. J. R. Hinton and others. Boston, 1851. 4°. . .
History of. D. Ramsay. Philadelphia, 1818. 3 v. 8°. . . . 6706
History of. Emma Willard. New York, 1831. 8°. . . . 7234
and Great Britain, late war between. J. F. Clarke. N. Y. 1848. 8°. 7812
and Great Britain, late war between. W. James. Lond. 1818. 8°. 11345

United States and Great Britain, late war between. C. J. Ingersoll. vol. 1. Philadelphia, 1845. 8°. 7538
and Great Britain, late war between. S. Perkins. N. H. 1825. 8°. 6902
House of Representatives, Debates in, on Treaties. Philadelphia, 1796. 2 v. 8°. 10520
Indian Wars of the. W. V. Moore. Philadelphia, 1840. 8°. . 6788
Interesting Events in the Hist. of. J. W. Barber. N. H. 1828. 12°. 6848
and Mexico, Mexican Hist. of the war between. N. Y. 1850. 12°. 7096
Internal Condition of, by a Russian. Tr. Baltimore, 1826. 8°. . 10655
Navy. See Navy and Naval.
New Views on the Constitution of the. J. Taylor. Wash. 1823. 8°. 11049
Notes on the, in 1838–40. G. Combe. Philadelphia, 1841. 2 v. 8°. 9566
Political and Civil History of the. T. Pitkin. N. H. 1828. 2 v. 8°. 7326
Progress of the. G. Tucker. New York, 1843. 8°. . . . 10691
Public Documents, including Messages, Reports, Correspondence, &c., from 1826–57. Washington, 1826–58. 82 v. 8°. . .

No. 10384–99. Reports, Petitions, &c., from 1826–31.
10400. Journal of the Senate, for 1827, 8.
10402. Annual Messages and Accompanying Documents, for 1835–47.
10407. Trial of Col. J. C. Fremont.
10408–18. Annual Messages and Accompanying Documents, for 1849–56.
10419. Report on the Commerce of British America, from 1829–51.
10420, 1. Report on Commerce and Navigation, for 1849 and '55.
10422. Report of an Exploration of Minnesota, in 1849, by J. Pope.
10423. Coast Survey Report for 1849.
11242. Sixth Census Report, and Abstract of each Preceding Census.
10424. Seventh Census Report.
10425–28. Report on Finances, for 1849–51.
10429. Coast Survey Report for 1851.
13097. Sketches accompanying the same.
10430, 1. Marcy's Exploration of the Red River, with Maps.
10432. Geographical Memoir of Upper California, by J. C. Fremont.; Memoir of a Tour to Northern Mexico, by A. Wislizenus; Report and Map of the Examination of New Mexico, by J. W. Abert.
10433. Reports of Scientific Investigations in relation to Sugar and Hydrometers.
10434. Treaty between the United States and Mexico.
10436. Military Reconnoisance in California and New Mexico.
10437, 8. Reconnoisances of Routes from San Antonio to El Paso.
10439–51. Patent Office Reports for 1844, '47–51, '53, '57.
10452, 52 1–2. Exploration of the Valley of the Amazon, by W. L. Herndon, and L. Gibbon.
10453. Report of the Exploring Expedition to the Rocky Mountains, Oregon and California, in 1842–44, by J. C. Fremont.
10454. Report of J. W. Foster, and J. D. Whitney, on the Geology, &c., of the Lake Superior Land District.
13086–91. United States Naval Astronomical Expedition to the Southern Hemisphere, in 1849–52, under J M. Gilliss.
13092–6. Coast Survey Reports for 1852–56.
13097. Sketches accompanying Coast Survey Report for 1851; Report on Meteorology, 1850. J. P. Espy.
13115, 6. Report of a Geological Survey of Wisconsin, Iowa and Minnesota, with Illustrations, by D. D. Owen.

Revolution in the. See American Revolution.
Resources of the. J. Bristed. New York, 1818. 8°. 7368
Seat of Government of. J. B. Varnum, Jr. Washington, 1854. 8°. 10087
Second Visit to. Sir C. Lyell. New York, 1850. 2 v. 12°. . . 8912
Senate of, Debates on the Judiciary, in the. Philadelphia, 1802. 8°. 10517
Sketches of Life and Manners in the. New Haven, 1826. 12°. . 8990
Speaker. Ed. J. E. Lovell. (Three copies.) Charleston, 1837. 12°. 3320
State Papers and Public Documents of, from 1789 to 1818. 12 v. 10471

U. States, Trav. in the. De La Rochefoucault Liancourt. Lon. 1799. 2 v. 4°. 10919
Travels in the, in 1849, 50. Lady E. S. Wortley. N. Y. 1851. 12°. 9826
Travels in North of. E. A. Kendall. New York, 1809. 3 v. 12°. 9527
Treasury Department, Origin, &c., of. R. Mayo. Wash. 1847. 4°. 13114
Unity of the Human Races. T. Smyth. New York, 1850. 12°. . . . 5721
Universal Biography. See Biography.
History, from Creation to 1820. A. F. Tytler, and E. Nares. New York, 1840. 6 v. 12°. . . . . , . 5546
See also History.
Mag. of Knowledge and Pleasure. vols. 21–91. Lon. 1757–92. 8°. 3821
Traveler. Charles A. Goodrich. Hartford, 1820. 12° 9228
Universalism as it is. E. F. Hatfield. New York, 1841. 12°. . . . 6129
Lectures on. J. Parker. New York, 1841. 12°. 6146
Universities, Eng. V. A. Huber. Tr. F. W. Newman. Lond. 1843. 3 v. 8°. 62
University Sermons. F. Wayland. Boston, 1849. 12°. 5405
Upham, C. W. Lectures on Witchcraft. Boston, 1831. 12°. . . . 4912
Life of H. Vane. Boston, 1834. 12°. 8071
Upham, E. History of the Ottoman Empire. Edinburgh, 1829. 2 v. 16°. 10015
Upham, T. C. Imperfect and Disordered Mental Action. N. Y. 1841. 12°. 5560
Interior, or Hidden Life. Boston, 1845. 12°. 5416
Life of Mad. de la M. Guyon. New York, 1847. 2 v. 12°. . . 8580
Ups and Downs in the Life of a Distressed Gentleman. W. L. Stone. New York, 1836. 18°. 1615
Urania, or the Use of Poesy, a Poem. B. Allen, Jr. New York, 1814. 18°. 2767
Ure, A. Cotton Manufacture of Great Britain. London, 1836. 2 v. 12°. 2975
Dictionary of Arts, Manufactures and Mines. N. York, 1843. 8°. 8811
Urquhart, D. The Spirit of the East. Philadelphia, 1839. 2 v. 12°. . 9008
Urquhart, D. H. Commentaries on Classical Learning. Lond. 1803. 8°. 2694
Urquhart, J. Memoirs and Select Remains. W. Orme. Bost. 1828. 2 v. 16°. 7757
Useful Works for the People. New York, 1843. 8°. 10663
Usury, Defence of. J. Bentham. London, 1818. 12°. 11187
The same. Philadelphia, 1796. 16°. 11154
Utah, Exploration of the Valley of the Great Salt Lake of, with Maps. H. Stansbury. (Two copies.) Philadelphia, 1852. 2 v. 8°. . 9401

V.

Vacation Rambles. T. N. Talfourd. London, 1845. 12°. 9790
Vagamundo, or the Attaché in Spain. J. E. Warren. N. Y. 1852. 12°. . 9828
Vale of Cedars. G. Aguilar. New York, 1851. 12°. 1198
Valentine's Eve. Mrs. A. Opie. Boston, 1827. 12°. 912
Valerius, a Roman Story. J. G. Lockhart. Boston, 1821. 2 v. 12°. . 701
Valerius Maximus. Dictorum Factorumque Memorabilia. Lipsiæ, 1830. 16°. 10615
Valley of Shenandoah. New York, 1824. 2 v. 12°. 639
Valpy, A. J. Gradus ad Parnassum. London, 1838. 12°. 2986
Van Amringe, W. F. Natural History of Man. New York, 1843. 8°. . 6322
Vanbrugh, Sir J., Dramatic Works of. London, 1840. 8°. 1794
Van Buren, M., Life and Polit. Opinions of. W. M. Holland. Hart. 1835. 12°. 8290
The same. 8337

Van Diemen's Land, Notes of Exile to. L. W. Miller. Fredonia, 1846. 12°. 9230
Van Halen, J. Narrative of Imprisonment in the Dungeons of the Inquisition. New York, 1828. 8°. 9418
Van Santvoord, G. Life of A. Sydney. New York, 1851. 12°. . . 8636
Van Schaack, P. Life. H. C. Van Schaack. New York, 1842. 8°. . 8131
Vane, H., Life of. C. W. Upham. Boston, 1834. 12°. 8071
Vasari, G. Lives of Painters, Sulptures, and Architects. Lon. 1850. 5 v. 12°. 5139
Vane, Sir H., (The Younger.) Life. J. Forster. London, 1838. 12°. . 9935
Varnum, J. B., Jr. Seat of Government of the U. S. Wash. 1854. 8°. . 10087
Vassor, M. le. History of the Reign of Louis XIII. Tr. Lond. 1700. 8°. 11453
Vaux, J. H. Autobiography. London, 1830. 16°. 7492
Vegetable Substances Used for Food. Boston, 1832. 12° 6209
Velleius Paterculus, C. Historia Romana. Lipsiæ, 1829. 16°. . . 10856
The same. 11297
Velvet Cushion, The. J. W. Cunningham. London, 1815. 12°. . . 1287
Venetian History, Sketches of. E. Smedley. New York, 1840. 2 v. 12°. 5859
Venetia. B. D'Israeli. Philadelphia, 1847. 8°. 5
Venice, History of. London, 1782. 8°. 7069
Vermont, History of. Z. Thompson. Burlington, 1842. 8°. . . . 7596
History of. S. Williams. Burlington, 1809. 2 vols. 12°. . . 7684
State Papers. Middlebury, 1823. 8°. 10470
Verona, Congress of. F. A. de Chateaubriand. Tr. Lond. 1838. 2 v. 8°. 7918
Verplanck, G. C. Discourses on American Hist., Arts, &c. N. Y. 1833. 12°. 782
The Doctrine of Contracts. New York, 1825. 8°. 10054
and others, Miscellanies. New York, 1833. 3 v. 16°. . . . 4289
Verri, A. Roman Nights, or the Tombs of the Scipios. Tr. N.Y. 1825. 2 v. 12°. 986
Vertot, Abbé de. History of the Revolutions in Sweden. Lon. 1711. 12°. 11458
Histoiré de Révolutions de Portugal. Paris, 1816. 18°. . . 10902
History of Revolutions in Portugal. Tr. London, 1754. 8°. . 11444
Vestiges of Civilization. New York, 1851. 12°. 473
of Creation, a Sequel to. New York, 1846. 8°. 5992
Vethake, H. Principles of Political Economy. Philadelphia, 1838. 8°. . 10932
Vicar of Wakefield. O. Goldsmith. Walpole, 1809. 12°. 1732
Vidocq, E. F. Autobiography. Tr. London, 1829. vols. 2–4. 12°. . 7504
Vienna, Congress of. D. D. de Pradt. Tr. Phil. 1816. 8°. . . . 11052
Vieusseux, A. Sayings and Deeds of Napoleon. London, 1846. 16°. . 7206
Views A-Foot. B. Taylor. New York, 1856. 12°. 9015
Viger, F. Tr. and Abridged. J. Seager. London, 1828. 8°. . . . 10084
Vignoles, C. Observations on the Floridas. New York, 1823. 8°. . . 9365
Villers, C. Spirit and Influence of the Reformation. Phil. 1833. 12°. . 6116
The same. London, 1805. 8°. 5388
Villette. C. Brontë. New York, 1856. 12°. 178
Village Patriarch. E. Elliott. London, 1833. 12°. 2259
Vincent, S. Exposition of the Catechism. New Haven, 1810. 12°. . 6610
Virgilius Maro, P. Opera. Lipsiæ, 1829. 16°. 10604
The same. Delph. Phil. 1827. 8°. 1885
The same. Ed. B. A. Gould. Boston, 1834. 12°. . . . 3044
The same. Tr. J. Dryden. New York, 1825. 2 v. 18°. . . 2776

Virgilius Maro, P. Opera. Tr. Dryden and others. N. Y. 1840. 2 v. 12°. . 5269
The same. New York, 1834. 2 v. 16°. 8747
Virginia, Debates, &c., of the Convention of, in 1788. Richm'd, 1805. 8°. 11081
Historical Collections of. H. Howe. Charleston, 1845. 8°. . 7250
History till 1781. J. W. Campbell. Phil. 1813. 12°. . . . 7442
History of, to the Present Time. R. R. Howison. Phil. 1846. 2 v. 8°. 7592
Notes on the State of. T. Jefferson. Phil. 1794. 8°. . . . 3294
Viri Illustres Urbis Romæ. C. F. L'Homond. New York, 1828. 18°. . 4952
Vision, The. Dante Alighieri. Tr. H. Carey. New York, 1845. 12°. . 2453
Vision of Columbus. A Poem. J. Barlow. Hartford, 1787. 12°. . . 1905
The same. 2430
The same. 2450
Visits to Remarkable Places, Old Halls, Battle Fields, &c. W. Howitt. Phil. 1841. 2 v. 12°. 9564
and Sketches at Home and Abroad. Mrs. A. Jameson. New York, 1834. 2 v. 12°. 1445
Vitruvius, Pollio M. De Architectura. Lipsiæ, 1829. 16°. . . . 10855
Vivian Grey. B. D'Israeli. Philadelphia, 1837. 2 v. 12°. . . . 1665
The same. Philadelphia, 1847. 8°. 5
Voiage and Travaile of Sir J. Maundeville. London, 1839. 8°. . . 9456
Voice, Philosophy of. J. Rush. Philadelphia, 1833. 8°. . . . 754
Voices of the Night. H. W. Longfellow. Cambridge, 1840. 12°. . . 2373
from Prison. Boston, 1847. 16°. 2068
from the Mountains and from the Crowd. C. Mackay. Bost. 1853. 12°. 1985
Volney, C. F. Travels in Syria and Egypt, 1783–85. Dublin, 1788. 8°. . 9488
Voltaire, F. M. A. de. The Age of Louis XIV. Tr. London, 1752. 2 v. 8°. 11408
Antobiography. London, 1826. 16°. 7481
The same. London, 1829. 16°. 7746
Henriade and Essai. Paris, 1829. 16°. 2076
Histoire de Charles XII. Boston, 1823. 8486
The same. New York, 1835. 16°. 8449
The same. Tr. Otsego, 1811. 16°. 8465
The same. 11419
Letters of Certain Jews to. Tr. Philadelphia, 1795. 8°. . . 5376
Life. J. Condorcet. Tr. London, 1787. 8°. 7951
Philosophical Dictionary. London, 1824. 6 v. 12°. . . . 9017
The same. London, 1765. 8°. 5617
Universal History. Tr. Edinburgh, 1777. 4 v. 12°. . . . 7144
and Rousseau against the Atheists. Tr. J. Akerly. N. Y. 1845. 12°. 5672
The same. 5676
Volume of Varieties. C. Knight. London, 1844. 16°. 7173
Vose, J. Compendium of Astronomy. Boston, 1834. 12°. . . . 6091
Voyage Round the World. G. Anson. Edinburgh, 1776. 2 v. 12°. . 8722
Voyages Around the World, Historical Account of. London, 1774. 4 v. 8°. 9206
Around the World. New York, 1844. 12°. 5220
to Various Parts of the World. E. Fanning. New York, 1838. 12°. 8932
and Travels, Account of. A. Fisher, J. Prior, and others. London, 1820. 8 v. 8°. 9220

W.

Wacousta, or the Prophecy. Major Richardson. Phil. 1851. 2 v. 18°. . 1712
Wachsmuth, W. Historical Antiquities of the Greeks. Ox. 1837. 2 v. 8°. 6933
Waddington, G. History of the Church to the Reforma. Lon. 1833. 8°. 5095
Wade, J. Essay on Junius, with his Letters. London, 1850. 2 v. 12°. . 5430
Wages, Essay on the rate of. H. C. Carey. Philadelphia, 1835. 8°. . 10759
Wakefield, E. G. England and America Compared. New York, 1834. 8°. 9177
Wakefield, Priscilla. Domestic Recreation. Philadelphia, 1805. 18°. . 4945
Tour through the British Empire. Philadelphia, 1804. 12°. . . 11931
Waldegrave, Earl of. Memoirs, 1754–58. Philadelphia, 1822. 12°. . . 7133
Waldie, Miss. Rome in the 19th Century. New York, 1827. 2 v. 12°. . 9608
Waldo, S. P. Life and Character of S. Decatur. Hartford, 1821. 12°. . 8349
Lives of American Naval Heroes. Hartford, 1823. 8°. . . . 8493
Memoirs of A. Jackson. Hartford, 1819. 12°. 8091
The same. Hartford, 1818. 12°. 8397
Tour of J. Monroe through the Eastern and Northern States in 1817. Hartford, 1818. 12°. 8738
The same. Hartford, 1820. 12°. 9010
Walk About Zion. J. A. Clark. Philadelphia, 1836. 12°. . . . 5677
Walker, A. On Intermarriage. New York, 1836. 12°. . , . . 3376
Walker, G. The Three Spaniards. New York, 1827. 2 v. 18°. . . 4638
Walker, J. Dictionary of the English Language. 18°. 4939
Philosophy of the Eye. London, 1837. 8°. 3258
Walker, S. Memoirs of A. Tassoni. London, 1815. 12°. 7720
Wallace, W. Continuation of History of England. See. Macintosh, J.
Wallace, Sir Wm. Life. J. D. Carrick. London. 8°. 50
Wallace, H. B. Art and Scenery in Europe. Philadelphia, 1857. 8°. . 468
Wallenstein, A., Memoir of. G. W. Haven. Boston, 1837. 12°. . . 2021
Wallenstein's Camp. F. von Schiller. Tr. G. Moir. Bost. 1837. 12°. . 2021
Waller, E. Select Poems, with Life, by E. Sanford. Phil. 1819. 16°. . 2120
Walpole, H. The Castle of Otranto. Philadelphia, 1840. 12°. . . 659
Hist'l Doubts on the Life and Reign of Richard III. Lond. 1768. 4°. 11266
Letters of. N. Y. 1833. 2 v. 18°. 11111
Memoirs of the Reign of George III. Philadelphia, 1845. 2 v. 8°. 7535
Reminiscences and Walpoliana. Boston, 1820. 18°. 4627
Walpoliana. London. 2 v. 12°. 3704
Walpole, R. Life and Administration. W. Coxe. Lond. 1800. 3 v. 8°. . 7958
Walsh, R. Residence at Constantinople during the Greek and Turkish Revolutions. London, 1836. 2 v. 8°. 9394
Walsh R., Jr. American Review. vols. 1–4. Philadelphia, 1811. 8°. . 2962
Appeal from the Judgments of Great Britain respecting the United States. Philadelphia, 1819. 8°. 6712
The same. 10981
Social, Literary and Political Didactics. Philadelphia. 1836. 2 v. 8°. 2995
Walton, I. Lives of Donne, Wotton, Hooker, &c. N. Y. 1846. 2 v. 12°. 8705
and C. Cotton. Complete Angler. London, 1836. 12°. . . . 10154

Walton, W. C. Memoir. J. N. Danforth. New York, 1837. 12°. . . 8323
Wandering Jew, The. E. Suë. New York, 1846. 2 v. 8°. . . . 41
Wanderings of a Tailor. P. D. Holthaus. Tr. W. Howitt. Lond. 1844. 12°. 8724
Wanostrocht, French Grammar. Boston, 1824. 12°. 3032
Recteil Choisi de Traits Historiques. New York, 1833. 12° . . 4855
War, The Art of. N. Machiavel. Tr. London, 1730. 4°. . . . 11251
Elements of. I. Maltby. Boston, 1813. 12°. 3344
Evils and Remedies of. 8°. 741
of 1812. History of. C. J. Ingersoll. Philadelphia, 1846. 8°. . 7538
of 1812. History of. S. Perkins. New Haven, 1825. 8°. . . 6902
of 1812, Notices of. J. Armstrong. New York, 1840. 2 v. 12°. . 6799
of Montrose. J. Hogg. Philadelphia, 1836. 2 v. 12°. . . . 1447
Warburton, E. Hochelaga, or Eng. in the New World. N. Y. 1846. 12°. 9618
Warburton, W. Divine Legation of Moses. London, 1742. 3 v. 8°. . 5637
Julian, or a Discourse Concerning the Earthquake and Fiery Eruption at Jerusalem. London, 1750. 8°. 11390
Letters. New York, 1809. 8°. 9758
Ward, Caroline. National Proverbs in Five Languages. Lond. 1842. 16°. 3060
Ward, H. G. History of Mexico. London, 1829. 8°. 9100
Ward, J. Lectures on Oratory. London, 1759. 2 v. 12°. . . . 2982
Ward, R. P. Fielding, or Society. Philadelphia, 1838. 12°. . . . 1332
Ward, S. Life. W. Gammell. Boston, 1846. 12°. 8061
Ward, W. Farewell Letters. New York, 1821. 12°. 6509
View of the Hist., Lit. and Relig. of the Hindoos. Hart. 1824. 12°. 7124
Warden, W. Voyage of Napoleon to St. Helena. N. Haven, 1817. 12°. 8399
Wardlaw, R. Christian Ethics. New York, 1835. 12°. 5652
Ware, H., Jr. On the Formation of Christian Character. Camb. 1831. 12°. 6210
The same. 6212
Life. J. Ware. Boston, 1846. 2 v. 12°. 8321
Works. Boston, 1846. 2 v. 12°. 5724
Ware, W. Julian, or Scenes in Judea. New York, 1841. 2 v. 12°. . 1322
Letters from Palmyra. Boston, 1838. 2 v. 12°. 9039
Life of N. Bacon. Boston, 1844. 12°. 8055
Probus, or Letters from Rome in 3d Century. N. Y. 1838. 2 v. 12°. 9613
Sketches of European Capitals. Boston, 1851. 12°. 8890
Warlock, The. Philadelphia, 1836. 12°. 266
Warner, Anna. Hills of the Shatemuc. New York, 1857. 12°. . . 1224
Queechy. New York, 1852. 12°. 1276
Wide, Wide World. New York, 1852. 2 v. 12°. 1277
Warner, J. F. Rudimental Lessons in Music. New York, 1845. 16°. . 10252
Warner, R. Literary Recollections. London, 1830. 2 v. 8°. . . . 731
Warren, J. E. Vagamundo. New York, 1852. 12°. 9828
Warren, J., Life of. A. H. Everett. Boston, 1838. 12°. 8052
Warren, S. Merchant's Clerk, and other Tales. New York, 1836. 12°. 647
The same. 1622
Now and Then. New York, 1848. 12°. 1485
Wars of Montrose. J. Hogg. Philadelphia, 1836. 2 v. 12°. . . . 1447
Warton, J. Essay on Genius and Writings of Pope. Lond. 1806. 2 v. 8°. 156

Warton, J., and T. Lives and Poems. Philadelphia, 1823. 18°. . . . 2146
Warton, T. Observations on the Fairy Queen of Spenser. Lond. 1807. 8°. 1833
History of English Poetry. London, 1840. 3 v. 8°. 712
Warton. Life of Sir T. Pope. 8°. 8512
Washington, G., Essay on the Character of. F. Guizot. Tr. Bost. 1840. 12°. 4585
Eulogies and Orations on the Life and Death of. Bost. 1800. 8°. 8489
and his Generals. J. T. Headley. New York, 1847. 2 v. 12°. . 8648
Life. W. Irving. New York, 1856–9. 5 v. 12°. 8657
Life. J. Marshall. Philadelphia, 1804. 5 v. 8°. 8216
The same, with an Atlas. Philadelphia, 1833. 3 v. 8°. . 7514
Life. J. K. Paulding. (Two copies.) New York, 1835. 2 v. 16°. 8771
The same. New York, 1840. 2 v. 12°. 5885
Life. J. Sparks. Boston, 1839. 8°. 7554
Life. M. L. Weems. Philadelphia, 1809. 12°. 8386
Maps accompanying a Life. Philadelphia, 1807. 4°. . . . 11258
Official Letters to Congress. New York, 1796. 2 v. 8°. . . . 11114
Pictorial Life of. Philadelphia, 1845. 12°. 7740
Political Legacies. New York, 1800. 12°. 4935
Religious Opin. and Character of. E. C. McGuire. N. Y. 1836. 12°. 6130
Revolutionary Orders, from 1778–82. Ed. H. Whiting. N. Y. 1844. 8°. 10654
Vie de. A. N. Girault. Philadelphia, 1835. 16°. 8452
Writings with Life, by J. Sparks. (vol. 1 miss.) Bost. 1834. 11 v. 8°. 10904
and Adams, Administrations of. Ed. G. Gibbs. N. Y. 1846. 2 v. 8°. 10936
Washington, or Liberty Restored, a Poem. J. Northmore. Balt. 1809. 12°. 11882
Water Witch. J. F. Cooper. Philadelphia, 1831. 2 v. 12°. . . . 350
The same. Philadelphia, 1841. 12°. 1257
The same. Philadelphia, 1831. 2 v. 12°. 1354
Waterbury, J. B. Book for the Sabbath. New York, 1840. 12°. . . 5669
Watson, J. F. Annals of Philadelphia. Philadelphia, 1830. 8°. . . 7317
Watson, (Bp.) Richard., Anecdotes of the Life of. Phil. 1818. 8°. . . 8485
The same. 8494
Apology for the Bible. 1796. 16°. 6424
Apology for Christianity. Boston, 1835. 8°. 4287
Chemical Essays. Dublin, 1786. 8°. 147
Watson, Richard. Life of J. Wesley. New York, 1831. 12°. . . 8353
Watson, Robert. History of the Reign of Philip II, of Spain. London, 1779. 3 v. 18°. 8228
Watts, I. Advice to a Young Man on Entering the World. Bost. 1808. 12°. 3907
Improvement of the Mind. New Brunswick, 1813. 8°. . . . 6343
The same. Boston, 1826. 16°. 4598
Logic. London, 1790. 8°. 454
The same. Boston, 1819. 12°. 3028
Lyric Poems. Boston, 1790. 12°. 2454
Lyric Poems, with Memoir. R. Southey. London, 1834. 12°. . 5782
Philosophical Essays on Various Subjects. London, 1733. 12°. . 6057
Scripture History. Ed. R. C. Shimeall. Philadelphia, 1831. 12°. 6156
Select Poems, with Life, by S. Johnson. Philadelphia, 1819. 18°. 2135
Waverley. W. Scott. Boston, 1834. 12°. 268

Waverley. See also Scott, Sir W.
Novels, Beauties of. Boston, 1828. 24°. 1750
Wayland, F. Elements of Moral Science. New York, 1835. 8°. . . 6396
Occasional Discourses. Boston, 1833. 12°. 6139
The Limitations of Human Responsibility. Boston, 1838. 12°. . 6111
Political Economy, Elements of. New York, 1837. 8°. . . 10692
The Present Collegiate System. Boston, 1743. 12°. . . . 4597
University Sermons. Boston, 1849. 12°. 5405
Waylen, E. Ecclesiastical Reminiscences of the U. States. N. Y. 1845. 8°. 7604
Wayne, A. Life. J. Armstrong. Boston, 1834. 12°. 8071
Weal and Woe in Garveloch. Miss H. Martineau. Bost. 1833. 18°. . 1676
The same. 1677
Wealth of Nations. A. Smith. Dublin, 1784. 2 v. 8°. 11109
Webbe, C. The Man about Town. London, 1838. 2 v. 12°. . . 143
Glances at Life. London, 1836. 12°. 1464
Webber, C. Gold Mines of the Gila. New York, 1849. 12°. . . . 9011
Weber, J., and others. Memoirs of Maria Antoinette. Tr. R. C. Dallas.
London, 1805. 3 v. 8°. 7815
Webster, D., Diplomatic and Official Papers of. New York, 1848. 8°. . 10963
Speeches. Boston, 1835–43. 5 v. 8°. 10993
Works of. Boston, 1851. 6 v. 8°. 10998
Life and Character of. J. Banvard. Boston, 1853. 12°. . . 8072
Webster, J. Travels in Crimea, Turkey, Egypt, &c. Lond. 1830. 2 v. 8°. 9145
Webster, N. Elements of Useful Knowledge. Hartford, 1812. 12°. . 3364
The same. New Haven, 1806. 12°. 4932
History of Animals. New Haven, 1812. 12°. 10173
Political Papers. New York, 1802. 8°. 10051
Webster, P. Political Essays. Philadelphia, 1790. 8°. 11113
Webster, W. Life of G. Monk. Dublin, 1724. 12°. 8315
Weekes, R. Poems on Relig. and Hist'l Subjects. New York, 1820. 12°. 1961
Weekly Magazine. Edinburgh, 1771. 8°. 2241
Register. Ed. H. Niles. vols. 1–35. Baltimore, 1811–35. 8°. . 4642
Weems, M. L. Life of F. Marion. Philadelphia, 1831. 12°. . . . 8388
Life of G. Washington. Philadelphia, 1809. 12°. . . . 8386
Weil, G. Biblical Legends of the Mussulman. Tr. N. Y. 1846. 12°. . 6175
Wellington, Duke of. Life. F. L. Clarke, and W. Dunlap. N. Y. 1814. 8°. 8540
Memoirs. M. Sherer. Philadelphia, 1833. 2 v. 12°. . . . 8394
and Sir R. Peel. Lives. (Two copies.) New York, 1852. 12°. . 8392
Wendeborn, F. A. View of Eng. Tr. by the Author. Dub. 1791. 2 v. 12°. 8733
Wept of Wish-Ton-Wish, The. J. F. Cooper. Phil. 1831. 2 v. 12°. . 352
The same. Philadelphia, 1841. 12°. 1256
Wesley, J. Life. R. Southey. New York, 1820. 2 v. 8°. . . . 8516
Life. R. Watson. New York, 1831. 12°. 8353
Works. New York, 1831. 7 v. 8°. 5317
Wesley Family, Memoirs of. A. Clarke. London, 1836. 2 v. 8°. . . 6451
West, Plea for. L. Beecher. New York, 1835. 12°. 6176
Winter in the. C. F. Hoffman. (Two copies.) N. York, 1835. 12°. 8928
Indies. See Indies.

West Indies, and other Poems. J. Montgomery. Boston, 1810. 18°. . 2754
Sketches of. J. Hall. Philadelphia, 1835. 2 v. 12°. 9046
West, B. Life and Studies. J. Galt. Philadelphia, 1816. 8°. . . 8204
Western Clearings. Mrs. C. M. Kirkland. New York, 1846. 12°. . . 9856
States, Notes on. J. Hall. Philadelphia, 1838. 12°. 8927
Westminster Assembly of Divines, History of. W. M. Hetherington. New York, 1843. 12°. 5671
Review. vols. 20–23, 35–72. (Continued.) N. Y. 1834–59. 8°. . 4358
West Point, Guide Book to. New York, 1844. 16°. 9314
Westward Ho. J. K. Paulding. New York, 1832. 2 v. 12°. . . . 1017
Westwood, J. O. Modern Classification of Insects. London, 1839. 8°. . 10134
Wetherell, E. See Warner, A.
Wexford Insurrection, Narrative of. T. Cloney. Dublin, 1832. 12°. . 11359
Whale, the Sperm, Natural History of. T. Beale. London, 1839. 12° . 3923
Whales, Treatise on. Edinburgh, 1837. 12°. 10198
Whaling Cruise, Etchings of. J. R. Browne. New York, 1846. 8°. . 9370
Voyage, Incidents of. F. A. Olmsted. New York, 1841. 12°. . 9816
Wharton, F. Treatise on Theism. Philadelphia, 1859. 12°. . . . 6464
What Cheer, a Poem. J. Durfee. Providence, 1840. 12°. . . . 2341
Whately, R. Dissertation on the Rise, Progress, &c., of Christianity. Boston, 1853. 4°. 10035
Kingdom of Christ. New York, 1842. 12°. 5696
Life and Writings of W. Pinkney. New York, 1826. 8°. . . 8198
Rhetoric. Boston, 1841. 12°. 3401
The same. New York. 16°. 4973
The same. (Two copies.) Boston, 1836. 12°. 8047
Wheeler, H. G. History of Congress. New York, 1848. 2 v. 8°. . . 7600
Whelpley, S. Compend. of History from Earliest Times. N. Y. 1814. 8°. 6735
The Triangle. New York, 1832. 8°. 5600
Whewell, W. Astronomy, &c., in Reference to Nat. Theol. Phil. 1833. 12°. 6485
History of the Inductive Sciences. London, 1837. 3 v. 8°. . . 412
Philosophy of the Inductive Sciences. London, 1840. 2 v. 8°. . 410
Whim and its Consequences. G. P. R. James. New York, 1848. 8°. . 49
Whimsicalities. T. Hood. New York, 1852. 12°. 1193
Whipple, E. P. Essays and Reviews. Boston, 1851. 2 v. 12°. . . 855
Whirlwind Storms, with Replies to Dr. Hare. W. C. Redfield. New York, 1842. 8°. 5949
White, G. Natural History of Selborne. New York, 1842. 18°. . . 5919
The same. Ed. E. Jesse. London, 1851. 12°. 5474
White, G. S. Memoir of S. Slater, with a History of the Rise and Progress of Cotton Manufacture. Philadelphia, 1836. 8°. 7857
White, H. K., Beauties of. Boston, 1827. 16°. 2072
Remains, with Life. R. Southey. Boston, 1823. 2 v. 16°. . . 2070
The same. Philadelphia, 1811. 2 v. 12°. 2412
Rogers, and others. Poems. Philadelphia, 1830. 8°. 1882
The same. London, 1830. 8°. 1869
White, James. Adventures of John of Gaunt, Duke of Lancaster. Dublin, 1790. 2 v. 16°. 7777

White, Joseph. Sermons Preached at Oxford, 1784. 1785. 8°. . . . 5618
White, W. Memoirs of the P. E. Church of the U. S. N. Y. 1836. 8°. . 5369
White, C. Essays in Literature and Ethics. Boston, 1853. 8°. . . . 465
White Jacket. H. Melville. New York, 1850. 12°. 546
Whitefield, G. Autobiography. London, 1830. 16°. 7750
The same. 7485
Memoirs and Sermons. J. Gillies. Middletown, 1838. 8°. . . 5348
The same. London, 1772. 8°. 8539
and Edwards, Revival in the Times of. J. Tracy. Boston, 1842. 8°. 5026
Whittier, J. G. Lays of My Home, and other Poems. Boston, 1843. 12°. 2448
Legends of New England. Hartford, 1831. 12°. 650
Old Portraits and Modern Sketches. Boston, 1850. 12°. . . . 875
Panorama, and other Poems. Boston, 1856. 12°. 1996
Whittlesey, C., Life of. J. Fitch. Boston, 1845. 12°. 8058
Wiclif, J. Life. C. W. Le Bas. New York, 1832. 16°. 8740
Wide, Wide World. S. Warner. New York, 1852. 2 v. 12°. . . . 1277
Wieland, or the Transformation. C. B. Brown. New York, 1798. 12° . 341
The same. Boston, 1827. 12°. 1425
Wieland, C. M. Oberon. Tr. W. Sotheby. London, 1826. 12°. . . . 2054
Wiggers, G. F. Augustinism and Pelagianism. Tr. R. Emerson. New York, 1840. 8°. 6378
Wilberforce, W. Correspondence. Ed. R. I. and S. Wilberforce. Philadelphia, 1841. 2 v. 12°. 5688
Life. R. I. and S. Wilberforce. London, 1839. 5 v. 12°. . . . 8276
The same, abridged. Philadelphia, 1839. 12°. 8350
Practical View of the Prevailing Religious System. N. York. 16°. 5223
The same. Boston, 1799. 12°. 4579
Wilbraham, R. Travels in Caucasus, Georgia, &c. London, 1839. 8°. . 9139
Wilcox, C. The Age of Benevolence. New Haven, 1822. 16°. . . . 11292
Remains, with a Memoir. Hartford, 1828. 8°. 5361
Wild Flowers, or Pastoral Poetry. R. Bloomfield. London, 1826. 12°. 2028
Wild Irish Girl. Miss Owenson. New York, 1807. 12°. . . . 673
The same. 366
Wild Sports in Europe, Asia and Africa. E. Napier. Lond. 1844. 2 v. 12°. 794
Wilderness, The. New York, 1823. 2 v. 12°. 980
and the War Path. J. Hall. New York, 1846. 12°. 243
Wilhelm Meister's Apprenticeship. J. W. von Goethe. Tr. T. Carlyle. Boston, 1828. 3 v. 12°. 1723
Wilhelm, S. Memoirs. E. Bickersteth. New Haven, 1819. 16°. . . 8451
Wilkes, C. Narrative of the U. S. Exploring Expedition, 1838–42, with an Atlas. Philadelphia, 1845. 6 v. 8°. 10628
Wilkins, J. Principles of Natural Religion. London, 1678. 12°. . . 6515
Wilkinson, J. G. Manners and Customs of the Ancient Egyptians. First and second series. London, 1837. 6 v. 8°. 9116
Wilks, S. C. Christian Essays. Boston, 1829. 12°. 6183
Will, Doctrine of, from Consciousness. H. P. Tappan. N. Y. 1840. 12°. 5700
Doct. of, applied to Moral Agency. H. P. Tappan. N. Y. 1841. 12°. 5701

Will, Enquiry into the Freedom of. J. Edwards. London, 1775. 8°. . 5622
Examination of Edwards on Freedom of. J. Day. N. H. 1841. 12°. 5702
Review of Edwards on Freedom of. H. P. Tappan. N. Y. 1839. 12°. 5699
Self-Determining Power of. J. Day. New Haven, 1838. 12°. . 6088
Willard, Emma. History of the United States. New York, 1851. 8°. . 7234
William IV, Life and Reign. G. N. Wright. London, 1857. 2 v. 8°. . 7680
William of Malmesbury. Chronicle of English Kings. Lond. 1857. 12°. 5441
Williams, C. R. Tour through Island of Jamaica in 1823. Lond. 1829. 8°. 9102
Williams, E. New York Annual Register. New York, 1836. 12°. . 11884
Williams, Helen M. Politics of France in 1793, 4. Lond. 1795. 3 v. 12°. 6830
Williams, James, an American Slave, Narrative of. N. York, 1838. 16°. 7756
Williams, John. Missionary Enterprise in S. Sea Islands. N. Y. 1837. 8°. 9183
The same. 9184
Life of Alexander the Great. New York, 1839. 16°. . . . 8758
The same. New York, 1841. 12°. 5509
Williams, J. B. Memoirs of M. Henry. Boston, 1837. 12°. . . . 7724
Williams, R., Life of. W. Gammell. Boston, 1845. 12°. . . . 8056
Memoir. J. D. Knowles. Boston, 1834. 12°. 8358
Williams, R. F. Secret Passion. London, 1844. 3 v. 8°. . . . 131
Shakspeare and his Friends. Paris, 1838. 8°. 129
The same. London, 1844. 3 v. 8°. 134
Youth of Shakspeare. London, 1844. 3 v. 8°. 137
Williams, S. History of Vermont. Burlington, 1809. 2 v. 8°. . . 7684
Williams, S. W. Middle Kingdom. (Two copies.) N. Y. 1848. 2 v. 12°. 9585
Williams, W. R. Miscellanies. New York, 1850. 8°. 5053
Religious Progress. Boston, 1850. 12°. 5414
Lectures on the Lord's Prayer. Boston, 1851. 12°. . . . 5703
Willis, N. P. Melanie, and other Poems. Philadelphia, 1837. 12°. . . 2411
Paul Fane. New York, 1857. 12°. 203
Pencilings by the Way. Philadelphia, 1836. 2 v. 12°. . . . 8998
Poetical Sketches. Boston, 1827. 8°. 1923
Romance of Travel. New York, 1840. 12°. 1664
Willis, R. S. Our Church Music. New York, 1856. 12°. . . . 10147
Willison, J. Sacramental Meditations and Advices. Hartford, 1815. 16°. 6645
Williston, E. B. (Ed.) Eloquence of United States. 5 v. . . . , 11011
Wilmot, G. Life. J. Burnet. London, 1820. 16°. 7775
Willoughby, Lady. Diary of, in Reign of Charles I. N. Y. 1848. 12° 8332
The same. New York, 1845. 12°. . . . 9843
Willson, G. Practical Arithmetic. Canandaigua, 1838. 12°. , . 3037
Wilson, A. Life. W. B. O. Peabody, Boston, 1834. 12°. , , 8069
and C. L. Bonaparte. Treatise on Ornithology. Edin. 1831. 4 v, 12°. 10175
Wilson, D. Palæmon's Creed Revie'd and Exam'd. Lond. 1762. 2 v. 12°. 6596
Wilson, H. Memoirs of Wonderful Characters. New York, 1841. 8°. . 8509
Wilson, James, Lectures on Law, Philadelphia, 1804. 3 v. 8°. . . 11020
Wilson, John. Lights and Shadows of Scottish Life. Phil. 12°. . . 3973
Miscellanies. New York, 1842. 3 v. 12°. 493
Noctes Ambrosianæ, Philadelphia, 1843. 4 v. 12°. . , , 865
The same. New York, 1857. 5 v. 12°. 496

Wilson, J. M. Tales of the Border. New York, 1848. 5 v. 8°. . . . 1078
Wilson, P. Introduction to Greek Prosody. New York, 1811. 12°. . 3030
Wilson, R. T. History of the Brit. Expedition to Egypt. Phil. 1803. 8°. 7221
The same, abridged. London, 1803. 12°. 8735
Windham, W. Speeches in Parliament, with Life. T. Amyot. London, 1812. 3 v. 8°. 10688
Windings of the River of the Water of Life. G. B. Cheever. New York, 1849. 8°. 6361
Wines, E. C. Trip to Boston. Boston, 1838. 12°. 8739
Two Years and a Half in the Navy, 1829-31. Phil. 1832. 2 v. 12°. 9619
Wing and Wing. J. F. Cooper. Philadelphia, 1842. 2 v. 12°. . . . 965
Winslow, B. D. Sermons and Remains. New York, 1841. 8°. . . . 5062
Winslow, M. Sketch of Missions. Andover, 1819. 12°. 6500
Winter Evenings. V. Knox. London, 1823. 3 v. 12°. 3700
Studies and Summer Rambles in Canada. Mrs. A. Jameson. New York, 1839. 2 v. 12°. 8925
The same. 8996
Winterbotham, W. History of the Chinese Empire. London, 1795. 8°. 6749
Winthrop, J. Journal of Settlement of Massachusetts. Hartford, 1790. 8°. 10804
Wirt, W. Memoirs. J. P. Kennedy. Philadelphia, 1850. 2 v. 8°. . . 7858
Life of Patrick Henry. Philadelphia, 1817. 8°. 7508
The same. Ithaca, 1850. 8°. 7920
The same. New York, 1835. 8°. 8599
Wisconsin, &c., Geological Survey of. D. D. Owen. Phil. 1852. 2. v. 4°. 13115
Wise, Lieut., Los Gringos; View of Mexico, California, &c. N. Y. 1849. 12°. 8920
The same. New York, 1850. 12°. 8921
Wise Men of Gotham. New York, 1826. 12°. 1639
Wiseman, N. Lect. on the Doctrines of Cath. Church. Lond. 1844. 12°. 5675
Wit, Flowers of. Hartford, 1825. 16°. 4294
Specimens of. D. Jerrold. Boston, 1858. 12°. 1195
Witchcraft, Lectures on. C. W. Upham. Boston, 1831. 12°. 4912
Trial for, or the Amber Witch. W. Meinhold. Tr. N. Y. 1845. 16°. 1596
Salem. R. Calef. Boston, 1828. 18°. 4623
Witherspoon, J. Essays on the Doctrine of Salvation by Grace, &c. London, 1765. 3 v. 12°. 5811
The Nature and Effects of the Stage, &c. New York, 1812. 12°. . 4578
Withington, L. The Puritan. Boston, 1836. 2 v. 16°. 4316
The same. 4571
Wittich, W. Curiosities of Physical Geog. 2d series. Lond. 1846. 16°. 7189
Wolcott, J. Works of Peter Pindar. 8°. 2360
Wolfe, C. Remains and Memoir. J. A. Russell. London, 1842. 12°. . 6499
Wolfert's Roost. W. Irving. New York, 1855. 12°. 543
Wolff, J. Narrative of a Mission to Bokhara. New York, 1845. 8°. . 9415
Wollaston, W. The Religion of Nature delineated. London, 1750. 8°. . 5641
Wollstonecraft, Mary. View of the French Revolution. Phil. 1795. 12°. 6836
Wolsey, T., (Cardinal.) Life. London, 1831. 16°. 9932
Life. J. Galt. London, 1846. 12°. 5491
Woman in America. Mrs. A. J. Graves. New York, 1843. 12°. . . 5216

Woman, Character, Education, Prerogatives, &c., of. Boston, 1837. 12°. 3029
Historical Picture of. T. H. Cornish. London, 1838. 12°. . . 3902
Noble Deeds of. Philadelphia, 1836. 2 v. 12°. 4930
Sketches of. 12°. 11476
Woman's Friendship. G. Aguilar. New York, 1851. 12°. . . . 1201
Women, Biograph. Memoirs of Illust. Mary Hays. Lond. 1803. 6 v. 12. 8404
of England. Mrs. S. Ellis. Philadelphia, 1839. 2 v. 12°. . . 4875
The same. Philadelphia, 1843. 12°. 8914
Characteristics of. Mrs. A. Jameson. New York, 1833. 12°. . 4230
History of. W. Alexander. London, 1782. 2 v. 8°. . . . 6925
of the American Revolu. Mrs. E. F. Ellet. N. Y. 1848. 3 v. 12°. 8632
of Israel. G. Aguilar. New York, 1851. 2 v. 12°. . . . 1196
Memoirs of Celebrated. G. P. R. James. Phil. 1839. 2 v. 12°. . 8325
Wonderful Characters, Memoirs of. H. Wilson. New York, 1841. 8°. . 8509
Wonders of the World, the Hundred. C. C. Clarke. N. H. 1821. 12°. . 8718
of the Universe. New York, 1831. 8°. 417
Wondrous Tale of Alroy. B. D'Israeli. Philadelphia, 1847. 8°. . . 5
Wood Leighton, or a Year in the Country. Miss M. Howitt. Phil. 1837. 12°. 1210
Wood, N. Practical Treatise on Railroads. Philadelphia, 1832. 8°. . 6024
Wood, W. M. Wandering Sketches to South America, &c. Phil. 1849. 12°. 8917
Woodbury, L., Writings of. Boston, 1852. 3 v. 8°. 10968
Woodcraft. W. G. Simms. New York, 1854. 12°. 569
Woodfall, W. Parliamentary Reports from 1794–8. Lond. 1794–8. 17 v. 10496
Woodstock. W. Scott. New York, 1826. 2 v. 12°. 603
See also, Scott, Sir W.
Woodworth, S. Melodies, Duetts, &c. New York, 1831. 16°. . . 2487
Woolman, J. Life. New York, 1845. 12°. 3000
Woolrych, H. W. Memoirs of G. Jeffreys. London, 1827. 8°. . . 11315
The same. Philadelphia, 1852. 12°. 8003
Worcester, Mass., History of. W. Lincoln. Worcester, 1837. 8°. . . 7558
Magazine. (vols. 1, 2.) Worcester, 1826, 8. 2533
Worcester, J. E. Ancient and Modern History. Boston, 1852. 12°. . 11454
Words of a Believer. F. De La Memnais. New York, 1834. 16°. . . 6217
Words, Study of. R. C. Trench. New York, 1855. 12°. . . . 4518
Wordsworth, W., Memoirs of. C. Wordsworth. Boston, 1851. 2 v. 12°. 7708
Poetical Works. Boston, 1834. 4 v. 12°. 2405
The same. London, 1836. 6 v. 12°. 2045
The same. New Haven, 1836. 8°. 1796
Prelude, a Poem. New York, 1850. 12°. 2001
Yarrow Revisited, and other Poems. New York, 1835. 12°. . . 2371
Working Man, Memoirs of a. London, 1845. 18°. 7200
Workman, J. Essays and Letters. New York, 1809. 12°. . . . 11168
World, The. J. Ferguson. London, 1823. 2 v. 12°. 3022
The same. London, 1823. 3 v. 12°. 3686
The same. London, 1794. 2 v. 12°. 4243
Age of the. R. C. Shimeall. New York, 1842. 12°. . . . 3312
of Art and Industry. Illustrated. B. Silliman, Jr., and others.
New York, 1854. 4°. . . . .

World, Geographical and Hist. View of. J. Bigland. Bost. 1811. 5 v. 8°. 6918
Geographical View of. J. Goldsmith. New York, 1826. 12°. . 9016
History of the, to the Conquest of the Romans in the East. Sir W. Raleigh. Edinburgh, 1820. 6 v. 8°. 7629
History of, to 1840. C. von Rotteck. Tr. Phil. 1840, 1. 4 v. 8°. . 6943
Second Journey Around the. Ida Pfeiffer. New York, 1856. 12°. 9590
Sacred History of the. S. Turner. New York, 1839. 3 v. 12°. . 5533
The same. 6874
The same. vols. 1 and 2. New York, 1833. 16°. . . 6251
Voyage Around the. G. Anson. Edinburgh, 1776. 2 v. 12°. . 8722
Voyage Around. W. S. W. Ruschenberger. Phil. 1838. 8°. . 9422
Voyage Around, 1806–12. A. Campbell. New York, 1819. 12°. 9803
Voyages Around the. E. Fanning. New York, 1833. 8°. . . 9095
World's Laconics. T. Edwards. New York, 1856. 12°. 516
Wortley, Lady E. S. Travels in United States. New York, 1851. 12°. . 9826
Wounds, Nature and Cure of. J. Bell. Walpole, 1807. 2 v. 8°. . . 426
Wrangell, F. Expedition to the Polar Sea, in 1820–3. N. Y. 1841. 12°. 5920
Wrangham, F. Evidences of Christianity. Edinburgh, 1828. 16° . . 10004
Wraxall, N. W. Hist. of France, from 1574–1610. London, 1814. 6 v. 8°. 7614
Historical Memoirs of His Own Time. London, 1836. 4 v. 8°. . 7610
Posthumous Memoirs of His Own Time. Philadelphia, 1836. 8°. . 7628
The same. London, 1836. 3 v. 8°. 7607
Wreath, The, a Collection of English Poems. Hartford, 1824. 16°. . . 3061
The same. Hartford, 1836. 16°. 3066
Wright, G. N. Life and Reign of William IV. London, 1837. 2 v. 8°. . 7680
Life and Times of Louis Philippe. London. 8°. 7842
Wright, S. Life. J. S. Jenkins. Auburn, 1850. 12° 8618
Wright, T. Queen Elizabeth and Her Times. London, 1831. 2 v. 8°. . 7876
Wuthering Heights. Miss E. Brontë. New York, 1857. 12°. . . 181
Wyat, Sir T. Select Poems, with Life, by E. Sanford. Phil. 1819. 16°. . 2118
Wycherly, W., and others. Dramatic Works. London, 1840. 8°. . . 1794
Wykeham, W. Life. R. Lowth. London, 1758. 12°. 8625
Wyoming, History of. C. Miner. Philadelphia, 1845. 8°. . . 6940
The Poetry and Hist. of. W. L. Stone and others. N. Y. 1841. 12°. 2217
a Tale. New York, 1846. 8°. 7
Wyse, F. America, its Realities and Resources. London, 1845. 3 v. 8°. 9390

X.

Xenophon. Ed. C. D. Cleveland. Boston, 1834. 12°. 3318
Cyropædia. Græce et Latine. Ed. T. Hutchinson. Phil. 1806. 8°. 11349
The same. Tr. M. A. Cooper. New York, 1841. 2 v. 12°. 5262
The same. vol. 2. (Three copies.) N. Y. 1831–6. 16°. . 8741
The same. Tr. M. Ashley. Philadelphia, 1810. 8°. . . 11342
Opera. Lipsiæ, 1829, 4°. 3 v. 16°. 10827
The same. Tr. A. Cooper and others. Phil. 1836. 8°. . . 11265

Y.

Yalden, T. Select Poems, with Life, by E. Sanford. Phil. 1819. 16° . . 2130
Yale College, Annals of. E. Baldwin. New Haven, 1831. 8° . . . 11338
The same. 11350
Catalogues of, 1817–42, &c. New Haven. 8°. 9716
Class of 1797, Memories of. J. Day and J. Murdock. New Haven, 1848. 8°. 12091
Yale Literary Magazine. vols. 1–24. (Continued.) N. H. 1835–59. 8°. . 4445
Yankee among the Nullifiers. E. Elmwood. New York, 1833. 12°. . 1672
Land and the Iron Horse. D. March. Hartford, 1840. 12°. . . 2218
Yarrow Revisited. W. Wordsworth. New York, 1836. 12°. . . 2371
Year Book of Daily Recreation and Information. W. Hone. London, 1833. 8°. 9723
of Consolation. Mrs. F. K. Butler. New York, 1847. 12°. . . 5714
Yeast, a Problem. C. Kingsley. New York, 1851. 12°. . . . 1223
Yemasse, The. W. G. Simms. New York, 1835. 2 v. 12°. . . . 685
Yellow Plush Papers. W. M. Thackeray. New York, 1853. 12°. . . 960
Youatt, W. Treatise on the Horse. London, 1842. 18°. 5937
Young, A. Chronicles of the Pilgrim Fathers. Boston, 1841. 8°. . . 6947
Young, A. W. Science of Government. Rochester, 1843. 12°. . . 11191
Young, E. Night Thoughts. Hartford, 1830. 18°. 2069
The same. 2431
Young, G. Scriptural Geology. London, 1840. 8°. 5973
Young, J. R. Advantages of Mathematical Study. Lond. 1846. 12° . 3307
Young Christian, The. J. Abbott. New York, 1833. 12°. . . . 6556
The same. 5247
Christian, Advice to. New York, 1831. 18°. 4612
Duke, The. B. D'Israeli. New York, 1831. 2 v. 12°. . . . 1270
The same. 1021
Men, Thoughts for. H. Mann. Boston, 1850. 16°. . . . 4979
Men, Advice to. W. Cobbett. New York, 1831. 12°. . . . 4980
The same. 4988
Men, Lectures to. H. W. Beecher. (2 copies.) Salem, 1846. 12°. 1158
Men, Lectures to. S. Graham. Boston, 1847. 16°. 6221
Youngs, J. Rise and Progress of Methodism. New Haven, 1830. 12°. . 6502
Yucatan, Incidents of Travel in. J. L. Stephens. N. Y. 1843. 2 v. 8°. . 9774
Central America, &c., Travels in. J. L. Stephens. New York, 1841. 2 v. 8°. 9779
Rambles in. B. M. Norman. New York, 1853. 8°. 9106

Z.

Zanoni. E. L. Bulwer. New York, 1842. 2 v. 12°. 1476
Zenaida. F. Anderson. Philadelphia, 1858. 12°. 559
Zillah. H. Smith. New York, 1829. 2 v. 12°. 615
Zimmermann, E. A. W. Political Survey of Europe. Dublin, 1788. 12°. 7687

Zimmermann, J. G. Influence of Solitude. Tr. London, 1797. 8°. . 431
Zincali, or the Gypsies of Spain. G. Borrow. London, 1841. 2 v. 12°. 11410
Zinzendorf and other Poems. Mrs. L. H. Sigourney. N. York, 1835. 12°. 2327
Zöology, &c., Lectures on. W. Lawrence. Salem, 1828. 8°. . . 752
of New Xork. J. E. DeKay. Albany, 1842. 4°. . . . 13098
Zóphiël. M. Brooks. Boston, 1834. 12°. . . , ... 2435
Zouch, T., Life and Writings of. P. Sidney. New York, 1809. 4°. . 11260
Zschokke. Tales. Tr. P. Godwin. New York, 1845. 12°. . . . 9849
Zwingle, U. Life. J. G. Hess. Tr. Lucy Aiken. Lond. 1812. 12°. . 8306

CLASSIFIED INDEX.

BIOGRAPHY.

Collections, &c.

No.

Mod. Brit. Plutarch. W. C. Taylor. 8030
Napoleon and his Marshals. J. T. Headley. 8301
Navigators, Early. 5531
Necromancers. W. Godwin. 8673
Niebuhr, G. B., Reminiscences of. F. Lieber. 8333, 8361
Orators of the Age. 8704
Painters, the Old. Mrs. H. Lee. 10199
and Sculptors. Cunningham. 6253, 5519
Philosophers, Ancient, by Fenelon. 5914
and Actresses. 506
Piozziana. 8308
Players, Lives of the. J. Galt. 8683
Plutarch. See Gen. Index.
Poets, British. R. Bell. 9945
See also Gen. Index.
English. R. Bell. 9945
English. H. F. Cary. 8092
English. S. Johnson. 7780
French. H. F. Cary. 8093
Italian. H. Stebbings. 8707
Italian. L. Hunt. 1170, 9850
Roman. L. Crusius. 7450
Uneducated. R. Southey. 8281
Popes. Ranke. 7352, 5144
Portraits and Sketches. Whittier. 875
Prisoner of State. Andryane. 8285
Public Characters. H. Brougham. 8701
Queens of England. A. Strickland. 7984, 8292
of Scotland. A. Strickland. 8023
Scotsmen, Biog. Dict. of. Chambers. 8139
Scottish Poets, Lives of. 2730
Writers. D. Irving. 8252, 8627
Self-Taught Men. Edwards. 8336
Signers of Dec. of Ind. Sanderson. 11299
of Dec. of Ind. Goodrich. 8596
Statesmen of the Time of George III. Lord Brougham. 8497, 8601
Second series. 8327
Third series. 7204
Swiftiana. 4310
Taylor and his Generals. 8094, 8703
Travelers, Celebrated. St. John. 5854, 6276
Walton's Lives. 8705
Washington and his Generals. Headley. 8648
Women, Celebrated. James. 8325
of the Revolution. Mrs. Ellet. 8632
Wonderful Characters. H. Wilson. 8509
Worthies of England. T. Fuller. 7906
of Ireland. R. Ryan. 8168

Lives of

Abeillard and Heloisa. J. Berington. 11256
Adams, J., Life of. 10971
Adams, John Q., Life of. Seward. 8017
Addison, Joseph. Lucy Aikin. 8576
Joseph. E. Sanford. 2127
Aikin, John. Lucy Aikin. 7926
Akenside, M. S. Johnson. 2140
Alcuin. F. Lorenz. 7734
Alexander the Great. J. Williams. 8758, 5509
Ali Pacha. 11314
Allen, E. Autobiography. 7773

No.

Allen, E. H. Moore. 7781, 8378
E. J. Sparks. 8068
American Lady. Mrs. A. Grant. 8679
Americus Vespucius. C. E. Lester. 7826
Anne, of Austria. Mad. de Mottville. 7783
Anson, Lord George. J. Barrow. 7896
Arminius, James. N. Bangs. 8459
Armstrong, J. 2143
Arnold, Benedict. J. Sparks. 8070
Arnold, Thomas. A. P. Stanley. 8319
Ashmun, Jehudi. R. R. Gurley. 7899, 8138
Augustine, St. Confessions. 614, 6145
Babajee. H. Read. 5693
Bacon, Francis. 6013
Bacon, Nathaniel. W. Ware. 8055
Balboa, V. N. de. 7774
Bannister, J. J. Adolphus. 7911
Barnett, Francis. Autobiography. 8444
Barnum, P. T. Autobiography. 8340
Barri, Mad. Du. Autobiography. 7506
Beattie, James. W. Forbes. 8518
Beckwourth, J. P. T. D. Bonner. 8016
Bedell, Gregory T. S. H. Tyng. 8309, 8681
Beethoven, Ludwig Von. I. Moscheles. 8272
Belisarius. Lord Mahon. 8411
Benvenuto Cellini. Autobiography. Tr. Roscoe. 5424
Berkeley, Eliz., with Autobiography. 7964
Berri, Duchess of. Dermoncourt. 7917
Blacklock, T. 2147
Blair, Adam. 11886
Blake, Robert. 2133
Blessington, Countess, Memoir of. Madden. 8020
Blucher, (Marshal.) Gneisenau. 7952
Boleyn, Anne. Miss Benger. 8245
Bolingbroke, Lord. 10780
Bolivar, Simon. Holstein. 8221
Bonaparte, Lucien. Autobiography. 8360
Bonaparte, Napoleon. Abbott. 7530
Napoleon, by an American. 7510, 8215
Napoleon. M. V. Arnault. 7763
Napoleon. Bourrienne. 8211
Napoleon. W. Hazlitt. 8652
Nopaleon. De L'Ardeche. 8135
Napoleon. J. G. Lockhart. 6630, 5506, 6639
Napoleon. J. Rapp. 7875
Napoleon. W. Scott. 8212, 7511
See also Gen. Index.
Boon, D., Life. J. M. Peck. 8065
Bowditch, N. 8042
Boyse, S. 2143
Bracciolini, P. W. Shepherd. 11252
Brainerd, David. J. Styles. 7457
David. J. Edwards. 8513, 5228, 8447
David. W. B. O. Peabody. 8050
Brant, Joseph. W. L. Stone. 7938
Brewster, W. A. Steele. 7874
Brontë, Charlotte. Mrs. Gaskell. 8345
Brown, Charles B. 1425
Charles B. W. H. Prescott. 8068
Brown, Sir T. 384
Bruce, J. F. B. Head. 5904
Brummell, George. Capt. Jesse. 8190
Brydges, Edgerton. Autobiography. 7929
Buchanan, Claudius. H. Pearson. 5238, 8034

No.

Douglass, F. My Bondage and My Freedom. 8298
Drake, Cavendish, Dampier, &c. 8762, 6615, 5531
Drury, Robert. 7484, 7749
Dryden, John. W. Scott. 3934
John. E. Malone. 1888
John. E. Sanford. 2125
Dwight, Timothy. W. B. Sprague. 8056
Dwight, Timothy, Jr. Thompson. 7733
Edward, the Black Prince. James. 8402
Edwards, Jonathan. S. E. Dwight. 7913
Jonathan. S. Miller. 8050
Eldon, Lord. H. Twiss. 7850
Eliot, John. C. Francis. 8045
Eliot, Sir J. J. Forster. 9933
Ellery, William. E. T. Channing. 8047
Ellwood, Thomas. Autobiog. 7755, 7490
Emerson, Joseph. R. Emerson. 8313
Emmet, Robert. J. W. Burke. 7732
Emmet, Thomas A. Haines. 7782, 8401
Erasmus. C. Butler. 8151
J. Jortin. 8246
Eugene of Savoy, Prince. Autobiography. 7752, 7487, 7741
Evarts, Jeremiah. E. C. Tracy. 7830
Evelyn, John. W. Bray. 7972
Exmouth, Admiral. E. Osler. 8287
Fanshawe, Lady Anne. Autobiog. 8282
Fenelon, F. de. M. de Bausset. 7947
F. de. C. Butler. 8087
F. de. Mrs. Follen. 6142, 6490
Ferguson, J. Autobiography. 775, 7485
Fichte, J. G. W. Smith. 8011
Finlayson, George. T. S. Raffles. 9458
Finati, J. 8463
Fisk, Wilbur. J. Holdich. 7868
Fiske, N. W., Memoir of. Humphrey. 6152
Fitch, John. C. Whittlesey. 8058
Fitzgerald, Edward. T. Moore. 8099
Follen, Charles. 5397
Foote, Samuel. W. Cooke. 8390, 8417
Foster, John. Ryland. 5183, 8255, 8570
Fouche, Joseph, (Duke of Otranto.) 8534
Fox, C. J. J. B. Trotter. 7459, 8250
C. J. Memoirs and Correspondence. Lord Russell. 8006
Fox, H. W. G. T. Fox. 8637
Francis I. J. Bacon. 7519
Franklin, Benj. Autobiog. 8423, 5552, 4570
Benj. Memoirs. 6029
Benj. J. Sparks. 6282
Frederica, Sophia Wilhelmina. Auto. 7498
Frederick the Great. J. G. Zimmerman. 8074
the Great. T. Carlyle. 8655
Frederick II. Lord Dover. 5857, 6632
Frederick III. J. Tower. 8573
Fremont, J. C. Bigelow. 8650
Frey, J. S. C. F. 8450
Fuller, A. A. G. Fuller. 5196
Fulton, Robert. C. D. Colden. 8202, 8484
Robert. J. Renwick. 8052
Fuseli, H. J. Knowles. 372
Gallaudet, Tribute. Barnard. 11311
Galt, John. Autobiography. 8097
Gardiner, James. P. Doddridge. 7776
Gates, Thomas R. 6602
Gay, J. E. Sanford. 2129

No.

Genlis, Madame de. Autobiography, 8514
George III. W. Belsham. 8224
George IV. G. Croly. 6274, 5517
Gerry, Elbridge. J. T. Austin. 7921
Gibbon, Edward. Autobiography. 7493
Edward. 444
Gifford, William. Autobiog. 7755, 7490
Girard, Stephen. S. Simpson. 8416
Godolphin, Mrs. Life of. J. Evelyn. 8639
Godwin, Mrs. M. W. 8379
Goethe, J. W. Von. Autobiog. 11377, 5158
Goldini, C. Autobiography. 7502
Goldsmith, O. 3635
Oliver. T. Campbell. 2142
Oliver. W. Irving. 5894, 536
Oliver. J. Prior. 8175
Good, John M. O. Gregory. 7726
Gorton, Samuel. J. M. Mackie. 8057
Gower, J. E. Sanford. 2118
Graham, Mrs. Isabella. 7739
Grammont, Count. A. Hamilton. 11312
Grant, Mrs. A. P. Grant. 8608
Mrs. J. S. W. W. Campbell. 8385
Granville, G. E. Sanford. 2130
Grattan, H. 7860
Gray, T. S. Johnson. 2141
Green, M. E. Sanford. 2130
Greene, Nathaniel. G. W. Greene, 8062
Gregory, O. J. M. Good. 7726
Gresham, Thomas. 7208
Griffin, Edmund D. W. B. Sprague. 5059
Edmund D. McVicar. (9477) 9474
Grimaldi, Joseph. C. Dickens. 8264
Grotius, Hugo. C. Butler. 8160
Guyon, Mad. 4610
Mad. T. C. Upham. 8580
Gustavus Adolphus. W. Harte. 7523
Hale, Matthew. G. Burnet. 7775
Hall, J. E. Sanford. 2119
R. O. Gregory. 5373
Halyburton, Thomas. 8341
Hamilton, Alex. J. Renwick. 5905
Alex. J. C. Hamilton. 7810
Hamilton, Lady Emma. 8257
Hampden, John. J. Forster. 9934
Hardwicke, P. R. Cooksey. 7797
Harrison, William H. J. Hall. 7768
Harte, W. 2141
Hausset, Mad. du. 8080
Hayden and Mozart. Bombet. 8043
Heber, Richard. Mrs. Heber. 7852
Hemans, Mrs. F. H. Chorly. 8575
Henry II. Lord Lyttleton. 8541
Henry IV. G. P. R. James. 8584
Henry the Great, 7961
Henry, Matthew. J. B. Williams. 7724
Henry, Patrick. W. Wirt. 7920, 7508, 8599
Patrick. A. H. Everett. 8053
Herbert, Edward, Lord. Autobiography. 7752, 7487, 8434
Herodotus. Dahlmann. 8254
Hill, Rowland. E. Sidney. 8368
Rowland. Porter. 7767
Hobart John H., (Bishop.) Berrian. 5111
Hogg, J. Bloodgood. 8648
Holberg, L. Autobiography. 7491
Homer, William B. E. A. Park. 5390
Homer, F. 8356

	No.
Shaftesbury, Earl of. G. W. Cooke.	7900
Sharp, George. C. Stuart.	8420
Shaw, C.	2143
Sheil, Richard L. T. McNevin.	10711
Shenstone, William. E. Sanford.	2136
Sherburne, Andrew. Autobiog.	7728, 8032
Sheridan, Mrs. Frances. Miss Lefanu.	8258
Sheridan, Richard B. T. Moore.	8351
See also General Index.	
Sherlock, T. T. S. Hughes.	5752
Shipp, J. Autobiography.	8469
Sidney, Algernon.	10644
Sidney, Philip.	8642
Philip. T. Zouch.	11260
Silvio Pellico.	1284, 8729
Slater, Samuel. G. S. White.	7857
Smith, Adam.	5189
Smith, (Capt.) John. G. S. Hilliard.	8069
(Capt.) John. W. G. Simms.	8338
Smith, Margaret. Journal.	3919
Smith, Miss Elizabeth. Bowdler.	8380
Smith, Mrs. Sarah L. E. W. Hooker.	8357
Smith, Sidney. Lady Holland.	7998
Smith, Sir S. E. Howard.	8143
Smollet, T.	2145
Somers, J. R. Cooksey.	7797
Somerville, W. E. Sanford.	2130
Southey, R. By his Son.	8132
Spencer, S. T. Raffles,	8075, 8090
Spenser, E. J. S. Hart.	29
Spurzheim. A. Carmichael.	8682
Stark, J. E. Everett.	8068
Sterling, J. T. Carlyle.	8002
Stewart, V. A. H. R. Howard.	8334
Stiles, E. A. Holmes.	8605
E. J. L. Kingsley.	8058
Stilling, Heinrich. Autobiography.	6
Stirling, Lord. W. A. Duer.	7871
Lord. E. Sanford.	2119
Strafford, Earl of. Forster.	9933
Sullivan, John. O. W. B. Peabody.	8055
Sully, M. de Bethune.	8523
Summerfield, John. J. Holland.	8157
Swartz, C. F.	5248
C. F. H. Pearson.	8619
Swedenborg, Emanuel. N. Hobart.	8044
Swift, Jonathan.	3945
Jonathan. W. Scott.	3935
Jonathan. D. Swift.	8270
Tai-Ping-Wang. Mackie.	8667
Talleyrand.	8172
C. K. McHarg.	8643
Tamerlane.	8095
Tasso, Torquato. J. H. Wiffen.	2457
Tassoni, A. S. Walker.	7720
Taylor, John. Autobiography.	8200
Taylor, Jeremy. R. Heber.	7715
Taylor, James B. Rice.	8626, 5237, 7762
Tecumseh and his Brother. Drake.	8344
Temple, William.	10491
William. T. P. Courtenay.	7840
Thelwall, J. Mrs. Thelwall.	7924
Thomas, E. S.	11395
Thomason, Thomas T. J. Sargent.	8324
Thomson, J.	2433
J. E. Sanford.	2134, 2397
Thoresby, R.	8505
Tickell, T. E. Sanford.	2130
Tindal, W.	5663
Tone, T. W. Autobiography.	7498
Tooke, John Horne. A. Stephens.	8232
Trenck, Frederick. Autobiog.	433, 8437
Trumbull, J. J. W. Stuart.	11316
Trumbull, J. (Col.) Autobiog.	7577
Uncas and Miantonomoh. Stone.	7760
Underhill, U.	8448
Urquhart, John. W. Orme.	7757
Van Buren, Martin. Holland.	8290, 8337
Van Schaack. H. C. Van Schaack.	8131
Vane, Sir Henry. C. W. Upham.	8071
Vane, Sir H., The Younger. Forster.	9935
Vaux, J. H. Autobiography.	7492
Vidocq, E. F. Autobiography.	7504
Voltaire, F. M. A. de. Autobiog.	7481, 7746
F. M. A. de. Condorcet.	7951
Waldegrave, Earl of. Autobiography.	7133
Wallace, Sir W. J. D. Carrick.	50
Wallenstein, A. G. W. Haven.	2021
Waller, E. E. Sanford.	2120
Walpole, Robert. W. Coxe.	7958
Walton, William C. Danforth.	8323
Ward, Samuel. W. Gammell.	8061
Ware, Henry. J. Ware.	8321
Warrren, Joseph. A. H. Everett.	8052
Washington, George.	8489
George. F. Guizot.	4585
George. W. Irving.	8657
George. J. Marshall.	8216, 7514
George. E. C. McGuire.	6130
George. Paulding.	8771, 5885
George. J. Sparks.	7554
George. M. L. Weems.	8386
George, Pictorial Life of.	7740
Watson, R.	8485, 8494
Watts, Isaac. S. Johnson.	2135
Isaac. R. Southey.	5782
Wayne, A. J. Armstrong.	8071
Webster, D. Banvard.	8072
Wellington, Duke of. M. Sherer.	8394
See also General Index.	
Wesley, John. R. Southey.	8516
John. R. Watson.	8353
Wesley Family. A. Clarke.	6451
West, Benjamin. J. Galt.	8204
White, Henry Kirke. Southey.	2070, 2412
Whitefield, George. Autobiog.	7750, 7485
George. J. Gillies.	5348, 8539
Wiclif, John. C. W. Le Bas.	8740
Wilberforce, Wm. By his Sons.	8276, 8350
Wilcox, Carlos.	5361
Wilhelm, Simeon. E. Bickersteth.	8451
William IV. G. N. Wright.	7680
Williams, Roger. J. D. Knowles.	8358
Roger. W. Gammell.	8056
Wilmot, J. G. Burnet.	7775
J. E. Sanford.	2124
Willoughby, Lady. Diary.	8332, 9843
Windham. W. T. Amyot.	10688
Wirt, W. Kennedy.	7858
Wilson, A. W. B. O. Peabody.	8069
Wolfe, C. J. A. Russell.	6499
Wolsey, (Cardinal) T.	9932
Cardinal T. J. Galt.	5491
Woolman, J.	3000
Wordsworth, W. By his Son.	7708
Working Man, a.	7200

	No.
Wright, S. J. S. Jenkins.	8618
Wykeham. W. Lowth.	8625
Yalden, T. E. Sanford.	2130
Zwingle, Ulrich. J. G. Hess.	8306

DRAMATIC LITERATURE.

COLLECTIONS, WORKS ON THE DRAMA, &c.

Annals of the Stage. J. P. Collier. 1109
Biographia Dramatica. 8856
British Drama. 1884
  Theatre. 2459
Defense of the Drama. 4315
Dramatic Art and Literature. A. W. Schlegel. 32, 94, 5194
  Literature. W. Hazlitt. 4588
  Miscellanies. T. Davies. 841
  Poets, Specimens of. 9845
English Comic Writers. Hazlitt. 87
English Stage. W. Hazlitt. 95
French Drama. Mad. de Bury. 6884
French Stage. T. Hook. 1135
Hindu Theater. (Trans.) 1826
Immolay. 2414
Lives of the Players. J. Galt. 8683
Living Plays. 2780
London Stage. 1929
Players, Thirty Years Among. Kohl. 9090
Plays. 2496
Plays. 11888
Reminiscences of the Stage. Kelly. 8488
Sardanapalus. 2081
Select Old Plays. Ed. Dodsley. 2228
Stage, Character of. J. Styles. 4568
Stage, Nature, &c., of. Witherspoon. 4578
Theatre, American, Hist. of. Dunlap. 409
Theatre of the Greeks. 10078

DRAMATIC WORKS OF

Æschylus. Tr. R. Potter. 3062, 5261, 2117
Aristophanes. Tr. T. Mitchell. 1846
  Tr. C. A. Wheelwright. 2113
Bacon, Miss D. Bride of Ft. Edward. 1569
Baillie, Joanna. 1820
Barrett, Miss E. B. 2013
Beaumont and Fletcher. 1804
  and Fletcher. Selections from. 5169
Bulwer, E. L. Duchess De La Valliere. 2392
  E. L. Not so Bad as We Seem. 340
  See also General Index.
Burgoyne, J. 1574
Butler, Mrs. F. 2391
Byron, Lord. Sardanapalus. 2319
Colman, G. 2114
Congreve, W. 1794
Dryden, J. 3047
Euripides. Tr. R. Potter. 3074
  See also General Index.
Farquhar, G. 1794
Fielding, H. 3594
Foote, S. 4312
Ford, J. 1786
Goethe, G. W. Von. 5160
Goethe, Faust. Tr. T. Anster. 2332
Goethe. Goetz of Berlichingen. 2735
Goldsmith, O. 3639
Haynes, J. 3071
Hillhouse, J. A. 1957
Hillhouse, J. A. Hadad. 1894, 1922
  J. A. Percy's Masque. 2458
James, G. P. R. 2409
Jonson, Ben. 2368
Knowles, J. S. Complete Works. 1907
  J. S. Select Works. 2482
  J. S. Love Chase. 2393
Körner, C. T. 8354
Lillo, G. 11982
Massinger, P. 1786
  The same. 6241
Milman, H. H. 2091
More, Hannah. 2269
Proctor, B. W. 1990
Schiller, F. 5155
Shakspeare, W. 1807
  See also General Index.
Sheridan, R. B. 5150
Sophocles. Tr. T. Francklin. 5271
  Tr. R. Potter. 1866
  See also General Index.
Talfourd, T. N. 2053
  T. N. Athenian Captive. 2334
Taylor, H. Edwin the Fair. 2089
  H. Philip Van Artevelde. 2484
Terentius. Tr. G. Colman. 2114
  Vanburgh, J. 1794
Wycherley, W. 1794

EDUCATION AND REFORM.

Academician. A. and J. W. Pickett. 3125
American Annals of Education. 2193
  Colonization Society. W. Jay. 11119
  Institute, Boston. 11679
  Institute, Lectures of. N. Y. Reports. 10069
Bacchus, Prize Essay. Grindrod. 514
Bennett's Letters to a Young Lady. 11283
Boarding School, The. 3974
Capital Punishment. G. B. Cheever. 6475
Catalogue. See General Index.
Christian Education. T. Babington. 6550
Collegiate System. F. Wayland. 4597
Colonization and Christianity. Howitt. 5635

ENCYCLOPÆDIAS AND PERIODICALS.

No.

Dictionary of Arts, &c. Ure. 8811
Biographical. Rose. 8834
of Dates. Putnam. 8885
of Lit. and Authors. Allibone. 9673
of Mechanical Science. 10918
Eclectic Magazine. 4677
Review. 3561
Edinburgh Annual Register. 3234
Edinburgh Encyclopedia, with Plates. 8472
Monthly Review. 3813
Review. 1802–34. 3754
Review. 1834–59. 4012
Emporium of Arts and Sciences. 2966
Encyclopædia Americana. 8818
of Antiquities. T. D. Fosbroke. 8793
of Arts, &c. 8112
Britannica. 10035
of Geography. Murray. 10915
Supplement. 10923
of Science and Lit. Brande. 8801
Farmer's Magazine. 3088
Foreign Quarterly Review. 4043
Foreign Review. 3556
Gazeteer of U. S. Morse. 9322, 9326
Universal. 9303
Gentleman's Magazine, The. 3402
Geographical Dictionary. Darby. 8899
Dictionary. McCulloch. 8805
Graham's Magazine. 3110
Gray's-Inn Journal. 4268
Harper's Magazine. 3715
Harvard Magazine. 12095
Home Missionary, The. 2245
Household Words. Dickens. 2208
Journal of Health. 11660
Knickerbocker, The. 4384
Literary Portfolio. 11681
Literary World. 3096
London Quarterly Review. 4326
London and Westminster Review. 4354
Memoirs of Libraries. 9720

No.

Memories of Literature. 3250
Metropolitan Magazine. 3112
Microcosm, The. 2244
Microscope, The. 11655
Mirror, The. 2493, 3690, 4270
Mirror Library. 1075
Missionary Herald. 2503
Monthly Review. 2590
Museum of Foreign Lit. and Science. 3221
Museum of Lit. and Hist. Register. 3247
Musical Cyclopædia. 10249, 10251
National Calendar. 1831, 4556
New England Magazine. 2942
New Englander. 4469
New York Annual Register. 11884
New York Review. 4090
New York State Gazetteer. 9123
Niles's Weekly Register. 4642
North American Review. 4100
North British Review. 4059
Parliamentary Register. 11095
Penny Cyclopædia. 9675
Penny Magazine. 3098
Philosophical Dictionary. 9017, 5617
Portfolio, The. 2949
Putnam's Monthly Magazine. 3738
Quarterly Review. 2814
Reflector, The. 2971
Religious Magazine. 2243
Retrospective Review. 4193
Southern Literary Messenger. 2155
Southern Review. 2955
Standard Library Cyclopædia. 5129
State Register. 4941
Universal Magazine of Knowledge and Pleasure. 3821
Weekly Magazine. 2241
Westminster Review. 4358
Worcester Magazine. 2533
Yale Literary Magazine. 4446

ESSAYS AND LITERARY MISCELLANIES.

Adams, Miss A. Journal and Correspondence. 4880
Adams, Mrs. A. Letters. 3377
Addison, J. Works of. 3640, 59
See also General Index.
Addisonia. 4308
Advancement of Society. Douglas. 6144
Adventurer, The. 3683, 11932
Age of the World. Shimeall. 3312
Amenities of Lit. D'Israeli. 721, 512
American Literature. Rice. 515
Literature. Simms. 854
Ancient Literature and Art. 470
Ancients, Essays, &c., of. Bacon. 3356
Anecdotes, Literary. 11697
Anne Queen, Court of. 7866
Antiquities of Great Britain. 1183, 5437
of Nations. 11298
Arnold, T. Miscellanies. 58
Bacon, F. Essays. 4631
See also General Index.
Bancroft. Miscellanies. 35

Barbauld, Mrs. A. L. Works. 4865
Beauties of Chesterfield. 4620, 11150
Bee, The. O. Goldsmith. 4629
Bibliomania. 425
Bollingbroke's Letters. 10779
Book of Conversation. 4965
Book for a Corner. Hunt. 1187
Boston Book. 700
British Essayists. 3664
British Prose Writers. 4627
Brookiana. 4306
Brougham, H. Miscellanies. 803
Bryant. Miscellanies. 4289
Bulwer, E. L. Miscellanies. 471, 478
Burke, E. Correspondence. 10701
Burns, R. Letters. 4628
Burns and Clarinda. Correspond. 4222
Byron, G. G. Correspondence. 3383
Cambridge, Conversations at. 3367
Carey, M. Miscellanies. 118
Carlyle, T. Essays. 844, 26
Chalmers, T. Miscellanies. 711

FINE AND USEFUL ARTS.

HISTORY.

No.

Mankind, Phys. Hist. of. Prichard. 405, 735
Marchmont Papers. 6686
Massachusetts Bay. Minot. 7372
  Bay, Colony of. Young. 7271
  Hist. of. Bradford. 11329
  History. Hutchinson. 6755
  Hist. Collections of. Barber. 6690
  Rebellion in. G. R. Minot. 6927
  Settlement of. Winthrop. 10804
Medes, History of. 7032
Mesopotamia and Assyria. Fraser. 5209
Methodism. J. Young. 6502
Mexican Revolution. Robinson. 9447
Mexican War, History of. 7096
Mexico, Conquest of. Prescott. 6949
  History of. Clavigero. 7210
  History of. Mayer. 7253
  History of. H. G. Ward. 9100
Michigan, History of. Lanman. 7244, 5913
  Hist. and Scientific Sketches. 7427
Middle Kingdom. Williams. 9585
Miller's Retrospect of 18th Century. 6923
Moguls and Tartars, History of. 7050
Monachism, British. Fosbroke. 5007
Moors in Spain, History of. Bourke. 11257
  in Spain, History of. Florian. 5253
Moreau, V. Campaigns. 8079
Naples, History of. 7070
  under Spanish Dominions. 5180
Napoleon Dynasty. 7845
Napoleon's Campaign in Russia, Events that followed. 6824
Nat. Philosophy, History of. Powell. 9955
Naval Battles. 11446
  History, English. Southey. 7449, 11478, 9927
  History, English. Brenton. 7261
  History of U. S. Cooper. 7639
Nestorians, or Lost Tribes. Grant. 6798, 7104
Netherlands, History. Grattan. 5836, 9988
  Revolt of. Schiller. 5154, 11469
  Troubles in the. Romans. 7437
New England, History of. Elliott. 7274
New Hampshire, History. Belknap. 6781
New Haven Colonial Records. 7240
  Haven Colony. Lambert. 11452, 7423
  Haven, Hist. Disc. Bacon. 7638
  Haven, Hist. Disc. Kingsley. 6684
New Jersey, Historical Collections. Barber and Howe. 6689
New London, History of. 12049
New Netherlands. O'Fallaghan. 7242
New York, Border War of. 11460, 11865
  York, Doc. History of. 10455
  York, History, in 1670. 11318
  York History. F. S. Eastman. 11468
  Political History. Hammond. 6961
North Carolina, Sketches of. Foote. 6952
Northmen in New England. Smith. 7107
Norwich, History. Miss Caulkins. 6768
Nova Scotia, History. Haliburton. 6931
  Scotia, History of. Martin. 5822
Nubia and Abyssinia. Russell. 6626, 8766
Ohio, Hist. Collections of. Howe. 7606
Ojibway Nation. Copway. 7106
Old Regime and the Revolution. De Tocqueville. 7393

No.

Origines. Drummond. 7586
Oregon, History of. T. Twiss. 7092
Oregon and California, History of. R. Greenhow. 7539
Orleans, House of. Taylor. 8000
Othman Empire, History of. 7056
Ottoman Empire, History of. Upham. 10015
Palestine, History. M. Russell. 5529, 6620
Paraguay, Reign of De Francia. 1551
  in the Reign of De Francia. 6736
Patriarchs, History of. H. Hunter. 8528
Paris and its Historical Scenes. 6204
Parthians, History of. 7087
Party, History of. 1666, 1832, 7624
Peloponnesian War. Thucydides. 7555, 5279
Peninsular War. R. Southey. 6656
  War, Annals of. Hamilton. 9524, 6803
  War, History of. Napier. 7559
  War, Memorials of. 10006
Pennsylvania, Hist. of. T. F. Gordon. 11362
  History. Proud. 6714
  Historical Collections of. 7251
  Hist. of Insurrec. in. Findley. 6767
Pergamus, History of. 7037
Persia, History of. J. B. Fraser. 6272, 5882
  History of. Hanway. 10921, 7051
  Sketches of. 9616
Persians, History of. 7032
Peru, Conquest of, by the Spaniards. 10020
  Hist. of Conquest of. Prescott. 7257
Philadelphia, Annals of. Watson. 7317
Philosophy, Ancient, Hist of. Ritter. 6315
  History of. 5915
  History of. W. Enfield. 6400
  History. Tennemann. 6372
Pilgrims, Chronicles of the. Young. 6947
Pirates, History. C. Johnson. 8374, 8376
Pitcairn's Island. J. Barrow. 6616, 5532
Plymouth, History of. J. Thatcher. 6802
Poetry, English, History. Wharton. 712
Poland, History of. 11377
  History of. 7076
  History of. S. A. Dunham. 9909
  Hist. of. J. Fletcher. 6622, 5527, 8761
  History of the Revolution in. 6964
Polynesia, History. M. Russell. 5210
Polynesian Researches. Ellis. 9295
Pompeii. 6205, 9629
Popery, History of. 6127
Popish Plot, History. 6601
Portugal, Civil Wars in. 6801
  History of. 7064
  History. S. A. Dunham. 9874, 5829
  Traits and Traditions of. 9288
Prideaux's Connexions. 6328
Protestants in France. 7265
Prussia, History of. 7077
Puritanism. Thomas W. Coit. 5775, 6187
Puritans, History. D. Neal. 7556, 5337
  and their Principles. E. Hall. 5020
Quebec, Campaigns against. Henry. 6835
Queen's County, L. I. Rev. Hist. of. 7420
Random Recollections of House of Commons. 8663
Rebellion, English. Clarendon. 6980
Rebellions in Scotland, 1638-60. Chambers. 10007
  in Scotland, 1689 and 1715. 10017

MATHEMATICS.

No.
Algebra. Davies. 3933
German. Michelsen. 4896
Key to Colburn's. 3313
Treatise on. Simpson. 3280
Arithmetic, Algebra, &c. Hopkins. 5096
Higher. Thomson. 3335
Treatise on. Lardner. 9956
Wilson. 3037
Calculus. Elementary. Morgan. 5096
Chemistry. 5099
Conic Sections. Dutton. 424
Engineering. Mahan. 11671
Geometry, Algebraical. 5007
Euclid. 11682
Plane, Solid, &c. 5097

No.
Geom. and Trigonometry. Legendre. 9730
Logarithms. F. Callet. 11666
Longitude Tables. Margett. 11988
Mathematical Repository. Leybourne. 2698
Study, Advantages of. Young. 3307
Mathematics, Philosophy of. 1067
Study of. Hopkins. 5096
Progress of. Playfair. 10035
Mechanics. Lardner and Kater. 5840, 9958
Renwick. 11668
Illustrations of. Moseley. 5256
Practical Geometry. Bonnycastle. 4560
Navigator. Bowditch. 1054
Surveying and Plane Trigonometry. 2688
Trigonometry. W. Hopkins. 5096

MEDICAL SCIENCE.

Adaptation of Nature to Man's Phys. Condition. T. Kidd. 6486
Anatomy, Introduction to. Paxton. 1068
Pathological, Treatise on. 11672
and Physiology. Cutter. 3920
System of. 2687
Animal Mechanism and Physiology. Griscom. 5543
Blindness. J. Kitto. 6883
Complex of Human Species. Smith. 3315
Constitution of Man. G. Combe. 4577
Deafness. J. Kitto. 7195
Digestion and Dietetics. A. Combe. 4974
Gastric Juice, &c. Beaumont. 401
Diseases. Sydenham. 9763
Diseases of the Mind. B. Rush. 2696
Dyspepsia, Forestalled and Resisted. Hitchcock. 4532, 3395
Economy of Health. J. Johnson. 4968
Examination of the Objections to Gall and Spurzheim. 4888
Eye, Philosophy of the. J. Walker. 3285
Health, Influence of Ment. Cultivation on. Brigham. 3287, 4886, 4877, 3924
Health and Long Life. Cornaro. 4622
and Longevity. 4621

House I Live in. W. A. Alcott. 4893
Human Voice. J. Rush. 754
Hydropathy, Hand Book of. Shew. 4521
Intermarriage. A. Walker. 3376
Man, Observations on. D. Hartley. 6341
Mechanism of the Hand. C. Bell. 6484
Medical Delusions. Hooker. 3308
Nervous System. J. A. Smith. 2989
Notes of a Professional Life. 9729
Philosophy of Living. C. Ticknor. 5887, 4957
of Sleep. R. Macnish. 4884
Phrenology. Fowler. 3336
J. S. Grimes. 3373
Spurzheim. 1056
Examined. T. Sewall. 11678
and Physiognomy. Spurzheim. 1059
Phys. History of Man. Prichard. 405, 735
Physiognomy, Essay on. Lavater. 3387
Outlines of. Redfield. 11652
Physiology, Animal and Vegetable. 5883
Applied to Health. Combe. 6271, 8768
Outlines of. Roget. 1071
Teeth, Struct. and Dis. Burdell. 11669
Wounds, Nature and Cure of. Bell. 426

MENTAL AND MORAL PHILOSOPHY.

Abercrombie's Intellectual Powers. 5540
Active and Moral Powers. Stewart. 4542, 6339
Aids to Reflection. Coleridge. 6133, 6430, 5350
Analogical Philosophy. Field. 739
Analysis of the Mind. Mill. 6319
Ancient Philosophy, Hist. of. Ritter. 6315
Berkeley G., Works. 6035, 6324
Body and Mind. Moore. 4240
Credulity and Superstition. 3927

Dissertations. Beattie. 6402
Elements of Thought. Taylor. 4587, 6410
English, Rev. of 1688. Mackintosh. 6302
Ethical Philosophy, Progress of. Mackintosh. 10035, 6302
Ethics. Aristotle. 755
Introduction to. T. Jouffroy. 713
See also General Index.
First Truths. C. Buffier. 5386
Health, Influence of Mental Cultivation on. 3287

No.
Hist. of Philosophy. V. Cousin. 6373
The same, with 2d series. 6345
Philosophy. W. Enfield. 6400
Philosophy. Henry. 5915
Philosophy. W. G. Tenneman. 6372
Hobbes, T. Works. 6310
How to Observe. Miss Martineau. 4887
Human Mind, Philos. of. Brown. 6374
Nature, Dignity of. Burgh. 3289
Soul, Nature of. Baxter. 6411
Appendix to the same. 5667
Hume, Philosophical Works. 6333
Hurd, R. Critical Notes. 6294
Critical Dissertations. 6295
Moral and Political Dialogues. 6296
Imp. of the Mind. Watts. 6343, 4598
Instinct, Dialogues on. Brougham. 7196
Intellectual Qualities. Abercrombie. 3354
Powers. Abercrombie. 5540
and Act. Powers. Reid. 6371, 6405
Kant, I. Metaphysical Works. 6344
Locke, J. Works. 6348
Logic. W. Duncan. 3024, 4981
Hedge. 4594
Mill. 396
I. Watts. 454, 3028
Mackintosh, Miscellanies of. 6302
Matter and Spirit. 6397
Mayo, R. Fiscal Bureaus. 13114
Melancholy, Anatomy of. Burton. 119
Mental Action. T. C. Upham. 5560
Discipline. H. F. Burder. 4241
Illumination. T. Dick. 6190
Philosophy. J. Douglas. 6320
Philosophy. Pearl. 4223
Mesmerism. Townshend. 3305
Modern Philosophy. Murdock. 4301
Moral Evidence. J. E. Gambier. 6229
Feelings. Abercrombie. 5874, 8765
Philosophy. J. Adams. 6306
Philosophy. D. Dewar 6337
Philosophy. C. Follen. 5399
Philosophy. Gisborne. 6408
Philosophy. Hutcheson. 4295
Philosophy. W. Paley. 6649

No.
Moral Philosophy. L. A. Sawyer. 6139
Philosophy. Smith. 6413
Science. Beattie. 6409
Science. Wayland. 6396
Sentiments. Smith.
6406, 12130, 5189
Morrell, J. D. Speculative Philosophy of Europe. 6323
Nature Adapt. to Const. of Man. 6110, 6382
Night Side of Nature. Cath. Crowe. 1150
No Fiction, Reviewed. F. Barnett. 8444
Novum Organon. Bacon. 5098
Opinions, Formation of. 4555
Philosophical Essays. D. Hume. 122
Essays. D. Stewart. 6342
Essays. I. Watts. 6057
Miscella. Cousin and Jouffroy. 768
Philosophy, History of. Lewis. 7180
of Future State. 6103
of Magic. Salverte. 3333
of Sleep. 1884
Phreno-Mnemotechny. Gouraud. 1072
Phys. Theory of Another Life. Taylor. 6511
Physician and Patient. 3004
Probability, Essay on. 5098
Progress of the Mind. Condorcet. 3971
Psychology. V. Cousin. 6347
F. Rauch. 6307
Society, Nat. Hist. of. W. C. Taylor. 3930
Soul and Body. 637
and Instinct. Paine. 6138
Plato on the. 6443
Power of the. Moore. 6173
Speculative Philosophy. F. Bowen. 789
Stewart, D. Works. 6364
Suicide, Reflections on. 11294
Truth, Essays on. J. Beattie. 4321
Understanding. Locke. 4614, 4637, 5221
Universe, Intellectual System of. Cudworth. 6308
Will, Doctrine of. H. P. Tappan. 5700
Edwards on, Exam. of. Day. 5702
Edwards on, Rev. of. Tappan. 5699
Freedom of. J. Edwards. 5622
Determining Power of. Day. 6088

NATURAL SCIENCE.

Agricultural Chemistry. Johnston. 6076
Chemistry. Liebig. 6050
Society, Transactions of. 10464
Albany Institute, Transactions of. 10643
American Geologists and Naturalists, Transactions of. 5960
Institute, Boston, Lectures before. 11679
American Institute, N. Y. Reports. 10069
Natural History. Godman. 10167
Animal Chemistry. Liebig. 6051, 6068
Kingdom. G. L. Cuvier. 10128
Mechanics. C. Bell. 5009
Animals, Geog. and Classification of. Swainson. 9971
Habits and Inst. of. Swainson. 9979
History of. N. Webster. 10173

Animals, Hist. and Hab. Kirby. 6385, 5488
Animated Nature, Hist. Goldsmith. 10111
Annual Reg. of Scientific Discovery. 6066
Anthology. Greek Collections. 1879
Architecture of Birds. 6203
Arkansas, Natural History of. 5984
Arts of Design in U. S., History of. 10107
Astronomer, Practical. Dick. 6093
Astronomical Exped., U. S. Naval. 13086
Astronomy. See General Index.
Bass Rock, Geology of. Miller. 6104
Bees, Natural History of. F. Huber. 10156
Birds, Architecture of. 6203
and Flowers. Mary Howitt. 2374
Natural History of. 5558
Natural History and Classification of. Swainson. 9973

ORATIONS AND ADDRESSES.

PHILOLOGY.

	No.
Greek Lexicon. Donnegan.	1066
Lexicon. Hedericus.	1055
Poets. Study of. Coleridge.	3045
Prosody. P. Wilson.	3030
Reader.	4883
Reader. Colton.	11653
Guide for Writing Latin. Krebs.	10791
Hebrew Grammar. Johnson.	11696
Lexicon.	10079
Hermes. J. Harris.	10076
Herodotus. Index to.	5433
Hieroglyphic System of Champollion. Greppo.	859
Hurd, Bishop R. Critical Works.	6294
Language, Treatise on. Johnson.	750
Latin Dictionary. Ainsworth.	1056
Dictionary. Mair.	3331
Exercises. Andrews.	3928
Grammar. Adam.	3389, 3396, 4849
Latin Grammar. Andrews' and Stoddard's.	3387
Grammar. J. Ross.	3390
Introduction to.	4960
Reader. Jacobs and Döring.	4850
Metro-English, Elements of. Roe.	10165
Museum Criticum.	415
Phalaris, Epistles of. R. Bentley.	378
Porson, R. Criticisms.	398
Porter's Rhetorical Reader.	3324, 4868
Shakspeare, Concordance to.	11680
Spanish Proverbs.	3306
Study of Words. Trench.	4518
Synonyms, English. Crabb.	1057
Francois.	3006
of New Testament. Trench.	4517
Translation, Essay on. Tytler.	155
Vocabulary of the U. S. Pickering.	10083, 11677

POETRY.

Collections, Works on Poetry, &c.

	No.
America, Poets of. Ed. K. Keese.	2328
Poets and Poetry of. Ed. Griswold.	1787
Female Poets. Ed. Griswold.	1789
American Poems.	2333
Poetry, Essays on. Brown.	3915
Poetry. Ed. S. Kettell.	2402
Poetry. Ed. Bryant.	5573
Ancients, Poetry of the. Peter.	1788
Ballads, Book of.	2357
Historical, &c. Evans.	1978
Pictorial Book of.	1844
Ballston Springs.	3053
Barnabee's Journal.	2491
Battle of Finnes-Burh.	2025
Beauties of Byron.	2074
of the Poets.	3054
of Shakespeare.	3081
of White.	2072
Biglow Papers.	1942
Bower of Spring.	11293
British Poets. Gee Gen. Index.	
Columbus, Vision of. J. Barlow.	1905, 2430, 2450
Connecticut, Poets of. Everest.	1857
Death's Doings.	98
Early English Poets. Ed. G. Ellis.	2015
French Poets. Cary.	8093
Echo and other Poems.	1883
Elegant Extracts.	1818
Extracts.	2107
Elijah and Elisha.	2488
Eolopoesis. (Am. Rejected Address.)	2005
English Poetry, History of. Wharton.	712
Poetry, Letters on. Aikin.	4929
Poetry, Lectures on. Neele.	864, 751
English Poets, Specimens of. Hunt.	9844
Europe, Poetry of. Longfellow.	1806
Fabliaux. Le Grand.	2002
Fairy Queen. E. Spenser.	1828
Queen, Observa. on. Warton.	1833
Flower of Innocence. Mrs. Tonna.	1709
France, Early Poetry of.	1898
Forget-Me-Not.	4619
German Poetry, Survey of. Taylor.	1850
Germany, Poetry of. Baskenville.	1938
Gospel Tragedy. A. Brockway.	2051
Greek Anthology.	1879
Greek Pastoral Poets.	
Poets, Study of. Coleridge.	3045
Growth of Poet's Mind.	2001
Horace in London.	1694
Icelandic Poetry.	1867
Imagination and Fancy. Hunt.	2410, 9844
Lay of the Scottish Fiddle.	2772
Lays of My House. Whittier.	2448
Literature, Pursuits of.	93
Maud, &c. A. Tennyson.	1950
Melaine. N. P. Willis.	2411
Minstrelsy, Ancient and Modern.	2066
of the Scottish Border.	1842
Mouse Trap, &c.	2379
New York Book of Poetry.	1825
Oberon.	2054
Odes upon Cash, &c.	2018
Oriental Poems. W. R. Alger.	1939
Othuriel. T. Aird.	1835
Oxford Prize Poems.	2492
Sausage.	1816
Panorama and other Poems.	1996
Passing Thoughts. Mrs. Tonna.	1708
Pentateuch, Poetry of. Caunter.	5027
Philo—an Evangeliad.	2340
Pizarro. A Tragedy.	1817
Pleasures of Imagination.	3058
of Memory, &c.	2084
of Religion.	2090
Poems, Amelia.	1937
Poetical Decameron. Collier.	4546
Dictionary. Hitchcock.	2500
Quotations. Ed. Addington.	2007
Poetry, Essays on. Beattie.	154
of the East. Alger.	1939
Poets, Thoughts on. Tuckerman.	5848
Pursuits of Literature.	93
Reliques of English Poetry.	1924

No.

Goldsmith, Oliver. 2142
See also General Index.
Gould, Hannah F. 2447
Gower, J. 2118
Grainger, James. 3139
Gray, Thomas. 1858
Thomas. Poems. 2716
Thomas. Select Poems. 2141
Halleck, Fitz Green. 1864
Fitz Green. Fanny, &c. 2339
Hayley, W. Triumphs of Temper. 11883
Heber, Richard. 3087
Richard. Palestine, &c. 2082
Hemans, Mrs. Felicia. 1837, 1880
Herbert, George. 2035
Hewitt, Mary E. 2352
Hill, George. 1823
Hogg, James. 2765
James. Queen's Wake. 2746
James. Songs. 2270
Holmes, O. W. 2333
O. W. Astræa. 2330
Homer. See General Index.
Honeywood, St. John. 2499
Hooper, Lucy. 1033
Horace. Trans. Francis. 5275
Howitt, Mary. Ballads. 2351
Mary. Birds and Flowers. 2374
Humphreys, David. 1917
Hunt, Leigh. 1841
Ives, Charles. 2338
Jenyns, S. 10770
Jerningham, Mr. 2434
Jones, Sir William. 2472
Jonson, B. 2368
Juvenal. Trans. Badham. 5292
Trans. Gifford. 1852, 1928
Third Satire. Trans. 2288
Keats, John. 1792
Kingsley, C. 1999
Klopstock, Odes of. 2260
Knight, Henry C. 2077
Körner, C. T. 8354
Ladd, Joseph B. 2229, 2348
Lamb, Charles. 1882, 1869
Charles. Poems. 2446
Landon, Miss L. E. 1798
Miss L. E. The Golden Violet. 2498
Miss L. E. The Troubadour. 2416
Landor, Walter S. 2223
Langhorne, John. 2142
John. Solyman and Almena. 2489
Linn, J. B. Power of Genius. 11936
Littleton, Lord. 2143
Longfellow, H. W. 1988
H. W. Courtship of M. Standish. 1943
H. W. Evangeline. 2020
H. W. Hiawatha. 1987
H. W. Voices of the Night. 2373
Lowell, J. R. 2455, 1997
J. R. Fable for Critics, 2347
Mackay. 1985
Mallet, David. 2138
March, D. Yankee Land and Iron Horse. 2218
Marston, J. W. 2346
Massey. 2355
Mickle, William J. 2146

No.

Milman, Henry H. 2031
Henry H. Nala Damayanti, &c. 1802
Milnes, R. M. 2280
Milton, John. 1814
See also General Index.
Montgomery, James. 2085, 1869, 1882
James. West Indies. 2754
Moore, Thomas. 2759, 2249
Thomas. Fudge Family in Paris. 3080
Thomas. Lalla Rookh. 2022
Thomas. Melodies, Songs, &c. 3076
Thomas. Loves of the Angels. 3077
Thomas. Tom Crib's Memorial. 3073
Moschus. Idyls. 1915
Motherwell, William. 2456
William. Posthumous Poems. 1954
Myers, Philip H. Ensenore. 1824
Northmore, T. Washington. 11882
Norton, Mrs. 2065
Mrs. Child of the Islands, &c. 5847
Mrs. Dream, &c. 5846
Odiorne, T. Progress of Refinement. 2479
Oliver, Isabella. 2449
Osborn, L. C. 2012
Osgood, Mrs. F. S. 2023
Ovid. 5277
Tristia. Tr. Arden. 1791
Tristia. Tr. Dryden. 8754, 5277
Owenson, Miss S. Wild Irish Girl. 366, 673
Pamell, T. 2774
Percival, J. G. 1932
J. G. Ohio. 2019
J. G. Dream of a Day. 2400
Persius. 2114
Trans. Drummond. 5292
Trans. Gifford. 1868
Phaedius. Trans. C. Smart. 5276
Pierpont, J. 2401
Pike, A. 2024
Pindar. Tr. Wheelwright. 5293
Pindar, P. 2360
Pitt, Christopher. 2133
Pollok, R. Course of Time. 1963
Poe, E. A. 532
Pope, A. 2768
See also General Index.
Porteus, B. Death. 4616
Praed, W. M. 2006
Prior, Matthew. 2128
Proctor, B. 1990
B. English Songs, &c. 2376, 1948
Ramsey, A. 2138
A. Tea-Table Miscellany. 2451
Ray, W. 4321
Read, T. B. New Pastoral. 1993
T. B. Sylvia. 1994
Robinson. Immortality. 2365
Richardson, G. F. 2979
Rogers, Samuel. 1869, 1882, 1900
Samuel. Italy. 2703
Samuel. Pleasures of Memory. 2084
Sands, R. C. 6290
Saxe, J. G. 1992
Schiller, F. Trans. 2364
F. Select Poems. 770
Scott, J. M. The Bluelights. 2778
Scott, J. 2144
Scott, Mrs. J. H. 2483

No.

Scott, Sir W. 2734
Sir W. Ballads and Lyrics. 2011
Sir W. Beauties. 2075
Sir W. Lay of the Last Mins. 2720
Sir W. Marmion. 1388
Sir W. Poems, Ballads, &c. 2758
Sir W. Search after Hapiness. 3068, 3082
Sears, R. Ballston and Saratoga. 3069
Shee, M. A. Rhymes on Art. 2445
Shenstone, William. 2136
Shippey, J. 1936
Sigourney, Mrs. Aborigines of Am. 2282
Mrs. Pleasant Memories, &c. 1157
Mrs. Zinzendorf, &c. 2327
Simms, W. G. Southern Passages and Pictures. 2326, 2415
Smart, Christopher. 2142
Smith, H. and J. 1918
Smith, Mrs. E. O. 2372
Smith, Seba. 2361
Smollet, Tobias. 2145
Sotheby, Wm. Constance de Castile. 3078
Southey, Robert. 1797
Robert. Roderick. 2756
Robert. Tale of Paraguay. 3085
Robert. Thalaba. 3063
Spear, C. Voices from Prison. 2068
Spenser, E. 1828
Sprague, C. and his Poetry. 6877, 1777, 1944
Sterling, J. 2225
Street, A. B. 1839
Frontenac. 2363
Swain, C. 3086
Tappan, W. B. 2052
W. B. Poems. 2480
Tasso. Tr. Fairfax. 7170, 9851
Tr. Hoole. 2428
Tr. Hunt. 2115

No.

Tasso, Tr. Wiffen. 2457
Taylor, B. Poems of the Orient. 2000
B. Rhymes of Travel, &c. 2356
Tennyson, A. 2276
Thackeray, W. M. Ballads. 1986
Theocritus, Idyls. Trans. 1915
Thom, Wm. 1913
Thompson, Wm. 2140
Thomson, James. 2134, 2397, 1855
James. The Seasons. 2433
Tickell, Thomas. 2130
Trench, R. C. 2454
Trumbull, J. 1895
J. McFingal. 3067
Tuckerman. 1991
Tupper, M. F. 2367
M. F. Proverbial Philos. 9852, 1951
Tyler, R. Ahasuerus. 2349
Umphraville, A. 11891
Virgil. Tr. Dryden. 2776, 5269, 8747
Warton, J. and T. 2146
Watts, Isaac. 2454
Isaac. Lyric Poems. 5782
Weekes, R. 1961
White, Henry K. 1882, 1869
Whittier, John G. 2488
John G. Legends of New England. 650, 2231
Wieland, C. M. Oberon. Trans. 2054
Wilcox, C. 11292
Willis, Nathaniel P. 1923
Nathaniel P. Melanie, &c. 2411
Panorama, &c. 1996
Wolcott, J. Peter Pindar's Works. 2360
Woodworth, Samuel. 2487
Wordsworth, William. 2405, 2045, 1796
William. Prelude. 2001
William. Yarrow Revisited. 2371
Young, E. 2069
E. Night Thoughts. 2431

POLITICS AND LAWS.

Adams, J. Works of. 10971
Africa, Ancient Nations of. 10686
Southern. 5820
America and American People. Von Raumer. 9105
Political Survey of. Everett. 9766
its Realities and Resources. 9390
American Constitutions. 11151
Laborer. Horace Greeley. 10928
State Papers. 10471
Americans in Social and Moral Relations. F. J. Grund. 2999
Ames, Fisher. Works of. 11047
Antiquities, Political, of Greece. 10966
Aristotle. Polites, Ethics, &c. 755
Army, British, Reg. and Orders of. 11690
British. List of Officers. 10050
of the U. S. Unif. and Dress. Folio
Artillery Tactics. 3323
Asia, Anc. Nations of. Heeren. 10683
Athens, Pub. Economy of. Boeckh. 7605
Austral-Asia. 5819
Banking in America. Gilbart. 10495
Banking, Practical. J. W. Gilbart. 10060
Banks and Money. G. Tucker. 10812
Bentham, J. Works. 10938
Benthamiana. J. H. Burton. 781
Blackstone's Com. 11185, 10745, 10712
Blue Laws of Connecticut. 11137
British Constitution. Brougham. 10055
British Treaties with other Powers. 11062
Burke, E. Works. 10485, 11089
Burlamaqui, J.J. Nat. and Pol. Law. 11177
Burr, A. Trials. 10734
California Convention, Debates in. 10435
Canada. 5818
Administration in. F. B. Head. 9115
Capital and Labor. C. Knight. 6885
Capital Punishment. Cheever. 6475
Carolinas, Campaign in. H. Lee. 7224
Chartism. T. Carlyle. 813, 863
China, Commercial Intercourse with. 5934
Civil Society, Hist. A. Ferguson. 753
Clay, C. M. Writings of. 10967
Cochrane, Lord T. History of Hoax and Trial of. 11193

RELIGION AND THEOLOGY.

SERMONS.

	No.
Edwards, J.	5379
Emmons, N.	5389
Follen, C.	5398
German Pulpit.	5030
Gisborne, T.	5598
Griffin, E. D.	5059
Hallam, R. A.	5403
Hare, A. W.	5308
Hawkins, E.	5036
Heber, Richard.	5331
Hobart, J. H.	5111
Horsley, S.	6393
Huntington, F. D.	5720
Irving, E.	10483
Johnson, Samuel.	4634
Kirk, E. N.	6194
Latimer, H.	5662
Logan, J.	5385
Love, C.	11875
Massillon, J. B.	
O'Beirne, T. L.	5351
Perkins, G. W.	5733
Plain Sermons.	5712
Pomeroy, J. L.	6174
Price, R.	5616
Rand, A.	6535
Robertson, F. D.	5407
Saurin, J.	5314
Seabury, S.	5101
Sherlock, T.	5752
Smith, Sidney.	5420, 375
South, R.	6326
Stroue, N.	5623
Summerfield, J.	5025
Taylor, J.	5333
Thomson, A.	6572
Wayland, F.	5405
White, Joseph.	5618
Whitefield, G.	5348, 8539
Winslow, B. D.	5062

RHETORIC AND CRITICISM.

Æsthetics, &c. F. Schiller.	1162
Schlegel.	5195
Age of Elizabeth, Lit of. W. Hazlitt.	4588
American Prose Writers. Griswold.	28
Aristotle, Rhetoric, Ethics, &c.	755
Art of Speaking.	3292
Belles Lettres. Rollin.	4908
Burke, Beauties of.	4946
Burns, Life and Land of.	8370
Byron, Conversations with. Kenedy.	3382
Conversations with. Medwin.	3898, 4853, 8081
Classical Learning. Urquhart.	2694
Classical Literature. R. Ray.	3288
Classics, Dissertation on.	3714
Cicero. De Oratore.	11684
Comic Writers, Lectures on. Hazlitt.	88
Course of Reading.	4867
Dramatic Art and Lit. Schlegel.	3294, 5194
Poets. C. Lamb.	9845
Elements of Criticism. Kames.	10806
Elocution. Murdoch.	10157
Book of.	4928
Essays on. J. Dwyer.	11878
Exercises. W. Enfield.	3042
Grammar. J. Barber.	3332
Lectures on. Sheridan.	3025, 3896
Eloquence, Princ. of. Abbé Maury.	5258
Eng. Composition, Prin. of. Booth.	3039
Literature. Chateaubriand.	75
Poetry, Letters on. J. Aiken.	49
Europe, Literature of. Hallam.	113
Literature of. Sismondi.	82, 5125
Fairy Queen, Essay on. Hart.	29
Queen, Observa. on. Warton.	1833
France, Mod. Lit. of. Reynolds.	9236
German Literature. Selections.	1070
Literature. Menzel.	509, 775
Romance. Carlyle.	1214
Germany, Literature in. Heine.	4897
Prose Writers of. Hedge.	27
Goethe, J. W. Von, Characteristics of.	4544, 4549
Goethe, Conversations with.	773
Grecian Wreath of Victory.	4944
Historical Proof, Process of. Taylor.	5074
Imagination and Fancy. Hunt.	2410, 9844
Indicator. L. Hunt.	523
Italian Literature. C. Herbert.	492
Literary Character Illustrated. D'Israeli.	1177, 3326
Literature, History of. Schlegel.	453
Influence of. De Stael.	4595
Longinus. De Sublimitate.	2692
Middle Ages. Literary History of.	5496
New Spirit of the Age. Horne.	8369
Noctes Ambrosianæ. Wilson.	865, 493
Oratory, Lecture on. J. Ward.	2982
Poetry, Eng. Lectures on. Neele.	864, 751
Essays on. J. Beattie.	154
and Gen. Lit. Montgomery.	5880
Poets and Poetry of Europe. Longfellow.	1806
Old, Conversations on.	4581
English, Lectures on. Hazlitt.	
Thoughts on. Tuckerman.	5848
Porson, R. Criticisms.	398
Portico. A Review.	2240
Quintilian. De Institutione Oratoria.	10366
Racine, and French Drama. Bury.	6884
Reading and Recitation. Barber.	4552
Rhetoric, Lectures, &c. H. Blair.	748
R. Whately.	3401
Art of. J. Holmes.	3296
Grammar of. Jamieson.	3343
Prac. System of. Newman.	4862
Philos. of. G. Campbell.	10814
Rhetorical Delivery. Porter.	3031, 3036
Roman Literature. Dunlop.	89
Schiller, Exam. of Works of. Follen.	8033
School, its Objects and Relations.	2993, 2994
Shakespeare, Criticisms on. Davies.	841
Notes on. Collier.	1145
Papers.	526
Slavonic Nations, Literature of.	828
Spanish Literature. Bouterwek.	5495

ROMANCE.

	No.
Confidence Man. Melville.	1225
Conformity. Mrs. C. E. Tonna.	1707
Coningsby. B. D'Israeli.	19
Consuelo. Mad. Dudevant.	918
Contarina Fleming. D'Israeli.	1635
Contrast. Regina M. Roche.	969
Cooper, J. F. Novels. See Gen. Ind.	
Corinne. Mad. De Stäel.	674, 20
Corse de Leon. James.	1281
Count Robert of Paris. Scott.	45
Countess and other Tales.	244
Court Conspirator. Sue.	49
Cousin Marshall.	10029
Crayon Miscellany. W. Irving.	540
Cricket on the Hearth. Dickens.	97
Crock of Gold. Tupper.	251
Crockfords, or Life in the West.	984, 1368
Crofton Boys. Martineau.	1679
Cromwell. H. W. Herbert.	1546
Croppy, The.	1314
Cruikshank at Home.	1624
Cyril Thornton. T. Hamilton.	1404
Darnley. G. P. R. James.	1046
David Copperfield. Dickens.	201
Death's Doings. Dagley.	98
Decameron. Boccaccio.	1745
De Foe, D. Novels, &c.	322
Deformed, The.	1252
Deerslayer. J. F. Cooper.	1264
Delaware, or Ruined Family.	1132
De Lilse, or the Sensitive Man.	628
Demarara. Harriet Martineau.	1674, 10021
Desultory Man. James.	1490
De Vere. R. P. Ward.	1025
Devereux. E. L. Bulwer.	1346
Diary of a Désennuyée.	1134
D'Israeli, B. Novels.	5
Doctor, The. R. Southey.	1531
Dollars and Cents. Amy Lothrop.	1279
Dombey and Son. Dickens.	7497
Domestic Recreation. Wakefield.	4945
Don Quixote. Cervantes.	1733, 127, 206, 1765
Doom of Devorgoil. W. Scott.	1424
Doomed, The.	311
Dream Life. Mitchell.	218, 214, 207
Dred. Mrs. Stowe.	173
Duke Christian. Jane Porter.	1336
Duty. Mrs. Roberts.	1683
Edgar Huntley. Brown.	1005, 1428, 1292
Edgeworth, Maria. Works.	100, 897
Elder Sister. James.	575
Elizabeth de Bruce.	956
Elkswatawa.	1238, 1241
Ella of Garveloch.	10022
Ellmer Castle.	1703
Emma. Jane Austin.	37
Emmeline. Mary Brunton.	949
English Fashionables Abroad.	617
Ernest Maltravers. Bulwer.	660
Errata. J. Neal.	1535, 643
Ethel. James.	576
Ethel Churchill. Miss Landon.	1549
Etonian, The.	2287
Eugene Aram. E. L. Bulwer.	1023, 1274
Evelina. Miss Burney.	1577
Fable for Critics. Lowell.	2347
Fables. J. La Fontaine.	1074

	No.
Fabliaux, or French Tales.	2002
Fairchild Family. Mrs. Sherwood.	185
Falsehood and Truth. Mrs. Tonna.	1705
Family Mansion. Mrs. Taylor.	4605
Fashionable World Displayed.	4913
Fast of St. Magdalen. Porter.	1358
Father as he should be.	1483
Feats on the Fiord.	7175
Fielding, H. Works.	3594
or Society. R. P. Ward.	1332
Fleetwood. W. Godwin.	1717
Floral Biography. Mrs. C. E. Tonna.	1202
Flower, Fruit and Thorn Pieces.	1659
Flower Garden. Mrs. Tonna.	1203
Fool of Quality, The. Brooke.	694
For Each and All.	10023
Forest of Arden. W. Gresley.	566
Life. Mrs. Kirkland.	9823
Fortunes of Nigel. W. Scott.	273
Foscarini, or the Patrician of Venice.	971
Foster Brother, The. T. Hunt.	6
Foundling of Belgrade.	369
Friends in Council. Helps.	3330
Four Sisters. Miss Bremer.	573
Fudge Doings. Mitchell.	209
Gaston de Blondeville. Miss Radcliffe.	611
Gentleman of the Old School.	233
Georgia Scenes. A. Longstreet.	1609
German Novelists. T. Roscoe.	1123
Ghost Seer. Schiller.	5157
Gil Blas. A. R. Le Sage.	11279
Giovanni Sbogarro.	1585
Gipsy, The. G. P. R. James.	1042, 1387
Glaucus. Kingsley.	10172
Glenarvon.	1400
Godolphin. E. L. Bulwer.	1486
Goethe. Novels and Tales.	5423
Governess, &c. Mrs. Sherwood.	189
Granby. Lister.	1377
Grandfather, The. Miss Pickering.	8
Great Metropolis, The. Grant.	1243
Greyslaer. C. F. Hoffman.	1497
Griffith Abbey. Mrs. C. Matthews.	1584
Guide to an Irish Gentleman.	6581
Gulliver's Travels. J. Swift.	338
Guy Mannering. Scott.	579, 1090, 286
Guy Rivers. W. G. Simms.	1506
Hajji Baba, Adventures of in England.	622
Hamlets, The. Harriet Martineau.	1027
Handy Andy. S. Lover.	14
Happiness ; a Tale for the Grave and Gay.	1726
Harcourts, The.	11152
Harry Franco. C. Briggs.	1499
Hawks of Hawk Hollow, The.	1504
Heads of the People. Jerrold.	47
Heart, The. M. F. Tupper.	251
of Mid-Lothian. W. Scott.	271
Heir of Wast-Wayland.	549
Heiress of the de Veres. Mrs. Marsh.	48
Helen Fleetwood. Mrs. Tonna.	1208
Henrietta Temple. B. D'Israeli.	145, 5
Henry of Guise. G. P. R. James.	1468
of Ofterdingen. Von Hardenburg.	1218
Milner. Mrs. Sherwood.	198, 184
Herbert Wendall.	1472
High-Ways and By-Ways.	1599

VOYAGES, TRAVELS, AND GEOGRAPHY.

WORKS IN FOREIGN LANGUAGES.

www.ingramcontent.com/pod-product-compliance
Lightning Source LLC
LaVergne TN
LVHW020237110826
845151LV00003B/949

* 9 7 8 1 4 2 5 5 3 0 0 7 5 *